Industrial Organization

Industrial Organization

second edition

JOE S. BAIN
University of California, Berkeley

JOHN WILEY & SONS, INC.   New York   London   Sydney

53690

Preface

This second edition of *Industrial Organization* is fundamentally similar in aim, concept, and organization to the first. Of course, statistical and related empirical information has been brought up to date—generally to the earlier 1960's. This has led to minor changes in conclusions in some instances. Similarly, recent developments in the application and interpretation of the antitrust laws have been recognized, along with changes in law and policy affecting some specific industries.

Otherwise, the book has grown mostly through the inclusion of more extended discussions of relevant aspects of economic theory. The main additions here include expanded introductory sections in Chapters 5, 7, and 8, that explore the *a priori* significance respectively of seller concentration, product differentiation, and the condition of entry; an extended discussion in Chapter 10 of theory about the importance of some phases of market performance; and a fuller treatment in Chapter 11 of the formulation and testing of hypotheses concerning the relations of market structure to market performance. These additions were made in part because of the comparative neglect of the theory of markets in many recent textbooks on price theory to which the current generation of students is likely to have been exposed.

Readers of the first edition will note some divisions of long chapters into two and other reorganizations of material in the interest of pedagogy. Finally, the book has been augmented by selective reference to and discussion of significant empirical findings and other writings in the field that have been published since 1958.

No encyclopedic coverage of the literature has been attempted. My view is that this book should serve as a basic text for an undergraduate course in Industrial Organization, being appropriately supplemented by such added readings as an instructor may choose. For a graduate course in the field, it should be useful as a "basic handbook" that should be heavily supplemented by readings in primary books and articles.

For such improvement of this work as may have been accomplished, I am heavily indebted for their suggestions to a number of colleagues and to many graduate and undergraduate students with whom I have worked in the last decade. I should like to express especial gratitude to Miss Alison Keith, who did nearly all of the statistical up-dating work needed for the revision, and to Mrs. Genevieve Tsaconas, who handled all of the typing in her usual impeccable fashion.

October, 1967   Joe S. Bain
Berkeley, California

Preface to the First Edition

This work is offered as a basic textbook in the area of economics usually designated as Industrial Organization. Its general subject matter is the organization and operation of the enterprise sector of a capitalist economy, with especial reference to the economy of the United States. It is primarily concerned with the economywide complex of business enterprises (excluding banking or other financial firms) in their function as suppliers and sellers, or buyers, of goods and services of every sort produced by enterprise. It does not deal with financial enterprises, or consider nonfinancial enterprises in their role as buyers in markets for primary factors of production such as labor.

My approach to the matters described is essentially external and "behavioristic"; I am concerned with the environmental settings within which enterprises operate and in how they behave in these settings as producers, sellers, and buyers. By contrast, I do not take an internal approach, more appropriate to the field of management science, such as would inquire how enterprises do and should behave in ordering their internal operations and would attempt to instruct them accordingly.

Being concerned in the main with the market behavior of enterprises, I have given major emphasis to the relative incidence of competitive and monopolistic tendencies in various industries or markets. Correspondingly, my primary unit for analysis is the industry or competing group of firms, rather than either the individual firm or the economywide aggregate of enterprises. Some attention, of course, must also be given to both smaller and larger units.

In analyzing the behavior of industries, I have drawn heavily upon accepted economic theory, and also upon the literature of the law affecting competition and monopoly, for identifications of significant phenomena to be investigated, conceptualizations, and hypotheses susceptible of empirical testing. Thus it is that I have organized the heart of my study in the following way. First, I have undertaken a rather detailed examination of (*a*) patterns of market structure, (*b*) types and forms of the market conduct of sellers and buyers, and (*c*) ultimate market performance, within the numerous industries of the American enterprise economy. Second, I have sought for demonstrable associations among the structure, conduct, and performance of industries, to the end of determining, for example, the extent to which market performance can be explained (or predicted) in terms of market structure or conduct, or market conduct in terms of structure. Finally, I have attempted to apply our findings in the aforementioned regards in an appraisal and critique of existing laws and derived public policies affecting enterprise monopoly and competition.

Although I have depended strongly upon received economic theory for concepts and hypotheses—and in fact deal with a range of issues roughly comparable to that encompassed by contemporary price and market theory—the present work is definitely not one in *a priori* price theory. The emphasis is dominantly on empirical study concerning issues raised by such theory, or on the implementation, application, and critical testing of such theory. It is not on the development and elaboration of *a priori theory* as such. In my treatment of empirical materials, moreover, my concern is not (as under one current fashion) to demonstrate the application of a theory the validity of which has already been assumed as axiomatic. Rather it is to implement the theory by determining objectively the relative actual importance of various situations which the theory imagines, and to test the theory by seeing whether its hypotheses or predictions can be confirmed or disconfirmed with factual data. Theoretical predictions are viewed only as hypotheses subject to critical testing, as is appropriate in a scientific endeavor.

In the treatment of market structure, conduct, and performance—and their interrelationships—I have abandoned, in the main, the common approach of studying all of these things together in a series of separate industry studies. Although the industry-study approach has a demonstrated entertainment value, it is seriously deficient in that it encourages a casuistic process of "generalizing from a single instance"; correspondingly is prone to engender confusion between accidental associations and fundamental tendencies toward associations; nearly always deals with too many parameters and variables for effective analytical handling; and provides no straight or passable road toward scientific generalizations.

In this work, therefore, I have chosen the alternative of cross-sectional treatments of numerous industries with respect to each of several selected dimensions of market structure, conduct, and performance; and of a search for generalizations regarding structure-performance and similar relationships through association tests involving substantial numbers of industry cases. The voluminous empirical materials drawn upon are thus in the main marshaled within a predetermined analytical framework emphasizing cross-sectional analysis, rather than as a series of industry case studies introduced to illustrate various situations and behavioral tendencies.

The book is organized along the following lines.* The first four chapters are introductory, devoted to the description of terms, concepts, and issues; to a survey of relevant theoretical constructs; to the general environmental background of American industrial organization; and to business size and overall concentration in the American economy. The succeeding eight chapters (5 through 12) constitute the core of the book, analyzing, on an empirical level, market structure, conduct, performance, and their interrelations in American industries. These chapters emphasize economics rather than political economy; their relationship to the discussion of public policies is that they describe and analyze systematically the economic problems with which policies affecting competition must deal. The last four chapters are devoted to a compressed analysis of American public policies affecting competition, including both antitrust policies designed to maintain competition and discourage monopoly, and a miscellany of other policies designed to restrict, prevent, or replace competition. This work differs markedly in content, organization, and intent from typical "government and business" textbooks, both in that it is centered in the main on the economics of industrial organization, considered initially

*The chapter references in this Preface to the first edition have been altered to reflect the slightly revised organization of the second edition.

apart from public policies affecting business, and in that its consideration of policies is largely confined to those affecting enterprise monopoly and competition. It likewise differs fundamentally in approach from textbooks emphasizing series of industry case studies.

The book has been written more or less according to the outline of an undergraduate year course in Industrial Organization which I have offered for a number of years. If it is used as the basis for a full-year course, it might seem appropriate to cover the first eleven chapters in the first semester and the remainder in the second. The book is of such a length that over a full year it could be supplemented lightly in the first semester by selected industry-study readings and by selections from recently published collections of articles in the field, and heavily in the second semester by added readings on public regulatory policies, including collections of judicial opinions in antitrust cases. For a one-semester course in Industrial Organization, the first eleven or twelve chapters seem to constitute a unit covering enough ground for fourteen or fifteen weeks of class meetings. Another possible procedure, for a one-semester course in which it is desired to attack policy issues, would be to assign selectively from the first twelve chapters and then to include the bulk of the last four chapters. I realize that the book is not written to fit numerous existing course outlines in the general field, but would of course be pleased if some such outlines were rewritten to fit the book.

As to acknowledgments, a primary obligation must be recognized to Professor E. S. Mason of Harvard, who in large part created and developed the modern Industrial Organization field and who introduced me to it in the 1930's. Thanks should also go to the Merrill Foundation, whose grant to support research underlying another book, since published, enabled me to develop as a by-product a large volume of empirical materials concerning manufacturing industries. Professor Richard Caves, a colleague at Berkeley, undertook a very helpful critical reading of the entire manuscript prior to its last revision. Finally, I am deeply indebted to my wife for her indispensable assistance in producing the manuscript in dittoed form for experimental classroom use.

Joe S. Bain

May 1959   Berkeley, California

Contents

Industrial Organization

1

Introduction

This book deals with the organization and working of markets in the United States, and thus with the "industrial organization" of the most important capitalist or enterprise economy in the world today.

Such an enterprise economy has distinctive characteristics that account for its name. In it, a multitude of privately owned and managed business enterprises play the central role in determining the course and character of economic activity. These enterprises (or companies or firms) develop and assemble natural resources, facilities for production, and labor forces; they determine what and how much is to be produced; and they distribute goods and services to users. They do all of this, moreover, independently and on their own private initiative, and without any important amount of centralized governmental planning, guidance, or control. Of course, there are other private and public decision-making units whose behavior interacts with that of private enterprises to determine the overall performance of the economy—including consumers, labor organizations, owners of resources, governmental credit and fiscal institutions, and some public enterprises. But the leading part is played by private business enterprises.

We are all, of course, interested in how satisfactory a job the American enterprise economy does in providing employment, producing goods, distributing income, and so forth— in what we call, for brevity, *the performance of the economy*. Since this economy-wide performance emerges mainly from the independent actions of many private enterprises, we should also be aware that how well the economy performs depends strongly on *the performance of business firms*. That is, the ways in which they behave and the results of their behavior have a dominant influence on the welfare of the whole economy. This being the case, the student, the average citizen, and the responsible public official alike should have a strong interest in their performance.

In centering its attention on industries or markets in the American economy, this book is naturally concerned with the performance of its business firms. A first task, therefore, is to explain just what this performance is or includes. Let us begin by pointing out that the performance of enterprises, however we measure it, is complex and has many aspects or dimensions. Thus we speak frequently of the numerous dimensions of business performance, noting that they reflect the varied functions of the business enterprise and its various interrelationships with the rest of the economy.

We may point out also that business firms perform in three distinct capacities:

1. As buyers in the markets for the basic factors of production: labor and natural resources.

2. As administrative units that organize productive facilities, materials, and labor, manage their use, choose techniques and methods of production, arrange financing, and so forth.

3. As sellers or buyers in the markets for goods and services that they produce or use. In this capacity, they determine outputs, prices, product designs, selling costs, and a number of related things—in other words, they make a complex of adjustments, in view of conditions of demand and supply, to the commodity markets in which they are active. (We generally emphasize the performance of enterprises as sellers in these markets, but their performance as buyers of outputs of other enterprises is also important.)

Because analyzing any one of these phases of performance is a big task, economists usually discuss them one at a time. We follow that practice here, and devote our attention almost entirely to the third aspect of enterprise performance just described—the performance that emerges from the activities of firms as sellers or buyers in the markets for produced goods and services. Discussion of business performance in factor markets is left to works such as those on labor markets, and treatment of internal management performance to the literature on management organization, production engineering, operations control, and the like. This volume is thus devoted to analyzing the *market performance* of business enterprise.

An analysis of this market performance, however, necessarily involves us also in considering other things concerning markets—particularly the *determinants* of the market performance of enterprise. This is because we should like not only to know how enterprises perform, but also to explain their performance. Why do enterprises perform as they do, and in particular why do some perform differently, or better or worse, than others? To answer these questions is to identify the determinants of enterprise performance, and to learn how variation in these determinants leads to corresponding variations in performance. This sort of knowledge is desirable because of its scholarly or scientific interest. It is also essential for the formulation of an intelligent public regulatory policy in the area often loosely designated as that of "monopoly and competition."

What things in general do determine the market performance of enterprise? Casual observation, common-sense, and formal theory all suggest that there are two main sorts of determinants. First, the organization or structure of an industry (or group of competing enterprises) exercises a strong influence on the performance of the industry. That is, *market structure* constrains and canalizes enterprise activities and their results; and variations in structure may lead to associated variations in performance. Second, the *market conduct* of enterprises—by which we mean policies, practices, and devices they employ in arriving at adjustments to the markets in which they participate—also influences performance. Thus we look initially to the characteristics of market structure and of market conduct as primary determinants of the market performance of enterprises, or of groups or industries of business firms.

There are then two tasks before us in addition to simply measuring and appraising market performance:

1. We must identify, describe, and classify the significantly different types of structure and conduct that are found in actual markets for goods and services, and determine the relative importance of each type within the American economy.

2. We must try to discover, through various analytical devices, any evident associations of market structure and conduct with market performance, in order to establish a pattern of causal relationship between structure and conduct on the one hand and performance on the other. This knowledge should enable policy makers to learn what sorts of structure and conduct are likely to lead to socially desirable market performance, and what kinds are not.

In trying to discover cause-and-effect relation of market structure and conduct to market performance, we luckily do not set out completely in the dark. Again, both common-sense notions and formal economic theory provide predictions concerning these relationships. We may thus profitably invest some time in trying to confirm or disconfirm relevant theoretical hypotheses bearing on the matter at hand, as well as engaging in some primarily inductive investigation. We will review some of the principal theoretical hypotheses in subsequent chapters.

The general plan of this book thus embraces first a description and analysis of: (*a*) the organization of the private-enterprise sector of the American economy, with special reference to the structure of the various markets in which goods and services are sold by business firms; (*b*) the market conduct of firms in the various markets; and (*c*) the market performance of these firms. Second, it includes also an exploration for associations or apparent causal links among market structure, conduct, and performance. Because of our ultimate interest in public policy this exploration is heavily oriented toward identifying those types of structure and conduct which are and are not likely to be associated with a socially satisfactory business performance. In currently popular terminology, we seek to identify the sorts of structure and conduct which are and not not conducive to *workable competition*.

Since the tasks of investigation and analysis just mentioned are undertaken in the light of a strong general interest in issues of public policy affecting business competition and monopoly, we finally consider the implications of our "scientific" study for governmental regulatory policy. In the last section of this book we consider, in turn, the public policy issues posed by our findings, their implications for the solution of such issues, the character and relative effectiveness of past and present policy measures designed to influence monopoly and competition, and desirable directions for future policy.

A Definition of Some Terms

Before proceeding further, let us pause to define and discuss briefly some of the terms we have introduced above and will use frequently in succeeding chapters. We must give particular attention to the crucial notions of market *structure*, *conduct*, and *performance*, but we should also define clearly, if briefly, some basic terms such as *enterprise*, *sector*, *industry*, and *market*, as well as that rather comprehensive and sometimes ambiguous term *workable competition*.

1. The Enterprise. By an enterprise we refer here to a privately owned business firm (owned either by one individual or jointly by several or many, as most corporations are), which engages in productive activity of any sort with the opportunity of making a profit.[1] Enterprises as defined thus include private firms engaged in manufacturing, whole-

---

[1]This is strictly the definition of private enterprise, which is generally denoted by the term "enterprise" without qualifying adjectives. Public agencies engaged in producing and possibly selling goods and services are often called "public enterprises"; we do not include them in the present definition of an *enterprise*.

sale and retail trade, supplying gas and electricity, construction, banking, and so forth; they do not include governmentally owned and operated productive operations, nonprofit organizations performing charitable services, and the like.

An enterprise has an owner or group of owners. It ordinarily has assets which it uses in performing its functions, including various facilities, materials, and cash. It also has a control group or management. The scope of a single enterprise is conveniently viewed as the total of assets and operations which because of common ownership is controlled by a single management. Whatever the legal technicalities (there are many in corporate organizations), all assets and operations under the ultimate legal control of a single management group fall in a single enterprise. Separate enterprises are different complexes of assets and operations that are under different ownerships and separate and independent managements.

2. *The Sector.* Enterprises are commonly referred to, as we have noted, as firms or companies, and, when legally incorporated, as corporations. The economy is populated by a very large number of separate firms, each controlled by a management that is ostensibly separate from and legally independent of that of every other firm.

Since most production in the United States is carried on by private enterprises, they engage in a wide range of activities, and these are often grouped under *sectors.* The principal sectors of private enterprise activity are:

Agriculture, forestry, and fisheries.
Mining and other extraction of mineral material.
Processing and manufacture.
Construction (for example, of roads, buildings, bridges).
Transportation.
Utilities (electric power, gas, etc.).
Communications (telephone, telegraph, radio, and television).
Distributive trades (wholesaling and retailing).
Service trades (hotels, dry cleaners, amusements, medical service, etc.).
Finance (banks, loan companies, insurance firms, etc.).

A very large number of firms operate in each of these sectors. Our interest in this book extends generally to all sectors of enterprise except the financial, which has characteristics and poses issues quite different from those encountered in nonfinancial enterprise. We speak hereafter of only the nonfinancial enterprise sectors of the economy, giving no systematic attention to banking and other financial organizations.

3. *The Industry.*   All of the firms engaged in any particular sector of productive activity have some common functions. At the same time they have many differences, and the differences are frequently dominant. In particular, firms in the same sector may produce quite different goods or services, fulfilling different needs of buyers and perhaps catering to entirely different groups of buyers. In a word, the products supplied by different firms may not be close substitutes (to buyers), and thus the firms may not be in any immediate sense in competition with each other. On the other hand, there may be within any sector various subgroups of firms making products which are close substitutes and are in competition with each other, although they are poor substitutes for outputs of other firms in the sector. Thus in manufacturing we would recognize that Chrysler Corporation, making automobiles, produces an output which is a distant substitute for that of U. S. Gypsum Co., making wallboard. But Chrysler's output is a close substitute for and in direct competition with the outputs of General Motors, Ford, and American Motors.

The firms (or, more strictly, outputs of firms) in any sector tend to fall roughly into subgroups of the sort mentioned, so that in each subgroup the outputs are relatively close substitutes for each other and relatively distant substitutes for all other outputs. Each subgroup is thus also a group of sellers potentially in more or less direct competition with each other. Any such subgroup may be called an *industry*—strictly a group of sellers or of close-substitute outputs who supply a common group of buyers.[2] Firms belong in the same industry if these conditions are fulfilled. They may fall in different industries either because they produce different products (for example fountain pens and shoes) or because they supply different groups of buyers (such as bakery bread buyers in New York and in Los Angeles). We may view the enterprise economy, or any sector of it, as made up of a large number of separate industries, recognizing of course that there are some overlaps and interrelations among industries which make the picture a bit complicated when we observe its details.

The reasons for our interest in the industry so defined are obvious. The industry is the primary focus of competitive forces; it is its structure which primarily conditions enterprise conduct and performance; it

[2]Since the industry is defined as a group of close-substitute outputs, a firm with a diversified output may, of course, be a member of two or more industries. Thus General Electric is a member of a washing machine industry, a heavy electric-motors industry, and so forth.

is the logical and convenient unit for study as we consider the conduct and performance of enterprise.

4. *The Market.*　A market is conveniently defined as a closely interrelated group of sellers and buyers. Therefore, we may define a market as including all the sellers in any individual industry, and all the buyers to whom they sell. On the "seller side" a market is coextensive with an industry as defined, but by including buyers it is also described in terms of the character and composition of its buyer population and of a geographical area in which the buyers are situated. The terms "structure of an industry" and "market structure" are therefore very similar in meaning, although the latter might comprehend a bit more. In speaking of structure here, we emphasize the broader term, market structure.

5. *Market Structure.*　What do we mean by market structure? According to Webster's Dictionary, "structure" means "form, or manner of building," "arrangement of parts . . . in a substance or body; the interrelation of parts as dominated by the general character of the whole, as the *structure* of society." In other words, by the structure of any complex thing we refer to the pattern in which its constituent parts are organized or put together.

Market structure refers to the organizational characteristics of a market, and for practical purposes to those characteristics which determine the relations (*a*) of sellers in the market to each other, (*b*) of buyers in the market to each other, (*c*) of the sellers to the buyers, and (*d*) of sellers established in the market to potential new firms which might enter it. In other words, market structure for practical purposes means those characteristics of the organization of a market that seem to exercise a strategic influence on the nature of competition and pricing within the market.

The most salient aspects or dimensions of market structure are:

(*a*) The *degree of seller concentration*—described by the *number* and the *size distribution* of sellers in the market.

(*b*) *The degree of buyer concentration*—defined in parallel fashion.

(*c*) *The degree of product differentiation* as among the outputs of the various sellers in the market—that is, the extent to which their outputs (though similar) are viewed as nonidentical by buyers.

(*d*) *The condition of entry* to the market—referring to the relative ease or difficulty with which new sellers may enter the market, as determined generally by the advantages which established sellers have over potential entrants.

The potential importance of each of these characteristics is fairly obvious. Seller concentration refers, for example, to whether the number of sellers in a market is *one, few,* or *many (monopoly, oligopoly, atomism)* and to the relative sizes of sellers with any given number. Theory and observation suggest that the character, intensity, and effectiveness of competition among sellers will be significantly influenced by the degree of seller concentration.

Buyer concentration has a similar significance in determining the character of competition among buyers and the character of the relationships between buyers and sellers that condition ultimate market performance.

Product differentiation refers, for example, to whether on one hand the products of competing sellers in a market are viewed as identical (homogeneous) by buyers, or, on the other hand, differences in quality, design, packaging, or reputation among the competing products lead various buyers to have various degrees of preference for certain of these products as compared to others. The extent to which competing products in a market are differentiated may clearly be expected to influence the competitive interrelationships of sellers in the market, their conduct, and their market performance.

The condition of entry, or height of barriers to new entry to a market, characterizes the extent to which established sellers have advantages over potential entrant sellers. It thus determines the relative force of potential competition as an influence or regulator on the conduct and performance of sellers already established in a market.

The numerous markets for goods produced by enterprises differ widely with respect to these aspects of market structure. As regards concentration, for example, we find markets with very high seller concentration, as in automobiles, where three domestic sellers supply about 90 per cent of the market, one other domestic seller 5 per cent, and several foreign producers the remainder; markets with "moderate" seller concentration, as in steel, where the four largest firms have about 58 per cent of the basic producing capacity and the next four about 18 per cent, with the remainder accounted for by about 72 smaller firms; and markets with low concentration, as in shoe production, where there are about 870 firms, and the largest 20 supply only about 43 per cent of the total market. In the case of product differentiation, there are markets in which there is substantial homogeneity of the products of competing sellers (cement, copper), relatively slight product differentiation (canned foods, wallboard), and a high degree of product differentiation (automobiles, fountain pens). Similar disparities among industries are found in buyer concentration and the condition of entry. Industries may thus be classified and subclassified according to their combinations of characteristics in the several dimensions of market structure. Once they have been so classified, we have some framework for testing notions concerning the influence of market structure on market conduct and performance.

Here we have confined our attention to four primary characteristics of market structure. Almost needless to say, other characteristics may also influence competitive behavior, and we may on occasion find it useful to extend the previous list. At times, market structure has been defined much more broadly—e.g., as "the economically significant features of a market which affect the behavior of firms in the industry supplying that market." So construed, market structure could embrace every objective circumstance—psychological, technological, geographical, or institutional—that might conceivably influence market behavior. According to this definition, every market has a multitude of characteristics, and every market is in some degree structurally unique. We do not espouse this concept of market structure here because a very loose and frequently ambiguous use of the idea of structure is involved, and also because meaningful intermarket comparisons and meaningful generalizations about the influence of structure on behavior are effectively forestalled if the content of "structure" is made so comprehensive that no two markets can be viewed as structurally alike.

6. Market Conduct. Market conduct refers to the patterns of behavior that enterprises follow in adapting or adjusting to the markets in which they sell (or buy). If firms are referred to as sellers, market conduct encompasses mainly:

(*i*) The "price policies" of firms, whether acting individually or collectively—effectively the aims they pursue and methods they apply in establishing what prices to charge, what outputs to produce, what product designs to choose, what sales-promotion costs to incur, etc.; and

(*ii*) The process or mechanism of interaction, cross-adaptation, and coordination of the policies of competing sellers in any market.

There are numerous dimensions or aspects of market conduct; a few significant ones are:

(*a*) The objective pursued and the method employed by a firm or group of firms in calculating or determining price and output. As to objective, is the aim for maximized group profits, maximized individual profits, or for a conventional or "fair" profit margin? As to method, are prices made by adding a certain margin to costs, or by other devices? And is a single price charged, or a set of discriminatory prices to different buyers?

(*b*) The product policy of the firm or group. Is product improvement or variation over time (via changing design) a part of the individual or collective market policy? If so, what is the character and orientation of the product variation policy?

(*c*) The sales promotion policy of the firm or group. Do advertising and other sales promotion play a significant role in the individual or collective market policy? If so, by what methods and according to what principles is the volume of advertising expenditure determined?

(*d*) Means of coordination and cross-adaptation of price, product, and sales-promotion policies of competing sellers. For example, is there:

1. Express collusion or agreement to arrive at common prices, or products, or sales-promotion outlays?

2. Tacit collusion based on established patterns of imitation, or of leading and following, as in the case of price leadership?

3. Defection from collusive agreements (express or tacit) by some or all sellers, via secret price cutting and the like, leading to "incomplete collusion"?

4. Interdependence of pricing and related adjustments, in the context of anticipation of reaction by rivals?

5. Complete independence, with individual adjustments undertaken without heed to possible reactions?

6. Exercise of predatory or exclusionary tactics directed against either established rivals or potential entrants?

The preceding list is long enough to exemplify the dimensions of behavior comprehended under the market conduct of sellers. Similar dimensions of market conduct for buyers may also be recognized. There are wide variations in conduct among different markets or industries, and markets might be classified according to the dominant patterns of conduct found in them. We are obviously interested in the extent to which the pattern of conduct may be systematically associated both with market structure (possibly to some extent a determinant of conduct) and with market performance (possibly to some extent determined by conduct).

7. *Market Performance.*   Market performance refers to the composite of end results which firms in any market arrive at by pursuing whatever lines of conduct they espouse—end results in the dimensions of price, output, production and selling cost, product design, and so forth. For firms acting as sellers, these results measure the character of the firm's adjustments to the effective demands for their outputs; for firms buying goods, they measure the quality of adjustments made by firms to the supply conditions of the goods they purchase. Whereas, for

example, conduct refers to whether a group of sellers arrived at prices through collusive agreement or through strictly independent action, market performance refers to what the margin of price above the cost of production turned out to be, and whether output was restricted in order to reap an excess profit, however the result was achieved.

One word of caution may be inserted briefly at this point. In general, it is not appropriate to measure the market performance of a firm or industry in terms such as its contribution to total employment in the economy, the total output of goods, or the stability over time of either. This is because (in the case of sellers, for example) the essential limits of the performance of enterprises within a capitalist economy are those of adjusting to whatever effective demands are present for their outputs, with the restriction that in so adjusting they must as a group at least "break even"—that is, not incur bankruptcy en masse and thus make private enterprise impractical. Market performance thus refers for sellers to the character of their adjustments to effective demands for their outputs within the limits just described. From a normative standpoint, the question is how well the adjustments made contribute to an effective performance for the entire economy.

The principal aspects of dimensions of the market performance of an industry include prominently:

(a) The relative technical efficiency of production so far as this is influenced by the scale or size of plants and firms (relative to the most efficient), and by the extent, if any, of excess capacity.

(b) The height of selling price relative to the long-run marginal cost of production and to the long-run average cost of production (usually about the same as long-run marginal cost), and the resultant profit margin.

(c) The size of industry output relative to the largest attainable consistent with the equality of price and long-run marginal cost.

(d) The size of sales-promotion costs relative to the costs of production.

(e) The character of the product, or products, including design, level of quality, and variety.

(f) The rate of progressiveness of the industry in developing both products and techniques of production, relative to rates which are attainable, and also economical in view of the costs of progress.

The performance of individual industries in dimensions such as these has an obvious bearing on the extent to which the economy as a whole will operate effectively in providing goods and distributing incomes. There is plenty of evidence, moreover, that performance varies significantly among markets, being more satisfactory in some and less so in others. Firms make various sorts of adaptations to the effective demands for their outputs, and some adaptations have better and some worse impacts on the operation of the whole economy. The character of these adaptations is measured by dimensions of market performance like those listed above. In order to obtain relevant knowledge, we need to measure and appraise enterprise performance in the many markets of the economy, and to classify markets according to the performance found in them. This sort of measurement, appraisal, and classification is also important for purposes of public policy, as a means of identifying those areas in which public interference or influence is needed in the interest of general welfare, and of determining the appropriate goals of such interference.

There are, similarly, two ways in which a study of market structure and conduct are important. It is interesting from a scientific standpoint to attempt to explain observed variations in market performance among industries in terms of accompanying variations in structure and conduct. Thus we may hope to learn to what extent different sorts of market structure and conduct lead to different sorts of performance. To do this, it is obviously necessary first to describe and classify types of market structure and conduct, and second to test for the associations of these types with the quality of market performance.

Moreover, a knowledge of the association of structure and conduct to performance is important for purposes of public policy. To be sure, performance is the essential thing from the standpoint of social welfare. But once it has been measured and appraised, and cases of unsatisfactory performance have been identified, we must ask what means of public interference should be employed to secure more satisfactory performance. At this point we find that direct regulation of performance (such as direct determination of price and output by a government commission) is not a generally workable means of regulating a free-enterprise economy. On the other hand, regulation of market structure and conduct is much more feasible and, in general, constitutes a workable mode of regulation. Then the feasible regulatory procedure aimed at securing satisfactory performance is to devise regulations which will secure market structures and patterns of market conduct which will lead to satisfactory performance. It is therefore clearly necessary, for purposes of public policy, to learn as much as possible of the associations of structure and conduct with performance, so that we will know the proper direction for a policy that deals with structure and conduct in order to influence performance. Since the guides of *a priori* theory in this regard are incomplete and uncertain, intensive empirical investigation of the associations in question is indicated.

8. *Workable Competition.*   The last basic concept to be explained in general terms is workable competition. The meaning of this term may be clarified by referring first to the operation of the whole economy. An economy as a whole (for example, that of the United States) performs in a certain way over time. The significant measures of its performance, from the standpoint of the material welfare of the populace are (a) the volume of employment it provides; (b) the efficiency of production, and thus the aggregate volume of output secured with any given volume of employment; (c) the relative stability, or freedom from fluctuations, of output and employment over time; (d) the rate of growth of output over time, or the rate of "progress"; (e) the composition of aggregate output as among alternative goods to be produced; and (f) the distribution of income among various potential income recipients. These are the principal dimensions of the aggregate performance of the economy.

With respect to each of these dimensions of performance, or the group of them in combination, it is possible to establish certain standards or norms of what would be the most satisfactory performance from the standpoint of the total populace. Thus we find that most people agree in wanting full employment, maximal efficiency, relatively stable output and employment over the years together with an optimal rate of growth of output, the avoidance of certain unnecessary and artificially contrived inequalities in income distribution, and so forth. These norms of overall performance are basic precepts from which the idea of workable competition is derived. By employing them we can appraise the aggregate performance of the economy and decide how far it falls short of the ideal.

Now the way in which the economy as a whole performs, or how well it performs relative to these ideals, is determined by many things, or many aspects of individual and group behavior. They include the behavior of enterprise, our subject of study here. But they also include the behavior, for example, of labor unions, of governmental and private credit institutions, and of individuals in determining whether to spend or save their incomes. From this complex of behavior, a complicated economic process of actions and interactions develops, and from it emerges the aggregate performance of the economy. Each of several sectors of the economy, including the enterprise sector, contributes to the outcome of this process, but the enterprise sector is only one of several important contributors.

The influence that the enterprise sector has on the aggregate performance of the economy is determined in important part by the nature of the adjustments or adaptations which enterprises make to the effective demands for their outputs as the total economic process generates these demands. (It also depends on the adjustments that enterprise buyers make to the supplies of outputs they purchase.) Depending on the character of their adaptations—that is, on their market performance—the aggregate performance of the economy is favorably or adversely affected.

It follows that workable (reasonably satisfactory) competition is revealed by, and is the result of whatever gives rise to, reasonably satisfactory or workable market performance—performance that enhances the aggregate economic welfare to a reasonable degree. *Ideal* performance is found in adaptations of enterprises to their markets which enhance to the maximum possible degree the attainment of the overall economic objectives relating to employment, efficiency, income distribution, and so on. "Workable" performance generally refers to adaptations of enterprises to their markets which reasonably approximate the ideal, or do not embody gross and important discrepancies from it.

To define workable market performance, it is necessary first to identify an ideal or norm for each of the important dimensions of performance. This must be done by determining, in each such dimension, the best adaptation which enterprises can make to their markets from the standpoint of contributing to the attainment of overall economic goals. Such determinations can really be arrived at, in the present state of knowledge, only by *a priori* theorizing concerning the relationships of enterprise actions to the total economic process. We do not venture into this area of theorizing here—it constitutes in itself a large and complicated field—but it is possible to illustrate the sorts of norms for market performance that emerge from such an analysis.

For example, ideals of market performance by individual industries in several leading dimensions would seem to be about as follows:

(*a*) *Price-Average Cost or Profit Margins.* In the absence of disturbances, they should move as long-run averages toward amounts just sufficient to pay normal interest returns on owners' investments, plus a "risk reward" to successful firms sufficient to offset the losses of unsuccessful ones. On the other hand, profit margins should be free to have short-run fluctuations (around the indicated long-term average) in response to changing market conditions, and also be free to exceed the minimal level for limited periods in order to reward innovators of new products and techniques for their contributions. In sum, persistent or long-run excess or supernormal profits are generally signs of unworkable performance.

(*b*) *Technical Efficiency.* All the output of an industry should be supplied by plants and firms of the most efficient scale, and none should be supplied by plants and firms of inefficiently large or inefficiently small scale. This implies among other things that the number and relative sizes of plants and firms supplying a market should be consistent with the attainment of technical efficiency. Furthermore, the firms of the industry should have an aggregate plant capacity adjusted to market demand in such a way that there is an absence of chronic excess capacity.

(*c*) *Products.* The general quality level of the products of an industry should be neither too high nor too low in view of buyers' desires relative to product quality. Products should not be excessively deteriorated, in the sense that they reach such a level that buyers would prefer to pay the extra costs necessary to improve quality. And they should not be excessively improved, enlarged, or made elaborate in the sense that buyers would prefer a lower quality product with the resultant saving in cost. A second criterion of desirable product performance is that there should be in any industry a more or less maximum variety of designs, qualities, and costs offered, so long as the production volume of the individual designs is large enough that inefficiently small-scale production does not offset the virtual advantages of variety.

Similar ideals may be established for other dimensions of performance, including selling costs, progressiveness, and so forth, but the preceding may be sufficient to illustrate the nature of performance norms. Although in some cases definition of a precise single ideal is difficult, it is ordinarily not very difficult to identify ranges of performance which lie outside the "acceptable."

Given these ideals, and given enough data, we can appraise the performance of any industry and estimate the extent to which, in various dimensions, its performance misses the ideal. We turn then to the notion of workable performance, which refers essentially to performance which does not diverge "too far" from the ideal. In setting the permissible limits of divergence, we must take into account the facts that our measurements of actual performance may be somewhat inaccurate, that in an uncertain world some divergences may result from accident rather than from design, and that some ideals may be imprecisely defined. Considering all of this, some *ad hoc* method of determining "limits of tolerance" for the divergence of actual performance from ideal performance as defined must be devised.

A common procedure is to view the more extreme divergences observed as definite signs of unworkable performance, to excuse very slight or minor divergences, and to reserve judgment about or require further evidence about those divergences lying between those two extremes. Applying this method of "horseback judgment," we might for example classify as having unworkable performance any industry with extreme divergence from ideal performance in one or more important dimensions; as having workable performance any industry having no more than minor divergences in any dimension; as probably having unworkable performance any industry with moderate divergences in several dimensions. This procedure will not lead to any neat and complete classification of industries, but it will permit some estimate of which are the "bad actors," the "very good actors," and the "doubtfuls."

So much for the primary meaning of workable competition—this is, workable performance. In terms of this standard of appraisal, cases may be identified in which some public interference to improve performance is, is not, and may be desirable. There is also, however, a derived meaning of workable competition, and this refers to patterns of market structure and conduct which may be expected to give rise to or be associated with workable performance. Some conformations of market structure as measured by such things as the degree of seller concentration, the extent of product differentiation, and the condition of entry may be conducive to good performance; and similarly there may be beneficial patterns of market conduct. Conversely, other patterns of market structure or conduct may be conducive to poor market performance. Thus we may hope to classify market structures and patterns of market conduct as "workably competitive" and "not workably competitive." The knowledge permitting us to do so is essential to a good public policy if, as we have suggested, public regulation must generally attempt to influence performance indirectly, via regulation of market structure and conduct. Then an intelligent policy would endeavor to identify market structures and patterns of conduct which were "not workably competitive," and to modify them accordingly.

Knowledge of what structures and patterns of conduct, or combinations thereof, are and are not workably competitive requires a knowledge of the association of structure and conduct to performance. This is one reason why the search for such an association is an important part of our study. And a thorough search, involving analysis of empirical data, is needed. There are some very simplified *a priori* theories concerning what may be workably and not workably competitive structure and conduct, but they are generally oversimplified, ambiguous on essential matters, and untested. Extended factual investigation is required.

We thus turn, beginning with Chapter 5, to a survey of the findings of relevant investigations bearing on the matters at issue—market structures, patterns of market conduct, market performance, and their interrelationships. This survey is followed by a discussion of public policy issues and modes of public regulation. First, however, we examine some preliminary matters, considering in Chapter 2 some indications of various theories concerned with industrial organization.

SUPPLEMENTARY READINGS

Mason, E. S., "Price and Production Policies of Large Scale Enterprise," *American Economic Review*, March 1939, pp. 61–74.

Clark, J. M., "Toward a Concept of Workable Competition," *ibid.*, June 1940, pp. 241–256.

Bain, J. S., "Workable Competition in Oligopoly," *ibid.*, May 1950, pp. 35–47.

2

Economic and Political Theories Concerning Industrial Organization

Three primary questions are posed in this book. What is the character of the market performance of the numerous industries within the private business sector of our economy? To what extent and in what ways is their market performance associated with the structure of their markets and the nature of their market conduct? And in what proportion of cases and in what degree do market structure, conduct, and performance in these industries fail to be workably competitive? These questions are important both scientifically and as a basis for appraising public policy toward competition and monopoly.

So far as possible we attempt to supply factual answers to these questions on the basis of available empirical evidence. Yet in doing so we are aware of our debt to *theory*—that is, to *a priori* speculations and hypotheses concerning matters in which we are interested. This debt is at the least very considerable, and perhaps overwhelming. Before considering factual findings, therefore, we will outline the content of relevant theory or theories, and explain the relationship of our investigations to them.

In view of our principal interests here, our major dependence is on economic theory. In this chapter we discuss this theory in broad outline. In subsequent chapters—dealing with various aspects of market structure, conduct, and performance—we examine relevant theoretical hypotheses in more detail.

There are three main aspects of our dependence on economic theory.

First, it provides us with a general orientation for investigation—with criteria of what should be investigated and what problems are significant. For example, economic theory furnishes a precise identification of market structure, conduct, and performance as an interrelated complex of phenomena that play important roles in determining aggregate material welfare in the economy.

Second, economic theory is the source of numerous hypotheses or predictions concerning the determinants of the economic behavior in which we are interested. It deals, for example, with the expected association of the market structure of industries to the market performance which emerges from them. Testing of these hypotheses with factual data provides a convenient beginning to an empirical investigation of the issues we have defined above, whether or not the *a priori* hypotheses received from economic theory are ever empirically confirmed. The development of empirically founded explanations of economic behavior necessarily proceeds from some working hypotheses, and economic theory is a fruitful source of these.

Third, economic theory is our only potentially reliable source of standards of what constitutes a satisfactory or workable market performance of business enterprises. The criterion of satisfactory market performance by enterprise is a favorable impact on total economic welfare. What sorts of performance have favorable and unfavorable impacts has in the present state of knowledge not been demonstrated empirically. It is known or guessed only through *a priori* theorizing concerning the probable interactions of various phenomena within the economy. We are thus definitely dependent on economic theory for norms of workable market performance—standards of evaluation to be applied to the observed performance of actual industries. Because of these three sorts of dependence on economic theory, it is natural that we should wish to survey the immediately relevant aspects of its content.

Although economic theory supplies the major orientation of our investigations, there are also other possible orientations for a study of industrial organization. The orientation provided by economic theory is largely toward the effects of industrial organization and behavior on the material welfare of the economy, measured by the output and distribution of goods. An alternative orientation is toward the effects of industrial organization, and particularly of change or evolution in it, on other aspects of social organization and activity. Frequently emphasized are its effects on political organization, the functioning of government, and the political and social status of various individuals and groups. Leading questions concern the effect of increasing industrial concentration on the working and viability of a democratic form of government, and the relationship between the rise of concentrated economic power and the concentration of political power in oligarchical governments.

Numerous *a priori* theories or doctrines have been advanced bearing on such matters. The reader is probably familiar, for example, with a persistent lay theory that concentrated big business undermines the foundations of a Jeffersonian democracy; with Marxian and neo-Marxian theories of the response of political and social organization to changes in industrial organization; or with the theory that a "managerial revolution" in big business is creating an elite of professional business executives who will supply the ultimate controlling oligarchy in society.

Although the political implications of developments in industrial organization indeed constitute an important subject for study, we do not emphasize these implications, or theories about them, in this book. We discuss a few such theories briefly later in this chapter, largely as a background for a later examination of the effect of political, as opposed to strictly economic, considerations in the development of public policies toward industrial organization. But for the most part our analysis and appraisal of industrial organization are developed from a limited viewpoint, emphasizing considerations of material welfare as reflected in the production and distribution of goods.

The remainder of this chapter is devoted first to surveying that part of the content of economic theory that is especially relevant to a study of industrial organization and, second, to some comments on relevant political theories.

Economic Theory: General Content

In this book, we do not refer to any and all theories concerning economic activity, but only to the conventional core of contemporary economic theory which deals with the working of capitalist or enterprise economies. This theory, which has a more or less uniform and agreed-upon content, is generally devoted to the following ends:

1. *Analyzing* the way in which an enterprise economy functions, or giving a systematic account of the mechanics of the operation of such an economy.

2. *Explaining* why it operates and behaves as it does, by establishing logical links between its behavior on the one hand and certain "fundamental determinants" of this behavior on the other.

3. *Predicting* how the enterprise economy will perform, and especially how its performance, or the performance of various parts or segments of it, will vary with changes in situations or circumstances.

4. *Evaluating* the performance of the economy—a process which in-

volves theorizing about what sorts of performance, both for the economy as a whole and for segments of it, will make the maximum contribution to attaining certain defined goals of social welfare.

The procedure or method of this economic theory is generally described as "deductive." That is, it first draws upon observation to formulate empirical generalizations concerning determinants of economic activity in the form of human psychology and motivation, technological conditions, institutional and legal framework, market structures, and so forth, and makes these generalizations into *assumptions* for theorizing. Then by a logical process it deduces from these assumptions how the economy will function and perform in various assumed circumstances. In this procedure, deductive logic is also used to ascertain the impact of various sorts of performance on various aspects of material welfare. Having this deductive form, economic theory can offer only *hypotheses* concerning the character, cause, and consequence of economic behavior. Empirical testing of these hypotheses is needed to confirm or disconfirm its predictions and evaluations.

In addition to having a definite method, conventional economic theory has a specific and limited orientation. It does not comprehend or attempt to explain all aspects of the behavior of individuals and groups engaged in economic activity, or to evaluate all aspects of their welfare. Matters of social status, cultural attitude, political repercussion from economic events, and the like are generally neglected by such theory. Thus the psychological attitudes of workers toward employers, and vice versa, the links between employment status and political party, the effects of routine factory as opposed to craft employment on individual and group psychology, and so on, are likely to be neglected. Generally, the political and sociological repercussions of economic organization and activity have not been considered in conventional economic theory; these matters are left to other theories or disciplines.

What conventional economic theory does emphasize are those phenomena which impinge directly on the determination of material welfare, represented in the volume of goods produced and the way in which it is distributed. As to performance, therefore, this theory is oriented to explaining and predicting those aspects of performance which directly affect material welfare. For the overall economy there is an emphasis on the general level of employment, the efficiency attained in production, the size and composition of total output, and the distribution of income. For segments of the economy, emphasis is correspondingly on such things as the relationships of prices to costs, the sizes of plants and firms, the relative levels of wages in different occupations, and the rate of flow of investment in new capital goods.

Similarly, conventional theory emphasizes those phases of conduct (that is, individual and group action in the economic sphere) which seem to be directly linked to the determination of performance in its material welfare dimensions, and neglects other phases of conduct. For example, it is concerned with how consumers allocate their expenditure among goods or how, given his cost, an enterpriser arrives at a selling price; but it is little concerned with the coffee hour as an experiment in group dynamics for the office force, or with the practice of nepotism in the selection of executives. Finally, in identifying and characterizing significant aspects of the structure of markets, firms, labor groups, and so on, it emphasizes only those aspects which seem likely to have a direct impact on the determination of conduct and performance in the dimensions directly linked with material welfare.

As such, this economic theory has a large content. Not only does it deal with the economy as a whole in broad terms, but it also has many special parts dealing intensively, for example, with the behavior of business firms, the organization and functioning of industrial markets, and the character and function of money and labor markets. Out of the total, there are two branches of economic theory that are especially useful to the student of industrial organization.

The first is generally called *price theory*, or the theory of the behavior of firms in markets. This theory undertakes to explain and to predict how business firms will behave as they participate in the industries or markets in which they sell (or buy) their goods. It comprehends among other things the analysis of market structure, market conduct, market performance, and their interrelationships. The second branch of theory may be designated as *general equilibrium analysis*. It traces and explains the interactions and interrelationships of behavior in the numerous segments or sectors of the economy, and the way in which these interactions determine the performance of the economy as a whole. It considers how performance in one sector—for example, price-cost relationships in any single industry—affects the overall level of employment, composition of output, and distribution of income. General equilibrium analysis is of crucial importance to us in that it provides a vehicle for appraising and evaluating the performancē of enterprises in various markets from the standpoint of their impact on total welfare.

General Equilibrium Theory

General equilibrium analysis is large and complex, and this is not the place to develop, justify, or criticize it. However, since it is our primary source of standards of what constitutes desirable performance by firms and industries, we briefly indicate how it is used to develop such norms.

A first step in establishing standards of desirable performance for segments of the economy (for example, firms and industries) is to define and assert the broad goals for the economy as a whole. With an emphasis on material welfare, these goals might include full employment, maximum efficiency in converting employment into output, equitable distribution of income, and so on. Such asserted goals essentially express value judgments—sometimes of a particular writer, more frequently of the society as a whole as a writer interprets them. There is probably broad agreement on certain goals, and less agreement on others, but normative appraisal of economic performance must proceed from at least tentative assertion of some broad goals.

The second step, and this is the one undertaken by general equilibrium analysis proper, is to relate "partial" performance—that by individual firms or industries, for example—to overall performance, and thus to determine what sorts of partial performance best contribute to the attainment of the specified goals. Thus norms or ideals of partial performance are developed, relative to which actual performance of firms, industries, or other segments of the economy can be appraised.

A part of the task of establishing these norms is relatively simple, and a part is not, by any means. The task is easy when we are considering an aspect of the performance of an individual firm or industry that is a simple fraction of the same aspect of performance for the whole economy. Then we can simply add arithmetically all individual industry performances in this dimension to get a total for the economy. For example, an obvious overall goal is maximum technical efficiency in production, including the provision of productive facilities and administrative units of the most efficient size and most efficient degree of integration. Since overall performance in this regard is in the main simply the sum of the individual performances of all plants and firms in the economy, norms of partial performances are easily derived: the plants and firms of each industry should ideally be of the most efficient size and degree of integration. Developing a partial norm for profits so far as they are judged by their effects on income distribution is similarly simple. Given an overall goal for the share of profits in income distribution, any firm or industry may be judged as contributing a fraction of the total result for the economy.

A more difficult task is encountered in establishing a norm for the rates of output of individual industries. Here, the relevant norm of overall performance for the economy defines the best allocation of resources among uses, or, in other words, the proportions in which all of the different goods that make up the total output of the economy should be produced if consumers are to get a maximum satisfaction from total output. It has been demonstrated by general equilibrium theory that the best proportionate production of all different goods—that is, the best composition of total output—should result if resources were allocated among the production of different goods in such a way that the value of the marginal product of each resource was the same in every line of production. The last or marginal hour of labor used in producing each good, for example, would add an output of that good which had the same value to consumers as the value to them of the added output of the marginal hour of labor used in producing every other good.

If this general norm is accepted, then a corollary norm for the rates of output of individual industries may be derived—essentially a norm of "allocative efficiency." In brief, if we assume all industries to be paying identical factor prices for each resource (e.g., the same wage rate for a given grade of labor), the composition of output would be ideal if all industries simultaneously set their rates of output at that level where the marginal costs of production of the various goods were equal to the selling prices of the goods. Finally, then, an output norm for each individual industry is that its output rate should be such that its marginal cost of production equals the selling price of its output—particularly in the long run. Such a rate of output is normative for each industry, provided that all or nearly all industries conform to this same norm. The output norm in question is then a goal to be sought for every industry, although its attainment by any one industry is truly normative only if all or most other industries also attain it, and if, in addition, factor-market imperfections do not allow different industries to pay appreciably different prices for the same productive factors or resources. While this norm is inescapably complex, it is nevertheless reasonably unambiguous and operationally useful.

The most difficult task is encountered with aspects of the performance of firms or industries which must be evaluated in terms of other indirect impacts they have on the overall performance for the economy. For example, we may wish to evaluate the profits of an industry from the standpoint of their impact on total employment in the economy, *indirectly* through their impact on the propensities of consumers and investors to spend money and thus maintain a steady flow of money income through the economy. The question in theory is what the predictable net impact is on spending of various rates of profit, and this cannot be unambiguously predicted. A similar problem is encountered if we attempt to evaluate the role of profits in inducing technological progressiveness, or of advertising expenditures in stimulating the flow of total spending. Where general equilibrium analysis must be employed to develop partial norms in cases like these, its indications are generally indefinite, or subject to wide ranges of uncertainty.

Since general equilibrium theory is our only available source of norms for individual firm and industry performance, we make do with what it offers. It supplies several reliable performance norms, concerning mainly technical efficiency in production and efficiency in the allocation of resources among uses. With respect to several other desired norms of market performance, the indications of the theory are either ambiguous or stated in such a form as not to be operationally useful. In this book we do not attempt to develop and justify specific norms, but in the main merely assert them as the occasion for evaluation arises.

Price Theory

Price theory explains and predicts the behavior and performance of business firms in the selling markets for the goods they produce (and in the buying markets for goods they purchase). It analyzes the rates of output at which firms and industries produce, how efficiently they are organized, the relation of prices charged to costs of production, their outlays on selling costs, their policies in designing and changing products, and so forth.

In so doing, price theory deduces the way in which production technologies, the psychological propensities and motivations of business firms and of consumers, and surrounding institutions interact to induce firms and industries to follow predictable patterns of market conduct and generate predictable patterns of market performance. It further predicts, through a process of deduction, how changes in surrounding circumstances should affect the performance of firms and industries. For example, price theory predicts the effect on price and output in a given industry of a decline in the unit cost of producing the good it supplies.

A very significant further use of price theory is to predict the way in which market conduct and performance in different industries will vary *because of differences in their market structures.* It thus provides hypotheses concerning associations of market structure with market conduct and performance—hypotheses that are clearly relevant to the empirical study of industrial organization.

Because the method of price theory is that of economic theory generally—that is, it proceeds by describing presumed determinants of behavior in a set of assumptions, and then deducing the consequences in conduct and performance of these assumed determinants—especial interest centers on the typical assumptions of price theory.

Conventional price theory depends heavily on three sorts of basic assumptions: concerning the psychology of buyers, the technological relationships of factors used in production, and the motivation of firms that produce and sell goods. The basic assumption concerning buyer psychology is that buyers' choice patterns among different sorts of goods are such that they will tend to purchase more of any good as its price is relatively lower, thus creating for any industry a typical reaction of buyer demand to price charged. The basic assumptions concerning technology depict the way in which the costs of production of firms tend to vary with changes in their rates of output. Important specific assumptions are that there is some tendency of costs per unit of output to decline as the plant or firm is expanded up to a certain size, and also that there is some variation of unit costs with changes in the rate of utilization of any plant of given size. The basic assumption concerning the motivation, or guiding principle of action, of firms in producing and selling outputs is that any seller (or buyer) will act to maximize his aggregate profits—adjusting price, output, selling cost, product, and so forth to further this end. This assumption is frequently held to oversimplify what is evidently a complex motivational pattern, but it is also defended as the most accurate simplified description of what most business firms try to do.

A more satisfactory and elaborate theory needs further assumptions about controlling conditions. These include assumptions concerning the degree to which buyers' demands for products respond to increases in sales-promotion costs, or the manner in which improvement or deterioration of products will affect production costs and buyer demands. Given such assumptions, deductive theorizing can produce more elaborate and realistic predictions of the market performance of enterprises under various controlling conditions.

Price theory requires a further set of assumptions, however. Early in the development of modern price theory it was recognized that the conduct and performance of firms and industries does not depend solely on the character of the demand, cost-output, and similar controlling relationships, plus the character of the motivation of firms (for example, profit maximization). These things depend also on the structures of the markets in which firms sell. Market structure may logically be expected to influence the market conduct of firms in seeking maximum profits and the market performance generated by this conduct. By affecting the character and intensity of competition among firms in the same industry, market structure shapes their conduct and performance.

Modern price theory has therefore identified and distinguished several different types of market structure which industries may have, and has explained and predicted how market performance should differ among industries with different types of market structure. It has classified market structures mainly according to:

The degree of seller concentration—whether the number of sellers in an industry is many, few, or one, and what their relative sizes are.

The extent of product differentiation—whether the products of competing sellers are uniform and identical, or are differentiated by design, branding, and so on.

The condition of entry to the industry—represented by the advantage that established firms have over prospective new entrant firms, and reflecting the force of potential competition as a regulator of the market conduct and performance of the established firms.

Given such a market classification, theory can predict how behavior will differ among classes of markets. It proceeds to deduce, for each category of market structure, (1) how firms will react to the basic demand, cost, and similar controlling conditions to determine their outputs, prices, selling costs, products, and so forth; and (2) how the competitive interaction of the policies of firms will operate, and what end market performance it will bring forth. This deduction obviously emphasizes the logic of profit maximization, the market processes of interaction as individual firms adjust to each others' actions, and the eventual equilibrium adjustment which should be reached.

Without developing this deductive analysis, we may summarize briefly some strategic predictions of price theory concerning the relationships of market conduct and performance to market structure. These theoretical predictions will be discussed further in subsequent chapters dealing with actual seller concentration, product differentiation, conditions of entry, and market conduct.

Market Structure and Performance—the Influence of Seller Concentration

A primary distinction among industries is drawn on the basis of seller concentration. The simplest familiar distinction is threefold:

I. *Atomistic industries,* in which many small sellers are in competition.
II. *Oligopolistic industries* (oligopolies), in which a few large sellers are in competition.
III. *Monopolized industries* (monopolies), in which a single seller supplies the entire output going to the market.

Price theory reaches the following conclusions about differences in market conduct and performance among these broad categories of industries.

1. In atomistic industries, each seller is so small that he will take the selling price for his output as given and beyond his control, and will simply adjust his output independently to the level which is most profitable at the going market price. Outputs will not be restrained in order to increase price, since no seller acting independently will have a perceptible influence on price. Collusive restraint of output by all sellers is ruled out by their large number.

When all sellers act in this way and market price reacts accordingly, the following market performance for the industry may be predicted. Industry output will be extended and price reduced to the point where the marginal cost of supplying added output is just equal to the price at which output sells. If firms may expand output indefinitely without increasing unit costs, or there is unimpeded and easy entry for any number of additional sellers, it also follows that long-run industry output will be extended and price reduced to the point where: (a) every firm is producing at the minimum attainable unit cost; (b) market price is equal to this minimal unit cost (which includes a normal profit); (c) industry output is the largest which can be sold at a price covering cost; (d) there are no profits in excess of the normal profits (interest on owners' investment). Atomistic competition is thus in theory the ultimate in competition, with the impersonal market a thoroughgoing regulator of enterprise action.

2. In monopoly, the single seller has complete control of the market price at which he sells (there is no competitive supply of goods in his market), and may raise it or lower it while effectively restricting or expanding the amount of product he sells. He is therefore in a position to choose a most profitable price relative to his costs, and will do so by restricting his output (relative to what the output in atomistic competition with similar costs would be) to a point which maximizes his aggregate profit and thus that of his industry. In general, the monopolist will, costs and other things being equal, produce less and charge more than an atomistically competitive industry would. Output will be smaller and selling price higher, and the monopolist will tend to earn an excess profit (one above a normal interest return on investment). *Monopolistic output restriction* and *monopolistic excess profits* tend to emerge. No definite or unique prediction can be made as to the technical efficiency of the monopolist as that is influenced by the scale of his operations, though desirable efficiency is quite possible.

3. Oligopolies—with a few large sellers—in some sense lie between atomistic competition and monopoly. There is still rivalry among sellers, as in atomistic markets, but each seller supplies enough of the total market output to influence market price with output adjustments at his command, and will thus anticipate reactions by his rivals to his output and price adjustments. Consequently, there is an interdependence, or nonindependence, of the price and output policies of rivals, and each will determine his price and output in the light of concurrent moves or induced reactions of rival firms. In this context, prediction of the market conduct patterns or price policies of firms or groups of firms becomes much more difficult. Indeed, unless price theory now adopts further assumptions, conduct patterns are theoretically indeterminate, and no single definite prediction can be logically deduced.

Alternative conduct patterns, however, are evidently possible, including: (*a*) effective express or tacit collusion among rival sellers, to act collectively "as a monopolist would"; (*b*) incomplete collusion, involving an incompletely successful attempt at effective collusion; (*c*) "stalemate," with each rival seller preserving any of a range of going policies rather than risking the danger of initiating a change and thus inducing reactions; (*d*) open rivalry, possibly culminating in market warfare to weaken or eliminate rivals.

Correspondingly, the market performance expected in oligopolies may range from about that attributed to single-firm monopoly to that attributed to atomistic competition, lying at either extreme or somewhere in between. In addition, it might comprehend a sort of dynamic instability of market structure, outputs, and prices. Similarly, there is a broad range of alternative possibilities predicted with respect to the efficiency in scale and number of firms in oligopoly, ranging from ideal technical efficiency to the incursion of wastes of insufficiently large or overlarge firms. It is clear that in its most simplified form, price theory is distressingly indefinite in its predictions of market conduct and performance in oligopolistic industries, because of the diffuse logical implications of the interpendence of a few rival sellers. We consider the predictions of more sophisticated theories of oligopoly in Chapter 5.

Market Structure and Performance— the Influence of Product Differentiation

Price theory draws a second distinction among industries on the basis of product differentiation, dividing them into:

A. *Industries with homogeneous products,* in which the products of all sellers are identical.
B. *Industries with product differentiation,* in which the products of various sellers are differentiated by design, quality, branding, etc.

This classification is combined with that based on seller concentration to produce an A and a B subcategory under concentration classes I and II above. Thus we recognize homogeneous and differentiated atomistic industries, and homogeneous and differentiated oligopolies.

It may be deduced that product differentiation broadens the scope of the sales policy or market conduct of the seller. What we have already said about atomistic and oligopolistic industries should apply generally to such industries when they have homogeneous (undifferentiated) products. If, instead, their products are differentiated, the following may also be predicted. First, the seller will have an incentive to undertake advertising and other sales-promotional expenditures to attract larger demands for his product, presumably regulating the volume of his expenditures so as to maximize his profit. Second, he will also have an incentive to adjust and vary his product in design and quality so as to secure the most profitable adjustment of production cost to demand and price. Third, the seller may be able to charge a price somewhat different from that of his competitors (an impossibility with homogeneous products), because of the allegiance of particular buyers to the products of particular sellers, and thus may exercise some "monopoly power" in restricting his own output in order to raise his own individual price.

Unfortunately, price theory has not been developed far enough to permit very definite predictions about the differences in market performance that result from these lines of conduct. About all that may definitely be deduced, in the present state of theory, is that with product differentiation: (a) there will be some sales-promotion costs, which raise the total cost and probably the price of supplying goods by some amount; (b) the level of selling cost in oligopoly may be less or greater than with atomism, other things being equal, depending on whether or not the oligopolists are "collusive" in determining the amount of their selling outlays; (c) any of a number of patterns of product quality, product variety, and product change over time may emerge, though purposive product change through time is generally encouraged; (d) the division of the market among sellers will be influenced by product differentiation, perhaps accounting for somewhat persistent differences in their sizes; (e) various patterns of price difference among competing sellers are possible, though not inevitable. These predictions are qualitative and rather indefinite, though they do tend to point out broad differences between homogeneous-product and differentiated-product markets.

Market Structure and Performance— the Influence of the Condition of Entry

Price theory also distinguishes industries on the basis of *the condition of entry* to them, or the height of barriers to the entry of new competitors. The condition of entry to an industry denotes roughly the advantages in terms of cost or selling price which established firms have over potential entrant firms. It may be measured by the degree to which established firms can persistently elevate their prices above minimal average or competitive costs without making it attractive for new firms to enter. Barriers to entry indeed exist, and they vary from industry to industry. Correspondingly, industries may be classified, for example, as having:

1. *Easy entry*—that is, no barriers to the entry of additional sellers.
2. *Moderately difficult entry*—that is, barriers to entry which are appreciable but not high enough to permit established sellers to set a joint monopoly price without attracting entry.
3. *Blockaded entry*—that is, barriers to entry high enough that established sellers can set a joint monopoly price without attracting entry.

The conditon of entry, or height of the barrier to entry to an industry, should in theory tend to influence its market conduct and performance in two ways. First, it places a long-run limit on selling price which established firms may choose not to exceed in order to forestall entry. This is a distinct possibility if the industry is oligopolistic and the established firms are thus large enough to take account of the effects of their price policies on entry. Second, the decision of established firms to exceed the limit price will induce entry, increase industry output, and probably tend in the long run to keep that price from being exceeded. Thus, in both ways, the force of potential competition as measured by the condition of entry influences market conduct and performance. Further theorizing concerning both the effects and the determinants of the condition of entry is considered in Chapter 8.

An Elementary Structural Classification of Markets

When industries are classified and subclassified on the basis of seller concentration, product differentiation, and the condition of entry, the following very elementary classification of industries by market structures emerges:

I. Atomistic industries
   A. Without product differentiation

B. With product differentiation
II. Oligopolistic industries
    A. Without product differentiation
        1. With easy entry
        2. With moderately difficult entry
        3. With blockaded entry
    B. With product differentiation
        1. With easy entry
        2. With moderately difficult entry
        3. With blockaded entry
III. Monopolized industries

(Note that atomistic industries are not subclassified according to the condition of entry, since entry to them is almost always easy.)

We have indicated very briefly above a number of ways in which market conduct and performance would theoretically be expected to differ among industries with the various combination of structural characteristics that are listed in this market classification. Extending the predicted association of the market structures of industries with their market performance requires that we adopt a somewhat finer and thus more elaborate subclassification of markets, particularly with respect to the degree of seller concentration within oligopolistic industries and to the condition of entry to them. When we do this, some development of the underlying theoretical analysis will also be required. These needed elaborations of the structural classification of markets, related theorizing, and the resulting more detailed predictions concerning the relations of market structure to performance are considered in Chapters 5, 7, and 8 in connection with discussions of actual seller concentration, product differentiation, and conditions of entry.

Empirical Investigation and Price Theory

The elementary predictions of price theory sketched above, together with somewhat more sophisticated predictions that are developed in later chapters, provide us with a substantial body of hypotheses concerning the association of market conduct and performance to market structure. In addition, the theory poses, but does not answer, a number of significant questions about market performance and its relation to market structure—questions that we may be able to answer through factual investigation. These considerations point to some obvious interrelationships between price theory on the one hand and empirical studies of industrial organization on the other. But let us explore this matter a bit more fully. What is the general relationship of price theory to the empirical investigation of industrial organization? How do we draw upon or otherwise apply theory as we begin to investigate facts?

There are numerous ways in which facts may be brought to bear on theory, or theory on facts. As we approach empirical investigation in the area of industrial organization, we are already heavily indebted to theory for an orientation of study and for an identification of phenomena to be investigated. Price theory has defined and clarified a general material welfare emphasis in approaching industrial behavior. It has defined market performance, showed it to be crucial, and identified its principal dimensions to be studied. Similarly, it has demonstrated the possible relevance of market structure and conduct in explaining performance, defined these things and identified their strategic dimensions, and suggested a plan for empirical study. Theory, therefore, represents a systematic advanced consideration of what is important to study, or what is relevant, as we examine a mass of empirical data.

But some more specific relationships between investigation and theory should also be recognized. A first purpose of our investigation is to implement price theory by determining the relative importance *in fact* of the various hypothetical structural situations which theory imagines. Price theory sets forth the possible broad categories of atomistic industries, oligopolies, and monopolies—and various subcategories of these broad groups—attaching some predictions of market conduct and performance to each. As a first step, it is interesting to determine how many and what proportion of actual industries in the American economy fit in each of these categories and subcategories, and to know the relative actual importance of atomism, oligopoly, difficult entry, product differentiation, and so on.

Given this knowledge, we might, if we were ready to accept without test the hypotheses of theory concerning market conduct and performance in each market category, simply stop there and conclude that conduct and performance in our various industries are as inferred from the theory. Some students of industrial organization have done approximately this. The procedure is not satisfactory, however, for several reasons.

First, the empirical measurement of market structure cannot always be entirely adequate and accurate, so that we cannot be certain of our empirical classification of industries. If we are not, empirical study of actual conduct and performance would be essential even if we depended implicitly on theoretical hypotheses. Second, theoretical predictions of conduct and performance are in several respects so vague, indefinite, or "iffish" that we desire to resolve the indefiniteness by systematically measuring actual conduct and performance in the strategic dimensions, thus answering questions not fully answered by theory. Third, even where theory is "definite" in its predictions, it is definite only in a qualitative sense (offering greater-or-less, higher-or-lower judgments). We may wish to implement its qualitative predictions with quantitative measurements, since the absolute magnitudes involved may be quite relevant as a basis for forming public policy judgements.

Finally, the predictions of theory are after all only hypotheses, and they could be inaccurate or wrong in various respects. This is not likely to be because of faulty logic in theoretical deductions, which have usually been thoroughly checked, but it might be due to faulty or insufficient assumptions. Attempts to test theory by confronting its predictions of conduct and performance with empirical evidence, and if possible thus confirming or disconfirming its hypotheses, are therefore in order.

The preceding obviously suggests several further aspects of the orientation of empirical investigation to price theory:

1. The systematic empirical study of market conduct and market performance (ideally in all industries, practically in a representative cross section of them) in order to supplement information on market structure with systematic data on conduct and performance.

2. The use of these data to find empirical answers to questions unanswered by price theory—to see what does happen in dimensions of conduct and performance with respect to which theoretical predictions are indefinite, ambivalent, or unavailable.(An example would be to appraise the actual impact of product differentiation on the character and development of products, or of high concentration on technological progressiveness.)

3. The use of the same data to give quantitative implementation to the qualitative predictions of theory. (For example, if theory predicts "higher" profits with higher concentration, the aim of empirical investigation would be to see how much higher such profits are in fact.)

4. The analysis of data on structure, conduct, and performance to test and, if possible, confirm or disconfirm the predictions of price theory. (Such testing may take the form in part of testing for predicted associations among structure, conduct, and performance, but it may also take other forms.)

5. The development and use of empirical findings in general as a basis for elaborating and reformulating theory in order to make it provide a more satisfactory explanation of observed phenomena. (This process may involve simply introducing added complexities into the

theory to make it more realistic; it could involve a basic revision of crucial assumptions.)

We proceed along all of these lines to some extent as we study industrial organization: drawing upon price theory for orientation, trying to answer some of the questions it poses, testing it critically, and also making suggestions for its improvement.

Political Consequences of Industrial Organization

Industrial organization, as we have seen, can be appraised theoretically from the standpoint of its impact on the production and distribution of material goods. Such an appraisal is a task of conventional economic theory. It can also be appraised in terms of its effects on social and political institutions, the politico-social relationships of individuals, and the nature and working of government generally. The second sort of appraisal, moreover, is not *of necessity* logically independent of the first. The material-welfare appraisals of conventional economic theory are appraisals of the working of a private enterprise system operating thorugh a complex of relatively unregulated free markets. The theory thus presupposes the maintenance of political institutions and a governmental system under which private enterprise and free markets will survive as the dominant basis of economic organization. But it does not itself analyze the conditions for the maintenance of this political and governmental setting. If now it were true that the very sort of industrial organization which economic theory analyzes tended to undermine and eventually alter or destroy the political basis for the economic system being analyzed, economic theory would have overlooked much. Its predictions would have at best a very temporary validity, and a theory of political-economic evolution would be required to elicit the longer-term implications of contemporary industrial organization.

Many economists faced with these possibilities have drawn solace from the fact that in the United States at any rate our political institutions, though always evolving, have showed a remarkable basic stability in the face of changes in industrial organization. Thus they believe that the political foundations for a private-enterprise market economy have not been and are not likely soon be overturned by the industrial organization which has evolved and is evolving. A neglect of the political implications of industrial organization is excused, therefore, not on the ground that these implications are unimportant, but on the ground that they are not such as to undermine the validity of the predictions (*vis a vis* material welfare) of conventional economic theories. This position seems to many economists, including the writer, valid to the extent that the predictions of conventional economic theory are likely to be generally meaningful and valid at least for the medium term of decades which most people contemplate. It leaves open the fact that a different order of theory is required to explain and predict the process of socio-politico-economic evolution extending over much longer periods of time.

However this may be, there is a body of theorizing with primary emphasis on the political and social implications of situations or changes in industrial organization. This theory should not be (and in practice is not) neglected in considering the overall merit of public policies affecting industrial organization. We do not attempt any comprehensive or formal survey of such theory here, but mention briefly two or three principal lines of thought which have been influential in the recent American scene.

A major line of thought especially persistent in the United States since its earliest days tends to emphasize the incompatibility of concentrated wealth, and thus of concentrated economic power and concentrated control of economic activity, with a viable and workable system of democratic government. Democracy finds its best setting, according to this idea, with a large electorate of persons (though one not necessarily including all the population) of relatively similar wealth, economic position, and power; and in particular in the absence of any oligarchy of relatively few very wealthy and powerful men whose position is higher than that of the rest of the electorate. A voting population made up entirely of small land-owning farmers in an agrarian country would do nicely; there would not be significant differences in wealth and power, nor in economic class, interest, or status.

According to this Jeffersonian ideal, the introduction of great disparities in wealth and in economic power is held to corrupt the working of democracy, particularly so far as the representative government, in both legislative and administrative branches, tends to become controlled or unduly influenced by the relatively few rich and powerful. If this happens, the different economic interests of these as opposed to other groups in society will lead them to favor and secure legislative and administrative policies in their interests and not in the interests of the bulk of the electorate.

In the elaboration and historical development of this theory, families of great wealth have come in for their share of attention. But a great deal of attention has also been given to our concentrated industrial organization, wherein a substantial fraction of industrial activity is controlled by a few hundred of our largest corporations, giving positions of considerable influence to the principal shareholders and to the managements of these corporations. The alleged working of the tendencies to which the theory refers is documented by reference to the influence on elections of large campaign contributions, the effects of lobbying and the purchase of "influence" in securing legislation or administration favorable to large economic interests, the periodic dominance of top executive positions in government by representatives of big business management, and so forth.

Taken in a mild form and without strong overtones of clairvoyance about future developments, this line of thought points to some of the apparent or possible political consequences of the development of concentrated industry and of the corresponding concentrated wealth and control. It generally characterizes these consequences as undesirable from the standpoint of the working of a democratic government. Other theories characterize parallel consequences on the sociological level.

The policy conclusion drawn from this line of theorizing is that concentration of the control of economic affairs, through concentrated big business or other similar concentrations, should be opposed *per se* as a matter of political principle. Its development should be limited, and existing concentration should be reduced as feasible. This is quite aside from the explicit impacts of various forms of industrial organization on the strictly material welfare of the populace. The preservation of (or reversion to) a situation in which economic units are very numerous, individually small, and relatively powerless, becomes an end in itself. The argument may be buttressed, moreover, by a general defense of atomism in economic organization as the safest choice in the long run, and also as most consistent with the spirit of democracy, because with atomism the impersonal controlling force of markets is dominant over all attempts of individuals to use power in controlling economic affairs. Generally, of course, the extent to which atomism is actually sought is tempered by considerations of the effects of industrial organization on material welfare.

It is not a long leap from the sort of analytical-descriptive theory just described to theories embodying prognoses of the concomitant evolutions of industrial and political structure. The familiar Marxian doctrine embodied among others the predictions (1) that the evolution of capitalism will involve inevitably ever higher concentration of ownership and control of industry (for reasons which on close analysis are not entirely convincing); (2) that a schism between the capitalist class and the worker class will develop and widen, the latter class being exploited economically by the former; (3) that the capitalist class will dominate the governmental system, securing national policies in their interests; (4) that a breaking point will come, with control passing ultimately to the working class under socialism. Neo-Marxian doctrines, aided by second guessing after the events of the interwar period in Western Europe, are likely to retain the Marxian notions about the steady march toward higher and higher concentration. But they point out that the breaking point may lead instead, at least temporarily, to the establishment of a dictatorial fascism in which the capitalist class secures a position of dominant power over other classes.

In the years accompanying and just following the maturity and collapse of German Nazism, it was fashionable to suggest that the development of industrial concentration in capitalism not only facilitated but led almost inevitably to the rise of fascist government. (The theory at least "explained" a couple of decades of experience for two countries.) More moderate and perhaps less doctrinaire theses point to the alleged fascistic tendencies inherent in the unchecked development of industrial concentration. In nearly all versions of Marxian and neo-Marxian theory, the process of concentration of power and control in industry, which is represented as almost indefinitely cumulative, is viewed as creating favorable preconditions for a revolution leading either to socialism or to fascism. We will not pause here to examine further variants of neo-Marxian doctrine concerning the interrelation of industrial and political development. Generally, such theories have been much more successful in rationalizing past events than in predicting future ones.

There is a theory of political development in the face of the observed evolution of industrial organization which is designed better to rationalize the last half-century's experience in the United States. This theory emphasizes a process of action and reaction wherein the rise of one economically and politically powerful group induces, or at any rate is matched by, the emergence of other opposing and equally powerful groups, so that a balance of power of opposing groups results, replacing the Jeffersonian type of democracy. Thus "big business" opposes "big labor," and we also have organized farm interests, organized small-business interests, and the like. In the working of markets, the bargaining of large opposing groups is viewed as a fairly adequate substitute, in terms of the performance it yields, for the impersonal market forces of atomistic competition. Similarly, the balancing of the power of these groups at the political level is viewed as not inconsistent with the continued effective and fair functioning of representative government in a democracy. The policy implications of this line of thought are that industrial and other types of concentration are not necessarily to be opposed *per se* on political grounds; rather, the problem is to encourage adequately representative power groupings and a balance of power and bargaining strength. It seems fair to say that the comparative merits of this economic and political system of "countervailing power," as it has been called, have not been thoroughly analyzed by the main proponents of the doctrine.

About these theories and others of the same order, several things may generally be said. They are essentially theories of historical development which emphasize, among other things, the impact of changes in industrial organization on the character of government, on the political relationships of individuals and groups, and on political behavior. They generally take the form of loose rationalizations of past experience and casual projections of this experience into predictions of future events. They are very difficult to "test" conclusively, though historical developments both consistent and inconsistent with such theories can frequently be detected. Finally, they refer in the main to a quite different range of social phenomena from those emphasizd in conventional economic theory. Both sorts of theory are correspondingly partial or restricted in their orientation and scope. Conventional price theory, for example, examines the working of markets within the going framework of political and social institutions, with those institutions operating as they do. The sort of theory we have just been discussing deals with the effects of developments in industrial organization on the development of the institutional framework, and on the way in which existing political and social institutions operate.

What is the relevance of these sociopolitical theories to the study of industrial organization? Like any other theories, they can, if accepted at face value, provide stereotypes in terms of which the significance of empirical information on industrial structure and its evolution can be appraised and evaluated. Similarly, they may serve as the basis of recommendations for public policy. Whether or not this is an uncautious procedure, they are in fact frequently so used.

More cautiously and more scientifically, these theories may be viewed simply as hypotheses to be tested through the extremely careful observation of political phenomena and their relation to economic phenomena, with the possibilities of confirmation, disconfirmation, elaboration, and revision of the theories all being open.

As noted above, testing these hypotheses is normally very difficult with the information ordinarily at hand. In any event, we do not attempt it in this book, nor do we report on the sort of empirical investigation on which such testing could be based. This important task must be left for other studies. We do, however, take some account of the relevant theoretical stereotypes as they bear on the explanation of the formulation of public policies toward business.

SUPPLEMENTARY READINGS

Chamberlin, E. H., *The Theory of Monopolistic Competition*, 1933.
Fellner, W., *Competition Among the Few*, 1949, Ch. 1.
Bain, J. S., *Price Theory*, 1952, Ch. 4–7.
Galbraith, J. K., *American Capitalism*, 1952.
Schumpeter, J. A., *Capitalism, Socialism, and Democracy*, 1942, Parts I and II.

3

Environment of American Industrial Organization

Our study of industrial organization centers on appraising the market performance of American business enterprise and on establishing its association with certain determinants. A principal hypothesis is that market performance may be systematically determined by market structure and market conduct. But the meaning of "determined" in this hypothesis is subject to interpretation.

Suppose that by market structure we mean simply the organizational characteristics of markets which establish various interrelations of sellers and buyers, and by market conduct the behavior patterns followed by enterprises in adjusting to their markets. Then we cannot mean that structure and conduct are the sole, sufficient, and complete determinants of the way in which enterprises perform. Any complex aspect of human behavior has many determinants, and this is true in the fullest sense of the market performance of enterprises. Market structure and conduct clearly represent only a small fraction of the total determinants of market performance.

When we suggest that they may "determine" market performance, the most we can mean is that, given the character of all the other important and perhaps more basic determinants, they "make a difference" in the performance that will emerge, or have some systematic influence on it. Given its many other important determinants, performance may be expected to differ somewhat from industry to industry in response to interindustry differences in market structure and conduct. We isolate and emphasize the influence on market performance of these particular determining variables because they appear to have an important differentiating influence and because, if we wish to influence performance via public policy, these determinants are to a considerable extent mutable and subject to deliberate modification. On the other hand, many more basic determinants of enterprise performance are relatively inflexible and slowly changing. Correspondingly, these are not subject to purposive modification in order to secure early revisions in performance.

The procedure of isolating the influence of certain strategic determinants of human behavior is not peculiar to the study of industrial organization. For example, we might explore the hypothesis that the number of hours required for a person to learn to operate an airplane proficiently depends on the person's age, sex, and height, and might test and find some systematic associations. In a given setting, or taking certain basic determinants as given, the age-sex-height combination might indeed have a systematic influence on learning speed for pilots. But it would also obviously be true that this ability depended on many other things as well, including things other than the individual's personal characteristics.

First, for the question to make some sense, we would have to have airplanes; the question is meaningless as applied to the population of the eighteenth century. Second, learning speed might depend a good deal on the physical environment and stage of economic and technological development in which the student pilots live, especially as this would determine their conditioning to mechanical apparatus. The design of airplanes in question, whether propellor- or jet-driven, should be taken into account. Finally, the culture in which the people in question have been brought up will have its influence. For example, is it a culture in which operating machinery, traveling fast, and flying are generally approved pursuits? The list of other basic determinants could be extended.

Our initial hypothesis, concerning the association of age-sex-height to learning speed for pilots, is thus meaningful only in the rather narrow setting given and on the assumption that many other determinants are given. It does not really explain everything about pilot learning ability, but only some things that make a difference, let us say, in the United States in the mid-twentieth century. Also, we have probably mentioned only part of the immediate personal characteristics of students that might be significant in this limited setting. Even so, the association of learning speed to age, sex, and height may be an interesting and important thing to know for purposes of the immediate future.

The same general order of limitations applies to explaining market performance through market structure and conduct. These things make a difference, assuming the going framework of events, but there are numerous other important determinants of performance which, for purposes of our study, we accept and assume to be more or less given. These include generally the physical, human, institutional, and cultural environment in which capitalistic economies, and particularly that of the United States, find their setting at this stage in time.

In the first place, to have market performance as defined, we must have markets, specifically free markets in which private enterprises buy and sell goods according to their own individual interests. This presupposes in general the governmental and institutional framework of capitalism as we know it. Investigation of market performance would be meaningless for a feudal society, or for a fully socialized society with governmental control of all production; it is meaningful only in some institutional settings, including our own. Furthermore, we presuppose a culture in which the pursuit of material welfare and the "commercial pursuit" of such welfare through seeking profit in private enterprise are generally approved and emphasized as proper goals for human beings. The human behavior we explain is that of people with certain main aims, motivations, and mores which we find now, but which have not been found universally at all places and times. Also, the results or performance which emerge from enterprise activity within the going institutional and cultural framework are conditioned and framed not only by market structure and conduct, but also by the fundamental physical environment (including the geography of the land, its resources, and so on), and by the going state of technology, accumulated scientific knowledge, and the characteristics of the human population.

All of these things are parts of the determining framework of the phases of economic behavior being observed. Within this framework, market structure and conduct are held to have some influence on the character of the market performance of enterprises. Thus before we start our study of contemporary market performance, conduct, and structure we should emphasize strongly the importance of the basic framework which we assume and within which our problem is set, and should consider, in brief review, some of the major outlines of this framework.

Institutional, Physical, and Technological Environment

Capitalism, according to a brief dictionary definition, is "the economic system of modern countries in which the ownership of land and natural wealth, the production, distribution, and exchange of goods, and the operation of the system itself, are effected by private enterprise and control under competitive conditions." On the understanding that the term "competitive conditions" is to be construed quite broadly, as referring to the general rivalry of enterprises for advantage in markets, this is a good capsule definition. Some aspects of the institutional framework implied, however, deserve emphasis.

The basic institution, recognized and supported in law, is that of individual private property in natural resources and in instruments of production, as well as in personal goods. Land, mineral resources, factories, stores, and capital goods in general may be and predominantly are owned by private individuals or groups thereof. This private ownership bestows on individuals the rights of exclusive use, of control of the manner of use, and of receiving such income, earning, or other advantage as redounds from the chosen use. Thus the productive natural resources and facilities are predominantly owned and controlled by private individuals, for such purposes as they elect—in the United States by a very large number of such individuals or associations thereof.

Correlative to the rights of private property in productive goods are implied responsibilties. That is, having the exclusive use and control of natural resources and capital goods, private individuals have the residual responsibility of supervising and directing the use of these things— to them falls the burden of "entrepreneurship" and of management of productive resources and goods. They must continually make the decisions as to how and for what the resources and facilities will be used. They may delegate management and decision making to employees, but the responsibility is ultimately theirs. Thus the decisions as to how production shall be carried on, and how its fruits are to be distributed and exchanged, are made piecemeal, in decentralized fashion, and without the control or coordination of higher authority, by many individual owners or ownership interests. They are made, moreover, in the light of whatever individual aims, motivations, and feelings of responsibility to others these owners have.

The basic resource which is not acquired as private property is human labor. Barring slavery, individuals or the perpetual rights to their services may not be owned by others; each person owns himself. Instead, labor may sell its services under a system of free contract. Since the productive facilities are in general owned by private individuals, this arrangement leads to the system of purchase and sale of labor services, with the individual owners or owner-groups acting as buyers and the individual laborers (or groups thereof) as sellers. In this way the owners of natural resources and capital goods, continually purchasing labor services to combine with the services of their inanimate property, also assume in general the responsibility of determining the manner and direction of use of labor resources. This is at any rate true except for those laborers—servants or psychiatrists, for example—who can sell their services direct to the final user without another employer acting as intermediary.

The ownership of property and direction and control of production, including most of the output of human labor, thus is the task of many individual owners or groups of owners, or of employees to whom they delegate these tasks. Each individual "ownership unit" of assets and operations falling under a separate control or management, legally separate from and independent of other such units, is identifiable as a business enterprise. A multitude of such private enterprises control and direct production activity under capitalism, and it is certain aspects of the performance of these enterprises with which we are concerned.

Private ownership plus free contract for labor alone, however, does not give us capitalism in its modern form. If every ownership unit were a self-sufficient farm which traded with no others and paid wages in kind from its produce, the economy would partake more of feudal than of modern capitalistic characteristics. Therefore, essential additional aspects of the technological and institutional organization of modern capitalism are: (1) Production is highly variegated and specialized, so that the individual enterprise produces only one or a few goods of many which are used, and thus produces not primarily for the use of its owners and employees but for exchange for the specialized outputs of other enterprises. (2) Exchange is accomplished largely through a highly developed monetary system in which goods are bought and sold for money; wages and owner incomes are received in money and then spent for goods, and money acts as a medium of exchange in nearly all transactions. The private enterprise emerges as an entity which predominantly buys labor, materials, capital goods, and so forth for money, sells its output for money, and garners an earning for its owners in the form of money ready to spend. Thus also emerge markets in the modern sense: closely interrelated groups of buyers and sellers exchanging goods or services for money.

To what we have already named must probably be added the prevailing culture and mores of the people who function within the system, since the viability and to a considerable extent the identity of capitalism depend on the attitudes, aims, and motivations of the people who participate in it. In general, capitalism has grown up and exists in a culture which accepts and approves the pursuit of material wealth as a main goal of human activity. Moreover, it approves the pursuit of material gain by each individual selfishly and more or less in rivalry with others. If each individual strives independently to enhance his own gain, he is doing a thing which is socially accepted and approved.

Correlatively, the pursuit of monetary profit by enterprises constitutes the pursuit of an acceptable goal. Furthermore, such commercial pursuits, especially if successful, generally have a status superior to or equal to that of other pursuits. The occupation of the businessman in general carries with it a prestige equal to or greater than that of the soldier, public official, teacher, or clergyman.

These attitudes provide a necessary basis for the patterns of behavior followed by people in their economic activity, and especially by the owners or managers of enterprises. Thus the aggressive pursuit of profit in rivalry with others, and correspondingly the aggressive endeavor to enhance profits by lowering costs, seeking new customers, and so forth, develop as corollaries of the basic cultural attitudes in question. In brief, the patterns of action which enterprises follow in responding to various market opportunities or situations which face them—what they *do* when presented with the responsibility of directing economic affairs—are in a general way determined by the surrounding culture. In attempting to explain market conduct and performance, we presuppose and take as given the basic culture which conditions people's attitudes, and correspondingly the typical aims, motivations, and restraints which guide and limit their actions. The explanations and predictions of market conduct and performance which we develop for American capitalism might in consequence have slight applicability to a "capitalism" set in a culture in which excessive material gain was shunned, wealth was sin, poverty was the ideal state, and quiet contemplation was supposed to occupy all time not needed to earn a bare subsistence.

Economic theory, discussed in Chapter 2, has attempted to grasp the simplified essence of the motivational patterns common to enterprises in capitalism by asserting (and then assuming for purposes of deductive argument) that enterprises in general will order and guide their operations in such a way as to *maximize their profits.* What goods to produce, the amount to be produced and sold, the prices to be charged and so on, will be determined by each enterprise in such a way as to maximize its profit. Productive activity will become organized and take its course as the result of many enterprises doing this in rivalry and independently, thus as a group responding to the demands of consumers for goods.

The profit-maximization hypothesis has long seemed to square fairly well with the apparent ethics and behavior patterns of capitalism. But it is undoubtedly oversimplified, and of late many psychologists, economists, and others have argued at length that human motivational patterns in business are much more complex, and that a more adequate representation of actual motivations is needed for purposes of theorizing. At the least, the evolution of social attitudes in the last century and a half has modified the mores and motivations of businessmen, so that there are many more express or implied restraints on behavior aimed at profit making than there used to be. Correspondingly, the character of enterprise responses to various market situations has presumably undergone modifications, so that the responses differ somewhat from those of a simple, unrestrained, socially amoral profit-maximizer. But how much do they differ, and in what ways? What is the contemporary motivational pattern? On these matters, we are still distressingly short of systematic information. Our economic theory (assuming profit maximization) must be recognized to be oversimplified and capable of producing only crude approximation predictions of actual economic behavior. Yet, speaking of contemporary capitalism in a broad way, it still seems fair to say that the pursuit of monetary profit constitutes a main motivation or ordering principle of action for business enterprises generally, and that, subject to increasing limitations and restraints which actually modify the meaning of "maximizing a profit," profit maximization represents some sort of rough central tendency of endeavors.

A final aspect of the institutional framework of capitalism concerns the role of government. With resources and productive facilities owned and operated by private individuals, the theoretical role of government in the economic affairs of capitalism is that of a referee of individual conflicts and of a rule-maker to place certain minimal restraints, in the public interest, on the unbridled pursuit of individual gain. Otherwise, *laissez faire* is assumed to be the rule, and certainly the government does not engage in or control production, directly regulate private enterprises or persons, or otherwise interfere much with individual action. At all times actually, however, and increasingly in the twentieth century, government's role has actually been a bit more extensive. It has acted as a subsidizer of selected industries or lines of private enterprise endeavor, as a limited participant in production, as a direct regulator of private enterprise in certain industries, and as a customer for the outputs of private enterprises. In addition, of course, its fiscal operations, including the exercise of taxing and borrowing powers, have considerable influence on the propagation and maintenance of the flow of income in the economy. Thus actual contemporary capitalism is not the "pure" capitalism of theoretical *laissez faire*; its character is modified as government plays an ever larger role. Yet we can say, with respect to the United States, that we still have an economy of relatively unregulated private enterprise, in which the bulk of production and distribution is guided by the largely unregimented independent actions of many private business concerns.

The student may well inquire why, in outlining the broad characteristics of modern capitalism, we have so belabored the obvious aspects of the system. The most important reason is that we should recognize clearly at the beginning that the setting with which we are so familiar markedly differs from visible alternatives, and that our analysis of economic behavior within this framework is largely one which has meaning for this setting only. When we discuss industrial organization, with emphasis on market structure, conduct, and performance, we are discussing phenomena of modern capitalism, and not of modern or past economies generally. It is only when we find an economy whose production is guided by the independent actions of a number of unregulated private enterprises, selling their outputs for money in highly organized markets, and manned by owners and managers whose aim is to maintain or enhance enterprise profits, that we encounter most of the problems posed in our study of industrial organization. And the conclusions we arrive at will certainly be almost entirely limited in their applicability to modern capitalistic economies.

To this point, we have not explored at all the details of modern capitalistic institutions, but have confined ourselves to the bare skeleton of the system. Much could be added on labor unions, farm cooperatives, social insurance, the banking system, restraints on international trade, and so forth. Most of this we assume as a part of the general background knowledge of the reader, and will bring up only certain matters as they become relevant to our discussion.

The Physical Environment of the American Economy

Economic activity never takes place in a vacuum. It is set on the land, is related to natural resources, and engages a population. What shape it takes depends on the physical and human geography to which it is related and responds. Thus it is with industrial organization as a phase of economic activity. Before we can analyze and understand the industrial organization of the American economy, we need to consider, at least briefly, the general character of the land space on which it is set, the resources on which it depends, the human population which it draws upon and serves, and its relationships to all these things.

The economy of the United States is set on a middle band of the North American continent, about 1200 miles wide from north to south and stretching east to west from ocean to ocean. Most of the continent not included in the United States consists of a subtropical area to the south and (southern Canada excepted) subarctic and arctic lands to the north. The economy is a semi-isolated unit, set off from the other major economies of the world by distance and water as well as by political boundaries; it derives a considerable internal unity from operating under a single national political jurisdiction as well as from the geography of the continent. As a unit, the economy is largely self-sufficient in basic resources and in production. Some minerals and fuels, and some agricultural and forest products, are drawn from abroad, and some manufactured goods are obtained from other industrial countries, but a preponderant share of the goods consumed in the United States are domestically produced, just as a similar share of its production is domestically consumed. This self-sufficiency, though in some degree encouraged by political barriers to international trade, results mainly from the balanced supply of most essential resources within the country, plus the high costs of transport to other continents. The population of the United States in 1967 was about 190 million.

Geographers frequently identify as many as twelve or thirteen principal "regions" of the United States, on the basis of terrain, climate, and the like. Using a grosser classification, we may divide the country into six main regions, on the basis of terrain and of principal economic activity:

1. *The North Atlantic Seaboard* region, including New England on the north and running south roughly through Maryland, bounded on the west by the Adirondack and Appalachian mountain systems, and including major coastal cities like New York, Philadelphia, Boston, and Baltimore. This area is predominantly devoted to manufacturing, although there is considerable agriculture in truck crops for the cities. It has relatively ample rainfall and water resources.

2. *The Middle West*, stretching from the edge of the seaboard region on the east to a bit beyond the Mississippi on the west, to include Minnesota, Iowa, and northern Missouri, touching the Canadian border on the north and extending south roughly to the Missouri and Ohio rivers. This region, including most of the Great Lakes area and having generally large rainfall and adequate water resources, is the rich center of American agricultural production, especially of the basic grains. But it is also the center of our coal mining and is heavily industrialized. We may speak of the North Atlantic Seaboard and Middle West regions combined as constituting roughly the northeastern quarter of the United States.

3. *The South*, reaching from the Atlantic on the east, through eastern parts of Texas and Oklahoma on the west, encompassing in this band all territory south of the North Atlantic Seaboard and Middle West regions, and thus roughly the southeastern quarter of the United States. Again, a generally moist region except for its western fringe, the South

is predominantly agricultural, with diversified crops but a heavy emphasis on growing cotton. In addition, there is a moderately important manufacturing area in the eastern part of the South, considerable forestry, and, toward the western part, the major petroleum deposits of the country.

4. *The Great Plains*, running south to north from border to border in a band roughly including the western parts of Texas and Oklahoma; Kansas and Nebraska; the eastern parts of Colorado, Wyoming, and Montana; and the Dakotas. This area is mainly agricultural but has more limited rainfall and water. It has a large wheat production and very large amounts of grazing land.

5. *The Rocky Mountains and the Intermountain Basin and Plateau*, west of the Rockies. This area includes a border-to-border band of territory 600 to 800 miles wide, reaching from the Great Plains on the east to the Sierra Nevada-Cascade mountains of the Pacific Coast on the west. This great "desert" is largely mountainous or arid, or both, and in general sparsely populated. Mining, especially of nonferrous metals, resort operation, sparse grazing, dry farming, and patches of intensive agriculture where irrigation water can be brought from the mountains are the principal occupations, but much of the land is substantially desert.

6. *The Pacific Coast*, including the western parts of California, Oregon, and Washington—the coast which is west of the Sierra Nevada and Cascade mountain chain. This is a sort of "island" economy of agriculture (largely irrigated on the basis of mountain rain and snowfall), forestry, petroleum production, and manufacturing.

The principal economic occupations of these regions reflect the locations of basic natural resources. This is patently clear in the case of the extractive industries—agriculture, forestry, mining, petroleum production—which generally are tied locationally to resource deposits.

Agriculture is based on fertile and adequately watered land, principally the low lands of the Middle West, South, and Great Plains areas, and forestry on forests as they remain, mainly at present the coniferous forests of the South and of the northern half of the Pacific Coast. A second main sort of extractive industry produces fuels and other sources of heat and power. The basic mineral fuel, coal (which supplies about half of the national energy requirements), is found in high grade mainly in (1) the northern and middle Appalachian fields, running from western Pennsylvania and eastern Ohio through West Virginia and eastern Kentucky; (2) the interior fields of Illinois, western Indiana, and western Kentucky; and (3) the southern Appalachian fields, largely in northern Alabama. The other main mineral fuel, petroleum (supplying 40 per cent of national energy requirements), comes in large part from the pools of the Texas, Oklahoma, and Gulf Coast area, and otherwise in the main from the Pacific Coast, Rocky Mountain, and Middle West regions. Hydroelectric power, the third main energy source (supplying about 10 per cent of national energy requirements), is developed about one-third on the Pacific Coast, one-third in the Southeast, one-sixth in the Northeast, one-eighth in the Rocky Mountain area, and negligibly elsewhere. A third category of extractive industry mines the major nonfuel minerals. Here we find the principal mineral ore, yielding iron, in large part in the Lake Superior regions of Minnesota, Wisconsin, and Michigan. The major nonferrous metal ores—copper, zinc, lead, aluminum—are less concentrated in locality, but come in considerable part from the Rocky Mountain and Intermountain Basin regions.

In these and similar resource locations, we find a sufficient explanation for the location of our extractive industries and for a part of the economic specializations of the various regions. Of a rural farm population of about 14 million persons in the United States in 1960, the Midwest, South, and Plains regions accounted for about 84 per cent, and the South alone for nearly 45 per cent. Two-fifths of the population of the South is rural, and a tenth of it is rural farmers. Nearly a third of the Middle West population is rural, and about a tenth is rural farmers. Similar relationships of occupation to region are found in coal and other mining, petroleum production, lumbering, and so on, although these occupations, of course, engage much smaller proportions of the population.

In a highly industrialized country like ours, however, manufacturing engages more of the population than do extractive industries, and the location of manufacturing industry is of dominant importance in the geographical picture. In the United States, almost 70 per cent of all manufacturing activity is concentrated in a major "manufacturing belt" running through the North Atlantic Seaboard and Middle West regions. If we run a line west from the middle coast of New England (above Boston) to Milwaukee on the western shore of Lake Michigan, loop south along the western border of Illinois to take in St. Louis, and proceed eastward along the Ohio River valley through West Virginia and to Chesapeake Bay, we have more or less defined this manufacturing belt. The area contained is about a tenth of that of the continental United States, but the population is nearly half that of the country as a whole. The area includes nine of the first ten industrial cities in the country.

Principal centers within the belt include (1) New England, emphasizing textiles, shoes, electrical and other machinery, and fabricated metal products; (2) the New York metropolitan area, with garment industries, petroleum refining, printing, and electrical machinery; (3) the Middle Atlantic area, with diversity of industry, including steel, refining, shipyards, garments, and instruments; (4) the northern New York, or Troy-Buffalo area, with steel, steel-using, chemical, and flour-milling industries; (5) the Pittsburgh-Cleveland area, with steel, rubber products, glass, chemicals, machinery, and machine tools; (6) southern Michigan, with motor vehicles and parts, machinery, and primary and fabricated metals; (7) the Chicago-Gary-Milwaukee area, with steel, farm machinery, machine tools, meat packing, and refining; (8) the St. Louis area, with diversified industry which particularly includes machinery, aircraft, and paper.

This main manufacturing belt clearly contains the heart of American manufacturing activity and also represents the center of city population and of markets for the country. The remaining 30 per cent of manufacturing activity is more or less scattered, but two-thirds of the remainder is concentrated in the South, in two belts. In the Southeast, from southern Virginia through the Carolinas and Northern Georgia and Alabama and into Tennessee, the important industries are steel, textiles, lumber, furniture, and tobacco products. In a series of nodes from Houston to Wichita there is diversified industry, with an emphasis on meat packing, flour milling, aircraft, petroleum refining, and chemicals.

The concentration of manufacturing in the northeastern quarter of the United States cannot be viewed in the main as an historical accident; it developed in response to systematic forces. Very important among these forces was the availability of fuel for the power and heat consumed in manufacture. With the bulk of good coal deposits located from the western edge of the North Atlantic Seaboard through the Middle West, and with coal heavy and expensive to transport, the development of major manufacturing activity more or less contiguous to the coal deposits was a predictable phenomenon. (One secondary manufacturing belt of the South is similarly based in part on important coal deposits.) Given this "resource-pull" attracting industry toward coal, plus the concentration of agricultural population and production in the Middle West as market and raw-material supply, plus the contiguous supply of iron ore around Lake Superior, the existing pattern emerged and tends to remain. The subsequent development of petroleum and hydroelectric energy resources in other regions has favored locational diversification of industry to some extent, but not yet enough to modify greatly the established pattern.

This geographical concentration of manufacturing is particularly strong in heavy or primary manufacturing industries using heavy materials—especially steel—and large amounts of heat and power. For such industries, localization of coal deposits favored a roughly corresponding localization of manufacturing plants. There are, of course, other categories of manufacturing industry which are less "resource-oriented," and more oriented to finding cheap labor supplies (garment manufacture) or to producing near populations and markets (bricks or ice cream). These latter industries frequently have geographically decentralized production, being dispersed according to the distribution of population. When we proceed to wholesale and retail distribution and to the service trades, we find industries almost completely market-oriented, with productive activity decentralized and locationally distributed according to population.

So much for the principal economic regions of the United States, their physical and occupational characteristics, and their resources. Industry has organized itself geographically mainly in response to the features of these regions. And so have the population, the demands for goods, and the markets. The population of the United States, roughly 180 million in 1960 was distributed about as follows by regions:

Northeast quarter (roughly the North Atlantic Seaboard and Middle West)	53 per cent
Southeast quarter ("the South")	25 per cent
Great Plains	7 per cent
Rocky Mountains and Intermountain Basin	4 per cent
Pacific Coast	11 per cent

Both productive activity and markets are regionally distributed in about these proportions, though there are differences among regions in per capita output and income. There is specialization by regions, and corresponding interregional exchange, in a well-defined pattern. The broadest outlines of this pattern depict the North Atlantic Seaboard as specialized in manufacture and an importer of agricultural and mineral products; the Middle West diversified with agriculture, fuel resources, and manufacturing; the South and the Plains specializing in extractive industry and supplying farm, forest products, and petroleum to the North while on balance importing manufactured goods; the Pacific Coast in the same general position but more nearly balanced between the extractive and manufacturing industries.

When we turn to the many individual industries, much more complicated and variegated locational patterns emerge. In the manufacturing industries, some of the general features are:

1. Heavily concentrated in the main manufacturing belt of the northeastern quarter of the country are the iron and steel industry and most industries making heavy products from steel (automobiles except for final assembly, agricultural implements, industrial machinery, railroad equipment, machine tools, major household appliances, and so on). Also located in this area are industries for nonferrous metal products, electrical machinery, boots and shoes, glass products, paper, and the like. In many of these industries production is much more concentrated geographically than the market for the goods produced. Also, producers in an industry may frequently be close enough together for all to be in general competition for a common national market.

2. There are some important industries with geographically concentrated production for which the locational center of production is elsewhere. Cotton textiles and manufactures, centered in the Southeast and the North Atlantic Seaboard, and lumber products, centered in the South and the Pacific Northwest, are two examples.

3. A number of industries are semidispersed roughly according to population, so that there are several major regional producing centers in different parts of the country. Examples are petroleum refining, flour milling, cement, and wallboard and plaster products. The national markets for the products of these industries are frequently segmented by regions, with different groups of producing plants largely specialized to different regions.

4. There are other industries which are widely dispersed according to population, with production close to nearly every center of population. These include the bakery goods, meat packing, beer, clay products, machine shop, printing, and numerous other industries; in them, there is a tendency for many semi-separate local markets to exist, each supplied by a different group of local producing plants.

The resulting variety in locational relations of producing plants to each other and to markets will appear, as we proceed, to be an important aspect of market structures.

The Technological Environment

As important as the supply of inanimate and human resources to an economy is the technology which it has inherited—the basic and applied scientific knowledge upon which its industrial arts are founded. The scope of our present technology is of course huge and advanced as compared to that of two centuries ago. It includes not only the knowledge of machines, devices, and processes for producing various goods, but also the design of a very large number of products which were unknown in a more primitive state of economic affairs. Basically, technology is knowledge or "know-how," but at any given time it is implemented by the availability of a varied complex of capital goods used in production.

The basic technological developments, upon which the emergence of the present form of industrial society was immediately based, include the steam engine, permitting the economical conversion of the heat of fuel into motive power; process machinery (first for spinning thread and weaving cloth) suitable for operation with this power; and the use of the steam engine for transportation power, in railroads and ships. From this beginning, technology has been improved and elaborated rapidly through time. In the provision of power, replacement of the piston steam engine with the steam turbine, conversion of steam and water power into electrical power through dynamos, and the development of producing machinery run by electric motors have all been important, as has been the development of various types of internal combustion engines. Another basic development was the introduction of new techniques of steel making—especially the use of coked coal in blast furnaces to extract iron from its ore, and of much more efficient contrivances to reduce iron to steel. Following upon the resultant general availability of cheap steel, we have witnessed a complex and varied development of steel machinery to perform various manufacturing tasks.

Parallel to these later developments have been two others of great importance—in chemical processes and in electricity and electronics. Chemical processes have been developed to exploit the chemical properties and reactions of various raw materials in order to produce useful and often novel goods: explosives, plastics, synthetic fibers, petroleum products, rubber goods, synthetic rubber, paper, and so forth. Similarly, electricity has been exploited through the development of electric motors, lights, heating elements, and communication devices, and in the development of chemical technology. More recently, electronics has applied the knowledge of electrical impulses to the development of numerous products and processes, embracing such things as radio, television, radar, automation in the control of machine operations in production, and computation. A new technique and source of power production is currently emerging from the development of atomic fission and fusion.

These technological innovations have left us with knowledge and possession of a fantastic array of products, devices, and processes, and it is from the resulting technology that our industries have drawn their present complex and variegated forms. Classification of industries by type of dominant technology is difficult because various sorts of technique are combined and interact in any industry. We will not comment here on technologies in the extractive industries or in industries in the transportation, communications, public utilities, or distributive and service trade sectors. In manufacturing and construction, some major groups of industries may be classified according to industrial technique as follows:

The Food Processing Industries. These mainly perform traditional and long-known functions such as converting grain to food, animals to meat and fat, vegetables to canned foods, milk to various products. In them, machinery is widely applied to tasks earlier performed by hand. Also, chemistry is applied to processing, and there is a proliferation of more highly finished end products. But in general the technology is comparatively simple and more slowly changing than in many other areas.

The Textile Industries. Initially, these spun natural fibers into thread and wove the thread into cloth. The basic machine techniques for spinning and weaving, employing steam and later electric power, were developed early and, although progressively improved, have not been fundamentally changed for a long time. They have been adapted to the use of synthetic fibers as these have become available.

The Apparel Industries. These sew cloth into clothes, and leather and other materials into shoes. Power machinery has been applied to assist workmen in the performance of many tasks, but these important industries have proceeded the smallest distance of any important industrial category away from handwork and toward mechanization and automation. A completely or largely machine-produced suit or shoe, for example, is still not a practical reality.

The Construction Industries. Housebuilding, industrial and commercial construction, road, bridge, and dam building all fall in this category. New mechanical devices, materials, and processes have been widely applied in these industries, including steel, cement, bulldozers, power saws, and so forth. Yet the development has been limited largely to better tools and new materials. Factory organization of production, with the drastic revision of process which often accompanies it has not developed, because of the nature of the functions performed and of the tying of individual construction tasks to different widely dispersed sites.

(If we take the food processing, textile, apparel, and construction industries together, we have encompassed food, clothing, and basic shelter as well as a good deal more. Although pervaded by machine and related techniques, the industries supplying these necessities generally feature a relatively simple and slowly progressing technology, and generally are not the areas dominated by gigantic enterprises based on huge aggregations of the most complex and advanced capital equipment. On food, clothing, and shelter the consumers of the United States spent about 67 per cent of their incomes in 1960.)

The Metal-Producing Industries. These extract the basic metals from their ores, purify them, and fashion the raw metal into primary products such as sheets, construction members, wire, pipe and so forth. In the steel industry, the technology features the application of heat from coal first to the ore to produce iron, and then to the iron to produce steel; and thereafter the use of machines in rolling and shaping the steel into final products. In some of the nonferrous metals industries, comparable techniques are employed, but in some—for example, copper and aluminum—the final stages of extracting metal from ore employ electrolysis.

The Metal-Fabricating Industries. These, in general, convert primary metal products into various products for final use. Basic to this group is the machine-tool industry, producing the equipment to be used in fabricating primary metal products into final products—such as machines for stamping metal into automobile body parts and cutting it into axles and gears. Built on this base are a wide variety of metal fabricating industries producing such things as automobiles, aircraft, railway equipment, farm machinery, industrial machinery, metal furniture, building materials, household appliances, and tin cans. The processes of these industries are largely mechanical, involving the heavy use of machinery to form metal into parts through stamping, grinding, and so on, and to assemble the parts into finished devices. Large-scale production in individual plants is common.

The Stone, Clay, and Glass Products Industries. These generally convert stones and earths, such as limestone, gypsum, silica, and clay, into a variety of end products through the use of heat and of machinery for pulverizing and combining the materials. Techniques are again mechanical, and in numerous cases relatively simple and slowly changing as, for example, in the production of bricks and cement.

The Forest Products Industries. This group is generally devoted to turning trees into lumber and lumber into various finished products. It usually employs rather simple and static mechanical techniques.

The Chemical Process Industries. These in general are based on a distinctive technology, emphasizing the use of chemical reactions to convert raw materials into various products. In many of them, chemical and mechanical processes are employed together or in sequence, and in general the chemical processes employ large-scale mechanical equipment. Principal products of the chemical industries include basic materials like acids and alkalis, chemical compounds like explosives and fertilizers, synthetic materials like plastics, synthetic fibers, synthetic rubber, and finished products like paper, gasoline, and rubber tires. Generally, these industries have techniques lending themselves to efficient use in very large individual plants.

Spending Patterns and the Response
of Industrial Organization to Them

An aspect of capitalist economic organization emphasized above is that production is directed, and composition of the total output of goods and services determined, by a large number of private enterprises, each of which seeks financial gain through selling in markets. The proportions in which flour and beefsteak and automobiles and typewriters and theater performances are produced—and the number and size of the enterprises in each of the many industries—is the result of a myriad of individual enterprise decisions. A reciprocal and equally important aspect of this economic organization is that in making their decisions, enterprises are guided by the demands of buyers for goods and services: by the way in which consumers and other buyers offer to spend their incomes. Let us therefore look briefly at the pattern of contemporary spending in the American economy and the adaptation of our industrial organization to it.

In 1960, the total of personal consumption expenditures of all people in the United States was apportioned among broad categories about as follows:

Housing and household operation	29 per cent
Food, beverages, and tobacco	28 per cent
Transportation	15 per cent
Clothing	10 per cent
Medical	7 per cent
Recreation	4 per cent
Personal care	3 per cent
Reading and education	2 per cent
Other	2 per cent

Of the total spent, about 65 per cent went for commodities and 35 per cent for services. It is evident that most consumer spending, or about 67 per cent, still goes for the "basic necessities"—food, clothing, and shelter. After accounting for these things plus transportation (largely automotive), only 18 per cent of the consumer's income is left for other things. The appearance may be deceptive, however, if we try to infer the pattern of industrial organization from these gross figures.

In the first place, each of the "necessity" categories of expenditure actually goes for a wide variety of different goods and services, many not requisite for bare subsistence. There is a complex of goods to which manufacture has contributed a great deal of preparation and finishing which in earlier days was done in the home. Food includes not only baked bread, meat, fresh, canned, and frozen vegetables and fruit, and so forth, but also soda pop, alcoholic beverages, cigarettes, restaurant meals, and other things. Housing and household operation begin with the house itself, but include expenditures on electric and gas utilities, stoves, refrigerators, vacuum cleaners, numerous other electrical appliances, furniture, and so on. In each broad category of expenditure we find a similar breakdown into many different lines of expenditure on different goods supplied by different industries.

In the second place, the expenditure referred to is only consumers' expenditure. Much of the money thus spent, and received by enterprises supplying consumer goods, flows through these firms to others by being respent on producer goods. About 60 per cent of the gross value of all output sold by American firms is purchased by other firms, generally for further use in production. The producer of electric refrigerators, included under housing, spends part of his sales income on sheet steel, electric motors, paint, refrigerant gas, and the like, thus feeding a second level of producer-good industries with a flow of income and creating a demand for their goods. The expenditure of consumers on canned peas will begin a flow of income supporting the retail grocer, his wholesaler, the food canner, the can-producing company, the manufacturer of can-making and canning machinery, the steel mill, the iron mine, the tin mine, the makers of mining and steel mill machinery, and so forth. When producer-goods industries are taken into account, the organization of productive effort into separate industries appears even more variegated and complex.

Taking all influences into account, the proportions of net national income originating in the several broad sectors of economic activity in the United States in 1963 were about as follows:

Agriculture, forestry, and fisheries	3.9 per cent
Mining	1.1 per cent
Manufacturing	28.7 per cent
Wholesale and retail trade	16.2 per cent

Contract construction	5.2 per cent
Transportation, communication and public utilities	8.1 per cent
Services	12.4 per cent
Finance, insurance, and real estate	10.2 per cent
Government and government enterprises	13.5 per cent
Other	0.7 per cent

Certain broad facets of our industrial organization stand out in these figures. Manufacturing industries made up by far the most important sector of enterprise activity, contributing nearly 29 per cent of national income. Wholesale and retail trade industries, dominantly engaged in distributing manufactured goods, contributed roughly another 16 per cent. On the other hand, all extractive industries, supplying manufacture with basic raw materials, accounted for only 5 per cent of national income, much less than the service trades or the finance sector. Transportation industries (confined here to railroads, airlines, bus lines, etc.), plus electric, gas, and similar utility industries, plus telephone, radio, and other communication industries accounted together for about 8 per cent of national income. Federal, state, and local governments, including governmentally owned enterprises, were fairly important suppliers of goods and services. The dominance of manufacture and the distribution of manufactured output in an industrial economy, however, is most striking.

The sectors of enterprise activity just listed are generally very broad. Each is broken down into many industries, with each industry supplying a particular good, service, or related group thereof in such a pattern that the outputs of different industries are typically not very close substitutes for each other. The most revealing breakdown of sectors would be into "theoretical" industries as defined in Chapter 1. Statistics of the Bureau of Census provide a grouping of sellers by industries which misses this goal somewhat, but the Census breakdown gives some rough notion of the manner in which broad enterprise sectors are divided into industries.

The service trades, for example, include hotels, personal services, commercial schools, advertising, other business services, repair shops, motion pictures, other amusement industries, physicians, hospitals, lawyers, engineers, education, religion, and other categories. Agriculture is divisible into numerous industries on the basis of crop; mining into numerous industries on the basis of the mineral produced. Thus it is with each sector listed.

The most diverse subdivision is found in manufacturing. The 1963 Census of Manufactures recognized 417 manufacturing industries. If we followed theoretical principles more strictly, the number would be at least doubled. Some notion of their variety may be gathered from a listing of the 42 Census manufacturing industries that were largest in point of dollar sales volume in 1958:

Motor vehicles and parts
Petroleum refining
Steel
Meat packing
Aircraft
Radios and related products

Fluid milk
Paper and paperboard mills
Bread and bakery products
Food preparations, miscel-
laneous
Newspapers
Aircraft engines

Saw and planing mills
Organic chemicals
Prepared animal feed
Canned fruits and vegetables
Cotton fabrics
Aircraft equipment

Refrigeration machinery
Paperboard boxes
Commercial printing

Structural and ornamental work
Inorganic chemicals
Pharmaceutical preparations

Tires and tubes
Cigarettes
Pulp mills
Shoes
Flour and meal
Beer and ale

Metal stampings
Paper products, miscellaneous
Tin cans
Rubber products, miscellaneous
Plastics material
Paints and varnishes

Periodicals
Dresses
Ready-mixed concrete
Tractors
Construction and mining machinery
Machine shops

This list, which might be shortened somewhat by a judicious combination of related categories, suggests the identity of the most important manufacturing industries. The 42 listed accounted in 1958 for about two-thirds of the total sales revenue of all manufacturing industries classified by the Census. At the other end of a full list, we would find among the smallest industries those producing suspenders, straw and felt hats, soda fountain equipment, floor and wall tile, pianos, umbrellas and parasols, and so forth. Thus the many manufacturing industries vary greatly in size, ranging in annual sales revenue from 5 to 10 billion dollars apiece for the very largest to under 10 million dollars apiece for the very smallest .

When, following the Census or any other reasonable classification, we list the numerous separate industries in the manufacturing sector and also in each of the other main sectors of the economy, a fact of considerable importance is made plain. The productive activity of enterprise is today broken down into the furnishing of a very large number of separate goods and services. The production of consumer goods is organized to supply a large number of different and distinguishable goods, fulfilling a similarly large number of separate and distinguishable needs or wants of consumers. Comparably, a large number of different producer goods fulfill a large number of distinguishable needs of producing enterprises. With production thus organized to fulfill many needs with different goods, we find that the outputs of different goods are generally not very close substitutes for each other, to either consumers or producers. Although all goods "compete for the buyer's dollar," there is no close substitution for consumers among cigarettes, soap, fountain pens, refrigerators, meat, haircutting, automobiles, and electric power for lighting—not close substitution in the sense that small or moderate changes in the relative prices of these goods would cause consumers to shift expenditure significantly from one good to another. Similarly, sheet steel, electric motors, metal-stamping machinery, copper tubing, paint, and insulation materials are likely to be poor substitutes for each other to the manufacturer of electric refrigerators.

This does not mean that in a Census classification of industries we will find a separate and semi-isolated product, close substitute for no others, in every Census industry. Considerable care is required to develop a classification of which this would be true. But the fact remains that such a classification can be developed, because of the general tendencies prevalent in the complex organization of the economy and in the substitution relationships among the multitude of goods and services produced. These tendencies give rise to the existence in the economy of a large number of semi-separate and semi-independent industries. In each industry, a group of rival or competing sellers supply close-substitute outputs to common buyers, and there is no equivalent competition (commonly negligible competition) between these industries. The individual industry, properly identified and defined, is thus a logical and convenient unit for studies focused on competition and monopoly, or on the character of market conduct and performance.

Industries may be classified in various ways—according to their technology, their geographical characteristics, the durability of their outputs, and so forth. We are especially interested in following chapters in a classification of industries according to their market structures, since these may be prime determinants of the market conduct and performance of enterprise.

Enterprise Ownership and Control
in the Modern Business Corporation

The capitalist economy, as indicated earlier, is based on the institution of private property. In modern times, such ownership has generally been in fee simple, without legal restriction on the rights of the owner to bequeath or sell the property to others. The rights and obligations of private property in productive goods are principally: (1) the right to exclusive use of the goods; (2) the right to receive the income or earning resulting from their use; (3) the implied obligation of supervising and directing their use—i.e., of exercising the functions of entrepreneurship and management. This complex of rights and obligations leads to an actual or hypothetical identity of the ownership class and the entrepreneurial or managing class.

This all would lead to a very simple system if property were always implemented in one-man ownership of each enterprise. If each business concern were an "individual proprietorship," with a single owner sharing ownership with no others, the owner would more or less naturally emerge as the entrepreneur or manager. Even though he delegated responsibility to employees, he would be so close to the business that all the responsibilities of management and all the rights of ownership could fairly be said to be vested in a single person. Even if businesses were organized in small partnerships, with two or three or four partners jointly owning the enterprise and sharing management responsibility, the situation would not be greatly different, although the practice of having some "active" (managing) and some "inactive" (investing) partners might alter the relationship of some owners to their business property significantly.

There are, in fact, many individual business proprietorships in the United States—over 9 million of them in 1962—and quite a few partnerships (932,000). The proprietorship is marked by the legal identity of the owner and his business concern. The owner *is* the concern, the latter having no legal being apart from him, and he as a person must make all contracts and incur all obligations for his concern, being fully responsible for its liabilities. The partnership involves a similar identity of the concern and the partners, the only difference being that in a "limited" partnership some, but not all, partners may be liable for the debts of the concern only to the amount of their investment in it, not compromising their personal wealth. Proprietorships and partnerships together are by far more numerous than the other main form of business organization, but they account for only about 22 per cent of all business done (as measured by sales revenue) in the United States. Another form of ownership organization is clearly dominant in the contemporary American economy.

This ownership institution is the business corporation. It deserves some attention here because as employed it has clearly altered (1) the character of ownership in business property; (2) the survival powers of the individual business concern; and (3) the extent to which owners retain the rights and obligations of property and, in particular, have the responsibility of performing the functions of entrepreneurship and management of business concerns. Since the roughly 1,300,000 corporations in the United States today do betwen 75 and 80 per cent of all business done, these implications of corporate business organization deserve some attention.

The corporation essentially is a device for associated joint ownership of a business concern by several or many persons. Furthermore, it enables the group of owners to constitute or establish an entity which has rights and liabilities at law distinct from those of the individual members of the owning group. "The corporation," in the eyes of the law, becomes a legal entity or artificial person which is in significant respects independent of and separate from any of the individuals who have shares in its ownership.

The corporation evidently represents some sort of extension of the institution of the partnership. In fact, the business corporation evolved historically from unwieldy partnerships, as the necessities of large-scale organization of business concerns required extensive joint ownership in individual concerns. But the corporation is not a partnership, as a review of its salient characteristics reveals.

First, the corporation is a "joint stock" company, in which small or large shares of ownership may be sold to individuals, the ownership right being confirmed in a stock certificate. This certificate shows the proportionate share of ownership and carries with it the right to receive a share in income as distributed by the corporation, as well (ordinarily) as the right to vote, usually in proportion to the ownership share, in the election of a management or on issues presented by management to the owners for decision.

Second, and definitely distinguishing the corporation from the partnership, the stock shares or certificates of ownership are freely transferable. Any shareholder may freely dispose of his shares to others, thus substituting another owner or other owners for himself, and the fact that he does this in no way impairs the existence of the business entity or unit which is the corporation. The incorporated business concern thus assumes an identity separate from that of any and all owners; it can survive them; it continues to exist although they "sell out" their interests, and so on. Potentially it is immortal, not depending for its existence on the continued existence of any human individuals. (Matters are much otherwise with partnerships, which legally dissolve and must be reconstituted to continue upon the death or withdrawal of a partner.)

Third, the corporation is endowed with "legal entity." It is an artificial person in the eyes of the law, separate from the persons of any shareholders, and as such can make contracts, incur debts, sue and be sued in the courts, and perform such other legally controlled commercial acts as a natural person might be entitled to do. It can do all these things in its own name, without the direct participation of the shareholding owners.

Fourth, and very important, the modern corporation is endowed with "limited liability." That is, the obligation of individual shareholders for the debts or liabilities which the corporation may incur is limited to a specified amount, usually the amount of money the shareholder has invested in the concern by purchasing shares, or has agreed to invest by subscribing to purchase shares. The separate identities of the owner and the business concern are thus more fully established; individual shareholders do not obligate their personal or other wealth by becoming owners, but only the wealth invested in the particular incorporated concern.

The corporation also embodies devices for the delegation of powers of management and control. The corporate charter—a permit from the government and a detailed agreement among shareholders—typically provides for the election of a broad of directors by the shareholders, ordinarily at intervals of a year. The board of directors assumes all powers of policy-making, direction, and management of the concern while it serves, though it must submit its record to shareholders at annual elections, ask for confirmation of its policies and procedures, and stand or fall according to whether or not it has satisfied the shareholders who are able to cast a majority of share votes. Thus a controlling or top managerial group is established who may or may not be shareholders themselves. Control is delegated to them and exercised semi-independently of individual owners.

The right to form a business corporation is not intrinsic in the simple right to own private property, but has been granted additionally by legislation. In recent times, the right to incorporate has been granted under free incorporation laws, which provide that a corporation may be formed by any group of responsible persons who register with a constituted administrative authority, pay a nominal fee, and receive a corporate charter specifying the purpose of the corporation, the capital it will be allowed to raise through sale of shares, the rights and obligations of the shareholders, and so forth. In the United States, business corporations are chartered by the several states, the corporation laws of which are roughly similar though not strictly identical.

The emergence of the business corporation has not simply made business ownership more complicated—it has actually altered the nature and content of private property in business in several ways. First, the income-receiving rights of owners have been changed. In the individual proprietorship, the right of the owner to income extends to that of filling his wallet from the cash register at any time—of drawing upon the business income at will—since the proprietor and his business are one and the same for all legal purposes. In the corporation, on the other hand, income-receiving rights of owners are reduced to those of receiving only such dividends as the elected board of directors declare as a means of distributing income. The receipt of income by owners is thus regularized and restricted, though of course, the dividend policy of the board of directors is subject to the control of shareholders with a majority of voting shares.

Income-receiving rights of owners have frequently been further altered by the establishment of two or more categories of stock shares, including "preference shares" (preferred stock) which have prior claim to the distribution of any earnings distributed up to a limited amount, any remainder being distributable residually to the holders of "common" stock. When holders of preference shares are also denied the right to vote in shareholders' elections, as is frequently the case, a class of quasi-owners, halfway between creditors and owners in their rights and powers, is established. Even without preference stock, however, the common shareholder is at best generally dependent for income on a directors' dividend policy supported by a majority of voting shares; a dissident minority of such shareholders ordinarily could force a different proportion of earnings to be distributed (through court action) only in the case of gross malfeasance or misfeasance by the directors.

Second, the corporation generally implements the use of borrowing, including borrowing through the sale of notes, bonds, and other certificates of debt, and thus the systematic acquisition of funds for investment from creditors rather than from owners. The creditors receive a prior right to income but no legal right to control except in case of default on the debt obligation. Thus the corporation, much more than the other forms of business organization, has the capacity to create an important class of non-owning investors, without rights of control. Correspondingly, another class of negotiable certificates or "securities" having income-receiving rights is created and becomes available for sale and trading.

Third, by the introduction of freely disposable stock shares as evidences of ownership, the ownership rights of shareholders have been reduced to a negotiable basis. The individual owner is no longer of necessity much tied to or identified with the incorporated business of which he owns a part. He can cease to be an owner at any time simply by selling his shares, or becomes a part owner in a new concern by buying some other shares. Ownership is thus reduced nominally, if the shareholder desires and often even if he does not, to the holding of a negotiable certificate entitling the holder to a share of distributed earnings. The owner's feeling of identity with, responsibility for, or interest in the operation of the concern in which he holds shares is thus easily weakened or erased. He is perhaps likely (following the advice of the National Association of Manufacturers in a sponsored textbook on economics) to express any serious disapproval of the operation or policy of his corporation simply by selling his shares. Thus a situation is created in which "separation of ownership from control" may easily emerge. That is, many or all shareholders may be passive investors, and the management of the corporation a quasi-autonomous control body which is only distantly responsible to the shareholders.

The Very Large Corporation and Its Control

These several changes in the character of private property in business are potential, and would not become actual if the business corporation typically remained quite small. Incorporation would then be primarily a slight revision in legal arrangements for one or a very few owners of a small concern. The business corporation, however, has found its distinctive function as a device for organizing very large business firms, which accumulate huge resources by selling stock to very numerous shareholders. And it is when the large or gigantic corporation emerges that the more significant potential implications of the corporate form of business organization are realized.

In Chapter 4 we consider in some detail the current extent of corporate size and of concentration of corporate wealth, but a few remarks here may serve to indicate what is meant by a large or giant corporation, and what its place in the economy is. Of the approximately 1,270,000 corporations in the United States in 1962, about 2,630 had more than $50 million of assets apiece, while another 8,330 had $10 million to $50 million in assets per corporation. Although these were only about 1 per cent of the number of all corporations, they jointly controlled about 76 per cent of all the assets of all corporations. A "giant" group alone (600 with above $250 million in assets apiece) had average assets per corporation of about $1 billion and jointly controlled over 46 per cent of all corporate assets. A considerable number of the very largest corporations now have assets of well over $1 billion apiece. A very important proportion of the business done in the United States is done by corporations so large that multiple ownership by very large numbers of stockholders is ordinarily necessary. In consequence, the potential changes in the character of property enumerated above tend to be realized.

The development of huge corporations has been greatly facilitated by a modification in incorporation laws which began shortly before 1900, permitting one corporation to hold stock in other corporations. This has given rise to the so-called holding company, which commonly controls several or many other corporations by holding majorities of their voting stocks. Use of the holding company device has permitted the organization of very large firms by unifying several corporations under a single management and control through purchasing their stock, or trading holding-company stock for their stock. For practical purposes, we ordinarily view a holding company and all of its controlled or subsidiary corporations as a single firm. The complex is under a single central control, even though a number of legally separate corporate entities exist within the complex.

The main implication of very large corporations for the character of private business property is the possible or probable separation of ownership from control. The very large corporation typically has a great number of shareholders, often running into or well beyond the thousands. It is estimated, for example, that on the average the largest 200 nonfinancial corporations have about 13,000 common stockholders apiece, in addition to many holders of preferred stock. For individual corporations the number of shareholders is as high as 650,000 and as low as a handful; for half of the 200 largest nonfinancial corporations the number of common stockholders is between 10,000 and 100,000. If we remember that it would take 1,000 people contributing $10,000 apiece to raise only $10 million for investment in a corporation, it is not surprising that even in corporations of only moderately large size it is common to have quite a number of shareholders.

If the number of shareholders is large, the proportional interest in the business of the average shareholder is correspondingly small, typically a small fraction of 1 per cent. Even a large absolute investment of several million dollars may give the shareholder a very small percentage interest in a half-billion- or billion-dollar corporation. Correspondingly, the average individual shareholder, under the usual system of one vote per share, has a miniscule voting power in the corporation, and little opportunity individually to influence the election of the board of directors, or the dividend or management policy of the company. He is in a position where the inducement to try to act as other than a passive investor is very small.

The lack of exercise of control power by the individual small shareholder is more fully explained, however, by the fact that ordinarily the great majority of voting stock is in the hands of relatively few individual shareholders, so that a large majority of shareholders combined hold together only a minority of the voting stock. In a study of the 200 largest nonfinancial corporations in the late 1930's, for example, it was found that on the average 5 per cent of the shareholders held 70 per cent of the voting shares, and 10 per cent of the shareholders about 82 per cent of these shares. The great majority of individual shareholders, even if they were somehow to act as a unified group, therefore typically lack even the theoretical power to control the corporation in which they have invested. To them, the annual shareholders' meeting does not actually represent an opportunity to influence the voting on anything, and they are, in general, truly in the position of passive investors. They retain the ownership right of receiving income (subject to the discretion of a board of directors which a majority of voting shares can elect), but they have more or less fully surrendered another right or responsibility of ownership, which is to direct and manage the property owned.

So far, however, we have simply the problem of balloting by a large constituency, plus that of the subjection of a minority of shares (and majority of shareholders) to the decisions of a majority of shares (and minority of shareholders). But the problem is more complex. Even the 3 to 5 per cent of shareholders who on the average control a majority of voting shares are numerous (5 per cent of 10,000 shareholders is 500), and on the average even these larger shareholders will hold individually small percentages of the total voting power. It is thus quite possible, in the typical absence in a corporation of any political machinery for discussing issues and organizing votes, that many of the larger shareholders will also be passive. Then control of the corporation will effectively fall either (a) to one or a few very large shareholders with a substantial minority of the voting stock, or (b) to the exitsing board of directors and management, which can maintain control by soliciting and obtaining the voting proxies of many relatively small shareholders.

What happens is a matter of fact, and investigations have been made of the facts of corporate control, although unfortunately they are largely restricted to the 200 largest nonfinancial corporations. A principal study (R. A. Gordon's *Business Leadership in the Large Corporation*) examines 176 of these 200 corporations as of the late 1930's. It finds that the least common situation in these giant corporations is that a person, family, or closely associated group of persons controls the corporation by virtue of a majority ownership of voting shares. In only 20 of the corporations (about 11 per cent of them) was there evident "majority control" based on stock ownership. (Such majority control, however, evidently becomes more common as we progress to somewhat smaller corporations than the 200 largest.)

The most common situation is that a person, family, or group actually controls the corporation (can elect and reject management) by virtue of a substantial minority holding of the voting shares—less than 50 per cent, and averaging 25 to 30 per cent. This appeared to be true in 98 cases, or 55 per cent of the total number studied. Such "minority control," of course, rests on the facts: (1) that a single shareholder or closely knit group of holders has a sizeable proportion of voting shares and far more shares than does any other interest; and (2) that all the remaining shareholders are sufficiently passive and unorganized that the dominant minority group (possibly assisted by the proxies of small shareholders) easily votes the majority of shares voted at stockholders' elections. Thus the dominant minority has *de facto* control of the corporation, although there is a hypothetical legal possibility that all the rest of the shareholders could combine to outvote the minority.

A third situation is that where there is *no* dominant group holding sufficient shares to control corporate elections, but rather a dispersion of shareholdings such that every stockholding interest is relatively quite small. This was found to be the case in 58 of the 176 cases, or 34 per cent of them. Cases of "no dominant group" have frequently been designated as instances of "management control"—control by the existing board of directors and officers of the firm, who are in turn as a group neither majority nor strong minority shareholders. This designation is based on the observation that in these corporations any shareholding person or group lacks either the power or the inclination to organize enough votes to carry an election. There is no available political machinery for organizing votes, and in the absence of a dominant shareholder group the existing management (however it first got there) is able to solicit and obtain the voting proxies of enough shareholders to vote the majority of shares voted at each meeting. Thus it can perpetuate itself in office or choose its own successors. In this event, control has more or less fully passed from owners in general to a largely non-owning professional management, and a part of the rights and duties of property— control and management—is fully shorn from the shareholders.

What do these three types of control—majority, minority, and management—ordinarily imply about the identity of those who actually guide corporate affairs and formulate the top policies to be followed in company management? Let us remember that "control" means only power to elect and reject the board of directors, officers, and management of the corporation; it does not necessarily mean active direction through participation in management.

In the "majority-control" cases, a family or other closely associated group holding a majority of the voting stock usually participates directly in top management, exercises active control, and discharges the functions of entrepreneurship. Non-owning professional management personnel is also employed, but in general the full functions of ownership (income-receiving plus management) are exercised by the owners of the majority interest in the corporation. Unless the majority shareholders desire to use their holdings as a basis for dominating management in their corporations, prudent investment policy would probably cause them, as passive investors, to disperse their holdings more widely among many corporations.

Where minority control exists, the relationship of the dominant shareholding group to active management is much more varied. At one extreme the dominant minority group acts very much like most majority-control groups, entering actively into the leadership and management of the corporation. At the other extreme, the control exercised by the minority is extremely passive, so that all or most leadership and policy-making functions are left to a professional management. The controlling minority does not enter at all into active management. Subject to the minority's approval in the most broad and general terms, the professional management formulates policy and exercises the functions of management. Of course, such management must keep the minority happy in order to survive, but in large part the entrepreneurial functions of ownership have passed to a group other than the owners. Between these extremes, we frequently find that the dominant minority does not participate actively in day-to-day management, but participates in and perhaps dominates the making of major policy decisions.

In cases of management control the situation is superficially simpler. No group of shareholders is actually able to elect or reject management, and the management group is able to perpetuate itself in office through use of the proxy machinery for obtaining share votes. The full functions of entrepreneurship and management are exercised by a quasi-autonomous group of professionals who are not important shareholders in the corporation. Actually, the situation is more complex because of the question of who these managements are and whom they represent. Are they simply professional managers with a primary or sole obligation to the shareholders of the corporation, or are they perhaps representatives of or obligated to interests not officially identified with the corporation by ownership? A principal possibility mentioned is that some such managements may represent investment bankers or other financial institutions that are creditors or financial advisors of the corporation. The questions posed are easy to ask, but no very satisfactory general answers have been developed. In any event, the separation of ownership from control and the reduction of shareholders to the role of passive investors have reached an extreme in the management-controlled corporations.

Taking majority, minority, and management-control cases together, the resultant overall degree of identification of management with ownership is statistically clear for the giant corporations. In the late 1930's, for 176 of the 200 largest nonfinancial corporations, the following was found. If management is defined as including all members of the board of directors plus all corporate officers, the average holding of stock by total management in these corporations was quite small. About 2.1 per cent of voting shares were held by all management combined in the average (median) case. In only 36 of the 176 cases did total management hold more than 10 per cent of the voting stock of the company (these 36 presumably including all or most of the 20 majority-controlled corporations). In 68 cases, total management held less than 1 per cent of voting shares; and in 120 cases, less than 5 per cent. Lumping management-control and passive-minority-control instances together, we find that corporate managements in the largest corporations generally do not own sufficient stock to control the corporations by virtue of their holdings. But while the percentage of stock shares held by management is usually small, the absolute dollar holdings may be large. Even a 1 per cent holding in a 200 million dollar stock issue is 2 million dollars, and a 5 per cent annual dividend rate on this 2 million would yield $100,000. Corporate managements thus frequently have significant financial stakes in the giant corporations, even though their proportionate holdings of stock are far too small to furnish a basis for control.

The Significance of Separation of Ownership from Control

What is the significance of the separation of ownership from control in the very large corporation? In the last thirty or forty years there has been a good deal of speculation about possible consequences, but we have not developed very much systematic information on the point. Many have suspected possible changes in the aims, motivations, and behavior of business entrepreneurship. Non-owning and quasi-autonomous managements, it has been suggested, may seek different ends for the corporation and act differently in seeking them than the traditional owner-manager would. The management may not be solely and selflessly devoted to enhancing the welfare of the collective shareholders; it may have other ends in mind, and alter its decisions accordingly.

Suppose we start with the notion that owner-managers would in general act so as to maximize the profit of the business, the value of their equity in it, or their total advantage or satisfaction. What might quasi-autonomous corporate managers not really controlled by the shareholders be likely to do that is different? A first answer is that they may not do anything different. They may serve as the trustees and simple servants of the shareholders interests in all matters affecting the corporation, maximizing the shareholders' interests as distinguished from their own or those of any other group. This is their legally correct role, and there is both legal and moral pressure upon them to perform it. There incentive to do so is reinforced when they hold large absolute (though small percentage) amounts of company stock, so that their personal incomes are importantly affected by the corporation income. It is also reinforced when executive compensation is significantly increased by bonuses that depend on the size of company profits. But other possibilities have been mentioned.

One of these is that a strict trusteeship management policy may be tempered somewhat by the pursuit of individual interests by the management group; the managers may alter corporate policy in order to further their personal advantage. One obvious avenue for such action is in the determination by management of its own compensation in salaries and bonuses—it may be inclined to "overpay" itself, perhaps innocently because it has an exaggerated impression of its own worth. Reports of legal actions or other protests by shareholders against allegedly excessive management compensation have occasionally been heard.

One writer has suggested that corporate managements, instead of trying to maximize profits (returns to ownership), may instead try to maximize the excess of revenues over basic costs, which excess they may then divide among executive bonuses or discretionary additions to their salaries, the cost of special perquisites to managers, expenditures on administrative staff, and remaining company profits.[1] Another possibility is that the management may seek to enhance its own prestige and power through fostering growth of the company, usually by reinvestment of earnings, when the shareholders would actually prefer to have more earnings distributed as dividends. It is true that corporate managements frequently have a fairly wide range of discretion in dividend policies and expansion policies. Whether or not and to what extent they

[1]Williamson, Oliver E., *The Economics of Discretionary Behavior: Managerial Objectives in a Theory of the Firm*, 1964, Chs. 3 and 4.

pursue policies different from those that owner-managers would follow is difficult to establish from available evidence. If they did pursue different courses, the basic motivation and behavior of entrepreneurship would have been at least somewhat altered because of the separation of ownership from control.

A more extreme possibility is that management may get far enough from strict promotion of the shareholders' interests that it views itself as sort of impersonal professional administration of the corporation, with obligations to numerous groups of whom the shareholders are only one. The notion of corporate management as a control group which arbitrates among the pressures of the various groups with which it deals—stockholders, labor unions, bankers, consumers, government—has sometimes been advanced. In this case, numerous corporate policies, including price, output, wage, and investment policies, might be expected significantly different from the policies of owner-managers. But it is much harder to predict how such a corporate management would think it should act, and would act, than it is to predict how a profit-maximizing owner-manager would behave. How much the theory of management just described is actually followed in large American corporations is really hard to tell.

A further possibility is that management might have specific obligations to, and act in the interest of, some group outside the corporation. Because members of investment banking firms are often importantly represented on the boards of directors of very large corporations, some students have suggested that (*a*) certain policies, especially in the financial sphere, may be slanted to favor certain banking interests, to the possible detriment of shareholder interests, and (*b*) the policies of ostensibly independent corporations may be coordinated in certain respects because their managements include members of the same investment banking firms. This would alter the character of entrepreneurial motivation, but again it is largely a matter of speculation rather than documented fact.

In summary, "management control" of corporations has several actual or possible implications. Without question, it raises the issue of ownership responsibility. The shareholders as owners are legally responsible for the management of their business firms, yet the non-owning managements have the actual powers of control. Second, questions are raised concerning the aims and motivations of quasi-autonomous managements. Do they differ from those of owner-managers, if so how, and what difference does this make for business behavior in general? Finally, there is the question of whether certain groups in the financial community constitute a sort of invisible control and coordinating mechanism in the world of large corporations, not based on ownership. These are intriguing questions, but unfortunately we do not have satisfactory answers to them. About the most we can do in studying industrial organization is to keep alert for evidences of the possible influences of modern corporate organization on the behavior of business concerns.

Problems Inherent in the Large Sizes of Corporations

Some other consequences of the corporate form of organization are not especially identified with the separation of ownership from control. As suggested above, the corporation has been preeminently an ownership device facilitating the organization and growth of very large business firms. Contemporary industrial organization, dominated by numerous very large individual concerns, could hardly have emerged lacking the corporation as a device for accumulating funds and delegating control and management.

In turn, very large size in itself appears to affect the way in which business managements function and respond to the forces of the market. It is a commonplace that any very large organization—be it a municipal or federal government, an army, a major religious group, or a business concern—acquires certain characteristics in becoming big that it would not have if it were small. Policy-making and administration far exceed the capacities of one or a few people, and the administrative organization necessarily becomes large. Some sort of chain of command must be established, with appropriate centralization and delegation of responsibility and decision-making power. An executive hierarchy emerges, and the larger it becomes the more there will be of formal rule-making, rule books or manuals, and departmentalization and specialization of control and administration. Almost inevitably also there emerges some sort of intra-organization politics and political organization, some form of professional bureaucracy as distinguished from "top" control, and some indefinite amount of "red tape." Communication within administration becomes a major problem, and formalization of communication through memoranda, committee meetings, and the like becomes a necessity.

All of these things may be efficiently handled, or inefficiently. In either case, control and administration are performed differently than in the small organization. Comparative inflexibility or slowness of response to changing situations is almost inevitable as the decision-making process is rigidified and formalized by manuals of rules, standing directives, and governing policies. Independence in decision-making tends to be suppressed below the top levels by obligations to standing rules or precedents. And the imperfections of interdepartmental communication tend to reduce the coordination of various parts of the decision-making process. As a result, the whole behavior of the decision-making organization is at least somewhat altered.

These things are pretty generally understood to be true of "the army" in any large country, and they are frequently held up as faults of "the government" or any of its large divisions. They are more or less equally true of gigantic business organizations, and with comparable consequences. The full range of these consequences has not been systematically studied, and we cannot report on them here. In our study of industrial organization, however, we should begin with an understanding that entrepreneurship, management, or business administration is frequently performed by very large organizations, and much differently than in a small concern where a single owner-manager runs the entire show from his desk. The influence of organizational size on market conduct must be appreciated and taken into account.

The preceding hardly exhausts the issues revolving around the modern business corporation. Numerous other questions both small and large might be mentioned; we have confined ourselves here to things especially relevant to our study. Therefore, we have not alluded to the general development of organized markets for corporate stocks or securities; to the complex role of investment bankers as middlemen in those securities and financial advisors to corporations; to the public regulation of stock markets and security issues for the protection of the investing public; to the underlying pathology of occasional misuses and abuses of corporate organization designed to advantage and enrich promoters and disadvantage and impoverish investors; or to the details of the legal evolution of the corporate form of organization. All these things and others like them must be left to other works.

Let us now extend our preliminary overview of the American business economy by considering the extent of business concentration in the economy as a whole.

SUPPLEMENTARY READINGS

Berle, A. A., and G. C. Means, *The Modern Corporation and Private Property*, 1932.
Mason (Ed.), E. S., *The Corporation in Modern Society*, 1959.
National Resources Committee, *The Structure of the American Economy*, Part I, 1939, Ch. I-V.
Gordon, R. A., *Business Leadership in the Large Corporation*, 1945, Ch. III-VIII.
Williamson, O. E., *The Economics of Discretionary Behavior: Managerial Objectives in a Theory of the Firm*, 1964.

4

Business Size and Overall Concentration in the American Economy

It is an established fact that there are in the American economy a considerable number of huge business corporations. One consequence of their existence which draws the most attention is that much of the economic activity in the country is controlled by "big business." The man in the street, his representative in Congress, and the economist are all concerned with the dominant position of very large corporate enterprises in the economy. But precisely what is it that concerns them?

Three main phenomena associated with huge corporations have been singled out for attention. One, revolving around the very large absolute sizes of firms, is the fact that each of a number of gigantic corporations puts very large amounts of liquid funds, productive equipment, and labor force under the discretionary control of a single management unit. The largest business corporations in the United States have assets in excess of a billion dollars apiece and hire tens of thousands of employees. Each very large corporation thus centralizes within its management a considerable absolute amount of economic power. A second and related phenomenon is that of the concentration of control of business activity within the economy as a whole in the hands of a comparatively few very large corporations, which together exercise discretionary control over a large proportion of all economic activity in the country. A third phenomenon, also related, is that within each of many individual industries within the economy, a very few large corporations control the bulk of assets, employment, and sales. That is, in many industries there is a high degree of seller concentration, which is likely to lessen the effectiveness of competition.

This last phenomenon reflects the impact of big business on the market structures of individual industries. The character of this impact, and its consequences, will be considered in Chapter 5, which deals with seller concentration as an aspect of market structures. In the present chapter, we emphasize mainly systematic factual information on (1) the absolute sizes of American corporations, and the degree of concentration of control of all national business in the hands of relatively few corporations, and (2) the extent and direction of changes in overall business concentration during the present century. If control of economic activity in the American economy is "concentrated," just how concentrated is it? And is it true or false, as is often alleged, that control of the economy is becoming progressively more concentrated over time?

Meaning and Measurement of "Concentration"

We cannot proceed far with presenting information on business concentration in the United States until we have defined "concentration" and indicated how it is best measured. Let us begin by noting that concentration as referred to by economists has two possible alternative meanings: (1) control of a large proportion of some aggregate of economic resources or activity *by a small proportion* of the units which control the aggregate; or (2) control of a large proportion of such an aggregate *by a small absolute number* of these units.

According to the first meaning, for example, control of one-half of an aggregate of $100 billion worth of assets by 1 per cent of the number of firms that control the assets reflects a given level of concentration regardless of whether the absolute number of firms involved is 1,000 or 10,000 (whether the 1 per cent of them that control half the assets are in fact 10 firms or 100 firms). According to the second meaning, control of one-half of the $100 billion in assets by 10 firms reflects a given level of concentration, regardless of whether these 10 firms represent 1, 5, 10, or 20 per cent of the total number of firms that control the assets. Which of these two general meanings of concentration deserves the most emphasis? The second meaning and corresponding measurement of concentration—which run in terms of the proportions of an aggregate controlled by various absolute numbers of firms—proves to be the more relevant one for purposes of economic analysis. This sort of meaning and measurement of concentration is emphasized here.

Having chosen this sort of measurement, we should note at once that concentration of control cannot properly refer to a qualitative state of things, so that all situations can be classified as either "concentrated" or "unconcentrated." Concentration or, more precisely, *the degree of concentration* is a variable which may assume any of a large number of values over a continuous range. How do we measure concentration as a continuous variable?

The economically most relevant measure of the degree of concentration refers to both (*a*) the absolute number of units which control a given economic aggregate, and (*b*) the size distribution of these units when the size of each is measured by the proportion of the aggregate that it controls. In the business economy, for example, the degree of concentration of control of all business assets by firms is described by the absolute number of firms and the proportionally measured size distribution of these firms (sizes being measured as fractions of the asset total). Full information on the number of firms and on the proportionate size of each would give us complete information on the degree of concentration of control of the aggregate in question. But this much information on the degree of concentration is typically unmanageable and difficult to interpret. To depict fully the degree of concentration of control of an aggregate of assets by 1,000 firms, for example, would require arraying them all in order of size and listing for each one the percentage of the asset aggregate that it controlled. This plethora of information would be hard to digest, even if it were reduced to a graphical form,[1] and comparison of the relative degree of concentration within two or more such arrays would be very difficult.

As a result, economists typically rely for convenient indicators of the degree of concentration in any sphere on simplified indices of concentration. These indices show the proportions of an aggregate controlled by various absolute numbers of firms. In measuring seller concentration within individual industries, for example, indices of the following sort are frequently used:

PERCENTAGE OF CONTROL

1963 Sales in:	Tire and Tube Industry	Meat Packing Industry
Controlled by the 4 largest firms	70	31
Controlled by the 8 largest firms	89	42
Controlled by the 20 largest firms	97	54
Controlled by the 50 largest firms	99	64
Total number of firms in the industry	105	2,833

[1] For any given absolute number of firms, arrayed in the order of their sizes, a line could be drawn relating the number of firms to the cumulative percentages of their aggregate assets controlled by successively larger numbers of them. This sort of line would summarize their number and proportionate size distribution, although it is not easily interpreted.

When this sort of concentration measure is used, the degree of concentration is not readily summarized by a single number, so that we might be able to say, for example, that the tractor industry had a concentration of "5" and the meat packing industry one of "3." We must instead specify, in as much detail as seems necessary, the proportions of the aggregate in question which is controlled by various absolute numbers of firms. Moreover, because the degree of concentration is then measured by a series of numbers, it is possible that one of two situations may be both more and less concentrated than the other, depending on the specific concentration index selected. Consider, for example, the following comparison of actual seller concentration in two industries:

PERCENTAGE OF CONTROL

1963 Sales in:	Transformer Industry	Synthetic Rubber Industry
Controlled by the 4 largest firms	68	57
Controlled by the 8 largest firms	79	80
Controlled by the 20 largest firms	93	100
Controlled by the 50 largest firms	98	—
Total number of firms in the industry	144	16

By the criterion of the percentages of sales controlled by the largest four firms ("top-level" concentration) the transformer industry is the more concentrated. But by the criterion of the percentages of sales controlled by the largest 20 firms ("lower-level" concentration) the synthetic rubber industry is the more concentrated (as it is, also, by the criterion of the total absolute number of firms in the industry).

Anomalies of this sort are encountered in a relatively small number of cases. Generally, an index of concentration referring simply to the percentages of an aggregate controlled by a given number of firms (such as the largest 4 or 8 in the case of individual industries, or the largest 200 when dealing with overall concentration in the economy), will give a relative concentration ranking of different situations which would be roughly sustained by indices referring to other absolute numbers of control units.

The sorts of concentration measures just referred to are generally available for individual industries, and we will refer to them further in the discussion of seller concentration within industries in the succeeding chapter. For the measurement of concentration of control of business activity in the entire economy, comparable sets of concentration indices are not available. However, we do have frequency distributions of firms by size classes, and these are presented in this chapter. Such frequency distributions impart a fairly good rough-and-ready picture of the pattern of concentration of control of broad aggregates of economic activity, and have the advantage that in addition they summarize information concerning the absolute sizes of firms.

Concentration of control within a given sphere, such as an industry or the whole economy, is usually measured with respect to one or more of three aggregates—business assets, business income or sales revenue, and labor force employed. The three corresponding concentration measures are primarily relevant to a matching variety of economic issues, but a given aggregate is often chosen as a basis for measuring concentration simply because it is the one for which the most adequate statistical data are available. In measuring concentration of control of business activity within the entire economy, we will emphasize control of total business assets (rather than business income or employment), largely because of the greater availability of data on business assets.

Business Size and Overall Concentration
in Recent Years

In this section, we present a statistical summary of prevailing business size and degree of concentration of control of all business activity in the United States. The meaning of the size of business firms, here measured by the amount of their total assets, is obvious enough to require no explanation. With respect to concentration, let us emphasize that what we are measuring is *concentration of control* of business assets within the economy as a whole, as distinct from concentration of ownership of these assets. The latter, concentration of ownership, would refer to the *personal* distribution of business wealth. To measure it, we would "look through" individual corporations or other firms to their individual shareholders, counting each shareholder as a separate ownership unit. In measuring concentration of control of business assets, on the other hand, we do not look through the corporation or unincorporated firm to its ultimate owners, but instead count each independent corporation or other firm as a single control unit. (In the case of corporations which are "holding companies" that own controlling share interests in other "subsidiary" corporations, we consider any holding company and all of its subsidiaries as a single corporate control unit.) We do this because in each separate corporation or other firm there is a single control group—the management—even though there may be a multiplicity of shareholding owners. Then we ascertain the number and size distribution of all business firms within the economy, size being measured by assets held. This number and size distribution provides an approximate measure of the general concentration of control over business wealth and activity. It depicts the distribution of "economic power," or the degree of concentration of discretionary control over the course of economic activity in general.

In deriving a first-approximation measure of overall business concentration, we would wish ideally to recognize as a separate control unit the management of each legally independent corporation or unincorporated firm, subsidiary corporations not being considered independent of the holding companies that control them. This is because each such management is ostensibly a sovereign unit controlling the assets held and income received by its firm. A measure of concentration derived in this way may somewhat understate the actual degree of concentration, however, for three reasons. First, it fails to recognize the existence of situations in which two or more legally separate corporations, with ostensibly independent managements, are legally or actually controlled by a single individual or family which owns either a majority or a dominant minority of the voting stock shares of the corporations. There may be an "invisible" centralization of control above the superficially independent managements of the corporations which is not reflected in our first-approximation measure of concentration. Second, it would also fail to reflect the effects on concentration of control which stem from cases in which one corporation is controlled by another by virtue only of dominant minority stock ownership, because no formal holding company-subsidiary relationship exists or is recognized. Third, it similarly fails to recognize the effect on concentration which may result from the common control of two or more corporations by a higher control group whose control power is not based on stock ownership. Therefore, any measure of the number of size distribution of control units that recognizes the management of every ostensibly independent corporation as a separate control unit is subject to some modification when such "concealed" lines of higher level control are taken into account. In a subsequent section, we will return to the matter of supercorporate controls and their possible effects on actual concentration of control. It is useful first, however, to employ the best concentration data available, which refer to ostensibly independent firms within the economy.

Concentration among All American
Business Corporations

The systematic data that are available on overall business concentration actually do not cover all business firms in the United States, but only all business corporations. They thus measure sizes of firms and the degree of concentration of control of incorporated business enterprises—the number and size distribution of business corporations. Corporations in the United States accounted for 78 per cent of all business gross income in 1962, and it is estimated that they owned at least 80 per cent of all business assets, since the ratio of their income to their assets is somewhat smaller on the average than the same ratio for unincorporated firms. Concentration of control within the sphere of incorporated business is somewhat higher than concentration of control of all business enterprise because corporations control only about four-fifths of business assets and at the same time are fewer and on the average larger than unincorporated firms. The following data on the degree of concentration of control of corporate assets are thus subject to "mental adjustment" if we wish to get an idea of the degree of concentration of control of all business assets.

One specific deficiency in the data on corporate concentration should also be noted before the data are presented. This results from the facts that the data are compiled from individual federal income tax returns filed with the Internal Revenue Service—each return representing one corporation—and that, under existing tax regulations, a holding company and its subsidiaries may and frequently do file separate income tax returns. When they do, they are tabulated as separate corporations, and the concentration data compiled by the Treasury Department correspondingly tend to understate the actual degree of corporate concentration by some amount. We will discuss the probable degree of this understatement below. Meanwhile, the data now presented fail to reflect the effect on corporate concentration of an uncounted number of unreported holding company-subsidiary relationships.

In 1962, the latest year for which data are available, about 1,190,000 active business corporations, accounting for 99 per cent of the sales income of all corporations, filed federal income tax returns with balance sheets showing the size of their assets. For them, the distribution by size of total assets was as follows:

Size of the Individual Corporation's Total Assets (in dollars)	Number of Corporations in the Size Class	Total Assets of All Corporations in the Size Class (in billions of dollars)
Under 50,000	506,738	9.6
50,000–100,000	206,039	14.8
100,000–500,000	350,650	76.9
500,000–1 million	58,065	40.2
1 million–5 million	49,262	103.9
5 million–10 million	8,564	59.9
10 million–50 million	8,336	171.8
50 million–100 million	1,204	84.2
100 million–250 million	828	128.9
Over 250 million	600	599.3
All Corporations	1,190,286	1,289.5 billion

Both the large number of business corporations in the United States, and the comparatively very small but absolutely substantial number of huge corporations stand out in these data. There were 1,428 corporations with assets in excess of $100 million apiece, and the average asset holding of these 1,428 was about $510 million. The resulting pattern of overall business concentration is better revealed if we convert the preceding table into a compressed one showing first the percentage of the total number of corporations which falls in each of several broad size classes, and second the percentage of all corporate assets which is found in each size class. When this is done, the following appears for the 1,190,286 corporations in question:

Size of the Individual Corporation's Total Assets (in dollars)	Percentage of the Total Number of Corporations in the Size Class	Percentage of the Total Assets of All Corporations in the Size Class
Under 100,000	59.9	1.9
100,000–1 million	34.3	9.1
1 million–10 million	4.9	12.7
10 million–100 million	0.8	19.8
100 million–250 million	0.06	10.0
Over 250 million	0.05	46.5

Several things are evident from these tabulations: (1) There is a very great dispersion among the sizes of individual corporations, which range from under $50,000 apiece in assets to above 250 million dollars apiece, with an appreciable number in the largest class running above $1 billion apiece. (2) The great majority of all corporations are quite small—for example 59.9 per cent of all corporations had less than $100,000 apiece in assets, and 94.2 per cent of all corporations had less than $1 million apiece. (3) But all these small corporations combined control a relatively small proportion of all corporate assets: the 94.2 per cent of the number of all corporations with assets under $1 million apiece (about 1,121,492 out of the total 1,190,286) together controlled only 11 per cent of all corporate assets. (4) Large and very large corporations are relatively few in number but control a very large majority of all corporate assets. To illustrate, there were only 10,968 corporations reporting assets above $10 million apiece (about 1 per cent of the number of corporations) but they controlled 76.3 per cent of all corporate assets. (5) There is an even less numerous group of "giant" corporations which together control over half of all corporate assets—for example, in 1962, there were only 1,428 corporations reporting assets above $100 million apiece, but they controlled 56.5 per cent of all corporate assets.

Concentration among Nonfinancial Business Corporations

The preceding tabulations, however, are merely direct reports of data from all corporate income tax returns. A critical appraisal of the origin and content of the data suggests that overall corporate concentration may be more effectively revealed if two revisions are made.

First, the aggregate of corporations to which the preceding tables refer includes both (1) "nonfinancial" corporations, which produce goods and services in manufacturing, wholesale and retail trade, public utilities, the service trades, mining, construction, and agriculture, forestry, and fisheries; and (2) "financial" corporations, engaged in banking, insurance, and real estate. It may be argued that assets held by nonfinancial corporations have a significance different from that of assets held by financial corporations. The assets of nonfinancial firms are by and large producing assets, accumulated in order to supply real goods and services—plants, machinery, goods inventories, working capital, and so on. The assets of financial corporations, on the other hand, are in considerable part either "just plain money" or the securities and credit obligations of nonfinancial enterprises. Aggregating the assets of nonfinancial and financial corporations for purposes of measuring concentration may thus produce a rather muddied picture of the effective concentration of control of producing assets within the economy. It is therefore desirable to segregate the two classes of corporations and to develop concentration data for nonfinancial corporations separately.

In 1962, the year referred to above, about 850,000 corporations out of roughly 1,190,000 were nonfinancial corporations. These had total assets of about $590 billion, out of the total for all corporations of about $1,290 billion. Financial corporations thus accounted for about 54 per cent of all corporate assets. For nonfinancial corporations alone, the size distribution of companies, in percentage terms, was as follows:

Size of the Individual Nonfinancial Corporation's Total Assets (in dollars)	Percentage of the Total Number of Nonfinancial Corporations in the Size Class	Percentage of the Total Assets of All Nonfinancial Corporations in the Size Class
Under 100,000	62.3	3.0
100,000–1 million	33.5	13.7
1 million–10 million	3.8	13.6
10 million–100 million	0.4	15.9
100 million–250 million	Under 0.001*	9.2
Above 250 million	Under 0.001†	44.6

*The absolute number of nonfinancial corporations with assets in the $100 to $250 million class was 345.
†There were 282 nonfinancial corporations with assets over $250 million.

For nonfinancial corporations alone, the relative concentration picture is roughly the same as already noted for all corporations, with the exception of the fact that large and very large corporations, with assets above 10 million dollars, control a slightly smaller proportion of total assets in the nonfinancial sphere than in the overall aggregate, and smaller corporations a slightly higher proportion. However, in the nonfinancial sphere there were only 627 corporations with assets above the $100-million line, and they controlled 53.8 per cent of all nonfinancial corporate assets.

Effect of Holding-Company Consolidations

A second revision should take into account holding company-subsidiary relations which are not recognized in the federal tax data. Rectified data recognizing all consolidations are not available for any year since the middle of the 1930's. But the general effect of so recognizing them may be judged from the analysis of rectified and unrectified corporate concentration data for 1933. In that year tax data showed 375 nonfinancial giant corporations (above $50 million in assets). This "giant" group in 1933 controlled 56.2 per cent of all nonfinancial corporate assets. When neglected holding company relations were taken into account, it was found that 102 of the 375 giants were actually subsidiaries controlled by the 273 others; in addition, these 273 companies controlled subsidiaries shown as separate corporations in smaller size classes. Attention was then centered on the 200 largest of these 273 nonfinancial corporations. It was found that they (all holding company affiliations having been recognized) controlled 57 per cent of all nonfinancial corporate assets, or about the same proportion which had been attributed to 375 giant firms before holding companies were consolidated with their subsidiaries.

We do not have comparable data for the 200 largest nonfinancial corporations in recent years. But overall concentration, as measured for example by the number of large corporations necessary to account for half of all nonfinancial corporate assets, probably declined noticeably from 1933 to 1962, even after we allow for the fact that the 1933 showing is biased upward because in severe depression years the proportionate importance of smaller enterprises seems to decline temporarily. If we were to project the 1933 findings to the 1962 data, we would guess that in 1962 it was possible that the 300 largest nonfinancial corporations controlled about 55 per cent of all nonfinancial corporate assets, all holding company-subsidiary consolidations being recognized. This is a hazardous extrapolation, however, and could easily be in error by several percentage points in either direction.

The meaning of the data on corporate concentration may be more fully understood if we now reconsider the relative importance of corporations as distinguished from unincorporated enterprises in the American economy. It has been noted above that corporations account for about 78 per cent of all enterprise sales income in the United States. If they control over 80 per cent of all nonfinancial business assets, as seems certain, this would mean that the 300 largest nonfinancial corporations control about 45 per cent of all nonfinancial business assets for all types of enterprise combined.

Varying Importance of Corporations and Corporate Concentration in Different Sectors of the Economy

This overall showing for the entire economy, however, conceals the fact that corporations, both large and small, are much more important in some sectors of the economy than in others. Moreover, the proportion of all assets controlled by a few large incorporated concerns varies widely among sectors. The corporation is dominant in the fields of public utilities (including transportation) and manufacturing, with corporations accounting for 90 per cent or more of all business done in each of these sectors. It is less important in wholesale and retail trade and in construction, where corporations do only about 60 per cent of all business done; still less important in the service trades, where corporations account for about 30 per cent of total sales volume; and of negligible importance in agriculture, in which corporations do only 6 or 7 per cent of all busines done. And in the sectors where the corporation is not dominant, much of the business is done by firms which are not only unincorporated, but also many and small.

Correspondingly, the dominance of the large corporation, and the high degree of concentration of control of business assets in the hands of a few firms, are not encountered throughout the American enterprise economy. They are predominantly phenomena of the manufacturing and public utilities sectors of the economy, which together account for about half the national output of goods and services supplied by private enterprise. In trade, construction, service, and mining industries, very large corporations are less important, and in agriculture their importance is very small.

The distribution of giant corporations among sectors reflects similar tendencies. Of the 200 largest nonfinancial corporations in 1933, 78 were in manufacturing, 48 in transportation, 48 in other public utilities, and only 26 in all other sectors combined. The place of these giant corporations in their respective sectors was as follows:

Sector	Number of Giant Corporations in the Sector, 1933	Proportion of Total Sector Corporate Assets Controlled by Giant Corporations
Transportation	48	92.6
Other public utilities	48	82.3
Manufacturing	78	45.5
All other sectors	26	15.5

The same impression is derived from the less adequate data for 1962. As was pointed out earlier, there were 627 nonfinancial corporations with assets above $100 million apiece (holding company consolidations not being fully recognized) in that year. The proportions of total corporate assets in the various sectors which these 627 corporations accounted for were as follows:

Sector	Number of Giant Corporations in the Sector, 1962	Percentage of Sector Corporate Assets Held by Giant Corporations
Public utilities including transportation	205	84.5
Manufacturing	316	57.1
Mining and quarrying	34	47.3
Wholesale and retail trade	55	17.5
Service trades	12	9.0
Agriculture, forestry, and fisheries	1	7.2
Construction	4	3.2

A high degree of concentration of business assets in the hands of the largest size of corporations occurs mainly in the utilities and manufacturing sectors, and 521 out of a total of 627 giant corporations are found in those two sectors.

A further finding worthy of emphasis is that the proportion of all corporate income or sales receipts controlled by the largest corporations is less than the proportion of all assets which they control. Thus in 1933 the 200 largest nonfinancial corporations controlled 57 per cent of all nonfinancial corporate assets but received only about 30 per cent of the total sales income of nonfinancial corporations. This lower proportionate control of income was found in each of the major sectors other than public utilities (exclusive of transportation). It seems attributable to the fact that the largest corporations find their most favorable environment in lines of production in which heavy capital investment relative to sales income is required.

In summary, we find that the corporation is the dominant form of business organization in the economy, with corporations accounting for about four-fifths of total business done in all sectors combined, for nearly all business done in the important manufacturing and public utility sectors, and for lesser proportions in other sectors. We find among the very numerous business corporations a wide dispersion in size, resulting in a fairly high degree of concentration of control of assets and income, such that in recent decades from 200 to 300 of the largest nonfinancial corporations have controlled over half of all the assets of nonfinancial corporations. The great bulk of nonfinancial corporations— over 95 per cent of them, or almost 815,000—are quite small, and altogether control only about 17 per cent of all nonfinancial corporate assets. The group of 627 "giant" corporations (holding company consolidations not being fully recognized) together with these very numerous "pygmy" corporations account for about 70 per cent of nonfinancial corporate assets. The fraction of assets unaccounted for by either group, moreover, points up a further finding of importance. There is a very sizeable group of middle-sized and large nonfinancial corporations, with assets ranging from $1 million to $100 million apiece, which numbers about 36,000 in all. These corporations account for roughly 30 per cent of nonfinancial corporate assets. Finally, a very large number of unincorporated enterprises account for about a fifth of all business activity.

Although there is considerable concentration of control of assets and income within the enterprise sphere, we must include about 40,000 corporations before we can account for 85 per cent of nonfinancial corporate assets or roughly two-thirds of all business assets, and the control of the remainder is very widely dispersed indeed. In all sectors other than the public utility sphere, where about two hundred gigantic corporations control 85 per cent of all enterprise assets, the pattern just described is generally found—a very large absolute number of enterprises must be included before we can account for a lion's share of all enterprise assets. This "other side" of the concentration picture deserves as much emphasis as does the importance of the 200 or 300 largest corporations.

The Significance of Overall Enterprise Concentration

What is the significance of these findings, generally or from the standpoint of an economic analysis of industrial organization? There are two main possible sorts of effect of the existing overall concentration of control of business: (1) on the distribution of economic and political power within the population; and (2) on the character and effectiveness of competition as a regulator of economic activity.

As to economic power, the management of each business enterprise has a certain power, or degree of discretionary control, over the use of the assets owned by the firm, over the labor force it employs, and over the pricing and distribution of the goods it produces. (The degree of discretion will be limited by the force of competition, and be less as the force of competition is greater.) If there is a relatively high degree of business concentration for the whole economy, this economic power is unequally distributed among all the numerous business firms in the economy. A very small proportion of all firms exercise the great bulk of all the economic power vested in enterprise managements. Moreover, a relatively small absolute number of managements alone exercise a very substantial quantum of this power. "A few men," if several hundred or several thousand are few, are extremely powerful in the conduct of our economic affairs.

This concentration of economic power has been deplored on two general grounds. First, it is held to be inconsistent with a democratic ideal of a wide dispersion of the control of economic affairs among a large proportion of the population. At the extreme, the existing concentration pattern is held to be so seriously inconsistent with democracy as to have substituted an oligarchical for a democratic control of economic affairs. However, if oligarchy means "control by a few," the statistics of business concentration seem to belie so extreme an assertion. Second, the existing pattern of distribution of economic power is held to imply a reduction in the effectiveness of competition. This, however, really shifts the argument from the power question *per se* to the analysis of competition and monopoly as related to market structures, and raises a distinct set of issues, to be treated in the next chapter.

As to political power, it is argued that even though in a democracy with universal suffrage we nominally have a "one-man-one-vote" or equalitarian distribution of such power, the actual political power of individuals varies with their wealth and with the quantum of economic activity they control. Thus political power becomes more unequally distributed as wealthy persons and the managements of large corporations have disproportionate influence on political elections through campaign contributions, on legislation through their well-financed lobbies, and on governmental regulatory policies as they succeed in staffing administrative authorities with persons sympathetic to their private interests. Following this line of argument, the relatively high degree of concentration of control of business wealth and activity is reflected in a roughly corresponding degree of concentration of political power, with consequences inimical to the best working of a democratic government. Furthermore, reduction of business concentration should be favored on political grounds alone, even if there were no obvious narrow economic grounds for sponsoring such a reduction.

This diagnosis of the political-power issue has been contested by other observers. Though not denying that considerable political power is exercised by a relatively few big business organizations, they hold that a countervailing political power is held by organized labor, organized farmers, organized little-business interests, organized government employees, and so forth. And they argue that bargaining on the political level among the various organized interest groups can and does produce a viable and equitable sort of democratic process. Whether or not the last is true, the character of the processes of democratic government have been altered through time to accord a very large role to the competition in the political arena of a few organized interest groups. Concentration of political power in big business is only one major phase of concentrations of political power generally. Reversion to a more primitive sort of democracy would require much more than just a reduction in business concentration.

Let us now return to the matter of concentration and competition. Does the existing degree of concentration of control over business decision-making, for the economy as a whole, lead to a reduction of the intensity and effectiveness of competition? The obvious answer to this question is that it is not overall concentration in an enterprise economy which determines the character and effectiveness of competition. The character of competition, so far as it is influenced by concentration, is determined by the degree of concentration within each of the many individual markets or industries which make up the aggregate enterprise economy. And we cannot easily infer from the overall concentration data we have just reviewed what the character of individual-industry concentration will be in each of the many specific markets in the economy.

If, indeed, all of the enterprises in the economy were in competition in a single market—which they decidedly are not—the observed degree of overall concentration is hardly high enough, or the number of enterprises small enough, that any significant departure from vigorous and effective competition would be expected. Three hundred large firms with a large share of enterprise assets perhaps reflect a significant degree of concentration of power within the whole economy. But three hundred large competing sellers plus a populous fringe of lesser ones in a single market would be ample to assure the absence of monopoly and the presence of effective competition in that market. If, therefore, the existing degree of overall concentration in some sense results in a diminution of competition, this is because it is reflected *in much higher degrees of concentration* in individual markets. This can result from the fact that individual large enterprises specialize in different and noncompeting industries or markets rather than all entering each market in competition with each other. The extent to which, given the overall concentration observed, individual-industry concentrations are high enough to imply a significant restriction of competition is a matter for factual determination in the next chapter.

Supercorporate Controls, Associations, and Collective Activity

Some students of business organization have contended that there is a substantially higher degree of concentration of control of business wealth in the United States than appears in a listing of the number and size distribution of apparently independent corporations. This contention rests in the main on three sorts of observation, and on inferences drawn from them. First, single individuals, families, or other closely associated groups of persons sometimes have controlling stock interests in several ostensibly independent corporations. They are thus in a position to impose a single control on the several companies and perhaps to manage them and coordinate their actions as subsidiary parts of a single entity. Second, each of several influential investment banking firms has "a common influence" over several or many ostensibly independent corporations by virtue of the fact that members of the banking firm are more or less continuously members of the boards of directors of each of the corporations in question. Thus they could possibly control or impose coordination on the policies of the several corporations. Third, various independent firms are common members of various associations, ranging from individual-industry trade associations to nationwide associations of manufacturers or merchants. These associations might be vehicles for some centralization or coordination of control of ostensibly independent enterprises. What is the factual basis of these observations, and how legitimate are the inferences drawn from them concerning further concentration of the control of business?

It is true that, throughout the population of large and small corporations, there are numerous instances in which a single person, family, or clique controls two or more corporations by virtue of holding either a majority or a dominant minority of the voting shares of such corporations. In these cases, each controlling individual or group is in a position to coordinate the activities of the several corporations controlled, and a single top control and administration over the combined assets and activities may be recognized.

For such groupings of corporations under common control to have any very significant effect on the overall concentration picture, however, the several firms controlled in common by a single interest will have in a considerable number of cases to be quite large corporations. For example, if a thousand single families each controlled three $1-million corporations apiece, the number and size distribution of corporate control units previously described would not be very significantly affected. Numerous instances in which single persons or families controlled several corporations in the $10-million, $50-million, or $100-million class would be required to effect a major revision in the overall concentration showing.

In fact, such instances are not very numerous, and for two good reasons. First, relatively gigantic personal or family wealth would be required to finance control of several very large corporations, and the number of persons or families with wealth of this magnitude is absolutely very small. Second, the very wealthy person or family in recent times is not predominantly disposed to keep its investments sufficiently concentrated in a few corporations that it can maintain voting control of them. Unless the person or family in question has an active interest in participating in business management or policy-making—which it frequently does not—its course as a "prudent investor" is to disperse its stockholdings widely among a fairly large number of dependable corporations, and to hold an insignificant fraction of the stock of any one corporation. By not "putting all his eggs in one basket," the wealthy individual or family gets the prospect of reduced risk, and a more stable flow of income, while at the same time retiring to the position of a passive income-receiving investor. This tendency is marked in recent decades, as the second, third, and fourth generation descendants of the business entrepreneur who initially accumulated the fortune become progressively more interested in things other than "grandfather's business."

Nonetheless, there are at least a few outstanding instances in which very wealthy families or groups do hold controlling stock interests in several large or very large corporations. There are no complete data on the incidence of this phenomenon, and thus we cannot accurately appraise its effect on overall concentration. Some indication of the magnitude of the effect was given in a study made during the 1930's of personal and family controls involving the 200 largest nonfinancial corporations and the 50 largest financial corporations. In this study, each of four families or groups was identified as controlling several of these 250 largest corporations. The Rockefeller group was found to have a "working minority" control in six oil corporations and one principal bank, with total assets of over $4 billion, accounting for about 17 per cent of the aggregate assets of the 107 largest industrial corporations. The Du Pont group was found to have similar minority control of the chemical firm Du Pont de Nemours, and of General Motors,

United States Rubber, and the National Bank of Detroit—total assets about $2.6 billion, and about 9 per cent of the aggregate assets of the 107 largest industrial corporations. (Antitrust action by the government has since forced the Du Pont interests to dispose of their holding of General Motors stock.) The Mellon group was found to have majority control of four principal industrial corporations (including the Aluminum Company of America), as well as "alliances" through participation of boards of directors with nine other giant corporations. The Mather group in Cleveland was found to have "minority voting interests" in four of the largest ten principal steel corporations, as well as majority control of second largest iron-ore mining company in the country.

Instances of this sort of centralization of control over groups of huge corporations apparently occur very rarely; if others than the four mentioned had been apparent, they would presumably have been brought forward in the study in question. Even a few such instances, however, can significantly increase the concentration of control over enterprise activity within the economy. Very roughly, the four groups in question in the 1930's apparently controlled together about one-seventh of the total assets of all manufacturing corporations in the United States.

The significance of this increased concentration of control, however, must be interpreted with care, because "control" is a rather complex commodity. Something like full coordination of the policies of the several corporations in a commonly controlled group is ostensibly possible. But that such a coordination will necessarily be accomplished is by no means certain. Observation of the role of "controlling" minority shareholders in these and other instances suggests that the extent to which potential powers of control and of intercompany coordination are exercised varies widely among cases. In some cases, the dominant minority shareholders seem to enter actively into the management processes of their corporations, thus exercising something like "full control." In others, the same sort of shareholders are moderatly passive, participating to a certain extent in the making of broad policy decisions but not entering into active management, or extremely passive, exercising no apparent control or management function other than the implied one of being able to approve or disapprove the existing managements of their corporations. On the average, the sort of control which is imposed, and the degree of intercompany coordination which is effected, appear to be much looser and much less comprehensive than the control and coordination which a large corporate management imposes on the operations under its jurisdiction.

A second sort of "centralization of control" of ostensibly independent corporations has been alleged to exist by virtue of the fact that partners or executives of each of several investment-banking firms regularly appear as members of the board of directors of several or many corporations, thus providing "interlocking directorates" among a group of corporations. To understand the underlying facts, and to be able to evaluate the allegation of centralized control of an "interest group" of corporations, it is necessary to look briefly at the role of the principal investment banking firms in corporate affairs.

The investment banker is primarily a first middleman in corporate security issues; as a first jobber or wholesaler he undertakes to market the stock shares or bonds of corporations. He may also underwrite, or guarantee at a specified price the sale of the corporate security issues he handles, and in general he serves as an expert financial advisor to the corporations which he serves in this capacity. Some of the necessary qualifications of the investment banker are a wide knowledge of the security markets, a thorough understanding of the problems of financing corporations, well-established connections with the principal large buyers of securities and with security "retailers," and ownership of or access to very large amounts of liquid funds.

An important fraction of the investment-banking service to the largest corporations is supplied by a few principal and prominent investment banking firms, situated mainly in New York, but also in financial centers like Chicago and Boston. Each of several principal investment-banking houses serves as investment banker to, and top financial advisor to, a considerable number of large corporations. The connection between an investment-banking firm and a corporation is typically one of long standing, so that a given group of corporations will have been continually associated with the same investment banker over a long period of years. Furthermore, partners or executives of a principal investment banking firm are frequently, though not always, elected members of the boards of directors of the corporations which they serve. Such investment bankers will not typically be in a majority on any board of directors, but they will be represented.

The circumstances leading to their initial election to such boards of directors are various. They may have been simply "invited in" by management as a means of giving principal financial advisors a place in the top policy-making group of the corporation. They may have played some role as promoters of a combine or merger through which the corporation was formed. They may have played a crucial role in a corporate reorganization when there were financial difficulties, and thus have a special interest in the subsequent financial success of the company. In any event, they are there on the boards of directors of numerous companies over long periods of time.

When all of this occurs, situations may be reached in which each of several corporations "have something in common"—that is, they all have the same investment banker, and perhaps in addition partners or executives of the same investment-banking firm are on all of their boards of directors. Thus a mechanism possibly exists for coordinating the policies of the several corporations, and even for imposing some sort of central "control" on them. These possibilities seem somewhat enhanced if, as is frequently the case, most of the large corporations under the "influence" of an investment-banking firm are "management-controlled"—that is, without any dominant group of controlling shareholders.

Some observers of corporate affairs and of the financial community have seized upon the bare facts described above as the basis for an allegation that each of several groups of corporations, each under the influence of or advised by a single investment-banking firm, constitutes an "interest group" under the common control of a single financial group. In a study made during the 1930's, the largest such "interest group" was held to be under the influence of the J. P. Morgan banking interests, as principally represented in the investment banking firm of Morgan Stanley & Co. The Morgan interests were held to have "partial control" of 13 major industrial corporations (including United States Steel, General Electric, and Kennecott Copper), 12 major utility corporations, 5 major railroad systems, and 5 large banks. The existence of "partial control" was alleged on the basis of the fact that the Morgan firm was investment banker to each of the corporations and that Morgan partners appeared on the board of directors of each. The total corporate assets thus allegedly controlled exceeded $30 billion and constituted important minor fractions of all assets invested in the public utility and railroad sectors of the economy. Two or three other important but lesser examples of "interest groupings" of corporations built around other principal investment-banking houses were also cited.

The full evaluation of these allegations of centralization of control is not possible with the evidence that is available. From what we do know, however, the following may be tentatively suggested. First, an interlock of directorates of several ostensibly independent corporations, whether involving members of investment-banking firms or not, is clearly not sufficient to provide a centralized *control* of the several corporations so long as the common directors do not have control of most (or any) of the individual corporations on whose boards they sit. The fact that the same person is one of a dozen directors on the boards of each of ten corporations, with a minority voting power on each board and no shareholding enabling him to control the election of any board, does not entitle him to control any of them, much less to control all of them as a group.

Second, it is not clear that the managements of the various corporations in these so-called interest groups have generally yielded up any important part of their sovereignty, or independent power of control, to the investment-banking interests who have minority representations on their boards of directors. And it is not clear that these investment bankers generally either have the power to impose a centralized control on the corporations they serve or would necessarily wish to impose it if they could. They are respected; their advice on financial matters is heeded; they are deferred to because of a dependence on their position and influence in financial markets. But all of this does not add up to centralizing control in their hands.

Third, the term "centralization of control" is therefore probably much too strong to describe the degree of coordination which may be imposed on the policies and actions of ostensibly independent corporations which are regularly associated with the same investment-banking firm. "Control" in the sense of power to issue orders for action and to insist that they be followed (such as is the power of any corporate management) does not appear to reside in the hands of these investment bankers.

Fourth, a more accurate estimate of the significance of interlocking directorates through investment-banking firms is that these interlocks, and these firms, (a) provide channels of communication between the managements of otherwise independent companies, and (b) provide a vehicle for the arrangement of coalitions, agreements, or treaties among otherwise independent firms. But such coalitions, if and when arrived at, do not generally involve the surrender of control to higher authority, or the yielding of sovereignty to a super-control group. Rather, they involve breachable agreements among independent control units which generally retain most or all of their sovereignty as parties to these agreements.

Thus it appears that the "interest groupings" identified as being built around investment bankers do not introduce *a structural change* which further centralizes *control* over corporate wealth and activity. Rather they are evidence of the existence of one sort of means for communication, and possibly for formation of coalitions, among independent corporate units. They possibly facilitate a certain variety of *market conduct* of independent companies (coalition or collusion on various matters), but they do not centralize control. This observation appears to apply to "groups" identified on the basis of interlocking directorates in general, and not just to those involving investment-banking interests.

It is not clear, moreover, that interlocking directorates, with or without the service of investment bankers, are crucial in providing a basis for coalitions or for collusive activity generally. There are myriad means or devices through which executives of different business firms associate, communicate, and arrive at agreements to coordinate their actions: the telephone, the business lunch, the service club, the golf course, and so on. The interlocking directorate is just one of these means, and probably not an indispensable one.

Nonetheless, considerable attention is sometimes given to another particular institutional device through which communication and possibly coalition among business firms is facilitated. This is the trade association broadly construed—either the association of firms operating in the same industry, such as the American Petroleum Institute or American Iron and Steel Institute, or the multi-industry association such as the United States Chamber of Commerce or the National Association of Manufacturers.

In this country, most principal industries have industry trade associations, and these associations are indeed devices for communication among member firms and frequently for the development of coalitions on various matters of common policy. In general, however, they are not devices for centralizing control powers, as is done in the legalized cartel. The American trade associations generally have not been and are not central control groups over their members (although similar associations in Europe have been). Even their usefulness as vehicles for arranging coalitions is severely limited by law. They should receive attention, however, in the general study of the collusive conduct of independently controlled firms which are members of a single industry.

In addition, there are various multi-industry associations, ranging from local chambers of commerce to a few nationwide business associations. In general, these associations do provide another vehicle for intercompany communication, though for the most part they have such large and diverse memberships that they are not very useful vehicles for specific coalitions of competing interests. They are probably most important as devices for fund raising for political propaganda "in the general interest" of business firms, and for influencing legislation and elections. In these capacities, however, they are generally not cohesive groups. Their secretariats frequently represent a position about which the total membership has varying and divergent views. The suggestion that they constitute in any meaningful sense either effective central control groups with power over members, or strong and unified coalitions, borders on the fantastic.

In summary, with respect to the possibilities of a control over enterprise wealth more centralized than appears from a listing of the number and size distribution of corporations, it appears that only in cases where a single family or closely associated group controls several very large independent corporations by virtue of stock ownership is there a significant increase in the concentration of control relative to that perviously discovered. There are not many of these cases, but three or four important ones can account for a perceptible increase in concentration. Common influences by investment-banking interests, interlocking directorates, and common membership in trade associations do not generally seem to provide an actual centralization of control over groups of otherwise independent firms. They do, however, provide vehicles which facilitate communication and coalition among independently controlled firms. Thus they are potentially important institutional bases for certain varieties of collusive or collective market conduct.

Changes through Time in Overall Business Concentration

The contemporary pattern of overall business concentration in the United States stirs our curiosity about such concentration in the past. Is the current situation one that has not changed much since the development of the American industrial economy, or was business concentration in earlier times less or greater? Have there been any long trends toward steadily increasing or steadily decreasing concentration? Are any historical tendencies leading us toward greater or less concentration of economic power?

Interest in these questions is stimulated not only by intellectual curiosity, but also by various popular "theories of history" which predict definite trends in the development of concentration. Marxian and related theories assert that a steadily increasing degree of concentration toward some monopolistic limit is natural and inevitable in a capitalistic economy. It is supposed to result from intrinsic properties of the process of technological development, and from the ultimate logic of profit seeking by business enterprise. The predictions of these theories, moreover, are allegedly confirmed by historical increases in business concentrations in the United States and in other countries with capitalist economies.

Although these theories actually comprise only assertions or conjectures about what has happened and is likely to happen to business concentration over time, they pose a definite set of questions for investigation. What has actually been the evolution of concentration over time? For what reasons did past changes in concentration occur? And, in view of the apparent reasons, may we logically expect progressively increasing concentration in the future?

We will not attempt to answer all these questions at this point. In this chapter, we will consider only the historical record of changes in overall business concentration in the United States, and of changes in concentration within several major sectors of the economy. At the end of Chapter 5 we will review the parallel record of changing seller concentration within individual industries. And in the latter part of Chapter 6, we will extend our discussion of the rationale of business concentration to develop explanations of past trends in business concentration and predictions of future ones.

An Overview of Concentration Changes since the Civil War

Tracing historical changes in American business concentration is difficult, and particularly so before 1930, because of the lack of adequate statistical data. Reliable statistical analyses of overall business concentration, of the sort we have reviewed for the 1930's and for 1962, are generally unavailable for earlier periods; for those periods we must rely at best on inferences drawn from scattered scraps of evidence. Even these scraps are substantially unavailable for times earlier than about 1870. We must thus limit or description to changes in concentration since the end of the decade of the Civil War.

This limitation is not unfortunate. It was largely after the Civil War that the American economy emerged in its present general form—embracing the continent, with its regions fully linked by rail transportation, and primarily industrial as opposed to agrarian in character. The problems of business concentration as we now understand them found the setting in which they exist largely after the Civil War.

In broad and rough terms, the sequence of changes in overall American business concentration for the last 100 years or more has been as follows:

1. Starting with a relatively unconcentrated business structure after the Civil War, the economy experienced a marked increase in overall business concentration from then until about 1905 to 1910, largely through a greatly increased concentration in the manufacturing sector.

2. From then until the early 1930's, business concentration increased further in a significant degree, but mainly because of a marked rise in concentration in the increasingly important public utilities sector, and, to a lesser extent, in the distributive trades sector. There was no further dramatic overall increase in concentration in manufacturing.

3. From 1933 to 1962, business concentration has remained relatively stable within the economy as a whole. Within the principal sectors, concentration either declined moderately or experienced little net change, although in the manufacturing sector there was a noticeable decline from 1933 to 1947 and a "recovery" to earlier concentration levels by 1954 (maintained through 1963).

A plateau of overall business concentration was generally reached by the middle of 1930's from which we have not departed, upward or downward, to any large extent. Thus we have now had much the same level of business concentration for about thirty years, although before 1933 there had been significant increases in concentration for more than half a century.

Any such simple depiction of historical changes in concentration is inadequate, however, because of the complexity of these changes. There are two major complications. First, the change in overall business concentration in the economy is an additive result of (*a*) changes in concentration in individual sectors of the economy (like manufacturing or public utilities or agriculture), and (*b*) changes in the relative importance of different sectors in the economy. Fully to understand any change in concentration for the whole economy, we must distinguish the differential changes which occurred in the component sectors.

For example, overall concentration may have increased over a certain twenty-year period even though agricultural and manufacturing concentration remained relatively constant, because increasing concentration in the public utilities sector created huge firms which controlled significant individual shares of business wealth. Furthermore, overall concentration may increase even without any increase in concentration within individual sectors, if only the sectors which were originally more concentrated become relatively more important in the economy than the less concentrated sectors. A decline in the share of business assets found in agriculture (a persistently unconcentrated sector) would increase overall business concentration even though concentration within each sector—e.g., agricultural and manufacturing—remained unchanged. This sort of complication is clearly found in American business history from the Civil War to date.

Second, the whole idea of change in concentration, as a statistical concept, is inherently complicated and potentially ambiguous. Consider the case of seller concentration in a particular market. It can be fully measured at any given time only by a complete description of the number and size distribution of all sellers in the market, but is commonly described by certain key indices of the proportions of the market supplied by certain absolute numbers of sellers. For example, in market A the first 4 sellers supply 60 per cent of the market, the first 8 supply 70 per cent, the first 20 supply 80 per cent, and there are 160 sellers in all. Now twenty years pass, and the concentration (or number and size distribution of sellers) has changed, but in a complex way. That is, the first 4 sellers supply only 50 per cent of the market, the first 8 supply 75 per cent, the first 20 supply 80 per cent, and there are only 110 sellers in all. Has concentration increased or decreased? Embarrassingly enough, it has done both. According to the criterion of proportion of the market controlled by four sellers it has decreased (from 60 to 50 per cent); according to the control-by-eight criterion it has increased (from 70 to 75 per cent); according to the control-by-twenty criterion it is unchanged (at 80 per cent); according to the total-number-of sellers criterion it has increased, since the number of sellers is reduced from 160 to 110.

What is fundamentally involved in this example, as in many actual cases, is that the number and size distribution of sellers (or number and size distribution of all corporations in the economy) may change in a complex way over time, so that the concentration of control may become simultaneously greater in one sense and smaller in another. The ambiguity is simply a reflection of the fact that "concentration" itself was not a simple and unambiguous idea at the outset. This complication has arisen in the evolution of business concentration in the United States. We cannot say merely that concentration increased or decreased in a certain period; we must specify the senses in which, or the measures by which, it did one or the other.

Let us now consider the recent evolution of American business concentration in a little more detail.

Changes in Concentration from the Civil War to 1905

Any precise appraisal of the changes in business concentration which took place during the first four decades after the Civil War is difficult. We lack any adequate statistics on concentration at the outset of the period, and statistics describing the situation in 1905 are not very much better. From certain broad indications, however, a general qualitative description of these changes can be developed.

At the beginning of the period, there was evidently a very much lower degree of overall business concentration than has ever existed since. Agriculture was proportionally much more important in the economy than it was to become, accounting for about a quarter of national income in 1870 compared to less than 4 per cent in 1963. Manufacturing, in spite of rapid growth since 1800, was still relatively unimportant, generating only about 16 per cent of national income as compared to about 29 per cent ninety years later. Since agriculture was highly atomistic in structure, with multitudes of very small firms, its relatively great importance made for relatively low overall concentration in the business economy. Even in manufacturing, moreover, concentration was generally much lower than it was to become, though of course greater than in agriculture. Huge industrial firms accounting for large shares of individual markets and significant shares of all business assets had not yet emerged. The structure of the manufacturing sector was, by present-day standards, relatively atomistic.

The same applied, in accentuated degree, to the distributive trades. Public utilities were yet to assume an important role in the economy. The only sector in which big business and relatively high concentration had emerged was in railroad transportation; most of the very large nonfinancial enterprises of the time were found in that sphere. Though precise statistics of concentration are unavailable for the period, two conclusions are inescapable. Overall business concentration was much, much lower than it was to become. The 200 largest nonfinancial enterprises of the time must have controlled a very minor percentage of all business assets. And, aside from the railroad sector, the concentration in individual sectors of the economy was predominantly low, ranging from extremely atomistic to only slightly concentrated. It was from this beginning that the dramatic changes in business structure of the later nineteenth century emerged.

The most important changes occurred in the manufacturing sector. Although the whole economy was growing, with rapid population increases and increasing productivity, manufacturing grew more rapidly than the rest, accounting for steadily increasing shares of national income and of business assets. At the same time, agriculture declined in proportionate importance. This rapid growth of manufacturing activity was accompanied by a substantial growth in the average size of manufacturing plants and firms. There was also a moderate increase in concentration of control in the manufacturing sector, as a relatively small proportion of manufacturing firms accounted for a relatively large proportion of the total growth in manufacturing plants. Until about 1896, however, the increase in manufacturing concentration had been gradual and relatively moderate, and had not reached the levels which were about to emerge.

There then occurred a major discontinuous change, or revolution, in American manufacturing concentration. This was accomplished in a so-called "merger movement"—a wave of several hundred major combinations of existing manufacturing firms to form much larger firms than had before existed. Actually begun at a relatively slow pace around 1880, this merger movement assumed major proportions after 1896 and continued at a rapid pace until about 1904. Writing at the latter date, Moody in his *Truth About the Trusts* indicated the scope of the changes this wave of business combinations had wrought. Since 1880, 318 major industrial combinations had occurred, together affecting about four-fifths of all existing manufacturing industries. They had assimilated about 5,200 separate industrial plants, and their total capitalization approximated 7 billion very uninflated dollars. It was estimated that the 318 resulting merger-produced firms held about 40 per cent of the manufacturing capital of the country. American manufacturing concentration had, by a process of numerous mergers, suddenly become much greater than ever before.

What is not so clear is how manufacturing concentration just after the merger movement, about 1905, compared to such concentration much later on, when it was accurately measured. To compare with Moody's horseback estimate that 318 "merger" firms held 40 per cent of manufacturing sector assets in 1904, we have statistics showing that the 133 largest manufacturing corporations in 1947 controlled about 44 per cent of all corporate assets,[2] and the largest 200 about 30 per cent of value added in the manufacturing sector. We also have the finding from Census data that in 1963 the 200 largest manufacturing corporations accounted for 41 per cent of value added in the manufacturing sector, which would suggest that they controlled over 55 per cent of all manufacturing assets. These later estimates imply that concentration in the manufacturing sector may have increased moderately from 1904 to 1947, and somewhat further by 1963, but the base concentration estimate for 1904 is imprecise and does not permit a reliable comparison.

In picturing the progress of business concentration from the Civil War to 1905, sectors other than manufacturing must also be taken into account. There seems to have been no significant increase in concentration in the agricultural sector—it remained extremely atomistic in structure. Since the share of national business output supplied by agriculture declined from about a quarter to about a fifth during the period, however, the influence of agriculture on the overall concentration picture diminished somewhat. Similarly, the sector of the distributive trades remained quite unconcentrated up to 1905. Evidence on developments in the public utility sphere is extremely scanty, but the sector was still relatively unimportant, and no dramatic general change in concentration took place. The only sector outside manufacturing that

[2]M. A. Adelman, "The Measurement of Industrial Concentration," *Review of Economics and Statistics*, XXXIII (1951), pp. 269–296.

seems to have contributed significantly to increased overall business concentration was that of railroads. After the Civil War the railroad network of the country, already well along in development by 1860, was filled in and extended, particularly to the South and the trans-Mississippi West. This resulted in the formation of more very large railroad companies and in the growth of companies which were already big. In addition, a number of important mergers in the railroad field further increased concentration in this sector.

In sum, the increase in business concentration in the United States between 1865 and 1905 was centered largely in the manufacturing sector and (to a lesser extent) in the railroad sector. The other sectors remained for the time being in a relatively unconcentrated state. The spheres of "big business" and high concentration were rather clearly distinguished from those of small enterprise and low concentration.

What effect did these developments produce on the degree of top-level concentration among business enterprises as a whole? Data bearing on this matter are unsatisfactory, but there is some support for a rough guess that by 1905 the 200 largest nonfinancial business firms controlled a share of all business assets between a half and two-thirds as large as that they held by 1929. That is, if the 200 largest firms in 1929 held about a third of all business assets (of both corporations and unincorporated firms), the 200 largest in 1905 probably held between one-sixth and one-fifth of such assets. Clearly, overall concentration had not reached a peak or semipermanent plateau by 1905.

Changes in Concentration from 1905 to 1935

What happened then, or in particular from 1905 to 1935?

Concentration-increasing merger activity slackened sharply after 1905—in part because of conditions in the security markets, and in part because of the initiation of a more aggressive enforcement of the antitrust law against monopolization. Concentration in a few industries was actually reduced by court decrees, under the antitrust law, requiring the dismemberment of dominant firms. In others it declined because of the growth of smaller firms. It was not until the postwar 1920's that a new, though lesser, wave of merger activity appeared, continuing throughout the decade. The magnitude and effects of this new move toward higher concentration require careful evaluation.

The dramatic increase in concentration of the 1920's was largely centered in the public utilities sector, especially in electric and gas utilities. The utilities sector expanded relative to the rest of the economy from the outset of the twentieth century. As it grew, very large firms emerged, because of the large capital investments required and because of the governmental practice of franchising single firms as legal monopolies in local markets for specific utility services. This general expansion was capped in the 1920's by a strong utilities merger movement, in which a number of very large firms were formed by combining or merging already large utility enterprises. Huge utilities holding companies were created, each with numerous operating subsidiaries. In general, the firms thus created were numerous enough and big enough that they effected a substantial increase in the proportion of nonfinancial business assets controlled by the largest 200 nonfinancial corporations.

Two scraps of evidence suggest the impact of the utilities merger movement on overall business concentration. First, as Berle and Means point out in *The Modern Corporation and Private Property*, there were about 20 public utility corporations that in one year or another during the 1920's were among the largest 200 nonfinancial corporations in the United States, and *which during the 1920's were acquired by other corporations also among the largest 200.* Mergers of this magnitude and number clearly had a dramatic effect on overall business concentration in the United States. Second, there were 35 public utilities corporations which were among the 200 largest nonfinancial corporations in both 1919 and 1928, and between these dates these on the average grew (in part by virtue of the mergers just mentioned) by 194 per cent—nearly trebling in average size of assets. The average growth of 115 other corporations which were among the top 200 on both dates, on the other hand, was less than 50 per cent between 1919 and 1928. The large utility corporation thus emerged as a dominant factor in overall business concentration during the decade of the twenties. There were 48 of them (exclusive of transportation companies) among the 200 largest nonfinancial corporations by 1933.

Changes in other sectors were distinctly less important, though developments in the distributive trades and manufacturing sectors deserve mention. The distributive trades had generally not been an arena for big business, or much affected by the merger movement, until the end of World War I. After 1919, however, there was a considerable movement toward the formation of chain stores or mass-distribution firms which produced a perceptible degree of concentration in this sector. In grocery distribution, for example, there were only two large chains in 1919, controlling together about 2 per cent of national grocery sales. By 1935, the five largest national grocery chains controlled about 26 per cent of national grocery sales, and some smaller chains held significant proportions. For other lines of distribution we lack adequate data, but it is known that between 1919 and 1935, a relatively few large chain-store firms obtained important shares of the total wholesale and retail volume in shoes, automobile accessories, variety goods, and drugs. This growth of big business in the distributive trades did not produce as high degrees of concentration within the sector as were reached in manufacturing prior to 1905 or in public utilities by 1929. But a significant degree of concentration was introduced in distribution, as the sector in part "caught up" with manufacturing in the matter of concentration.

The picture in manufacturing was much more mixed. There is some evidence that concentration within the sector as a whole increased a bit. For example, somewhat fewer plants and firms accounted for a quarter or a half of all manufacturing workers at the end of the period than at the beginning. Furthermore, the manufacturing sector was affected perceptibly by the merger movement of the 1920's. For example, there were 14 industrial corporations that were members of the largest 200 nonfinancial corporations at some time during the 20's, which were acquired by other members of the largest 200 during the decade. In addition, there were many mergers involving manufacturing firms of somewhat lesser size.

This evidence, however, does not necessarily lead to the conclusion that concentration, as usually measured, increased significantly for the sector as a whole. The rise of large firms in manufacturing during this period occurred mostly in industries which had been small at the time of the first merger movement, and industries which had become rather concentrated in the earlier period were not in general comparably affected. Furthermore, continuing expansion of large manufacturing firms in the older industries did not necessarily increase concentration in those industries, for their markets were generally growing rapidly, and so were their competitors. Lacking direct evidence on the point, we are not in a position to conclude that the manufacturing mergers of the 1920's increased concentration within the manufacturing sector as a whole.

The combination of these individual-sector changes in concentration for public utilities, the distributive trades, and manufacturing (given the facts that other sectors such as agriculture and contracting remained relatively atomistic and that the railroad sector increased somewhat in concentration), led to a significant increase in the overall concentration of control of business assets. By 1930 and thereafter the 200 largest nonfinancial corporations controlled a share of all nonfinancial business assets from 50 to 100 per cent greater than in 1905. However, this marked increase in top-level concentration of control of aggregate business activity between 1905 and 1935 was due mainly to the utilities merger movement, and in much smaller degree to increasing concentration in the distributive trades. Not every sector of the economy had been moving steadily toward higher concentration, and in the very important manufacturing sector any net change in concentration appears to have been relatively slight. The question was thus posed, as the prosperous 1920's ended and the country began to emerge from a severe depression by about 1935, whether other episodes such as the utilities merger movement of the twenties would appear to produce further increases in overall concentration.

Changes in Concentration from 1935 to 1963

During and immediately after the participation of the United States in World War II (roughly from 1942 through 1948), numerous predictions were made that overall business concentration in the United States had been and was undergoing another significant increase. The war and postwar phenomena of World War I and of the 1920's were being repeated, it was said, with the result that even fewer firms would control even more business activity in individual sectors and in the economy as a whole. The bases for these assertions were numerous, but principally they included the following.

First, many observers believed that there was some sort of irresistible historical trend toward ever-increasing concentration, as evidenced by the "steady increase" of concentration since the Civil War, and that wars and postwar booms helped to keep the trend going. Second, it was noted that during the actual period of World War II hostilities, when a large fraction of American industry was converted to war production, the little-business sector of the economy declined in population and importance. In some industries, moreover, war contracts were let by the government so as to give the dominant firms larger shares of production than they had previously enjoyed. Third, it was predicted that, the government having built a great deal of extra plant capacity, the largest firms would succeed in acquiring a disproportionate share of this surplus war plant and thus increase their relative hold on producing capacity. Finally, it was noted that there had been a perceptible wave of mergers, including acquisition of small firms by larger ones during the war and immediately thereafter, and many concluded that these mergers would also increase concentration. *Quod erat demonstrandum,* concentration was increasing once again.

Unfortunately for the reputation of the prophets, the prediction does not seem to have been realized. First, one careful statistical comparison has shown that the share of all manufacturing-sector assets controlled by the largest 139 manufacturing corporations actually declined from 49.6 to 45.1 from 1931 to 1947.[3] From 1947 to 1954, the share of all manufacturing value added accounted for by the 150 largest manufacturing companies rebounded from 27 to 34 per cent (of value of shipments by about a third as much), and thereafter increased only slightly, to 37 per cent, by 1963. From 1931 to 1963, concentration in the manufacturing sector as a whole evidently increased only slightly. Thus the plateau of manufacturing concentration which was approached about 1905 and reached by 1931 has not been seriously departed from, in spite of wars and little merger movements. Second, concentration in the utilities field has apparently decreased somewhat, because of the growth of smaller firms and of the dissolution of some of the largest ones under the provisions of federal legislation passed during the 1930's. Third, in the other sectors, including the distributive trades, no general upward or downward trend in concentration is evident, though there are many diverse movements in individual industries. Fourth, the little-business sector of the economy was rapidly repopulated with the close of the war, and is now proportionally at least as important as it was before.

Finally, for the economy as a whole, concentration of control by a relatively few giant corporations has apparently declined somewhat. Statistics cited earlier in this chapter suggest tentatively that in 1962 the 300 largest nonfinancial corporations controlled about the same share of all nonfinancial corporate assets (roughly 55 per cent) as the largest 200 nonfinancial corporations controlled in 1933. Thus we arrive at the conclusion that overall business concentration certainly has not increased since the early 1930's. We seem at least temporarily (now for three decades) to have reached some sort of a rough plateau in overall concentration. An ever-upward trend is not in evidence.

A word of explanation may be in order as to why various observers prophesied incorrectly regarding concentration changes during the 1940's. First, the "historical theory" that concentration will continue increasing evermore was at the outset fairly questionable, both on *a priori* grounds and in the light of a careful reading of the evidence prior to 1935. But it did encourage some observers to seize on and attribute undue importance to scraps of evidence which seemed to support the theory. Second, the wartime decline of the small business sector and increase in the importance of the largest firms in producing for government contracts turned out to be transitory phenomena. The small-business sector bounced back vigorously after the war, and such smaller firms as suffered in the allocation of war contracts generally reestablished themselves in the civilian market with great facility. So far as

[3]Adelman, *op. cit.*

surplus war-plant disposition went, the variety of policies followed did not seem to foster increasing concentration. Either the smaller firms got their share, or they built new plants after the war sufficient on the average to maintain or increase their market positions. Finally, the concentrating force of mergers and acquisitions seems to have been offset by the deconcentrating forces of the growth of markets and the vigorous expansion of smaller firms. The postwar merger movement does not seem to have been big enough to do any more than approximately restore prewar concentration. Thus we find fairly stable overall business concentration for the last 30 or 35 years.

The preceding completes our description of changes in overall business concentration in the United States since the end of the Civil War. Both the earlier eras and episodes of rapidly increasing concentration and subsequent long interval of relatively stable concentration require explanation and interpretation. Such an explanation will be suggested in the latter part of Chapter 6, following our description toward the end of Chapter 5 of changes in seller concentration in individual manufacturing industries.

SUPPLEMENTARY READINGS

Adelman, M. A., "The Measurement of Industrial Concentration," *Review of Economics and Statistics*, November 1951.

Nelson, Ralph L., *Concentration in the Manufacturing Industries of the United States*, 1963.

Nutter, G. W., *The Extent of Enterprise Monopoly in the United States, 1899-1939*, 1951.

Thorp, W. L., and W. F. Crowder, *The Structure of Industry* (T.N.E.C. Monograph 27), 1940.

5

Market Structures: Seller and Buyer Concentration in Individual Industries

Let us turn now from overall business concentration to concentration within individual industries. Economic theory predicts, as we noted in Chapter 2, that the market conduct and performance of firms will be influenced by the structures of the markets in which they sell and buy. It also indicates that one of the strategic aspects of the market structure of any industry is its degree of seller concentration—the number and size distribution of sellers in its market. Correlative importance may be attached to its market's degree of buyer concentration. In this chapter we begin our examination of market structures by considering in turn:

1. The basic theoretical reasons for believing that seller and buyer concentrations are important.

2. The contemporary status of actual seller and buyer concentrations in American industries.

3. Changes during the present century in the degree of seller concentration in these industries.

In succeeding chapters we will also examine two other aspects of individual-industry market structures.

The Basic Theoretical Predictions

The degree of concentration of control of all business activity, or of any broad sector of it, is significant mainly as an indicator of the distribution of general economic and political power among business firms. It is not primarily relevant as an indicator of the probable character of competition. If concentration is to be viewed as a structural determinant of competition, it is the degree of concentration *within groups of competing firms* which will presumably be the strategic influence. Our attention is thus directed to the degree of concentration within individual industries.

This is because the myriad of business firms in the economy do not all really compete with each other, except in the distant and dilute sense that all of them are trying to attract buyers' dollars. Competition in the relevant sense occurs when a number of firms offer to a common group of buyers a group of products that the buyers view as close substitutes. (A hallmark of close substitutability among the products in a group is that noticeable changes in the selling price of any one product will significantly affect the selling prices or sales volume of the others.) In fact, the total output of business firms is broken up into a large number of product groups, with direct competition or close substitutability among the products within each group, but without direct competition between the products of different groups. Furthermore, individual firms typically specialize in supplying one or a few products, and each firm directly competes with only a limited number of other firms—those that offer products which are close substitutes for its own. Correspondingly, the economy-wide complex of enterprises may be viewed, roughly and generally, as being broken into a large number of separate "industries" of competing firms. It is the concentration within each of these industries that should be of primary importance in influencing the character and results of inter-firm competition.

Theory concerning the influence of business concentration on the market conduct and performance of firms begins with the preceding logical postulates and empirical observations. Precisely what importance does it attribute to concentration within individual industries? We have already noted in Chapter 2 that price theory invokes the concept of seller concentration to identify the extreme possible concentration found with single-firm monopoly (one firm supplying the entire output of an industry), and then to classify all other industries according to their seller concentration into two broad groups:

1. Atomistic industries, in which seller concentration is very low. Strictly, these are industries wherein the number of sellers is large and

wherein every seller supplies so small a proportion of industry output that his own changes in output or price cannot perceptibly affect the price or sales volume of the other firms in his industry.

2. Oligopolistic industries, in which seller concentration is high. Strictly, these are industries in which the number of sellers is small and in which every seller supplies a large enough proportion of industry output that his own changes in output or price will perceptibly affect the prices or sales volumes of the other firms in his industry.

We have also noted in Chapter 2 that price theory predicts that the market conduct of firms will differ between atomistic and oligopolistic industries in the following way:

1. In atomistic industries, every seller views the industry-wide market selling price for his output as given and not subject to his influence. He therefore independently produces that output which will yield him a maximum profit at that price. Concerted action by competing sellers collectively to control industry output and selling price is impossible because of the large number of sellers, their small individual sizes—and because of the resulting fact that every seller would find it advantageous to violate any collective output-restricting agreement and could do so without inviting retaliatory action from others.

2. In oligopolistic industries, on the other hand, each seller supplies a large enough share of industry output that his adjustments will influence the market selling price. He therefore anticipates reactions by rival sellers in the industry to his own price or output adjustments, and determines these adjustments accordingly (that is, in the light of induced adjustments he expects by his rivals). Or, more broadly, all sellers in the oligopolistic industry recognize a mutual interdependence of their price-output decisions, and therefore act interdependently rather than independently in adjusting their prices or outputs. Moreover, they find concerted action for collective control of industry-wide price and output practicable. This is because the fewness of sellers makes a price or output agreement feasible, and also because any defector from an agreement would noticeably affect the prices or sales volumes of his rivals, attract their attention, and invite their retaliation. Given the foregoing, many patterns of market conduct are possible in oligopolistic industries, ranging from collusive joint monopoly pricing and market sharing at one extreme to market warfare at the other.

The preceding is a framework of elementary hypotheses concerning atomism and oligopoly. Within this framework, what is the significance of seller concentration within individual industries?

The Distinction between Oligopoly and Atomism

First is the fact that seller concentration determines whether industries are atomistic or oligopolistic. At any rate, it obviously does this except when the number and size distribution of sellers is on the border line where it is difficult to infer whether or not mutually recognized interdependence will be significant. This raises the following question: How high does seller concentration need to be before mutually recognized interdependence of sellers emerges and, conversely, how low does it have to be for sellers to neglect rivals' reactions and act independently?

In qualitative terms, the theoretical answer is that oligopolistic interdependence exists if each of two or more sellers in the industry has a large enough market share that a small proportional increase in his own volume of sales, made at the expense of other sellers in the industry, will result in a noticeable proportional decrease in the sales of the other sellers. Suppose, for example, that an industry has only two sellers, each supplying 50 per cent of the same market, and that one of them, seller A, increases his sales volume by 10 per cent at the expense of the other, perhaps by a small price cut sufficient to generate this increase. Then the other, seller B, will suffer about a 10 per cent decrease in his sales volume. He will notice it, identify its source, and will presumably react by changing his price. Moreover, his reaction will have a noticeable effect on the sales volume of seller A. Then oligopolistic interdependence (operating circularly or two ways between the two sellers) exists. Suppose alternatively that the industry has five sellers of equal size instead of two. Now a 10 per cent increase in sales volume by one at the expense of all the others will reduce the sales volume of any one of the others (on the average) by only about 2½ per cent. But their loss in sales will still be noticeable and identifiable as to source, and reactions would be induced. Oligopolistic interdependence still exists, but it is not so strong as if there were only two sellers. Now suppose still further that the industry has 101 sellers of equal size. A 10 per cent sales increase by any one of them at the expense of all the others (given, let us say, a price reduction just sufficient to induce this increase) will reduce the sales of any of the others by only about one-tenth of 1 per cent. It seems unlikely, in actual markets in which slight variations in sales volumes due to many causes are always occurring, that this slight loss of sales would be either noticed or identified as to source by the other 100 sellers. Reactions of rivals to individual-firm price and output adjustments would not ensue or be anticipated, and each seller would tend to act independently without taking account of such reactions. Oligopolistic interdependence would not be present; an atomistic market structure would prevail instead.

The distinction between oligopolistic and atomistic industries is easy as long as we choose extreme examples—either *very few* large sellers (like 2 or 5) or *very many* small sellers (like 100 or 1000). The trouble comes with the in-between case of "moderately few" or "fairly many" sellers, with moderate but not large shares of the market held by the larger sellers. Where do we draw the line? Suppose an industry had 20 equal-sized sellers (with 5 per cent of the market apiece), so that a 10 per cent sales increase by one at the expense of the others would reduce the sales of each of the others by about one-half of 1 per cent. Is this enough to be noticed, so that oligopoly would exist? If not, how much higher a seller concentration would be required to introduce oligopoly? Or should we consider 50 per cent increases in individual sellers' sales at the expense of rivals as likely enough that the effect of an adjustment this large should be considered in appraising the possible existence of oligopolistic interdependence? Precisely where in the range of varying seller concentration do we draw the line between oligopoly and atomism?

This question has no simple quantitative answer, and thus we are unable to draw any precise quantitative line between oligopolistic and atomistic markets. The same answer, moreover, is not necessarily applicable to all situations. Whether a given sales loss to a rival will be noticed and identified as to source in a particular industry should depend a good deal on the general degree of instability of industry sales due to other causes. Thus a certain degree of seller concentration might be sufficient to produce oligopolistic interdependence in an industry with a very stable market, but not do so in one with an unstable market. Therefore, we can make fairly certain statements about the presence or absence of oligopoly only with respect to comparative extremes of high and low concentration, and must guess about the middle. Guess, that is, until market conduct and performance in the middle range are investigated in detail.

In spite of the manifest impracticality and general meaninglessness of any attempt to establish a clean *a priori* dichotomy of actual oligopolistic and atomistic industries, several economists have nonetheless made such an attempt. One prominent classification names industries in which the largest four sellers supply more than half of industry output "monopolistic" (by which is evidently meant "having the monopolistic tendencies loosely attributed to oligopolies"), and industries in which the largest four sellers supply less than half of industry output "competitive." Although the 50 per cent line (referring to the combined market shares of the largest four sellers) is not entirely implausible, it seems to have been chosen mainly because 50 lies halfway between zero and 100. The classification has no clear merit in distinguishing monopolistic from competitive pricing tendencies.

Another suggested classification names as "oligopolistic" all industries in which the largest eight sellers together supply one-third or more of industry output, leaving all less concentrated industries in the "atomistic" category. This dichotomy draws the line low enough down on the concentration scale that industries with even very slight degrees of oligopolistic interdependence are classified as oligopolies.

Degrees of Seller Concentration within Oligopoly

The discussion has proceeded far enough to show that a simple two-fold classification of industries as either oligopoly and not-oligopoly, or as representing "monopoly" and "competition," will not do. It has also pointed to a further significant aspect of seller concentration to which our empirical findings are related: Within the sphere of oligopolistic industries, differences in the degree and pattern of seller concentration may be expected to result in differences in the market conduct and performance of sellers.

Given the fact that oligopolistic interdependence of sellers is something that varies by degrees, theoretical logic suggests two related things. First, other things being equal, oligopolistic interdependence becomes stronger as seller concentration becomes higher, or weaker as seller concentration is less. Second, therefore, the higher the degree of seller concentration within oligopoly, the greater is the probability of the adoption of joint monopoly price and output policies by rival sellers. Conversely, the lower the degree of seller concentration in oligopoly, the greater is the probability of some active rivalry among sellers and of departures from joint monopoly policies in the direction of competitive (atomistic) price and output determination.

A very broad range of market situations may be considered as in some sense potentially oligopolistic. Oligopoly is present in any market in which two or more sellers have large enough market shares mutually to recognize their interdependence with others—regardless of whether or not there is also a fringe of small sellers who do not recognize mutual interdependence with each other or with the larger sellers. Across this broad range of oligopolistic market situations, therefore, there is a wide variation in both the strength and pattern of oligopolistic interdependence of sellers, corresponding roughly to the variation in the degree and pattern of seller concentration.

Therefore, instead of attempting to classify industries as either oligopolistic or not, we should develop a classification of markets which, in addition to distinguishing industries of truly atomistic structure, distinguishes a number of subcategories of oligopolistic industries according to degree and pattern of seller concentration. And in drawing it up, seller concentration should be measured not only by some simple index such as the proportion of the market controlled by the first four or eight sellers, but also by other characteristics of the number and size distribution of sellers. Among the several subcategories in such a market classification, market conduct and performance might be expected to differ because of differences in seller concentration and in the corresponding strength and pattern of oligopolistic interdependence.

General Rationale of Oligopolistic Behavior

But why, a bit more precisely, should market conduct and performance be expected to respond to variations in seller concentration among oligopolistic industries? To answer this, we must explore briefly the theoretical reasoning that establishes the causal linkage which runs from degree of seller concentration, through strength of mutually recognized interdependence, to market conduct and performance. This line of reasoning is roughly as follows.

Given an industry in which there is mutually recognized interdependence among some or all of the member sellers each seller may be expected to have two conflicting desires. First, he has a virtual desire to act cooperatively with all rival sellers to establish an industry price and output which will yield maximum joint profits to all sellers—a joint monopoly price and output. This wish to attain a joint profit-maximizing price is simply one to secure the largest total profit "pie" to be divided among all the rival sellers in the industry.

Second, however, each seller also has a virtual desire to increase his own share of industry joint profits and his own total profit at the expense of rival sellers in the industry, even though in so doing he causes industry joint profits to be lower. Thus he is ready to act independently in setting price and output, and antagonistically to the interests of rival sellers, to the extent that this action will enhance his own profit. This latent antagonism and the disposition to pursue independent rather than collective pricing and related policies are explicable by the fact that each seller in a oligopolistic industry represents an independent ownership interest with aims fundamentally antagonistic to those of his rivals.

In sum, therefore, each seller in an oligopolistic industry has conflicting desires to pursue respectively joint profit-maximizing and independent profit-maximizing market policies. "What happens" will depend on the relative strength of the two motivations in individual market situations.

The structure of the oligopolistic industry, and in particular its degree and pattern of seller concentration, may be expected to influence strongly the comparative force of the two motivations in determining market conduct and performance. Under one extreme set of structural conditions, more or less "automatic" choice by all sellers of a joint profit-maximizing price and output policy, with no independent and antagonistic action, might be expected. These conditions are: (1) The sellers are few enough and all have large enough market shares to recognize mutual interdependence. (2) In addition, their proportions of total industry sales (shares of the market) at any common price are equal. (3) Their "cost conditions" are identical—i.e., each has the same relationship of cost of production to output—so that they have an identical view of the level of the most profitable joint price.[1] (4) Any price or output change by any seller[2] will be immediately known by and draw an instantaneous response from his rivals, with the result that no independent move by any seller can gain him, either temporarily or permanently, any increase in his share of the market. If all of these structural conditions were fulfilled in an oligopoly, no seller therein could ever gain any advantage from independent, antagonistic action. The joint profit-maximizing motivation should be the only operative one; and all oligopolists should concertedly arrive at and maintain a joint profit-maximizing or joint monopoly price.

If these extreme structural conditions are not all fulfilled, however—and in practice they never are—individual sellers find various reasons for departing from strict joint profit-maximizing policies and for undertaking independent and antagonistic actions. If the sellers have unequal market shares or differing cost conditions, there may not be an automatic agreement on the most profitable common price. Then the effective price may be set anywhere within a range that depends on the relative market shares, cost conditions, and other attributes of individual sellers. If independent price and output adjustments are not immediately known to rivals, who thus do not respond to them very quickly, individual sellers may be disposed to undercut joint profit-maximizing prices (perhaps by making clandestine price concessions to individual customers) in order to gain temporary or even semipermanent increases in their market shares. This practice may not only tend to result in bidding actual prices to some point below the joint-

---

[1] Assuming that each depends for his revenues and profits on the sale of his own output.

[2] Or any change in his product or his sales-promotion outlays.

monopoly level, but also may deter the rival firms from establishing a joint monopoly price to begin with, if it makes price cutting too attractive.

Or suppose that some of the sellers in the market have such small market shares that their individual price and output adjustments do not significantly affect the market positions of larger sellers or induce them to change their prices or outputs. Then the smaller sellers may undercut prices established by the larger ones in order to better their positions. In so doing, they will be limited mainly perhaps by higher costs or by the inferior positions of their products in the preference rankings of buyers. The pursuit of such policies by a competitive fringe of sellers in an oligopolistic industry may deter the larger sellers of the oligopolistic core from attempting to set price at or near a joint-monopoly level and may bid prices below this level if it is initially set there.

In sum, there will be in the usual oligopoly a counter-pull between joint profit-maximizing and independent profit-maximizing motives. The resultant market conduct and performance of the industry may lie at or near a joint monopoly level, at or near a competitive level, or anywhere in a potentially wide range between these levels. The ultimate influence of the degree and pattern of seller concentration on actual conduct and performance should be exercised through its influence on the relative importance of independent or antagonistic price and output policies, as opposed to joint profit-maximizing policies, pursued by sellers in the industry.

In this connection, two specific aspects of the degree and pattern of seller concentration should influence the comparative importance of independent and joint action within oligopolies:

1. *The degree of seller concentration, as reflected in the number of sellers and the proportions of the whole market supplied by individual sellers.* The higher the degree of seller concentration, the greater should be the tendency toward cooperative action to establish a joint profit-maximizing industry price and output. And the smaller should be the incentive for individual sellers to pursue independent competitive policies that are designed to enhance their market shares and profits at the expense of their rivals.

The reasons for this are clear. First, as sellers are progressively fewer in number, it becomes progressively easier for them to arrive at and sustain express or tacit agreements to pursue joint profit-maximizing price and output policies. (Agreements are generally harder to secure and maintain as there are more parties to them.) With fewer sellers, then, the probability of securing concerted pursuit of joint monopoly policies is enhanced. Moreover, sellers are more likely to enter into such express or tacit agreements when their numbers are small because mutual adherence to agreements is then more likely to be secured. That is, "violation" of agreements through independent, antagonistic actions of individual sellers is less likely to occur.

This smaller likelihood of independent, antagonistic policies being pursued with fewer sellers is in fact the second reason that higher seller concentration favors joint profit-maximizing policies. Why is the likelihood of independent action less? As the number of sellers is smaller and the fractions of the market supplied by individual sellers are larger (for each one or on the average), any given percentage gain in sales volume by one at the expense of the others results in a large and more noticeable loss to each of the others, and is more likely to invite retaliation. For example, if there are only three sellers of equal size in an industry, an independent move by one (such as a clandestine price cut to some large buyers) that increases his sales volume by 10 per cent will tend to reduce the sales volume of each of his rivals by about 5 per cent. It is therefore very likely to be noticed and to draw retaliatory price cuts from them. But if there are 11 sellers of equal size, such an independent move by one to increase his sales volume by 10 per cent will reduce the sales volume of each of his rivals by only about 1 per cent, and is less likely to draw attention or to induce retaliatory action. Retaliatory reactions by rival sellers to the independent, antagonistic action of any one seller is thus progressively more likely as the sellers are fewer in number and supply larger individual fracions of the market. Also, the scope of independent action that is unlikely to draw retaliation becomes smaller as sellers are fewer. And, since independent, antagonistic actions by any seller tend to be profitable to him only so far as they do *not* elicit retaliatory reactions by rivals, the probability of individual sellers undertaking independent actions at all becomes less as seller concentration is higher, and greater as seller concentration is lower.

If we add together these two consequences of higher seller concentration—first that it facilitates arrival at agreements on joint profit-maximizing policies and second that it discourages independent, antagonistic policies because rivals are more likely to react to them—we arrive at the conclusion stated above. As seller concentration in oligopoly becomes higher, there is an increased tendency toward joint profit-maximizing policies and away from independent. antagonistic policies. As seller concentration becomes lower, independent actions tend progressively to undermine joint profit-maximizing policies.

This is a sound qualitative conclusion. But we are still left without a quantiative indication of how high a degree of seller concentration is ordinarily needed to support dominantly joint profit-maximizing policies, or of how low a degree of concentration will suffice to make antagonistic policies dominant. As a consequence, subclassifications of oligopolistic markets according to quantitative degrees of concentration are essentially experimental, pending the establishment of empirical relationships between degrees of seller concentration on the one hand and market conduct and performance on the other.

2. *The presence or absence of a competitive fringe of small sellers in an oligopolistic industry, and its quantitative importance if it is present.* In a great many oligopolistic industries, two things are true, First, some but not all of the sellers supply sufficiently large individual fractions of the market that they recognize their mutual interdependence, have propensities to agree on joint profit-maximizing policies, and are deterred in some degree from independent and antagonistic actions by the threat of retaliation. Second, there are also present some small sellers (ranging from few to relatively many), each of whom supplies so small a fraction of the market that his own price and output adjustments will not noticeably affect the welfare of other sellers in the industry, large or small—although his welfare is likely to be affected by market adjustments of the larger sellers. Mutually recognized interdependence between such small sellers and any others is thus lacking. They are correspondingly prone to pursue independent price and output policies that maximize their advantage, given the policies being pursued by the dominant larger sellers. They are inclined to do so, that is, unless the dominant sellers can induce them to observe pricing or market-sharing agreements. The pattern of seller concentration just described is generally designated as involving an oligopolistic core with a competitive fringe of sellers, and the consequences of the pattern for market conduct and performance are potentially quite significant.

In effect, several or many small sellers in the industry tend to take advantage of whatever joint profit-maximizing or other policy sellers in the oligopolistic core pursue. They do this by charging prices that are lower by the amount most profitable to them, thus enhancing their market shares. And their propensity to do so tends to deter the oligopolistic core of sellers from setting price as high as the joint profit-maximizing level. It encourages them to set it at such a lower level that the smaller sellers cannot progressively enlarge their shares of the market at the expense of the large firms. The dominant sellers, that is, are encouraged to pursue price policies which will "contain" the smaller sellers to a limited and at any rate not rapidly increasing share of the market.

Does this mean that with a competitive fringe, oligopolistic prices will tend to be dragged down to the competitive levels associated with atomistic market structures? Not necessarily, and not even most probably.

The reason that it may not is that very often the small sellers of the competitive fringe have competitive disadvantages as compared to the larger firms—most frequently in the form of higher levels of production cost or of products which are "inferior" in the judgment of buyers. (This product inferiority means that they can sell significant amounts only at prices noticeably below those of their larger rivals, and larger amounts only at prices still further below. The matter will be discussed further in Chapter 7.) Given the advantages of lower costs, relatively higher selling prices, and much larger market shares at equivalent prices (the latter two because of the "superiority" of their products), the larger sellers of the oligopolistic core of the industry may well be able to establish prices which, though below the joint profit-maximizing price for the industry, are well above their own costs. Thus they may earn a partial monopoly profit while at the same time confining the small sellers to limited market shares. Competitive pricing thus does not necessarily result. But the industry should come closer to it as the disadvantages of the smaller sellers are less and as their collective share of the market is greater.

The other side of the coin obviously is that the existence of a competitive fringe—in degrees varying with the competitive disadvantages of member sellers of the fringe and with their aggregate market share—tends to result in industry prices which are lower and outputs which are larger than they would be if there were no such fringe. The actual and threatened competitive action by sellers in the competitive fringe acts as a check on joint monopoly pricing by the sellers of the oligopolistic core. It therefore seems obvious that in devising an experimental sub-classification of oligopolistic industries according to concentration, we should distinguish them according to whether or not they have competitive fringes of small sellers and also according to the size of these competitive fringes.

The preceding has set forth the main line of theoretical reasoning that supports the prediction that the degree and pattern of seller concentration in an oligopolistic industry should importantly influence its market conduct and performance. We could extend this line of theorizing to consider the influence of equality as opposed to inequality of size of the principal sellers in oligopolistic industries, of the presence or absence of a "dominant" firm as a seller, and so forth. The elementary framework of hypotheses so far presented, however, should serve as a sufficient background for a presentation of empirical data on actual seller concentration.

In succeeding pages, we will present a fivefold classification of oligopolistic industries according to seller concentration, recognizing both the degree of seller concentration and the presence or absence of a significant competitive fringe of sellers. First, however, we should consider some questions concerning the reliability and meaningfulness of available statistical data purporting to show seller concentration in individual industries.

Contemporary Seller and Buyer Concentration in American Industries

The main purpose of this section is to present a body of available information concerning actual seller concentration—and buyer concentration as well—in American industries. Statistical data measuring such concentration should give us some notion of the relative prevalence of oligopolistic and atomistic industries in the United States, and of the variety of subtypes of oligopoly that are encountered. The data upon which we rely most heavily for an overall picture of seller concentration, however, are developed primarily from the Census of Manufactures, and these data for various reasons do not measure with systematic accuracy the theoretically relevant seller concentration within industries that we have been discussing above. This is largely because the definition of "an industry" employed by the Census of Manufactures does not systematically conform to the appropriate theoretical definition of an industry. Therefore, the Census often measures concentration within a group of sellers which is either too small or too large to make the concentration measure meaningful. It is thus necessary, as a preamble to the presentation of Census data on seller concentration, to explore the deficiencies of and systematic biases in these data.

Definitions of the Industry and of Seller
Concentration—Theory versus the Census

The seller concentration that is directly relevant to market conduct and performance is concentration within industries defined in a certain way. Each industry should be recognizable as a group of products that are close substitutes to buyers, are available to a common group of buyers, and are relatively distant substitutes for all products not included in the industry. This is a "theoretical industry."

Firms make products, and a firm is a member of a given theoretical industry to the extent that it supplies output within the given group of close substitute products. A single firm producing several products which are not close substitutes for each other is a member of several theoretical industries. A theoretical industry is therefore primarily a group of products, not a group of firms. It is only derivatively a group of firms, which are included in the industry (whole or split) just to the extent that they supply given products.

What we seek primarily in measuring actual industry concentration is seller concentration within theoretical industries thus defined. We want in each case a measure of the number and size distribution of firms supplying a given group of close-substitute products, the size of each firm being measured by the proportion of output it supplies within the given product group. To arrive at such a measure, we need first to devise a master grouping of actual products and actual firms that follows the theoretical principle in question, and then to measure concentration for each group established. Do we have such a grouping available or can we devise one? If not, what sort of grouping is available, and what sort of statistical data on seller concentration?

The general answer to the first question is that we do not have available a master "industry" grouping of products and firms which conforms closely to the theoretical principle stated, and we are not in a position easily to devise one. The task of developing the required grouping would be huge, involving a manifold investigation and determination of the substitution relationships among all the several million enterprise outputs in the economy, and an establishment of at least several thousand "theoretical industry" groups on the basis of findings. Measuring concentration for each of the groups thus established would further require determination of the contribution of supply to each group of every enterprise making a product included in it. This task is so large and difficult that it has never been undertaken, and is not likely to be in the near future.

What we do have available instead are certain so-called industry groupings of firms and their outputs employed by several federal agencies (notably the Bureau of Census and the Bureau of Internal Revenue) for summarizing financial and other data concerning business firms that they collect. These groupings do not employ the "theoretical" concept of the industry described above; a simpler grouping is expediently chosen. The industry definition chosen by the Bureau of Census and other agencies, which we will hereafter refer to as the "Census industry," is that an industry is simply "a branch of trade." This means in general that it is identified as a group of firms (or divisions of firms) which either (*a*) produce similar products, or (*b*) employ similar processes. Such Census-industry groupings have been developed rather fully for the manufacturing sector of the economy (primarily in the Census of Manufactures), and less fully for other sectors. For the manufacturing sector only, systematic measures of seller concentration within individual Census industries have been calculated for five disparate years (1935, 1947, 1954, 1958 and 1963).[3] These are the data we have at our disposal as we seek to learn the *relevant* degrees of seller concentration within industries—concentration within "theoretical industries." Of what use are the Census data in this endeavor? And in particular, (*a*) do the Census industry groupings generally correspond to theoretical industries, and (*b*) does concentration as calculated for Census industries generally correspond to "theoretical concentration"? And, therefore, do Census concentration data have some meaning as estimates of the degrees of concentration within theoretical industries?

Generally, the Census industry does not conform at all closely to a theoretical industry, though it may in a small minority of cases. The main reasons for the divergence between Census and theoretical industry groupings are that, as "a branch of trade," (*a*) the Census industry very frequently includes several or many products that are not close substitutes for each other, and (*b*) it less frequently excludes products which are evidently close substitutes for products it includes. It is thus very often "too broad" a grouping from the theoretical standpoint, and less often "too narrow" a grouping. In more detail:

1. The Census industry frequently lumps together firms with similar processes, even though these processes result in the production of several or many products that are not close substitutes for each other. For example, one Census industry classification is "blast furnaces and steel mills" and includes firms with the indicated facilities. Yet the products produced by these firms and facilities are extremely variegated, including steel strip, plate, wire, pipe or tube, heavy construction members, etc. In general, none of these products is a good substitute to buyers, or in use, for any of the others. Clearly, several theoretical industries have been lumped together in a single "overinclusive" Census industry. This sort of aggregation of nonsubstitute products occurs in the case of a large proportion of Census industries.

2. The Census industry uniformly includes all the outputs or sellers

---

[3]See footnote 4 of this chapter for further comments on the definition and scope of Census industries.

within the United States which are identified with the designated "branch of trade." If there is a single national market for the products involved, so that all included outputs are available to a common group of buyers (sold nationally in general), this method of grouping does no violence to theoretical principle. But frequently the sellers are not all in the same locality or region, and high shipping costs relative to the value of the product (or perishability of the product) confine any seller to supplying only a single region or locality within the United States. In these cases the products of all sellers included in a Census industry are *not* available to a common group of buyers. Rather, the Census industry is "geographically segmented" into a number of regional or local subgroups of sellers. Each subgroup supplies close-substitute products to a common group of buyers, but the products of different local or regional groups are not close substitutes to buyers. Then the Census industry, as a nationwide grouping, clearly aggregates several theoretical industries, and again is "too broad" or overinclusive in definition. The inclusion of all "bread and related products" in the country in a single Census industry is a typical example of this.

3. The Census industry sometimes is defined "too narrowly," by excluding from it products which evidently are close substitutes for the products included, and is thus "underinclusive". This appears when the "beet sugar" and "cane sugar" industries are established as separate Census categories, even though the two products are in practice not significantly distinguished in use or by users, or when cotton, wool, and synthetic fabrics are set up in separate Census industries. It also appears, although infrequently to a significant extent, because imports from foreign sources are not registered in the Census. In those cases where imports are important, a part of the relevant outputs or supplies are omitted from the Census industry. The "pulp mills" Census category is a case in point. The Census includes only United States mills, but a larger proportion of our supply comes from abroad.

4. Given these sorts of aberrations of the Census from the theoretical industry, there is nonetheless a residuum of cases in which the Census industry obviously corresponds, at least in a rough and ready way, to a theoretical industry. These are cases in which the Census industry (*a*) includes a single product or sort of good, with all outputs of it evidently being close substitutes; (*b*) does not exclude any close substitute products (domestic or imported); and (*c*) is not geographically segmented, but rather includes a group of sellers supplying in common a single national market. Some Census industries which apparently meet all of these qualifications are "salt," "cigarettes," and "locomotives," but

all such cases combined do not constitute a large proportion of Census industries.[4]

The next question is what, theoretically, can be made of measures of seller concentration which are calculated for Census industries? Are such measures generally meaningless, or are they susceptible to theoretical interpretation? An analysis of this issue suggests the following:

1. *When the Census industry happens to correspond to a theoretical industry*, as it does where it includes only close substitute products with a unified national market and does not exclude any close substitutes, the concentration as calculated for the Census industry is also concentration for a theoretical industry. For example, the Census finding that in 1963 in the cigarette industry the four largest firms supplied 80 per cent of national output and the largest eight firms 100 per cent is meaningful as an indication of concentration within a theoretical industry supplying cigarettes. This is because the Census industry corresponds closely to a theoretical industry.

2. *When the Census industry is underinclusive*, so that it omits products that are close substitutes for those included, the concentration as calculated for the Census industry is generally *greater* than that for the corresponding theoretical industry. The theoretically relevant degree of concentration tends to be exaggerated.

Suppose, for example, that there are two textile fabrics, which we will call A and B, and that they are very close substitutes for each other—buyers regard them as practically interchangeable at going prices. All outputs of both A and B should thus be regarded as falling in a single theoretical industry. Suppose also that different sets of firms supply A and B textiles, and that the degree of seller concentration (and total output) in each textile is as follows, for the four largest firms in each:

[4]All of the preceding refers to the so-called "four-digit" Census grouping (designated by a number of four digits), since this is the one which most closely conforms to common sense and theoretical notions of "an industry." The Census also presents data for broader groupings (e.g., the two-digit group of stone, clay, and glass products, encompassing numerous four-digit industries), and for narrower groupings (e.g., plate glass, a five-digit group included under the four-digit industry designated as flat glass). In general, the broader groupings (less than four digits) are so broad as to have little significance for the analysis of theoretical industry concentration. The narrower groupings (five digits and more) make some meaningful distinctions among nonsubstitute products included in the four-digit industries, but too frequently separate close-substitute products into different categories, and also take no account of geographical segmentation of markets. Any close study of Census concentration data, however, should include an examination of the various fine subdivisions of Census industries by individually designated products.

TEXTILE A (Total annual output— 100 million sq. yd.)		TEXTILE B (Total anual output— 100 million sq. yd.)	
Identity of Firm	Percentage of the Market for A Supplied	Identity of Firm	Percentage of the Market for B Supplied
Firm 1	30	Firm 11	30
Firm 2	20	Firm 12	20
Firm 3	10	Firm 13	10
Firm 4	5	Firm 14	5
Percentage supplied by the first 4 firms	65	Percentage supplied by the first 4 firms	65

Now suppose further that the Census treats the producers of fabrics A and B as separate industries (even though their outputs are close substitutes). The Census will then tell us that in fabric industry A concentration is such that the largest four sellers supply 65 per cent of industry output; also that concentration in fabric industry B is such that the first four firms supply 65 per cent of industry output. But what is the true concentration picture in terms of theoretical industries?

First, all eight firms are members of the same theoretical industry, since all produce close substitute outputs. Second, the total outputs of fabrics A and B being the same, it is easily calculated that, of the output of the theoretical industry (A plus B), firms 1 and 11 produce 15 per cent apiece, and firms 2 and 12 produce 10 per cent apiece, so that the true theoretical concentration for the textile industry is such that only 50 per cent of industry output is supplied by the first 4 firms, instead of 65 per cent. The Census concentration figures thus exaggerate the true or theoretical degree of concentration. This is because the proportions of given *fractions* of a theoretical industry output controlled by given firms will generally be larger than the proportions they control of the whole output of the theoretical industry.

This bias in the measurement of concentration (encountered when Census industries are underinclusive) will be avoided only if the same firms operate in all the Census industries which compose a theoretical industry and if, in addition, each controls the same proportion of output in each such Census industry. In the preceding example, that is, if firms 1, 2, 3, and 4 not only controlled 30, 20, 10, and 5 per cent respectively of textile fabric A output, but also 30, 20, 10, and 5 per cent of textile fabric B output (instead of having B supplied by four different firms), the degree of concentration by four firms as calculated for either A or B would be the same as that for the theoretical industry including A and B—i.e., 65 per cent by four firms. But this degree of "balanced diversification" of firms among underinclusive Census industries with close substitute products does not occur frequently enough to alter the observation that underinclusive Census industry classifications generally lead to an exaggeration of true theoretical concentration.

3. *When the Census industry is overinclusive*, including several products which are not close substitutes to buyers generally, or several regional groups of sellers and their similar outputs which are not in competition with each other, then concentration as calculated for the Census industry is generally *smaller* than that for the component theoretical industries which the Census industry includes. The theoretically relevant degree of concentration tends to be understated.

Suppose, for example, that we find included in a single Census industry two nonsubstitute products groups (say, electric toasters and electric blankets), or alternatively two regional groups of outputs of sellers of the same sort of product, not in competition with each other (dry cleaning in San Francisco and dry cleaning in Boston). Let us refer to the two products, or the two regional groups, as C and D. Suppose further that different sets of firms supply markets C and D, and that the degree of seller concentration (and total output) in each market is as follows, for the four largest firms in each:

MARKET C Toasters or San Francisco Dry Cleaning (Total annual output— $10 million value)		MARKET D Electric Blankets or Boston Dry Cleaning (Total annual output— $10 million value)	
Identity of Firm	Percentage of the Market for C Supplied	Identity of Firm	Percentage of the Market for D Supplied
21	40	31	50
22	30	32	20
23	15	33	10
24	5	34	5
Percentage supplied by the first 4 firms	90	Percentage supplied by the first 4 firms	85

We know (by assumption) that C and D are separate theoretical industries, without significant substitutability between their respective outputs. Thus the true or theoretically relevant concentration in market C is measured by the finding that 90 per cent of value of output is controlled by the first 4 firms; in market D, the first 4 firms control 85 per cent. What does the Census do by aggregating C and D into a single Census industry? It will show that of the C and D output values combined (each being half of the total), firm 21 controls 20 per cent, firm 31 controls 25 per cent, firm 22 controls 15 per cent, firm 32 controls 10 per cent. Thus the first 4 firms in C plus D control 70 per cent of the Census industry output value. Since the true theoretical concentration for the two component theoretical industries is measured alternatively by a 90-per-cent-by-4 and an 85-per-cent-by-4 firm control, the Census concentration measure understates the true theoretical concentrations. This is because the proportions of a given theoretical industry output controlled by given firms will generally be larger than the proportions they control of some aggregate of the outputs of several theoretical industries included in a Census industry.

This bias in the measurement of concentration from Census data, encountered when Census industries are overinclusive, will be avoided (exactly or roughly) if it happens that the same firms operate in all of the component theoretical industries included in the Census industry, and if, in addition, each controls the same proportion (exactly or roughly) of the outputs of the several component theoretical industries. If in the preceding example, the first 4 firms in both C and D had been the same (firms 21, 22, 23, and 24), the Census measure of concentration for C plus D would have showed that the first four firms in the Census industry controlled 87½ per cent of Census industry output—at least a satisfactory average of the theoretical concentrations in the two component theoretical industries.

In general, if the firms operating in an overinclusive Census industry have a more or less "balanced diversification" among all of the nonsubstitute regions or products included in the Census industry (producing similar proportions of total output in each), the seller concentration calculated for the Census industry will be at least roughly representative of the true theoretical concentration in each of the various component theoretical industries. If, on the other hand, such firms are "specialized" to producing most or all of their outputs in only a part of the theoretical industries included in a Census industry, the seller concentration calculated for the Census industry will tend to understate the true concentration within the component theoretical industries.

Examination of overinclusive Census industries (which include the majority of all of them) suggests that both sorts of situation are encountered in substantial number. That is, in a considerable number of the overinclusive cases, roughly balanced diversification of firms among different products and regions included in the Census industry results in a Census measure of seller concentration roughly approximating true concentration within component theoretical industries. In more numerous cases, specialization of firms (absolutely, or as a matter of emphasis) among component theoretical industries results in a Census measure of seller concentration which understates true concentration in the component theoretical industries.

Certain general conclusions thus emerge concerning the analytical significance of measures of seller concentration calculated for Census industry groupings. First, Census industries are frequently broader or more inclusive than theoretical industries in that they include product groups which are not close substitutes for each other, or regional or local output groups of a given product which are not close substitutes. In fewer cases, Census industries are narrower or less inclusive than theoretical industries, excluding products which are close substitutes for those they include. In some small proportion of cases, Census industries roughly correspond to theoretical industries.

Second, overinclusiveness of Census industries, the predominant tendency, tends generally to result in measures of seller concentration within Census industries which understate the degrees of concentration within component theoretical industries. This understatement is encountered so far as firms included in the Census industry specialize, relatively or absolutely, in only a part of the products or regions which the overinclusive Census industry contains. It is avoided so far as the firms have a more or less balanced diversification among the products or regions included.

Third, underinclusiveness of Census industries correspondingly leads to seller-concentration measures which tend to overstate the degrees of concentration within the relevant theoretical industries. But such underinclusiveness and overstatement appears to occur much less frequently than overinclusiveness and understatement.

Finally, there is as a result some net average tendency for Census-industry concentration measures to understate the degree of seller concentration within the numerous theoretical industries into which existing firms should be grouped. We are not in a position to estimate in precise quantitative fashion the average degree of understatement which is involved. It is probably significant but moderate, and perhaps on the average sufficient to raise by five to ten percentage points the measures of the proportions of industry outputs controlled by the largest four sellers, as we hypothetically convert from Census to theoretical industry groupings.[5]

Census Statistics on Seller Concentration
in American Manufacturing Industries

We are generally interested in the patterns of individual industry seller concentration in all of the sectors of the American business economy. Actually we have available reasonably detailed concentration data only for individual Census industries in the manufacturing sector, the most recent year reported being 1963. Let us look first, therefore, at these Census measures of the degree of seller concentration.

The Census of Manufactures for that year lists 417 manufacturing industries for which there are comparable data on sales volume by individual firms. Seller concentration in these Census industries is measured by indices of the proportions of total value of shipments for the industry supplied by the largest 4 firms, largest 8 firms, largest 20, and

[5]It should also be added that measures of seller concentration computed for over-inclusive Census industries also frequently tend to conceal, through an averaging process, the true variation of seller concentration among component theoretical industries. Suppose, for example, that a Census industry R includes a product X and a non-substitute product Y, supplied by different firms as follows:

PRODUCT X (Total annual output— $1 million value)		PRODUCT Y (Total annual output— $1 million value)	
Identity of Firm	Percentage of X Supplied	Identity of Firm	Percentage of Y Supplied
41	40	51	15
42	20	52	10
43	15	53	5
44	10	54	5
Percentage supplied by the largest 4 firms	85		35

The concentration measures for the two theoretical industries are respectively 85 and 35. The concentration measure for Census industry R, including both of them, will be 45 (the percentage of combined sales made by firms 41, 42, 43, and 51). This measure of 45 conceals the fact that there are two theoretical industries with concentration measures of 85 and 35. There is also a downward bias in the Census-industry concentration ratio, previously noted, since the *average* concentration measure for X and Y is 60, not 45. This example suggests that the dominant tendency toward overinclusiveness in Census industries tends both to conceal variation in theoretical-industry concentration, thus understating the degree of dispersion of concentration among theoretical industries, and to understate average degrees of concenration.

largest 50. For purposes of summarization, major emphasis is placed on the proportion of industry shipment supplied by the first four firms in the industry.

When the 417 comparable Census manufacturing industries are classified according to the proportion of industry shipments supplied by the largest four sellers in 1963, the result is as shown in the following table.

Manufacturing Industries in Which:	Number of Industries in Each Concentration Class	Percentage of the Number of Industries in Each Concentration Class
76 to 100% of industry shipments were supplied by the largest 4 firms	32	8
51 to 75% of industry shipments were supplied by the largest 4 firms	81	19
26 to 50% of industry shipments were supplied by the largest 4 firms	161	39
0 to 25% of industry shipments were supplied by the largest 4 firms	143	34
Total	417	100.0

In about 8 per cent of Census manufacturing industries there was a very high degree of seller concentration, with the largest 4 firms supplying more than three quarters of industry output in each case. In about 19 per cent of such industries, concentration, though lower, was still high, with the largest 4 firms supplying between one-half and three-quarters of industry output in each case. In about 34 per cent of these industries, seller concentration as measured by this index was quite low, the first 4 firms together supplying a quarter or less of industry output. And for the remainder (the 39 per cent of industries in the third concentration class), concentration was moderate to relatively low, the largest 4 sellers supplying between a quarter and one-half of industry output in each case.

It may be noted that industries of lower concentration are on the average somewhat larger industries (with greater individual value of shipments) than those of higher concentration. This is apparent from

Census concentration data for 1958 (value of shipments data not having been calculated as yet for 1963). In that year, whereas the percentages of the number of industries in the four successively lower concentration classes were approximately 9, 22, 39, and 30 per cent,[6] the percentages of the total value of shipments in the same classes were approximately 8, 15, 39, and 38 per cent. Perhaps this is because, on the average, a larger industry has room for more sellers; a large seller of given absolute size in it will have a smaller proportion of the total market.

Before we attempt to interpret these and other seller concentration figures, we should take some account of the probable bias in Census-industry concentration measures as compared to those which would apply to theoretically valid industry groupings. In general, as we have seen, Census concentration data should not be taken at face value; they probably have on the average a downward bias, understating true or theoretical seller concentration. How much they understate it, we do not know exactly, the detailed studies which would tell us never having been made. But it would seem safe to say that a rectified set of concentration measures conforming to theoretical principle would very probably find perceptibly more than 10 per cent of the number of manufacturing industries with concentration above the 75-per-cent-by-4-firm line, more than 25 per cent of the number of industries in the 51-to-75-per-cent-by-4 group, and perceptibly less than 30 per cent of the number of industries in the lowest concentration category. Actual or theoretically relevant seller concentration by industries is at least a bit higher than appears from Census data.

The preceding classification of all manufacturing industries according to seller concentration should be examined in the light of the theoretical argument presented in the first section of this chapter. Drawing upon that argument, one might hazard the guess that in the highest concentration category (where more than 75 per cent of each industry output is supplied by the largest 4 sellers), firms should have a maximum tendency to agree on a joint profit-maximizing price, and a minimum propensity to pursue independent and antagonistic policies. A net tendency toward joint monopoly in market conduct and performance is predictable. In the lowest concentration category (where 25 per cent or less of each industry output is supplied by the largest 4 sellers), effective joint profit-maximizing action appears unlikely, and competitive market conduct and performance of the sort associated with atomistic

[6]The differences in the percentages of industries in the four classes as between 1958 and 1963 cannot be regarded as significant because a revised industry classification was employed in the 1963 Census of Manufactures.

market structures might be expected. What of the middle concentration categories? In industries where the largest 4 sellers supply from 51 to 75 per cent of industry output, joint monopoly tendencies still appear probable, but there is an enhanced likelihood that these tendencies may be tempered or restrained by the independent, antagonistic policies of individual sellers. And where the largest 4 sellers supply from 26 to 50 per cent of industry output, the mutually recognized interdependence of sellers may still be strong enough that strictly independent action is counterbalanced by some tendency toward concerted action for maximum joint profits. Therefore, market conduct and performance might be expected to lie somewhere between monopolistic and competitive limits.

The foregoing, of course, is strictly *a priori* speculation, and can be confirmed or disconfirmed only by empirical tests for the actual association of seller concentration to market conduct and performance—considered later in Chapter 11. In any event, the average person who inspects the statistics of seller concentration just presented in the context of the earlier theoretical argument should be convinced of one thing. It would be meaningless to establish arbitrarily any twofold classification of industries which designated all above a certain concentration line (such as 50 per cent control of the market by the largest 4 sellers) as oligopolistic or monopolistic, and all below that line as competitive. A number of subcategories of oligopoly must be recognized, corresponding to different degrees and patterns of seller concentration, in addition to a category of atomistic industries.

The fourfold Census classification just presented is, of course, better than a dichotomy. It permits us to recognize, in a rough and ready fashion, three subcategories of "oligopolistic" industries with seller concentration ranging from "high" to "moderately low," as well as a category of unconcentrated or approximately atomistic industries. This Census classification, however, has two definite deficiencies. First, the lines between the seller-concentration classes are arbitrarily drawn. Second, and more importantly, the classification is strictly in terms of the proportion of industry output supplied by the largest 4 firms—in terms of one measure of "top-level" sellers concentration. Not reflected in the classification are both the size distribution of the largest 4 sellers in any industry, and the number and size distribution of remaining sellers other than the largest 4. It should therefore be useful to devise a classification of industries according to seller concentration which overcomes some of these deficiencies.

A Tentative Classification of Industries
According to Seller Concentration

We are not in a position to present here a definitive classification of this sort, since we lack the requisite detailed data. We can, however, use typical examples to suggest a severalfold classification which takes account not only of the degree of top-level concentration, but also the total number of sellers in the industry and their size distribution in general. Let us attempt this by starting with a category of the most highly concentrated industries and working down.

At the top of the seller-concentration range we find relatively few industries with very high concentration of total output in the hands of the largest 3 or 4 firms, and a small total number of firms. Let us assign these to a category I-*a* of oligopoly, designated as "very highly concentrated." A familiar and important member of this category is the passenger automobile industry. In 1964 this industry contained altogether only 4 active firms of perceptible size in the United States, and a degree of seller concentration was revealed by the following figures:

TYPE I-*a*   AUTOMOBILE INDUSTRY

Passenger-Car Producing Firms	Percentage of New Passenger Cars Sold in the U.S., 1964
General Motors	49.1
Ford	26.0
Chrysler	13.8
American Motors (Rambler)	4.7
(First 4 firms)	(93.6)
Foreign producers and other	6.4
Total	100.0

Here we observe domination of the industry by four sellers, all with large though differing shares of the market, these constituting a very highly concentrated oligopoly. In addition, there is a scattering of foreign and small domestic suppliers, of which only two or three have perceptible market shares, and a very small number of sellers altogether. Oligopolistic interdependence may be presumed to be at a practical maximum in such cases. Other familiar industries qualifying for inclusion in this most highly concentrated category would include those producing, as of 1963, primary aluminum (7 sellers in all—1 very large and 2 others supplying most of the remainder of the market), and cellulose fibers (8 producers in all, with the largest 4 accounting for 82 per cent of industry sales and the other 4 for the rest.)

A second category, which we tentatively view as a subclass of the first and thus number I-*b*, also has very high concentration of output in the hands of the largest 3 of 4 firms. But either somewhat more sellers have important market shares, or there is a more numerous competitive fringe of smaller sellers. The cigarette industry is a familiar example of this class, as indicated by the following data:

TYPE I-*b*   CIGARETTE INDUSTRY

Cigarette Producing Firms	Percentage of U.S. Cigarette Production, 1965
R. J. Reynolds	32.4
American Tobacco	26.3
Brown and Williamson	13.1
(First 3 firms)	(71.8)
Philip Morris	10.5
P. Lorillard	9.0
Ligget & Meyers	8.3
(First 6 firms)	(99.6)
6 other firms	0.4
Total	100.0

Other members of this category would include (for 1963 output): electric light bulbs (92 per cent by 4 firms, 96 per cent by 8, 99 per cent by 20, and 52 firms in all); gypsum products (84 per cent by 4, 97 per cent by 8, 99 per cent by 20, and 60 firms in all); and telephone and telegraph equipment (92 per cent by 4, 96 per cent by 8, 99 per cent by 20, and 65 firms in all).

The similarities between classes I-*a* and I-*b* are more significant than their differences. They differ mainly in that members of class I-*b* are likely to have somewhat more sellers apiece and in that added small sellers together supply a small fraction of the market. In both cases, the existence of a very high degree of mutually recognized interdependence among the principal sellers is unquestioned. There is some possibility, but not a probability, that the competitive fringes of small sellers, where they are found, will affect the character of competition somewhat. Actually, the disadvantages in cost and in buyer evaluation of their products that the small firms suffer in these cases are such that their presence probably has slight actual or potential influence on industry conduct and performance.

A slightly lesser degree of concentration is found in industries which we will call "highly concentrated," and label as Type II. These, of which there are a good many in the American economy, are distinguished from Type I in that the proportion of the market controlled by a few large sellers though still big is perceptibly less, and in that the competitive fringe of smaller sellers is usually more numerous and collectively controls more of the market. In general, this class is typified by roughly 85 or 90 per cent control of the market by the first 8 sellers, by from 65 to 75 per cent control by the first 4, and by a competitive fringe of small sellers usually ranging in number from 20 or 30 to more than 100. A good example of this category is the tire and tube industry, for which available data show the following:

TYPE II   RUBBER TIRE INDUSTRY

Tire-Producing Firms	Percentage of U S. Passenger-Car Tire Plant Capacity, 1965
Goodyear	25.6
Firestone	22.8
U. S. Rubber	13.8
Goodrich	13.1
(First 4 firms)	(75.3)
Armstrong	8.3
General	3.5
Mansfield	2.8
Cooper	2.1
(First 8 firms)	(92.0)
30 other firms	8.0
Total	100.0

Among other industries falling in this general category for 1963 are transformers (68 per cent of total sales by 4 firms, 79 per cent by 8 firms, 93 per cent by 20 firms, and 144 firms in all); and household laundry equipment (78 per cent by 4 firms, 95 per cent by 8 firms, 99 per cent by 20 firms, and 31 firms in all). In general, oligopolistic interdependence among the largest six or eight firms in the industries designated as Type II must still be very strong. But control of as much as roughly 85 or 90 per cent of the market involves 7 or 8 firms instead of 3 or 4, and the members of the competitive fringe, not fully restrained by oligopolistic interdependence, are either relatively larger, more numerous, or both.

As Type III oligopolies we may recognize industries of "high-moderate" concentration, in the sense that the first 8 sellers will ordinarily control roughly 70 to 85 per cent of total output, and the first 4 roughly 50 to 65 per cent, with the total number of sellers ordinarily being larger than in the preceding categories. If concentration in the steel industry is measured in terms of the distribution among firms of basic capacity to produce steel ingots, this industry typifies the category.

TYPE III   STEEL INDUSTRY

Steel-Producing Firms	Percentage of U.S. Basic Ingot Capacity, 1960
U.S. Steel	28.2
Bethlehem	15.5
Republic	8.6
Jones & Laughlin	5.5
(First 4 firms)	(57.8)
National	4.7
American Rolling Mill	4.6
Youngstown	4.5
Inland	4.4
(First 8 firms)	(76.0)
7 other firms with 1 per cent or more apiece of national ingot capacity	10.6
65 other firms with less than 1 per cent apiece	13.4
Total	100.0

Here we note a perceptibly lessened degree of top-level concentration. Though it is still certainly enough to produce a substantial degree of oligopolistic interdependence among the few largest firms, a significant share of the market is supplied by a substantial number of smaller firms. This competitive fringe is clearly stronger and more important than in categories previously described. Other industries in this category are exemplified (in 1963) by the aircraft industry (59 per cent by 4 firms, 83 per cent by 8, 99 per cent by 20, and 82 firms in all), and by the ball and roller bearing industry (57 per cent by 4, 76 per cent by 8, 91 per cent by 20, and 93 firms in all).

A next category of industry as we proceed downward in the concentration scale might be labeled as having "low-moderate" concentration (Type IV)—with roughly 35 to 50 per cent of the market controlled by 4 firms, roughly 45 to 70 per cent by 8, and with a large number of sellers in all. Of familiar industries with large outputs, the meat-packing industry is a prominent representative of this class. If concentration is measured in terms of proportions of the total national nonfarm slaughter of meat animals (by both wholesale slaughterers and meat retailers) the picture in 1947 was very roughly as follows:[7]

TYPE IV   MEAT-PACKING INDUSTRY

Meat-Packing Firms	Approximate Percentage of National Nonfarm Slaughter, 1947
Swift	15.5
Armour	13.5
Wilson	5.0
Cudahy	4.0
(First 4 firms)	(38.0)
Morrell	2.0
Hormel	1.5
Rath	1.5
Kingan	1.5
(First 8 firms)	(44.5)
Over 2,000 other firms	55.5
Total	100.0

[7]In the case of the meat-packing industry, calculation of seller concentration for each of several principal regional markets probably would be more meaningful, but the same general order of seller concentration by regions would evidently be observed.

Comparable data are not available for later years, but the concentration pattern in the meat packing industry has evidently not changed very much. Data from the 1963 Census of Manufactures show 31 per cent of meat packing done by the 4 largest firms, 42 per cent by the 8 largest, 54 per cent by the 20 largest, 64 per cent by the 50 largest, with 2,833 firms in all supplying the market.

Other industries falling in this same category in 1963 included, for example, printing ink (48 per cent controlled by 4 firms, 63 per cent by 8, 77 per cent by 20, and 216 firms in all); wallpaper (33 per cent by 4, 48 per cent by 8, 75 per cent by 20, and 77 firms in all); and lubricating oils (36 per cent by 4, 48 per cent by 8, 65 per cent by 20, and 311 firms in all).

By the time we have reached a degree of concentration as low and a total number of sellers as great as are found in our Type IV of industry, there is a legitimate question as to whether we still have "oligopoly." Various students have differed on this matter. The question is whether the classification should rest on structural characteristics of the market, or on various observations and theoretical predictions of the conduct and performance of sellers in such industries. According to structural criteria, there is still "some oligopoly" in these markets. That is, there is a moderately concentrated oligopolistic core with a large competitive fringe. Of the largest three or four or more sellers, each is large enough that the market adjustmnts of one will perceptibly affect the others and presumably induce reactions. Thus recognized interdependence among sellers (the hallmark of oligopoly) is present, even though 30 to 60 per cent of market output is supplied by sellers each of whom is so small that his own market adjustments will not perceptibly affect others. Following structural criteria, we call this sort of industry oligopolistic, though it is clearly a quite different sort of oligopoly from that characterized under Types I and II.

Following instead the certain criteria of observed or theoretically predicted performance, some students have tended to characterize our Type IV industries as "competitive" rather than oligopolistic. They have done so on the ground that the independent competitive action of the large competitive fringe in these industries should force the whole industry, including the large sellers, to perform roughly as an atomistic industry would. Granted that industries in this category may be expected to and do perform differently than highly concentrated oligopolies, we are hesitant here to accept their classification as "competitive" or "the same as atomistic." Neither theory nor observation is conclusive on this point. It seems safer to classify such industries as a variety of "low-grade" oligopoly, and leave it to be determined how they act.

In fact, an even lower degree of concentration than what attributed to Type IV industries may still be identified as being other than atomistic and as having in it elements of oligopoly. This would be found in industries (according to our classification) with less than 35 per cent of the market controlled by 4 firms, and generally less than 45 per cent by 8, but with the largest sellers controlling more than a few per cent of the market apiece. Generally, such industries have a competitive fringe of a very large number of small sellers. The flour industry exemplifies this Type V of industry, as shown in the following table:

TYPE V   FLOUR-MILLING INDUSTRY

Flour Firm	Percentage of National Flour-Milling Capacity,* 1966
International	8.1
Pillsbury	7.4
Peavey	5.7
General Mills	5.3
(First 4 firms)	(26.5)
Colorado	4.7
Seaboard	4.2
Nabisco	3.3
Econo-Flo	3.3
(First 8 firms)	(42.0)
First 20 firms	66.7
385 other firms	33.3
Total	100.0

*Concentration of output in the flour industry is somewhat greater than concentration of capacity.

Other members of this category would include the women's shoe industry, the canned fruit and vegetable industry, and the paint industry. In these industries, generally the largest 4 sellers control on the average from 6 to 8 percent apiece of the market and the next largest 4 sellers 2 to 4 per cent apiece; nearly all remaining sellers control about 1 per cent apiece or less of the market. The total number of sellers will ordinarily range from more than a hundred up to well over a thousand. The force of oligopolistic interdependence is presumably slight in Type V industries.

Finally, we come to industries which are clearly "atomistic" for all practical purposes. In them, no seller is large enough to be likely to have a recognized interdependence with others. Examples of this Type VI of industry would include the women's suit and coat industry, with 2,481 sellers in 1963 and with the 4 largest sellers together supplying only 8 per cent of the market and the largest 50 only 28 per cent; most of the other garment and clothing industries; most wood-product industries; and others.

The preceding sixfold classification of manufacturing industries according to the degree of seller concentration is largely experimental or pragmatic. But it is oriented to theory and systematic observation in that it tries to distinguish structural patterns which might theoretically be expected to, and on occasion have been observed to, generate different sorts of market conduct and performance. Either fewer or more than six classes might be required to draw all important distinctions among industries on the basis of seller concentration. However, a classification of the sort just described has the merit of recognizing that oligopolistic industries have wide differences in the degree and pattern of seller concentration, that may be expected to lead to corresponding differences in the character of market conduct and performance. Precisely what these latter differences are remains to be determined, and this determination is complicated by the fact that conduct and performances are influenced by characteristics of market structure in addition to seller concentration.

Seller Concentration in Industries Outside the Manufacturing Sector

For sectors other than manufacturing, we cannot present so adequate a statistical picture of seller concentration by industries. But we can make some appraisal based on qualitative information and on scraps of specific evidence.

A complicating factor as we consider concentration in the nonmanufacturing sectors is that all or parts of some of them are subject to governmental regulations and actions designed to restrict or eliminate competition. This tends to diminish the significance of seller concentration as a determinant of market conduct and performance. For example, industries with a "competitive" structure so far as concentration is concerned may be regulated into behaving in a "monopolistic" fashion. In spite of this complication, we will adhere to reporting patterns of seller concentration as they are, and note separately the existence of competition-restricting regulation.

One broad sector in which seller concentration by industries is generally very high is that including transportation, communication, and other public utility industries. Generally, each of these subsectors is broken up into numerous theoretical industries, distinguished on the basis not only of the type of service provided, but also of geography. There are numerous noncompeting regional or local industries in most cases. Thus in the production of electric power or the provision of local telephone service we would recognize numerous seperate regional or local markets, each corresponding roughly to a theoretical industry; in transportation, we would at least distinguish freight and passenger transport initially, and would then identify numerous separate theoretical transportation industries on the basis of locality, region, or route. The following would then appear with respect to seller concentration in individual industries:

1. Electric power utilities and natural or manufactured gas utilities—very high concentration in any single market, typically was a single-firm monopoly.

2. Local telephone service—the same.

3. Interstate or long distance telephone service—very high concentration, approaching single-firm monopoly.

4. Telegraph—the same.

5. Radio and television, as regards either local markets or national network service—either high or very high seller concentration.

6. Passenger transportation other than local, including rail, air, and highway—high or very high concentration in almost every market, even after all competing railroads, airlines, and bus companies have been taken into account.

7. General freight transportation, including rail, truck, and domestic (coastal or inland) water transportation—from high to moderate concentration in individual markets.

8. Urban street transportation—single-firm monopoly or very high concentration in any market.

9. Petroleum transportation by pipelines and tankships—high or very high seller concentration by markets.

In nearly all of these cases, general freight transportation possibly excluded, there is an absence of any competitive fringe of small sellers; one or a few large sellers occupy the entire market. Entry to these fields is generally restricted by public authorities which grant franchises necessary for operation, so that the fewness of sellers is deliberately pre-served. With the exception of radio and television, prices are deter-mined or must be approved by public agencies, with the dual or alternate purposes of preventing excessive charges to the public and of preventing interfirm competition from denying firms a "reasonable" return on their investment.

A sector in which moderate or high seller concentration by industry is less frequently encountered is mining. The two largest industrial sec-tors in the mining category are those producing the main fossil fuels, bituminous coal and petroleum (including natural gas). The bituminous coal industry is definitely atomistic, with several thousand sellers, none of them large. The petroleum-producing industry, logically divided into several regional industries, is in each case moderately concentrated, with 10 to 20 sellers supplying about half the output, and a multitude of smaller sellers the remainder. In most oil-producing states, however, the rate of petroleum production is restricted (and its price thus raised) by governmental authorities established to promote conservation of petroleum. In the mining of metallic ores, high or very high concentra-tion is the rule. This clearly applies to the principal industries mining iron, copper, aluminum, lead, and zinc ore. Nonmetallic mining of stone, sand, gravel, clay, and so forth is generally conducted by indus-tries of rather unconcentrated or atomistic structure.

In the numerous industries included under agriculture proper (ex-cluding forestry and fisheries), the typical situation is one of atomistic market structure: there is no significant degree of seller concentration. This is true of each of the agricultural industries producing the major grain and fiber crops (wheat, corn, cotton, etc.), other major food ma-terials (such as meat animals, peanuts, soybeans, milk), and most fruit and vegetable crops except for a few limited specialties. There are in any such agricultural industry a very large number of small sellers, none of which supplies a significant fraction of the total industry out-put. Here, then, is a sector which is atomistic or competitive in the structural sense almost throughout.

However, the agricultural sector has been favored by wide-spread governmental interference designed to modify or prevent the working of competitive market forces, and the presumptive effects of atomistic market structure on market conduct and performance have thus been in some degree mitigated or forestalled. Under present practice in the United States, much of agriculture is atomistic in structure but not "atomistically competitive" in conduct and performance, because of direct governmental interferences with supply and price, and governmentally sponsored cartels of private producers. But the atomistic structure of agricultural production retains a somewhat modified significance, in the sense that the working and results of various governmental interference schemes are importantly influenced by this structural pattern.

Close relatives of agriculture proper are the forestry and fishery industries. These, like agriculture, are by and large atomistic in structure, though in certain regional forest industries a low-moderate concentration in the hands of a few firms, together with a large competitive fringe, is noted.

We might look further for a refuge of atomistic competition in the distributive trades—the wholesalers and retailers of all sorts of goods from groceries to automobiles. An adequate structural appraisal here is hardly contained in the observation that there are thousands or tens of thousands of grocers, automobile dealers, and so forth in the United States, and that most of them are small. The distributive trade sector must be divided and subdivided and resubdivided before we arrive at the individual industry. There is first a general distinction between wholesaling and retailing, except in lines where the two are integrated in single firms. Then either of these (let us take retailing as an example) is divided into numerous separate lines, like grocery stores, houseware and appliance stores, building materials stores, service stations, drug stores, automobile dealers, ladies' clothing stores, men's clothing stores, liquor stores, and so on, each providing a distinct sort of distribution service. Finally, the sellers in any such line must in general be divided into numerous local industries, since the primary characteristic of the distributive trades—that the service sold must be performed at the point of use or delivery—means that retailers in different localities are not in competition with each other and are not members of the same theoretical industry. Thus we arrive at industry units at least as small, for example, as the Philadelphia automobile dealer industry or the San Francisco Bay area grocery industry, and even finer subdivisions are probably in order. Correspondingly, the significant measures of seller concentration in the distributive trades which we seek are measures of concentration within local competing groups in individual lines of distribution.

The seller concentration picture, as thus construed, is not uniformly one of extreme or approximate atomism, and includes numerous cases of moderate or low-moderate oligopolistic concentration, together with a substantial competitive fringe of smaller sellers. This is true, at least, for cities and metropolitan areas; higher concentration will generally be found in towns, villages, and rural areas. Speaking of the city or metropolis and of retailing, several patterns are observed among the different trades, such as the following:

1. Fairly high concentration of sales in the hands of a few sellers, and a limited competitive fringe—for example, variety or "5-and-10-cent stores," auto supply stores, fluid milk distribution.

2. Moderate to low-moderate concentration with a limited total number of sellers—for example, building materials dealers, new-automobile dealers.

3. A moderately to highly concentrated oligopolistic core of a few sellers, plus a large competitive fringe—as with groceries, where one or two nationwide chain-store firms plus a few local chains will control over half of total sales in an area, the rest being distributed among very numerous small grocers.

4. From low-moderate concentration to atomism, with a large total number of sellers—seen in clothing lines, housewares and home appliances, and liquor (except where there are state liquor "monopolies").

Retail distributive-trade industries as a group tend to be less concentrated than manufacturing industries, and in an important proportion of them something approaching atomism is found. But there is another important proportion in which moderately concentrated or low-grade oligopoly, with a substantial competitive fringe, occurs, just as it does in many manufacturing industries. In wholesaling, the picture is less well delineated, but in general concentration in wholesaling in any line will run substantially higher than it does in retailing in the same line.

Like agriculture, but to a lesser extent, the distributive trades are the subject of some governmentally sponsored interference with competitive market conduct. This appears principally in the form of the so-called "fair trade" (resale price maintenance) laws of most of the states, which cover not much more than a tenth of all retail goods sold. In addition, there is frequently price-fixing by state authorities of wholesale and retail prices of milk and liquor.

Statistics of seller concentration in contract construction are quite inadequate. The picture is intrinsically complicated because of the necessity of distinguishing general (total-project) contractors from various types of subcontractors engaged in electrical work, plumbing, plastering, and the like. With respect to subcontractors and to general contractors engaged in residential construction in any metropolitan area, the total number of sellers is usually large and the degree of concentration from quite low to atomistic. In the construction of large projects, including roads, freeways, bridges, dams, and large commercial and industrial buildings, however, the number of eligible contractors is ordinarily very much smaller (in part because of the restrictive effect of high bonding and other requirements), and seller concentration apparently ranges from moderate to quite high. A fair share of the contract construction industries thus appears to fall somewhere in the oligopoly category.

The service trades present a miscellaneous picture with respect to seller concentration in individual industries or markets, though perhaps one tending dominantly in the atomistic direction. At one extreme we find motion picture production and distribution, in which there is a high degree of oligopolistic concentration. At the other are such lines as local dry cleaning and laundry service, barbershops, gardeners, and housemaids, with atomistic structure industry by industry. In-between cases might include hotels, with low-moderate concentration among a few big hotels plus a substantial competitive fringe in most urban markets. Generally, the bulk of service-trade industries tend in the atomistic direction, and this sector has not been much subject to governmental interferences with competition.

Since we are concerned in this book mainly with nonfinancial enterprise, we will not comment at any length on concentration in the financial sector, including banking, insurance, and real estate. A variety of concentration patterns is found in industries in this sector.

When all sectors in addition to manufacturing are taken into account, what is the incidence of potentially significant degrees of seller concentration in the whole enterprise economy? In manufacturing, potentially significant seller concentration is encountered in a dominant proportion of industries, although among these concentration ranges from quite high to barely enough to introduce some oligopolistic interdependence. For the rest of the economy we find that high seller concentration is typically encountered in transportation, utility, and communication industries and in some mining industries. Moderate or low-moderate oligopolistic concentration, with large competitive fringes, is found in many distributive-trade industries, in petroleum production, in some branches of contract construction, and in a few service trades. Atomistic structure pervades nearly all agricultural industries, forestry and fisheries, much of contracting, coal mining, and most of the service-trade industries. Oligopolistic market structures of one variety or another are extremely common, and where they are not, their absence is frequently compensated for by governmental interferences with competition.

Buyer Concentration in Individual Markets

In speaking of concentration as an influence on the character and results of competition among enterprises, we have so far emphasized seller concentration within individual industries. Let us now consider the correlative importance of the degree of buyer concentration: the number and size distribution of the buyers who make up the market which a given industry of sellers supplies.

In the American economy, departures from substantial atomism are much less common on the buying sides of markets than on the selling sides. In the great majority of industries, the suppliers face markets made up of many buyers, all relatively small. Seldom are there a few large individual buyers, each of whom purchases a significant fraction of industry supply. A significant degree of buyer concentration—or oligopsony—is much less frequently encountered than is oligopoly among sellers. Nonetheless, oligopsony is found in an important minority of cases, and the extent and character of buyer concentration in them deserves at least brief mention.

Where it does occur, oligopsony has potential consequences more or less congruent with those of oligopoly. That is, the purchase of significant shares of a market supply by a few large buyers creates a recognized interdependence among them, which may restrict their tendency to compete for supplies. Express or tacit collusion among them may grow up, and they may thus have a tendency to act jointly or collectively to exercise their "monopsony" (buyer's monopoly) power to depress buying prices and increase their own profit, generally at the expense of the sellers who supply them. Even without collective action the individual large buyer may by virtue of the bargaining power inherent in his large volume of purchases be able to negotiate lower prices in imperfect markets.

This is in contradistinction to the situation which prevails with atomistic buying. With many buyers, all relatively small, each buyer purchases so little that he cannot influence the price at which he buys, either by restricting his purchases or by bargaining with sellers. Instead, he will take the price fixed by sellers or by market forces as given to him and will independently adjust his purchases on the supposition that he cannot influence the price. Correspondingly, sellers with price-determining power, such as oligopolistic sellers, can simply establish a uniform market price for all buyers and let them adapt to it, without being subject to price-influencing policies on the part of buyers.

The possibility that there is oligopsony in various markets obviously introduces another basis for distinguishing and classifying markets, and leads to a somewhat elaborated set of theoretical predictions concerning market conduct and performance. Generally, we can recognize the following important categories as distinguished on the basis of both seller and buyer concentration:

1. Markets with many small buyers and many small sellers—or *fully atomistic markets.*
2. Markets with many small buyers but with a significant degree of seller concentration—*simple oligopoly.*
3. Markets with a significant degree of buyer concentration and many small sellers—oligopsony plus atomistic selling, or *simple oligopsony.*
4. Markets with a significant degree of buyer concentration *and also* a significant degree of seller concentration—oligopoly plus oligopsony, or, as it is sometimes called, *bilateral oligopoly.*

The general direction of theoretical predictions of conduct and performance tendencies in these categories is easily anticipated. We will not pause long to consider simple monopoly, simple monopsony, or bilateral monopoly structures, since these are seldom encountered in markets for commodities. (They are frequently approximated in labor markets.) Briefly, the expectation with ordinary monopoly is for unilateral price determination by the one seller, with a tendency to restrict supply in order to raise price above a competitive level; with ordinary monopsony, we anticipate unilateral price determination by the one buyer, with a tendency to restrict purchases in order to depress price below the competitive level; with bilateral monopoly, the prospect is for price and output determination by bargaining or negotiation between the buyer and seller, with the price arrived at being hypothetically variable over a range admitting both supercompetitive and subcompetitive prices.

The predictions for cases involving oligopoly, oligopsony, or both, follow a similar course, since in general oligopolies are expected to have some "monopolistic" tendencies, and oligopsonies to have "monopsonistic" tendencies. Thus we might, on the basis of theory, expect:

(a) *In fully atomistic markets* (many small buyers plus many small sellers)—independence of action on the part of each buyer and each seller, none being able to influence price, and price and output determined competitively by the impersonal market forces represented in the aggregate of individual supplies and demands forthcoming.

(b) *In ordinary oligopolistic markets* (with many buyers)—some control over price by large sellers, no control by buyers, and some general tendency (varying importantly with the degree of seller concentration) for large sellers collectively to elevate price somewhat above the atomistic level while restricting supply.

(c) *In ordinary oligopsonistic markets* (with many sellers)—some control over price by large buyers, no control by sellers, and some general tendency (varying significantly with the degree of buyer concentration) for large buyers collectively to depress price somewhat below the atomistic level while restricting purchases.

(d) *In bilateral oligopolies* (with significant buyer concentration and seller concentration)—full control over price in the hands of neither buyers alone nor sellers alone, express or tacit bargaining on price between buyer-seller pairs or between groups of buyers and of sellers, and some general tendency for the power of large sellers and that of large buyers to offset each other, so that price deviates from the atomistic level less than it would with oligopoly alone or oligopsony alone. That is, the "countervailing power" of large buyers and of large sellers may tend to blunt both monopolistic and monopsonistic tendencies, though arrival exactly at an atomistic market outcome is not generally to be expected. Comparative degrees of seller and buyer concentration should have some influence on the outcome.

Given these theoretical possibilities, what is the nature and extent of the incidence of concentrated buying in the American economy and its impact on market structures? Systematic statistics on buyer concentration are unfortunately not available, but some general qualitative observations are possible.

First, as indicated above, for all industries in all sectors, the predominant pattern is one of atomistic buying. This is in part because many markets are those in which goods and services are sold directly to consumers for use, and because the consumers of any good or service are generally numerous and small. Moving back a stage in the process of production and distribution, a close approximation to atomistic buying is also found in a major fraction of manufacturing industries. Although firms in those industries that produce consumer goods do not in general sell directly to consumers, their markets are frequently made up of large numbers of distributive firms which purchase from them. Unconcentrated buying is also faced by a high proportion of manufacturing industries which sell producer goods. They sell either to the many producers in a single unconcentrated manufacturing industry, or to firms in a wide variety of other manufacturing industries. Similar unconcentrated buying is encountered also by many producer-good industries outside of manufacturing. Atomistic buying, or an insignificant degree of buyer concentration, is thus faced by the great majority of all industries in all sectors of the economy combined.

There remains, however, an important minority category of industries in whose markets a significant degree of buyer concentration is present. Since the significance of buyer concentration or oligopsony may be expected to differ according to whether or not there is also significant seller concentration or oligopoly, we may separate these industries with concentrated buying into two classes: those with atomistic selling, or simple oligopsonies, and those with a significant degree of seller concentration also, or bilateral oligopolies. The precise extent of either of these categories is not known from available data, but some general comments and some examples may be offered.

Concentrated buying from industries made up of a large number of small sellers appears to be encountered mainly in some of the agricultural and mining industries. An outstanding example in agriculture is found in the leaf tobacco market, in which a very large number of small tobacco growers sell the bulk of their output to 6 major cigarette manufacturers. Here a high degree of oligopsonistic concentration is juxtaposed with an atomistic selling market. High or moderate buying concentration is also ordinarily encountered in the farm markets for fluid milk, and low-moderate buying concentration in the markets for meat animals (the members of the meat-packing industry being the principal buyers). In general, a significant minor share of total agricultural output passes through markets with some degree of oligopsonistic concentration, although only in a few cases is this concentration very high. In the mining sector, a moderate to high degree of buyer concentration is encountered in most markets for crude petroleum, wherein a few large refiners with specialized transport facilities at their disposal are typically the only available buyers for the crude-oil output of a large number of relatively small producers. A similar pattern is encountered in the markets for some mineral ores. In such instances, where oligopsony is combined with unconcentrated selling, special questions concerning possible deviations from competitive pricing standards arise, just as they do with ordinary oligopoly.

Bilateral oligopoly, or concentrated buying versus concentrated selling, is most frequently found (when it is found at all) in markets for manufactured goods—either for producer goods sold by one set of manufacturers to another, or for consumer goods sold to large distributive firms. Bilateral oligopoly is not the most common form of market structure in either of these sorts of market, but there are instances of it in each. Among producer-good industries, concentrated buying faces concentrated selling in a number of markets for basic metals or metal products. In the steel industry, for example, a moderately concentrated oligopoly of sellers faces moderate or high buyer concentration in the markets for steel strip and sheet (a large share of which is purchased by a relatively few large automobile and appliance makers), for tin-plated steel (the bulk of which is purchased by two tin-can makers), and for rails. Roughly comparable buyer concentration occurs in the markets for primary copper and basic copper products, for some other nonferrous metal products, and for a number of automobile parts or components, where a few parts makers sell their output to a few automobile manufacturers. Markets in which manufactured goods are sold to distributive firms under conditions of bilateral oligopoly are found largely in lines in which a few "mass distributors" (usually with chain-store operations) have secured significant proportions of the national distribution volume. Since the largest 9 grocery chain-store firms in the United States together control about 29 per cent of all grocery-store sales, some low-moderate degree of oligopsonistic concentration occurs in the markets for most processed food items. With the industries supplying these items generally having moderate or low-moderate seller concentration, a not very concentrated pattern of bilateral oligopoly ordinarily emerges. A similar pattern is found for some manufactured consumer-good items outside the food lines, in which chain-store plus mail-order firms like Sears, Roebuck and Montgomery Ward account for significant shares of the total market volume. Usually, the bilateral oligopoly which occurs in markets involving manufacturers as sellers and mass distributors as buyers seems to be of a "low-grade" variety, involving no more than low-moderate concentration on either the seller or the buyer side of the market.

Summary

The preceding characterization of seller and buyer concentration within individual industries throughout the economy discloses numerous different patterns of market structure. Variety rather than uniformity of structure, in the dimensions of concentration, is the keynote. Within this variety we note the existence of several significantly different sorts of oligopolistic selling—distinguished on the basis of the degree of seller concentration—as well as the broader distinction between oligopoly and atomism as forms of organization of the seller side of markets. In addition, the picture is complicated, in a minority of cases, by the coupling of oligopsonistic buyer concentration with either atomistic or oligopolistic selling.

The effects on market conduct and performance of these variations in concentration patterns have been predicted in an extremely rough fashion by *a priori* economic theory, and we have referred to such predictions. A satisfactorily precise knowledge of these effects, however, can come only from systematic empirical study of the relationship of market conduct and performance to market structure. We therefore reserve further comment on this matter until we have looked at empirical findings concerning the character of market structures in other dimensions, and concerning typical patterns of conduct and performance associated with various structures.

Changes in Concentration in Individual Industries

In the last section of Chapter 4 we presented a general description of changes in overall business concentration in the United States from about 1870 to date—and also of changes in concentration in principal sectors of the economy, such as manufacturing, public utilities, the distributive trades, and agriculture. Highlights of the picture drawn there were that, given the impetus of the great merger movement from 1880 to 1905 and of a lesser merger movement during the 1920's, together with internal growth of large firms: (1) Overall business concentration increased greatly from the end of the Civil War until the early 1930's, but then reached a plateau from which it has departed only by declining slightly. (2) Such a plateau in the manufacturing sector was reached or approached as early as 1905, but in the public utility and the distributive trades sectors only at the end of the 1920's or somewhat later. (3) In the period from 1947 to 1963 the only significant sectoral change measured has been some increase in the proportions of all manufacturing activity carried on by the largest 25, 50, and 100 firms, this representing in large part a "recovery" of manufacturing sector concentration to the levels of the 1930's.

Now we will extend that discussion by considering briefly the trends over the same period in seller concentration in individual industries. This is not necessarily a redundant exercise, because changes in individual-industry concentration do not at all exactly mirror changes in concentration in the economy as a whole or in broad sectors of it. Growth of individual firms which increases overall or sector concentration may not be reflected in increased concentration in any individual industry. This may be because the firms grow by diversifying to enter new industries or by increasing their vertical integration, or because their proportionate growth is no greater than that of the industries in which they operate, so that it does not increase seller concentration in industries. Conversely, increased concentration in numerous individual industries through the growth of their larger firms need not increase top-level concentration in a sector or in the whole economy if the industries and their principal firms are comparatively small or are of declining relative importance over time, or if opposite changes in seller concentration occur in other industries or sectors. Some independent attention to changes in individual-industry concentration is thus justified. Because of the lack of adequate data on changes in industry concentration in any other sectors, we will confine our attention here entirely to manufacturing industries.

The great merger movement from 1880 to about 1905, the impact of which on overall business and manufacturing sector concentration has been noted in Chapter 4, had the predictable effect of dramatically increasing concentration in the great majority of the then established manufacturing industries in the United States. It has been noted that during this period there were about 318 major industrial combinations and that they involved about 80 per cent of all existing manufacturing industries. How high were the degrees of seller concentration which were brought about in the industries involved? Information relative to this question is rather incomplete, but some indications are available. Moody's *Truth About the Trusts* reports that of the 92 largest individual companies formed by mergers before 1905, 78 controlled 50 per cent or more of their respective industries, and 26 controlled 80 per cent or more of their industries. This contemporary report suggests directly that single-firm domination of individual industries emerged at least in a significant minor proportion of manufacturing industries, and indirectly that oligopolistic seller concentration was created in a similar or larger proportion of them. Nutter[8] and Adelman[9] confirm this impression by estimating that as of approximately 1900 to 1905, about one-third of the value of all American manufacturing output originated in industries in which the largest 4 sellers supplied 50 per cent or more of industry output—a somewhat greater share than in 1947. By the same token, however, two-thirds of manufacturing output evidently originated in industries with lesser seller concentration—roughly the same proportion as found in 1963.

Putting together all scraps of available evidence the following seems to have been true by about 1905: (1) Concentration in manufacturing industries as measured by the proportion of individual industry output supplied *by the largest single firm in the industry* was probably on the average at an all-time peak, and somewhat greater than in the 1920's or at present. (2) Concentration as measured by the share of individual industry output supplied by the largest 3, 4, or 5 firms was probably, on

[8]G. Warren Nutter, *The Extent of Enterprise Monopoly in the United States, 1899-1939*, Chicago, 1951, Ch. III.

[9]M. A. Adelman, "The Measurement of Industrial Concentration," *Review of Economics and Statistics*, **XXXIII**, 4 (Nov., 1951), p. 291.

the average, about as it has remained since. (3) Concentration as measured by the fractions of industry outputs supplied by the largest 10 or 20 firms may well have been lower than it later became and is now. Subject to these qualifications, individual-industry concentration in manufacturing reached a plateau around 1905 from which it has not departed very much to date.

The second and lesser merger movement of the 1920's, which had very important effects on concentration in the public utilities sector, had an important impact on industries in the manufacturing sector only in a highly selective fashion. The emergence of large firms and high individual-industry concentration during the 1920's was centered in "newer" industries which had been relatively immature and small at the time of the first merger movement and had grown rapidly since. Thus the petroleum refining, automobile, radio equipment, food-packaging, and chemicals industries all experienced increasing seller concentration after 1920, as did the motion picture industry in the service trades sector. There was a good deal of "catching up" by manufacturing industries that had missed the merger train before 1905.

But manufacturing industries that had become rather concentrated in the earlier period were in general not comparably affected. As noted in Chapter 4, expansion of large firms in these industries, by merger or internal growth, did not necessarily increase their concentration, since their markets and their competitors were also growing rapidly. Many such expansions, including those accomplished by mergers, were so offset by market growth that the market shares of the expanding firms—and thus the degree of concentration in their industries—declined or failed to increase. For example, the United States Steel Corporation, with 65 per cent of the steel market in 1900, grew steadily until 1935 and emerged with only about 35 per cent of the market. On the average, the deconcentrating force of market expansion and growth of lesser competitors tended to counterbalance the concentrating force of mergers and expansions by large firms in American manufacturing industries during this period. (There were, of course, many individual increases and decreases in concentration—usually moderate—in individual industries).

This impression is confirmed by the findings of Nutter[10] and Adelman[11] that the percentage of manufacturing output produced by industries in which the largest sellers supplied 50 per cent or more of industry output either did not change significantly or declined from around 1905

[10]*Op. cit.*
[11]*Op. cit.*

to 1937 or 1947. Nutter estimates that this percentage declined from 32 to 28 by 1937; Adelman finds that it fell from 33 to 24 by 1947.

Comparison of Adelman's and Nutter's findings suggests that there was probably some minor downward shift in average top-level seller concentration in American manufacturing industries from the middle 1930's to 1947. This suggestion is supported by comparing 4-firm concentration ratios for all manufacturing industries as computed respectively for 1935 and 1947, although changes in industry definitions and other procedures employed by the Census of Manufactures between the two dates precludes a definitive comparison. In any event, it appears clear that, on the average, seller concentration in individual industries did not increase and probably decreased slightly from 1935 to 1947, in spite of the impact of World War II and a minor merger movement during the 1940's.

From 1947 until 1958, the latest date for which comparable measures of seller concentration in manufacturing industries have been computed, there are somewhat conflicting indications as to the direction of change (if any) in average seller concentration for manufacturing industries. The findings support the tentative conclusion that no statistically significant change took place over this period. An analysis by the Bureau of the Census shows the following for industries which were comparably defined in 1947, 1954, and 1958:

PERCENTAGE OF THE TOTAL VALUE OF SHIPMENTS IN
352 MANUFACTURING INDUSTRIES WHICH ORIGINATED IN
INDUSTRIES IN 4 SELLER CONCENTRATION CLASSES

Percentages of Industry Shipments Supplied by Largest 4 Firms	Percentage of Total Value of Shipments Originating in Each Concentration Class for:		
	1947	1954	1958
75–100	10.0	9.3	7.9
50–75	13.7	15.4	14.7
25–50	36.3	35.6	39.4
0–25	40.0	39.7	38.0

These data suggest a slight decline from 1947 to 1958 in the proportion of shipments originating in the most highly concentrated manufacturing industries, and a slight increase in the share originating in industries of middle-range concentration.

From data prepared by Shepherd on the percentages of employment in manufacturing industries in various seller concentration classes, for all manufacturing industries, the following condensed comparison of 1947 and 1958 can be developed:[12]

PERCENTAGE OF ALL MANUFACTURING EMPLOYMENT IN 5 SELLER CONCENTRATION CLASSES OF INDUSTRIES

Percentage of Industry Shipments Supplied by Largest 4 Firms	Percentage of Manufacturing Employment in Each Concentration Class For:	
	1947	1958
80–100	3.0	3.7
60–80	8.5	10.3
40–60	22.9	18.8
20–40	34.2	35.2
0–20	31.4	32.0

These data suggest a slight increase from 1947 to 1958 in the importance of industries with seller concentration above the 60-per-cent-by-4 line (from 11.5 to 14.0 per cent of total manufacturing employment), with a corresponding decrease in industries in which the largest 4 sellers supply from 40 to 60 per cent of industry output. But the movements are not large, and Shepherd is probably justified in his conclusion that no statistically significant change occurred.

In concluding this brief discussion of changes in seller concentration in individual manufacturing industries, let us for a moment shift attention from average trends of change for many industries in the last eighty years to patterns of change for individual industries, and pose the following questions: Are there ascertainable any typical patterns of evolution of seller concentration for individual industries? And how stable or unstable has seller concentration in individual industries been in the last several decades, following the merger movements of the late nineteenth century and of the 1920's?

The question concerning patterns of evolution in concentration in individual industries has never been extensively and intensively studied, but observation of a fair sampling of available case histories suggests the following. No single pattern of evolution of concentration typifies all industries; instead, at least a small variety of different patterns is descernible.

One prominent pattern finds that the industry in its "youthful" stage

[12]William G. Shepherd, "Trends of Concentration in American Manufacturing Industries, 1947-1958," *Review of Economics and Statistics,* **XLVI,** 2 (May, 1964), pp. 200–212.

(while its product is gaining wide acceptance and its basic technology is being developed) comes to be populated by a fairly large number of relatively small firms; that in its early maturity, concentration increases to some peak level of from very high to moderately high seller concentration; and that thereafter concentration declines for a period of time to a point somewhat lower than the peak and levels off to remain relatively stable in the mature industry. In the process of increase of concentration to a peak, it has not been uncommon for a single dominant firm to gain a dominant market share which is then yielded in part to a few larger rivals, so that a "big" 3, 4, or 5 firms emerge as an oligopolistic core supplying most or much of industry output.

A significant but less prominent pattern of evolution is about like that just described except that the level of concentration reached in the early maturity of the industry is not subsequently lessened by increases in the mature industry to a higher plateau and is thereafter relatively stable. (Instances in which concentration progressively increased to substantially monopolistic dominance of the industry by a single firm are extremely rare in American industrial history.) The complex causal factors which account for these patterns of evolution will not be discussed here, but some of them may become apparent in Chapter 6, which deals with explanations of concentration, and in Chapter 8, which discusses the condition of entry of new firms to industries.

A quite different pair of patterns of evolving concentration has been observed in a smaller number of industries—featuring in their early stages the establishment of a monopolistic or dominant firm that controls substantially all industry output. Such "early monopoly" patterns have generally developed because a single firm acquired a strategic patent on a process or product, or a monopolistic hold on a group of related patents, which enabled it to exclude competitors. Less frequently, the acquisition of a monopolistic control of a strategic natural resource has played the same role. Subsequent evolution of concentration in these cases has generally followed one of two courses. The dominant firm has continued to dominate the industry (rarely), or concentration has decreased as the single-firm monopoly gave way to a highly or moderately concentrated oligopoly of firms (more frequently). Expiration of strategic patents, development of competitive processes or products, and governmental antitrust actions to dissolve monopolies have all been instrumental in bringing about deconcentration. Single-firm dominance of an industry has occasionally been disguised when a dominant firm holding strategic patents has licensed several other firms to use them, but essentially has retained monopolistic control of industry price and output.

By no means all industries, however, have followed the patterns of evolution in concentration so far described. In many, the level of seller concentration attained in the early maturity of the industry has been appreciable but not high, and further developments have seen this level of concentration either sustained or subsequently increasing or decreasing somewhat. And in numerous others, a more or less atomistic structure has persisted for long periods. Numerous subpatterns of change in concentration differing slightly from those enumerated above may also be identified.

A motif common to most of the evolutionary patterns mentioned is that in "mature" industries, with familiar and established products and more or less settled basic technologies, seller concentration tends to become comparatively stable, or rather slowly changing through time. This bears on the second question posed earlier, concerning the comparative stability of seller concentration in individual industries in the past three decades. By and large, seller concentration in a substantial majority of manufacturing industries has been comparatively stable, though almost never static. In them, comparisons of top-level seller concentration in 1935, 1947, 1954, 1958, and 1963 reveal that changes in the share of the industry controlled by the 4 largest firms typically does not increase or decrease by as much as 5 percentage points in one or even two decades, though minor changes in concentration are very common. This tendency reflects the fact that the bulk of our industries in any recent time have been relatively mature. It also results from the fact that other structural changes which might engender rapid changes in concenration (such as revolutionary changes in techniques, products, or buyer preferences) really affect only a small proportion of industries in any period of one or two decades. A further consideration is that there is some counterbalancing of concentration-increasing forces (e.g., mergers) and concentration-decreasing forces (e.g., growth of markets).

On the other hand, more rapid shifts in seller concentration have been encountered in a significant minority of industries. These include notably relatively "new" industries in such areas as electronics and chemicals, which are still in the process of rapid evolution of seller concentration. They also include older industries in which other structural changes have upset the balance of forces which had maintained a previously established general level of concentration. In a minority of our many manufacturing industries, therefore, significant changes in seller concentration—ranging from 5 to 10 or more percentage points in the shares of markets controlled by the 4 largest firms—have occurred in periods as short as a decade.

The complex flux of minor and major changes in seller concentration in individual industries is consistent with, but qualifies, our earlier observation that "average" concentration in American manufacturing industries has not changed a great deal since 1935. Counterbalancing minor and major changes in individual industries have left the overall average picture above the same.

Another type of flux related to seller concentration may be mentioned in concluding this discussion. This is the shifting in the comparative market shares of individual sellers—and particularly of the largest sellers—in individual industries. Although seller concentration in an industry as measured by the proportion of the market supplied by the largest 4 or 8 firms may be quite stable over time, the relative market shares of these firms may shift, their ranking in order of size of market share may change, and some firms earlier among the largest 4 or 8 may be replaced by others. Such shifting in relative positions of firms, though not ubiquitous, is extremely common. A study based on the 1947 and 1958 Census of Manufactures, for example, shows that out of 204 selected manufacturing industries, in only 38 were the same 4 firms the largest in both 1947 and 1958. And in 25 of these cases the size ranking of the unchanged "big 4" had changed. In 166 of the 204 industries, one or more of the "big 4" of 1947 had been replaced by a previously smaller firm by 1958.[13]

This sort of shifting around of relative market shares of firms does not alter the force of mutually recognized interdependence if the degree of seller concentration remains relatively unchanged, as it typically does. Nor does it qualify the significance of observed degrees of top-level seller concentration. A situation in which firms A, B, C, and D together supply 70 per cent of a market in 1947, and are ranked in size in the order given, is not fundamentally altered if in 1958 firms B, A, C, and E supply 70 per cent of the market (E having replaced D in the "big 4" and B having moved ahead of A in market share). The influence of oligopolistic interdependence on market conduct and performance should be the same. Thus it would be easy to overstress the importance of the shifting of the ranks and market shares of individual firms in any industry, if this shifting is not matched by appreciable changes in the degree of seller concentration. What this shifting does reflect importantly when it occurs is the evident continuing rivalry for market shares among the member firms of industries, even in the most distinctly oligopolistic industries. We will return to this matter in Chapter 9.

---

[13] A similar flux over time in the identities and size rankings of the 100 largest industrial firms in the United States has been noted. See Norman R. Collins and Lee E. Preston, "The Size Structure of the Largest Industrial Firms, 1909–1958," *American Economic Review*, LI, 5 (Dec., 1961), pp. 986–1009.

SUPPLEMENTARY READINGS

Stigler, George J., "A Theory of Oligopoly," *Journal of Political Economy*, **LXXII**, 1 (Feb., 1964), pp. 44–61.

Nutter, G. W., *The Extent of Enterprise Monopoly in the United States, 1899-1939*, 1951.

Adelman, M. A., "The Measurement of Industrial Concentration," *Review of Economics and Statistics*, **XXXIII**, 4 (Nov., 1951), pp. 261–296.

Shepherd, William G., "Trends in Concentration in American Manufacturing Industries, 1947-1958," *Review of Economics and Statistics*, **XLIV**, 2 (May, 1964), pp. 200–212.

Concentration Ratios in Manufacturing Industry, 1958, Parts I and II. Report prepared by the Bureau of Census for the Subcommittee on Antitrust and Monopoly of the Committee on Judiciary, United States Senate. Washington, 1962.

Concentration Ratios in Manufacturing Industry, 1963, Part I. Report prepared by the Bureau of Census for the Subcommittee on Antitrust and Monopoly of the Committee on the Judiciary, United States Senate. Washington, 1966.

6

The Rationale of Concentration — Efficiency and Other Considerations

The foregoing description of contemporary patterns of concentration in American industries, coupled with a brief history of changes in concentration, inspires interest in three related questions. First, what economic and other forces have determined the degrees of concentration attained in the industries in today's economy? In other words, how are existing patterns of industry concentration explained? Second, viewing the interval from 1870 to date, what changes in concentration-determining forces initially acounted for dramatic increases in concentration in a broad spectrum of industries, and in the past 30 years brought about a comparatively stable average degree of concentration in these industries? What concentration-increasing forces were at work in the earlier period, and what countervailing forces have subsequently tended to stablize concentration? Third, given the logic of the interaction of these two sorts of forces, should we anticipate increasing, decreasing, or stable industry concentration in the future?

We begin this chapter by analyzing the first broad issue, concerning the general rationale of existing concentration. The structure of this analysis is strongly influenced by the economist's central concern with efficiency—in this case the "technical" efficiency of the organization of industries. Technical efficiency is measured by the level of unit costs of production attained by an industry in supplying any output it produces; the degree of technical efficiency is measured by the relationship of attained unit costs to the minimum attainable unit costs of production.

With respect to efficiency so defined, the following specific questions are considered:

1. What general effects will the sizes of firms in individual industries, and derivatively the degrees of concentration in them, have on the efficiency attained in production and distribution?

2. To what extent does the pursuit of profits by firms lead them to assume sizes consistent with maximum efficiency, and what limits would the tendency of firms to attain efficient sizes place on degrees of concentration attained in individual industries?

3. What proportions of the outputs of individual industries must firms typically supply in order to secure the greatest possible efficiency in production?

4. To what extent in fact are American manufacturing industries alternatively:

(a) So highly concentrated that they are inefficient because their firms are inefficiently large?

(b) More concentrated than is required for maximal efficiency but nonetheless just as efficient as if their firms were somewhat smaller and concentration somewhat lower?

(c) Concentrated only to the minimum degree required for maximal efficiency?

(d) Insufficiently concentrated for purposes of efficiency, so that their firms are of inefficiently small size?

The fourth question deals with the extent to which the attainment of efficiency in sizes of firms in fact explains or justifies existing degrees of concentration in our manufacturing industries. Because our general answer to it is that existing concentration is by no means fully justified by considerations of efficiency, we then turn to an exploration of determinants of industry concentration other than the pursuit of efficiency. Numerous additional determinants being discovered, we thereafter offer a generalized explanation of existing concentration patterns, in which the pursuit of efficiency is identified as only one of many determinants. Some explanations of past changes in and recent stability of concentration, and some observations on possible further changes, are then derived from this analysis.

Economies and Diseconomies of Large-Scale Plants and Firms

Basic to all of the following discussion is one elementary fact. For a firm in almost any industry, the degree of efficiency in production will be systematically influenced by the size that the firm attains. And the effects of the size of a firm on its efficiency result from: (1) *Economies of large-scale plants* that are practically always available. (2) Possible further *economies of large-scale or multiplant firms*. (3) Possible *diseconomies of very large-scale firms*.

Let us consider these in turn.

Economies of Large-Scale Plants

The economies of large-scale available to the typical firm are at least mainly economies of large-scale plants—of larger factories, or stores, or electric generating stations. As the plant (generally defined as an aggregate of productive facilities at a single location) becomes larger up to some point, the firm operating it is able to obtain lower costs per unit of output. This is because larger plants permit it to exploit mass-production techniques that involve (*a*) the specialization of labor to specific narrow tasks; (*b*) the use of specialized machinery and other capital equipment, including units of equipment which are available in only very large minimal sizes; and (*c*) the specialization of management and supervising personnel to narrow and detailed tasks. Exploitation of all these opportunities as the plant becomes bigger will result in lower unit costs. For example, a cement plant with a capacity of 500 million barrels of cement per year may have a cost of $3 per barrel of cement, whereas one with a capacity of 1 billion barrels per year may attain a cost of $2.50 per barrel, and a still larger plant producing 2 billion barrels per year may have a cost of $2.25 per barrel. Unit cost declines (or efficiency increases) as the plant becomes larger.

But this is true only "up to a point" in the growth of the plant: unit costs do not generally become indefinitely lower as the plant becomes indefinitely larger. The economies of specialized labor, equipment, and management can be fully exploited or realized by making the plant "just about so big"—by increasing its size up to some finite and limited point. Further increases in its size beyond that point will not generally result in further cost reductions. To refer to the preceding example, it might be found that whereas a cement plant became more and more efficient as its size was increased up to a 2-billion-barrel capacity, further increases in its size would not reduce its cost at all. A 4-billion-barrel plant, for example, might have the same $2.25 per barrel cost as a 2-

billion-barrel plant. Thus, in general, the size of the plant influences cost and efficiency in this way. Larger plants will result in lower costs up to some critical scale of plant, so that there is some minimal scale of plant which will be more efficient than any smaller plants. But further increases in the size of plant beyond this *minimum optimal scale* will not result in further increases in efficiency.

Neither will they result in decreases in efficiency—i.e., in higher unit costs at some scale larger than the minimum optimal—unless distribution costs as well as production costs are counted and unless, in addition (*a*) average unit costs of transportation for delivery become appreciably higher with production centralized at one location than with production dispersed among several locations, and (*b*) production can be carried on at more than one location without production-cost disadvantages that offset virtual savings in distribution costs.

The typical possible relationships of unit cost of production and distribution to the size of a plant are illustrated diagrammatically in Figure 1. In the absence of net diseconomies in delivery costs with centralized production, the scale curve (*AC*) relating unit costs to the scale of plant is described by the line *defg*. This shows that as the plant is enlarged from smaller scales, unit costs decline until it reaches the scale

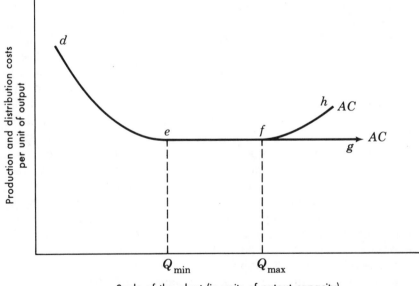

Figure 1

designated by Qmin—the minimum optimal scale—and that as the plant is further enlarged, unit costs remain constant at the optimal level. If enlargement of the plant beyond a certain point results in diseconomies in net delivery costs which could be avoided by building a plant at another location, the plant scale curve is described by the line *defh*, which shows that unit costs including those of distribution rise above the optimal level if the scale of plant exceeds Qmax. Thus the range of optimal scales available lies only between Qmin and Qmax, rather than being indefinitely large beyond minimum optimal scale.

This economic or technological law concerning economies of large-scale plants seems rather universally applicable to all sorts of productive operation; larger plants will always be more efficient than smaller plants *up to a point*. But among industries, depending on the character of the production techniques used, this "point" may vary widely. In some industries, a plant of very large scale, producing a very large quantity of output per period of time, may be required for maximum efficiency; in others, rather small-scale plants may be just as efficient as much larger ones.

The most significant difference among industries with respect to the output capacity of plants of minimum optimal scale is the difference *in the proportion of total industry output* which a single plant of minimum optimal scale will supply. What percentage of all goods bought from the industry will be produced by one such plant when it is fully utilized? In some industries, the output of a minimum optimal-scale plant will supply a fairly large fraction of the market faced by the industry. For example, in automobile production a single integrated plant complex of minimum optimal scale will probably supply as much as 10 per cent of all passenger-car output for the American market. In other industries, the percentage of industry output supplied by a single optimal plant will be more modest (for example, about 5 per cent in the case of cigarettes), and in still others, the percentage will be quite small (for example, 1 per cent or less in the manufacture of shoes or of flour).

The size of an optimal plant expressed in these terms (that is, as a percentage of total industry output supplied) obviously depends both on the extent of economies of large plants and on the size of the market which the industry supplies. The larger the market, the smaller a percentage of it a plant of given optimal size will supply; the greater the plant-scale economies, the larger the percentage of a given market an optimal-scale plant will supply. Given these two interacting determinants, there is a wide range of difference among industries with respect to the share of the industry market which is or would be supplied by a single plant of minimum optimal scale.

These differences are extremely significant, moreover, in determining *the minimum degree of seller concentration* which will be required in an industry to attain maximum efficiency, so far as efficiency is influenced by plant size. The larger the share of the market a plant of minimum optimal scale will supply, the fewer is the number of plants which can efficiently supply industry output. And if a plant cannot ordinarily be owned by more than one firm, the smaller is the number of efficient firms or sellers which the industry can accommodate. If in industry A, one plant of minimum optimal scale can supply 25 per cent of industry output, then the industry can at the most accommodate only 4 plants (and firms) of efficient scale, and seller concentration will be quite high if efficiency in plant scale is to be attained. In industry B, on the other hand, it may be that one plant of minimum optimal scale will supply only 2 per cent of industry output, in which case as many as 50 firms of efficient scale can coexist in the industry, thus making much lower seller concentration consistent with efficiency. The pursuit of efficiency, or lowest unit costs, may thus lead to widely differing degrees of concentration among different industries.

Ordinarily, of course, the size of a plant of minimum optimal scale as related to the size of the market will only determine the *maximum* number of plants and firms which can exist in an industry consistent with maximum efficiency. Since plants can usually be either somewhat or much larger than the minimum optimal scale without reducing their efficiency, the number of plants and firms can usually be fewer than this maximum—and the degree of seller concentration correspondingly higher—with unimpaired efficiency of plant size. Thus in industry C, the size of a plant of minimum optimal scale may be such that it will supply 4 per cent of the market, so that the industry cannot accommodate more than 25 plants and firms of optimal efficiency. But it may also be true that, in industry C, a plant five times as large, and thus supplying 20 per cent of the market, is just as efficient as one supplying 4 per cent. Then the industry may also have only 5 plants and firms and still have optimal efficiency in plant operation. In brief, the economies of large-scale plants in an industry only determine the maximum number of sellers and minimum degree of seller concentration consistent with efficiency, and leave open the possibility of higher degrees of concentration having comparable efficiency.

It should further be noted that the total importance of plant-scale economies in any industry will depend not only on the size of a minimum optimal plant as related to the size of the market, but also on the extent to which the production costs of plants of smaller than minimum optimal scale exceed those of optimal-scale plants. For example, in each of two industries we might find that a plant of minimum optimal scale would supply 6 per cent of the market. But in one industry a plant of half-optimal scale (supplying 3 per cent of the market) might have costs per unit of output only 2 per cent higher than those of an optimal plant, whereas in the second industry a plant of half-optimal scale might have unit costs 15 per cent higher than those of an optimal plant. (In the former case, the sector *de* of the plant scale curve in Figure 1 would be comparatively flat or slowly declining from *d* to *e*, and in the latter it would be more steeply declining, as it is drawn in that figure.) Clearly the penalty in terms of reduced efficiency for having a plant of less than optimal scale is much greater in the second case than in the first. Given such differences among industries, the size of the minimum optimal plant will be a stronger influence on the degree of seller concentration in an industry if the difference in efficiency between plants of optimal and suboptimal scale is great.

Economies of Large or Multiplant Firms

In addition to being able to reduce its costs per unit of output by expanding plant scale up to a certain point, the firm may also find that costs can be somewhat further reduced by growing large enough to manage and operate several optimal-scale plants, or at any rate by acquiring a total productive capacity that is some multiple of that of one plant of minimum optimal scale. These further possible economies are not those of the large plant, but are additional to them, and may be designated as *economies of the multiplant firm*. Such economies, if realized, are likely to be largely (1) economies of large-scale management, (2) economies of large-scale distribution, or (3) pecuniary economies of large-scale buying from suppliers. In some industries, economies from the centralized and coordinated management of several plants are claimed to be present. In some, operation of multiple plants may reduce costs of delivery freight if several branch plants are geographically scattered so as to be near different buying markets, and may also permit the building up of an efficient volume of sales through each of a number of geographically separate distributive centers. (Existence of such distributive economies presupposes that the firm for some reason—perhaps more effective sales promotion—finds it advantageous to distribute its output over a wide geographical area, such as the entire national market.) And in some again, the bulk-buying power of a multiplant firm in acquiring materials for use in manufacture, merchandise for resale, etc., may permit it to bargain for lower buying prices than smaller firms can obtain.

If such economies are available, increase of the size of the firm beyond that of one minimum optimal-scale plant will result in a reduction of unit costs of production and distribution below those of the one-plant firm. Thus in a given industry it might be found that a plant supplying 3 per cent or more of the market had the lowest attainable unit costs so far as costs are influenced by plant size—at, let us say, $2.00 per unit of output. But a two-plant firm (supplying 6 per cent of the market) might have slightly lower costs, at $1.97 per unit, and a four-plant firm (supplying 12 per cent of the market) might have still lower unit costs, at $1.95 per unit. The reduction in costs is the result, let us say, of more efficient distribution.

Like economies of a large-scale plant, however, economies of the multiplant firm will not continue to be realized indefinitely as the firm grows indefinitely larger. They will be "exhausted" or fully exploited at some finite size of firm, and beyond that size the firm will not become more efficient by adding still more plants. A four-plant firm in the preceding example might attain costs of $1.95 per unit and be more efficient than smaller firms, but a firm with six, eight, or twelve plants might be no more efficient than one with four, and also have unit costs of $1.95, the available opoprtunities for cost reduction having been fully exhausted at the four-plant size.

A scale curve for a firm that realizes multiplant economies (but does not encounter any diseconomies of very large scale) is illustrated in Figure 2. The first segment of this firm scale curve reading from the left

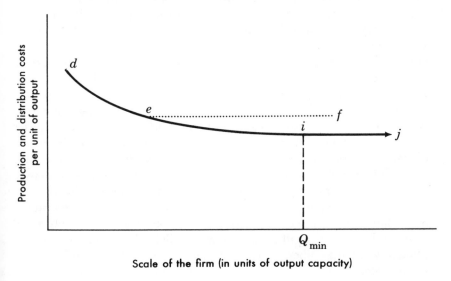

Scale of the firm (in units of output capacity)

Figure 2

(segment *de*) is also the plant scale curve, which by assumption reaches minimum optimal plant scale at *e* and is then horizontal at larger outputs (the total plant scale curve is *def*). Beyond the minimum optimal scale of one plant, however, the firm realizes multiplant economies until it reaches the scale Qmin at *i*, some multiple of *e*. So long as diseconomies of the very large firm are not encountered, the firm in becoming larger than Qmin then experiences neither decreases nor increases in unit costs, so that the firm scale curve as a whole is described by *deij*.

If economies of the multiplant firm are available in an industry, of course, firms will have to be larger and fewer in order to minimize costs, and the minimum degree of seller concentration which is consonant with maximum efficiency will be correspondingly higher. So far as firms tend to seek optimal scales of operation, economies of the multiplant firm should tend to increase seller concentration.

To this point we have suggested that, as the typical business firm is enlarged from the tiniest conceivable size (let us say, zero size) up to some critical size, it will progressively attain lower and lower production and distribution costs per unit of output. These economies of increased scale of the firm will result from certain economies of large-scale plant, and perhaps further from certain additional economies of the large-scale, multiplant firm. In order fully to realize such economies, the firm will need to grow to some critical minimum size or scale, at which scale unit costs become as low as they can get. This critical size may be designated as the minimum optimal scale of the firm (the word "optimal" meaning here simply "lowest-cost-per-unit"). If the firm becomes larger than the minimum optimal scale that rules in its industry, we have so far discussed no reason why its unit costs will therefore become either higher or lower—at scales in excess of the minimum optimal scale it may maintain the same level of efficiency attributed to a firm of minimum optimal scale.

The output of a firm of minimum optimal scale, expressed as a percentage of the total output absorbed by the market of its industry, varies widely among industries because of variations among industries in the character of production technique, the size of the market, the geographical character of the market and the importance of transport costs, etc. Correspondingly, the attainment of optimal efficiency in different industries will require widely differing degrees of seller concentration. Some industries can have a relatively large number of relatively small firms and have them all attain optimal scale; others can have only a relatively small number of relatively large firms if all are to be of optimal scale. Of course, if firms can exceed minimum optimal scale by any amount without reducing efficiency, then any industry can be highly concentrated and also efficient.

Possible Diseconomies of Large Firms

But can firms grow indefinitely large, beyond the minimum optimal scale, without suffering a loss of efficiency? Are there or are there not *diseconomies of very large scale* which affect firms as they grow beyond a certain size, and thereafter make them progressively less efficient as they get still larger? This is a remaining question of considerable importance. It bears on the issue of whether, in any industry, the degree of seller concentration that is consistent with efficiency can be any more closely determined than as lying between (*a*) the lower limit of the concentration found when each firm is of minimum optimal scale, and (*b*) the upper limit of control of the whole industry by a single-firm monopoly.

Neither theorizing nor the collection of evidence has so far given any conclusive answer to this question. Some theorists have advanced the hypothesis that diseconomies of very large-scale production will be encountered as the firm grows, probably because of the unwieldiness of management and administration in very large organizations. Others have held that such potential diseconomies are not or need not be experienced, given the available techniques of management organization demonstrated in the largest firms. Attempts to ascertain differences in efficiency between the very largest business firms and somewhat smaller (but still large) firms in various industries have not been conclusive, though the bulk of evidence is consistent with the hypothesis that the gigantic firms are in general neither more nor less efficient than the firms which are simply large. Taking into account all opinion and evidence, we are generally left with three alternative possibilities concerning the incidence of diseconomies of very large scale, and three corresponding alternative relationships of the scale of the firm to its efficiency.

Possible Relationships of Firm Scale to Efficiency

First, it is possible that diseconomies of very large scale begin to be encountered at a scale no larger than that at which economies of large scale are exhausted or fully exploited (that is, as soon as minimum optimal scale is reached). Then, as the firm is enlarged progressively, unit costs of production no sooner cease to fall than they begin to rise. This would result in a relationship of unit costs to the scale of firm of the sort shown in Figure 3. The firm would become more efficient as it grew

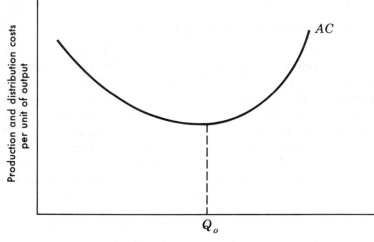

Figure 3

toward a size to produce the output Q_o per unit of time, and less efficient if it exceeded that output. Thus it would have a single unique
optimal scale (the scale to produce Q_o) and could be neither smaller or
larger than that if it were to attain maximum efficiency. The scale curve,
or line relating unit costs to scale of firm would thus be of a U or
rounded dish shape.

Second, it is possible that diseconomies of large scale are eventually
encountered, but only at a scale significantly larger than the minimum
optimal scale at which the firm first fully exploits its economies of large
scale. Then there would be a finite range of alternative scales, between
the minimum optimal scale and a larger one, at all of which the firm
would be equally efficient with minimized unit costs. But at scales exceeding the larger (or "maximum optimal") scale it would become less
efficient. This would result in a scale curve for the firm like that shown
in Figure 4. The firm could find the lowest attainable cost by reaching
the minimum optimal scale sufficient to produce the output Qmin. It
could also have the same minimized unit costs at any larger scale between Qmin and a maximum optimal scale of Qmax—which might be
a small or a large multiple of Qmin. But if its scale became larger than
Qmax, its unit costs would rise and it would become less efficient. There
would thus be a "neutral range" of possible alternative scales at which
the firm could be equally efficient at a minimized cost level.

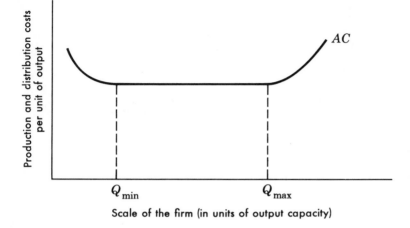

Figure 4

A third possibility of course is that, after reaching minimum optimal scale, the firm might expand "indefinitely," or at any rate over any range of sizes relevant in the actual market situations observed, with neither increases or decrease in unit cost. Its scale curve would then be represented as in Figure 5, already anticipated in the curve *deij* in Figure 2. Carried to the extreme, this curve would represent a situation in which any scale of firm between the minimum optimal scale and, let us say, a scale sufficient for one firm to monopolize the industry, would be equally efficient.

Which of these possibilities is realized in fact, or which is most frequently realized? Evidence suggests that the possibility illustrated in Figure 3 is not commonly found in fact, and is perhaps realized very infrequently if ever. That is, we will seldom if ever find firms with a single unique optimal scale. Diseconomies of very large scale are typically encountered, if at all, only at scales substantially greater than the minimum optimal scale of a firm. This is in spite of the fact that *a priori* theories of pricing and market structure have usually represented the scale curves of firms as having a U shape, possibly because this assumption facilitated the drawing of conclusions regarding unique equilibrium market adjustments of the number and size of firms.

This possibility being rejected, most or all real cases probably fit the pattern of either Figure 4 or Figure 5. That is, there is typically some range of scales larger than the minimum optimal scale—either a limited range or an indefinitely long one—over which the firm will have unit costs just as low as it gets at the minimum optimal scale. In the in-

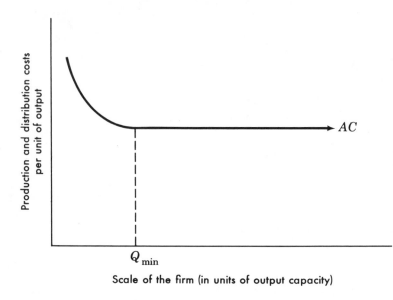

Figure 5

stances observed, actual firms have evidently not become so large that we are able to tell whether the second or the third pattern applies. Over the observed range of firm sizes, the largest firms appear not yet to have become big enough to suffer perceptible diseconomies of very large scale.

This finding has clear implications for the determinacy or indeterminacy of efficient degrees of seller concentration in various industries. It says in effect that in general the *minimum* degree of seller concentration which will be efficient is one which permits each firm to attain minimum optimal scale, and that this degree of seller concentration will vary among industries according to the importance of scale economies and the size of the market. It says also that seller concentration may ordinarily be higher over some substantial range than the minimum efficient degree of seller concentration (if this involves more than one seller), without impairing efficiency—and perhaps even as high as the concentration associated with single-firm monopoly. The degree of seller concentration consistent with best efficiency is thus indeterminate within a substantial range, corresponding usually to the range of indeterminacy of the most efficient size of firm. Firms operating in the typical market thus enjoy considerable leeway, or room for maneuver, in establishing an efficient degree of seller concentration and efficient sizes for their operations. They can, without impairing efficiency, attain a degree of seller concentration considerably higher than the minimum degree required for efficiency.

Economies of Vertical Integration

So far we have talked about how efficiency is influenced by the size of the firm as measured in terms of the output of its end product—for example, about the effect on costs of the size of an automobile producer measured by its output of passenger cars. This dimension of size is often called *horizontal size* ("across the market"); correspondingly, we have been appraising the effects of horizontal extension or growth of the firm on its efficiency. There is, however, another dimension of size and another direction for the growth of the firm—"vertical" growth or extension via integration of preceding or succeeding productive processes. For example, a steel firm producing steel ingots by feeding pig iron into an open-hearth steel furnace may grow not only horizontally by equipping to produce more ingots, but also by *vertical integration*. Either through new construction or through acquisition from others, it may integrate "backward" to secure facilities to produce its own pig iron, or "forward" to secure facilities for rolling or drawing its steel ingots into semifinished products such as steel sheets or wire. Again, a firm engaged in petroleum refining may integrate backward to secure its own crude oil supply, or forward to acquire its own wholesale storage and distribution depots in various local markets for refined petroleum products.

Some such integration may give rise to economies in production, reflected in the fact that the integrated firm can perform a series of successive productive functions more efficiently than they could be performed by a number of individual firms each of which performed only one function. Economies of vertical integration are especially apparent in cases where technologically complementary productive processes can be brought together in a single plant. For example, the integration of making pig iron, converting iron into steel, and shaping of steel into semifinished products—all in a single plant—permits considerable savings in the total fuel requirement for heating the iron and steel. If all functions are performed in a single plant, neither the pig iron nor the steel ingots have to get cold and then be reheated before passing to the next productive process. Some economies of vertical integration are also claimed in instances where the firm performs successive functions that are not technologically complementary and are not subject to unification in a single plant—for example, production of the components of a machine, assembly of the components into a finished machine, and distribution of the machine. In such cases, economies are usually attributed to improved coordination of the rates of output at the successive stages (through placing them under one management), consequent reduction of intermediate inventories, and elimination of the expense of purchase-sale transactions in moving goods from one stage to the next. In addition, pecuniary economies may result if the firm can, by integrating backward or forward, eliminate the payment to suppliers or customers of profits in excess of a basic interest return on the added investment required to integrate.

Yet it does not appear that all vertical integrations are economical. Whether or not they will be depends strongly on the nature of the productive processes or functions at various stages; on whether or not the production of the end product will absorb most or all of an efficiently produced output of a potentially integrable component or raw material; and on the comparative extent of economies of horizontal scale in production at successive production stages. For example, tin can manufacturers have not found it economical to integrate backward to produce their own steel strip for tin plating, largely because their demand for steel products is only a minor fraction of the total, and because steel firms producing a variety of end products can attain economies of scale in steel production which permit them to sell steel strip to the can-makers at a price (including a profit) lower than the can makers' cost of producing steel would be. And manufacturers of breakfast food do not find it economical to integrate forward into grocery wholesaling or retailing, since their own product is only a small fraction of the total merchandise which must be handled by grocers, and specialized distributive firms which engage in assembling the different products of a large number of food processors can do the distributive task more efficiently.

All we can say in general is that vertical integration is economical in certain cases. There is no evident general tendency for economies to be realized with integration. In some cases, integration may have a neutral effect on costs, neither increasing or decreasing the unit cost of the end product.

So far as firms are impelled to or desire to minimize their costs, they will tend to undertake cost-saving vertical integrations. These will tend to increase the sizes of the firms, though not necessarily their shares of the market for the end product that they supply. A petroleum refinery supplying 15 per cent of the total market demand for gasoline from its industry, for example, might integrate backward to acquire enough crude oil production to feed the refinery, and thus become a larger firm, but still only supply 15 per cent of the gasoline sold in the market.

Of course, firms may also undertake integrations that have neutral effects on costs, if they can derive some other advantage from integration, such as increased power to exclude new competitors. Thus the degree of integration and its resultant effect on the sizes of firms are not determinate even if all uneconomical types of integration are avoided. The degree of integration consistent with efficiency is indeterminate over the range of possible integrations which would have neutral effects on costs.

A further important point is that the development of integration may result in an increase of the minimum horizontal scale at which, in the interest of overall efficiency, some of the integrated productive functions must be performed. Suppose that one of two integrated processes has a "larger" minimum optimal horizontal scale than another, so that, at minimum optimal scale, it either (*a*) requires more raw material than a minimum-optimal-scale operation at a preceding production stage will supply, or (*b*) delivers more output than a minimum optimal-scale operation at a succeeding production stage will require. Then the preceding or succeeding production stage will need to be increased above its own minimum optimal level in order to get the greatest overall efficiency. This is true, at any rate, unless "outside" sources can be used efficiently to make up a deficit in supply, or outside outlets can be used to absorb a surplus of output. In brief, there must be in an integrated operation a "reconciliation" of the horizontal-scale optima of the related stages, generally requiring for best efficiency an increase of the scale of operations above the minimum optimal for the stages with the smaller minimum optimal scales.

For example, it might be true in automobile production and distribution (the following figures are to some extent hypothetical) that the passenger-car manufacturer found a definite advantage and possibly an economy in integrating (1) the production of components (engines, body parts, etc.), (2) the assembly of components into finished automobiles, and (3) the wholesale distribution of his particular brand of automobile on a nationwide scale. Now he might find, at these various stages: (1) that the minimum optimal scale for the production of major components was such that he should produce components for 1,000,000 autos per year, or about 15 per cent of the total market; (2) that the minimum optimal scale for an assembly plant alone would require only 100,000 units per year, or 1.5 per cent of the market; and (3) that for economical nationwide distribution (freight costs being considered), he would need at least three regional assembly plants, with a combined capacity totaling 4.5 per cent of the market. Given these three considerations, what is the most efficient size for an integrated firm? If there are no *diseconomies* of very large-scale production or distribution, the minimum efficient scale is clearly one to supply 15 per cent of the market, with the equivalent of ten assembly plants of minimum optimal scale. The *critical* optimal scale is the largest (that found in component production), and this critical scale is imposed on the whole integrated operation if overall efficiency is to be maximized. In general, we may expect that the process of integration imposes requirements of greater scale for optimal efficiency on some of the stages of production absorbed by integration.

We have now considered the first question bearing on the relationship of efficiency to the degree of seller concentration attained in markets—concerning the effects of the sizes of firms, and correlatively of degrees of industry concentration, on efficiency as measured in terms of unit costs of production and distribution. A systematic relationship of firm size to efficiency, and thus of industry concentration to efficiency, is firmly predicted. We come then to our second question—concerning whether the pursuit of efficiency by firms leads them toward efficient sizes, and also the extent to which this pursuit does and does not result in a uniquely determined degree of concentration in any industry.

Pursuit of Efficiency as a Determinant of Concentration

Business firms that attempt to maximize their profits will have some virtual tendency (other things being equal) to minimize their unit costs, and thus to seek scales of operation within the optimal range. The main issue is whether, given this tendency, competition will actually force firms to attain optimal scales in order to survive. An alternative possibility is that they will have effective options as to the scale and comparative efficiency they attain, and will be able to operate at nonoptimal scales if they find it more profitable to do so. Which is the case? The answer is that the firm's alternatives depend on the structure of its market.

Effectively, there is only one sort of market situation for which theory predicts that all sellers will ultimately be forced by competition to attain optimal scale. This situation is such that (*a*) there are many sellers, each so small as to supply an insignificant fraction of the market for industry output; (*b*) scale economies are "unimportant" so that at its minimum optimal scale a firm will supply only a tiny fraction of the market, thus making possible the survival of a large number of small firms under the pressure of competition; and (*c*) diseconomies of the large-scale firm are "important," so that if a firm tries to grow large enough to supply a perceptible fraction of the market, its costs per unit of output increase above the optimal level. In addition, the products of all firms in the industry should be standardized or homogeneous, so that buyers in no way distinguish the outputs of different firms or prefer one to another. And there should be no barriers to the entry of new firms or to the exit of existing ones.

For this situation, it is theoretically predictable that market competition will in the long run tend to force the price of the product down to the level of the minimum attainable average cost of production, to force all surviving firms (which will remain many and small) to adopt scales within the optimal range, and to bring about such a combination of the number and size of firms that total industry output will equal the aggregate amount demanded by buyers at a price equalling the minimized average costs. This result will come about through a process in which all firms within the industry independently adjust their scales and outputs relative to an industry price which no one of them can control, with the aim of maximizing profits; in which some added firms enter the industry so long as price exceeds minimal average cost and offers the prospect of excess profits; and in which some established firms leave the industry if price is below minimal average cost and losses result. Sellers will then in the long run be forced to attain optimal scales, and the degree of seller concentration will tend "automatically" to become consistent with maximum efficiency in size for every firm in the industry.

If any condition enumerated for this special market situation is not fulfilled, an "equilibrium" result of the sort just outlined is less than completely forced by competition. Suppose, for example, that all of the conditions mentioned are fulfilled except for the fact that diseconomies of large-scale firms are not important over a wide range (so that any firm can attain optimal efficiency either at a very small scale or up to a much larger scale). Then the number of firms is no longer forced to remain large. Firms may grow or combine without loss of efficiency until their sizes are large and their number is few. Thereupon, the force of interfirm competition may be restricted to permit periodic elevation of price above minimal average cost, and existing firms may be permitted or induced to attain inefficiently large scales (if diseconomies of the very large-scale firm are ultimately encountered). Excessive entry, possibly including entry at nonoptimal scales, may also be attracted, creating transitional excess capacity. Easy entry always ultimately should tend to erase each aberration from optimal scales and competitive price, but aberrations could recur repeatedly. Thus dynamic market instability with possible recurring departures by some firms from the most efficient scale is possible if diseconomies of the large-scale firm are not a stringent limiting factor on firm size. Similarly, nonfulfillment of the condition that the outputs of all firms be homogeneous (so that competing products are differentiated) may require some modest qualification of our earlier conclusion, even if all the other conditions of atomistic competition with easy entry are fulfilled.

However, the important category of situations in which exactly or approximately optimal scales *are in no meaningful sense forced* is characterized by the alteration of competitive conditions in all of the following respects: (*a*) there is some barrier to new entry, or disadvantage of potential entrant as compared to established sellers; (*b*) diseconomies of large scale are "unimportant," so that firms can economically expand to sizes sufficient to supply significant shares of the market; and (*c*) the number of sellers either is initially small or [because of (*b*) just above] can become small without loss of economies. This general category of situations subsumes (1) both those in which economies of large scale are unimportant and those in which they are important, and (2) both those in which the products of competing sellers are homogeneous and those in which they are differentiated.

Efficiency in Oligopolistic Industries

A common characteristic of these situations is that if a small number of sellers (a high degree of seller concentration) either already exists or develops, the oligopoly of firms faces an altered type of competition in which sellers do not perforce adjust independently to a market price beyond their control. There is lacking any impersonal, automatic market force to drive them to any particular adjustment. Instead, they act interdependently, and perhaps collectively, in setting prices; are able within some range to exercise discretionary control over their prices; and are not forced by an automatically moving market price to adopt some particular scale of operations. Furthermore, because of the barrier to the entry of new sellers, the established sellers are presistently able (if competition among them is somewhat restricted) to maintain prices somewhat above the level of minimal average costs without inducing entry to drive their prices down. They then may be able to survive while operating at nonoptimal scales, and may have a range of choice as to whether to operate at optimal scales or at scales smaller or larger than the optimum. If product differentiation is also present within the industry, this range of choice for various individual sellers may be broadened.

In some of the cases falling within this category, an oligopolistic degree of seller concentration would emerge more or less automatically as a result of competition even if sellers were initially many and small.

If there are important economies of the large-scale firm, so that to approach optimal scale a firm must supply a significant fraction of the market, atomistic competition among many firms will lead all to expand. This expansion will drive price down until only large-scale firms can survive, eliminating all but a few firms, and will thus "automatically" produce an oligopolistic or concentrated market structure. Also, the existence of substantial product-differentiation advantages favoring a few established sellers over all others within or outside the industry may result more or less automatically in the domination of the industry by these few, and in a high degree of seller concentration. Furthermore, any other sorts of substantial barriers to entry protecting any few sellers established in an industry may permit them to exclude all competitors and to perpetuate a high degree of seller concentration. But all that is automatic in these situations is the emergence of a high degree of seller concentration. Adaptation of all firms to optimal scales is by no means forced or guaranteed, since intraindustry competition in oligopoly does not necessarily force it, and entry (being at least somewhat impeded) cannot.

In other situations in this category, the development of large firms and high seller concentration is not automatic, but "optional." That is, firms that do not encounter diseconomies of large scale may choose to become large and impose high seller concentration on an industry, even though they are not impelled or automatically induced to do so. These will generally be cases in which there are no important scale economies (or diseconomies), no advantage protecting any few established firms against the others, but some barriers to entry that give all established firms advantages over potential entrant sellers. Then there is nothing to "force" an increase in the sizes and a reduction in number of firms if they are initially many and small. But they have the option of accomplishing these changes by individual growth or by combination or merger. And given the protection of a general barrier to new entry, they may find it profitable to do so. Such "nonautomatic" developments of oligopolistic seller concentration, frequently by mergers, may be in fact equally as important as the "automatic" developments.

We thus envisage an important category of cases in which a relatively few large sellers either must or may emerge to control relatively large shares of individual industry markets, behind the protection of some barrier to the entry of added sellers. In these situations prices can and frequently will exceed the level of costs attainable at optimal scale, and sellers are not generally forced to operate at optimal scales in order to survive. But even if not forced to do so, will they?

If we consider this question in its most general terms, the answer is necessarily indefinite. On the one hand, there is a virtual advantage to any firm in an oligopolistic industry in attaining a scale within the optimal range—big enough to attain minimal average costs and not so big that diseconomies of large scale are encountered. On the other hand, there may be serious impediments to the attainment of such a scale by each firm in the industry if that is its desire. In addition, some firms may find it profitable to operate at nonoptimal scales. (This is because efficiency is only one of the factors influencing the profitability of the enterprise.) As a result, some or all firms in any industry in this category may remain indefinitely at either suboptimal or superoptimal scales. Generally, persistence of at least some firms at suboptimal scales may result from the dual condition that they are unable individually to secure sufficient market shares to support optimal-scale operations, and that the resulting "undersized" firms do not merge with each other or with larger firms to the end of attaining optimal scales. They may fail to do so because of their inability to agree on merger terms, or because of legal barriers.

Commonly, the market shares of established firms in an oligopolistic industry are not all equal, and only some of them are undersized. In almost any oligopolistic industry, including those in which the products of rival sellers are viewed as generally homogeneous, there is enough actual market imperfection or product differentiation that different sellers will secure different shares of the market. Even though they may sell ostensibly identical products at identical prices, some will have larger market shares and some smaller. And it is quite possible that, in the course of evolution of market structure, some of them will and some will not secure sufficient market shares to support operations at minimum optimal scale. This possibility is clearly increased as the degree of differentiation of the rival products increases, and as more definite buyer preferences for one seller's product as compared to another's emerge. Therefore, some of the firms in an industry may be "undersized" from the standpoint of efficiency because of inability to attract enough customers, although given a certain restriction of competition and a certain barrier to entry, they may find their operations profitable.[1]

Given the possible existence of at least some firms in the industry at suboptimal scales, an obvious "rationalization" of the structure of the industry might be accomplished if the undersized firms would merge with each other or with larger firms, combining their shares of the market in order to be able to support plants and firms of optimal scales.

[1]It is also hypothetically possible that all firms in an oligopoly might be undersized, but this occurrence is so rare in fact that we will not discuss it.

Other things being equal, such "rationalization" mergers should reduce unit costs and increase the combined profits of the participants in the mergers. And, other things being equal, we should expect profit-seeking enterprises to arrange and carry through such mergers. But will they, and will undersized firms thus in the long run tend to disappear?

There are three principal reasons why they *may not*. First, presuming a desire to merge for increased efficiency with increased size of firm, mergers may be discouraged or prohibited by law. In the United States, Section 7 of the Clayton Act forbids mergers which may tend substantially to lessen competition in any line of commerce. Depending on judicial interpretation of the law, it may stand in the way of mergers which would increase efficiency, *if* the increase of seller concentration resulting from the mergers is such as to have the probable result of seriously lessening competition. This more or less specific prohibition is backed by that of the Sherman Act against "monopolization" of an industry by one firm, or by several acting in concert.

Second, consummation of a merger essentially requires that the parties to it arrive at mutually agreeable terms for merging, and such an agreement may not be forthcoming. If one firm "sells out" to another, the owners of the selling firm giving up participation in the industry, there must be an agreement on the price of the sale, and it is quite possible that the potential purchaser and seller may be unable to agree on a price. An "undersized" firm may continue in operation because no other firm in the industry is willing to pay as much as it demands for its property and business. If two or more firms consider "combining forces" by bringing their operations under a single unified ownership and management, there is a similar problem of terms concerning the fraction of ownership, control, and income-receiving power that each of the initially separate ownership-management groups attains. It is hypothetically and actually quite possible that the agreement necessary for a merger will not be reached, even though the earning power of the merger firm would justify it because of increased efficiency.

Third, it is possible, in markets with considerable product differentiation among rival sellers, that some relatively small or "undersized" firms may find it most profitable to remain that way. This could be because they can attract only rather limited shares of their markets (but at very attractive prices), catering to customers who prefer their special brands or designs, and because they could not combine production with others while still maintaining their distinctive market positions. Large-scale production would imply either loss of valuable product identity, or a production of the specially identified product in excess of the demand for it at attractive prices.

The preceding suggests why the operation of at least some firms in an industry at suboptimal scales may persist in spite of the available opportunity of merging to increase firm size. By the same token "oversized" firms, so large that they have encountered diseconomies of very large scale, may also find it profitable to persist without "spinning off" excess facilities to get down to a size allowing lower unit costs. This may happen because certain firms can command exceptionally large market shares at attractive prices, and can more than overcome their disadvantages in unit costs by the extra revenue from sales. In general, therefore, oligopolistic industries will not automatically move to "rationalize" their structures so that every firm is within the range of optimal scales—at least so long as competition within the industry is somewhat restricted and there are some barriers to new entry. Both "undersized" and "oversized" firms may persist, and do so with profit.

On the other hand, there is a considerable probability that the firms producing the bulk of the output in an oligopolistic industry will ordinarily attain reasonably efficient scales. There is apparent in nearly all such industries a relation of scale to efficiency such that a fairly wide range of different sizes of firms will be equally efficient. After the firm reaches and passes its minimum optimal scale (giving it the lowest attainable unit costs) it can in general become either somewhat or much larger without influencing these costs perceptibly one way or another. Thus a firm might attain lowest unit costs at a minimum optimal scale sufficient to supply 5 per cent of its market, but might be able to grow tenfold to supply 50 per cent of the market without raising unit costs. The firm may ordinarily attain a considerable range of sizes which are all of approximately equal efficiency.

As a result, the task of attaining efficient size, either through command of a sufficient market share by the firm or through merger, is much simplified. No one specific size of firm is needed; any of a considerable range of sizes will ordinarily do. In spite of certain difficulties encountered in altering size by internal growth or by merger, the chance of reaching efficient size by some route is much increased as the "target" size expands from a "bullseye" to "the side of a barn." Further, the chance of firms reaching excessive size, or encountering diseconomies of very large scale, becomes relatively slight, since in general so much expansion beyond minimum optimal scale is possible without loss of efficiency.

Attainment of efficient firm sizes is also made probable because the threat of entry by new firms ordinarily places limits on the extent to which established firms can maintain inefficient scales and survive.

Some barriers to entry are generally present in oligopolistic markets, permitting established firms to elevate prices somewhat above minimal average costs without attracting new entry. But these barriers are not indefinitely high, and the maximum price which can be maintained without attracting new entrants will ordinarily exceed minimal average costs only by some certain moderate amount. This means in effect that in most oligopolistic markets, firms whose unit costs are importantly elevated because of severe "undersize" or severe "oversize" will be unable to charge prices sufficient to cover their elevated costs without attracting new entry. They will ultimately be unable to survive at their inefficient sizes if they charge prices low enough to forestall entry, and also unable to survive in the face of new competition if they attract it through higher prices. More importantly, this threat of entry therefore furnishes a special extra inducement for inefficient established firms to attain reasonably efficient scales. The pressure to be efficient in order to "beat out" potential new competitors and still make a profit may well swing the balance to induce efficiency-increasing mergers which might otherwise not take place.

Finally, the secular growth of most markets is a sort of corrective force which tends to permit undersized firms to grow to efficient scale with the market. Although at some given time a number of firms in an industry may have insufficient market shares to support operation at minimum optimal scale, growth of the market may permit them to attain or more closely approximate efficient scales by simply holding their original percentage shares of the market (and to do even better than this if they can capture disproportionate shares of the new customers). Steady economic expansion—a significant environmental condition of American industries over many years—thus tends to reduce the incidence of uneconomically small operations in oligopolistic industries. By contrast, of course, the occasional declining industry is more likely to be plagued with overcrowding and inefficiently small-scale operations.

On balance, then, we can draw these conclusions about the attainment of efficient scales by firms in oligopolistic industries: (a) An evolving adjustment of the size and number of firms so that each attains optimal scale is not automatic or forced—a range of other possibilities is left open. (b) "Rationalization" of inefficient market structures if they arise is also not automatic, and there are some strategic impediments to a process of rationalization. (c) But in view of the virtual advantages of rationalization, of the typical existence of a fairly wide range of alternative scales of optimal efficiency, of the threat of entry of new firms, and of the secular growth of markets, there should be a net probability that the firms supplying the bulk of output in most oligopolistic markets will attain reasonably efficient scales.

Two conclusions concerning seller concentration follow. First, *the degree of seller concentration found in an oligopoly should on the average, or most probably, be consistent with the production of the bulk of industry output by firms of reasonably efficient scale.* But in some oligopolistic industries there may be either excessive concentration (with oversized firms supplying much of the output), or insufficient concentration (with undersized firms producing a significant fraction of the output). And even in the industries where the bulk of output comes from firms of efficient scale, there may well be a fringe of inefficiently small firms supplying a minor fraction of industry output.

Second, *in most oligopolistic industries a fairly wide range of different degrees of seller concentration may be equally consistent with efficiency in scale on the part of the member firms.* This of course is because, for any firm, there is ordinarily a fairly wide range of scales, between the minimum optimal scale and a considerably larger one, over which the firm will be equally efficient. Correspondingly, the requirements of efficiency in scale of firms ordinarily permit a fairly wide range of variation in the degree of seller concentration in oligopolistic industries. This holds, at any rate, unless the minimum optimal scale of the firm is very large indeed (for example, sufficient to supply a third, a half, or more of the market), and this situation is encountered very infrequently. We are thus led to consider, in a later section of this chapter, other forces influencing the degrees of seller concentration actually attained.

Before turning to these, a word may be said about the determination of degrees of vertical integration accomplished by firms as industrial structure is determined. Very much the same remarks apply here as applied to the determination of horizontal firm size and horizontal concentration. First, there will be possibility of integration by the firm (acquiring or combining with supplier firms or customer firms) which has (a) positive economies or savings in cost; (b) no effect on costs; or neutral economies; and (c) diseconomies or inefficiencies. Atomistic market structure with unrestricted competition will tend to force, or make "automatic," efficiency-increasing integration. It will provide no deterrent to integration having no effect on costs, and will tend to deter inefficient integration. In oligopoly, no particular sort of integration will be fully forced, but there should be a net tendency to effect efficiency-increasing integrations. There should also be a tendency to integrate where efficiency is not affected if there are other advantages (not connected with costs) to the integration. And even inefficient integration is possible if it has offsetting advantages. There is thus a wide range of possible integration patterns that may develop, including importantly integration with no cost advantages but significant advantages of other sorts.

In developing theoretical predictions of the influence of the pursuit of efficiency on industrial market structures, we have emphasized this influence as it operates in the two most common sorts of markets—those which are atomistic (with many sellers) and those which have become oligopolistic. Of much less practical importance (except as hypothetical alternative) is the market supplied by a single monopolistic firm. What of the consistency of single-firm monopoly with efficiency? In general single-firm monopoly will emerge and survive only if (*a*) economies of large scale are so overwhelming that one firm can supply the market much more efficiently than two or more could, thus giving the single firm dominant control with a relative immunity to new entry; or (*b*) a single firm can impose impassable barirers to the competition of others— for example, by monopolizing strategic resource supplies or obtaining exclusive patent control of requisite techniques; or (*c*) a governmental body grants to a single firm an exclusive franchise to supply a given market (as in the case of some public utilities). The potential efficiency of monopolies obtained in these various ways is fairly obvious. If a monopoly is based on some barrier to entry other than scale economies (resource control, patents) it may get big enough to encounter dis-economies of very large-scale production, and provide less efficiency than several smaller firms could. However, it may also very well not encounter such diseconomies, and be just as efficient as smaller firms would. The strategic question here will be whether or not diseconomies of very large scale production are encountered in the particular case. With franchised monopolies, the same conclusion applies, except that the official cause for public franchising of monopolies is ordinarily that there are overwhelming scale economies which make the franchising de-sirable.

Actual Scale Economies and Diseconomies in American Manufacturing Industries

The preceding theoretical discussion, couched in qualitative terms, should whet our interest in obtaining some pertinent information. One part of this information concerns the quantitative importance of economies of large scale plants and firms in American industries, and takes the form of answers to the following questions:

1. How "important" are scale economies in our various industries? And, in particular:
    (a) How large are the minimum optimal scales of plants and firms, expressed as percentages of the total capacities required to supply the various markets?
    (b) What decrease in efficiency is experienced if plants and firms firms are smaller (in various degrees) than their minimum optimal scales?

2. What evidence is there of the incidence of diseconomies of very large-scale firms—of firms becoming so big that they are less efficient than smaller ones?

3. In the light of answers to the preceding questions, how concentrated do our industries need to be and how concentrated can they be if all firms in them are to be of reasonably efficient scale?

These questions have been examined closely by research economists only for a scattering of industries in the manufacturing sector, and our tentative answers here are necessarily confined to the indications from such a sample. Taking the preceding questions in order, we present the following brief summary of relevant findings.

The evidence presented is based on a study of twenty selected manufacturing industries made by the writer.[2] These include industries supplying many of the more important producer and consumer goods, and range in seller concentration from "very high" to "low-moderate," though in a preponderance of the cases there is from high-moderate to very high seller concentration. They might thus be expected to represent, on the average, instances in which scale economies of the more important sort would be experienced. The findings are essentially a reflection of "engineering estimates" (made by executives of firms engaged in the industries) of the true or net relationships of the scales of plants and firms to efficiency. They are relationships, that is, of scale to efficiency for plants or firms which are not obscured by random differences in rates of utilization, techniques employed, wages or material prices paid, and so forth. Also, the estimates in general rest on the assumption of the going or customary pattern of vertical integration of plants in the various industries in question.

In examining the importance of scale economies, we have distinguished the plant problem from the firm problem, and will report first on the extent of economies of large plants. A first but only partial indicator of the importance of plant scale economies in an industry is the

[2]Joe S. Bain, *Barriers to New Competition*, 1956, Ch. 3.

size of one plant of minimum optimal scale, expressed as a percentage of the total plant capacity needed to supply the common market faced by sellers in the industry. This market may either be the entire national market if all sellers supply it in common, or a geographical or product submarket—the largest of those found, for purposes of these calculations—if the national market is segmented into several noncompeting submarkets on the basis of region or product. For example, in the case of the cigarette industry, which has essentially a unified national market supplied by all sellers in common, we inquire what percentage of national market demand would be supplied by one cigarette plant of minimum optimal scale. (The estimate is 5 or 6 per cent.) In the petroleum refining industry, where the national market is broken into several regions and each supplied by an essentially separate set of plant facilities (so that there are several "theoretical" industries instead of one), we inquire what percentage of the demand in the largest regional market (that of the Atlantic seaboard) would be supplied by one refinery of minimum optimal scale. (The estimate is about 4 per cent, but would be a bit higher for some smaller regional submarkets.)

For the twenty industries studied, the degree of importance of plant-scale economies, as measured in these terms, varies widely. In fact, the most striking aspect of the findings is the great and pervasive *diversity* among industries with regard to the significance of economies of the large plant. In six industries, one plant of minimum optimal scale should supply 10 per cent or more of the market, with the figure running as high, at maximum estimate, as 20 per cent or more in two of these cases: automobiles and typewriters. (The other industries are fountain pens, tractors, copper, and gypsum products.) In five industries, one plant of minimum optimal scale should supply, on the basis of mean estimate, 5 or 6 per cent of the market. (Included here are cigarettes, soap, rayon fiber, farm machinery, and steel.) And in nine industries, the percentage of the market supplied by one plant of minimal optimal scale would be less than 5, this group including at least three instances (flour milling, liquor distilling, and fresh meat packing) where less than 2 per cent of the market would be supplied by one plant of minimum optimal scale.

Any conclusion about the net importance of plant scale economies, however, should be withheld until a second indicator of this importance is taken into account. This is the extent to which unit costs are higher with plants of suboptimal scale, as shown by the shape of the plant scale curve that relates unit costs to scale of plant as scale is increased from zero up to a minimum optimal scale.

Suppose, for example, that we find two industries in each of which one plant of minimum optimal scale will supply about 5 per cent of the market. This is true for cigarettes (referring to the unified national market) and for cement (referring to the largest of several regional submarkets). On the basis of this showing alone, plant scale economies would seem to have the same moderate importance in each industry. But suppose that in one of the industries there is a relatively steep plant scale curve, so that operation at suboptimal scales will elevate costs significantly, whereas in the other case there is a rather flat plant scale curve, indicating only a slight elevation of unit costs at suboptimal scales. For example, in the cement industry, a plant of one-half optimal scale (supplying 2½ per cent of the market) is estimated to have unit costs about 12 per cent higher than those for an optimal plant, and a plant of one-fifth optimal scale (supplying 1 per cent of the market) would have unit costs 35 per cent above the optimal level. On the other hand, in the cigarette industry it is estimated that although the minimum optimal scale is the same (5 per cent of the market), a plant of half-optimal scale would have unit costs only 1 per cent above those of the optimal plant, and one with one-fifth optimal scale (supplying 1 per cent of the market) would incur unit costs only 2 per cent above the optimal level.

It is clear that, though the minimum optimal scale is the same in the two cases (in terms of percentage of total market supply), plant scale economies are actually much more important in the industry with the steep plant scale curve (cement) than in that with the shallow plant scale curve (cigarettes). This is because with the steep curve efficiency requirements are approximately met only at or near the minimum optimal scale, whereas with the very flat curve the size of plant is really of rather slight importance in determining overall efficiency, and plants can range from quite small to very large without significantly affecting unit costs. Thus we must take simultaneous account of the magnitude of the minimum optimal plant scale and of the degree of upward variation of costs as the plant is reduced to smaller scales, in order adequately to appraise the net importance of plant scale economies.

For the sample of twenty industries mentioned earlier, therefore, engineering estimates were also sought on the relative steepness or flatness of the plant scale curves. The general indication of these estimates is that, in a preponderance of cases, plant scale curves tend to be at least moderately flat (and sometimes very flat), so that plants of half-optimal scale would experience no more than a 2 or 3 per cent elevation in unit costs and plants of quarter-optimal scale no more than a 5 or 6 per cent elevation. In a small minority of cases, on the other hand, plant scale curves are fairly steep (as in the cement industry, just mentioned, or the rayon fiber industry). In the bulk of cases, then, the relative flatness of plant scale curves virtually diminishes the importance of plant scale economies, or makes them in effect less important than would be tentatively indicated by a simple examination of minimum optimal scales. Taking both the magnitude of the minimum optimal scale of plant and the shape of the plant scale curve into account, the twenty manufacturing industries studied were grouped in the following way with respect to the importance of plant scale economies:

1. *Two* industries had "very important" plant scales economies, in the sense that minimum optimal plant scale exceeded 10 per cent of total market capacity, and that unit costs would be elevated by 5 per cent or more at half-optimal plant scale. (These industries produced automobiles and typewriters.)

2. *Five* industries had "moderately important" plant scale economies, in the sense that minimum optimal plant scale was in the neighborhood of 4 to 6 per cent of total market capacity, and that unit costs would be elevated by at least 5 per cent at half-optimal plant scale. (These indusries produced cement, farm machinery, tractors, rayon, and steel.)

3. *Nine* industries had unimportant plant scale economies, either because the minimum optimal scale was small, or because the plant scale curves were quite flat back to rather small scales, or for both reasons. (These industries produced cigarettes, liquor, petroleum products, soap, rubber tires, shoes, flour, meat, and canned goods.)

4. *Four* industries were not classified because of lack of sufficient information (copper, gypsum products, fountain pens, and tin cans), but at least two of them seem likely to have either moderately important or very important plant scale economies.

These findings are of course only for a sample of twenty manufacturing industries, somewhat disproportionately weighted (as compared with the total population all manufacturing industries) in the direction of industries of moderate or high seller concentration. Nevertheless, some tentative indications emerge which are potentially applicable to manufacturing industries in general.

First, the importance of plant scale economies varies widely among different manufacturing industries, and even among different manufacturing industries of high seller concentration. The degree of importance ranges from numerous cases in which such scale economies are of negligible importance to fewer cases in which they are substantially important. Not all industries, or even all concentrated industries, can be "painted with one brush" in this respect.[3]

Second, the incidence of plant scale economies requiring relatively high seller concentration for reasonable efficiency in production and distribution (on the basis of one efficient plant per firm) is relatively slight. Only in two to four industries out of twenty, or 10 to 20 per cent of the observed cases, were plant scale economies so great that production for the market needed to be concentrated in ten or fewer plants for purposes of efficiency. In the remaining cases—80 to 90 per cent of them—optimal plant scale economies could be realized with much lower degrees of plant concentration (with twenty to several hundred plants per industry).

Third, we must look, therefore, for justification or explanations of high seller concentration in areas other than economies of large scale plants, although there will evidently be a small minority of cases in which such economies do require high plant and seller concentration for purposes of productive efficiency.

Another aspect of our first general question concerns the actual importance of economies of the multiplant firm. To what extent is it true that the growth of the firm to sizes where it controls more than one plant of minimum optimal scale results in reduction of unit cost of production and distribution—thus making the minimum optimal scale for a firm, in terms of plant facilities controlled, larger than the minimum optimal scale of one plant? For example, suppose an integrated steel plant has a minimum optimal scale of 1 million tons per annum of ingot capacity, in the sense that plants smaller than this will be less efficient, and larger plants no more efficient. Is it nevertheless true that a steel firm large enough to operate four such plants, with a total annual ingot capacity of 4 million tons, will realize lower unit costs than a one-plant firm? And if it will, how much lower will its costs be? As we have indicated above, there is a conflict among various theoretical answers to this sort of question. Some theorists hold that there are economies of the

---

[3]Some recent attempts have been made to identify either the optimal or the minimum optimal scales of plants in various industries by determining the size class of plant (in a frequency distribution) in each industry which over time (e.g., from 1947 to 1958) was coming to supply larger proportions of industry output. (See T. R. Saving, "Estimation of Optimum Size of Plant by the Survivor Technique," *Quarterly Journal of Economics*, LXXV, 4 (Nov., 1961), pp. 569–607; and L. W. Weiss, "The Survival Technique and the Extent of Suboptimal Capacity," *Journal of Political Economy*, LXXII, 3 (June, 1964), pp. 246–261). Unfortunately, the assumptions of these analyses are vague, much of the available data do not yield meaningful results, and the resultant findings are of questionable relevance to the problem at hand.

multiplant firm and others deny it; empirical evidence is essential to resolve our doubts.

Although no comprehensive evidence bearing on this issue is available, the study of the sample of twenty manufacturing industries already mentioned suggests three tentative answers to the general question. First, economies of the multiplant firm are at least sometimes encountered, in the sense that such a firm in some settings realizes somewhat lower unit costs of production and distribution than a one-plant firm could. Second, however, there is no general tendency in this direction that applies in all or nearly all industries. We find a substantial fraction of industries in which such economies are not present, and in which the one-plant firm is as efficient as the multiplant one. Again, we cannot "paint all industries with one brush." Third, where economies of the multiplant firm are encountered, they are ordinarily quite slight in magnitude. In these cases, the unit costs of production and distribution of the firm with several plants (whatever number appears to be required for greatest efficiency) are typically only 1 or 2 per cent below those of a firm with one plant of minimum optimal scale. Even where there are some large-firm economies, then, they are not very important, since the scale curve for the firm, beyond the size of one plant, is typically quite flat.

To report specific findings for the twenty-industry sample briefly, meaningful estimates concerning multiplant economies were obtained in twelve of the cases, but not for the other eight. For six of the twelve for which estimates were obtained, the existence of any significant multiplant economies was denied, even though in three of these six industries the larger firms had attained substantial multiplant development. For the remaining six of the twelve cases, some multiplant economies were claimed to exist—to the extent that a firm with three to ten plants would be more efficient than a one-firm plant. But the extent of unit-cost reduction attributed to such multiplant development was generally estimated as "small," "slight," or not exceeding 2 or 3 per cent.

Where multiplant economies were claimed, they were generally attributed either to economies of large scale management or to economies of large scale distribution. The latter sort of economies, however, were generally predicated on the assumption that the firm would operate to supply all parts of the national market (thus reaping advantages from disparately located regional plants or from large sales volumes through various regional wholesaling centers). And it is not clear that such nationwide distribution by the single firm is an essential precondition of productive and distributional efficiency. Moreover, in half of the six instances in which multiplant economies were claimed, they could be exploited by a firm having one plant in each of several disparate geographical markets, thus not necessarily increasing its proportionate hold on, or the degree of seller concentration in, any one market.

The apparent overall "importance" of economies of large scale—as this importance might be reflected in the degrees of seller concentration essential for efficiency in production and distribution in various markets—is thus only slightly increased by taking into account economies of the multiplant firm. In some minor fraction of cases multiplant economies will justify, for purposes of efficiency, a substantially higher degree of seller concentration than would be justified by economies of the large plant alone. But ordinarily the savings in cost from higher concentration in these cases would appear to be quite small.

This conclusion is tentatively confirmed by the findings of a thin scattering of studies which, rather than developing engineering estimates of the relationship of firm size to efficiency, have compared the unit costs simultaneously attained by firms of different sizes in each of several manufacturing industries. Focusing on the relative efficiency of "small," "medium," and "large" firms in the industries examined, these studies have generally found that the largest two or three firms in the industry, typically with extensive multiplant development, on the average have unit costs which are not significantly different from those of "medium-sized" firms with efficient-sized plants but without extensive multiplant development. On the other hand, "small" firms—generally with one undersized individual plant apiece—on the average have significantly higher unit costs than "medium-sized" and "large" firms.[4]

These studies and the engineering estimates mentioned previously also bear on our second general question, which concerns the possible incidence of diseconomies of the very large scale firm. These would be reflected in a rise in unit costs due to such things as the "intrinsic inefficiencies of very large-scale management." Although the data accumulated so far are quite inadequate, the findings based on them are generally negative. Within the observed ranges of firm size, diseconomies of the very large firm do not seem to have been encountered. Although the very largest firms observable in various industries are not visibly more efficient than their somewhat smaller rivals, neither are they demonstrably less efficient. Occasional differences in profit rates favoring medium-sized as compared to large firms are encountered, but the considerations other than efficiency that affect the firm's rate of profit are numerous and important enough that no meaningful conclu-

[4]The findings of such studies are summarized in A. D. H. Kaplan, *Small Business: Its Place and Problems*, 1948, Ch. V.

sion regarding relative efficiency can be drawn. We thus tentatively conclude that diseconomies of the very large firm do not represent a significant phenomenon within the range of firm sizes attained to date. The typical scale-curve pattern for both the plant and the firm is one of declining unit costs with increasing scale up to some minimum optimal scale, and constant unit costs at the optimal level as the plant or firm grows to successively larger sizes within the relevant range. (This sort of scale curve was represented in Figure 5 earlier.) Consequently, diseconomies of the firm of very large scale do not appear to be a significant determinant of the degrees of seller concentration which are efficient in various industries—imposing no upper limit on efficient degrees of concentration.

Relationship of Actual Industry Concentration to that Required for Efficiency

A second sort of important quantitative information concerns the varying extents to which American industries are less concentrated than is needed for efficiency, concentrated only to the minimal degree required for firms to be of reasonably efficient scale, and more concentrated than that. The major specific question, in the light of general observations of industrial structure, is to what extent existing firms are larger than need be for efficiency, and correspondingly to what extent concentration in various industries is greater than the minimum required for efficiency.

An answer to this question again has not been developed for a large sample of industries, and again we must rely on the study of the sample of twenty manufacturing industries referred to in the preceding section. For this sample, we have sought an answer specifically by examining the scales of the largest four firms in each industry. The general indications are as follows:

First, there is a very significant multiplant development in most of the twenty industries but not in all of them. That is, the largest four firms in an industry usually but not always have scales which are substantially greater than that of one minimum-optimal plant. When the average size of the first four firms of each industry was expressed as a multiple of the size of one plant of minimum optimal scale in that industry, the following results appeared:

1. In *six* industries, the average size of the first four firms was such that each could control from 9 to 24 plants of minimum optimal scale.

2. In *nine* industries, the average size of the first four firms was such as to allow each from 3 to 8 plants of minimum optimal scale.

3. In *five* industries, the average size of the first four firms was such that each could control from 1 to 2 plants of minimum optimal scale.

Since the first firm will on the average be at least twice as large as the fourth firm, the extent of multiplant development for the largest firm in most industries was larger than indicated by the preceding four-firm averages, and the multiplant development for the fourth largest (or even third largest) firm was less than the average indicate.

Extremes of multiplant development were not systematically associated with high degrees of seller concentration. In three of the six industries with the greatest multiplant development (canned goods, flour, and shoes, in which the average size of the first four firms was such as to support, respectively, 18, 24, and 22 plants of minimum optimal scale apiece) seller concentration was in the low-moderate range. On the other hand, in the other three industries with great multiplant development (liquor, tin cans, and rubber tires, where the average size of the first four firms was such as to support, respectively, 13, 17, and 9 minimum optimal plants apiece) seller concentration was high or very high. Further to complicate the picture, three of the five industries with the smallest degrees of multiplant development (copper, typewriters, and automobiles) all had very high seller concentration. In them, very large plants rather than extensive multiplant development of firms accounted for the high degree of seller concentration.

If the possibility of actual economies to multiplant firms is tentatively put aside, and we refer to plant economies alone as the efficiency justification for concentration, it would appear from our sample of manufacturing industries that the size of the leading firms in most though not all industries is substantially greater than is required for efficiency. Correspondingly seller concentration in most industries is either moderately higher or much higher than required for efficiency. A dismemberment of large multiplant firms into fragments each roughly the size of one optimal-scale plant would reduce seller concentration moderately or greatly without a loss of efficiency.

The preceding is only a provisional judgment, however, based on the assumption that multiplant economies do not exist or are insignificant. We must therefore inquire how much the judgment should be revised if "alleged" multiplant economies are taken into account. On the basis of our twenty-industry sample, we would be led to conclude that some revision of the judgment is in order, because there were some cases in which existing multiplant development was held to have an efficiency justification. In a majority of cases, however, unnecessary firm size and unnecessary seller concentration would still be found.

The findings on this point in brief were as follows. In five of the six industries with extreme multiplant development (9 to 24 minimum optimal plants apiece for the first four firms in canned goods, flour, liquor, tin cans, and rubber tires), no multiplant economies were claimed in engineering estimates, although their existence was positively denied only in the instance of the canned goods industry. In the sixth of these industries (shoes) some multiplant economies were claimed, but only enough to justify an average size for the first four firms of one-seventh to one-fourth as great as actually attained. The general indication in this group is that all or much of existing multiplant development by the largest firms lacks a justification on efficiency grounds, and that "unnecessary" seller concentration is present in an acute degree.

Of the nine industries with moderate multiplant development by large firms (3 to 8 minimum optimal plants apiece for the largest four firms), there were five in which asserted multiplant economies, though slight in estimated magnitude, would roughly justify the average size of the largest four firms on efficiency grounds: the cement, steel, gypsum product, soap, and cigarette industries. For the other four of these nine industries, the existence of multiplant scale economies was positively denied in two cases (petroleum refining and meat packing), and they were not claimed in the other two.

Thus, for six out of fifteen industries with either moderate or great multiplant development, a rough justification of existing firm sizes and degrees of seller concentration was based on economies of the multiplant firm; for the rest of these industries, no justification was presented. Finally, for the five industries with slight multiplant development (1 or 2 minimum optimal plants apiece for the four largest firms), no justification of firm sizes on the basis of multiplant economies was presented, but multiplant development was insignificant in two or three of these.

The findings from this small sample of industries could hardly be hoped to be exactly representative of tendencies present in manufacturing industries in general. But they lend support to the thesis that in at least half or more of all such industries the leading firms are in a significant degree larger than necessary for the attainment of efficiency in production and distribution. Seller concentration is, in a corresponding sense, unnecessarily high. On the other hand, we must recognize that the picture is definitely mixed as among industries, and that no one sweeping generalization regarding the efficiency justifications of existing concentration is applicable to all.

Determinants of Industry Concentration Other than the Pursuit of Efficiency

The theoretical discussion earlier in this chapter suggested that although the tendency of firms to seek efficient sizes should result in degrees of industry seller concentration falling within certain broad limits, the exact degree of seller concentration attained is not determinate even if efficiency considerations are the only ones influencing market structures. A considerable range of degrees of seller concentration will ordinarily be consistent with efficiency. In the immediately preceding section, findings of fact were presented which suggested that in a majority of manufacturing industries, concentration has developed which is significantly greater than the minimum required for efficiency. Both theory and empirical study thus suggest that we should look for other forces, in addition to the pursuit of efficiency, that determine more precisely the degrees of concentration actually attained in various industries.

In general, firms will be interested in determining their sizes, and thus the degrees of seller concentration within their industries, in such a way as to maximize their profits. Consistent with this, we have seen that firms may in general tend to seek efficient sizes, because this tends to reduce costs and, other things being equal, to increase profits. The drive to increase profits accounts for an approach to degrees of seller concentration which are consistent with optimal efficiency. But if the increase of profits is the master motive, firms may also tend to vary their sizes, and the degrees of seller concentration within their industries, for other reasons than that of simply reducing costs. Firm size and industry concentration may be altered whenever this will tend to increase profits, whether the alteration reduces costs or not. We must therefore look for other connections between profit opportunities on the one hand and firm sizes and industry concentration on the other.

Desire to Restrict Competition

Two such connections stand out, both linking higher profits with large firm size and higher seller concentration. First, firms may be able to increase profits by restricting competition among themselves. And they may be able to do this best by attaining, through mergers or otherwise, a market structure in which there are relatively few firms and a relatively high degree of seller concentration. This is because in a concentrated oligopolistic industry (or at the extreme in a monopoly) competition will ordinarily be less intense and effective than when there are many firms, so that maintenance of a price substantially in excess of costs will be much easier to accomplish. There is thus a "monopoly" motive for mergers or other devices for increasing seller concentration.

Second, individual firms may be able to better their competitive positions and their profits by increasing the effectiveness of their sales-promotion activities, and may be able to do this by increasing the scales of their operations up to some point. That is, firms may encounter or anticipate "advantages of large scale promotion" by becoming big enough to promote sales on a rather large scale. These advantages are reflected in their ability to obtain higher prices, larger sales volumes, or, in general, more advantageous relations of sales revenues to promotional costs. The advantages of large-scale sales promotion are not essentially connected with the reduction of unit production and distribution costs, and not necessarily connected with the reduction of sales-promotion costs per unit of output.

The tendency to increase firm size and seller concentration in order to restrict competition (for example, by the firm's merging with one or several of its principal competitors, or by driving competitors from business with predatory tactics) knows no certain limits. Given no opposing forces and no alternative ways of accomplishing the same end, concentration in every industry might well increase progressively until all firms were combined into one (or only one survived), and each industry was controlled by a single-firm monopolist. There are, however, opposing forces, and there are alternative ways of restricting competition.

One principal opposing force in the United States is that of law. Increase of concentration in any industry up to the point of single-firm monopoly, especially via merger or predatory elimination of competitors, would almost certainly violate either Section 2 of the Sherman Act or Section 7 of the Clayton Act or both, and pertinent legal prohibitions have been clearly in effect since strategic judicial interpretations of the Sherman Act were made between 1905 and 1912. Sellers in an industry may legally strive for at least moderately high degrees of concentration via mergers or otherwise, but hardly for monopoly or any very close approximation to it.

A second opposing force is that of the intrinsic difficulty on the part of potential participants in mergers in agreeing upon terms, and of their intrinsic reluctance to yield up control or sovereignty to a larger firm in which they would have only partial interest or control. A merger to reduce competition may be profitable in prospect, but can the potential participants agree upon the division of the spoils? This matter is always uncertain, and correspondingly just how far mergers-for-monopoly will proceed is uncertain.

Combined with these opposing forces is the consideration that competition among firms may be restricted to a satisfactory degree without actually arriving at or closely approaching single-firm monopoly in the industry. Collusive agreements, or tacitly collusive market conduct as among several independent firms, may effectively restrain or suppress competition. If only a fairly high degree of seller concentration is attained, this may be accomplished with relative certainty. Therefore, the member firms of an industry, once it has reached a fairly high degree of seller concentration, may find no special necessity of combining further to restrict competition, since the attenuated competition of concentrated oligopoly may permit satisfactorily large profits. Finally, of course, combinative activities that would produce firms with serious inefficiencies of very large scale would have a disadvantage which might discourage them, although this does not seem to be a serious limiting consideration in practice.

This combination of "restraining forces" on merger or other activity that is undertaken to increase concentration makes it highly uncertain just how far seller concentration within industries will be increased in order to reduce competition. The relative strength of these restraining forces and the intrinsic drive to restrict competition by increasing concentration is likely to vary from industry to industry and from time to time (especially as interpretations of the law change over time).

All that we can say in general is that there is some latent tendency to restrict competition by the device of increasing concentration, ordinarily by merger, up to some point. So far as this latent tendency becomes actual, seller concentration is likely on the average to become higher than it otherwise would—and to be increased up to some limit, whether or not economies of the large-scale firm are realized. We thus find a possible force, of unappraised net strength, tending to push industries toward higher concentration. This force may well encourage higher degrees of concentration than are needed at the minimum for efficiency, pushing industries toward the higher limit of the range of efficient degrees of concentration, and could even account for uneconomically high concentration. Alternatively, of course, the competition-restricting motive for increasing concentration may in some cases simply reinforce an existing efficiency-increasing motive for the same increase in concentration, making the increase doubly probable. It may be added that mergers to restrict competition have a much better chance of occurring in cases where the participant firms are protected by or can impose some significant barrier to the entry of new sellers.

Advantages of Large-Scale Sales Promotion

The second link mentioned between higher profits and larger firm size involves the possible advantages of large-scale sales promotion.

These advantages are likely to be restricted mainly to firms in industries producing consumer goods, the sales of which are effectively promoted by advertising or other "selling" devices. These include durable goods which require maintenance and repair services that may be provided by the manufacturers. In industries of this sort, some of the most effective "media" for advertising are such that the advertising message automatically reaches potential consumers over the entire nation or at least over a substantial region. Nationally distributed periodicals and "network" television and radio are examples of such media. In order fully to exploit such exceptionally effective media, the firm needs to distribute its product on a nationwide (or regionwide) basis, making it available to buyers in all localities covered by the media. If it equips itself to do so, it can possibly obtain a more profitable relationship of price and sales volume to promotional cost than it otherwise could.

But to do so, it must become big—and perhaps bigger than would otherwise be desirable—not only in terms of the absolute size of its advertising outlays, but also in terms of its productive capacity. Thus, given the existence of a preferred group of advertising media covering broad areas, the firm may find a net advantage in large-scale advertising on a nationwide or regionwide basis, tied to large-scale production and distribution to a nationwide or regionwide market. Unit production costs may not be reduced thereby, but the relationship of sales revenues to sales promotion plus production costs may very well be improved.

How large a firm's optimal size from the standpoint of effective sales promotion will be, relative to its optimal size from the standpoint of efficiency in production, will depend on the facts of the individual case. But one clear possibility is that the firm may find an individual profit advantage in becoming much larger in order to exploit sales-promotion media than it would need to if its main goal were simply to minimize the unit costs of production and physical distribution. In some industries producing durable goods which require servicing—e.g., automobiles—a similar advantage may be reaped from having a reasonably dense nationwide or regionwide network of distribution outlets and servicing stations, with a comparable increased requirement for scale in production.

In industries of this sort, the actual or suspected availability of advantages of large scale sales promotion may frequently lead to the development of larger-scale firms, and higher degrees of seller concentration, than would otherwise result. It is difficult to appraise the net strength of this concentration-increasing force. It should also be noted that realization of the advantages of large-scale sales promotion may involve "distributive integration" by manufacturers—vertical integration involving acquisition of large networks of distributive and servicing facilities.

Barriers to Entry

So far in discussing those profit-increasing opportunities of increased firm size and industry concentration that are not tied directly to productive efficiency, we have emphasized mergers and allied devices to reduce competition, and expansion of firms for effective sales promotion. Both sorts of development tend to increase industry concentration and generally to encourage the development of oligopolistic market situations. However, if oligopolistic situations are to be not only created in these ways but also effectively maintained, there must in general be some barrier to entry, protecting the relatively few remaining large firms from new competition. These barriers are needed so that they can obtain prices at least somewhat above the competitive level without attracting a flood of new competitors.

Considering the matter of impediments to entry further, high seller concentration may emerge more or less naturally without any particular necessity for mergers, or for exploitation of the opportunities of large-scale sales promotion, if any one or a few firms in an industry can obtain some long-term strategic advantage over all actual and potential competitors. Such an advantage will permit the one or a few firms to dominate the market and to exclude rivals from effective competition. This would occur if they were able, because of their positions or possessions, to exact higher prices or produce at lower costs than their actual or potential competition to such an extent that they could make profits (perhaps very goods ones) while charging prices at which competitors would make losses and be unable to survive. Such an ability is the essence of any barrier to entry, and a barrier having these consequences in some degree will generally protect any stable oligopoly. The additional thing suggested here is that, in the cases of some industries, the barrier to entry, instead of being just a general protection to a considerable group of established sellers (who may with its protection manipulate their market structure), will be a protection that favors just one or a very few sellers over all others and permits them to dominate a market. Then the barrier to entry comes to play a leading role, as distinguished from a passive protective role, in the process of determination of the degree of seller concentration within an industry.

Significant barriers to the entry protecting one or a few firms in an industry seem to have resulted mainly from their possession of three sorts of institutional advantage:

1. *Patents giving them exclusive rights over strategic productive techniques or product designs.* These place actual or possible competitors at a substantial disadvantage in cost or price if they must use inferior techniques or produce inferior products, or must pay high royalties for use of the patented techniques or products. Under our patent law, a firm may secure a 17-year patent protection on a newly invented technique or product—plus possibly prolonged protection from "improvement" patents. This can give one or a few firms that are fortunate enough to develop or secure a strategic patent or group of patents a long time to establish a dominant position in a market.

2. *A virtual monopoly over the supply of some essential resource used in production*—for example, of a mineral ore used in making a metal. Where geographical and other conditions make it possible for one or a few firms to acquire ownership of most or all of the relevant supply of a necessary resource, they may dominate the industry and exclude competitors, who either cannot operate at all or must incur prohibitive costs from using resources of inferior grade.

3. *A product-differentiation advantage over all other actual and potential sellers.* The fact that buyers in general strongly prefer the products of the one or a few firms to any others permits these firms to secure all or nearly all of the market at profitable prices, while others in competition with them can or could secure little if any of the market with profit. This sort of advantage develops from the simple allegiance of buyers to particular brand names—usually built up by prolonged and persistent persuasive advertising—and from the dependence of buyers on the "reputations" of certain sellers producing complicated and expensive durable products (such as automobiles or pianos) which the buyer purchases infrequently and is not able to evaluate accurately. Possession of this sort of advantage by one or a few sellers may enable them to become large and dominate their market, even though scale economies in production may be of no particular importance.

When and where among industries these several sorts of advantage favoring one or a few sellers will occur is a matter determined by a variety of circumstances specific to the industry: the opportunity for major inventive improvement in techniques or products; the natural limitation on the supply of and geographical distribution of the deposits of certain natural resources; and the susceptibility of buyers to persuasive advertising appeals and product "reputations," for example. The fact is that they have occurred and do occur from place to place and time to time. When and where they do, one or a few sellers are able, by excluding competition, to monopolize or "closely oligopolize"

an industry and to reach very large firm sizes. As long as they do not encounter serious diseconomies of the very large-scale firm, they find it
profitable to do so.

It may be added that these special advantages to one or a few firms
are not necessarily perpetual. Patent grants finally expire; alternative
resource deposits are discovered; buyer preferences may ultimately become fickle. But while the advantages are in effect, they may account
for the development of high seller concentration in various industries,
and in many cases this high concentration may in one way or another
be maintained long after the initial strategic advantages have ceased
to exist.

Legal Considerations

In the preceding account of forces leading to the development of
substantial degrees of seller concentration within industries, we have
referred to restraining or deterring forces supplied by the law. Particular mention has been made of the antitrust laws—mainly embodied in
the Sherman Act and Clayton Act in the United States—as deterrents to
mergers that would increase industry concentration beyond some point.
The Sherman Act has also provided deterrents to the achievement of
monopolization (or dominant market control by a few sellers) through
the use of exclusionary and predatory tactics in competition with other
firms. The interpretation of these laws has varied over time (since their
passage in 1890 and 1914, respectively), and thus the character and
strength of their deterrent effects has varied. At all times since about
1905, however, there has evidently been some substantial discouragement to concentration approaching full monopolization of industries
(especially if accomplished through exclusionary or predatory tactics),
and in recent years a somewhat more stringent discouragement of
merger activity has been in force. This, then, is part of the legal framework within which enterprises operate in revising their sizes and the
degrees of seller concentration within their industries—a part which has
generally somewhat restrained otherwise "natural" tendencies to increase concentration within industries.

The effect of the antitrust laws, however, has not always been restraining. In the period between its passage in 1890 and about 1905, the
Sherman Act was construed by the courts roughly as (*a*) prohibiting
agreements in restraint of competition among independently owned
competitors in an industry, but (*b*) *not* prohibiting the merger of these
same competitors into a single firm. This paradoxical interpretation was
considerably modified about 1905. But it has been suggested that in the
fifteen years prior to that date, the "legal framework" of the Sherman

Act actually encouraged mergers and the increase of concentration as a legal means of reducing competition. And the merger movement of those fifteen years has had lasting effects on the structure of American industries.

Other aspects of the legal framework, of course, have influenced or conditioned the manner in which concentration has developed over time. We have already alluded to the importance of the patent law in establishing protected positions for certain sellers in certain industries. The revision of corporation laws in the later nineteenth century to permit "holding companies"—that is, the acquisition of a controlling stock interest in one corporation by another corporation—greatly facilitated mergers by providing an easier device for combining companies. And the protective tariff laws, by excluding foreign competition in numerous industries, have provided a more favorable climate for the restriction of competition through domestic mergers. Further discussions of the framework of legal prohibition, privilege, and regulation must be left for the latter part of this volume.

Financial Considerations

So far we have looked for explanations of the development of seller concentration in industries largely in the logic of the profit-seeking activities of the firms. That is, they seek certain sizes and concentration patterns that are more economical and thus more profitable, or simply more profitable for one reason or another—but specifically in the sense of being more profitable to them, the firms engaged in the industry. We must now take account of the possible influence of "outsiders"—of individuals or firms who stand to make a profit or to increase their earning power not from operating within the affected industry, but from arranging, facilitating, or servicing the combination of firms within the industry.

The principal group usually referred to here is made up of financiers, including "promoters" and investment bankers. In the arrangement of most mergers, there are dollars to be earned in the form of commissions paid to investment bankers for handling the requisite exchanges or sales of corporate securities, and in the form of promoters' fees or rewards for their services. Certain service costs are inescapable in handling the financial details of any merger, and will be incurred even if the merger has been decided upon, as a profitable move, by the firms operating in the industry.

What is referred to here, however, is that these functionaries (investment bankers, promoters), instead of simply supplying their services as demanded by firms in an industry which wish to merge, may in some cases take a leading or active role. That is, they may initiate, arrange, and carry through mergers primarily because they can profit from so doing through their commissions and fees, even though the mergers do not necessarily increase the profitability of the firms engaged in the industry. Thus "the tail may wag the dog," and mergers may take place because they provide financial profits to "outsiders."

The possibility of this happening is clear—given the details of the intricate world of corporate securities and control arrangements—and instances have been cited of mergers which seem to have been conceived of and executed primarily with financial profits of outsiders in mind. The wave of public-utility mergers of the 1920's seems to have been influenced at least occasionally by considerations other than the effects of the mergers on the operating profits of the utilities involved. On the other hand, very numerous mergers seem not to have been influenced by such considerations. The actual incidence and importance of strictly "financial considerations" in accounting for merger activity in general is hard to appraise. We must simply count these considerations as another influence, of unascertained strength, on the development of concentration patterns within the American economy. Whatever its strength, it was undoubtedly greater in the period from the end of the Civil War to about 1930 than it has been subsequently.

Another influence on the development of seller concentration not directly linked to the pursuit of operating profits by the firms in the industries concerned may also be mentioned. Concentration may sometimes be increased in an industry by some firms acquiring others mainly because the acquiring firms have a lot of money to spend. As we have seen in Chapter 3, the organization of the large corporation is such that the corporate entity, controlled by a management with various possible relationships to the shareholding owners, earns profits that the management may then distribute entirely or in part to shareholders in the form of dividends. But typical corporate dividend policies favor distribution of only a fraction of earnings, and retention of the remaining fraction in the firm, usually for the stated purposes of assuring liquidity in the face of unfavorable contingencies, and of expansion of the firm. The typical large corporation is thus usually in the process of accumulating a pool of liquid funds from undistributed profits, and these funds become available for investment at the discretion of management.

In many or most cases, investment of earnings will take place within the firm as it acquires added physical assets for the purposes of expansion. But in some cases, alternative sorts of investment may seem more desirable—investment in government bonds, purchase of a portfolio of earning business securities, or short-term loans. Presumably corporate managements are looking for the best available earning yield on their liquid capital, risk being allowed for.

One of the possible avenues for investment of such funds may be that of buying out a competitor (thus effecting a horizontal merger) or perhaps of buying out a supplier or customer firm (vertical integration). That is, acquisition of a controlling or complete interest in other firms may promise the best available yield on the funds available for investment. And this may be the "best investment" even though the merger effected does not promise to increase the combined profit-earning power of acquired and acquiring firms. Thus acquisitions amounting to mergers may take place simply as the result of some firms looking for attractive places to invest excess funds. Mergers of this sort are likely to be especially frequent in times of great prosperity, when corporate earnings run high and there are large quantities of funds left for investment after all conventional dividend payments have been made to shareholders.

If such a merger involves two or more firms in the same industry, it of course tends to increase seller concentration in that industry. If vertical integration is involved, concentration in any one industry is not necessarily increased, but firm sizes are and so is overall concentration in the economy as a whole. Such acquisitions, however, are not necessarily limited to horizontal mergers with competitors and vertical integration with suppliers or customers. Equally possible—and frequently observed in the last twenty years—is the "conglomerate" acquisition, in which a firm operating in one industry acquires a firm which operates in quite another industry. (The process whereby a firm expands internally by building new facilities to enter an industry other than the one in which it is currently engaged is a closely parallel phenomenon, explicable in similar terms.) We thus encounter two additional phenomena—the "diversification" merger (usually by acquisition), and the "diversification" internal expansion of the firm. Both involve creation of a firm straddling two or more separate and not necessarily related industries.

The reason for diversification mergers and expansions is not necessarily limited to the desire of a firm to find the most profitable investment of surplus funds, although this is certainly an important consideration. Also involved may be the desire of the acquiring or expanding firm to "spread its risks" over two or more industries, and of course there may or may not be some economies of the large-scale diversified firm to be realized. Whatever the reason, diversification mergers and expansions tend to increase overall economic concentration without generally affecting concentration within individual industries. And the availability of excess funds for investment in the hands of corporations provides an added motive to all three sorts of increase in concentration—by horizontal, vertical, and conglomerate combination and expansion.

General Economic Growth

Let us return to one final force which tends to restrain or attenuate the development of concentration within markets and the economy as a whole: the growth of the economy and of individual markets. We have seen that there are at work certain forces which may be roughly labeled as "concentration-increasing"—including the desire to attain efficiency in production and distribution or advantages in sales promotion, the desire to restrict competition, the possession of special advantages by limited numbers of firms, and so forth. We have also seen that there are certain deterrent forces which limit the development of concentration, such as the antitrust laws and the intrinsic difficulties of developing agreements on merger terms. The additional countervailing force is the growth of the economy and of the various industries within it.

Suppose that the economy and its various individual markets grow steadily, as on the average they have in this country since its inception. Then principal firms which have attained a given absolute size at some point in time will thereafter control smaller and smaller percentages of their markets, and of economic activity generally, unless they themselves can continue to grow as rapidly as their markets or as the economy. Thus *concentration*, as measured by their percentage shares of the sales in the market or of the business investment in the economy, will tend to decrease unless they can "keep up."

For example, we might find in 1910 that each of three firms supplied 25 per cent of the output of industry X, each having a scale to produce one million units per annum of good X, so that among them they supplied three-fourths of the total market output of four million units. Now, between 1910 and 1950, the market for good X may have doubled in size, so that eight million units are demanded each year. If the three firms have simply maintained their original absolute scales (sufficient for one million units of output per year), they will in 1950 supply only 12.5 per cent apiece of the market—or in the aggregate 37.5 per cent—and seller concentration will probably have decreased as new firms entered the industry to supply the extra demand. Even if each of the three firms has grown to produce 1.6 million units per year, they will control individually only 20 per cent apiece of the market, or collectively 60 per cent, and again seller concentration will have probably decreased. To keep industry concentration as high as it was in 1910, these firms would have to grow as fast as the market (or double their sizes in forty years), thus maintaining the same percentage shares of the market. And they may not succeed in doing this. The same principle applies, in the case of overall economic concentration, to the growth of the firm relative to the growth of the entire business economy.

Therefore, progressive growth of the economy and its individual markets is virtually a concentration-reducing force, which in general can be counteracted only if the larger firms in an industry or in the economy can themselves grow with the same rapidity. For concentration to increase, such firms need to grow with greater rapidity than the individual market or the economy as a whole. In terms of expansion, the larger firms must "run very fast to stay in the same place" as measured by percentage control of markets or larger economic aggregates. If they do not do so, expansion of smaller competitors and the entry of new ones will reduce concentration even though the absolute sizes of the larger firms are not declining, or are increasing at an insufficient rate. Parenthetically, the larger a market becomes, the less seller concentration is required or justified by the pursuit of given economies of large-scale production or advantages of large-scale sales promotion.

General Explanation of the Development of Concentration

We can now summarize our answers to the first question posed at the outset of this chapter: What sorts of forces determine the degree of industry concentration which is attained, or "explain" existing concentration patterns? One thing stands out clearly—there is no one simple force determining concentration and no especially simple explanation. Instead, there is a multiplicity of considerations determining both the degrees of concentration which will be reached in various industries, and the degree of overall concentration in the whole economy. The same variety of considerations determines the directions and rates of change of concentration as it evolves through time.

The constellation of forces involved may be summarized as follows:

1. There is a general drive by firms in the various industries to attain efficient sizes by exploiting existing economies of large-scale production and distribution. This tends to bring about degrees of seller concentration (and patterns of vertical integration) which are at least roughly consistent with technical efficiency. The inclination to move toward efficient market structure, sometimes said to reflect mainly *technological considerations*, tends to bring degrees of seller concentration in the

various markets within certain limits. That is, industries tend to become concentrated enough to exploit available economies of large-scale production, and not so concentrated that firms become inefficiently large. But pursuit of this tendency in the usual industry allows a substantial range of alternative degrees of seller concentration to develop. The degree of seller concentration ordinarily is not at all closely determined by technological considerations alone.

2. Parallel to the pursuit for technical efficiency, there is a drive on the part of firms in some industries (largely supplying consumer goods) to develop scales which are most effective or profitable for sales promotion. This may lead to the development of larger firms and higher degrees of seller concentration than would be required for technological reasons alone—and also to more vertical integration. Response to these *sales promotion considerations*, however, still does not leave the degree of seller concentration at all closely determined.

3. In addition, there is a group of "concentration-increasing" forces that are always at work with one degree of vigor or another. These are stimuli for firms to increase concentration progressively without any necessary limit, either within the industry or through the growth of firms exceeding the bounds of single industries. Chief among them are:

(a) Drives to restrict competition by reducing the number of firms, whether by mergers or by elimination or exclusion of rivals— either at the horizontal level of one industry, or by vertical integration. These may be called, for convenience, *monopolization considerations*.

(b) Tendencies for certain firms to acquire dominant market positions and thus impose high seller concentration because of their acquisition and possession of strategic advantages over all actual or possible competitors. These advantages include patent controls over strategic techniques or products, monopolistic ownership of strategic resource supplies, and strong buyer preferences for their products as compared to those for actual or potential competitive products. These *specific entry barrier considerations* are important in explaining the development of high seller concentration in a number of industries.

(c) Tendencies of "outsider" financial interests to perpetrate mergers (within industries or across industry lines) in order to reap financial profits from the formation of mergers. And, parallel to these, tendencies of corporations with large liquid funds to acquire other firms, within or outside their own industries, mainly as a means of investing these funds. Both tendencies may be included under the head of *financial con-*

siderations. Both are concentration-increasing in essence, though they do not always result in increased concentration within individual industries.

4. Opposing these concentration-increasing forces are certain concentration-deterring ones. These tend to check, limit, offset, or discourage increases in concentration. The most important of them are:

(*a*) *Legal considerations,* principally the antitrust laws and especially the Sherman Act and the Clayton Act. These tend to place certain limits on mergers, on extremely high concentration, and on the development of high concentration through the employment of predatory and exclusionary tactics toward actual or potential competitors.

(*b*) *Enterprise sovereignty considerations.* These are forces virtually deterring mergers, and inhere in the difficulty of potential parties to mergers in agreeing on terms. Fundamentally, they are attributable to the reluctance of individual ownership-management units to yield up their sovereign controls over their operations to a larger combined unit.

(*c*) *Market-growth considerations.* The steady growth of markets and of the economy tend to reduce concentration unless the larger business units grow as rapidly. It offsets the virtual concentration-increasing effects of the merger and internal growth of larger firms.

5. Operation of all these considerations or forces of course takes place within a certain institutional and legal framework. Important parts of this include the tariff laws, the tax laws, and the laws governing incorporation of businesses (as well as the patent law and the antitrust law, already discussed under the heading of more positive influences). *The legal framework* has at least a conditioning influence on the results, in terms of concentration that will ensue from the operation of the various positive forces or considerations enumerated.

What happens to business concentration within an industry is a result of the simultaneous operation of all these various complementary and opposing forces. Exactly what patterns of concentration will emerge at any particular date cannot be predicted *a priori* unless we acquire more information than we now possess concerning the relative strength and detailed nature of the various forces.

As to changes in concentration, the relative force of various concentration-increasing or concentration-deterring forces may alter significantly through time. Scale economies may become more or less important because of technological changes. Entry barriers based on patent or resource control may wither away, or new ones may emerge. Product developments may undercut old product-differentiation barriers to entry. Legal restrictions on concentration may be tightened or slackened. Markets may grow more or less rapidly. The future course of changes in concentration cannot be foreseen until changes in all these dimensions can be predicted, and their probable consequences appraised.

In our present state of knowledge, therefore, we cannot fully explain or rationalize the evolution of concentration in the past, or accurately predict its future course. Identification of the various forces at work, however, provides us with a better understanding of the complex phenomena of structural change observed in the past, and a better basis for appraising alternative possibilities of future development.

Moreover, this analysis of complex forces enables us to reject two incomplete and erroneous theories about economic concentration, and to make some sort of probability judgment about the relationship of existing concentration patterns to economic efficiency.

1. *It is not true* that there will be a never-ending process of increasing concentration, involving fewer and fewer firms controlling more and more of individual industries and of the economy. The desire to combine and concentrate to restrict competition is to be sure always operative, and it is reinforced in a degree by other considerations favoring higher concentration. But there are powerful opposing or countervailing considerations, including law, market growth, and protection of enterprise sovereignty. It is quite possible that over time these will tend to balance or overbalance the drives toward increasing concentration so that, in the net, concentration will not increase and may even decline over time. The experience of the last thirty years is consistent with predictions to this effect.

2. *It is not true* that existing degrees of business concentration are adequately explained as the simple result of adjustments to attain maximum efficiency in production and distribution. They are in part the result of adjustments to attain maximum profits, in a context where profits are influenced by things in addition to efficiency. In part they result from other things, such as financial and legal considerations. As a result, existing degrees of business concentration necessarily reflect the operation of many considerations in addition to that of technological efficiency. Although market structures may still turn out to be relatively efficient on the average (since the limits of efficient structure are fairly broad), the precise degrees of concentration attained are likely to reflect importantly the operation of these other forces.

3. Although the degrees of seller concentration observed in various industries are reasonably efficient, the numerous concentration-increasing forces, other than the pursuit of efficiency, seem to have been strong enough that concentration often tends to be higher than the minimum required for efficiency. Industries probably tend to be "more concentrated than necessary" for efficiency—and the larger firms bigger than necessary—because of the operation of monopolization, sales-promotion, and financial motives, and because of specific entry barriers favoring a few firms in certain industries. Even inefficiently high concentration is not ruled out in some proportion of cases. We return to evidence on this matter in a later chapter.

Explanations of Changes in American Business Concentration since 1870

The preceding analysis is useful in interpreting the history of changing business concentration in the United States since the Civil War. We will not attempt here to analyze this history in any detail, and consider only the explanation of several broad changes:

(*a*) The rapid growth of concentration (featuring the great merger movement) from 1870 until about 1905.

(*b*) The relatively slower and more selective increase of concentration from 1905 to about 1935.

(*c*) The relative stability of concentration since 1935.

The Period from 1870 to 1905

From the end of the Civil War to about 1905, the dramatic increase in concentration was centered in the manufacturing sector. A large proportion of manufacturing industries had their structures drastically revised by the growth of certain firms and especially by mergers. What accounted for this more or less revolutionary change? As might be expected, a number of forces operated at once, reinforcing each other to produce the recorded outcome.

First, there were considerable changes in technology in many industries, generally featuring new mechanical devices and the development of factory mass production. These had the effect of greatly enlarging the minimum optimal sizes of plants. A result was that, to realize efficiency under the new techniques, fewer and larger plants and thus higher concentration were required.

Firms responded to these technological opportunities by attempting to expand rapidly. But if all had expanded to the new larger sizes which had become efficient, excessive capacity would have resulted and losses would have ensued until part of the firms had been eliminated. This in fact occurred to a certain extent. To avoid this result, firms had a considerable incentive to merge with each other, thus enabling them to concentrate their combined production in a smaller number of enlarged plants. Thus they realized the economies of increased scale without developing serious excess capacity. Merger, in other words, was a device for facilitating expansion of plant sizes without developing a serious amount of excess capacity and without requiring some firms to be eliminated from the market.

Technological change, therefore, coupled with business expediency, accounted for some of the increase in concentration observed. It provided a partial explanation for many of the individual mergers. But the evidence hardly suggests that it accounted or could account for all of the mergers or all of the increase in concentration. This increase was on the average substantially greater than was required for technological reasons.

Second, therefore, we must recognize that monopolization motives undoubtedly played an important role. Elimination of competition via mergers was an evident aim in numerous instances. This force was probably unusually strong at the time. The tendency of competitors to expand in order to realize newly available technological economies of large scale was producing, or would potentially produce, excess capacity and more severe competition. Also, the unification of local and regional markets through completion of the railroad network was bringing into competition with each other firms that had previously been isolated by barriers of distance and transport cost. For both reasons, a "defensive" desire to restrict a competition of unaccustomed vigor reinforced any latent "offensive" desire to monopolize industries. The drive to restrict competition through mergers evidently carried the degrees of seller concentration in many industries well beyond the minimum required for efficiency.

The operation of the monopolization drive, moreover, was not seriously restrained by laws during the strategic interval, and in fact was probably encouraged. The Sherman Act was not passed until 1890, and from then until 1905 it was interpreted to the effect that restraint of trade or monopoly effected by merger was not prohibited by law, although loose-knit agreements to restrain competition were prohibited. Thus firms felt that they were not only legally permitted to merge, but encouraged to merge as an alternative to restraining competition by agreement. The *Northern Securities* decision of 1904 changed this interpretation of the Sherman Act, but by then the great merger movement had run its course. And subsequent interpretation of the law was not such as to require the "unwinding" of most of the mergers which had already taken place.

In addition, other factors contributed in at least some degree to the increase of concentration via merger or other means. In a few cases, acquisition of dominant control of strategic mineral deposits served as the pivot for the emergence of a dominant firm in an industry, either by growth or by merger with rivals that also needed access to the mineral. In at least a few cases, patent control provided a similar basis for dominant control or a pivot for a crucial merger. And in numerous cases, the financial profits of investment bankers in arranging mergers were at least a contributing factor in the consummation of mergers. On the other hand, advantages of large-scale sales promotion, and market control based on buyer preferences for certain brands, had by 1905 apparently not as yet become important factors.

A significant facilitating factor was the revision of corporation laws around 1890 to permit holding companies—in particular, the merger of two or more companies by one acquiring a controlling stock interest in the others. This greatly eased the process of merging, and also set the stage nicely for the realization of financial gains by investment bankers and other "outsiders." Thus we discover, in the period from 1870 to 1905, a multiplicity of forces favoring the increase of concentration, and a minimum of restraining factors.

The Period from 1905 to 1935

From 1905 to about 1935, and especially in the decade of the 1920's, concentration in the manufacturing sector did not increase very much, but increased concentration in the public utilities and distributive-trade sectors resulted in a significant increase in overall business concentration. Why was there this retardation in the increase in concentration, and why did most of the increase in concentration affect only the sectors noted?

In the manufacturing sector, there were many signs of activity which might have been expected to produce, other things being equal, a substantial further increase in concentration. There were numerous mergers, including a fair number involving the largest firms. Large individual firms grew in size even without merging. Several new industries developed almost from the outset with a few firms in a dominant position. And the same forces which had operated to produce the greater increase in concentration before 1905 were still at work, albeit with somewhat diminished force. Technological changes on the average continued to favor still larger plants for efficient production. The desire to restrict competition by merging presumably still remained in force. Financial motives for promoting mergers still survived.

Furthermore, added considerations favoring concentration were coming into play with the emergence of a more unified national market and the increasing use of national media for advertising. Buyer-preference advantages to the holders of heavily advertised brand names, and advantages of large-scale sales promotion, were clearly instrumental in establishing and maintaining high concentration in a number of industries. Yet, although concentration increased in some manufacturing industries between 1905 and 1935, in others it decreased, and no very large average change took place in "top-level" concentration (as measured by the percentages of markets controlled by the first few firms in various industries). Why, in spite of all the favoring considerations, did manufacturing concentration fail to make significant progress?

The answer lies partly in the inheritance from 1905—that is, concentration in manufacturing industries that was already on the average quite high. The pushes for higher concentration—and especially the monopolization push—had already been pretty well spent, and the desires behind them pretty well satiated by the great merger movement prior to 1905. Except for "stray" industries or new industries, the work of concentration was already done or overdone. The persistence of some moderate drive toward further concentration was unlikely to produce such spectacular results in the thirty years following 1905 as in the thirty years preceding it. Concentration was frequently already high enough to result first in satisfactorily restricted competition, and second in firms big enough to adjust internally the numbers and sizes of their plants so as to realize increased economies of plant scale without upsetting the balance of capacity and demand.

More importantly, two concentration-deterring factors began to play a more vital role. First, the very rapid growth of most manufacturing markets through the years in question created a great deal of room for the entry of new sellers and the expansion of smaller sellers—both concentration-reducing phenomena. It meant that concentration would decrease unless the principal sellers on the average expanded as rapidly as their markets. The record shows that they tried to, and on the average just about succeeded, but generally they did not succeed in growing more rapidly than their markets. Thus a great many mergers involving principal firms, together with internal expansion by these firms, on the average just about offset the concentration-decreasing effects of market growth, and held concentration at about the same level. In a number of industries, to be sure, concentration increased. But in at least an equal number the firms which were dominant in 1905 after the great merger movement experienced by 1935 a decline in the percentage of the market they controlled, growing on the average less rapidly than their markets grew.

Second, legal deterrents to increasing concentration began to have some effect after 1905. To be sure, they were not strong deterrents, but they had some force. After 1905, the Sherman Act was judicially interpreted as making restraints of trade and monopolization through mergers at least potentially illegal. Although the use of predatory and exclusionary tactics by the dominant firm against competitors (as well as dominant market occupancy) was necessary to perpetrate a Sherman Act "monopolization" offense, a considerable uncertainty was created as to the legality of moves which would further concentrate already concentrated industries. The net attractiveness of mergers or other devices of accomplishing very high concentration to reduce competition was undoubtedly less, even though no clear and definite prohibitions of given degrees of concentration emerged from the interpretation of the law. Furthermore, Section 7 of the Clayton Act as passed in 1914 forbade mergers via stock acquisitions that tended to reduce competition. Although this provision was subsequently emasculated by judicial interpretation (mergers via asset acquisitions were exempted), it probably also had some deterrent force during the crucial period of the 1920's. In addition, of course, various events transpired which favored deconcentration. In particular, strategic patent grants expired in some industries, favoring the entry of new firms and the reduction of concentration.

Given these countervailing forces, plus the lessened vigor of the drive toward further concentration, the degree of concentration in manufacturing industries did not on the average increase significantly in the thirty years after 1905. Concentration in the public utility sector and in the distributive trades, however, did increase considerably.

In the public utilities industries, the major considerations seem to have been (1) the rapid growth of the sector to a position of such importance in the economy that it commanded major attention from the high practitioners of corporate finance; (2) a development of technology that greatly increased economies of large-scale plants (and of firms controlling physically interconnected plants) in such lines as electric power production; and (3) the possibility for promoters and investment bankers to reap large financial gains from organizing and servicing huge public utility holding companies. Thus, for a variety of reasons, a considerable public utilities merger movement was launched in the 1920's, greatly increasing concentration in this sector and considerably increasing overall concentration in the economy as a whole. Except that it involved a new sector of the economy, this merger movement was perhaps not very different in its rationale and its results than the manufacturing merger movement prior to 1905. However, two differences in detail may be noted. First, the concentration accomplished for the sector and the industries in it was higher. Second, financial considerations seem to have played a relatively more important role. In part because the rates of public utility firms are generally regulated by public authorities, mergers in this field received little attention from the administrators of the antitrust laws.

In the distributive trades, the increase in concentration involved the development of large chain stores and other mass distributors. Here the dominant factor seems to have been the introduction of a major technological change. This change exploited the economies of the operation by a firm of a large number of retail stores and of the vertical integration of wholesale and retail functions, and the introduction of "streamlined" retail services (eliminating counter service, consumer credit, and delivery). Exploitation of this technological innovation seems to have accounted in large part for the rise of chain stores and the increase of concentration in the distributive trades.

In the period from 1905 to 1935, therefore, we observe (1) the relative satiation of the desire for increased concentration in the manufacturing sector, in spite of some continuing pressure in this direction; (2) the incipient emergence of a balance between concentration-increasing and concentration-deterring factors in that sector; and (3) the selective continuance of increasing concentration in two sectors which had not been greatly affected by the great merger movement that occurred before 1905.

The Period from 1935 to Date

In the period from 1935 to date, a balance of countervailing forces (encouraging and discouraging further increases of concentration) seems to have been struck more fully in nearly all sectors of the economy. Market growth and legal restraints seem to have been sufficient for the most part to offset the virtual tendencies toward higher concentration. The growth of markets has generally proceeded at a spectacular rate. Legal restraints have tended to become more stringent, with more severe interpretation of general antitrust law and with the amendment of Section 7 of the Clayton Act in 1950 to provide a much stronger deterrent against competition-reducing mergers. New legislation aimed at lessening the advantages of chain stores, and specific legislation aimed at dissolving (and preventing the emergence of) public utility holding companies that lack some economic justification in efficiency have also been significant. Thus while the usual concentration-increasing forces are still at work (though possibly technological changes of the past twenty years have not especially favored more concentration), and while large firms still grow and firms still merge with each other, countervailing forces seem to have struck a rough balance with forces tending to increase concentration. Rather than increasing apace, concentration has barely been holding its own.

Prospect for Changes in Concentration

What will happen to the degree of business concentration from now on, or for the next several decades? Perhaps nothing. We have experienced a "balance of forces" (concentration-increasing and concentration-discouraging) for the last thirty years, and this situation may well continue.

On the other hand, changes may take place that will alter the balance. In particular, the framework of legal limitations is always subject to deliberate alteration. Antitrust restrictions on mergers and on concentration could be relaxed to the point where considerable increases in concentration would almost certainly ensue. They could also be strengthened to the point where deconcentration of existing market structures could be accomplished on a broad scale. It is not our purpose at this point to predict what will happen in this respect, or recommend what should happen.

The virtual tendency to concentrate in order to restrict competition presumably remains more or less constant. Barriers to entry due to patent and resource control may continue to emerge, but in no predictable pattern. The same applies generally to other concentration-increasing forces. They are present, but evidence no long-run tendency over time. As to technology, future developments might of course favor either increased or decreased concentration. There seems to be no way of predicting which, but on the negative side we can say that there has been no observable long-run, irresistible march toward a technology that favors higher and ever higher concentration for purposes of efficiency. Technological changes have been episodic in character, and any general drift toward higher concentration requirements for efficiency has been for several decades at least fully offset by market growth.

Finally, of course, market growth has been and will continue to be important. Aside from legal restraints, it has been principally responsible for offsetting numerous concentration-increasing tendencies for many decades. If we can anticipate comparable rates of growth in the future, increasing concentration is much less probable than if we cannot, because a static economy is much more susceptible to increasing concentration than a dynamically growing one.

SUPPLEMENTARY READINGS

Burns, A. R., *The Decline of Competition*, 1936, Ch. 1.
Robinson, E. A. G., *The Structure of Competitive Industry*, 1935.
Bain, J. S., *Barriers to New Competition*, 1956, Ch. 3.
Kaplan, A. D. H., *Small Business: Its Place and Problems*, 1948, Ch. 5.

7

Market Structures: Degree of Product Differentiation within Industries

Although concentration is the dimension of market structure that has traditionally been most emphasized, other aspects of structure may be comparably important in influencing market conduct and performance. One of these is the *degree of product differentiation* within the industry. As suggested in Chapter 2, the degree of product differentiation refers to the extent to which buyers differentiate, distinguish, or have specific preferences among the competing outputs of the various sellers established in an industry—for example, among the various brands of toothpaste, or the various makes of electric refrigerators. In technical terms, it measures the degree of imperfection of "substitutability" (to buyers) of the various outputs of an industry. As such, the degree of product differentiation has important influences on the competitive relationships of the established member sellers of an industry.

In this chapter, we will discuss its nature and importance by considering in turn (1) the theoretical definition of product differentiation, theory concerning its sources, and theoretical predictions concerning its effects on market conduct and performance in individual industries; (2) evidence concerning the frequency of occurrence and the varying strength of product differentiation in American industries; and (3) the relationships of product differentiation to seller concentration in and the condition of entry to such industries.

Theory Concerning Product Differentiation

As already indicated, product differentiation refers in some sense to an imperfection in the substitutability—to buyers—of the outputs of competing sellers in an industry. In other words, buyers have developed preferences for certain competing products over others. Let us examine this notion a bit more closely.

First, the concept of product differentiation within an industry is dependent on the basic concept of an industry. An industry has been defined as a group of outputs (and of the sellers of those outputs) that are sold to a common group of buyers and that are, to these buyers, close substitutes for each other but relatively distant substitutes for all other outputs. The outputs included in a single industry are thus initially defined as close substitutes *inter se*, and as poor substitutes for all other outputs in the economy.

The close substitutability of the outputs of different sellers in the same industry generally results from the fact that they are all varieties of the same sort of good or service—of cigarettes, of farm tractors, of cement, of laundering—with similarity in form or function and fulfilling the same sort of specific want or need of buyers. It results also from the fact that considerations of seller and buyer location and shipping cost permit all the outputs included to be effectively offered to a common group of buyers. Conversely, the relatively distant substitutability of seller outputs in different industries is generally a result of the different sorts of goods fulfilling different wants or needs of buyers (cigarettes versus penicillin). Also, a lack of substitutability results when groups of outputs are physically similar, but for geographical reasons can be offered only to different groups of buyers (Boston bakery bread and Los Angeles bakery bread would fall in different industries). Generally, we take a provisional view of the outputs of all sellers in the economy as being grouped in a large number of disparate industries.

In technical terms, the degree of substitutability of any two different outputs, whether in the same industry or different ones, should be measurable by the "cross-elasticity of demand" between the outputs. This cross-elasticity measures the responsiveness of the sales volume of one output to a small change in the price of the other. Strictly it is the ratio of the percentage change in the amount buyers demand of output A to the percentage change in the price of output B which induces the change in the demand for A, the price of A being held unchanged.

Between close substitutes, a small reduction in the price of output B will produce at least a perceptible reduction in buyers' demands for output A, because buyers will shift from A to B as the price of B declines. Between distant substitutes, on the other hand, a small price reduction for output D will not perceptibly affect the demand for output C, since it will not induce buyers to shift significantly from C to D.

Generally, then, the outputs of sellers included in any single industry will have at least finite and perceptible cross-elasticities of demand for each other (and perhaps infinitely large ones), whereas the cross-elasticity of demand between outputs in different industries will be very, very small, or approach zero. This is reasonably clear and precise, except that it must be added that any cross-elasticity measure must refer to given initial going prices of the two outputs involved—generally prices at which they are both being bought in the market or markets involved.

Returning to the individual industry, all the outputs included in it are at least close substitutes to buyers, but they are not necessarily perfect substitutes. At one extreme they may be perfect substitutes ("homogeneous") in the sense that all buyers regard the outputs of all sellers as identical, and have no preference for one as compared to others. (This may be the case when all sellers produce perfectly standardized goods with identical qualities or specifications, and where the buyers are well informed and not subject to persuasion by brands, advertising, and so forth.) In this event, the cross-elasticities of demand between different pairs of outputs will "approach infinity" (a very small price reduction for one will tend to attract all of the buyers away from any other), and the various outputs will be bought simultaneously only at a single identical price. Among the numerous industries in the economy, a substantial number are found to approximate homogeneity or perfect substitutability of competing outputs. In these industries there is, to a close approximation, no product differentiation.

In numerous other industries, however, the substitutability of competing outputs is imperfect. An imperfection of substitution between outputs will be registered generally in the fact that various buyers prefer various different outputs to others and have different scales of preference among outputs. As a result, some buyers will buy one output instead of others if the prices are identical (and some other buyers another output), and probably they will be willing to pay at least slightly more for a preferred output in order to obtain it. In general, the cross-elasticity of demand between various pairs of outputs will then be perceptible and finite, but not infinite. A small price reduction for one output will attract some but not all of the customers away from other outputs, and a small increase in the price of one output will cause it to lose some but not all of its customers to other outputs. Also, competing outputs may be sold, simultaneously and compatibly, at perceptibly different prices, depending on their ratings in the preference systems of buyers.

One condition implied above must be present to give product differentiation its full meaning. This is that different groups of buyers rank various competing outputs differently on their scales of preference. Some buyers will prefer one output and some another at identical or comparable prices. Some will be willing to pay a price premium to get a certain output whereas others would require a price concession to be induced to buy it. Among buyers preferring a given output, some will prefer it more strongly than others, or be willing to pay a higher price for it relative to other outputs. These circumstances, moreover, will tend to account for some specific, and generally unequal, division of the market among competing sellers, and also for the possibility of such a division occurring either with identical or with unequal prices for their outputs. If, on the other hand, all buyers had identical preference ratings of competing outputs, we would be much closer to simple uniform "grading" of these outputs than to full-fledged product differentiation.

Sources of Product Differentiation

The sources of product differentiation within an industry encompass all considerations which may induce buyers to prefer one competing output to another. The most obvious ones are differences in quality or design among outputs. One brand of shoes may have better materials and workmanship than another, or one make of automobile may feature soft spring suspension and a "box on a box" body design while another features stiff spring suspension and a "fastback" body. In either case, different buyers may rank the competing outputs differently. One buyer may prefer one automobile design and another the other design, or one may be "quality-conscious" and willing to pay a considerable price premium for quality shoes, whereas another is "price-conscious" and will accept the lower quality if there is only a relatively small price concession.

A second source of product differentiation is the ignorance of buyers regarding the essential characteristics and qualities of the goods they are purchasing. This is likely to be an important consideration in the case of goods bought by consumers (as distinct from those bought by producers, who are generally better informed), and particularly in the case of durable consumer goods that are infrequently purchased and are complex in design or composition.

Let us consider the significance of buyer ignorance. Regarding meat, canned vegetables, bread, stockings, and similar goods purchased repeatedly at short intervals, a housewife is likely to obtain a reasonably good knowledge of the quality and other characteristics of competing outputs, and to arrive at a reasoned and informed choice among alternatives. But with respect to automobiles, major electrical appliances, home-movie cameras, and the like—all complex in design and very infrequently purchased—the average consumer is likely to have only the sketchiest notion of the relative performance, reliability, and other essential characteristics of competing brands, and is in effect ignorant or uninformed. In this situation, he is likely to rely on the reputations of the various products or their sellers: on popular lore concerning the performance and reliability of past outputs of a seller, on whether or not the seller has remained in business for a long time, and so forth. This reliance on seller or product reputations by consumers is a further important source of preferences favoring some seller outputs as compared to others.

Third, buyer preferences for certain products are developed or shaped by the persuasive sales-promotion activities of sellers, and particularly by advertising. Inextricably interconnected with brands, trademarks, or company names, advertising and other sales promotion may of course be primarily "informational" in its impact (thus tending to build a product differentiation based on a knowledge of the relative designs, qualities, and prices of competing outputs). But in fact the bulk of advertising is instead primarily "persuasive." It is aimed at creating product preferences through generally phrased praises of the attributes of various outputs (Winstons taste good, like a cigarette should), or simply through dinning into the potential buyer's mind an awareness of the product through endless repetition. Thus an important category of product differentiation is built primarily on a nonrational or emotional basis, through the efforts of the "ad-man."

Fourth, the possibility of developing significant product differentiation through advertising—whether or not the good is durable or the buyer ignorant—is greatly enhanced for so-called "gift goods" or "prestige goods." These include generally products that are frequently purchased on special occasions as gifts for others (like fountain pen and pencil sets given as graduation gifts), and those that though not given away are similarly bought with the motive of gaining the admiration or gratitude of others (like liquor bought to serve to guests whose respect or admiration the host would like to cultivate). In the case of such products, there is a maximal opportunity for "name brands" which are heavily advertised and also widely known to be relatively expensive. They establish preferred positions in the preference scales of some part of the buyers in a market.

Finally, some product differentiation may result from differences in the locations of sellers of the same sort of good, which result in various buyers in the market being situated at different distances from different sellers. Such locational differences among sellers, however, are the source of true product differentiation only if two other conditions are fulfilled. One is that there are, from the standpoint of the usual buyer, significant differences among sellers in the costs of either having the good delivered or picking it up—different costs in terms of money, inconvenience, or time. The other is that buyers pay or suffer these delivery or pickup costs in such a way that they pay different "full" prices (prices at sellers' locations plus monetary or other costs of delivery or pickup) to sellers located at different distances from them. Then the products of differently located sellers become imperfect substitutes to buyers; differently located buyers will have different scales of preference among different sellers; and an effective locational product differentiation exists. These conditions are most usually fulfilled in various retail distributive industries, where differences in store locations result in the sort of differentiation noted.[1]

In the case of some products, of course, two or more of these five sources of product differentiation may be simultaneously present, in which event high degrees of effective product differentiation tend to develop. The first four sources mentioned, for example, seem to be operative in the case of automobiles.

The preceding list of sources could be extended—to include for example, the function of attractive "packaging" in attracting customers— but we have covered the primary bases of most existing product differentiation.

Effect of Product Differentiation on Market Conduct and Performance

We are interested in product differentiation as a dimension of market structure primarily because of its influence on the market conduct or performance of sellers in the industries where it is found. This influence will stand out more clearly if we first consider the consequences of a complete or approximate absence of product differentiation, a condi-

---

[1]If the first condition—significant interseller differences in delivery or pickup costs—is not fulfilled, locational product differentiation will not exist. If the first condition is fulfilled but the second is not—so that buyers in a single market do not absorb the differences in delivery or pickup costs among differently located sellers, but pay the same full delivered price to all sellers—the different locations of sellers do not tend to make their products imperfect substitutes to buyers. Then locational product differentiation is not apparent. Rather, differences in seller locations are compensated for by geographical price discrimination among buyers (in terms of delivered prices less delivery costs). Of course, wide differences in the locations of sellers may result in their supplying different regional markets, thus being members of different theoretical industries.

tion found when all sellers in the industry produce substantially identical or homogeneous outputs among which buyers make no significant distinction and have no significant preferences.

First, all sellers will be able to sell only at a single identical price, and price differentials among their outputs will be unable to persist. No seller will be able to raise his price above the general market level of price and hold his customers, and any seller will be forced to match the price reductions of his rivals in order to hold his customers.

Second, the market shares of various individual sellers will be determined not by systematic buyer preferences but at random or as a result of a past sequence of historical developments in the establishment and growth of firms. The individual firm is generally not well protected in its going share of the market by any specific structural conditions, and is potentially vulnerable to losses in proportionate control of the market because of the growth of other firms, their pricing policies, and so forth.

Third, advertising and other sales promotion by individual sellers will be generally ineffective in increasing or maintaining their market shares, or in securing preferred prices, since buyers view the competing outputs as effectively perfect substitutes for each other. (If sales promotion becomes effective, product differentiation has been introduced.) The same applies to alterations in product design or quality by individual sellers to gain market-share or price advantages. Competition among sellers is thus essentially confined to adjustments in price or in quantity of output offered for sale. "Nonprice" competition through advertising or product variation is not an available alternative. Not many markets reach the polar extreme of absolutely no product differentiation, but in numerous industries there is little enough product differentiations that the preceding tendencies are at least roughly approximated.

When the products of the various sellers in an industry are significantly differentiated, the market situation is changed in all of the respects just mentioned. With regard to pricing, two things stand out. First, sellers are not bound to sell their products at a single common price. Different buyers or groups thereof prefer different products, or, more generally, assign different rankings on their schemes of preference to the various products available. Each seller is then faced with a market in which some buyers either prefer his product to all others or rank it relatively high in their preference schemes, others who prefer it less strongly or rank it lower, others who prefer other products or assign it an even lower preference ranking, and so forth. Therefore, each seller acquires at least a small measure of independent jurisdiction over the price of his product. He can raise it at least slightly above those of his competitors (or raise it relative to their prices) without losing all of his customers, and can reduce it at least slightly to a level below those of his competitors (or cut it relative to their prices) without attracting away all or most of their customers.

This degree of independence in pricing by individual sellers does not necessarily result in their selling at a variety of different prices. If their products are on the average about equally preferred (though by different groups of buyers), and if each seller's individual price reduction will greatly expand his sales at the expense of competitors (and his individual price increase greatly reduce his own sales), the forces either of atomistic competition or of oligopolistic rivalry will tend to make the prices of all sellers in the market at least approximately equal. It is quite possible, however, that when the competing products are not about equally preferred, or when product differentiation is so strong that small individual sellers' price changes will not have large effects on their shares of the market, a variety of different prices will simultaneously be charged by different sellers, each then securing a determinate and relatively stable share of the market.

This brings us to the second main point about pricing in product-differentiated markets. It is quite possible that of the several or many sellers in the market, some—perhaps very few—will enjoy generally superior positions in the preference schemes of most or all buyers, while the others have products that are generally considered inferior or less desirable. Some sellers, in other words, may enjoy a general product-differentiation advantage over others in the market. In this event, the less advantaged sellers may be unable to sell any output—or alternatively unable to sell enough output to save them from crippling diseconomies of very small-scale production—unless they charge prices perceptibly lower than those of their more advantaged rivals. The outcome then is likely to be that some sellers, enjoying product-differentiation advantages, will regularly sell at prices higher than those of their rivals, so that two or more different prices will prevail among the competing products. The resulting price differentials will reflect general differentials in the ranking of products in the preference schemes of most or all buyers, even though the strength of preference for the "superior" products varies among buyers.

There may obviously be a number of reasons for the persistence of these inter-seller price differentials. One is that some of the products in a market may be intrinsically superior in quality, design, or workmanship—or perhaps larger, thus more desirable, and also costlier to produce. Another is that buyers may view some products as superior in one respect or another even when they are not, because of established product reputations or brand names, successful persuasive advertising, and so forth. In fact, a not uncommon pattern in product-differentiated markets finds a group of heavily advertised products with established brand names selling at a given top level of prices, and another group of products that are much less advertised selling at appreciably lower prices. Correspondingly, the two groups of products may respectively attract buyers who are "quality-conscious" (or are susceptible to advertising appeals) and who are "price-conscious," at least as a matter of emphasis. Further discussion of the rationale of inter-seller price differentials seems unnecessary, given our earlier analysis of the sources of product differentiation.

Let us now consider the market shares of individual sellers in product-differentiated markets. Generally, systematic schemes of buyers' preferences among products (the same that confer some independent price differentials among them) tend at any time to determine the share of the market that each seller will secure, given the relative prices of the various sellers. Many sorts of division of the market among sellers may emerge. It is logically possible, but statistically very improbable, that all sellers would have equal advantage in securing and retaining buyer preferences, so that when all were charging the same price, all would have identical shares of the market. (In this case, the charging of the same price by all would definitely tend to be encouraged either by atomistic competition or by oligopolistic rivalry.) Much more likely is a determinate division of the market through which, if charging identical or closely similar prices, different sellers secure appreciably different and perhaps greatly different shares of the market—these shares being determinate in any given state of buyer preferences. Even in atomistic markets, the shares of the many individual sellers are likely to differ appreciably. In oligopolistic markets, differences among the market shares of the principal sellers are highly probable because of product differentiation, as are much wider differences between the shares of the dominant firms and those of any competitive fringe of smaller sellers.

In fact, the ability of a few firms in an industry to secure strong product-differentiation advantages over all others has frequently been a primary reason for the emergence of oligopolistic market structures, including those with high seller concentration. Similarly, the persistent product-differentiation disadvantages of a number of other firms in the industry, resulting in their being able to secure only small individual market shares, is a principal explanation of the persistence of a competitive fringe of small sellers surrounding an oligopolistic core of a few large ones. Oligopolistic market structures are frequently stable because of patterns of product differentiation that stabilize market shares.

The market shares of the several large and perhaps numerous small sellers in an oligopolistic market are of course not necessarily (or usually) determined with all sellers charging identical prices. The relative prices of the sellers and their respective market shares are generally codetermined, subject to the prevailing schemes of buyer preferences. Many patterns are logically possible, of which a few typical ones may be mentioned. One involves an oligopoly of several large sellers only (no competitive fringe) with differing market shares if their prices are identical, and with their prices in fact being identical or approximately so—largely because an independent price reduction by any one seller would affect the sales of his rivals enough that they would match his price cut. Another involves an oligopolistic core of sellers each of which secures a large share of the market, together with a fringe of small sellers that individually can secure small market shares when charging the same price as their larger rivals—and with the small sellers profitably charging this same price. A third is similar except that (1) if the small sellers charged the same price as their large rivals, they could secure either no market shares or shares so small that diseconomies of small scale would deny them profits, and (2) when the small sellers charge prices somewhat lower than those of their large rivals, they can secure somewhat larger but limited market shares at which they can make profits so long as the prices of their large rivals are high enough. A stable market situation potentially results, provided that the product-differentiation disadvantages of the small sellers confines them to small and not progressively expanding individual shares of the market. And it is likely to result because the large sellers are restrained from raising their prices to such a level that the small ones could profitably undersell them by enough to enable them to expand their collective share of the market significantly. Numerous other sub-variant patterns of market sharing and price policies can readily be imagined.

The last matter to be considered is that of sales promotion and product policy. In product-differentiated markets, sellers are encouraged to try to increase their market shares or better their relative selling prices by advertising and otherwise engaging in sales promotion activity. Similarly, they are induced to establish levels of product quality and product designs which will increase market shares, make possible higher selling prices, or generally improve their profit positions—and to vary their products over time through improvements or style changes intended to have the same effects. Sales-promotion policies and product policies thus become essential parts of the market conduct of sellers in these industries. Moreover, the several or many sellers in a product-differentiated industry tend to pursue sales-promotion and product policies rivalrously or competitively (except as restrained by oligopolistic interdependence), so that advertising competition and product competition—or, in general, nonprice competition—emerge as supplements to and substitutes for price competition. The character and intensity of such nonprice competition becomes an important aspect of market conduct.

In summary, product differentiation in an industry exerts an influence on pricing, on the determination of market shares, and on the scope of market conduct open to sellers. It also brings to the fore as important some distinctive dimensions of the market performance of firms, including:

1. The size of sales-promotion or selling costs, and the extent to which selling costs are incurred to persuade rather than inform buyers.

2. The level of product quality, which may be judged as excessive, deficient, or satisfactory in view of the alternative costs of producing alternative qualities of product.

3. The frequency with which products are varied over time, evaluated in view of the costs of various frequencies of variation.

4. The variety of qualities and designs of products supplied by the industry, relative to the variety of consumer tastes for different qualities and designs.

We will not attempt here to outline systematically the predictions of price theory concerning the market-performance tendencies of product-differentiated industries in these respects—in part because it would be a lengthy task and in part because the predictions themselves are mostly indefinite or ambiguous. Some general comments, however, may be in order.

The importance of the impacts of product differentiation on market conduct, and thus on market performance, will of course depend on the degree or intensity of product differentiation, on its particular pattern in individual cases, and also on whether differentiation occurs in conjunction with low or high seller concentration. Rather than speaking of all product-differentiated industries as members of a single group with common tendencies, it is useful to divide them into subgroups on various bases, such as: (1) general intensity or importance of product differentiation—great, moderate, or slight; (2) primary basis of product differentiation—product design, branding and advertising, or service to customers; (3) character of the distribution of buyer preferences among competing sellers—whether heavily favoring a few sellers as compared to all others, or distributed among all sellers in a roughly even fashion; (4) number of sellers in the market. Recognizing these distinctions, numerous categories of product-differentiated markets could be recognized. Without attempting here to set forth a formal classification of these categories, the general influence of the underlying differences may be noted.

All of the potential effects of product differentiation are likely to be more strongly felt if the general degree or intensity of product differentiation is great. Interseller price differences are likely to be more important, and the market shares of individual sellers less sensitive to transitory influences, including price variations. Price competition is likely to be of much less importance than nonprice competition, costs being adjusted relative to comparatively insensitive prices rather than prices to costs. If, on the other hand, product differentiation is relatively moderate or slight, a closer similarity of the prices of competing products, a smaller proportionate emphasis on nonprice as compared to price competition, and a greater potential instability of market shares is likely to be noted. As to performance, the size of sales-promotion costs and the effect of product quality and frequency of product variation on production costs are likely to be more serious issues as product differentiation is more intense.

The basis of product differentiation will tend to be reflected in the types of nonprice competition that are emphasized in an industry. Where product differentiation is based mainly on brands and advertising, competition via sales promotion will loom large and the size of selling costs will tend to be a principal issue. Where product design is the primary basis of differentiation, product competition, involving periodic improvements or other variations in the products of competing sellers, is likely to be important. Then major performance issues tend to concern the levels of product qualities and costs, the variety among competing products offered, and the costs of frequent product changes. Where customer service is the key to product differentiation, integration of distributive facilities by manufacturers is likely to become an important phase of conduct, and the costs of integrated distributive systems an important performance issue.

The influence of the distribution of buyer preferences among sellers is clearly significant in establishing different patterns of seller concentration and differential advantages among competitors. And whether product differentiation occurs in an industry with many small sellers or a relatively few large ones (a matter ultimately determined by this distribution of buyer preferences) is important because the degree of seller concentration is likely to influence the character of nonprice rivalry and its performance results in the dimensions of product determination and selling costs.

Very roughly it may be suggested that, with product differentiation among many small sellers in an industry, independent policies of individual sellers undertaking sales promotion and designing and varying products will tend to result in a substantial variety among competing products and in sales-promotion costs of different firms. Price competition is likely to be liberally admixed with nonprice competition, offering buyers a considerable variety of genuine alternatives. When product differentiation is conjoined with higher seller concentration, on the other hand, the interdependence of competing sellers is much more likely to result in parallelism of product and sales-promotion policies, and in a much reduced variety of genuine product and price alternatives open to buyers. Also, the substitution of intensive and expensive nonprice competition for price competition in such concentrated markets may raise acute issues of excesses in product and sales-promotion costs.

Evidence Concerning Actual Product Differentiation

How important is product differentiation in the various sectors and industries of the American economy? Systematic data based on measurement of the relevant indicators—for example, the cross-elasticities of demand of competing products—are unavailable. We have no government reporting service that supplies data on this dimension of market structures. Nevertheless, some judgments about the apparent incidence of product differentiation may be made, beginning with a broad appraisal of its occurrence in the principal sectors of business activity.

Product differentiation within industries is based generally on the opportunity for producing significantly different designs and qualities of the good in question, the comparative ignorance of buyers with respect to the merits of various alternative products, and the susceptibility of buyers to persuasive appeals concerning the alleged superiority of the outputs of individual sellers. If this is the case, a first general rule (subject to a number of exceptions) is that product differentiation tends to be more important in consumer-good industries and less important in those supplying producer goods. Producer-buyers tend to make it their business to be well informed about the qualities and properties of the goods they buy, and are thus less susceptible to the persuasive appeals of sellers. In addition, their task is frequently simplified by the fact that numerous producer goods are standardized, uniform raw materials, the suppliers of which find little opportunity for introducing physical product differentiation among their outputs.

Thus in the numerous producer-good industries in the sectors of agriculture, forestry, fisheries, and mining, for example, product differentiation is generally of negligible or slight importance. The good produced by competing sellers in an industry in any of these sectors is likely to be more or less standardized or uniform, at each of a few standardized grades and qualities. And efforts of sellers to introduce product differentiation have generally been unsuccessful. In most but not all of these sectors there is atomistic market structure in addition to approximate product homogeneity in the individual industry—an approach to theoretical "pure competition"—as in industries producing grain crops, or in bituminous coal mining.

Among manufacturing and processing industries, on the other hand, there is an important incidence of product differentiation, primarily in numerous industries supplying consumer goods. The consumer-buyers of these goods often tend to be poorly informed, and especially so when the goods are complex and intricate in design and function. Even when the goods are not complex, buyers are frequently susceptible to persuasive advertising appeals. In addition, many types of consumer goods can be purposefully varied or differentiated in design or quality by their producers in ways the significance of which is not easily understood by consumers. Goods like cigarettes, soap, and liquor are strongly differentiated through the use of persuasive advertising appeals; goods like autos and electrical appliances evidence differentiation resting strongly on product design and on the ignorant consumer's dependence on the seller's reputation; goods like gasoline and rubber tires display a differentiation which rests in considerable part on the character of the manufacturers' distributive and service facilities. In these industries, moreover, product differentiation more frequently than not is found in conjunction with high to moderate degrees of seller concentration, reflecting a distribution of consumer preferences that has come to favor heavily, industry by industry, a relatively small number of sellers.

In other consumer-good manufacturing industries, by contrast, product differentiation—though generally present in some measure—is of relatively slight importance. This seems to be especially true of basic "necessity" goods in the area of food, clothing, and household supplies. These are relatively simple in character and function, and the housewife (as principal consumer-buyer) purchases them repeatedly and frequently. Thus we find that in the industries producing fresh and processed meats, groceries of most sorts, children's shoes and clothing, and the like, the efforts of competing sellers significantly to differentiate their products have not ordinarily been very successful. Effective product differentiation has generally remained negligible or slight. Thus the establishment of brands and their support by advertising is not automatically efficacious in creating strong product differentiation within a consumer-good industry; other circumstances must also be propitious.

In manufacturing industries making producer goods, product differentiation is most frequently slight or negligible, and for the usual reasons—expert buyers, and goods which may be produced to standards or specifications. Basic industrial raw materials such as steel, copper, cement, and industrial chemicals, for example, clearly come under this heading. Buyers purchase to specification or rely on established grades, and generally do not prefer one seller's output to another sufficiently to induce them to pay a higher price for it. The slight buyer preferences that do introduce some element of product differentiation generally rest on such details as ancillary services which the seller performs for buyers, promptness in filling orders and making deliveries, and so on. But in the case of producer goods for which the provision of services by the manufacturer is an important element of the transaction (often when the producer buyers are typically rather small firms), and of producer goods that are large and complex devices (specialized machinery of various sorts), product differentiation may become as important as it is in consumer-goods categories. This would be true, for example, of large, complex farm machinery and of business office machines of various sorts.

Other sectors of the enterprise economy may be characterized more briefly with respect to the incidence of product differentiation.

1. *Wholesale and Retail Trade* (groceries, clothing, drug stores, etc.). In the numerous retail distributive industries identified with various product lines and localities, product differentiation based on type and quality of service offered by the retailer and on the convenience of his location to the buyer is generally quite important. Product differentiation is evidently less important in the wholesale markets in which retailers purchase from wholesale distributors.

2. *Service Trades* (barber shops, dry cleaners, entertainment enterprises, etc.). Product differentiation is again important, for the same general reasons as those that apply to retailing.

3. *Contract Construction.* In large-scale construction for industry or for governmental agencies, where contracts are let after a process of bid-

ding to specifications, product differentiation is a minimal factor. In the residential construction or housebuilding field, product differentiation based on design and location is generally important.

4. *Finance* (including real estate firms, insurance companies, banks, etc.). A mixed picture is found as among various industries, with product differentiation important in some cases and not in others.

5. *Public Utilities and Transportation.* In most utility industries, including those in the electric, gas, and communications fields, local monopoly supply by a single firm typically forestalls the emergence of product differentiation between competing sellers. In the transport field, product differentiation among the services of competing types of carriers and between competing carriers of the same type is present, but is evidently more important in the field of passenger transportation than in that of freight transport.

Product Differentiation in Manufacturing Industries

The preceding survey provides only a rough general impression of the incidence of product differentiation in broad groups of industries. To get a more definite impression, we must examine individual industries, with attention to the wide range of differences in intensity, basis, and detailed pattern of product differentiation. In this connection we can present the results of our study of twenty manufacturing industries (and some of their segments) alluded to in the preceding chapter.

In this sample of industries, an appraisal of the relative importance of product differentiation was made on the basis of various visible evidences of its causes and effects in terms of the size of sales-promotion costs, the existence of distinct design and quality differences among competing products, the occurrence of product improvement and variation by sellers as a device of competition, the sensitivity of sellers' market shares to variations in products and in sales promotion campaigns, and the existence of significant differential advantages of some sellers over others in terms of the relationship of their selling prices to their costs of production and sales promotion. Considering all such evidence, the industries were ranked, for purposes of comparison only, as having "great," "moderate," "slight," or "negligible" product differentiation. Correspondingly, the bases of product differentiation were identified primarily as product design, quality, or reputation, advertising, and service to customers. We also added a notation concerning the degree of seller concentration in the industry, following the classification of Chapter 5.

I. INDUSTRIES WITH "GREAT" PRODUCT DIFFERENTIATION

Industry	Principal Basis of Product Differentiation	Seller Concentration in Industry
Cigarettes	advertising	very high
Distilled liquor	advertising; product quality	high
Automobiles	product design and reputation; customer service with controlled distributive outlets; advertising	very high
Heavy complex farm machinery and tractors	product design; customer service with controlled distributive outlets	high
Fountain pens ("quality" or high-priced field)	advertising; product design	very high
Typewriters	customer service; product design; advertising	very high

II. INDUSTRIES WITH "MODERATE" PRODUCT DIFFERENTIATION

Industry	Principal Basis of Product Differentiation	Seller Concentration in Industry
Petroleum refining	advertising; customer service through controlled or subsidized distributive outlets	high (in most regional markets)
Rubber tires	advertising; customer service with controlled or affiliated distributive outlets; product design	high
Men's shoes (high-priced or "quality" field)	advertising; controlled or affiliated distributive outlets	high moderate
Metal containers (tin cans)	customer service, including leasing of machinery etc.; product design	high
Flour (consumer market sales)	advertising; customer service	high moderate

III. INDUSTRIES WITH "SLIGHT" PRODUCT DIFFERENTIATION

Industry	Principal Basis of Product Differentiation	Seller Concentration in Industry
Steel	customer service	high moderate
Meat packing (processed meats)	advertising; product quality	low moderate
Fountain pens (low-priced field)	advertising; product design	moderate
Men's shoes (low-priced field)	advertising; controlled or affiliated distributive outlets	low

IV. INDUSTRIES WITH "NEGLIGIBLE" PRODUCT DIFFERENTIATION

Industry	Seller Concentration in Industry
Copper	very high
Cement	low moderate
Rayon yarn and fiber	high
Canned fruits and vegetables (bulk fruit and vegetable lines)	low
Flour (commercial and industrial, or producer-good, market)	low
Meat packing (fresh meats)	low moderate

Some Specific Examples

The basis, character, and influence of product differentiation in the preceding categories may be made clearer by discussing an example from each: automobiles from that of "great" product differentiation barriers; petroleum refining from that of "moderate" differentiation; and steel and "industrial" flour from the categories of "slight" and "negligible" product differentiation.

Passenger automobiles in the United States are currently produced almost entirely by four firms—the Big Three of General Motors, Ford, and Chrysler, and one firm of smaller size, American Motors (Rambler). They supply all but about 6 per cent of the American market for automobiles, the remainder coming primarily from several European producers. Seller concentration, as noted in Chapter 5, is exceptionally high, with the Big Three together accounting for almost 90 per cent of sales—a total divided, in recent years, to allot about half of the total market to General Motors, a quarter to Ford, and 15 per cent Chrysler. The largest European supplier (of the Volkswagen) has not consistently exceeded a 3 per cent share of the American market.

Product differentiation, which is generally recognized as having a maximal importance in this market, is evidently based both on physical product differences and on a number of other considerations. The physical product structure of the industry has long been built around four loosely defined price classes, identified as "low," "low-medium," "high-medium," and "high." There is a typical price difference of several hundred dollars between adjacent classes, and corresponding systematic interclass differences in the gross specifications of engine size and horsepower, overall length, wheelbase, weight, and (to some extent) quality or refinement in construction. The outputs of each of the Big Three, each generally offering at least one brand or make in each price class correspondingly reflect some intrafirm product differentiation. Thus General Motors offers Chevrolets in the low- and low-medium-price classes; small Pontiacs, Oldsmobiles, and Buicks in the low-medium-price class; larger models of each make in the high-medium-price class; and Cadillac in the high-price class. The other two large firms generally follow suit. The surviving "independent" (American Motors) has attempted to produce in two or more price classes so far as it could attain sufficient sales in each. European producers have since World War II sold mainly in a fifth size and price class (low-priced "compact"), now also entered by all four American producers.

Product differentiation among different sellers in the same or adjacent price classes depends to a noticeable extent on physical differences in body design and appearance, in design of engines, transmissions, running gear and suspension systems, and so forth. There are indeed perceptible differences among competing products at most times. But the fact that all sellers generally follow product policies of protective imitation of their competitors has generally kept these differences within a rather narrow range, and on a superficial rather than a fundamental level. Thus, at most times, the similarity among competing brands in appearance, engine design, power, and the like is, from a technical standpoint, perhaps more striking than the difference, considering the almost unlimited variety of design alternatives open to the automobile manufacturers. It is correspondingly true that the importance of the physical product differences which do exist is the result in considerable part of the exaggeration of their importance in advertising claims. Sellers make persistent attempts to persuade the buyer (who on the average is poorly equipped to evaluate such a large and complex mechanism as the modern automobile) of the unique and superior characteristics of their several fundamentally very similar products.

The automobile buyer's typical state of relative ignorance about the properties of what he buys is related to a second important basis for product differentiation in the market—the dependence of the buyer on the established reputation of the manufacturer for producing automobiles of high quality, dependability, and durability. Purchasing this large and complex mechanism very infrequently, so that he has a very limited chance for trial-and-error experiments, and spending a great deal for each unit purchased, the buyer is prone to depend on the long-established reputations of given products and their sellers as his insurance against making a mistake. Thus each of the Big Three, and to a lesser extent American Motors or Volkswagen, tends to have the allegiance of a "loyal following" of automobile buyers who prefer a particular seller and product for the reason noted, and who buy on faith in its reputation.

Another important aspect of the psychology of the buyer is reflected in his "conspicous-consumption" motives in purchasing an automobile. New automobiles in particular are goods not only to be put to a functional use, but also to be displayed as tokens of eminence, taste, and ample income to one's neighbors and associates and to strangers. In the operation of these motives, the American buyer typically seems to want to acquire brands of automobiles which are "popular," or highly regarded by a large proportion of the population, and thus to imitate the bulk of other buyers in his choice of an automotive badge of distinction. Thus there tends to be a certain snowballing of buyer preferences for particular brands, and a correspondingly increased ability of long-established, large-volume brands to maintain their market positions through time, even in the face of strong product competition from less favored competitors.

A final important basis of product differentiation in the automobile industry is found in the nationwide systems of retail distributors and connected service garages which the established sellers control. Each principal manufacturer has such a network of "dealers," generally made up of independent firms which are tied to a single manufacturer and to one or more brands by terms of a franchise requiring that they deal exclusively in the specified brand or brands. By performing the dual functions of personally promoting sales and of providing specialized maintenance and repair service, the dealers in each manufacturer's network significantly differentiate his delivered product from those of his competitors. They do so in each locality according to the popularity, aggressiveness, and reliability of individual dealers, and nationally according to the adequacy of geographical coverage of the country.

The resulting pattern of consumer preferences gives each manufacturer a preferred hold on some group of buyers at any time, and to a considerable extent over long periods of time. It is also such as to give the Big Three a much-advantaged position compared to other sellers, and to give General Motors the greatest advantage of all. This is reflected in the market shares usually obtained by the various sellers, and in the difficulties of since defunct independents after 1930 in holding market shares large enough to permit production at an economical and profitable scale. Thus we observe the demise after 1950 as passenger-car producers of Willys, Kaiser-Frazer (a short-lived newcomer after World War II), Packard, and Studebaker, and the shrinkage of sales of Nash and Hudson which led to their merger into American Motors. As we retrace the path of industry development further back in time, we find it strewn with the bones of numerous other independents that failed to survive in the face of product differentiation favoring the few largest firms. The preferred position of the Big Three rests in some part on each of the bases detailed above, but perhaps more largely on reputation, conspicuous consumption motives, and superior strength and size of dealer systems than it does on demonstrable superiority in design or quality of products. Independents have generally encountered difficulties in keeping up with the Big Three in the matter of product design only after their market shares and profits had sunk so low that they had difficulty in financing periodic improvements and design changes.

There is no lack of evidence of the effects of product differentiation in the automobile industry, although significant price differences between competitors is not one of them. Exact identity of competing prices in a given price class is not found, but in general they are closely similar, class by class, for the high-volume models. This is true of the Big Three products, and the main relatively recent exception involves the pricing of the independent Nash, Hudson, Studebaker, Willy, and Kaiser products after World War II. There was observable then some tendency for the independents to announce, for their products of given gross specifications of weight and horsepower, prices which were significantly above those of comparable products of their Big Three competitors, although the final net retail prices at which sales were consummated by dealers probably showed smaller differences. In any event, currently competing products are evidently enough differentiated to give the individual seller a noticeable measure of independent discretion in determining his price, and the failure of greater price differentials to appear is apparently the result of the deliberately adopted market strategies of the principal firm.

The consistent disparity among the market shares of the various sellers is of course a primary evidence of the incidence of product differentiation. Differential positions of advantage are also evident in the relative evaluations of the products of different sellers when they reappear on the market as used cars. In measuring the "depreciation" in value of the various makes over given time intervals after 1950 as the difference between the original quoted retail price and the average resale value at retail one or two years later, we found typically that General Motors products had the lowest depreciation, Ford and Chrysler somewhat larger depreciation, and independent makes the largest depreciation. For the period 1950 to 1952, for example, for standard four-door sedans of the 1950 model sold in the northeastern quarter of the United States, we found that in the low-price class General Motors (Chevrolet) suffered a $70 decline in retail value, whereas Ford, Plymouth (a Chrysler product), and Studebaker suffered declines of $180, $201, and $302 respectively. Or, in the low-medium-price class, the average two-year decline for three General Motors makes (Pontiac, Oldsmobile, and Buick) was $234; for Chrysler's Dodge and de Soto, $387; for Ford's Mercury, $412; and for the average of Nash, Studebaker, and Hudson, $447. Comparable results were generally observed in the other price classes.

On the surface, at least, these figures would appear to suggest; (a) that the "cost-of-owning" a new automobile of a given price class—especially for the owner who traded in his slightly used car for a new one with considerable frequency—increased as we progressed downward from General Motors products through those of successively smaller American firms; (b) that the manufacturers of the less favored makes, in order to have stayed in the market, must have enjoyed the allegiance of substantial groups of buyers who preferred their products enough actually to pay more for them than it was necessary to pay for other products of similar size and specifications. This propensity of buyers may of course have resulted in part from lack of adequate information on the "cost-of-owning" various makes, but evidently was explicable also in terms of systematic preferences for given designs, reputations, and dealer-service outlets.

A final strong evidence of the importance of product differentiation is the leading role played in the market policies of all American automobile manufacturers by progressive and frequent improvements or variations in the design of their products. Periodic revisions of body style and mechanical design—generally each year, with major changes every two or three years and minor ones in between—are the major expression of interfirm rivalry in the industry, with competition in price very little in evidence. Although protective imitation of rivals keeps these successive changes from effecting dramatic long-term differences in the designs of competing products, year-to-year changes by individual sellers are frequently sufficient to cause significant short-term fluctuations in relative market shares. In the race of product competition, finally, small sellers have suffered damaging and sometimes fatal disadvantages, because their relatively small sales revenues and profits have not permitted them to finance product developments and changes at the same rate as have their major rivals.

In sum, strong product differentiation is a leading aspect of the structure of the automobile industry, and has a dominant influence on its market conduct and performance.

The principal product of the *petroleum refining industry* is gasoline, to which we will confine our attention in considering product differentiation in this field. Generally, this differentiation is much less striking than in the automobile industry, but it is still signficant.

The American petroleum industry is broken up into several fairly distinct regional markets, and we may select the Pacific Coast market of five far-Western states as an example. In this market we find seven large or "major" refiners producing about 80 per cent of the gasoline sold, and about twenty or more smaller "independent" refiners (including small subsidiaries of large eastern refiners) supplying the remainder. Although there is perceptible product differentiation among competing "major" brands of gasoline, and somewhat more differentiation between "major" and "independent" brands, it does not seem to be based primarily on physical differences among competing products. The chemical and physical compositions of the gasolines sold under the "major" brands and at least part of the "independent" brands are highly similar. Improvements in any one brand are rapidly matched by corresponding changes in the others, and their functional or performance characteristics are close to identical. This is true within each of the two principal grades of gasoline, "regular" and "premium" (distinguished mainly by octane rating and adaptability to use in very high-compression engines). The main distinction between the products of the majors and some of the lesser independents has frequently been that the independents did not produce the higher grade of gasoline.

As a result, consumer attachments to the products of particular refiners seem to rest mainly first on the persuasive effects of brand advertising claiming superior quality, and second on the distributive and automotive service facilities offered by the various refiners. Advertising alone does not loom as large as it does in some other industries (those producing liquor, cigarettes, and soap, for example), its cost generally not exceeding 2 per cent of the sales revenue of the major refiners. Nevertheless, it is apparently a sufficient force to create at least slight consumer preferences among major brands, and, in the case of a substantial fraction of buyers, somewhat stronger preferences favoring the majors over the independents.

It is through the various refiners' maintenance of chains of exclusive-dealing service stations, however, that effective product differentiation seems to be mainly supported. Each of the major refiners has acquired and supports a network of retail outlets, dealing exclusively in his gasoline and more or less covering the common marketing area. A minor fraction of such service stations are actually owned and directly operated by the refiners (only one of them emphasizes this device strongly). The more typical arrangement is that the refiner exercises considerable control over his numerous retail dealers through various contractual devices, including "agency" agreements and leasing arrangements covering land or physical facilities or both. The refiner typically takes the initiative in getting such service stations established in attractive locations and in an appropriate density relative to the buying population of the locality. And, through the adjustments of margins and rental charges, he subsidizes dealers to the extent necessary to defray the costs of well-located land, attractive plant, and adequate labor force. Thus each major refiner in effect establishes and controls his own retail distributive system. Independent refiners often do the same but on a smaller and generally less lavish scale, frequently confining distribution to a limited geographical area and usually not attempting to support retail operations using such expensive land and physical plants.

The bases of the product-differentiating effects of controlled systems of service stations are evidently several. They are vehicles for the prominent display of refiners' brand names on the streets and highways, and thus indirectly a means of advertising. They provide varying degrees of convenience in location or accessibility of products to various buyers. And they are used to offer numerous free or nominally priced automotive services to the buyer in connection with his purchases of gasoline, with some differentiation in the quality of service among different individual outlets or chains thereof. Thus different refiners' products are effectively differentiated according to the relative density of outlets, the relative convenience of service-station locations, and the relative quality of supplementary services offered. On such bases, each of the major refiners succeeds in attracting the allegiance of some substantial fraction of the buyers in the market. The independent refiners also have their smaller followings, but in general there is a dominant preference for major products (prices being equal), based in part on the smaller density and less attractive locations of independent outlets and on the less elaborate service ordinarily offered.

Thus product differentiation has some significance in the petroleum refining industry. But it is not as important as it might be. The main evidences of its effects, aside from the incursion of direct and indirect promotional costs, are the persistent and fairly stable disparity in the market shares of the various majors and of those of the major and independent groups of refiners, and the ability of the major refiners as a group to obtain slightly higher prices for their products than can the independents as a group. But the sensitivity of market shares to price differences suggests that competing products are rather close substitutes to many buyers, and that advertising and product competition has by no means relegated price to a secondary position in market adjustments.

One evidence of this is the fact that differences among the quoted gasoline prices of the different major refiners generally do not persist. Identity of major refiners' prices is more or less continually maintained, aided by the device of all competing majors following the price changes of the major "price leader" promptly and exactly. A general opinion in the industry is that product differentiation is not strong enough to permit any major producer persistently to secure a perceptibly higher price than his major rivals. Such price differences as do emerge are the generally transistory and results of localized price cutting at the retail level. Second, although the majors have been generally able to maintain their market shares while securing a small price differential above independent competitors, these shares have proved in the past to be quite sensitive to the size of this major-independent differential. If the differential is eliminated, independents begin to lose most of their usual market shares to the majors; if it is widened much beyond established limits, the independents gain buyers significantly at the expense of the majors. These and other evidences strongly suggest that, all in all, product differentiation is at most of moderate importance in the petroleum refining industry, and does not dominate market behavior to the extent that it does in some other industries.

The steel industry evidences product differentiation which is rather slight. With high-moderate seller concentration (as indicated in Chapter 5), the industry supplies as its end products a variety of "finished" steel products such as sheets, strips, plates, pipe, and wire. Each type of product is generally produced to well-established specifications or standards, and there is substantially no physical differentiation among competing products. Such product differentiation as does emerge is based on personal sales representation by the various sellers, on promptness in filling orders and making deliveries, and on the provision of various technical services to steel buyers and users. But this differentiation is generally not such as to give any seller the ability to charge a higher price than those of his competitors, and buyers generally are ready to change sellers to secure perceptible price concessions. It probably is true that the slight product differentiation in evidence helps stabilize the disparate market shares of various sellers in the short term, but over longer periods relative market shares have shifted significantly, and the shares of larger sellers do not seem to have been much protected by the product preferences of steel buyers.

The flour industry—or specifically that principal market for the industry output in which wheat flour is sold to commercial bakery concerns and other industrial users—may be characterized as having negligible product differentiation. Wheat flour is a standardized product (in each of several grades and types), and commercial-industrial buyers evidently "buy to price," without giving much attention to the identity of the selling firm, so long as it is known to meet the requisite product specifications. Industry sources say that the loyalty of industrial users to particular suppliers is generally not worth 5 cents per hundred pounds in price differential. Competition among flour-milling concerns in this market is apparently thus little influenced by considerations of product differentiation, and centers on price. (A much different situation is evident in the consumer market for flour, where branding and advertising have a very substantial importance.)

Product Differentiation and Seller Concentration

These examples give a somewhat more detailed notion of the character of product differentiation in individual markets, and of its varying importance from industry to industry. Let us return from them to the preceding classification of a sample of manufacturing industries in terms of the importance of product differentiation.

Considering it in conjunction with the earlier classification of industries according to seller concentration (in Chapter 5), we find implied an industry classification successively in terms of two leading characteristics of market structure: concentration and product differentiation. Combining the two principles of classification, numerous possible categories and subcategories of industry appear: industries of high seller concentration with (*a*) important, and (*b*) unimportant product differentiation; industries of moderate seller concentration with (*a*) important, and (*b*) unimportant product differentiation; and so on. In each subcategory of industries eventually established, the particular combination of degree of seller concentration and of product differentiation might be expected to have some unique influence on the character of market conduct and performance of sellers.

This matter will be considered at a later point. For the present, a further question may be raised as to whether, in the markets observed or in markets generally, there is some significant interrelationship between the degree of seller concentration and the degree of product differentiation. For example, is higher seller concentration generally associated with important product differentiation and low seller concentration with unimportant product differentiation; or, conversely, does important product differentiation predispose toward high seller concentration?

On this issue the indications from our sample of manufacturing industries are not necessarily conclusive. The sample is heavily weighted with industries of high or moderate seller concentration, and does not give us much chance to observe the varying importance of product differentiation in industries of relatively low seller concentration. Drawing upon casual observation of numerous cases not included in the sample, however, the following generalizations may be offered.

First, high or very high seller concentration can easily develop in various industries, other conditions being favorable to such a development, even though product differentiation is negligible and has no significant impact on the formation of market structure. This is because the emergence of high concentration can be encouraged by a number of circumstances in addition to the development of strong product differentiation—by the existence of great economies of large-scale production for the firm, or by exclusion of all but a few firms through strategic control of essential patents or of natural resource deposits necessary for production. Thus we will find at least some highly concentrated industries with little product differentiation (the copper, rayon, and gypsum products industries, for example) along with highly concentrated industries with strong product differentiation (autos, cigarettes, and typewriters).

Second, great product differentiation in a market does usually seem to lead to or be associated with high seller concentration. This tendency, apparent in samples studied, evidently results from the fact that very strong product differentiation in practice typically assumes a pattern in which a very few sellers come to be strongly favored over all others in the preference patterns of consumers, and are thus enabled to secure and retain major shares of the market. Conversely, it appears that industries of moderate or low seller concentration typically evidence only moderate or slight degrees of product differentiation. When product differentiation is less intense, it appears that a larger number of sellers have a chance to gain significant shares of the market.

In summary, there is no simple direct correlation between the degree of product differentiation and the degree of seller concentration in an industry, but great product differentiation is evidently one of several forces predisposing toward high seller concentration.

Product Differentiation and the Condition of Entry

To this point we have emphasized the degree of differentiation of the products of the various sellers already established in an industry, thus emphasizing the usual meaning assigned to "product differentiation." Such differentiation evidently has significant effects on the character and intensity of competition among established sellers, and on their market performance.

There is a second and different type of product differentiation, however, that may also affect conduct and performance in various markets—namely, the differentiation between the products of established sellers and those of potential new entrant sellers. In effect, we must look also to the character and distribution of buyer preferences between established products and company names on the one hand, and newly introduced products and sellers on the other. The existence of this sort of product differentiation clearly influences the degree of advantage that established sellers may have over new entrants, the force or importance of "potential competition" as a regulator of the behavior of established firms, or, in brief, the height of barriers to new entry to an industry. This aspect of product differentiation is considered, along with other barriers to the entry of new sellers, in the following chapter.

SUPPLEMENTARY READINGS

Chamberlin, E. H., *The Theory of Monopolistic Competition*, 1933, Ch. III–VI.
Bain, J. S., *Barriers to New Competition*, 1956, Ch. 4 and Appendix D.

8

Market Structures: Condition of Entry to Individual Industries

A structural determinant of market conduct and performance that is at least as important as any other is the condition of entry to individual industries. It measures the height of the barriers to the entry of new competitors to an industry—of the disadvantages that new sellers face if they try to compete in the industry.

Therefore, the influence of the condition of entry on market conduct and performance is somewhat different from that of the two dimensions of market structures already discussed. Both seller concentration and product differentiation among established sellers in an industry presumably influence the market relationships among these sellers. They determine whether there is oligopolistic interdependence among them or atomistic independence, and the degree of substitutability of their rival products. The condition of entry to an industry, on the other hand, determines the competitive relationships *between established sellers and potential entrant sellers*, and thus in a sense the force of potential or latent competition by new entrants. The character of the condition of entry—or height of barriers to entry—to an industry may strongly influence both the conduct and performance of established sellers and the stability of the seller concentration and product differentiation within the industry.

In this chapter, we consider in turn:

1. Theory concerning the character and consequences of the condition of entry to individual industries.

2. Evidence concerning the actual condition of entry to a variety of American industries.

Discussion of the actual relationship of the condition of entry to market performance is deferred to Chapter 11.

Theory Concerning the Condition of Entry

Economic theory concerning the condition of entry is fairly complex, and here we will present only a condensed and simplified version of it.[1] On the following pages, we discuss:

(*a*) The definition and measurement of the condition of entry.

(*b*) The determinants of the condition of entry (in other words, the sources of barriers to entry).

(*c*) The predicted influence of the condition of entry on market conduct and performance in individual industries.

Definition and Measurement of the Condition of Entry

A definition of the condition of entry rests on an initial distinction between (1) firms already established in an industry and supplying output to its market (hereafter *established firms*), and (2) firms not already established in the industry that which might enter by building new plant capacity[2] and using it as sellers in the industry (hereafter *potential entrant firms*). In loose terms, the condition of entry is then defined as the "disadvantage" of potential entrant firms as compared to established firms—or, conversely, the "advantage" of established over potential entrant firms.

Somewhat more precisely, the condition of entry refers to the extent to which, in the long run, established firms can elevate their selling prices above the minimal average costs of production and distribution (those costs associated with operation at optimal scales) without inducing potential entrants to enter the industry. If the established sellers in an industry have some advantage over potential entrants, they will be

[1]For a fuller exposition see Joe S. Bain, "Conditions of Entry and the Emergence of Monopoly," *Monopoly and Competition and Their Regulation* (E. H. Chamberlin, Ed.), 1954; and Bain, *Barriers to New Competition*, 1956, Ch. 1.

[2]New entry as defined is not accomplished if a firm previously not in an industry simply acquires the plant of an already established firm and operates it; that is, the mere change of ownership of existing plant capacity does not constitute new entry as that term is understood here. If an outside firm does acquire existing plant in an industry, therefore, it "enters" the industry only to the extent that it then adds to the plant capacity it has acquired.

able persistently to set selling prices at least somewhat above the level of minimal average costs (and supply smaller than competitive outputs) without making it attractive for other firms to enter. This is because potential entrants, with their disadvantages, could not make satisfactory profits either at such prices (if the prices are not expected to change because of entry), or at lower prices expected to prevail after their new outputs were added to market supply.

The highest selling price that established sellers in an industry can persistently charge without attracting new entry may be referred to as "the maximum entry-forestalling price." Then *the condition of entry is measured numerically as the percentage by which the maximum entry-forestalling price exceeds the minimum attainable average costs of established firms.*

Entry to an industry will not occur if selling prices do not exceed the maximum entry-forestalling level. Conversely, if established sellers set prices higher than this level, or at an "entry-inducing" level, potential entrants will be induced to enter the industry in spite of their disadvantages and will anticipate satisfactory profits after so doing. Somewhere in the progression of successively higher possible selling prices in any industry we will encounter the largest possible entry-forestalling price, followed immediately by the smallest possible entry-inducing price. For example, with minimal costs for product A at $1.00 per unit, any price charged up to $1.10 may be sufficiently low to forestall the entry of added sellers, so that $1.10 is the maximum entry-forestalling price. But prices above $1.10 per unit will induce entry, so that $1.11 is the minimum entry-inducing price. Then the numerical measure of condition of entry is 10 per cent.

A further word should be said about the meaning in this definition of the minimal average cost relative to which the maximum entry-forestalling price is measured. For production and distribution costs this refers to the lowest attainable average costs—those which the firm would have if operating at the optimal or most efficient scale of production and without any chronic excess capacity. (It would tend to do this in the long run under conditions of theoretical atomistic competition.) So far as sales-promotion costs are incurred, it is difficult to set a similarly definite competitive standard, since even a competitive firm may spend more or less on promotion and correspondingly be able to charge higher or lower selling prices. This difficulty in definition may be dealt with by defining the condition of entry in terms of the percentage excess of (*a*) the maximum entry-forestalling selling price per unit of output *minus* the average promotional costs per unit accompanying it, over (*b*) minimum attainable average costs of production and distribution.

Greater precision can and should be introduced into the preceding rather rough definition of the condition of entry—and the need for it is occasioned by the facts that:

(*a*) Different established firms in an industry frequently have differing degrees of advantage over potential entrants—reflected in some established firms having advantages over others—so that different firms already in an industry will effectively have different maximum entry-forestalling prices (or the same entry-forestalling price but different minimal average costs). Therefore, we should distinguish the "most advantaged" established firms in an industry—those with the highest ratio of maximum entry-forestalling prices to minimal average costs—from other established firms.

(*b*) Different potential entrant firms often have differing degrees of disadvantage as compared to the most advantaged established firms in an industry that they might enter. Consequently, we should distinguish the "least disadvantaged" potential entrants from other potential entrants, and if possible rank potential entrants according to the degrees of their disadvantage (from least through successively greater disadvantage).[3]

Given these circumstances, the "immediate" condition of entry to an industry should be defined in terms of the advantage of the most advantaged established firm or firms over the least disadvantaged potential entrant or entrants. It should be measured by the percentage excess over its minimal average costs of the highest selling price that the most advantaged established firm (or firms) can charge without inducing the least disadvantaged potential entrant (or entrants) to enter the industry. (As we will see later, the immediate condition of entry at any time will potentially exercise the strategic proximate influence on the pricing policies of established firms.)

The "general" condition of entry to an industry should correspondingly be measured as the series of values of the immediate condition of entry which would emerge if, successively, individual potential entrants entered the industry one by one in the order of increasing disadvantage (beginning with the least disadvantaged one, followed by the next least disadvantaged one, and so forth.) The general condition of entry to an

---

[3]Potential entrant firms may have initially differing degrees of disadvantage which would remain unchanged after the least disadvantaged potential entrant had actually entered the industry. But also, where scale economies are a deterrent to entry (as discussed below), the disadvantages of remaining potential entrants, though not initially different from any others, would increase after one or more potential entrants had actually entered the industry. That is, entry to an industry by additional firms may become more difficult if economies of the large-scale firm are important.

industry will be measured by a series of constant or unchanging values only if all potential entrants are equally disadvantaged initially, and if also economies of the large-scale firm are unimportant. In the following abbreviated theoretical discussion, we will unless otherwise noted be referring either to immediate conditions of entry, or to general conditions wherein all potential entrants are equally disadvantaged.

The condition of entry, thus measuring the ability of established sellers to secure supercompetitive prices without attracting new competitors, is evidently an important characteristic of the structure of any industry. Although in practice it is frequently difficult to measure precisely from available data, it can be meaningfully estimated and comparisons of conditions of entry to different industries can be made. Let us next consider the typical determinants of the condition of entry.

Sources of Barriers to Entry

The existence of a condition of entry to an industry that permits established firms to elevate price at least somewhat above minimal average costs without inducing new firms to enter obviously reflects the existence of some barrier to entry—some source of disadvantage to potential entrants as compared with established firms. In general, these barriers to entry are of three types:

1. *Product differentiation advantages of established over potential entrant firms.*

2. *Absolute cost advantages of established over potential entrant firms.*

3. *Advantages of established over potential entrant firms due to economies of large scale firms.*

Although two or more of these types of barrier to entry may combine to determine the condition of entry in a single industry, we will begin by discussing them separately, and also initially consider each one on the assumption that the other two are not present in the case at hand.

The established firms in an industry may enjoy a product-differentiation advantage over potential entrants because of the preference of buyers for the products of established firms over new ones. If so, any potential entrant may be unable to secure a selling price as high (relative to average costs) as established firms can when selling their products in competition with the entrant.

The resulting disadvantage to the entrant can be reflected in three alternative ways. First, it may be that established firms can charge prices above minimal average costs and the competing entrant would be able to charge only a lower price that does not cover his average costs. Second, it is possible that to secure a comparably favorable price, the entrant would have to incur sales-promotion costs per unit of output greater than those of established firms, again having average costs greater than his price. Finally, even if neither of these disadvantages is incurred so long as the entrant supplies a limited fraction of the market, he might be unable, at comparable prices and selling costs, to secure a sufficiently large market share to enable him to support an economically large production and distribution organization. Excluded from realizing available economies of large scale production and distribution, he might again find his average costs above his selling price, even though established firms were receiving prices in excess of minimal average costs.

In any of these circumstances, established firms have the power to elevate their prices by some amount above their minimal average costs without making it attractive for new firms to enter the industry. It is true of course that if a potential entrant did enter in the face of such disadvantages, these might tend to diminish and perhaps eventually vanish after a period of years during which his product gained acceptance and respect among buyers. Therefore, the duration of his product-differentiation disadvantage, as well as its initial and subsequent sizes, is to be reckoned in computing the net barrier to entry. The net deterrent effect on his entry might be calculated by averaging his declining disadvantages over all the years of his prospective operation (with appropriate discounting of more remote years), to arrive at that maximum excess of the prices of established firms over their minimal costs that would suffice to forestall his entry.

For example, an entrant firm might anticipate that for the average of the first ten years after his entry his selling prices would have to be 10 per cent below those of his rivals. But after ten years (and up to thirty years, which we will suppose is as far as he looks ahead) he would expect no disadvantage. This situation would probably not permit established firms to elevate prices above average costs by as much as 10 per cent without inducing entry. But they might well be able to make the early losses of entry unattractive, and deter entry, by setting their prices persistently only 4 to 5 per cent above average costs.

The preceding may be clarified by analyzing in a simple theoretical model the operation of a "pure" product-differentiation advantage of established firms in determining a maximum entry excluding price. (The advantage is "pure" in the sense that no economies of the large-scale firm are present and that established firms have no absolute-cost advantages over potential entrant firms, and also have no absolute-cost

differences among themselves.) In this case, the long-run average cost
or scale curves of all established firms and all potential entrants—showing the long-run relation of average costs of production and distribution
to rates of output—are identical and also are horizontal (showing no
change in average cost with variation in scale of firm). The scale curves
of both the most advantaged established firm and the least disadvantaged potential entrant[4] are thus shown by the single line *ac* in Figure 6.
Sales promotion costs are assumed to be absent.

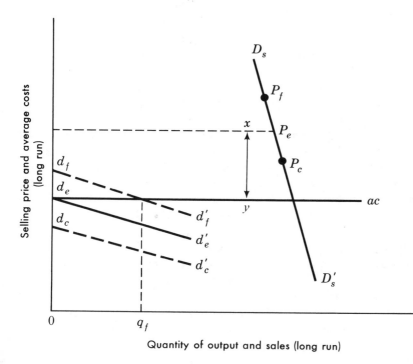

Figure 6

Let us now suppose that the demand curve for the output of the most
advantaged established firm, showing the long-run relationship of his
sales volume to the price he charges, is $D_s D_s'$ in Figure 6—this relationship being drawn on the assumption that all other established firms
always match his price changes so as at all times either to charge the
same price as his or to charge prices having the same ratios to or differentials from his. (All established firms, let us say, change prices concertedly and concurrently to maintain the same interfirm price relation-

---

[4]And, by assumption, of all established firms and all entrants.

ships.) The question posed is how high a price the most advantaged firm can charge persistently without inducing the most advantaged potential entrant to enter the industry.

With no scale economies present, entry can be forestalled only if the established firm's price is such that there is no output (however small) that the potential entrant can sell at a price exceeding his average cost, ac. If the established firm has a pure product-differentiation advantage, he can set some price above his minimal average cost (also ac) and leave the potential entrant in a position where there is no output he can sell profitably. Let us suppose that the product-differentiation advantage is such that the maximum entry forestalling price is P_e in Figure 6. Then when this price is charged by the established firm, the demand curve for the potential entrant's output (drawn on the assumption of no re-action of established firms' prices to his entry)[5] will lie at $d_e d_e'$, showing that even at the smallest possible output the entrant could not gain a price above average cost.

The established seller's price P_e, however, is the highest price that will forestall all entry. If he charged a higher price P_f, the demand curve for the potential entrant's output would lie at $d_f d_f'$. He would then be attracted to enter and could make a profit by selling any output between zero and $0q_f$. (His profit-maximizing output would lie between zero and $0q_f$, and his corresponding price above ac.)[6] And if the established seller instead charged a lower price P_c, the demand curve for the potential entrant's output would lie at $d_c d_c'$, whence he would not enter—but the price P_c would be lower than necessary to keep him from entering. The height of the immediate (and possibly general) product differentiation barrier to entry in Figure 6 is thus measured by the excess of P_e over ac (of the maximum entry forestalling price over minimal average cost), or the distance xy. (If there were no product-differentiation barrier to entry, P_e would lie at the level of ac.)

The model just presented becomes more realistic if we relax the as-sumption that there are no economies of the large-scale firm and sup-pose instead that there are some such scale economies, although the out-put of a firm of minimum optimal scale is nevertheless such a small fraction of industry output that entry at that scale would induce no price reactions from established sellers. (Consideration of the effect of important scale economies *per se* on the condition of entry is thus still

[5] A valid assumption since the entrant would add so small a fraction to industry supply in this case that he would engender no price reactions from established firms.

[6] Precisely, he would choose the price and output at which his marginal revenue, derived from $d_f d_f'$ (but not shown on Figure 6), was equal to ac (and thus to his marginal cost).

excluded.) If some such relatively negligible scale economies are present, the barrier to entry resulting from a product differentiation advantage of established firms can be noticeably heightened even though the preference of buyers for their products is no stronger. This is because, if they suffer diseconomies of very small scale, potential entrant firms will require higher prices at small outputs in order to make production profitable. Therefore, established sellers can raise their own prices further and still forestall entry.

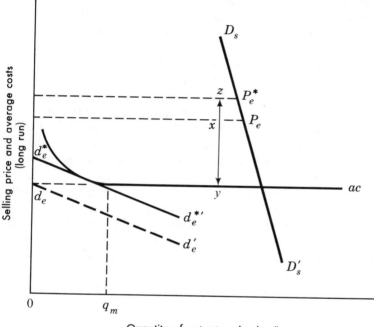

Quantity of output and sales (long run)

Figure 7

The argument is illustrated in Figure 7, which depicts the situation shown in Figure 6 exactly except that the common scale curve, ac, now shows some economies of the large scale firm up to a relatively small long-run output—$0q_m$, the minimum optimal scale. When the most advantaged established firm now charges what the maximum entry excluding price would be in the absence of scale economies—that is, P_e, as in Figure 5—resulting in the potential entrant's demand curve lying at $d_e d_e'$ as previously, it is clear that a still higher price set by the established seller will exclude entry, since $d_e d_e'$ is now not close to the backward-rising ac. In fact, the established seller can now set some higher price such as $P_e{}^*$, which will result in the demand curve for the potentrial entrant's output lying higher at $d_e{}^*d_e{}^{*\prime}$—just enough higher that his selling price barely equals cost at his most profitable output. Only if the established seller's price exceeded $P_e{}^*$ would the potential entrant's demand curve shift upward from $d_e{}^*d_e{}^{*\prime}$ to allow him (in view of diseconomies of very small scale) a profit at some output. Therefore, the maximum entry excluding price is higher because of diseconomies of very small-scale production even though the product preferences favoring established sellers are no greater. The effective barrier to entry— now measured in Figure 7 by the distance yz rather than by xy—is higher. When really important scale economies are encountered, as we will see later, they may interact with product-differentiation advantages of established firms to erect very high barriers to entry.

Further theoretical models and diagrams could be developed to illustrate the operation of higher sales-promotion costs (rather than lower selling prices) for the potential entrant in establishing comparable product differentiation barriers to entry, but the foregoing should suffice.

The possible sources of product-differentiation barriers to entry are fairly clear: (1) the accumulated preferences of buyers (often under the influence of long-sustained advertising) for established brand names and company reputations, either generally or except for small minorities of the buying population; (2) the exclusive control of superior product designs by established firms, through patent protection; (3) the ownership or control of favored systems of distributive outlets by established firms, in circumstances where alternative distributive systems can be established, if at all, only at a cost disadvantageous to the entrant. We will turn later to evidence on the importance of product-differentiation barriers to entry.

The second main type of barrier to entry reflects the "absolute" advantage, for one reason or another, of established firms in the matter of production and distribution costs. Their costs, at any comparable scale of operation, may be at a lower level than those of potential entrants. If this is so, they can obtain prices which are some amount above their own costs while potential entrants, competing with them, could not cover costs and so would not enter the market. (Again, the prospective duration of the entrant's disadvantage affects the calculation of the net resulting barrier to entry.)

The principal potential bases for such advantages to established firms seem to be the following: (1) control of superior production techniques by established firms, maintained either by patents or by secrecy; (2) exclusive ownership by established firms of superior deposits of resources required in production; (3) inability of entrant firms to acquire necessary factors of production (management services, labor equipment, materials) on terms as favorable as those enjoyed by established firms; and (4) less favored access of entrant firms to liquid funds for investment, reflected in higher effective interest costs or in simple unavailability of funds in the required amounts. Any one or more of these circumstances can place the costs of potential entrant firms on a higher level and permit established firms to elevate selling prices somewhat above their own minimal average costs without making operations profitable for entrants and thus without inducing entry.

The case of "pure" absolute cost barriers to entry (unalloyed with economies of the large-scale firm or with product-differentiation advantages of established firms) is illustrated in Figure 8. The long-run average cost or scale curve of the most advantaged established firms is ac_s, and that of the least disadvantaged potential entrant is ac_e—the higher level of ac_e reflecting the absolute cost disadvantage of the potential entrant at any scale or rate of output. Clearly, the established firm may set his selling price as high as (but no higher than) ac_e without inducing entry, since the entrant would find production unprofitable at that price but profitable at higher prices. The maximum entry forestalling price is thus P_e (equal to ac_e), and the height of the barrier to entry is measured by the distance xy.

Absolute cost disadvantages of potential entrants, of course, may not always be unrelated to the scale of operations; they may increase as the scale of the potential entrant increases. This is especially likely, per-

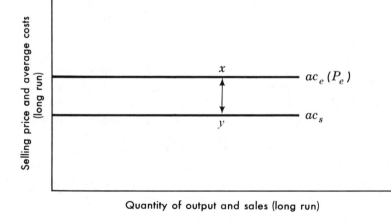

Quantity of output and sales (long run)

Figure 8

haps, if the disadvantage is reflected in the entrant's interest costs of securing funds for investment—a disadvantage which is likely to be greater as larger amounts of funds are sought.

Then the absolute cost disadvantage might be as illustrated in Figure 9, where again ac_s is the scale curve of the established firm and ac_e that of the potential entrant. (The existence of some economies of the large scale firm—not necessarily great enough that the added output of an entrant would induce reactions by established firms—is also depicted in Figure 9.) The potential entrant firm is depicted as having a scale curve which lies progressively farther above that of the established firm at progressively larger scales, because of absolute cost disadvantages that

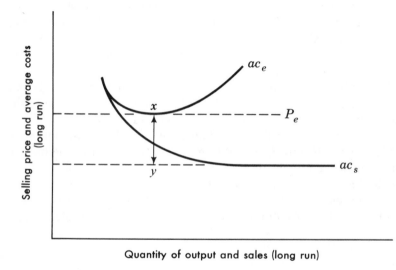

Quantity of output and sales (long run)

Figure 9

increase with its scale (and that result in its experiencing diseconomies of increasing scale beyond a scale corresponding to x on Figure 9). In this case, the maximum entry-excluding price would correspond to the lowest level of average costs that the potential entrant could attain at any scale, and would thus be P_e. The height of the barrier to entry is the difference between P_e and the level of minimal average cost of the established firm, measured by the distance xy on Figure 9. It should be emphasized that P_e is unequivocally the maximum entry-excluding price only on the suppositions (1) that the entrant could secure a market share at least as large as that corresponding to output x and sell at the same price as established firms (he would have no effective product differentiation disadvantage) and (2) that his entry with an output as large as x would induce no reduction in market price by established firms (economies of the large-scale firm would not *per se* provide a deterrent to entry).

The third sort of barrier to entry may result from the fact that economies of the large-scale firm in the industry are such (*a*) that an entrant of minimum optimal scale (smallest scale at which lowest unit costs are attained) would supply a significant fraction of industry output, and (*b*) that at appreciably smaller scales, the entrant would have appreciably higher than the lowest attainable unit costs (would suffer significant diseconomies of small scale).

In the "pure" case of a barrier to entry due to scale economies (with no absolute-cost or product-differentiation barriers, and established and potential entrant firms supplying a homogeneous output), this situation would be reflected in the fact that the scale curve of every established and potential entrant firm was as illustrated by ac in Figure 10. Any firm's output corresponding to minimum optimal scale (Q_{min}) would be a significant fraction of that total industry output (Q_I) which would be demanded at a price ($P = ac$) equal to minimal average cost (Q_I being codetermined by the demand curve for industry output, D_ID_I'). At progressively smaller scales than Q_{min}, any firm's average

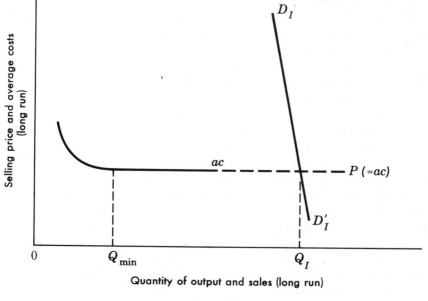

Quantity of output and sales (long run)

Figure 10

costs would increase progressively and by significant amounts. In Figure 10, Q_{min} is depicted as one-fourth of Q_I, so that four firms of minimum optimal scale could supply all industry output. But for scale economies to impede entry, it could be a larger fraction of Q_I, or a somewhat smaller one (so that the industry could accommodate fewer or more firms of minimum optimal scale), as long as Q_{min} was a large enough fraction of Q_I that its addition to total industry output would significantly reduce the market price of that output.

Now if economies of the large-scale firm are significant in the sense just described, established firms are likely to be able to set their selling price at least somewhat above the level of minimal average costs (P in Figure 10) without attracting entry, because one of the following situations is likely to be faced by any potential entrant firm:

1. It could enter at minimum optimal scale (or larger), secure a corresponding share of the market for industry output, and thus add enough to total industry output that selling price for that output would decline significantly. This price decline would occur, that is, unless established firms reduced their combined outputs by an amount about equal to the entrant's addition to output. In this case, however, it is probable that the potential entrant firm would not expect established firms to react to its entry by reducing their outputs sufficiently to leave industry output unchanged. If they did not, its entry would cause the selling price for the enlarged industry output to fall. The post-entry selling price would therefore be lower than the pre-entry price.

Assume that the potential entrant firm conjectures that this price decline would occur because of its entry. Then established firms should be able to set a maximum entry-forestalling selling price that exceeded minimal average costs by the amount that the potential entrant firm expected this price to fall as a result of its entry. (If such a price were set, the potential entrant would expect that the price which would prevail after his entry would yield him no profit.)

2. It could enter at any of a number of scales somewhat smaller than the minimum optimal one but still large enough to add appreciably to industry output, secure corresponding shares of the market, and again conjecture that established firms would not reduce their pre-entry outputs by enough to keep the price for industry output from falling. The anticipated post-entry price would be below the pre-entry price, but probably below it by progressively less as the scale of entrant was progressively smaller. In addition, the potential entrant would incur average costs of production which were above minimal average costs—by increasing amounts as its scale was made smaller—because of dis-

economies of small-scale production. In this case, established firms should be able to set a maximum entry-forestalling price that exceeded minimal average costs by an amount equal to (*a*) the expected reduction in this price resulting from entry, plus (*b*) the excess of the potential entrant's average costs over minimal average costs.

3. It could enter at some scale smaller than the minimum optimal one—either large enough to add appreciably to industry output or small enough not to do so—secure a corresponding market share, but conjecture that established firms would not reduce the pre-entry price perceptibly as a result of entry. It would expect, that is, that they would reduce their combined outputs by as much as the entrant's addition to output. (The likelihood of this conjecture by the entrant firm should increase as its proportionate market share was smaller.) Though not expecting industry price to fall as a result of his entry, the potential entrant would incur average costs of production above the level of minimal average costs. Established firms should therefore be able to set a maximum entry-forestalling price that exceeded minimal average costs by the same amount that the potential entrant's average costs would exceed them.

The first two situations are represented diagrammatically together in Figure 11. There *ac* is the scale curve of the potential entrant, already familiar to the reader. The curve *pp′*—not familiar—represents (by its varying distances from the horizontal axis) the excesses of the pre-entry over the post-entry prices that the potential entrant firm expects to be associated with its entry at various scales—or, in other words, the varying amounts by which the price for industry output are expected to fall as a result of its entry at varying scales. If we now add these expected differences between pre-entry and post-entry prices to the average costs of the entrant at each possible scale, we obtain the maximum entry-forestalling price at every scale of entry. This is done diagrammatically by adding vertically to the values on *ac* the values on *pp′*, to obtain the curve $P_eP_e{}'$, which shows the relationship of the maximum entry-forestalling price to the scale of the potential entrant. Assuming that the entrant firm is free to vary its scale, moreover, $P_eP_e{}'$ shows by the lowest price on it, $P_e{}^*$, the maximum entry forestalling price resulting from scale economies. No higher price could be entry-forestalling, because at any higher price the potential entrant firm could enter at the scale Q_e and expect a post-entry price in excess of its average costs. The height of the barrier to entry is *xy*.

In the general situation represented in Figure 11, the key to the determination of the maximum entry-forestalling price is found first in the

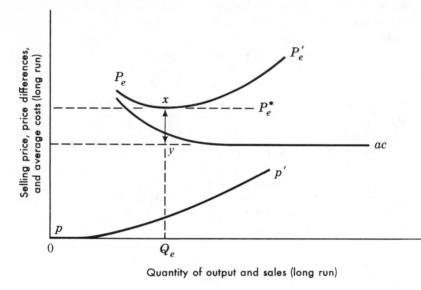

Quantity of output and sales (long run)

Figure 11

potential entrant firm's general conjecture that after its entry established firms would not restrict their outputs by enough to maintain the
pre-entry market price for industry output. It is found further in the
entrant's specific conjectures concerning how much industry output
would in the net increase, and the market price for it correspondingly
fall, as a result of its entry at various scales. The general conjecture is
comparatively pessimistic, and more so the less that the entrant firm
expects established firms to reduce their outputs as a result of its adding
a given amount to industry output.

But this is not the only conjecture the entrant firm may have. In the
third situation just discussed, we indicated the possibility that it may
entertain the more optimistic conjecture that established firms would
maintain the going industry price unchanged in the event of its entry,
essentially by reducing their collective output by an amount equal to
the entrant's output and market share.

This third situation is represented in Figure 12. There ac is again the
scale curve of the potential entrant firm. $D_{e1}D_{e1}'$ shows a possible demand curve for the potential entrant firm's output. It is drawn on the assumption (appropriate to a pure oligopoly) that the entrant and all
established firms would always charge identical prices, and on the further assumption that the entrant's expected market share is insufficient
to let it operate profitably at minimum optimal scale. $D_{e2}D_{e2}'$ shows the

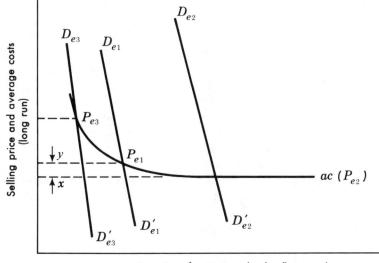

Figure 12

potential entrant firm's demand curve on the alternative assumption that its expected market share is great enough to allow profitable operations at a minimum optimal or larger scale. (If the industry output is undifferentiated, the alternative DD' curves show the market shares of all firms after one more firm enters.)

Suppose that the expected market share of the potential entrant firm is as shown by $D_{e1}D_{e1}'$. Then, if the entrant firm expects pre-entry market price to be maintained after its entry (and if it cannot undercut it without drawing matching price cuts from the other firms), the established firms can set a maximum entry-forestalling price of P_{e1}, which is above minimal average costs. If the potential entrant firm expects a post-entry price of P_{e1} or lower, it cannot operate profitably with the market share shown by $D_{e1}D_{e1}'$, and will not enter. The height of the scale-economies barrier to entry is then measured by the distance xy.

Suppose alternatively that the entrant firm's expected market share is shown by $D_{e2}D_{e2}'$. Then it can operate profitably at or somewhat beyond minimum optimal scale and produce at minimal costs. The established firms therefore cannot elevate market price perceptibly above P_{e2} (equal to minimal average cost), and there is no scale-economies barrier to entry. (But there would be if the potential entrant expected a post-entry price lower than the pre-entry one, as supposed in Figure

11.) In industries where no product-differentiation or absolute-cost barriers to entry are also present, and where potential entrants optimistically expect pre-entry market price to be maintained, scale economies tend to impose a barrier to entry only after the industry has enough firms in it that the addition of one more firm would leave all firms with market shares too small for profitable operation at optimal scales.

The preceding analysis makes it plain that the height of the barrier to entry to an industry (if any) that results from significant scale economies alone is a function of the conjectures of potential entrants concerning the reactions of established firms to their entry. The barrier may be higher or lower as these conjectures are more pessimistic or more optimistic. Since we are in no position to predict just what the conjectures of potential entrants will be, there is logically considerable uncertainty about how high a barrier to entry will result from the presence of scale economies of a given magnitude, though very important scale economies should probably provide some deterrent to entry.

It should also be noted that there may be some difference between (1) the "actual" barrier to entry due to scale economies, which depends on the actual conjectures of potential entrants concerning the reactions to entry of established firms, and (2) what established firms think that the barrier to entry is (how high they think the maximum entry-forestalling price is), this depending on their conjectures concerning the conjectures of potential entrants about their reactions to entry. This oligopolistic interdependence of crossed conjectures adds further uncertainty to the effects of significant scale economies on the price policies of established firms, as we will see later.

We have now considered product-differentiation, absolute-cost, and scale-economies barriers to entry. In any particular industry, one or more of the three types of barrier to entry may exist (sometimes in complex combination), and as a result some total or aggregate barrier to entry will determine the condition of entry, or the degree to which established firms can elevate their selling prices above minimal average cost while still forestalling entry. We will not go further with theory that analyzes the interaction of two or more entry barriers in the same industry except to note that the combination of important product-differentiation disadvantages of potential entrant firms with significant economies of large scale production may result in exceptionally high barriers to entry.

Suppose that, because of product-differentiation disadvantages, the least disadvantaged potential entrant firm can secure only a rather small share of the market, though it can secure it (and because of oligopolistic interdependence perhaps must secure it) at the same selling price as established firms. (This is unlike the case of "pure" product differentiation disadvantage illustrated in Figures 6 and 7, where the entrant has a price disadvantage as well.) And suppose further that economies of large scale (conversely diseconomies of small scale) are such that with the market share the entrant firm can secure, it will have average costs far above the minimal level. Then established firms may be able to set maximum entry-forestalling prices that are very high relative to minimal average costs. This possibility is illustrated in Figure 12 by the relationship of $D_{e3}D_{e3}'$—showing the putative minor market share of a potential entrant with product differentiation disadvantages— to his scale curve, ac. Even if the potential entrant entertains the optimistic conjecture that the pre-entry market price will not react to his entry, established firms could forestall entry while charging the high price P_{e3}. The aggregate barrier to entry is far higher than the mere sum of component barriers individually attributable to product differentiation and to scale economies.

There will presumably be a wide range of different conditions of entry among different industries, varying from those in which barriers are so high that entry is effectively blockaded almost regardless of the price policies followed by established firms, to those in which there are practically no barriers to entry at all.

The extreme at this latter end of the range is completely "easy" entry, with no barriers and with new entry being attracted if established firms persistently raise their selling prices at all above their minimal average costs. With such "easy" entry, it will of course be true that established firms enjoy no product-differentiation advantage over potential entrants, and no absolute-cost advantage, and that economies of scale are sufficiently unimportant that an optimal-scale firm will supply an insignificant percentage of total market output. As we depart from these polar easy-entry conditions in one or more of the three dimensions, the condition of entry becomes progressively more difficult.

Influence of the Condition of Entry
on Market Conduct and Performance

What effects should the condition of entry to an industry have on the market conduct and performance of its member firms? The theory predicting these effects is unusually complex, and the variety of predictable influences correspondingly great. Here we will attempt only to present a rough outline of the more significant predictions of this theory, beginning with some elementary propositions.

First, the immediate condition of entry to an industry clearly determines how far above minimal average costs established firms could raise their selling prices without inducing the entry of one or more added competitors. This follows from the definition of the immediate condition of entry as the excess of the maximum entry-forestalling price (that which would forestall the entry of the least disadvantaged potential entrant or entrants) over minimal average costs. If the immediate barrier to entry is very low or nonexistent, established firms could persistently set selling price only slightly or not at all above minimal average costs (above a competitive level) without attracting new competition. If the immediate barrier is high enough, they could establish a fully monopolistic selling price, that would maximize total profits for the industry and very substantially exceed minimal costs, without inducing new competitors to enter the industry. And if the immediate barrier is substantial but not as high as the industry profit-maximizing price, they could set a selling price below the fully monopolistic but well above the competitive level without attracting new competition.

Second, the general condition of entry to an industry—represented by the succession of immediate barriers to entry that would be (or are) encountered as successive potential entrants were (or are) attracted to enter the industry—effectively establishes an upper limit on the amount by which industry selling price can in the long run exceed minimal average costs, whatever pricing policies established firms may pursue. This is seen most simply where there is a "constant" general condition of entry to an industry, such that the immediate barrier to entry remains unchanged at a given level regardless of how many added firms enter the industry. (That is, the excess of the maximum entry forestalling price over minimal average costs is the same for all potential entrants and would be unchanging as a series of them successively entered the industry.) Then any endeavors of established firms (their numbers growing if new entry is indeed attracted) to establish a selling price higher than the constant maximum entry forestalling price will attract new competitors and competition sufficiently that these endeavors will fail. In the long run, industry price will be no higher than the constant maximum entry-forestalling price. This long-run ceiling price, of course, might be equal to minimal average costs or might exceed it by various amounts.

Suppose, however, that the general condition of entry to an industry is not constant but "progressive"—is represented by a succession of immediate barriers to entry that are successively higher as added firms successively enter the industry. Then the long-run upper limit on industry selling price corresponds to the immediate barrier that would prevail when, with any conceivable pricing policies by established firms, no additional firm could profitably enter the industry. That is, potential entrants facing successively higher immediate barriers to entry might conceivably be attracted successively to enter the industry by entry-inducing prices set by established firms, until the established firms were only "breaking even" at the most profitable price and would incur losses if they raised price further. Then entry would necessarily cease, since any added firm would find operation unprofitable. The ultimate ceiling on price would correspond to the price then prevailing and would forestall further entry.

Third, the hypothetical long-run ceiling price that the general condition of entry to an industry imposes will be no means necessarily be attained, though it cannot in the long run be exceeded. This is because either (a) competition among established sellers keeps price from reaching this ceiling, or (b) established firms elect to establish entry-forestalling prices at a stage when higher prices would allow both them and an added entrant or entrants to make profits. To elaborate on point (b), established firms may set "limit prices" to forestall further entry well before the industry becomes so crowded with firms that none can make an appreciable profit.

Fourth—and this is a corollary of the third proposition—the firms populating an industry at a given juncture may under varying circumstances persistently set (or be able to obtain) a selling price which is alternatively below, equal to, or above the maximum entry-forestalling price corresponding to the immediate condition of entry. If they set or are only able to secure a price below or equal to the maximum entry-forestalling price, the structure of the industry should be stabilized to the extent that the number of competing firms in it will not increase. But if they persistently set or are able to secure a price above the immediate maximum entry-forestalling price, and thus attract entry, the structure of the industry will be unstable. Seller concentration will be reduced, the intensity of competition may increase, and a stable market structure will not be reached until further entry is not being attracted.

Fifth, the effects of both the general and any immediate condition of entry to an industry on the price policies and other market conduct of established firms in the industry will tend to differ distinctly between industries which are alternatively:

(a) Atomistic, or with seller concentration sufficiently low that no individual firm can appreciably influence the market price for industry output and that collective action by competing firms to control this market price is impossible, and

(b) Significantly oligopolistic, or with seller concentration sufficiently high that at least some firms in the industry are large enough to influence industry price (in particular, put upper limits on it by setting a price that competitors cannot profitably exceed) and that collective action by rival firms to determine a common market selling price is feasible.

In atomistic industries, each individual seller (and thus all sellers) will tend to take no account of the possible influence of his price or output adjustments on entry, because he will correctly believe this influence to be negligible. Sellers in such an industry thus pay no attention to the condition of entry, or to the entry-forestalling or entry-inducing effects of their price and output adjustments. Therefore, their independent competitive policies result in the emergence of a market-determined price that either does not attract entry (perhaps induces some exit), or does attract it until price is brought down to the level of the minimal average costs of the most-disadvantaged or marginal entrant. It follows that in atomistic industries the condition of entry is simply one of the market forces that "automatically" determine long-run equilibrium market prices. Theory thus offers no very striking hypotheses concerning the effect of the condition of entry on pricing in atomistic industries.

The situation is much different in the case of significantly oligopolistic industries. In these, as we have seen, the established firms can collectively determine a market price above the level of minimal average costs. In addition, any principal firm can place an upper limit on industry price, because its rivals will not exceed its price for fear of its capturing significant parts of their shares of the market. When this is true, either a group of oligopolistic sellers acting collectively, or any principal seller "calling the tune" for the market, should logically take definite account of the condition of entry in setting the selling price for industry output. Specifically, the price-determining firm or group of firms should ascertain or estimate:

(a) How high a market price for industry output it can establish without attracting entry—that is, the level of the maximum entry-forestalling price.

(b) Whether it (the group of established firms or a principal firm) can make greater long-run profits by (1) charging a limit price that excludes entry, and keeping all industry profit for itself perpetually, or (2) setting a higher price that will attract some entrants into the industry, and sharing total industry profit thereafter with additional firms.

If the price-determining firm or group expects higher long-run profits from a limit-price policy that excludes entry, it will presumably pursue such a policy and set price at the maximum entry-forestalling level. If it does not, it will set a higher price and attract entry. And successively more numerous firms will then do likewise until a point is reached (given the general condition of entry) where it is most profitable to exclude further entry by limit pricing, or until increased intra-industry competition brings price to or below the then prevailing limit level.

Whether or not the established firms in an oligopoly will set selling price so as to exclude entry will obviously depend on the height of the barrier to entry. As the maximum entry-forestalling or limit price is progressively greater than minimal average costs, the greater will be the likelihood that established firms will charge limit prices and exclude entry. The lower the limit price, the greater is the probability that a higher price will be charged and new entry thus attracted. But whether or not a limit price is set will obviously also depend on three other things, as estimated by the established firms:

How much entry (or how many entrants) would be attracted by an entry-inducing price policy, and thus how much of a share of the market established firms would lose to new entrants.

How much (if at all) competition in the industry would increase as the result of induced entry, and thus how much (if at all) market price in the industry would decline as the result of entry.

How long would be the "lag period" between the time that established firms set an entry-inducing price and that when entrants became established as competitors—a period during which established firms could reap the extra profits of an entry-inducing price without having to share them with the entrants.

It is clear that as the share of the market to be lost to entrants is larger, as the adverse effect of entry on industry price is greater, and as the lag period in question is shorter, the greater should be the disposition of established firms to set an entry-forestalling limit price when there is a barrier to entry of a given height. It is also evident that the decision of established firms in an industry as to whether to charge an entry-excluding limit price or a higher one should depend directly on their somewhat uncertain conjectures concerning all three of the things just enumerated and concerning the actual height of the maximum entry-forestalling price. In the light of all of these conjectures, established firms in a significantly oligopolistic industry should make their decision.

And, in view of all conjectures, such firms should find that the barrier to entry is one of four general types, designated as follows:

1. *Blockaded Entry.* The maximum entry-forestalling price is so high as to be above the full joint monopoly price at which the established firms would maximize total industry profits. In this case, they would disregard the condition of entry and tend to charge a fully monopoly price which still was too low to attract entry. Industry structure and price should not be destabilized by entry.

2. *Effectively Impeded Entry.* The maximum entry-forestalling or limit price is below that which would maximize total industry profits and above minimal average costs, and the established firms expect that it will yield them greater long-run profits than a higher price which would attract entry. In this case, they would charge a limit price that was below the full monopoly level but appreciably above the competitive or minimal average cost level. Again, industry structure and price should not be destabilized by new entry.

3. *Ineffectively Impeded Entry.* The limit price is below that which would maximize total industry profits and above minimal average costs, but low enough that the established firms expect that they can make greater long-run profits by charging a higher price and inducing entry. In this case, they would charge an entry-inducing (perhaps fully monopolistic) price, and some entry would take place. Thereafter, several possibilities ensue. The industry after some entry might stabilize with effectively impeded entry and with the sellers now in it charging a limit price to discourage further entrants. It might become unconcentrated enough that competition held price below a level which would induce further entry, and thus have a stable structure. Or the increasing number of sellers in it might progressively pursue entry-inducing price policies until the industry was overstocked with undersized firms and had excess plant capacity. After this, some structural revolution involving severe competition and the elimination and consolidation of firms might reestablish the *status quo ante*, and the same process could begin again. In the last eventuality, dynamically unstable market structure and prices are predictable.

4. *Easy Entry* (No Barriers to Entry). Though the conditions are far from the most propitious, oligopolistic market structures can emerge in spite of easy entry—for example, through merger movements. They may be encouraged especially if the established firms can exploit lag periods during which they can charge high prices and enjoy high profits before a flood of entrants becomes established to bring prices down. In this case, the established firms would presumably establish monopolistic prices and profits for limited periods of time, and induce considerable entry. Thereafter, the prognosis is either for dynamically unstable market structure and prices—the last possibility considered under type 3

above—or for "deterioration" of the structure of the industry into one of atomistically low concentration, where it might stabilize.

The foregoing complex of hypotheses concerning the relation of the condition of entry to market conduct and performance in oligopolistic industries with high seller concentration generates some tentative predictions of a rough and ready sort, as follows:

(*a*) With very high barriers to entry (that probably blockade entry), fully monopolistic pricing policies should be expected, and these price policies should be persistently pursued without new entry occurring.

(*b*) With high or high-moderate (but not very high) barriers to entry, persistent stable limit-pricing policies that establish prices noticeably below monopolistic levels but appreciably above competitive levels should be found, and market structures should not be altered by new entry.

(*c*) With moderate to low barriers to entry, and with negligible ones, periodic high prices and large profits are likely to emerge, followed by induced entry, and further followed by excess plant capacity. The long-run result may be dynamically unstable market structures and prices, or alternatively stabilization with a comparatively unconcentrated and competitive industry.

Predictions of this sort must be appropriately qualified to take account of inter-industry differences in the lag periods required for entrants to become established, and of related considerations. Moreover, the predictions refer specifically only to oligopolies in which seller concentration is sufficiently high so that collective control of market price by the sellers is possible, or a principal seller or a few large ones can effectively determine the market price. In less concentrated oligopolies, it is possible or probable that intra-industry rivalry will keep prices below maximum entry-forestalling prices, not only when barriers to entry are high or moderately high, but also when they are relatively low. Thus the condition of entry to an industry and its seller concentration interact to help determine market conduct and performance.

One further note may be added to this abbreviated theoretical discussion. So far, we have referred entirely to the possibility of oligopolists deterring entry through restricting their selling prices to entry-forestalling levels, and to their decisions as to whether or not the corresponding limit prices would yield them the greatest long-run profits. In oligopolistic industries wherein the barriers to entry depend importantly on product-differentiation advantages of established firms, they may alternatively (or concurrently) deter entry by increasing their advertising and other sales promotion costs to certain levels, and may determine whether or not it is more profitable to forestall entry in this way than not to. Moreover, they may be concerned with codetermining selling prices and sales promotion costs at such related levels as will yield the greatest long-run profit while forestalling entry.[7]

So much for theoretical predictions of the effects of the condition of entry on market conduct and performance. Let us now turn to empirical evidences of the heights of barriers to entry in various industries in the economy.

Actual Conditions of Entry in Sectors and Industries of the American Economy

No systematic body of data exists that refers to conditions of entry for large numbers of industries in the various sectors of the economy. Thus we cannot turn to a Census compilation of measurements, as we could when seeking information on degrees of seller concentration in manufacturing industries. A similar lack of data has been noted with respect to product differentiation, but at least casual observation of relevant market phenomena gives us some rough notion of the incidence of significant product differentiation. This sort of observation, however, is seriously deficient as a basis for judgments concerning the absolute and comparative heights of barriers to entry in different industries. Detailed study of many individual industries is required to arrive at meaningful estimates of this dimension of market structures.

Because there is no mass-production of the relevant data by governmental agencies, economists must develop their own data through painstaking research. We are prepared here to present in the main only tentative findings on the twenty manufacturing industries referred to in Chapters 6 and 7, and to hazard some inferences from these findings. First, however, some general comments on evident conditions of entry in sectors outside manufacturing may be offered.

Barriers to Entry in Sectors Other than Manufacturing

In the extractive sectors of agriculture, forestry, and fisheries, entry barriers to the various component industries seem to be in general low or negligible. Product-differentiation barriers seem to be generally absent; economies of scale typically are not significant; and "absolute-cost" barriers based on monopolistic resource control, patents, or capital

[7]Cf. Oliver E. Williamson, "Selling Costs as a Barrier to Entry," *Quarterly Journal of Economics*, **LXXVII**, 1 (Feb., 1963), pp. 112–128.

requirements for entry are usually negligible. In these sectors, atomistic market structures (very low seller concentration) are commonly conjoined with very easy entry. In the mining sector the same general situation is found for certain important minerals, such as bituminous coal and (to a lesser extent) crude petroleum. For some other kinds of mining, however—for example copper, iron, and nickel ores and sulfur[s]— entry is severely impeded by the close holding by established firms of known ore deposits of good quality.

In the wholesale and retail distributive trades, barriers to entry again are ordinarily quite low. Absolute-cost barriers, including those stemming from capital requirements, are ordinarily slight, and economies of scale not an important deterrent to entry, in spite of small but perceptible advantages enjoyed by large-scale chain-store organizations in some principal distributive fields. Existing product-differentiation patterns give the stronger firms at least transitory advantages over new entrants, but these are not of such a magnitude as to create significant net barriers to new entry. The continual high incidence of new entry (and exit) in these fields tends to support these judgments.

Another sector in which entry barriers are ordinarily low is contract construction. Except for that area of contracting which requires large technical organizations and sizeable financial resources on the part of the firm (major bridges, large office buildings, big dams), entry typically appears to be very easy.

Finally, entry to most of the service industries is relatively easy. This is clearly true of laundries, dry cleaners, barber shops, night clubs, and automotive service garages, for example. In some other industries in this sector—motion picture production and distribution, for example—scale economies, large capital requirements, and product differentiation of various sorts may impose appreciable barriers to new entry.

In the public utilities sector, including transportation, communications, and utilities "proper" like electric and gas companies, very difficult or fully blockaded entry is frequently encountered. This is perhaps primarily because franchises from governmental authorities are required for operation in nearly all of the industries in this area, and because these franchises are generally issued to only one or a few firms in any given market. In addition, of course, scale economies and capital requirements are frequently so important as to raise equivalent nongovernmental barriers to entry. Difficult or blockaded entry is found in rail transportation, in electric and gas utilities, and in telephone, tele-

[s] For findings concerning coal, nickel, and sulfur, see H. Michael Mann, "Seller Concentration, Barriers to Entry, and Rates of Return in Thirty Industries, 1959–1960," *Review of Economics and Statistics*, **XLVIII**, 3 (August, 1966), pp. 301–302.

graph, television, and radio communications. Perhaps the main exception is found in highway freight transportation or trucking, where technological conditions and governmental policy combine to make entry a good deal easier. In the industries in this sector with difficult entry, high entry barriers are generally combined with monopolistic or highly concentrated seller control of individual markets and also with some governmental regulation of market conduct and performance.

Finally, in the "finance" sector (including insurance and real estate firms) the entry picture seems to be mixed, ranging from one of easy entry for the local real estate firm, for example, to one of rather difficult entry into the life insurance industry.

Barriers to Entry in Manufacturing Industries

Some more definite information concerning conditions of entry is available for the sample of twenty manufacturing industries referred to in preceding chapters (actually for twenty-three industries and separable segments of industries). The data refer to barriers to entry in the early 1950's (usually 1952); although the heights of these barriers remain roughly unchanged to the present date in nearly all of the industries, they have since changed appreciably in one or two cases, as will be noted below.[9]

The principal findings concern:

1. The absolute and comparative heights of the aggregate barriers to entry—that is, barriers resulting from scale economies, absolute cost advantages, and product differentiation advantages combined—in the individual industries and groups thereof.

2. The relative importance of the three main sources of barriers to entry.

The aggregate heights of barriers to entry to the industries were classified and defined as follows:

Very high, or such that established firms could persistently elevate their selling prices above minimal average costs by 10 per cent or more while still forestalling entry.

Substantial, or such that the maximum entry-forestalling price exceeded minimal average costs by roughly 6 to 8 per cent.

Moderate to low, or such that the maximum entry-forestalling price exceeded minimal average cost by no more than 4 per cent, and frequently by only 1 or 2 per cent.

As of about 1952, the twenty-three industries or industry segments were distributed among these entry-barrier categories as follows:

[9]From Bain, *Barriers to New Competition*, Chs. 3–6.

A. *Industries with Very High Barriers to Entry*
Automobiles
Cigarettes
Tractors
Typewriters
Distilled liquor
Fountain pens ("quality" grade)
B. *Industries with Substantial Barriers to Entry*
Copper
Farm machinery (large and complex)
Petroleum refining
Steel
Soap
Shoes (men's high-priced and specialties)
C. *Industries with Moderate to Low Barriers to Entry*
Cement
Farm machinery (small and simple)
Fountain pens (low-priced)
Gypsum products
Tin cans
Rayon
Shoes (women's and men's low-priced)
Tires and tubes
Flour (commercial)
Canned fruits and vegetables
Meat packing

The last three industries listed appeared to have extremely low barriers to entry, generally or in their major segments.

Six industries or industry segments were found to have very high barriers to entry, six to have substantial ones, and eleven to have entry barriers that were moderate to low. One conclusion that can be drawn from these sample findings is that there is a wide variation in the condition of entry among industries, with barriers to entry ranging from quite high to low or negligible. Concerning the comparative incidence of entry barriers of various absolute heights among American manufacturing industries as a whole, however, the findings for this particular sample of industries do not necessarily provide a reliable guide.[10] This is in part because difficulties of measurement precluded any very pre-

[10]Mann (*op. cit.*, pp. 302–305) has made some estimates of barriers to entry to ten additional manufacturing industries, for which the proportions of industries with very high, substantial, and moderate to low barriers are roughly the same as found for the 23 industries just listed.

cise classification of industries according to the absolute height of the barrier to entry. More importantly, the sample of industries is somewhat biased in the direction of including a disproportionately large number of industries with from moderate to high seller concentration, and may therefore have the related bias of overstating the comparative incidence of "very high" and "substantial" barriers to entry. Neverthless, it would appear that industries differ one from another with respect to the condition of entry about as significantly as they do with respect to seller concentration.

It is not possible to establish any simple relationship of "very high," "substantial," and "moderate to low" barriers to entry as defined above, to "blockaded," "effectively impeded," "ineffectively impeded," and "easy" entry conditions as defined in a preceding section of this chapter. This is because we lack strategic information on the lengths of the time periods beginning when established firms in the various industries might charge entry-inducing joint monopoly prices and ending when entrants would become established in the various markets, and also on the relationships of these joint monopoly prices to minimal average costs. Rough guesses might be made, however, to the effect:

1. That in industries with "very high" barriers to entry, as defined, the condition of entry is probably either "blockaded" or "effectively impeded."

2. That in most industries with "moderate to low" barriers to entry, as defined, the condition of entry is probably either "ineffectively impeded" or "easy."

3. That in industries with "substantial" barriers to entry, as defined, the condition of entry is probably either "effectively impeded" or "ineffectively impeded," depending largely on the values of other relevant variables. Some evidence bearing indirectly on these speculations is presented in Chapter 11.

Comparative Importance of Different Barriers to Entry

Further findings from the study of the sample of industries concerned the relative importance as impediments to entry of scale economies, absolute-cost advantages of established firms, and product-differentiation advantages of such firms. Several things stand out.

First, economies of the large-scale plant and firm more frequently than not are the source of at least perceptible barriers to entry. In more than half the cases observed, the proportion of the market which an entrant would have to supply in order to attain reasonable efficiency is large enough to provide at least a noticeable deterrent to entry. Thus, in ten of sixteen industries for which revealing data could be developed, at least a moderate impediment to entry—sufficient in itself probably to permit established firms to elevate prices from 2 to 4 per cent above minimal average costs without attracting entry—was found to result from scale economies. On the other hand, higher barriers to entry did not frequently result from scale economies. In only three of the ten cases just cited (automobiles, typewriters, and tractors) were scale economies evidently great enough to permit established firms to elevate prices by 5 per cent or more above minimal average costs while forestalling entry.

Scale economies thus appear to be a fairly pervasive source of rather mild barriers to entry to manufacturing industries, although there are perhaps almost as many cases in which they are unimportant from this standpoint as cases in which they have a limited importance. And scale economies are probably a relatively infrequent source of high barriers to entry, having this influence in probably no more than 15 per cent of all manufacturing industries. This, at any rate, is the tentative indication of the sample study, based on estimates of (*a*) the minimum optimal size of firm, expressed as a percentage of total capacity supplying the market; (*b*) the extent to which unit costs are elevated if the firm is smaller; and (*c*) the probable repercussions within the industry to the entry of new firms of various alternative sizes.

Second, product differentiation advantages of established firms are typically a somewhat more frequent source of at least moderate barriers to entry than are scale economies, and a much more important source of high barriers to entry. In all but three of thirteen consumer-good industries (or industry segments) that were examined, product-differentiation barriers to entry were adjudged to be either moderate or high, and in four of the thirteen cases they were rated high. (Consumer-good industries producing automobiles, cigarettes, quality fountain pens, and distilled liquor were found to have high product differentiation barriers; those producing rubber tires, soap, high-quality men's shoes, petroleum products, consumer-brand flour, and specialty canned goods were found to have moderate product-differentiation barriers.) In addition, high product-differentiation barriers to entry were also found in three producer-good industries (producing typewriters, tractors, and large farm machinery) and moderate barriers in one other (the metal container industry). Thus product-differentiation advantages of established firms loom larger than any other source of barriers to entry, and especially large as a source of high and very high barriers.

These advantages generally reflect the ability of established firms to secure higher selling prices, lower promotional costs, or market shares more adequate for supporting an efficient scale of production operations. This superiority of established firms in turn typically hinges in important or major degree upon the susceptibility of buyers to persuasion through heavy advertising or other sales-promotion effort. The highest barriers are further frequently linked with complexity and durability of the product, often associated with poor consumer ability to evaluate products; the integration of retail dealer service organizations by the manufacturer; and the evident importance of "conspicuous consumption" motives in the psychology of the consumer.

Third, "absolute-cost" advantages of established firms, aside possibly from those connected with large capital requirements, do not appear (from the industries sampled) to be a frequent source of important barriers to entry. In most industries, entrants would be at a nominal and transitory disadvantage in acquiring talented management personnel, production know-how, and perhaps other essential ingredients of an efficient productive operation, but in almost no case did these disadvantages appear to impose more than a slight barrier to entry. The principal candidates as sources of important absolute-cost advantages to established firms would seem to be control of strategic patents covering productive techniques and equipment, and dominant control of natural-resource deposits essential to production. In only three of the twenty industries sampled did these considerations apparently raise significant barriers to entry. Control of mineral ore deposits did so in the steel and copper industries, and less important resource control plus some significant patent holdings did so in the gypsum products industry. Throughout all the other industries sampled, neither patents nor resource control seem to provide significant deterrents to entry currently, although patents have been important in this respect in earlier years in several industries.

The sample is probably not adequately representative of all manufacturing industries in this respect, especially as regards patents, since it is possible to name offhand at least several industries in the chemical, electrical, and electronic fields in which patent control currently imposes severe barriers to entry. The generalization can probably be sustained, however, in that in the overall scene patent and resource control are much less frequent sources of significant barriers to entry than are either scale economies or product differentiation.

The preceding reference to absolute-cost barriers to entry does not take into account the possible entry-impeding effect of large capital requirements. It is widely believed that the requirement of a very large lump of liquid funds for investment by an entrant firm essentially constitutes some sort of a barrier to his entry, the common-sense argument being that potential entrants simply cannot raise enough money to finance effective entry, or that in any event established firms can raise money for expansion more easily and cheaply than potential entrants can raise it for entry. Thus potential entry is discouraged and established firms retain their hold on the industry. This argument seems especially plausible if we think of industries in which, let us say, $100 million are needed to establish an efficient firm, and conjure up a mental image of the typical potential entrant as an unknown "little man" with total personal assets of $10,000 or as a small group of persons with less than $100,000 to their combined names. The argument seems less conclusive, of course, if we picture the possible entry of a large going industrial corporation, with assets of $500 million or more, into a new industry—for example, of General Electric into automobile production, or of American Tobacco into petroleum refining (both strictly imaginary examples). Here a comparative disadvantage of the potential entrant in acquiring funds for entry is clearly less apparent.

If, however, we examine the reasoning behind the belief that large capital requirements deter entry, two things stand out. First, it seems frequently or usually true that when very substantial sums would be required for investment by the entrant, the firmly established concerns already in an industry can obtain funds more easily and at a lower net interest cost than nearly all potential entrants. Also, they are usually paying less for the use of funds they currently have invested than entrants would have to pay for the equivalent. They have superior access to the security markets and other sources of funds, and their "credit ratings" with prospective lenders or investors are superior because of their established positions. Thus the lower cost of money to the established firms places their total average costs of production below those of most potential entrants, and raises a corresponding barrier to entry.

Second, very large amounts of capital simply cannot be raised at all, in any conceivable fashion, by a very large percentage of all the individuals, groups, or business concerns who might otherwise be considered likely potential entrants to the usual manufacturing industry. Therefore, the ranks of the effective potential entrants are often greatly thinned by capital requirements, and the probability of finding one or more ready to enter in response to a given inducement is greatly reduced, though usually there will be some potential entrants left who could, if sufficiently attracted, "raise the money."

All this is reasonably clear. The difficulty is that we are in no position, in our current state of information, to estimate just how much of a barrier to entry (however measured) is imposed by the existence of capital requirements of given sizes. All that we can say is that there may be and probably is some *perceptible* barrier to entry (as reflected in the ability of established firms to elevate prices without attracting entry) inherent in large capital requirements.

On this rather uncertain backdrop, it may be noted that capital requirements for efficient entry to a considerable proportion of manufacturing industries are indeed quite large. To establish a firm with just one plant of the most efficient size in 1951 would have required, for a sample of eighteen manufacturing industries: (*a*) $125 to $650 million per one-plant firm in five industries; (*b*) $10 to $75 million per one-plant firm in six industries; (*c*) $2.5 to $10 million per one-plant firm in four industries; and (*d*) under $2 million per one-plant firm in three industries. It does not seem unreasonable to speculate that some added deterrent to entry may have resulted from capital requirements at least in the cases where more than $10 million was the required "ante," and these accounted for over half of the cases sampled. Capital requirements are thus an added potential deterrent to entry, though one of substantially unascrtained force and importance.

Summarizing with respect to the relative importance of various types of barriers to entry to manufacturing industries, it appears generally that product-differentiation barriers are the most frequent in occurrence (and especially if we refer to high barriers); that scale economies are of slightly lesser importance as an impediment to entry, and also usually have less extreme effects in impeding entry; and that absolute-cost barriers (including those resulting from patents and resource ownership but excluding capital requirements) are distinctly less important. Large capital requirements may impose an added barrier to entry in a considerable proportion of manufacturing industries. This identification of the source of high barriers to entry may appear pertinent when we consider the feasibility of measures to revise market structure by reducing entry barriers.

Examples of Conditions of Entry in Specific Industries

The source and character of conditions of entry to particular industries may be better understood if we consider a few examples in somewhat more detail. Let us therefore look briefly, as of about 1952, at the automobile and distilled-liquor industries as examples with very high entry barriers, at the steel and soap industries as examples with substantial barriers, and at the gypsum-product and meat-packing industries as examples with moderate to low barriers.

In both automobile and distilled-liquor industries, product differentiation between the outputs of established and potential entrant firms plays or played a significant role in impeding entry. In the automobile industry, scale economies and very large capital requirements are also significant contributing factors.

A high degree of differentiation among the products of established automobile firms, in a pattern generally favoring General Motors products over all others and "Big Three" products over the remainder, has been noted in Chapter 7. This differentiation seems attributable in part to the uninformed consumer's reliance on established firm and product reputations, in part to the "conspicuous consumption" psychology of buyers, in part to physical design differences, and in part to the character, size, and quality of the distribution-service networks which are controlled by the various established firms.

The product-differentiation disadvantages of potential entrants have the same sources as those of the one remaining smaller domestic auto firm, but would be greater. The experience of the attempted entry of Kaiser-Frazer to the industry just after World War II (under circumstances which were seemingly very propitious) illustrates the difficulties which a firm attempting entry to the industry would encounter. Before the Kaiser-Frazer firm gave up and abandoned passenger-car production in the early 1950's, it suffered all of the expected disadvantages in extreme degree. Lack of consumer acceptance of the new and unknown product resulted in inability to maintain a market share sufficient to support efficiently large-scale production. There was an actual decrease in consumer acceptance over a critical period of years. The used-car trade-in values of its products were far inferior to those of established makes—for example, the two-year depreciation in retail value of a 1950 Kaiser sedan in the Northeast was 36 per cent of original sales price, as compared to 24 per cent for a Studebaker, 15 per cent for a Buick, and 5 per cent for a Chevrolet. Finally, the firm was unable to build an effective nationwide network of financially strong and experienced automobile dealers to promote sales and offer service. As a result, the new entrant concern was, after the first couple of years, absorbing increasing operating losses ranging upward from $10 million annually, and apparently at last decided not to throw further good money after bad in an attempt to establish a foothold in the industry.

From this experience and from a general appraisal of entry possibilities by industry sources, the extent of the product-differentiation barrier to entry into the automobile industry is judged roughly as follows. First, because of the crushing disadvantage in initial consumer acceptance, in resale or trade-in values of its product, and in developing an adequate network of retail dealers, the most favored potential entrant firm would sustain in various forms (such as price concessions or subsidies to tottering dealers) a net price disadvantage, compared to the "Big Three," of at least 5 per cent of factory retail price on the average the first ten years. If it operated with this disadvantage, the most that the entrant could reasonably expect to gain, at the end of ten years, would probably be 3 to 4 per cent of the market (210,000 to 280,000 units per annum) if the total demand for autos were seven million per year.

Second, during the first half and perhaps most of the ten-year break-in period, the average annual output of the entrant would be so small that it would encounter significant diseconomies of small-scale production—especially in the matter of retooling costs for model changes—and these would result in "break-in" losses. An average loss of $15 million a year for ten years is easily in prospect, incurred in the face of a substantial probability of ultimate failure.

In sum, the total product-differentiation disadvantage of the potential entrant seller in the automobile industry is evaluated as at least 10 per cent of selling price for the first ten years, with ultimately successful entry then not being assured. Ability of the major established sellers to hold prices persistently a considerable distance above minimal average costs without attracting entry seems correspondingly to be implied.

Entry is further impeded in the automobile industry by scale economies and by large capital requirements. Economies of large-scale production in the industry are very important largely because the firm must or does, for reasons of maintaining the differentiation of its product from others, engage not only in assembly operations but also in the production of its own major components, especially engines and bodies. And although for assembly-plant operations scale economies are relatively unimportant, they are quite important in component production. For the most efficient production, therefore, a firm would need an integrated plant complex, consisting of single plants for the production of each of several major components and a number of assembly plants—and its total output capacity would need to be from 300,000 to 600,000 or more passenger cars per year, or roughly 5 to 10 per cent of total industry capacity. Operations at significantly smaller scale than 5 per cent would evidently experience a significant disadvantage in production costs. Because of these scale economies, the entrant would either have to be inefficiently small (even after breaking in), or large enough to induce repercussions in industry pricing.

Finally, capital requirements for entry are large. It is estimated that a firm with a plant of efficient size as just described would require an initial investment of from $250 to $500 million and might in addition need to invest another $150 million or more in "break-in" losses, all in the face of a substantial risk of ultimate failure. All things considered, barriers to effective new entry to the American automobile industry seem very high and perhaps insuperable, particularly if we are referring to mass production of automobiles of the standard American production type. The principal established firms have great latitude in selecting their price and product policies without much attention to the threat of new competition.

The only entry of a sort that has appeared to have even a moderate chance of success is that of foreign manufacturers into the "little car" field, which was for some time neglected by the producers in Detroit. Given this early neglect, followed by Detroit's response with lines of "compact" cars, all foreign makes combined have so far captured only about 6 per cent of the American market. The more successful foreign sellers have done so profitably because their large sales elsewhere in the world market have enabled them to attain efficient scales of production. General indications, however, are that such competitors are in the long run unlikely to capture more than a limited corner of the American market, and holding that part over time may be difficult.

In the period from about 1935 to about 1952—that is, following the repeal of the "prohibition" amendment to the Constitution and until six or eight years after the end of World War II—the distilled-liquor industry was also one in which established sellers were protected by very high barriers to entry. Seller concentration was high and increasing, with eight largest firms accounting for 71 per cent of industry sales in 1935 and 88 per cent in 1947. In more detail, the concentration picture in 1947 appeared as follows:

Firm	Percentage of U.S. Liquor Sales in 1947
Seagrams	24.9
Schenley	22.1
National	15.9
Walker	11.9
(First 4 firms)	(74.8)

Firm	Percentage of U.S. Liquor Sales in 1947
Publicker	6.8
Glenmore	2.3
Brown-Forman	2.1
Park & Tilford	2.1
(First 8 firms)	(88.1)
136 other firms	11.9
Total	100.0

Among the established sellers, there was a pattern of product differentiation which conferred a great advantage on the "Big Four" distillers over all others, and a lesser advantage on the four next largest firms. Since at that time whiskey was by far the most important product of the industry—accounting for about 85 per cent of all liquor sales—product differentiation in the whiskey market may be emphasized while we neglect lesser liquor markets. Excluding Scotch and other imported whiskeys, which then supplied very small shares of the market, whiskeys fell (and still fall) into four main classes: (1) "bonded" American whiskey, generally 100-proof straight bourbon whiskey that has been aged four years or more; (2) aged "straight" American whiskey, similar to "bonds" but further diluted with water; (3) "blended" American whiskey, a mixture of "straight" whiskey and neutral grain alcohol; and (4) "Canadian" whiskey, a blend of component whiskeys and other spirits having a somewhat different taste from American whiskey.

There were recognizable differences in potency and taste among these principal types of whiskey, and there existed a variegated difference of consumer preferences among them. In addition, within each "type" there were recognized differences among competing products—differences in taste, quality, uniformity of taste and quality over time, and so forth. The major basis of whiskey product differentiation, however, was found in brand names and heavy advertising. At least 5 per cent of distillers' sales revenues was expended on advertising for many years, with cumulative effects on consumer preferences. As a result, in 1951 the top twenty-five brands accounted for about 75 per cent of all whiskey sales, and of these brands twenty belonged to members of the Big Four and one each to the five next largest sellers.

One evidence of the importance of product differentiation in the liquor industry was the persistent disparity in the market shares of competing sellers, evidenced especially in the dominant combined share of the Big Four. A more striking evidence was the advantage which the Big Four generally held in selling price or in the ratio of advertising costs to sales revenues. In the market for high-quality bonded whiskeys, their principal brands commanded a retail price premium of about 75 cents per "fifth" over the comparable brands of the next largest sellers. In the large-volume market for blended whiskies, a general distinction was drawn between "A" and "B" blends, the former containing less neutral spirits and selling at retail at about 40 cents per fifth over the latter. In 1952, when six brands of "A-blend" whiskey dominated the market, all were produced by one or another of the Big Four distillers, and no smaller distiller had been able successfully to enter the "A-blend" field. The ratio of price to production plus sales promotion costs was evidently more favorable for "A" than for "B" blended whiskeys, but it was said that the smaller sellers "could not make an A-blend." That is, whatever the physical qualities of their products, they could not secure perceptible sales volumes at prices above the "B-blend" level. Furthermore, the smaller distillers held their minor shares in the "B-blend" market only by incurring larger unit advertising costs than the Big Four, or by offering special price discounts to liquor wholesalers and to taverns in order to attract their business.

The same forces that accounted for this intra-industry differentiation appeared to place the potential entrant in a worse relative position than the relatively small and weak independents which were already established. Entry at a substantial scale, comparable to that of the smallest of the Big Four, was considered inconceivable by industry sources, because of the overwhelming difficulty of the entrant in securing a sufficient market share in competition with established brands. It was estimated that entry at a smaller scale (for example, large enough to supply from 2 to 5 per cent of the market) could be accomplished, if at all, only at the expense of accepting, for a very long period of time, substantially lower net selling prices than the principal established firms. That is, the entrant would presumably have had to accept—through extra promotional costs or through price concessions to wholesalers and retailers—a net price (after promotion costs) about 15 per cent below that received by the Big Four, and would have needed to do so for an indefinitely prolonged period. Even a very substantial excess of existing prices over minimal average costs was therefore insufficient to make new entry very attractive.

Scale economies did not appear to add perceptibly to this barrier to entry in the liquor industry. An optimally efficient distillery operation would not have had to supply as much as 2 per cent of the total market, and even an operation supplying as little as one-third of 1 per cent would not have suffered serious cost disadvantages.

Capital requirements, however, were fairly high, especially because of the need for investing in aging stocks of whiskey. An investment of $30 to $42 million was estimated to be required to support an operation supplying 1½ per cent of the national market. In addition, the established firms in general and the Big Four in particular possessed through most of the period in question (1935 to 1952) a substantial absolute-cost advantage over potential entrants through their holdings of most of the available supplies of aged whiskey—these supplies being scarce first in the 1930's after nearly 15 years of Prohibition, and then during and immediately after World War II because of severe governmental restrictions on whiskey production. Therefore, unless the potential entrant after 1947 was prepared to mark time while he aged his own whiskey for four years, he would have a hard time securing or would pay premium prices for the raw material essential for making a competitive whiskey product.

Barriers to entry to the distilled-liquor industry were thus very high during World War II and in the six or eight years immediately thereafter. As we will see later, however, these barriers were appreciably lowered in succeeding years by a number of factors.

The steel industry is generally thought of as one extremely large-scale production, so that it might be expected that economies of large-scale production would be the source of substantial barriers to entry. Actually, such scale economies seem to provide at most only moderate barriers in the American industry. To be sure, an integrated steel plant of optimum size for mass-producing standard steel products is absolutely very large, with a capacity ranging from 1 million to 2½ million ingot tons per anum, according to various estimates. Production costs would be significantly higher for plants which were of substantially smaller capacity than a million tons—for example, up as much as 5 per cent at a half-million-ton capacity. Furthermore, some small added economies for the multiplant firm with two to eight plants under a single management are claimed by some sources.

On the other hand, the American steel industry is very big, with a total capacity above 150 million ingot tons per annum, so that one efficient plant would not provide a very large percentage of total capacity. And although a multiplant firm of efficient size (maximum estimate) would provide a more sizeable percentage, the cost disadvantages of a one-plant firm would be relatively slight. In general, an entrant firm supplying no more and possibly less than 2 per cent of national steel output, or around 5 per cent of the output in the largest regional markets, would be likely to suffer at most only slightly from diseconomies of small-scale production as compared to the biggest firms. Thus it is estimated that the impact of an efficient unit of entry on total industry supply would be quite moderate, that appreciable price reactions by established firms would be unlikely, and that the scale of production needed for efficiency would thus provide no more than a very modest deterrent to new entry.

The situation is otherwise so far as the capital requirements for entry at efficient scale are concerned. An investment of $250 to $650 million would be required for one integrated plant of most efficient scale, and correspondingly more for the establishment of a multiplant firm. The roster of financially eligible potential entrants must thereby be considerably reduced.

The principal barrier to entering the steel industry, however, is the scarcity of high-grade reserves of iron ore and the close holding of known reserves by established steel firms. The principal economical sources of iron ore for American steel making are in the Lake Superior region, and these are almost entirely owned or contractually controlled by existing established firms. In addition, close control is similarly developing with respect to new ore sources as they are opened, including Canadian and other foreign ore deposits, and domestic taconite deposits. As a result there is, in times of good demand for steel, substantially no open or spot market for ore in which a new firm could purchase its requirements from year to year. Absolutely requiring an assured supply of ore over a long period of years, the entrant could establish himself only either (a) by discovering and developing a new ore deposit, (b) by "buying into" some established company group now controlling ore, at a price set by the established firms, or (c) using an inferior grade of ore with correspondingly higher costs of obtaining steel. Whatever his choice, it would appear that he would be at some substantial absolute-cost disadvantage as compared to established firms, except in the very unlikely event that he should make a lucky discovery of a presently unknown major ore deposit.

Taking into account the combined impact of scale economies, capital requirements, and shortage of ore supplies, the aggregate barrier to entry to the steel industry must be rated as at least substantial. The preceding applies to entry to the mass production of standard steel products with integrated facilities. Entry into the semi-integrated production of specialty steels, depending on scrap steel or purchased steel ingots for a raw material, can be made at a smaller scale and with much less comparative disadvantage to the entrant.

In the soap industry, the two major barriers to entry are scale economies and product differentiation, though capital requirements also are other than negligible. Scale economies appear moderately important. A plant of most efficient scale for producing both detergents and the more traditional fatty-acid soaps would, according to estimate, supply from 4 to 6 per cent of the national demand for soaps; a plant half this size would have unit costs of production perhaps 3 per cent higher. In addition, slight added economies, mostly of distribution, are predicted for a firm with two or three optimal-scale plants. Scale economies of this magnitude should be sufficient to raise a slight-to-moderate barrier to entry. Along with this may be considered the fact that an investment of $13 to $20 million would be required to establish a single plant of the most efficient size.

The major potential barrier to entry, however, might be expected to stem from product differentiation. Although physical product differentiation within any of the various recognized types of soap (light-duty detergents, heavy-duty detergents, liquid dishwashing compounds, etc.) is not apparently a factor of major importance, it is well known that the promotion of brand names by very heavy advertising is a major aspect of the market behavior of soap firms. Advertising costs generally run at the astonishingly high level of 10 per cent or more of sales for the principal firms. The resultant pattern of product differentiation secures over 80 per cent of the soap market for the "Big Three" of the industry (Procter & Gamble, Colgate, and Lever Brothers), and most of the rest of the market for six smaller firms. But it is not such apparently as to give any brand or seller a preferred position in the matter of selling price. The housewife buyer apparently shops with a major attention to price, and the actual brand attachments of consumers are generally characterized as slight or ephemeral (a situation much in contrast to that found in the markets for distilled liquor or cigarettes). In consequence, typical sales promotion tactics feature the systematic use of special prices, coupons allowing a reduction in price, and so forth. In summary, the intensive and expensive efforts of sellers to differentiate their products and develop strong brand preferences on the part of consumers seem to be in large measure self-canceling, and less successful than might be imagined except in the matter of more or less stabilizing the widely disparate market shares of different sellers.

Potential entrants could still, of course, suffer a perceptible product-differentiation disadvantage as compared to established firms as a group, and apparently they do. To establish its product, a new firm must expect for a period of some years to incur significantly higher sales-promotion costs per dollar of sales than established firms incur to maintain their market positions. This disadvantage appears to raise at least a moderate barrier to entry, permitting established firms to hold prices somewhat above their minimal costs without making entry attractive. The force of the disadvantage is somewhat mitigated, however, by the fact that new entrants have periodically been able to ease their way into the industry by introducing new types of products (like special soaps for automatic dishwashers), and the possibility that such product innovations will continue to make easier entry possible seems fairly good. On balance, therefore, we are inclined to rate the product-differentiation barrier to entry to the soap industry as only moderate, and the aggregate barrier to entry from all sources as only "substantial" rather than "very high."

The gypsum products industry (producing chiefly plaster wallboard and building plaster) is interesting because of significant changes in its barriers to entry over the last twenty years. Up to about 1950, it would have had to be rated as having a substantial or very high barrier to entry; thereafter, the aggregate barrier seems to be no more than moderate.

The change came about principally as a result of an antitrust action affecting the use of patents that covered the design of plaster wallboard, which accounts for about 70 per cent of the sales revenue of the industry. (Calcined bulk plaster and uncalcined gypsum have long been unpatented products.) Until a court decree which concluded this antitrust action in 1951, the United States Gypsum Co. had for a long time controlled the strategic patents covering the design of plasterboard so superior to any unpatented type that competition by producing substitute designs was not feasible. U. S. Gypsum was therefore able to monopolize the market at will, excluding all competitors, or alternatively to offer patent licenses to a restricted number of other firms (in return for royalty payments), under the terms of which it could determine the number and relative market shares of competing sellers and, indirectly, fix the selling price for the industry. It elected to do the latter, licensing five other sellers, reserving about 55 per cent of the market for itself, and completely foreclosing further entry. Licensees, in fact, were frequently able to acquire or absorb nonlicensed competitors. Until 1951, therefore, entry to the industry was in effect blockaded through this exclusive patent control of a superior product design, and the product-differentiation barrier to entry was indeed very high.

With the court decree in 1951 (issued because U. S. Gypsum was found to have violated the antitrust laws through its restrictive licensing scheme), the company was required thereafter to offer nondiscriminatory and nonexclusive licensing, at reasonable royalty rates and to all applicants, of all the patents it then held or might acquire for the next five years. This, together with the fact that its most important patent expired in 1954, has effectively removed any significant product-differentiation barrier to new entry. Any remaining barrier of this sort inheres in the 1-per-cent-of-sales royalty rate still charged for patent licenses, and in apparently very slight buyer preferences among competing brands.

Information on the importance of scale economies in the industry is too scanty to support any generalizations along this line. Capital requirements, however, are evidently on the low side, $4 to $6 million being judged sufficient to establish one efficient plant. The main added barrier to entry would result from (*a*) initial disadvantages of a new firm in acquiring requisite production "know-how" of a complicated sort, often protected by secrecy, and (*b*) some scarcity of high-grade gypsum-rock deposits not already held by established firms, probably placing new firms at some net disadvantage in the matter of raw-material costs. Adding up all individual barriers, the aggregate barrier to entry at present hardly seems to exceed the "moderate" level.

The meat packing industry, our last example, clearly represents the category of slight to negligible barriers to entry. Scale economies are of minimal importance. A plant of the most efficient size should not have to supply more than one thousandth of the national market in the area of fresh meat packing, or 2½ per cent of the market in canned and processed meats. Much smaller plants are only very slightly less efficient, and there are no evident net economies to multiplant firms. These estimates are in part corroborated by findings that in the matter of profits the so-called medium-sized firms of the industry, each supplying from 1 to 2 per cent of the market, do as well as or better than the largest four or five firms, each of which supplies from 5 to 15 per cent of the market. Evidently neither scale economies nor capital requirements are the basis of a deterrent to entry. Fresh meat packing can be entered at reasonably efficient scale with an investment of at most a few hundred thousand dollars, and diversified meat packing, including processing, with a few million.

Product differentiation likewise does not impose a significant barrier to entry. In the field of fresh meats, brand attachments of consumers are generally recognized to be either very slight or absent; an entrant firm will suffer no perceptible disadvantage because of his products being distinguished from those of established sellers. In processed meats, brand names are held to have some importance, but still a rather slight one. It is estimated that the maximum disadvantage of the entrant would be in higher sales-promotion costs during a "break-in" period of a year or two. In summary, the aggregate barrier to entry to the meat packing industry is negligible for the fresh-meat field, and only slight for the processed-meat field.

Changes in the Condition of Entry Over Time

The condition of entry, like seller concentration and the degree of product differentiation, has been treated as a structural characteristic of the industry because like them it is ordinarily a relatively stable, semi-permanent, or at most slowly changing aspect of the market environment within which firms operate. In any industry, it tends to remain relatively unchanged over considerable periods of time, so that it may be legitimately regarded as a relatively long-term determinant of the character of market conduct and performance. Certainly the condition of entry is not subject to such frequent or ephemeral variations over short periods of time that it would be so variable as to provide no explanation of long-term patterns of conduct and performance. The stability of the condition of entry to an industry evidently results from the slowly changing character of scale economies in most industries, from the relative longevity of most absolute-cost advantages (such as patent holdings and resource control), and from the durable character of established consumer preferences between established and potential entrant products.

On the other hand, conditions of entry to industries in general do change somewhat over time, and in some instances they change quite markedly within relatively brief intervals. Changes in the importance of scale economies or in the extent of the product-differentiation advantages of established firms seem generally to be gradual, although their cumulative effect over many years may be substantial. Rapid lowering of barriers to entry are more likely to result from the expiration of strategic patents, from the voiding of the force of such patents through antitrust decrees, or from the undermining of strategic resource controls through the discovery of important competitive resource deposits that are available to newcomers. Rapid increases in entry barriers (as well as undermining of old barriers) often have resulted from innovations of product or technique, frequently covered by protecting patents. In reviewing the history of a number of industries over a period of thirty years, we find, in addition to gradual changes in the condition of entry, fairly rapid and important changes in 10 or 15 per cent of the cases. Moreover, the observed changes are often the result of purposive activity on the part of established sellers to increase their protections against entry (through developing and patenting new techniques or products, for example), or of potential entrants to break down existing barriers.

A few examples may serve to illustrate the variety of circumstances that can lead to significant alterations in the heights of barriers to entry to individual industries. The effects of changes in the importance of scale economies on the condition of entry is well illustrated in the automobile and steel industries.

In the infancy and early youth of the automobile industry, producers were primarily "assemblers" of components—including engines and bodies—purchased from other suppliers, and they employed assembly techniques with which "optimal" efficiency was attained at very small scales. Scale economies provided no significant deterrent to a wave of early entrants to the industry. Thereafter, assembly-line and related mass-production techniques were progressively introduced, including techniques for the mass production of engines, body stampings, and so forth. When the drive to differentiate their products caused a number of automobile producers in the 1920's to integrate engine and body production within their firms, the minimum optimal scale of an integrated firm using new mass-production techniques both for components production and assembly became large enough to supply an appreciable fraction of the market. Scale economies have ever since provided a significant barrier to entry to the industry.

In the period after the postwar reconstruction period following World War II, however, earlier lowering of tariffs on imported automobiles had reduced the entry-deterring effect of scale economies in the American market by permitting foreign producers (like that of the Volkswagen) to supply minor fractions of the American market from large-scale plants built to supply a much larger output to the world market. The product-differentiation advantages of the established American firms, however, still kept high the barrier to entry to the American market.

In the steel industry, progressive introduction in the late nineteenth and early twentieth century of blast furnaces using coke, Bessemer and open-hearth steel furnaces, continuous rolling mills, and other new facilities greatly increased the importance of scale economies for the integrated steel firm and provided a very significant deterrent to entry. Since then, the scale of a steel plant of minimum optimal scale has certainly become no smaller, but the size of the domestic market has increased manyfold. As a result, a steel plant of minimum optimal scale now supplies a very small percentage of the market rather than a substantial one, and scale economies no longer impose a significant barrier to entry.

The incidence of a change in absolute-cost barriers to entry is also seen in the case of the steel industry. When the United States Steel Corporation was formed by merger in 1901, it acquired most of the known high grade deposits of bauxite ore on the continent, and a few other firms acquired the rest. Thereafter, as noted earlier, the inaccessibility to potential entrants of requisite iron ore supplies of high grade has imposed a major barrier to entry to the American steel industry. In the period since the reconstruction of Europe and Japan following World War II, however, earlier reductions in tariffs on steel have invited the influx of foreign supplies, until at present foreign producers are supplying an appreciable minor fraction of the American market. These foreign suppliers are drawing on iron ore reserves that have not been generally accessible to potential entrant firms that might have produced steel in this country. As a result, the barrier to entry to the American steel market (if the entry of foreign steel producers is included) that depended on the close holding of domestically available iron ore deposits by established American firms has been appreciably reduced. The situation could be returned to the *status quo ante*, of course, by a revision in American tariff policy.

Barriers to entry depending on the product differentiation advantages of established firms are perhaps somewhat more subject to change over time than those depending on scale economies or absolute cost advantages—though this propensity seems to depend on the bases of production differentiation advantages in individual industries. The creation of a product differentiation advantage through the patenting of a superior product, or its loss because a patent expires or is effectively voided by antitrust action, of course occurs from time to time. Both events occurred in the case of the gypsum products (more broadly, wallboard) industry, with the initial acquisition by the United States Gypsum Company of a series of patents protecting a wallboard product superior to all substitutes, and its later loss of patent control of the product as a result of antitrust action (referred to earlier).

In the fountain pen industry, a huge product-differentiation advantage over potential entrants, which Parker and Sheaffer long held and assiduously nurtured by advertising, has been seriously eroded since World War II by a genuine product innovation in the shape of the ballpoint pen. The demand for traditional gold-nibbed fountain pens has declined severely, and a number of new entrant firms (and previously very small established firms) have been able to compete successfully with Parker and Sheaffer in the ballpoint field. The barrier to entry to the industry producing self-fueled writing pens has clearly been reduced.

Product-differentiation barriers to entry to the distilled-liquor industry appear to have been seriously reduced in the last ten or twelve years,
in large part because of a simple shifting of consumer tastes that undermined the drawing power of the major whiskey brands of the Big Four
sellers. This shift has involved first a significant rise in the proportion of
distilled-liquor sales commanded by gin and vodka. These are products
for which brand attachments were never strong and which can be produced with little or no aging, both circumstances making the way for
potential entrants to the industry much easier. It has also involved a
similar increase in the market share of Scotch whiskey, much of it sold
under a variety of brands not controlled by the principal American
distillers. As a result, the market share of American whiskey—the strong-
hold of the Big Four—has declined very significantly, and the product-
differentiation advantages which they held in the form of established
brands of this whiskey have become correspondingly less important.
This advantage has been further eroded by a shift within the market
for American whiskey (i.e., bourbon) away from bonded whiskey and
blended whiskey, in which the Big Four enjoyed their largest product
differentiation advantage, toward "straight" whiskey, in which the Big
Four had less firmly entrenched brand positions. This last shift has been
facilitated by the termination of the period of scarcity of aged stocks of
American whiskey, and the emergence of a situation in which smaller
firms and potential entrant firms could acquire as much aged whiskey
as they could sell in the form of "straight" bourbon.

The fact that barriers to entry to the distilled-liquor industry have
been lowered greatly since about 1952 is attested to by considerable
new entry to the industry and by declining seller concentration in it.
From 1947 to 1963, the combined market share of the four largest firms
declined from 75 to 58 per cent, and that of the eight largest from 86 to
74 per cent. Predictably, profit rates earned by firms in the industry have
also declined markedly.

Whatever their cause, rapid and important changes in the condition
of entry to industries introduce new structural situations. In the new
situations there are frequently induced repercussions both in the degree
of seller concentration and in market conduct and performance. Therefore, in appraising the role of market structure as a determinant of market conduct and performance, we must keep in mind that structure itself
is subject both to slow evolution over time and to episodes of dramatic
change in some instances, rather than being completely stable over intervals of many years.

Condition of Entry, Seller Concentration, and Product Differentiation

The condition of entry provides a third major basis for classifying industries according to their market structures. As with seller concentration and product differentiation, we have seen that there is a wide range of differences among industries in this structural dimension. A further question is whether, among industries, there is a high degree of association or correlation of the condition of entry with the degrees of seller concentration and product differentiation. Are high entry barriers systematically associated with high seller concentration and lower barriers with lower concentration, or are barriers to entry generally higher as the degree of product differentiation is higher?

Some degree of association between the height of entry barriers and the degree of seller concentration might be anticipated, on the ground that higher barriers will typically protect a few principal sellers from all competitors, and thus foster and maintain high-seller concentration. The actual association observed in our sample of twenty-three manufacturing industries or segments thereof bears out this prediction in part. In all six industries with very high barriers to entry, the degree of seller concentration is either high or very high. Also, in all six cases with low-moderate or low seller concentration, the barriers to entry are either moderate or low. Thus it appears from the sample that very high entry barriers are generally conducive to higher seller concentration, and that low concentration generally emerges only when entry barriers are not high.

But the association is not complete, for it appears that high seller concentration can and does also exist without the protection of very high barriers to entry. Thus five industries classified as having either very high or high seller concentration were protected only by "substantial" entry barriers, and four such industries only by moderate barriers.[11] We conclude that the correlation between the condition of entry and the degree of seller concentration is so imperfect that each dimension of structure should be awarded separate and independent importance in making a structural classification of industries.

Again, some association between the degree of product differentiation in an industry and the height of its barrier to entry might be expected, since product differentiation is one of the three principal sources of impediments to entry. This expectation is borne out by the fact that strong product differentiation is either the dominant factor or a strong con-

---

[11]In the remaining two cases, high-moderate concentration was associated with either substantial or moderate entry barriers.

tributing factor in impeding entry in all six of the preceding sample of industries that were found to have very high barriers to entry. But as might also be expected—since scale economies and absolute-cost considerations also influence the condition of entry—there is no "one-to-one" correspondence between product differentiation and the height of the barrier to entry. In a fair proportion of cases with either "substantial" or "moderate" barriers, the impediment to entry has little to do with product differentiation; also, moderately important product differentiation may be associated with entry barriers of varying heights, depending upon the force of other supplementary influences. Product differentiation and the condition of entry should thus be considered as quasi-independent and quasi-separate dimensions of market structure.

Other Dimensions of Market Structure

Having defined market structure as embodying those organizational characteristics of a market or industry that determine the character of seller-to-seller, seller-to-buyer, and similar relationships and thus influence the nature of competition in the market, we have in this and two preceding chapters considered the structures of American markets in four leading dimensions: the degree of seller concentration, the degree of buyer concentration, the degree of product differentiation, and the condition of entry. These dimensions of structure have been emphasized because they appear to be the most important conditioning influences on market performance.

The list of probably or possibly relevant dimensions of market structure, however, does not end with the four mentioned. There are numerous other characteristics of individual industries that may be called "structural," either in a narrow, precise sense or in a more broad and loose sense, and that obviously have some influence on the character of market conduct and performance.

Using "structure" in the broadest possible sense, every technological, institutional, geographical, legal, and psychological characteristic of the selling firms of an industry, its buyers, and the framework within which both operate might be considered as dimensions of the market structure. And, in a sense, the complete "structure" of each industry, thus construed in its myriad dimensions, should in a sense fully "explain" conduct and performance in that industry.

But structure in this sense would provide no useful explanation of differences among industries in conduct and performance, since each industry would present in some degree a unique structural situation. The classification of industries for purposes of generalization would be impossible. We would have no way of knowing which structural differences among industries accounted for the observed conduct-performance differences. It is thus expedient for scientific as well as for policy purposes to emphasize a very few apparently leading dimensions of market structure, and to look for their roles in explaining inter-industry differences in behavior, whatever the further influence may be of the special, peculiar characteristics of numerous individual industries.

Thus we will not extend our analysis and investigation of market structures here to include further dimensions of structure or further environmental characteristics of individual industries. If we were to extend our list a little further, however, the following industry characteristics might deserve attention: (1) the geographical structure of the market, with reference to the pattern of seller locations and buyer locations, considered in the light of the importance of the transportation costs of delivery; (2) the degree of durability of the product in use; and (3) the "trend of demand" for industry output—whether it is secularly growing, declining, or remaining more or less stable. Distinguishing industries on these criteria might offer added explanations of observed differences in market conduct and performance.

SUPPLEMENTARY READINGS

Bain, J. S., *Barriers to New Competition*, 1956, Ch. I–VI.
Sylos-Labini, P., *Oligopoly and Technical Progress*, 1962.

9

Market Conduct in American Industries

The market structure of an industry is a strategic part of the framework, environment, or "situation" within which its member firms engage in profit-seeking activities. Of these activities, an important proportion is frequently characterized as comprising the market behavior or market conduct of the firms. And market conduct within any industry ultimately generates some sort of market performance, or set of end results, that may be measured in several dimensions. In Chapters 5, 7, and 8 we have suggested that an industry's market structure influences or helps determine the market conduct and performance of its firms. We have also presented some theoretical predictions concerning the influences that seller and buyer concentration, product differentiation, and the condition of entry are likely to have on conduct and performance. In this chapter we give much more detailed attention to both the hypothetically possible and the actual market conduct of firms, and to the relationships between market structure and market conduct.

As already noted in Chapter 2, market conduct refers mainly to two closely interrelated phases of the business enterprise behavior. For the firms in any industry acting as sellers, these are:

1. The manner in which, and the devices and mechanisms by which, the different sellers in the industry coordinate their intrinsically rivalrous decisions and actions, adapt them to each other, or succeed in making them mutually consistent—as they react to demands for their products in a common market.

2. The character of pricing policies and related market policies that the sellers in the industry adopt, assessed in terms of the individual or

collective aims or goals that they pursue as they determine their selling prices, their sales-promotion outlays, the designs and qualities of their products, and so forth. Because the aims of market policies are frequently implemented by and perhaps reflected in the methods that firms use in determining prices, selling costs, and the like, these procedures also comprise a part of market conduct.

Essentially subsumed under the character of market policies and the devices and mechanisms of rivalry and coordination is a subphase of market conduct that probably deserves to be singled out. This is:

3. The extent of the use, if any, by established firms in the industry of "predatory tactics" designed to weaken or eliminate established competitors, and of "exclusionary tactics" aimed at discouraging the entry of potential new competitors—and the character of such tactics if they are employed. Although the dividing line is sometimes hazy, predatory and exclusionary tactics are generally distinguishable from the "normal" market policies pursued and devices of competition and coordination used by the firms of an industry.

In the language of the law as applied in antitrust action, the market conduct of sellers embodies the composite of "acts, practices, and policies" of sellers in arriving at and in some way coordinating their several decisions as to what prices to charge, what outputs to produce, what selling costs to incur, what product designs to offer, what actual or potential competitors to discourage, and so on. The potential scope and content of the conduct of buyers is parallel, although the actual variety of buyers' conduct patterns is much smaller. Throughout most of this chapter we refer to the market conduct of sellers only, thereafter appending some remarks on the conduct of buyers.

Market conduct so construed is evidently a complex thing, encompassing numerous major and subsidiary dimensions of enterprise behavior. It would not be rewarding to explore it in detail in every one of its aspects. Here we will abbreviate and simplify (to a certain extent oversimplify) discussion of it by considering separately in the succeeding main sections of the chapter:

1. Determination of selling prices and outputs by sellers.
2. Determination of selling costs and products by sellers.
3. Predatory and exclusionary tactics of sellers.
4. The market conduct of firms acting as buyers.

In the first two of these sections, we will discuss in turn (though in greater detail in the section on pricing) the following:

(*a*) Types and modes of inter-seller coordination, cross-adaptation, and rivalry. The major emphasis here will be on whether or not the market policies of rival sellers are arrived at in a completely independent fashion, and, if not, which of a variety of patterns of interdependent, collusive, or concerted action is pursued.

(*b*) Alternative principles or aims of the market policies of sellers. The primary questions here concern whether the guiding aims of these policies are joint profit maximization by an industry's sellers as a group, independent profit maximization by individual sellers, some hybrid of the preceding two aims, or any of several alternative aims.

(*c*) "Combined" patterns of the market conduct of sellers, incorporating both modes of rivalry and coordination and goals of policy.

(*d*) The relationship of market conduct to market structure.

(*e*) Empirical evidence of actual patterns of market conduct.

The succeeding sections on predatory and exclusionary tactics and on the market conduct of buyers are much briefer and center mainly on actual patterns of conduct.

Sellers' Conduct in Determining Prices and Outputs

For both individual sellers and cooperating groups of sellers, a matter of first importance is the determination of the selling price of the product and of the quantity of output that will be produced and offered for sale.

In logic, the two decisions are strictly interdependent. In a given situation, that is, determination of a selling price implies a corresponding unique determination of output sold, and vice versa. Suppose that buyer incomes, propensities to spend, and preferences among different goods are given, as are products, sales-promotion outlays, and the prices of other products. Then there is presumably a unique relationship, for any firm or industry, between the selling price charged for output and the quantity of output buyers will purchase. At each alternative price some specific alternative quantity will be bought, and conversely, each specific quantity offered for sale will command a corresponding price.[1]

---

[1]For example, the demand for product A in a given situation may be such that buyers will take 10,000 units per month if the price is $1.00 per unit, 11,000 units per month if the price of 95 cents per unit is charged, and 12,500 units per month if the price is 90 cents per unit. Now if sellers set a price of 95 cents per unit, they have effectively determined their saleable output (inventory accumulation or decumulation aside) at 11,000 units per month. If, conversely, they do not set a price at all but simply produce and offer 11,000 units of output for sale for what it will bring, buyer demands will tend to bring the selling price of this output to 95 cents.

Nonetheless, sellers do have a choice of procedure in making the price-output decision, between announcing a selling price and then supplying whatever output buyers choose to take at that price, or deciding to produce and offer a certain output for whatever price it will bring.

Both procedures are used at one place or another in the business economy. But the practice of setting price, and leaving output to be determined by market demands at that price, is far more common than that of setting output and leaving price to be determined. Preference for the price-setting approach stems in part from a normally prevailing uncertainty as to how much can be sold at a given price, or as to what price buyers will pay for a given output. Sellers then find it less risky to their profits to gamble on how much they can sell at a price than on what price they can get for a given output. Furthermore, by fixing a price rather than an output, possibly disruptive variations in price among different buyers, attributable to imperfections in the market or to exercise of bargaining power by individual buyers, are minimized.

In the great majority of markets, therefore, we will find sellers approaching their price-output problems by calculating and announcing selling prices. The alternative policy of determining outputs to be offered and "letting price take care of itself" is found usually only in industries of relatively atomistic structure, in which the individual seller faces a well-publicized going market price for all industry output—a price that will not be much influenced by the quantity he decides to produce and offer for sale.[2] These are mainly extractive industries like those in agriculture, lumbering, and crude petroleum production.[3]

Whether it is price or output that is directly determined by sellers in an industry, however, two interrelated questions arise concerning their conduct. First, do they act independently or interdependently in making their decisions? Second, what aims do they pursue and what methods do they follow in determining prices and outputs?

---

[2] This going and generally known market price in turn may result either from the operation of highly organized central markets for the goods in question, or from the domination of the market by a few large buyers, who simply determine and announce a fixed buying price.

[3] The main exceptions to this rule would appear to be found in the operation of comprehensive collusive agreements in some oligopolistic industries, by the terms of which output quotas are assigned to most or all of the participating sellers as a means of sharing the market. But even in many of these cases, one or a few dominant sellers have been without quotas, this leaving them in a position to fix price and to supply the residual output (over and above the total of quota outputs) demanded at that price.

Independent, Collusive, and Quasi-Collusive
Price and Output Determination

The layman's first question about competition in an industry is almost automatically something like this: "Do the sellers in industry really compete by acting independently in setting their prices or outputs, or do they just get together and agree on what prices they will charge or what outputs to produce?" In asking it, he often implies the existence of a sort of black-or-white dichotomy between "independent, competitive" pricing on the one hand, and consensual, collective, or collusive pricing on the other.

Unfortunately for the economist's peace of mind, things are not this simple. Both collusion and independence are matters of degree, and there is a wide variation of degrees, types, and forms of either. Correspondingly, *complete collusion* and *complete independence* are in a strict sense only extreme or polar types of conduct that mark the two ends of a wide spectrum of conduct patterns. Most actual patterns lie at various places between the two extremes and embody elements of both collusion and independence. As a result, we must recognize and identify at least several major patterns of market conduct (so far as the character of interseller relationships is involved), ranging from the collusive pole to the independence pole.

Complete independence in the conduct of sellers in an industry refers to a conduct pattern with two essential characteristics. First, each firm makes its price or output decisions unilaterally and without engaging in prior consulation with or entering into any form of agreement with its competitors. After each makes any unilateral price or output decision, it observes what the others have done and may then competitively revise its decision, so that a process of competitive adjustments is potentially generated.

But the absence of collusion alone is not sufficient. For although each of several rival sellers acts unilaterally, all may be strongly interdependent because each supplies a large enough fraction of the common market that his own price or output adjustments would significantly affect the sales and profits of his rivals. They would be expected to react to his adjustments with counter-adjustments of their own, and each would therefore temper or modify his own price and output adjustments in the light of the anticipated reactions of rivals. Then a distinct mutually recognized interdependence of rival price and output policies would be found, with a variety of interesting potential consequences not necessarily dissimilar to those of collusion. This has been suggested in the first part of Chapter 5, in the discussion of oligopolistic market structures.

Second, therefore, complete independence of seller conduct requires also that, in making his unilateral price-output decisions, each individual seller takes no account of possible reactions of rivals to these decisions. This is tantamount to saying that under complete independence he assumes that neither his rivals' prices nor their outputs will be induced to change significantly by any contemplated adjustments in his own price or output. For this to be true, of course, it must also be true that his own price or output adjustments will have negligible effects on the prices or sales volumes of his rivals—that the general level of price and output in the market as a whole will not be much influenced by the action of any individual seller. The necessary structural condition for complete independence of market conduct, therefore, is that the industry should be made up of a large number of small firms, no one of which supplies or is likely to supply a significant fraction of total industry output.

The other pole of conduct in price-output determination is complete collusion among the rival sellers in an industry. Collusion in general implies that the sellers in some manner arrive at an understanding as to what price to charge or what outputs to produce, or both. If collusion is not only complete but "perfect"—as it sometimes almost has been in some European cartels—it embodies the following elements: (*a*) all sellers in the industry are included in the agreement; (*b*) the agreement is definite, and enforceable on all parties to it; (*c*) it covers both the price to be charged and the quantity of output to be produced by each agreeing seller, the output allocations being calculated so as to minimize the aggregate cost of producing the indicated industry output; (*d*) it also incorporates a formula for distributing the profits of the combined operations among the agreeing of parties, not necessarily in proportion to their assigned individual outputs and sales; (*e*) all parties rigorously adhere to the terms of the agreement. In this sort of perfect cartel, all agreeing sellers would operate essentially as if controlled by a single monopolistic firm.

Collusion is complete, however, if fewer conditions than those just named are satisfied. In effect, the following three should suffice: all sellers in the industry are parties to the agreement; all rigorously adhere to its terms; and the agreement embodies an unambiguous mutual understanding which fixes the price or prices to be charged and/or the individual outputs to be produced. (Determination of individual market shares at an agreed-upon price may not be covered.) Other things being equal, complete collusion would seem to provide a feasible maximum chance for the establishment of a joint monopoly price and output by rival sellers. But it will not necessarily support such a price policy, for reasons that were suggested in Chapter 5 in our discussion of oligopolistic markets and later will be developed further.

A completely collusive agreement does not have to be either an express agreement in writing or an express oral agreement arrived at through direct consultation. It may instead be a tacit agreement or "unspoken understanding," arrived at through the rival sellers' experiences with each others' behavior over time, repeated until all sellers tacitly understand that they will act together uniformly, in a well-defined and regular manner, in determining prices and outputs.[4]

Between the poles of complete independence and complete collusion there lie a wide variety of conduct patterns embodying some blend of collusion and independence. These "in-between" patterns may be characterized as involving *incomplete collusion,* which is marked by a failure to fulfill one or more of the three conditions sufficient for complete collusion—namely, all sellers being parties to price or output agreement, all adhering to its terms, and the terms being unambiguous. The great bulk of all observed conduct pattern lie somewhere within the in-between range of incomplete collusion—with elements of collusion and elements of independence. A variety of types of incomplete collusion can be identified, of which we may (by simplifying greatly) recognize three:

[4]Thus, for example, a group of sellers may all adopt, and tacitly agree to continue using, a uniform "rule of behavior" which if followed is equivalent to an agreement to fix uniform prices. A common version of such a convention is found in so-called "price leadership" systems, in which a principal seller (usually the largest) takes the lead in making any change in prices in the industry, and in which all the rival firms regularly follow his lead in each price change and always charge prices identical to his. If this convention is unambiguously understood by every seller in the industry, and always followed rigorously and without exception, the pattern of conduct is one of complete price collusion implemented by tacit agreement. We will see shortly, however, that many or most forms of price leadership are subject to imperfections which do not permit them to qualify as systems of complete collusion.

As suggested in Chapter 5, there are some minimal structural conditions for the emergence and survival of complete collusion as a pattern of market conduct. The most important of these—a necessary but not sufficient condition—is that the number of sellers in the industry shall be sufficiently small, and the degree of seller concentration sufficiently high, that it is feasible for agreements including all sellers to be arrived at, and further that there is a reasonable probability that all of the sellers will abide rigorously by the agreement. Agreements are practically impossible to arrive at if the number of sellers involved is large and unwieldly. Furthermore, for agreements (if arrived at) to be viable, in the sense that all participants observe their terms, the individual sellers must be few enough, and control large enough individual market shares, that the defection of any of them from the terms of an agreement would perceptibly affect the welfare of his rivals, and invite attention and retaliation. Lacking this prerequisite, collusion if attempted will generally be incomplete and possibly unstable.

1. *Incompletely Observed Collusion.* There is a collusive agreement among sellers (express or tacit) aimed at fixing prices or outputs, but it is not rigorously observed by some or all of the sellers. There are defections from or violations of the agreement, frequently in the form of clandestine price cutting under uniform announced prices. This results in actual prices which fail to correspond closely and at all times to agreed-upon and announced prices, and may also result in sellers initially agreeing on lower prices than otherwise.

2. *Collusion with Indefinite Terms of Agreement.* There is an express or tacit collusive agreement among sellers affecting prices or outputs, but its terms are at least somewhat ambiguous, or ambiguously understood by some or all sellers. Therefore, the price and output policies of individual sellers are likely to be somewhat at variance, and perhaps somewhat influenced by independent decision-making.

3. *Collusion with Incomplete Participation of the Industry Members.* There is an express or tacit agreement among sellers affecting prices or outputs, but not all of the sellers in the industry are parties to the agreement, or even nominal adherents to it. Thus, there is a group of agreeing sellers (normally the large principal firms of the industry), and a group of nonagreeing "independents" (normally sellers with small market shares) who act independently in adjusting to the collusive actions of the agreeing sellers, and who possibly follow divergent price policies.

In addition, we must recognize a pattern of market conduct that is closely related if not strictly "collusive"—namely:

4. *Interdependent Action without Agreement.* There is no express agreement, and really not a sufficiently sustained uniformity of action over time to permit inference of a tacit agreement. But either some or all of the sellers in the industry, acting unilaterally without the guidance of an agreement or of a mutually accepted traditional convention for price-output determination, condition their decisions in the light of anticipated reactions of some or all rivals. For example, they may raise prices only if they anticipate that rivals will roughly match their actions, and cut them only when it is desirable to do so even in the face of anticipated matching price cuts by rivals. Thus, although we do not find "collusion," we ascertain a significant departure from complete independence of action as previously defined.

The preceding appear to be the principal variant types of quasi-collusive, quasi-independent seller conduct. But they are not mutually exclusive, nor is it always clear in which category a particular observed conduct pattern belongs. And a given conduct pattern may belong in two or more of the categories at once. For example, we may find a pattern of incompletely collusive conduct which qualifies for inclusion in the first category because the agreement is not rigorously observed by its adherents, in the second because the terms of the agreement are somewhat ambiguous, and in the third because some sellers in the industry are not even nominal adherents to the agreement. A single sort of imperfection, of course, may be dominant in various individual cases.

Difficulty is encountered especially in distinguishing between interdependent action without agreement (4) and incomplete collusion of various sorts (1, 2, or 3). Suppose that each of the several sellers in a concentrated industry follow "conspicuously parallel" price policies, implemented by a loosely observed system of price leadership in which all the rivals of the largest firm nearly always (but not quite always) follow the announced price changes of the largest firm, almost never changing their quoted prices except by following the leader, and thus charge prices that nominally are nearly always identical. And suppose also that some of these sellers occasionally or frequently make unofficial or semi-secret-secret concessions from their quoted prices to some of their customers. The economist observing this conduct may be hard put to say whether this is incomplete tacit collusion on the one hand, or interdependent action without agreement on the other. And the issue of which it is seems largely a semantic one, without substantive importance. The semantic issue may become crucial, however, in an antitrust suit in which the sellers are accused of illegal collusion in restraint of trade under the Sherman Act. The prosecution would invariably argue that there was an express or tacit agreement (illegal), whereas the defense would argue that the parallel action had no basis in agreement and that each seller acted independently (legal).

The relatively small significance of the lines between categories is emphasized if we recognize that within each of the four types of conduct pattern designated there can be a wide range of different subpatterns. With collusion (types 1, 2, and 3) there may be a wide range of different degrees of incompleteness in the collusion. Defection from the agreement may range from slight and occasional to significantly large and persistent. If there is ambiguity in the terms of the agreement, this again may range from slight to very significant. And a failure of some sellers to subscribe or adhere to the agreement may involve only a few sellers of insignificant size and with no real influence on the market, or a vigorous group of "independents" supplying a significant fraction of total market output.

In the same vein, interdependence without agreement may range from the very strong interdependence of a very few large sellers to the comparatively slight interdependence in an industry of low-moderate concentration. In effect, we may expect to find under each of the four forms of nonindependent conduct a variety of subpatterns ranging from "close-to-monopolistic" (conspicuously concerted or parallel collective action, as if under the control of a single firm), to "close-to-competitive" (dominated, as a matter of emphasis, by true independence of action). And it is not possible to say *a priori* that one form of hybrid conduct is generally "more monopolistic" in its tendencies than another.

It might therefore be more meaningful to classify hybrid market conduct patterns not according to whether they are "collusive" and to the sorts of incompleteness of collusion, but according to the degree of incompleteness of collusion and the degree of seller interdependence. Although this is abstractly quite possible, such a classification has little operational usefulness because of the great difficulty encountered in classifying actual cases according to this principle. The finer distinctions required for such a classification cannot be successfully made in practice by observing conduct *per se*, but only by observing the market performance to which the conduct gives rise.

Specific Forms of Collusive and Interdependent Behavior

Having identified general types of conduct patterns, we may now recognize some specific forms which collusive and kindred activity commonly take. The detailed forms are so numerous that a full catalogue of them would be boring, but a few commonly encountered ones deserve a brief description.

A first form is the direct agreement of sellers to fix prices or outputs at specified levels. For example, all sellers agree to charge a single common price, or to produce only certain assigned output quotas. Such agreements are typically "express" in character, based on direct consultation, communication, and exchange of promises, though the actual agreement may be oral rather than written. Complete collusion may result from such agreements, but so may various sorts of incomplete collusion.

Direct and express agreements are not frequently discovered in the United States (so far as they exist, they are concealed), because the antitrust laws prohibit them. The examples that are familiar have often revolved around the licensing of patent rights. For example, the holders of patents have in some instances attached conditions limiting output or fixing price to the licenses which permitted sellers in an industry to use the patented production technique or produce the patented product, this on the theory that the legal monopoly inherent in the patent grant gave the resulting agreement immunity from the antitrust laws. (Court decisions of the past several decades have tended to undermine this theory.)

A second form of collusive action—and a very common one in the American economy—is price leadership (and "followership"). In its simplest form it involves the adoption by some or all of the sellers of an industry of the following sort of uniform "rule of behavior." One seller (usually the largest) is the "price maker" or price leader for the industry, establishing the price which all conforming firms will charge and initiating all price changes. The other sellers who conform to the rule charge prices identical to that of the leader (or prices related to his price in a rigid fashion), and always follow the price increases and decreases of the leader. The pattern of conduct is generally implemented by public quotation or announcement of selling prices by the leader and his followers.

If the price-leadership convention is rigorously followed, the ostensible conduct pattern is the same as if the sellers had agreed to charge uniform prices at a level fixed by the leading firm. Actually, of course, adoption and continued observance of the convention may rest on an express agreement among the conforming sellers to follow the rule of behavior in question, and the leader's price may be determined by secret consultation among the agreeing parties. Evidence of such direct consensual action not being found (and it seldom is), it is more usual to recognize price leadership as a form of tacit collusion, resulting from the existence of an unspoken agreement. The notion of tacit agreement, however, is itself somewhat nebulous, and it seems perhaps equally appropriate to designate the conduct pattern in question as one of interdependent seller action without basis in agreement.

Price leadership may of course implement either complete collusion or collusion that is incomplete in various ways and degrees. Failure of some sellers in the industry to observe the convention is possible, and a pattern at least occasionally observed is one wherein the large, principal sellers of the industry follow a price leader, but a fringe of small sellers do not. Under some price-leadership schemes in operation for many years, sporadic defections from the leader's price have been encountered when a usually conforming follower failed to follow a lead to a higher price or initiated an independent price cut. And a common pattern is one in which all followers nominally adhere to the leader's price by announcing identical prices, but regularly make secret or unannounced price concessions to individual buyers.

Under this last pattern, the size of the average difference between actual and quoted prices may influence the price leader in setting the quoted price. If price concessions become persistent and large, he may be induced to lower the quoted price in order to "recognize" the actual state of the market. If there are almost no concessions at all, and perhaps some unofficial premium prices being secured, he may recognize the market by raising the quoted price. If the price leader reacts in the indicated fashion, we may discover what has been called "barometric price leadership," in which the price leader acts as a sort of barometer who recognizes, in his price quotations, the effective results of price rivalry in the market. It has been mistakenly argued by some that barometric price leadership is generally associated with competitive pricing of the sort attributable to atomistic markets. In fact, since oligopolistic interdependence may be far from fully undermined by the price concessions that influence the barometric leader, pricing somewhere in a range betwen competitive and monopolistic levels is at least equally probable.[5]

The possibilities for the undermining of price leadership by independent price concessions are often anticipated and occasionally dealt with by the development of supplementary collusive uniformities (express or tacit) among the sellers, aimed at averting various sorts of nonuniform price concessions. These include uniformities in the functional classification of customers for purposes of allowing price discounts, in the sizes of discounts granted customers of a given class, in the structure of "quantity-discount" schedules, and so forth. Where sellers are disparately located and freight costs of delivery are high, a common uniformity involves adoption of uniform methods for calculating the delivered prices (at destinations of shipments) that buyers will be charged—to the end that the delivered prices of all sellers at any delivery point will be uniform. The so-called basing-point system of prices, under which all sellers calculate any delivered price as the factory price at the designated "basing point" factory or mill which is nearest the buyer, plus freight from that nearest basing point—regardless of the location from which the actual shipment takes place—is a common device for securing uniformity in delivered prices. In general, numerous supplementary collusive uniformities are present in markets in which price leadership implements reasonably complete collusion.

A third form of collusive conduct that occurs with some frequency involves the mutual adoption by rival sellers of a different sort of rule of

---

[5]For discussion of this issue see J. W. Markham, "The Nature and Significance of Price Leadership," *American Economic Review*, **XLI** (1951), 891–905; and J. S. Bain, "Price Leaders, Barometers, and Kinks," *Journal of Business*, **XXXIII** (1960), 193–203.

behavior. In effect all sellers adopt a uniform accounting system for determining their costs of producing one or more products, so that their costs, as calculated according to the same rules, will be identical or closely similar so long as the wage rates, material prices, and so on that they pay are the same. Furthermore, all sellers determine the relationship of their selling prices to their costs by using a uniform formula (for example, the addition of a uniform percentage to production cost). Then their "independently" determined prices will turn out to be closely similar and perhaps identical. This kind of collusion, usually based on at least some express consensual activity, can be reasonably complete, but of course it can be quite incomplete also. In addition to defections from the prices arrived at by using the adopted formulas, and nonadherence by some sellers to the formulas, there is ordinarily at least some uneliminable ambiguity in the resultant agreement on prices, so that the collusion which is arrived at by this route is likely to be significantly incomplete.

Let us now turn to conduct patterns involving interdependent seller action without agreement. A recognized interdependence exists among a group of sellers in an industry when each of them in turn controls a sufficient share of the common market that his price changes (or output adjustments) will have a significant effect on the selling prices or sales volumes of the others, so that competitors will react to his price-output adjustments. Each of the sellers then recognizes this and sets or alters his price or output in the light of anticipated reactions by his rivals. This recognized interdependence, when it occurs, may involve all of the sellers in an industry or only some of them. For example, the large sellers in an industry may have a mutually recognized interdependence, but the members of a fringe of small sellers may not recognize interdependence either with each other or with the large sellers. Also, the interdependence which does exist may be strong or weak, tending generally to be stronger as the degree of seller concentration is higher, as argued in Chapter 5.

When recognized interdependence is significantly present, true or complete independence of action by the individual sellers is no longer rationally to be expected. Each interdependent seller presumably makes his price-output decisions only in the light of anticipated reactions of his rivals, and the composite of their several policies comes to comprise an interdependent whole. If price determination is the matter at issue, for example, the individual seller is likely (*a*) to wish to arrive at a most profitable level of selling price; but (*b*) to be willing to raise his price significantly above the going industry level only if he anticipates that his rivals will then make similar price increases, so that he does not lose customers to them; and (c) to undertake significant and open price cuts only in the anticipation that his rivals will more or less match those cuts, this precluding him from appropriating their customers by virtue of a lower price. Thus the prices of the interdependent rivals are likely to move more or less together, and on the average stay in a more or less balanced relationship, although they may attain various different levels. Two things are clear. The scope for truly independent action, and for its influences on industry price, is smaller as the degree of interdependence is greater, and vice versa. And there is always some amount of uncertainty as to how pricing will develop, in view of each seller's dependence, in making his own policies, upon conjectures concerning the reactions of rivals.

This uncertainty is not infrequently resolved by schemes of express or tacit collusion of the sorts described earlier. But this is not always the case, and we observe numerous markets in which interdependent sellers, without the use of agreements or comparable devices, act unilaterally in a manner far different from that associated with complete seller independence. The resulting rationale of conduct can be described in various terms.

One appropriate concept is that of "implicit bargaining." Every publicly announced price (or output) change that an interdependent seller makes is implicitly an invitation to his rivals to react in some acceptable way, or, in other words, an implicit bargaining offer made without direct communication. (Will you match my price increase? If not, I will withdraw it.) This being so, an implicit bargaining process to fix a mutually acceptable level of selling price may automatically emerge among the rival sellers, possibly culminating in a tacit agreement on price. We thus see the inevitable blurring of the line between "tacit collusion" and "interdependent action without collusion." The principal identifiable difference is perhaps that with the latter no repetitive routine of action or mutually adopted uniform rule of behavior is in evidence.

Another concept is that of the "game". Individual sellers may be viewed as engaging in a game of strategy and tactics, each calculating his moves so as to maximize his advantage subject to restricting or minimizing the risk he takes. There is a "games theory" which predicts possible outcomes of such games. One—but only one—of the definitely possible outcomes is coalition or collusion among the opposing players to exploit a third party—that is, the buyer. Whatever names we give it, we recognize there a sort of conduct which is in general somewhere intermediate between complete collusion and complete independence.

Patterns of interdependent conduct are not infrequently bolstered by supplementary collusive activities which assist sellers in making their policies. Such activities typically involve the systematic exchange of information among rival sellers as to what price they are charging or intend to charge, what volume of sales or advance orders they are experiencing, and so forth. Information of this sort from some sources is essential to effective interdependent action, since one seller can hardly react intelligently to the policies and market experiences of others until he knows what those policies and experiences are. And truly independent pricing action by the individual seller is encouraged as long as he can keep his price adjustments secret from his rivals at the time they are made and for some interval thereafter, but discouraged if all rivals are keeping each other informed of their moves in the market at all times. Thus we find in many markets various systems for the exchange of trade information among rival sellers, under so-called plans of "open" competition. Given a sufficient exchange of information, sellers may proceed unilaterally to establish their own prices, and the net result may be action comparable, for example, to that obtained with incomplete collusion. That this is probable has been recognized by the courts under the antitrust laws, which have frequently found elaborate schemes for the exchange of trade information among sellers to be evidence of an illegal conspiracy aimed at restraining competition.

Aims and Methods of Price Determination

In pursuit of the task of identifying the principal alternative types of seller conduct in determining prices and outputs, we have so far recognized several main patterns of interseller relationship or coordination. Characterization of a conduct pattern in these terms alone, however, is not a complete or necessarily meaningful description, because it deals with only one aspect of the pattern of market conduct. To describe satisfactorily any given conduct pattern, we must specify not only the degree and type of interseller coordination, *but also the aims that the sellers involved pursue in deciding what outputs to produce and what prices to charge*, and the methods "of price calculation" that the sellers individually or jointly employ.

Our remaining task in identifying alternative patterns of market conduct must thus proceed along the following lines. First, we must identify the main alternative aims and methods of price-output determination that sellers in various settings may or do employ. Second, we must attempt to ascertain the possible and probable associations of the aims and methods of price determination with the character of the pattern of interseller coordination—so that we may determine, for each type of

interseller coordination, what aims and methods of price-output determination ordinarily are or may be sought or employed.

Let us first consider the general alternative aims or goals of price
determination that sellers may seek to attain in determining prices and
outputs. Simplifying greatly and abstracting from numerous matters of
detail, the following alternative aims may be distinguished:

1. *Joint Profit Maximization.* The aim, subscribed to in common by
the sellers in the industry, is the coordinated adjustment of all prices
and outputs to the point that will yield the largest aggregate of profit
to all firms combined. (Typically in the absence of a perfect cartel,[6] the
aim is actually the largest aggregate profit obtainable subject to the con-
straint that each seller derives his own profit only from his own sales,
and that various sellers thus secure market shares that are not necessarily consistent with minimizing the aggregate cost of industry output.
This constrained maximization tends to yield a slightly smaller profit
than a perfect cartel could secure.) For firms operating through time,
this means the largest aggregate of all present and future profits of all
firms, the profits of more remote years being appropriately discounted
to allow for waiting and risk.[7]

The pursuit of joint profit maximization by a group of firms implies
a coordination, by some device, of all individual firm actions for the
common purpose of obtaining the greatest combined profit. It also implies suppression of rivalrous moves by individual firms such as might
be aimed at enhancing the profit of one firm at the expense of the total
profits of all. The implied procedure of calculation of the joint profit-
maximizing price and output involves (*a*) assessing the effect of
simultaneous and parallel variations of selling price by all sellers on
their combined quality of sales and sales revenue; (*b*) assessing the effect of sales and output variations (corresponding to price variations)
on their combined aggregate cost of production; and (*c*) finding that
particular combination of price and output which should yield the maximum excess of aggregate group revenues over aggregate group costs.
If all the firms of an industry observe the principle of joint profit maximization, they should be acting at least roughly "as a monopolist would."

Joint profit maximization by all firms in an industry, however, need
not involve seeking the largest possible profit for the industry. It should
do so persistently or in the long run if the established firms can maxi-

---

[6]See p. 307.

[7]Where the effects of alternative price-output policies on profits are uncertain,
simple profit maximization would dictate a course of action producing the largest
mean probable value of aggregate time-discounted profits, regardless of the degrees
of uncertainty surrounding the various mean probable values.

mize industry profits without attracting a significant entry of new firms to share these profits with them—that is, if in the terms employed in Chapter 8 entry is *blockaded*. It should do so for short periods if the barriers to entry are so low that established firms prefer the immediate high profits of entry-attracting prices to the very low long-run profits obtainable at a price low enough to forestall new entry—that is, if in the same terms entry is *ineffectively impeded*. But if there is a moderate or substantial barrier to entry, high enough to allow considerable profits without attracting new entrants but not high enough to permit maximization of industry profits without new entry occurring, established firms may maximize their own long-run joint profits by charging a "limit price." This is just low enough to forestall further entry, and lower than the price that would maximize industry profits. Entry, in the terms of Chapter 8, is *effectively impeded*. In such situations, the price consistent with joint profit maximization is lowered (and the size of industry output enlarged) because of established sellers' reactions to the threat of new entry.

In sum, we recognize three versions of joint profit maximization: long-run maximization of total industry profits with blockaded entry, short-run maximization of industry profits with ineffectively impeded entry, and long-run maximization of the joint profits of established firms with effectively impeded entry.

2. *Independent Profit Maximization.* The aim of the individual seller is to adjust his price or output so as to maximize his own profits, without regard to the effects of his adjustment on the profits earned by his rivals or by the industry as a whole. Correlatively, each seller pursuing this aim sets his price unilaterally and without consultation with his rivals, with whom he has no express or tacit agreement. This independence of the individual sellers' market adjustments, however, is not sufficient to assure that his aim is independent profit maximization.

A further necessary attribute of independent profit maximization is that the individual seller, in adjusting his price or output to secure a maximum profit for himself, does not take account—or at any rate full account—of any possible changes in his rivals' prices and outputs that his own adjustments might induce. In its full-fledged or extreme form, independent profit maximization would involve each firm acting on the assumption that its own price or output adjustments would induce no perceptible reaction by its rivals. When pursued, it implies that individual firms act selfishly to enhance their individual profits, disregard the effects of their collective price or output adjustments on total industry profits, and in so doing reduce to a competitive level the prices and profits of their rivals, of themselves, and of the industry as a whole.

In a less extreme or attenuated form, independent profit maximization may only involve each firm acting on the assumption that its own price and output adjustments will not be both fully and promptly matched (or otherwise reacted to) by its rivals. Therefore, the individual seller "strikes out alone," for example, in lowering his price or extending his output, with the expectation that his rivals will not instantaneously and exactly move in a parallel fashion. Independent profit maximization in its less extreme forms may thus be pursued by individual firms even though induced reactions of rivals to their unilateral adjustments are expected—provided:

(*a*) that the occurrence or magnitude of the reactions is uncertain,

(*b*) that "full matching" by rivals of independent price or output adjustments is not expected,

(*c*) that some significant delay in induced reactions is expected (as, for example, when independent price reductions are made secretly), or

(*d*) that the individual seller simply disregards probable rivals' reactions, or alternatively welcomes them as he seeks warfare in the market.

The obvious tendency of this sort of attenuated independent profit maximization, when pursued by many, most, or all firms in an industry, is toward a competitive lowering of prices and extension of outputs in some degree, relative to the prices and outputs that would result from joint profit maximization.

3. *Mixed or Hybrid Profit Maximization.* The aims involved here embody both joint profit maximization and independent profit maximization. In markets with a significant degree of seller concentration and oligopolistic interdependence, it should not be at all uncommon that the sellers involved are motivated simultaneously in various degrees by desires to maximize joint profits and desires to maximize individual profits at the expense of rivals. That is, there may be attempts at joint action oriented toward obtaining the largest combined profit, qualified or modified by individual attempts of various sellers to enhance their own positions to the ultimate detriment of group profits. This sort of ambivalent aim of pricing, discussed earlier in Chapter 5, is logically consistent with an interdependence of sellers that is significant but not strong enough to impose "automatically" a full joint profit-maximizing rationale.

Some typical mixtures of pricing principles may be found in industries:

(*a*) where some large sellers strive for joint profit maximization but some small competing sellers act more or less independently;

(*b*) where pricing aimed at joint profit maximization is undercut by secret defections of some or all sellers;

(*c*) where the danger of such undercutting discourages jointly acting sellers from trying initially for a price high enough to maximize joint profits.

Market conduct guided by such a hybrid aim tends to bring about somewhat lower prices and larger outputs than conduct oriented only to joint profit maximization (specifically to any of the three types of joint maximization mentioned), though the resulting prices may be lower by widely varying amounts.

4. *A "Maximin" of Profits.* What is implied here is a somewhat different version of the aim of maximizing "advantage" by the decision-making unit, whether this unit be a firm or a group of firms. Roughly, its aim is to obtain the largest possible profit consistent with a minimized risk of loss. More precisely, in any situation in which the profit outcome of each alternative course of action is subject to some uncertainty (possible outcomes ranging from worse to better), its aim would be to select that course of action (for example, that price or output) which would secure for it the largest profit if "the worst happened" under each alternative course. That is, the decision-making unit would seek the maximum of minimum possible gains, or "maximin" of profits. The implied course of action to be selected would be identical to that of simple profit maximization only in special or limiting cases.

The maximin pricing principle could be applied by a group of firms acting in solid concert, or by individual firms acting unilaterally. It is ordinarily thought to be most appropriate to explaining the unilateral actions of interdependent firms. Although its price-output outcomes are not usually predictable in precise terms, they would appear to lie mainly in the range of those attributable to hybrid (quasi-joint, quasi-independent) profit maximization.

5. *A "Fair" Profit.* Instead of trying to maximize anything, the firm or group of firms may aim simply to earn a "fair," "satisfactory," or "customary" rate of profit (a profit aggregate which bears a satisfactory or customary ratio to sales revenue or to investment). The specific content of this aim is intrinsically vague and ambiguous, however. What is fair or satisfactory cannot really be defined in terms of any unique principle, and will be a subjective matter to the specific firms involved and particular to the individual industry. (All's fair in love and war.") Were this pricing principle generally employed, a variety of *ad hoc* and arbitrary profit goals would be pursued by different industries.

So much for alternative general aims of pricing. Related to these aims are the methods employed in calculating what price to charge or output to produce—the formulas through which the target prices are computed. Again we must simplify, but the following general alternatives are most often mentioned:

1. The seller or group of sellers calculates the price to be charged and output to be produced by using "marginal" techniques. That is, it evaluates each possible price adjustment, or corresponding adjustment of output sold, from the standpoint of (*a*) the marginal changes it produces in the total sales revenues of the firm or group of firms, and (*b*) the marginal changes that simultaneously occur in the firm's or the group's aggregate costs of production. Then, if, for example, profit maximization is the goal, the decision-making unit would lower price (from some hypothetical high beginning level) and extend output so long as the resultant marginal addition to total revenue of the unit exceeded the resultant marginal addition to total cost. It would fix price and output just at the point where a further lowering of price and extension of output would add more to total costs than to total revenue. (Effective direct use of this technique would require that the sellers have much detailed information on the effects of successive price reductions on the physical volume of sales.)

2. The seller or group of sellers may arrive at selling prices by adding an established and inflexible percentage rate of profit to the costs of production per unit of output as calculated in some way. The most common measure of unit costs for this purpose is one of what unit costs would be at some "standard" or average expected rate of output—of "normal" costs.

3. The sellers may follow a similar cost-plus-margin formula for pricing, but vary the size of the margin in response to changing market conditions (for example, to the going level of demand for the product as related to available productive capacity).

4. Some sellers in an industry may arrive at price by imitating the prices of competitors. This is hardly a complete pricing method for a whole industry, since there must initially be a nonimitator who is imitated, and what *his* method of pricing is becomes crucial. But it may well describe the conduct of many individual sellers in many industries.

This list of general pricing methods or formulas could be extended, but to no particular purpose if our aim is generalization rather than particularization. One might inquire, indeed, as to why we should give much attention to the mechanical trivia of methods of price calculation, when the main issue concerns the aims of price calculation which are implemented, by whatever detailed device, by sellers in various types of market situation. This query is especially pertinent in view of the fact that the second and third methods of price calculation just listed (involving the addition respectively of a fixed and a flexible margin to a normalized unit cost) may easily be employed to arrive, at least approximately, at the same prices that "marginal" calculations would yield—although they could also result in arriving at different prices. In brief, very little can ordinarily be inferred from the ascertainable character of pricing-calculating methods *per se.*

Two reasons for giving some attention to pricing methods nevertheless deserve mention. First, supposing that some guiding aim of pricing has been consciously chosen by the firm or group, the accuracy or precision with which the aim is pursued may be significantly influenced by the price-calculating method employed in pursuing it. In particular, employment of typical simple pricing formulas may result in arriving at prices that are only very rough, average crude approximations to those aimed at. Second, it is frequently impossible for the investigator to learn what aim of pricing has been pursued in a given industry. Then he may wish to fall back on available evidence concerning pricing methods or formulas, and try to infer aims from them. As noted, however, there is a sufficient lack of simple relationship between aims and methods that definite inferences are hard to draw.

Total Patterns of Seller Conduct
and Their Predictable Significance

Having reviewed the major alternatives open to sellers with respect to two main aspects of their market conduct—the character of interseller coordination within the industry and the aims and methods of price calculation—we face a further task in distinguishing and evaluating alternatives. First, we must attempt to "put together" the two aspects of conduct in order to determine what variety of "total patterns" of conduct are open to sellers in various industries—patterns of conduct described in terms both of the character of interseller coordination and of the aims and methods of price calculation. Second, we must attempt to assess the implications of each identifiable total pattern of conduct, to the end of determining the extent to which different patterns are likely to have different consequences for market performance.

The two problems posed have frequently been "solved" by the application of simplified, heroic, and not very careful assumptions, with the following conclusions:

1. Complete collusion is "evidently" entered into in order to facilitate joint profit maximization, and this aim is generally pursued where col-

lusion is complete. Therefore, complete collusion tends to lead to a maximum of monopolistic output restriction and price raising.

2. Complete independence is evidently associated with independent, competitive profit maximization by each seller, and thus leads to an absence of monopolistic output restriction and price raising, or to the feasible maximum industry output and the feasible minimum price.

3. Incomplete collusion and interdependent action without collusion tend to be associated with or reflect either hybrid profit maximization or maximin pricing goals with performance results somewhere between those of complete independence and those of complete collusion—that is, with some monopolistic output restriction and price raising above the competitive level, but not as much as with complete collusion.

If this simple formulation could be accepted without serious qualification, we would have an easy means of distinguishing among the different observable patterns of interseller coordination in terms of their significance for market performance. Unfortunately, the formulation is very seriously oversimplified, and the following qualifications must be considered.

With respect to complete collusion, both the detailed meaning and general validity of the assumption that sellers involved generally try to maximize their joint profits may be questioned.

First, if they do set prices and outputs so as in some sense roughly to maximize their joint profits, the height of price and degree of output restriction consistent with this aim may vary quite widely according to the height of the barriers to entry to the industry. With entry essentially blockaded, the joint profit-maximizing price might be very high; with only moderate barriers to entry, it might be significantly lower (though still high enough to allow some long-run excess profit). Joint profit-maximizing policies in various cases of complete collusion may lead predictably to widely varying degrees of monopolistic price raising and output restriction.

Second, it is certainly conceivable that the terms of the agreement arrived at with complete collusion may not be such as to permit maximization of the joint profits of the agreeing sellers. Any virtual drive toward a joint profit-maximizing price may be tempered by the selfish, antagonistic motivations of individual sellers, who may be unwilling to agree upon such a high price because either (*a*) their rivals are more likely to violate the agreement by undercutting the high price, with resultant losses to them, or (*b*) their weaker rivals might grow fat on the accumulated profits resulting from the high price and become more dangerous antagonists in the future. Therefore, the final terms of an agreement with complete collusion, reflecting these considerations, may very well specify a price lower than a joint profit-maximizing one and result in a lower joint profit. This may be attributed to an essential admixture of individual profit-maximizing with joint profit-maximizing aims in pricing (to hybrid profit maximization), or to an application of maximin principles by each party to the agreement.

The preceding is deducible without introducing the possibility that the collusive sellers, instead of applying a maximizing rationale of any sort, simply might have an arbitrary or customary rate of profit as the goal of their agreement. If this were true, the potential results of complete collusion would be even more various.

Let us next turn to incomplete collusion in its several varieties. Are the intrinsic performance tendencies of this broad category of conduct likely to differ from those of complete collusion, and if so, in what ways? The main thing that distinguishes incomplete from complete collusion is that, when a degree of independence of action by some or all sellers is introduced, there probably will be an added emphasis on independent as opposed to joint profit maximization. Whatever the collusive pricing aim would have been with complete collusion, the aim is hybridized with the independent, competitive pursuit of individual profits by individual sellers.

If this is so, any completely collusive conduct pattern which becomes incomplete in one of the ways noted should have a general tendency to generate a "less monopolistic" performance—toward some lowering of price and extension of industry output as compared with the putative performance of complete collusion in the same setting. Incomplete collusion should thus probably lead on the average to a less monopolistic performance than complete collusion.

But only on the average, and not in such a way that all or nearly all industries with incomplete collusion will have lesser monopolistic tendencies than all or nearly all industries with complete collusion. The reasons for this are twofold. First, the high-water mark of completely collusive prices below which the incompleteness of collusion drags price (by some amount) is not itself uniform and fixed for all cases: it is a mark that will vary widely among cases. In some instances, the "complete collusion" price which incompleteness of collusion undercuts may be a very high one, corresponding to joint profit maximization with a complete barricade of entry. In other cases it may be a much lower price, corresponding to joint profit maximization with a significant threat of entry or to hybrid profit maximization by the completely collusive sellers. Therefore, one incompletely collusive price (undercutting a high completely collusive price) may in the net actually be higher

relative to costs than another completely collusive price that is at a reduced level because of threat of entry or of interseller conflicts shaping
the terms of the agreement. We should thus anticipate many instances
in which the performance under incomplete collusion is more monopolistic, as judged in terms of height of price and restriction of output,
than the performance in many other instances in which collusion is at
least nominally complete. The ranges of possible performance results of
complete and incomplete collusion *overlap* to a very significant degree.

Second, collusion may be incomplete in a wide range of possible degrees. Secret price concessions in violation of an agreement may range
from sporadic to persistent. The sellers that refuse to participate in an
agreement may range from a few insignificant ones to a number of some
significance, and so forth. Correspondingly, the predictable performance with incomplete collusion may vary nearly all the way from that
attributable to complete collusion to that attributable to complete independence of action. *On the average*, incomplete collusion is likely to
lead to a more competitive performance than complete collusion. But in
numerous individual instances, noticeable incompleteness of collusion
may be insufficient to produce performance results that are practically
distinguishable from those of complete collusion. Unless informed in
detail as to the aims and methods of price calculation employed in individual instances of complete and incomplete collusion (which we typically are not), we are in a poor position to predict, except in a broad
average sense, differences in the performance tendencies of incomplete
and complete collusion.

The same general dilemma is encountered in appraising the performance possibilities if interdependent seller action without collusion.
Here, with the degree of interdependence variable within wide limits
and depending roughly on the degree of seller concentration, "anything may happen." At one extreme (that of a very few large sellers
occupying the whole market, and all strongly interdependent) the effective rationale of action may well turn out to be joint profit maximization. Close to the other extreme (with moderately low concentration)
interdependence may place only a slight drag or brake on truly independent profit-maximizing action, with performance approaching but
not quite reaching the competitive standard. In between—and there is
a very wide range of in-between—an extensive variety of performance
tendencies may be observed, reflecting various hybrids of joint profit-
maximizing and independent profit-maximizing tendencies, or, alternatively, the application of maximin principles by the several individual sellers. Interdependent pricing without collusion may range all
the way from extremely monopolistic to extremely competitive. And

unless we are able to identify in detail the aims pursued and methods of price calculation applied in various individual cases (which we usually are not) we are in a poor position, at the level of prediction, to differentiate the performance tendencies of interdependent action from those of complete or incomplete collusion.

We have less difficulty in distinguishing the performance tendencies of complete independence of action. In the generally atomistic market structures in which such independence is found, adjustment of individual prices or outputs in order to maximize individual profits or at any rate to enhance them, without regard to the reactions of competitors or to the consequences of parallel independent actions by all sellers in the industry, seems to be the prevailing motif. The predictable consequences of this motif are "competitive" performance results from the industry: a feasible maximization of industry output and minimization of industry price. Only if all of the independently acting sellers followed an arbitrary rule of setting price enough above normal average costs to yield a customary or "fair" profit—and stuck to this rule to the extent of not competitively revising prices to enhance individual advantage—would the predictable performance outcome be different.

Let us now summarize our conclusions with respect to the predictable performance tendencies of market conduct conforming to the principal alternative patterns of interseller coordination:

1. Because of the potential wide variation in pricing aims pursued under complete collusion, incomplete collusion in its several varieties, and interdependence of sellers without collusion, a very wide range of alternative performance possibilities may be attributed to each pattern— a range roughly from the full monopolistic pole to near the competitive pole. These ranges of possible performance evidently overlap so thoroughly that it is difficult to distinguish meaningfully the predictable performance consequences of the three patterns of interseller coordination, except in a broad average sense. In individual cases, performance can be accurately predicted from market conduct patterns if we know the detailed pricing aims pursued and method of price-calculation applied, but ordinarily we do not have this information.

2. In terms of broad statistical averages, we might expect incomplete collusion, and possibly interdependent action, to lead to somewhat more competitive results than complete collusion. But, in view of the wide dispersion of individual tendencies around the central averages, this prediction is not especially useful in dealing with individual cases.

3. A convincing and useful distinction can be drawn, given the amount of relevant information available, between the performance tendencies of completely independent seller action on the one hand and

all forms of nonindependent action on the other. The former should lead in the great bulk of cases to more competitive results.

4. Such distinctions as can be made practically among different patterns of nonindependent market conduct have slight value as the basis for case-by-case predictions concerning market performance. Essentially this is because the detailed evaluation of any total conduct pattern—including an identification of the detailed aims pursued and methods of price calculation employed—ordinarily is not possible without (*a*) examining the connected market performance itself, and (*b*) then *inferring* the crucial characteristics of the conduct pattern from the observed performance.

As soon as this is recognized, we see that descriptions of conduct *per se* in individual cases have little independent significance in analyzing market behavior or predicting performance. For a knowledge of performance, *as well as a full description of the character of conduct itself*, we ordinarily need to examine market performance directly.

In the preceding, we have said much more about the alternative basic aims of pricing than about the methods or formulas which sellers apply in calculating prices. This is because, if the seller or sellers in an industry are pursuing some aim in determining prices, the methods or routes by which they arrive at these prices are relatively inconsequential and do not deserve emphasis in a general analysis. Only if the choice of a method supersedes the choice of an aim, or if a method is blindly pursued and the governing aim is whatever may be inferred from the method, does the method assume a role of general importance.

The question of method attracts our attention, therefore, only because a scattering of casual studies of a few industries in American and England have produced the following tentative findings. First, sellers observed do not seem to follow price-calculating procedures of the sort attributed to profit-maximizing sellers in textbooks on economic theory. That is, they do not expressly balance the marginal increments to cost against the marginal increments to sales revenue for each possible extension of output, in order to determine that precise price-output combination which will yield the largest profit. Second, they most frequently appear instead to calculate what price to charge by simply adding some profit margin to their average costs of production (or to what these average costs would be at a long-run average expected output). The profit margin added is frequently described as fair, conventional, or satisfactory. Third, the findings in question generally cast little light on whether and to what extent the margins added to cost differ among industries, and on whether the margins are inflexibly applied, or varied with changing conditions of overall demand and supply. (Evidence from other sources, however, suggests strongly that actual profit margins vary widely among industries, and that the margin added is at least very frequently flexible and responsive to changing market conditions.)

What do these findings, if true and widely applicable, imply about the character and rationale of price-calculating processes? One interpretation is that they reveal that sellers in general do not pursue profit maximization as a goal, but instead aim for more or less arbitrary profits or profit margins. Then conduct patterns and resulting performance would tend to be rather haphazardly determined, and not easily susceptible to logical analysis and explanation. It is of course at least hypothetically possible that this is true, but in terms of all available evidence not very probable. Even if in many cases prices are nominally determined by adding a profit margin to average costs, this does not warrant the inference that the aim of profit maximization (joint or separate) has been abandoned in favor of some really different alternative.

In fact, the procedure of arriving at price by adding a profit margin to average costs can be at least roughly consistent with pursuit of any of the maximizing principles we have discussed, provided that the profit margins added vary significantly from industry to industry. Firms in all industries could be "margin-adders" while simultaneously pursuing a full variety of alternative pricing aims. If all sellers in one industry (or their price leader) add a certain rigid high margin to costs in determining price, this can be roughly consistent with long-run joint profit maximization in a situation where entry is blockaded. If in another industry they add a more moderate margin, this can be roughly consistent with joint profit maximization subject to the threat of entry, the margin being just short of high enough to attract new entry. In a third industry, a margin yielding less than maximum joint profits may simply reflect a balance between conflicting drives toward joint and independent profit maximization. The arguments just presented are fully applicable to any pattern of conduct observed, whether collusive, incompletely collusive, interdependent, or independent. The fact is that margin-adding as a price-making device does not contradict or even seriously bring into question the hypothesis that a variety of maximizing aims of price making are systematically being pursued.

The main qualification to the preceding is that if the firms of an industry pursue a *rigid* margin-adding policy—always adding the same uniform margin to normal average cost in order to determine price, regardless of the current rate of output demanded or of other immediate market considerations—they can generally at best attain only a crude or long-run average approximation to the prices which would maximize joint or separate profits. Except under very special limiting conditions of demand and cost variation, precise month-to-month or year-to-year profit maximization (of whatever sort) would require some variation of the margin with variations in demand and in the rate of output. However, appropriate choice of a certain rigid margin is potentially quite consistent with a long-run average approximation to a profit-maximizing price. And if the margins applied are indeed varied with varying market condtions, the pricing procedure in question is potentally consistent with fairly precise maximizing policies.

We conclude in general that neither the essential pricing aims being pursued in an industry nor the character of its total conduct pattern is revealed by information of the sort ordinarily available on the methods or formulas of price calculation employed.

Market Conduct and Market Structure

We have argued that a classification of different patterns of market conduct of the sort that can be developed from available evidence provides a poor basis for predicting market performance. That is, it is not possible to link a distinct class of performance with each objectively distinguishable broad class of market conduct.

In *a priori* theory, of course, we may envisage a three-stage sequence of causation running from market structure to market conduct to market performance. That is, structure is systematically associated with or determines conduct; and conduct, as determined by structure, determines performance. Therefore, structure is associated systematically with performance by the link of its systematic association to conduct. But as we try through empirical investigation to implement or verify this sort of explanatory-predictive hypothesis, we find that actual patterns of market conduct cannot be fully enough measured to permit us to establish empirically a meaningful association either between market conduct and performance, or between structure and market conduct. It thus becomes expedient to test directly for net associations of market structure to market performance, leaving the detailed character of the implied linkage of conduct substantially unascertained.[8]

[8]For example, suppose we wish to test the prediction that structure A should lead to conduct pattern B which should lead to performance pattern C, whereas structure J should lead to conduct pattern K which should lead to performance pattern L. We thus are testing for an A to B to C relationship, and a different J to K to L relationship. But we cannot independently measure either B or K in precise enough fashion to verify the predictions fully. Nonetheless, we have something simpler to test—namely a prediction that A leads to C and that J leads to L. This can be tested if we can get adequate objective information only on market structure (A and J), and market performance (C and L), even though market conduct is practically unmeasurable. One of the three steps can be skipped for purposes of empirical testing, and the results of the test may still meaningfully confirm or disconfirm the essential predictions.

In spite of the fact that detailed appraisal of patterns of market conduct may thus not be strictly essential to our analytical purposes, we should inquire whether there are either theoretically predictable or empirically observable associations between the market structure on the one hand and market conduct on the other.

On the level of either observation or *a priori* prediction, there does not seem to be any very close association between patterns of interseller coordination and the character of market structure. Once we have recognized that there is a more or less axiomatic correspondence of atomistic market structure and complete independence of seller action, and turn to nonatomistic structures and nonindependent seller conduct, systematic structure-conduct relationships are difficult to predict or observe. The principal relevant dimensions of market structure would seem to be the degree of seller concentration in the industry, the condition of entry, and the degree of product differentiation. The main alternative conduct patterns are complete collusion, incomplete collusion of several varieties, and interdependent action without collusion. In general, almost any of these conduct patterns might theoretically be expected to be associated with any market structure outside the atomistic range. And empirical observation bears out this prediction.

High seller concentration, for example, does not lead inevitably to complete collusion. Sometimes this association is found, but in other high-concentration cases interdependent action without collusion is the evident pattern. Conversely, moderate seller concentration is not systematically associated with any special conduct patterns. Instances of complete collusion, incomplete collusion, and interdependent action without collusion are all discoverable in industries in this category. Nor does the degree of product differentiation or the condition of entry seem to have very much to do with the pattern of interseller coordination chosen.

A few general tendencies, however, may be noted:

1. High or very high seller concentration seems to be accompanied by interdependent action without evident collusion more often than does moderate seller concentration. And obvious and detailed collusive arrangements seem to appear with the greatest frequency in industries of only moderate concentration. This is perhaps because simple interdependence cannot be so fully relied on to effect mutually desirable market behavior when the number of sellers is larger and the degree of their interdependence less.

2. Where there is evident collusion, it tends to be incomplete in

various ways more frequently in the less concentrated than in the more concentrated industries.

3. Really high degrees of product differentiation, with any given degree of seller concentration, tend to be linked with simple interdependence without collusion (as distinct from collusion) much more frequently than lesser degrees of product differentiation. This is probably because with highly differentiated products an exact matching of the prices of rival sellers is not a prerequisite for effective joint action to exploit the market. But there are many highly concentrated industries with nominally strong product differentiation in which fairly close collusion for determination of a single uniform price is observable.

4. The height of barriers to entry does not appear to have, nor would it be predicted to have, much influence on the pattern of interseller coordination.

From a maze of these and other tendencies, no clear pattern of relationship between market structures and patterns of interseller coordination emerges. And, one might inquire, why should it? The several alternative patterns are potentially just alternative routes to the same goal, whatever the particular goal may be. ("There is more than one way of skinning a cat.") The particular choice of the device for ordering nonindependent seller action is relatively inconsequential and perhaps haphazard, since any of the devices, in a particular structural setting, can lead to roughly comparable performance results.

The crucial question, on the other hand, concerns how the aims of price determination that are pursued are related to market structure. Regardless of the apparent patterns of interseller coordination, does the choice between joint profit maximization, hybrid profit maximization, maximin pricing, and so forth, turn on the character of market structure? To this question, as we have already implied, we are not in a position to give an answer based on direct empirical observations of market conduct.

We do have available, however, as suggested in Chapters 5, 7, and 8, some theoretical hypotheses about how nonindependent price-calculating principles should be related to market structures, along the following lines:

1. High seller concentration should favor the pursuit of genuine joint profit maximization more than moderate or low seller concentration, because of the constraining force of a higher degree of interdependence among sellers.

2. More moderate seller concentration should be more conducive to

hybrid profit maximization—or its equivalent in maximin pricing—with the pursuit of individual profits significantly undermining the pursuit of joint profits.

3. The height of the barrier to entry should significantly influence the height of the price that will accomplish joint profit maximization for all established sellers. Therefore, so far as sellers strive for maximum joint profits, variations among industries in the height of entry barriers should tend to be accompanied by variations in the height of price relative to cost. But where the profit-maximizing aim is distinctly hybrid, the influence of the height of barriers to entry may be considerably weakened by that of independent pricing action.

4. So far as price-output determination by the industry is concerned, the degree of product differentiation should probably not have a significant influence on the aim of price calculation that is pursued.

The truth of such predictions cannot easily be checked by direct observations of market conduct in various structural situations—as we have already emphasized. There is a set of derived predictions, however, that are more susceptible to empirical check. That is, *if* high concentration tends to lead to joint profit maximization as an aim of conduct, it should also tend to lead to comparatively high prices and profits and comparatively great restriction of output on the level of performance. *If* moderate concentration tends to be associated with hybrid profit maximization on the level of conduct, it should tend to lead to lower prices and profits and larger outputs than high concentration. If higher barriers to entry mean that joint profit-maximizing prices are higher, then, at least among highly concentrated industries, high barriers to entry should lead to relatively higher prices, higher profits, and smaller outputs than moderate barriers. In effect, a series of predictions of the relationships of market structure to market performance are derived from predictions of structure-conduct associations. These predictions of structure-performance relations are much more easily susceptible to check. We will consider various empirical tests of predicted relationships between structure and performance in Chapter 11.

General Evidence on Actual Market Conduct in Determining Prices; Some Examples

In light of the dubious analytical significance of objective descriptions of market conduct, no great emphasis on empirical findings concerning actual conduct patterns seems justified here. This is probably just as well, because the available evidence on market conduct is, except for a very few industries, extremely scattered and incomplete. It may be useful, nonetheless, to review the principal sorts of evidence that are available.

A first source of "evidence" is the experienced observer's general impressions of conduct tendencies in a great many industries, based on his superficial appraisal of visible manifestations of conduct over a long period of years. This sort of observation in the main supports a gross distinction between tendencies of market conduct in atomistic and non-atomistic markets. In general, there is a group of industries (more outside the manufacturing sector than in it) which have atomistic or close-to-atomistic structures and in which the evident tendencies of conduct are those of complete or nearly complete independence of individual-seller action. There is also a populous and variegated group of industries that are in some degree oligopolistic in structure. In this group a variety of patterns of nonindependent seller conduct are observed, embracing complete collusion, incomplete collusion, noncollusive interdependence, and so forth. But it is generally not possible to make precise identifications of specific nonindependent conduct patterns in individual instances, to associate specific conduct patterns with specific market structures, or to ascertain the relationship of conduct to performance.

The casual observer, of course, may attempt to remedy the deficiency in his knowledge by theorizing about what he would find in detail if he looked more closely, but this leads to unverified hypotheses and not to the empirical findings we are interested in. Broad casual observation, therefore, has not been a very useful source of satisfactorily precise empirical knowledge concerning different patterns of market conduct, their determinants, and their results.

A second type of evidence on patterns of market conduct is derived from superficial observation of a more systematized sort: the rapid, organized survey of a large number of industries which seeks for easily visible indicators of the character of conduct (and also, perhaps, of structure and performance). In appraising conduct, such surveys of necessity rely heavily on general allegations and judicial findings in cases under the antitrust laws, on testimony in Congressional committee hearings, on a scattering of special industry studies by governmental agencies, and on unsifted trade lore or gossip.

A good example of this sort of survey is found in *Monograph No. 21* of the Temporary National Economic Committee (1940). So far as the study emphasizes market conduct (it simultaneously considers structure and performance), it makes identifications like the following. The extractive industries in agriculture, lumbering, fishing, and bituminous coal mining, as well as manufacturing industries producing the several major textiles, clothing of all sorts, and leather, are ostensibly classified as having complete or close-to-complete independence of action by all sellers. Price leadership is found to exist, or to have existed at some time, in the steel, cement, agricultural implement, petroleum refining, copper, lead, newsprint, glass container, and cracker industries—this leadership having been supplemented regularly or sporadically by direct agreements affecting prices at least in the cases of steel and petroleum refining. Furthermore, either price agreements or market-sharing agreements are found to have existed, at least sometimes, in the electric lamp, sulfur, gypsum product, radio equipment, chemical nitrogen, potash, typewriter, eyeglass, cheese, anthracite coal, meat packing, cigarette, asphalt shingle, and power cable and wire industries. As to interdependent action without collusion, this is identified as existing or having existed at least in the automobile, electric equipment, chemicals, and rayon industries, whereas interdependent action bolstered by supplementary collusive uniformities is found in such industries as those producing flour, household furniture, cottonseed oil, steel window products, snow fence, and a few others.

Unfortunately, an assortment of miscellaneous information of the preceding sort has little application in serious analytical pursuits. The coverage of industries is scattered and haphazard, and the identification of the dominant conduct pattern is often inaccurate or questionable. More troublesome is the fact that the classification is in essence so gross as to lump together in a single class significantly different patterns of conduct (based on significantly different structural situations), and to fail to distinguish, within given broad conduct patterns, distinct subvarieties with potentially different consequences for performance. For example, neither with price leadership nor with other price and market-sharing agreements is there any general way of telling if the collusion in question was incomplete in the individual cases, and if incomplete, to what extent. Nor is there any systematic indication of the relative force, case by case, of joint profit maximizing as distinct from independent-profit-maximizing action of sellers.

Scraps of other evidence indeed suggest that the classifications presented evidently have lumped together very unlike instances of market conduct. Placed in a single category is price leadership apparently representing reasonably complete collusion, as in copper or glass containers, and price leadership that reflects significantly incomplete collusion, as in cement or petroleum refining—with corresponding significant variations in underlying market structures. Another broad category— price or market-sharing agreements—includes agreements that were tight, well-observed, and effective in securing joint action (cigarettes, gypsum products) and agreements so incomplete that the significance of their existence may be questioned (meat packing, anthracite coal). And, in a single category identified as having interdependent action without direct collusion on price or output, we find the automobile industry with very high seller concentration and interdependence and little independence of pricing action; the rayon industry with somewhat lower concentration, less interdependence, and more influence of independent action on pricing; and the flour industry with slight interdependence and a dominance of independent pricing action. It makes little sense, and subtracts from rather than adding to our understanding of market phenomena, to throw assortments of such unlike items into single classificatory baskets.

We thus turn to a third general source of evidence on patterns of market conduct—more intensive, or "deeper," studies of conduct in particular industries. In these there is a systematic search for all relevant details of observable conduct and, presumably, greater precision in identification and classification. Because of the large amount of time required to investigate any one industry thoroughly, we have available at this time detailed descriptions of conduct for no more than fifteen or twenty industries. Almost all are in the manufacturing sector. These do not provide a solid basis for empirical generalizations concerning the sources and consequences of different conduct patterns among industries in general. It may be useful, nevertheless, to review a sampling of detailed findings of this sort in order to appraise their possible utility in developing analytically significant classifications of patterns of market conduct. In this review, we will confine ourselves entirely to studies of nonindependent (collusive or interdependent) conduct in six manufacturing industries.

First we may consider a group of four industries, with special reference to their history during the 1930's, in each of which there was ostensible evidence of well-developed collusion, but also evidence (of the sort almost invariably found on close examination) that this collusion was in some degree incomplete.

The first case is that of the electric light bulb industry, producing a variety of incandescent electric lamps among which the most important was the large, tungsten-filament lamp for general household and commercial lighting use. This industry had been dominated since shortly after its inception by General Electric, whose market power inhered in its initial control or subsequent acquisition of a number of basic patents covering the design of electric lamps and of lamp-making machinery. Its general policy was not to try to reserve to itself a single-firm monopoly in electric lamp manufacture in the United States, but rather to share its patent monopoly with a small number of other firms to which it issued restricted licenses for the use of patented designs and devices. It was through the restrictive provisions of these licenses that a collusive agreement of every licensed producer with General Electric, and implicitly of all licensed producers with each other, was developed in the industry.

.The G.E. licensing scheme had evolved through various stages after its official inception in 1912, and in 1927 it took on the following form. General Electric licensed one large producer, Westinghouse, and six small producers to make lamps of one sort or another under its patents. The conditions of the licenses were generally (a) that a sales quota of lamps, expressed as a percentage of G.E.'s lamp sales, was established for each licensee; (b) that on production and sales within its quota, each licensee would pay to General Electric a modest royalty fee based on sales revenue; and (c) that on production and sales in excess of quota, each licensee would pay a steep and essentially prohibitive royalty rate to General Electric. In addition, Westinghouse was bound to follow G.E.'s prices and terms of sales on lamps, although the six small licensees were not so bound. From inception of the 1927 agreement, the combined quota provisions of the several licenses had the effect of dividing the American domestic market for large tungsten-filament lamps approximately 61 per cent to General Electric, 21 per cent to Westinghouse, 13 per cent to four smaller licensees combined, and the remaining 5 per cent to unlicensed domestic producers and foreign imports. (Other licenses, to Westinghouse and two other small licensed producers, apportioned the output of miniature electric lamps.) To this point we observe a fairly complete and enforceable collusive agreement to determine outputs, market shares, and (inferentially) prices of lamp bulbs for producers supplying 95 per cent of the American market. The only visible sign of incompleteness of collusion was the assortment of unlicensed domestic and foreign producers, who were not parties to the greement. They supplied 5 per cent of the market, although under substantial competitive disadvantages because of lack of access to the strategic patents.

Further departures from complete collusion, however, became evident as the 1930's proceeded, principally because of the expansion of unlicensed competition. The most important basic patents held by G.E. expired, leaving its "patent hold" on the industry resting mainly on "improvement" patents and some patents on lamp-making machinery. Thereafter, unlicensed foreign producers (especially Japanese), aided by favorable foreign exchange rates as well as patent expirations, temporarily invaded the market to a significant extent. Imports exceeded 9 per cent of American domestic sales of large tungsten-filament lamps in 1932 and remained above 4½ per cent as late as 1937. (Imports were down to a fraction of 1 per cent of the market by 1941.) More important, at least 25 unlicensed domestic producers expanded during the 1930's to capture about 14 per cent of the domestic market for large tungsten-filament lamps by 1941—this at the long-run expense mainly of the smaller licensees of G.E. and of foreign firms, and to a lesser extent of G.E. and Westinghouse.

Throughout this period, General Electric was the recognized price leader for the industry. Westinghouse was a legally bound follower, and the rest of the industry followed G.E.'s leads generally but with competitive price differentials. During the 1930's General Electric made a number of price reductions on lamp bulbs reflecting reductions in production costs, and also made other selective price reductions in apparent response to the pressure of unlicensed competition and to the threat of further entry of unlicensed producers. (It further engaged in the introduction of a line of second-grade light bulbs at reduced prices, to counter unlicensed foreign and domestic competition.)

We thus observe, in the decade of the 1930's, a pattern in the American light-bulb industry of incompletely collusive conduct, with departures from complete collusion centering on the development of a fringe of unlicensed and nonagreeing firms sufficient to supply almost 15 per cent of the market. We also see superficial evidence that the agreeing firms, led by G.E., responded to the increased competitive threat by making price adjustments. But how serious or meaningful were the departures from complete collusion, and did they result in a serious undermining of a joint profit-maximizing policy on the part of G.E. and its licensees? This is clearly not apparent from any reading of the record of market conduct as such, and we need to look at market performance really to appraise the significance of the observed conduct pattern. Before looking at performance to see what this pattern of conduct really implied, let us consider a second instance.

This is the case of the petroleum refining industry of the Pacific Coast in the period of 1936 to 1940. We are concerned here with a substantially isolated regional market made up of five far-western states (California, Oregon, Washington, Arizona, and Nevada), supplied almost entirely by a group of petroleum refiners located in California. The dominant product (in terms of value) was gasoline. As we pick up the record of conduct in this industry in 1936, we find the market supplied by seven integrated "major" companies which together sold about three-fourths of the gasoline to buyers in the five-state area, and 50 or more small, generally nonintegrated refiners that together accounted for the remaining one-fourth of domestic gasoline sales. The majors' market shares ranged from that of Standard Oil of California with about 20 per cent of the market to that of Texas Corporation with about 6 per cent; the largest "independent" refiner supplied about 4 per cent of the market, but all except four independents had market shares below 1 per cent apiece.

In 1936, the industry had a long history of gasoline price leadership by Standard, with almost invariable and exact followership (in terms of announced prices) by the other six majors. However, there was no consistent followership by many of the small independent refiners, most of whom, even in stable times, sold their gasolines at a price somewhat below that of the majors. Moreover, they engaged in frequent forays of competitive price cutting. In the past, episodes of prolonged competitive price-cutting by the independents had induced a lowering of the leader's price and had precipitated vigorous price wars between the majors and the independents.

The price leadership pattern continued in 1936 and thereafter, with at least nominally rigorous adherence by the major-company followers. But it was now allegedly supplemented by market-sharing and price-maintaining agreements between the majors and the independents, the latter being represented by an Independent Refiners' Association. (These allegations were contained in an indictment under the antitrust laws charging illegal restraint of trade; they were not tested in court because the defendant majors and independents entered a plea of *nolo contendere*—that is, refused to defend, but without express admission of guilt—and accepted penalties and a decree enjoining further action of the sort alleged.) The essence of the alleged agreement was that all members of the Independent Refiners' Association accepted gasoline output quotas and agreed to maintain their prices at a level equal or in a certain ratio to that set by the majors' price leader. In return, the majors agreed to purchase from the independents, at specified attractive prices, all of their quota outputs which they could not sell at the agreed-upon prices.

This agreement was apparently or allegedly in effect from April, 1936, to the end of May, 1940. During this interval, the majors purchased unusually large amounts of independent gasoline (much of which they in turn exported or marketed domestically). They bought about half of the total independent output, whereas they had bought almost none of it previously. Independent price cutting (with some exceptions to be noted below) was virtually eliminated. The wholesale gasoline price throughout the period, as set by Standard as price leader, was higher than it had averaged since the end of 1931 and much more inflexible;

from April, 1936, until the end of May, 1940, it was changed only once, by a half-cent-per-gallon increase in March, 1937.

If description of this episode is halted at this point, we seem to observe a complex and well-organized collusive arrangement among nearly all the sellers in the market, which might closely approximate complete collusion. Some departures from complete collusion, however, are notable. First, some potential instability in the arrangement was propagated by the entry of new independents into production and into the agreement (they usually entered by opening previously shut-down facilities), this phenomenon in part accounting for the growth of the independent share of the market by several percentage points between 1936 and 1940. Second, as the period proceeded a number of stronger independents broke away from the agreement to sell (or the practice of selling) gasoline to the majors. They produced without reference to quotas, agressively marketed their gasolines at prices significantly below those of the majors, and thus expanded their individual shares of the market. Third, there is some evidence of the use of secret wholesale price concessions by some or all of the majors, in part through the device of various allowances or subsidies to retail service stations that purchased from them. However, neither independent price competition nor clandestine price cutting by majors was sufficient to induce a reduction of the posted prices of the leader and other majors. Posted prices were not reduced until May, 1940, after the conclusion of the antitrust suit and the evident abandonment of large-scale purchasing of independent gasoline by the majors.

How serious or meaningful were these departures from complete collusion? Did the collusive scheme implement joint profit maximization for the majors or for the industry as a whole, or did it simply stabilize prices at a low level? And can we answer these questions by examining the pattern of conduct alone, without reference to evidence of structure and performance? Let us defer these questions as we consider a third instance, that of the cigarette industry.

This is essentially a single-product industry with a relatively few sellers supplying a common national market. In 1930, the beginning of the decade examined here, the Big Three of American Tobacco, R. J. Reynolds, and Liggett & Myers (principal brand names than Lucky Strike, Camel, and Chesterfield) together supplied 91 per cent of the market, and the only other seller of consequence was P. Lorillard (Old Gold) with another 7 per cent of the market. Five small firms which later expanded their sales at least for a while were identified as supplying together 1.2 per cent of the market.

Since 1923, Reynolds with Camel had been the effective price leader for the industry, all other sellers of any consequence following its lead precisely in terms both of list prices and discounts to dealers. At the outset its leading position was attributable to the fact that it held the largest single share of the market (nearly 42 per cent in 1925). Thereafter, as American Tobacco came to enjoy a slightly larger share than Reynolds, the latter's retention of the leadership position has been attributed to the fact that its management preferred a somewhat lower price for the industry than did its principal rivals. It could thus "call the tune" by setting a price its rivals could not safely exceed and did not wish to undercut, and could be pretty sure that its rivals would welcome and follow its price increases when it made them.

Throughout the 1930's, this price leadership pattern continued, with American, Liggett, and Lorillard following nicely, and also Philip Morris, as during the decade it introduced a new cigarette and secured a sizeable market share (about 7 per cent by 1940). The only significant exception is that in the first two months of 1933, American Tobacco with Lucky Strike led two sharp price cuts for the industry, and the other principal manufacurers of the "standard" brands, including Reynolds, followed in step. Otherwise, Reynolds was the leader for all price changes until 1946, and we have the appearance of a smoothly operating price leadership system, in which the one episode of apparent disagreement over price (in 1933) was resolved by American's temporarily assuming the role of a "downward" price leader. A "new member" to the system, Philip Morris, could be assimilated and acquire some of the market shares previously held by the Big Three without engendering any independent or competitive pricing action.

This superficially complete tacit collusion on pricing, however, became significantly incomplete during the 1930's because of vigorous competitive action by a group of smaller firms that introduced cut-price cigarettes made of tobacco of somewhat lower quality. In a setting of depressed business, drastically lowered consumer incomes, and lowered tobacco costs, Reynolds led the price of standard-brand cigarettes in mid-1931 to its highest level since 1921, corresponding to 14 or 15 cents per pack inclusive of the then prevailing federal tax, and the price remained there until the beginning of 1933 (close to the bottom of the great depression). Given the resulting wide spread between tobacco leaf costs and cigarette prices, plus the severe shortage of consumer incomes, several previously very small firms, including Brown & Williamson, Axton-Fisher, Stephano, and Larus, introduced a variety of brands of cigarettes to retail at 10 cents per package, definitely breaking with the price line of the large standard-brand producers. They were so successful that by the end of 1932 the ten-cent brands had secured about 23 per cent of the cigarette market, almost entirely at the expense of the largest three or four companies.

Thereafter, the tacitly collusive price of these largest companies reacted to competition when American led the price through two steep cuts early in 1933 (as previously noted), this being followed by three moderate price increases led by Reynolds in 1934, 1937, and 1940. By 1940, the standard-brand price was almost as high as it had been in 1931, but tobacco costs had increased since that time. The reaction of the standard-brand producers to the price competition of the ten-centers arrested and reversed the expansion of the latter's market shares, so that by 1939 they supplied less than 18 per cent of the market. By 1948, cut-price brands accounted for an insignificant fraction of cigarette sales, and the only remaining "independent" of any importance (Brown & Williamson) survived by emphasizing standard-brand production at prices conforming to those of the industry leaders.

We observe here a neat example of fairly tight tacit collusion in pricing among a concentrated oligopolistic core of firms, plus the independent, competitive pricing action of a relatively few independent small firms. There is persuasive evidence that the level at which the tacitly collusive price was set was significantly influenced and limited by the threat of aggressive independent competition. Cigarette prices, though collusively determined, appear to have been held below the industry profit-maximizing level in part because of the rivalry and independence of action of a limited group of independents that were not disposed to follow the Reynolds-American lead in setting cigarette prices. Knowing this, we must again raise the question of just what in the way of industry performance results can be inferred from the existence of this conduct pattern. And again we defer attention to this question while we look at a final instance of collusive conduct, in the steel industry.

The steel industry of the United States may be broadly construed as encompassing all firms operating steel works and rolling mills in the country, with their outputs (as supplied to buyers) comprising mainly a variety of basic steel products such as sheets, strips, bars, plates, wire, pipe, and so forth. The principal firms of the industry are fully integrated to include within the single firm iron ore production, blast furnace operations to produce iron, steel furnace operations to turn iron into steel, and a variety of finishing facilities to roll, draw, or otherwise shape steel into the assortment of basic producers alluded to above. Lesser firms may be only semi-integrated in that they operate only steel furnaces and finishing facilities, or may not produce a full line of finished basic products.

There is some regional segmentation of the steel industry, with plants in each of several producing regions having, because of high transport costs for finished steel, a substantial competitive advantage in selling to (but not exclusive control of) contiguously located buyers. The main producing regions are three: the area of western Pennsylvania and eastern Ohio running roughly from Pittsburgh to Cleveland to Buffalo, the Chicago area, and the Atlantic seaboard area in the general vicinity of Philadelphia. Much smaller production areas center around a half-dozen other points, including Birmingham (Alabama), Colorado, and the coast of California.

The largest firm in the industry, United States Steel, has plant facilities in every producing region of consequence; other producers are more specialized in region, and progressively so as they are smaller. Of the national aggregate of basic steel-producing capacity in the 1930's (that is, capacity to produce steel ingots from which the basic finished products are made), U. S. Steel controlled about one-third, the first four firms controlled somewhat less than two-thirds, the first eight firms somewhat over three-quarters, the first fifteen firms about 90 per cent, with around 60 smaller firms accounting for the remainder.

Since shortly after its organization in 1901, U. S. Steel had been the recognized price leader for the industry, and it continued in this role during the 1930's and subsequently. That is, its quoted prices were in general closely matched by the quoted prices of all other steel producers of significance, and it initiated all quoted-price increases or decreases for the industry. The effectiveness of this means of obtaining concurrent and parallel pricing action by the firms of the industry was secured by their mutual adoption of strategic supplementary uniformities in their pricing policies. First, all firms followed the same schedule of price differentials employed by U. S. Steel in relating the various prices of specific finished steel products (sheet, plates, wire, etc.) to the basic quoted price for steel ingot. Therefore, by establishing for the industry a basic quoted price for steel which was matched by all others, U. S. Steel also in effect established a common quoted industry price for each of the principal mass-produced finished steel products. Second, inter-firm uniformity on delivered prices (at the point of delivery, including freight) was secured by all firms following U. S. Steel in the adoption of a uniform basing-point system. Under this system, the delivered price at any delivery point was calculated by all sellers as the mill price (that is, U. S. Steel's price) at the nearest mill designated as a "basing point," plus freight costs from that basing point to the point of delivery, regardless of the actual origin of the shipment or the actual freight cost incurred. Mutual adherence by all sellers to the same basing-point formula (and the same basing points) in calculating delivered prices resulted in their following U. S. Steel's delivered price for each product at each possible delivery point. It eliminated such price competition as might have resulted from individual firms offering lower delivered prices to nearby customers than firms with more distant mills might offer.

In sum, the steel industry had long been the scene—and was in the 1930's—of a fairly elaborate tacitly collusive system of price determination, revolving around the price leadership of U. S. Steel. Nor does the collusion seem to have been significantly incomplete either because of ambiguities in the terms of the tacit understanding or because of non-participation by any very important fringe of small sellers. (Information on the latter point, however, is inadequate.) The major evident departure from complete collusion was that of secret price shading—the granting of price concessions below the quoted price to various individual buyers—by some or all of the sellers in the industry. The incidence of this price shading, however, was apparently variable with the state of the market, or the relation of demand to available capacity. In the first half of the 1920's, and again in 1941 and 1942, for example, with relatively good demand, price concessions were very infrequent and on the average extremely small. But in 1939 and 1940, when there was considerable excess capacity available, significant price shading affected as much as 70 or 80 per cent of all steel tonnage sold, and the average concession on all sales exceeded 5 per cent of quoted price. For most of the decade of the 1930's, upon which we focus attention here, detailed findings are not available, but since in much of this period there was a short demand for steel and much unutilized capacity, a high incidence of price shading was probably experienced.

There is some evidence also that U. S. Steel, as the price leader, reacted somewhat "barometrically" to the size and frequency of secret price concessions, being encouraged to lower the quoted price if concessions became very frequent and severe, and to raise the quoted price if concessions were unimportant, thus sensing and reacting to the sentiment of its constituency of followers concerning the level of uniform quoted price that they were willing to observe. And it is quite possible that the height of the leader's price was at all times essentially limited by the threat of nonfollowership or of widespread secret price cutting if the price were made "unrealistically high." That is, the threat of independence of individual seller action, as well as its actual emergence in secret price concessions, probably influenced the level of the tacitly collusive quoted price which all sellers nominally followed.

As to the actual pricing record of the 1930's, it is observable that U. S. Steel made a succession of reductions in its quoted prices from 1929 to

1935, as the general business depression deepened, and a subsequent succession of increases (interrupted by a decrease in 1938) up to 1940, arriving then at a quoted price slightly higher than that which had prevailed in 1929. Throughout the period the industry operated with a substantial shortage of demand and with excess capacity, though there was a trend toward improving demand after 1934. To what extent the price leader's moves were themselves led by the frequency and size of price concessions has not been closely ascertained. However, it is not evident that the tacitly collusive quoted price established by the leader was simply a barometer of underlying competitive conditions. It seems to have exercised its own strong influence on the level of price and output in the market for steel.

With this fourth instance of incompletely collusive market conduct, we return again to the crucial questions regarding what can be inferred from the observed pattern of conduct *per se*. In the case of the steel industry, what can be inferred about the effective aims of price determination—about the extent to which joint profit maximization for the industry was implemented, or the extent to which independent pricing action and the threat thereof lowered steel prices toward a competitive level? Or, as regards performance, should we predict that the steel price leadership system led to monopolistic excess profits and restricted output?

More generally, given the record of conduct for the electric light bulb, Pacific Coast gasoline, cigarette, and steel industries, do we have any foundation, *on the basis of available evidence concerning market conduct alone*, for predicting which of these industries should have evidenced the more monopolistic performance and which the more competitive? Or for predicting in which cases the incompleteness of collusion, reflecting independence of individual seller action, should have more seriously undermined the maximization of joint profits for sellers in the industry?

The answer to these latter questions, in the opinion of the writer, is simply "no"—negative in these industries, and also more generally in most industries to be encountered. Available evidence on conduct patterns *per se*, even in intensively studied cases, does not ordinarily reveal enough to support meaningfully precise inferences about the aims price-calculation pursued, or predictions of the associated market performance. In each of the four studies at hand, we find express or tacit collusion, and significant incompleteness of this collusion. Knowing only what is evident about conduct, there is no clear basis for differentiating the four in terms either of predicted performance or of inferred aims of price calculation.

Yet, if we "peek" ahead at performance, there is considerable evidence that there did indeed emerge a variety of distinctly different performance tendencies. Wide divergences in industry profit rates are generally good rough indicators of corresponding differences in the degrees of monopolistic output restriction and price raising, or of the differing extents to which joint profit maximization has been accomplished by the sellers in the industries compared. Confining ourselves here to profit rate evidence, we note that from 1936 through 1940:

1. General Electric profits on sales of light bulbs ranged between 20 and 30 per cent per annum of capital invested in light-bulb production, with Westinghouse showing a profit rate only slightly lower and the licensed smaller firms a rate above the industrial average.

2. The profit (after taxes) of the principal cigarette firms was about 14.4 per cent per annum of owners' capital investment, or equity.

3. The corresponding average profit rate on owners' equity for the major Pacific Coast petroleum refiners was apparently under 6 per cent per annum.

4. The average profit rate on equity of a group including nearly all principal steel producers for the same period was 4.9 per cent per annum.

In effect, we find two of the four industries with profit rates so low as to suggest an approximately competitive adjustment of price to cost (petroleum refining and steel), one with a distinctly supernormal profit rate suggestive of a substantial degree of monopolistic price raising (cigarettes), and one with an even higher profit rate to the principal firms (electric light bulbs). Although profit rates for any short period of years are subject to many influences other than the character of market conduct and the effective aims of price calculation, these profit differences are so gross as to suggest a distinct difference in effective pricing goals and performance tendencies as between light bulbs and cigarettes on one hand, and petroleum refining and steel on the other, in the latter half of the 1930's.

As suggested, these differences are hardly predictable from a reading of available evidence on market conduct alone. On the other hand, it is quite easy, once the performance evidence is known, to "infer" the unobserved and perhaps unobservable characteristics of conduct from the performance that it generated—to remark casually, for example, that collusion after all was not very seriously incomplete and joint profit maximization not too seriously undermined in the cigarette industry, whereas collusion was evidently quite incomplete and joint profit maximization seriously undermined by independent action in the steel industry. But this is only to say that we know performance once we have looked at it, and not that performance can be adequately predicted or inferred from observable conduct.

In the same vein, we might have been able in these cases to predict performance from the market structure of these industries, without much reference to detailed patterns of conduct. For example, the fact that the electric-light-bulb and cigarette industries both had very high seller concentration and very high barriers to entry, whereas in petroleum refining and steel there was only high-moderate seller concentration and only moderately high barriers to entry, might serve as a basis for inferring (from conventional *a priori* theory) that extreme monopolistic pricing tendencies were more likely to emerge (through whatever route of conduct) from the first two industries than from the second two. But here again the inference or prediction is not based on observable market conduct.

This observation is reinforced if we turn briefly to two instances of interdependent, but apparently noncollusive, market conduct of sellers. A first concerns the passenger automobile industry, the Big Three members of which in the 1930's supplied a little less than 90 per cent of the industry output, with five or six much smaller firms accounting for the remainder. As regards pricing, there was little if any evidence of collusive activity—even of tacit collusion such as might be implemented through price leadership. Prices were in general determined annually, with the introduction of the "new model," by each seller, and not otherwise changed except for end-of-the-year discounts to dealers to encourage clearance of inventories before the next year's model was introduced. Each seller apparently determined his own price without consultation with, or exchange of cost or other information with, his rivals. The widely reported formula for determining price involved determining what the average cost per automobile would be if sales volume were at a standard equal to that of some "average year," and then adding a certain conventional profit percentage to this standard average cost. It is not known whether or to what extent the profit margins added or the relation of standard to capacity volume varied among firms.

After this initial determination of the price for a year, each firm then apparently looked at what prices the others were announcing, and revised its prices accordingly to arrive at an approximate competitive matching of prices for each "price class" of automobiles. At times, this process amounted to all firms roughly matching the prices of the firm with the lowest announced prices. For a period, the Ford Motor Company was viewed as a sort of price leader for the industry by virtue of the fact that its idea of the best price lay at the low end of the alternatives. This has not always been true, however, and for 1957 models, for example, we observe the Ford Motor Company revising its previously announced prices upward on Ford brand autos to match General Motors' higher announced price of Chevrolet. No distinct leadership pattern has generally been in evidence, but rather one of parallel pricing policies and formulas plus some ironing out of resultant inter-firm price differences. Generally, automobile prices have responded fairly sensitively, year to year, to changes in the costs of labor and materials, but not to the level of demand.

This pricing pattern, then, is apparently not collusive, although strongly influenced by the interdependence of the principal rival firms. What it should lead to in the way of performance, either absolutely or as compared to the four cases of incomplete collusion discussed above, is hardly predictable from the observable aspects of market conduct *per se*. The facts are that we find an industry with persistently high excess profits and every evidence of monopolistic output restriction leading in the direction of, though probably not fully reaching, joint profit maximization for the established firms. The 1936–1940 average profit rate on equity for all firms except Ford (after income taxes) was 16.3 per cent—among the highest earned in important American manufacturing industries. The annual average profit rate on investment in motor vehicle production alone (before nominal income taxes) for the 11 years from 1927 through 1937 (fully including the great depression) was about 28½ per cent for Chrysler and 35½ per cent for General Motors, while the most profitable independent (Nash) made about 37 per cent per annum on investment for the same period.[9] These profit data provide a basis for inferring that interdependence among the rival automobile firms was very strong and led in the direction of joint profit maximization. Or, these profit results might have been predicted as probable in view of the market structure, which featured very high seller concentration and the extreme barriers to entry protecting established sellers. But the evidence on market conduct alone would not permit us to predict performance in the industry, or its difference from performance in industries with various collusive conduct patterns.

A final instance which may be briefly mentioned is that of the flour industry. This is not a very concentrated industry. In 1935 the largest eight firms supplied only 37 per cent of industry output, and there were

[9]Available profit data on the Ford Motor Company, not a publicly listed corporation at the time, are unreliable.

about 1,000 firms in all. However, the largest firms, including General Mills, Pillsbury, and several others, had sufficient market shares to create a significant degree of recognized interdependence among them. Although express collusive action was not in evidence in this industry, the recognition of interdependence and the endeavor to make this interdependence "work" to control or suppress independent pricing action had been in evidence through trade-association activities directed toward discouraging sales below cost, issuing to all sellers suggested "industry-average" costs on which prices should be based (by adding a suggested margin to the suggested cost), recommending the use of standard and uniform terms of sale, etc. The pricing policies of individual firms were presumably arrived at in the light of such recognized interdependence as existed, and with the aid of such supplementary collusive "props" as were from time to time introduced.

This, then, is an instance of interdependent pricing, but to what result? If we examine the evidence on performance, we find close-to-competitive profits (in the 1930's and later) for the industry as a whole. Even the largest and most-advantaged firms had an annual average profit rate of only 7.6 per cent from 1936 to 1940. Market conduct, it may be inferred from performance evidence, was in actuality dominated by independent pricing action and motives of independent profit maximization, in spite of various endeavors to avert or modify this tendency. Or, we might predict from the relatively low seller concentration of the industry, and its low entry barriers, that the structure would lead to competitive pricing and low profits, more or less regardless of the details of conduct. But from the evidence on conduct alone, nothing much could be inferred *a priori*, and the details of the conduct pattern are substantially without analytical interest or significance.

Sellers' Conduct in Determining Selling Costs and Products

The preceding pages have discussed the market conduct of sellers in arriving at one range of strategic decisions, those concerning the selling prices to be charged or quantities of output to be offered for sale. These are not the only decisions ordinarily required of firms in adjusting to their selling markets; two related types of decision must also frequently be made. These concern:

(*a*) The amounts to be spent on sales promotion, and the specific applications of these expenditures to various promotional devices.

(*b*) The design and quality of the product to be offered, and the extent and frequency of variations of the product to be undertaken through time.

The numerous aspects of the conduct of firms making these decisions are conveniently grouped and designated under the labels of *sales-promotion policy* and *product policy*. Both sorts of policy presumably aim to increase, or to prevent the reduction of, the demand for the output of the decision-making unit, whether this unit be the firm or the industry. If profit maximization is the overriding goal, the aim would be to seek increases (or prevent reductions) of demand through these policies so long as the resulting additions to (or losses avoided of) sales revenue exceeded the connected additions to sales promotion or production costs.

Product and sales-promotion policies, however, are not equally important in all industries. In some, products are relatively fixed and not susceptible to much profitable variation (as in the case of electrolytic copper, sulfuric acid, or building bricks). In some (like those just mentioned, or cement, or cotton gray cloth) advertising and other sales promotion may be relatively pointless because of the unavoidable homogeneity of the outputs of competing sellers plus the fact that buyers are thoroughly informed and price-conscious. On the other hand, such policies are important in most or all industries in which product differentiation and variation are feasible, and especially in consumer-good industries, which typically face poorly informed buyers.

Both sales-promotion policy and product policy are essentially multidimensional, and more complex than price policy. Sales promotion policy includes the complex design of promotional campaigns (involving, for example, choice of advertising media to be used, or the emphasis of the promotional "message") as well as a determination of how much to spend. Product policy can embrace the alteration of product design in any of numerous dimensions. An automobile can be made lighter or heavier, shorter or longer, higher or lower, more or less powerful, *et cetera ad infinitum*. Policy decisions can be made to alter product quality over a wide range, and the seller faces multiple choices with respect to the rate and frequency of product change through time.

Market performance in cognate respects is correspondingly multidimensional, but for purposes of simplification it is convenient to emphasize only:

(*a*) The size of selling costs in ratio to total costs or revenue, whatever the applications of the expenditures; and

(*b*) The character of the quality-cost combination attained for the product (level of quality as connected with resulting level of product cost) relative to alternative quality-cost combinations, plus the frequency of product change and the cost of this frequency relative to alternative frequencies and their connected costs. Correspondingly, we may emphasize mainly those aspects of market conduct or policy that bear on the determination of these major aspects of selling-cost and product performance.

In appraising conduct in these respects, we may again emphasize (*a*) the pattern of interseller coordination within the industry that affects the determination of sales outlays and products, and (*b*) the aims pursued and methods employed by individual sellers or groups thereof in determining sales promotion and product policies. And again, before assessing empirical evidence on actual sales-promotion and product policies, we may inquire first what are the main alternative patterns and aims available; second what are the predictable performance consequences of the major alternatives; and third how choice among these patterns and principles may be related to market structure.

Alternative Patterns and Aims of Conduct

Regarding alternative patterns and aims, we can save time by referring to the alternatives identified for price-output determination, since they are fully applicable here. That is, as regards interseller coordination, sales promotion or product policies can be determined by the sellers of an industry with complete collusion, with incomplete collusion, interdependently without collusion, or with complete independence. And the effective aim pursued in arriving at these policies can be one of joint profit maximization, independent profit maximization, hybrid profit maximization, or maximin calculation. Similarly, the use of simplified formulas to direct policy is not unknown, at least in the determination of advertising expenditures. Also, as to total patterns of sales promotion or product policies, any nonindependent pattern of seller coordination can conceivably implement any of a considerable range of aims, so that the ranges of predictable performance results (in the selling-cost and product dimensions) of complete collusion, incomplete collusion, and noncollusive interdependence overlap so seriously that it is difficult to draw meaningful distinctions among them in terms of their consequences. However, completely independent determination of sales promotion and product policies by individual firms—linked in general with atomistic market structures—probably has performance tendencies clearly distinguishable from those of noninedependence in determining selling outlays and products.

Our identification and broad interpretation of hypothetical alternative patterns of conduct in sales promotion and product determination are thus so far conveniently parallel to their counterparts in price-determining conduct. As we probe further, however, it appears that the parallelism cannot be fully maintained.

First, it is not easy to identify from available evidence various specific forms of collusive conduct (complete or incomplete) involving sales-promotion and product policies. Aside from the occasional joint action of firms through their industry trade associations to standardize their products as to specification or quality (an action that might implement the suppression of product rivalry), no assortment of forms of collusive activity is apparent. The probable reason for this is that noninde-pendent market conduct in the spheres in question takes the form in most cases of noncollusive interdependence of policies (even though there may be collusion on price in the same industries). Probable as it may be, it leaves the way open for the determination of sales outlays and products in pursuit of a wide variety of alternative aims, depending on the degree of interdependence in the market and sellers' reactions to it.

Second, the predictable consequencs in terms of market performance of pursuing different aims in determining selling outlays and products cannot be read from the parallel analysis of aims of price determina-tion. The necessary separate theorizing about these consequences is complicated and we will not pursue it here, but a few conclusions based on such theorizing may be stated:

1. In situations of oligopolistic interdependence, a joint profit-maxi-mizing determination of individual and total sales-promotion outlays by the member firms of an industry "acting as one" will tend to lead to a certain reduction of total selling outlays relative to most alternatives, because outlays designed to secure customers at the expense of rivals (or to prevent the loss of customers to agressive rivals) will be elimi-nated. But total elimination of sales-promotion outlays is not to be ex-pected, since considerable promotion may improve the earnings of the industry as a whole by attracting buyer expenditure away from other industries. Even a monopolist might do considerable advertising for this reason.

Similarly, a joint profit-maximizing product policy adopted in com-mon by all members of an industry might be expected to restrict the extent of product improvement and the frequency of product changes over time, relative to most alternatives, because of the elimination of product rivalry or competition by which individual firms would other-wise attempt to gain at the expense of their rivals. But again, elimina-tion of progressive product improvement or of relatively frequent product change is not necessarily implied by a joint profit-maximizing policy. The industry as a whole may benefit from a fairly aggressive policy of product improvement and variation. For example, it is not entirely clear that the well-known "product competition" in the automobile industry, involving frequent improvements or variations of products by several sellers, reflects an overall product policy which is substantially different, in its broader aspects, from the policy which a profit-maximizing single-firm monopolist controlling the whole industry would pursue.

2. With a hybrid profit-maximizing aim in oligopoly (where joint profit-maximizing action is at least somewhat modified or undermined by independent actions aimed at gaining customers at the expense of rivals), we should expect somewhat larger sales-promotion outlays than in the first case, and a greater rate and frequency of product improvement or variation through time. This conclusion is qualified, however, to the extent that the character of such quasi-independent product and promotional policies will be affected by the concurrent character of price determination. If there is effective collusion on price, the increase in selling outlays and rates of product change will tend to be accentuated; if there is considerable price competition, this may in a sense replace the emphasis on sales-promotion and product competition. The preceding applies generally also to maximin determinations of selling costs and products by individual firms.

3. With independent profit-maximizing determination of selling costs and products, and a maximum of competition in these respects, we should expect a further enlargement of selling outlays and further emphasis on product improvement and change, *if other things are equal.* Actually, they usually are not equal, and therefore the conclusion does not hold. That is, truly independent profit-maximizing determination of products and selling outlays will be found generally in atomistic industries, wherein the same maximizing principle as applied to pricing leads to a maximum of price competition. This price competiton serves as both a substitute for and restraining force on sales-promotion and product competition, so that sales outlays and product improvements may in the net be at least as low as they would be with joint profit-maximizing product and promotion policies.

4. Which of these and other alternative patterns of predicted performance is most desirable from a social standpoint is not obvious on the surface, until definitions of normatively ideal levels of selling outlays and products are supplied from another analytical framework. It might be indicated that if there is some general tendency to excessive selling costs and excessive rates and frequencies of product change, it is

probably most accentuated in oligopolistic industries where hybrid profit maximization is the effective governing principle of product and promotional policies—especially if price competition has been suppressed by effective collusion on price.

5. The level of selling outlays and the rate and frequency of product changes that correspond to joint profit maximization, or that in any event may be undertaken, in some cases may be increased in order to heighten the barriers to the entry of new sellers to the industry. (In these instances the pseudo-rivalry of established sellers toward potential new sellers results in independent action by the former to gain at the expense of the latter—thus bringing this sort of conduct generally into the fold by hybrid profit maximization.)

Another preliminary matter concerns the relation of conduct patterns in determining sales-promotion outlays and products to the market structure of the industry. Only a few very elementary observations can be supported here. First, of course, full independence of individual firm action and independent profit-maximizing policies are associated almost entirely with industries of very low seller concentration or atomistic structure. Second, among all other industries, or those with one degree or another of oligopolistic interdependence, interdependent action without obvious collusion in determining selling outlays and products seems to be the general rule. The applicable aims of policy range from joint profit maximization to a hybrid maximization in which independence of action oriented to individual profits plays a strong but not entirely dominant role. If there is a further predictable tendency here, it is that action is likely to be more oriented to aims of joint profit maximization as seller concentration is higher and interdependence greater, and to aims of independent profit maximization as concentration is lower and interdependence less. Third, increased selling outlays and higher rates and frequencies of product change may be associated, within oligopolies, with industries in which barriers to entry other than product differentiation are unimportant. In these industries, such aggressive policies become essential for protecting established sellers against entry.

Evidence on Sales-Promotion and Product Policies

Actual evidence of the intrinsic characteristics of market conduct at the level of sales-promotion and product policies is so scanty that it is almost nonexistent. To be sure, it is not difficult to ascertain and recite the usually entertaining details of the superficial aspects of these policies in a number of industries. For example, it is easy to describe at length the policies of annual model change and progressive product enlargement and improvement pursued by sellers in the automobile industry, or the continuing conflict of rival advertising campaigns in the cigarette or soap industries. But it is not ordinarily possible from such recitals (whatever their entertainment value may be) to ascertain much about the fundamental aspects of the patterns of conduct pursued— whether or to what extent they are in essence collusive as opposed to independent, and to what extent they are oriented to or influenced by considerations respectively of joint and independent profit maximization.

In appraising the fundamental character of actual sales-promotion and product policies, therefore, we are forced to observe market performance in the matter of the size of selling costs and the behavior of products, and so gain knowledge of the aims of conduct largely by inferring them from this performance evidence. Market conduct in these respects, therefore, or what we can find out about it, has little independent analytical significance for purposes of prediction. It may be interesting, nevertheless, to indicate briefly the sorts of things that can tentatively be inferred about sales-promotion and product policies from evidence concerning selling-cost and product performance.

First, in oligopolistic industries of relatively high seller concentration, sales-promotion and product policies seem to reflect, more frequently than do price policies, significant elements of independence of action by individual sellers, and significant though limited departures from the pursuit of joint profit-maximizing aims. That is, there is in such industries more often an important element of competition or rivalry among firms on the sales-promotion and product levels than on the level of price.

To be sure, complete independence of policy-making in these respects—of the sort in which the individual seller would attempt to enhance his own profits at the expense of rivals without regard to their probable reactions—seems never to be found in these highly concentrated industries. And whatever the apparent excesses of selling cost or of product improvement or variation, they are in observed cases less than those to which truly independent action would almost certainly lead. On the other hand, significant elements of independence in determining selling outlays or products very frequently seem to result in selling outlays or expenditures for product improvements or change that are evidently well in excess of the joint profit-maximizing level, even in many industries where collusion on price seems to be in effect.

For example, in the soap and typewriter industries, neither of which shows evidence of much price competition, selling costs amounting to roughly 10 and 25 per cent of sales revenue respectively for all firms in each industry seem clearly to be in excess of what a profit-maximizing monopolist would spend. However, they are possibly less than truly independent action by individual sellers would produce. Or, on the product level, the history of the rubber tire industry in the latter part of the 1920's and at some subsequent times suggests that competitive product development has resulted in a reduction of the overall earnings and profits of the industry, largely through increasing the durability of the product so greatly as to result in a substantial reduction of demand. In these and numerous comparable cases, some balance between independence and interdependence, or between competition and co-operation, has been struck in devising selling and product policies, even though in the same cases there has frequently been rather effective collusive or parallel action on pricing.

The picture, however, is not so clear with respect to some smaller proportion of highly concentrated industries. In these the ostensibly competitive sales-promotion and product policies of the sellers do not obviously add up to a total industry policy seriously at odds with the profit-maximizing policies of a single-firm monopolist in the same situation. For example we may ask (though we are unable to develop a definite answer) whether the expenditure of about 5 per cent of sales revenue on the average for advertising by firms in the cigarette and distilled liquor industries—in spite of the fact that the individual sellers incur them with an eye to maintaining or increasing their market shares—really much exceed the level consistent with maximizing industry profits through building demand for cigarettes or liquor as a whole. This speculation is given some sustenance when we observe that each of three of the four principal firms in the liquor industry offers a variety of "competing" brands, usually takes pains not to reveal that these brands are produced by the same firm, and aggressively advertises each brand as if it were in competition with the others. Or, we may inquire whether the composite of aggressive product policies of the firms of the automobile industry—involving large expenditures for steady product change or improvement and for annual model changes—is not at least roughly consistent with maximizing industry profits, since these policies sustain demand by continually imposing a "forced obsolescence" on vehicles previously sold. The interdependence of large sellers, in short, may in numerous cases restrain competitive sales-promotion and product policies to the point where the total industry policy does not differ too greatly from that of a profit-maximizing monopolist.

A second general observation concerns identification of obvious major forms of product and sales-promotion policies. In industries where product policy is an important item, at least three patterns are noticeable.

First, there is a considerable range of industries making consumer durable goods in which the common policy of sellers in the industry is to make successive improvements and other changes in design at a rapid rate over time. These improvements are introduced through periodic (usually annual) "model changes," incorporating alterations in both design and style. The outstanding example here is the automobile industry, but the pattern is also followed in other industries producing large consumer durables, such as electrical household appliances. The presumptive orientation of such policies is not only (or even mainly) competition among the rival firms, but also the endeavor to sustain industry sales volume by making units already sold outdated in function or out of style. Notable aspects of this policy are that products are improved (or enlarged) rapidly through time—possibly improved to excess in the light of connected costs, and that the high frequency of style and other changes increases overall costs and prices, relative to the alternative of less frequent changes.

Second, there is another group of industries producing consumer goods which regularly engage in periodic alterations or variations of their products, of the sort not necessarily identifiable as improvement, in order to stimulate consumer demand. The regular introduction of "selling features" in fountain-pen or electric shaver design, or of "new" soaps (pastel-colored, perhaps)—ordinarily trivial alterations of product which serve as a fulcrum for advertising effort—exemplifies this sort of policy. Again, the policies may be either genuinely rivalrous or consistent with joint profit maximization for the firms in the industry. This sort of policy is usually more expensive in the matter of connected advertising costs than in added product costs.

Third, we find in other industries a more deliberate product development policy, featuring occasional rather than periodic changes in product, and not connected with "model changes" at specified time intervals. Examples of this are found in the petroleum refining, rayon, and metal container industries. In its superficial aspects, at least, this policy is not so "competitive," and it is generally less expensive relative to the results achieved in the way of product improvement.

The most interesting differences among sales-promotion policies are in the amounts spent relative to sales revenue, and here of course we observe a wide range of practices. Promotional costs run from 5 to 10 per cent of sales in the industries that emphasize promotion most heavily (although occasionally higher ratios are found), to 1 or 2 per cent in most producer-good industries. As to form of promotional policy, advertising through television, radio, newspaper, billboard, and direct-mail media is the most common. In some industries, however, maintenance and subsidization of distributive outlets and service facilities as promotional devices are the major instruments of policy.

A fourth general observation is that in industries of low-moderate or low seller concentration, there is generally evidence of a lessened emphasis on sales-promotion and product-change policies. This is probably linked to the greater pressure of price competition as an alternative to promotional or product competition, and also might occur because the smaller margins between price and cost that prevail provide less funds for, and make less attractive to the individual competitor, very large expenditures on promotion and product development. It is quite possible in these cases that overall expenditures on sales promotion and product variation are less than a profit-maximizing single monopolist would undertake.

The preceding generalizations are essentially inferences drawn from the observation of market performance in the selling-cost and product dimensions. We will comment further on these aspects of performance in Chapter 10.

Predatory and Exclusionary Tactics of Sellers

The two broad dimensions of market conduct considered so far embrace the "acts, practices, and policies" of sellers in determining first price and output, and second sales promotion outlays and product designs and qualities. A third dimension of market conduct also deserves mention—namely the "acts, practices, and policies" of sellers that are aimed at (*a*) gaining advantage over, weakening, controlling, or eliminating competitors, or (*b*) discouraging or preventing the entry of new competitors to the market. These phases of conduct are conveniently labeled—drawing upon the language of the law under the antitrust statutes—as "predatory and exclusionary" (and also "coercive") tactics. We wish here to include, however, all manifestations of this generic type of conduct, whether or not they have been recognized as violating existing law.

These phases of conduct are generally expressions of rivalry and "independence," since they comprehend actions of one firm or group of firms that are directed against other firms or have the effect of disadvantaging others, though not necessarily at the expense of the aggregate profits of the industry. The creation or protection of favorable market shares and profit margins for the firms engaging in the predatory or exclusionary tactics is the ordinary rationale of these tactics, which thus also aim at the elimination or limitation of the market shares or profit margins of other firms. Correspondingly, the main purpose and effect of this sort of market conduct is typically the creation and protection of a given degree and pattern of seller concentration in the industry, and/or of a given condition of entry that is favorable to the protection of the desired concentration pattern. The secondary or derived effects of this kind of conduct are found in the market performance tendencies inherent in the market structure which is created and maintained.

The alternative types or forms of predatory and exclusionary tactics are extremely numerous. Among them, some distinctions are drawn at law—loose and fundamentally ambiguous—between (*a*) aggressive predation and exclusion, inferentially stemming from the direct purpose or intent of weakening, eliminating, or excluding competitors, and (*b*) "normal, prudent business practices" that have the aforementioned effects but simply reflect the routine exercise by established firms of the selfish advantages which inhere in their market positions. Because tactics falling in the former category are generally illegal under the antitrust statutes, whereas those classified under the latter category may not be, tactics of the former sort are uncommonly observed in recent decades. Most actual "predatory and exclusionary" tactics qualify, or try to qualify, under the second heading. However this may be, we will not attempt there to draw any hard line between the two major sorts of predatory and exclusionary conduct, since the line is ill-defined and without much analytical significance.

Forms of Predatory and Exclusionary Conduct

Some of the principal forms of predatory and exclusionary conduct, and examples of them, are:

1. **Predatory price cutting,** aimed at weakening or eliminating established competitors. Included here we find:

(*a*) *Selective price discrimination* among various geographical market areas or other customer groups, undertaken by a larger firm to weaken or eliminate a smaller firm which sells to a particular area or customer group. This is implemented by the larger firm's cutting price in the small competitor's market without cutting price in the whole market served by the larger seller. This sort of tactic has been appropriately labeled by Corwin Edwards as "discriminatory sharpshooting." It was allegedly used, for example, by the old American Tobacco Company prior to 1907 as a means of eliminating small local competitors in the pipe- and chewing-tobacco markets, and later allegedly employed by some of the large chain grocery stores in the 1920's in attacking independent competition in particular localities.

(*b*) *General price warring*, through which some firms, generally the larger ones in the industry, invoke drastic temporary price cuts, frequently below the level of immediate or variable costs. These price cuts are made in order to weaken or eliminate competitors who have lesser financial resources with which to bear losses, and to capture or recapture all or part of the market shares of these competitors. In the early 1930's in the Pacific Coast petroleum industry, for example, the seven major integrated firms periodically initiated gasoline price wars of this sort in order to recapture market shares which forty or fifty smaller firms had taken from them through much more minor price reductions over a period of time.

2. **Monopolization of raw material supplies or distributive outlets,** aimed either at limiting the market shares of established firms or at excluding the entry of new firms. Involved here are two major sorts of activity: acquisition by one or a few large firms of dominant control of necessary raw-material supplies (usually natural resource deposits), and similar acquisition of dominant control of distributive outlets needed by any manufacturer to market his goods. The result is to restrict or eliminate the access of smaller established firms or of potential entrants either to needed materials or to indispensable established marketing channels.

Vertical integration of the major established processing or manufacturing firms is involved. This includes "backward integration" into the ownership or control of resource deposits or other material supplies, or "forward integration" into the ownership or control of distributive facilities. (The integration, to exclude others, must of course proceed far enough that nonintegrated material supplies or distributive outlets no longer remain available, on attractive terms, to established or potential competitors.) Thus actual or potential competitors may be excluded or operate at a disadvantage. Or they may become "dependencies" of the integrated firms, using the latter's material supplies or distributive facilities on terms that place them at a financial disadvantage and restrict their possibilities of competitive expansion. There have been and are many instances of this sort of predatory or exclusionary tactics, usually identifiable as "normal, prudent business practices" by the larger firms. We may mention as examples:

(*a*) The progressive acquisition, from 1910 to 1940 or later, by the Aluminum Company of America of most available attractive deposits of aluminum ore (bauxite) and of uncommitted hydroelectric sites to generate the cheap power needed for aluminum production, a policy which forestalled the threatened entry of competitors to its monopolized domestic market.

(b) The practice of the principal established automobile producers (until very recently) of "tying up" nearly all of the available retail auto distributive facilities under a system of franchises by the terms of which the individual automobile dealer agreed to market only the products of the contracting manufacturer. This erected a considerable barrier to the entry of new automobile manufacturers.

(c) The joint acquisition or control by roughly the largest 20 petroleum refiners in the United States of nearly all trunk pipelines and most tankship facilities for transporting crude oil and refined products for the American market. This practice for a long time placed nonintegrated and independent crude oil producers and refiners in a position either of being denied access to economical petroleum transport, of paying a "penalty rate" for its use, or of having to undertake overwhelming financial outlays to equip themselves with transport facilities.

Generally involved here is the exploitation by vertically integrated firms of their advantages, inherent in integration, over nonintegrated firms.

3. **Various adverse uses of the inherent advantages of vertical integration.** There is a variety of specific ways in which large integrated firms in an industry can design their policies so as to disadvantage, weaken, eliminate, or exclude nonintegrated competitors. These usually emerge when the nonintegrated firms must purchase materials, supplies, or merchandise for resale at prices or on terms controlled by integrated firms, by virtue of the fact that the integrated firms are the principal available suppliers. Thus the nonintegrated firms incur higher costs or less favorable terms for materials, supplies, and so on, than their integrated competitors. In competition, therefore, they can realize smaller profits or no profits while their integrated competitors prosper. Some principal examples of this variety of phenomena are:

(a) *The price squeeze.* This can develop when the integrated firms of an industry produce both a raw material and a finished good made from the raw material (though they may purchase a part of their raw material requirements), and when the nonintegrated competitors produce only the finished good and must both sell the finished good at a price competitive with that set by the integrated firms, and buy their raw materials at a price also set or controlled by the integrated firms.

In this situation, the integrated firms *can* set raw material prices in such a relationship to finished good prices that nonintegrated competitors are "squeezed" and will operate with a minimal profit or a loss, while the integrated firms, which produce at least a good part of their own raw materials at costs below prices which the nonintegrated firms must pay, can at the same time prosper.

During the 1920's, for example, the Aluminum Company of America (Alcoa) was both the sole American supplier of basic aluminum ingot used in making certain finished aluminum products, and also a principal producer of these finished products. Certain other firms produced finished products only, which they made from aluminum ingot purchased from Alcoa. It has been alleged that during this period Alcoa set the selling price for aluminum ingot so high relative to its prices for certain finished products that the non-integrated finishers were "squeezed" to a nonprofit position, while Alcoa, essentially only paying its own production costs for the ingot it used, could prosper mightily from its integrated operation.

(b) *The semi-squeeze.* The term "price squeeze" is generally used to refer to an administered narrowing of the margin between a raw material price and a derived finished-good price to such an extent that the nonintegrated finished-good producer will make no profit or a loss. Obviously, integrated firms with nonintegrated competitors can (and frequently do) establish somewhat more liberal margins between the raw material prices at which they supply those competitors and the finished goods prices which those competitors must meet—margins sufficient to allow the nonintegrated firms some profit. But at the same time, the integrated firms may still be charging for raw materials sold to others a price well in excess of their own costs of production. In this way they may enjoy overall ample profit margins and develop and maintain strong financial positions, while their nonintegrated competitors are held in relatively weak profit and financial positions, have their possible growth retarded, and are unable to engage in strong price competition at the finished-good level.

For example, this sort of "semi-squeeze" apparently developed from the policy of General Motors, which is not only the largest American producer of motor vehicles, but has also been the largest supplier of automotive components or parts to the nonintegrated or less integrated small independent firms outside of the "Big Three" (while they survived). General Motors' stated policy has been to price its parts at levels sufficient to yield from 20 to 30 per cent per annum on the capital invested in parts production. In others words, it has set parts prices high enough to include a very substantial supernormal profit. It sold parts to outsiders at such prices, and also "sold to itself" (that is, to its own automotive vehicle divisions) at the same prices. Since the latter sales represented in essence only internal bookkeeping calculations, General Motors reaped a much larger supernormal profit overall on the integrated production of vehicles than its less integrated small competitors. For whereas General Motors really paid for parts only its own costs of producing them (inclusive of a normal profit), the nonintegrated firms that it supplied paid this cost plus a substantial supernormal profit. This sort of pricing policy was evidently one of the things that tended to keep the independents of the auto industry weak and poor. Yet it appeared to reflect nothing more than the "normal, prudent" pursuit of the advantages inherent in its integration by an integrated firm like General Motors.

(c) *Supplying of nonintegrated competitors on unequal terms.* Manipulation of prices to effect a squeeze or a semi-squeeze is not the only means by which integrated firms can disadvantage nonintegrated competitors who depend upon them for supplies. Supplying them on nonprice terms that are relatively unfavorable or restrict their competitive ability may also help the integrated firms to maintain market control.

A good example of this sort of practice appeared in the 1940's in an antitrust suit against the principal integrated motion-picture firms. These firms were integrated from production ("movie-making") through exhibition (operation of movie theatres throughout the country). They had as competitors nonintegrated exhibitors or movie-theatre operators in most cities. It was the common practice of the integrated movie firms to reserve the "first-run" exhibition market to themselves or their own theatres. They supplied films to the nonintegrated exhibitors on terms which restricted them to exhibiting any film only after a substantial waiting period following the first-run showing of the film in the integrated theatres. Since the major integrated firms were the predominant source of supply of movie films, independent exhibitors were thus excluded from the lucrative first-run exhibition market. A composite of such practices, including the one just mentioned, was found to constitute illegal joint monopolization of the first-run exhibition market, and numerous revisions of market structure and conduct were ordered by the courts. Yet the line between such illegal predation and exclusion on the one hand, and normal, prudent business practice to exploit the advantages of integration on the other, is thin and hazy.

4. **Tying arrangements and other restrictive contracts.** Without actually integrating forward to acquire ownership or full control of their distributive outlets or other buyers, large firms in an industry may successfully establish a policy of selling to buyers only on contractual terms that exclude competitors from selling to the same buyers. We have already noted, under (2) above, the practice of writing "exclusive dealing" contracts, whereby the distributor-buyers of a manufactured good are bound to deal only in the products of a single manufacturing supplier. If this policy is successfully pursued by several large firms in an industry, the access of smaller competitors to buyers and to established distributive channels may be severely restricted. In addition, two other sorts of restrictive contract, used to the same general effect, may be mentioned:

(a) *The tying contract*, whereby the buyer or user of one good supplied by a manufacturer is bound, as a condition of purchasing or using this first good, to purchase all of his requirements of other, connected goods from the same manufacturer. If one or a few firms are the sole suppliers of the first good, and it is essential to buyers, these suppliers may be able to exclude other competitors from supplying the secondary or connected goods, since all prospective buyers of these latter goods will come to be bound by tying contracts.

A classical example of this practice arose prior to 1912 in the case of the A. B. Dick Company, which was the sole supplier (under patent protection) of mimeographing machines. It sold or leased these machines only on the condition that the users purchase all of their requirements of mimeograph paper and ink from A. B. Dick, thus excluding competitive paper and ink suppliers from the given market. Later examples include the leasing of gasoline-pump equipment to service stations by petroleum refiners on the condition that the service stations involved purchase all their gasoline from the pump-supplying refiner. Such practices have not generally been found illegal if a number of sellers in an industry all follow the same policy in competition with each other.

(b) *The full-requirements contract.* A close cousin of the tying contract, the full-requirements contract is occasionally used by the supplier of industrial goods to bind the buyer to purchasing all of his needs of a given good from the single supplier, as a condition of obtaining an assured supply and also, ordinarily, of receiving supplementary services from the supplier. Such contracts, for example, were widely employed prior to 1950 by the largest two manufacturers of tin cans, who in return gave their buyers (such as food-canning companies) advisory services and favorable leases on can-closing machinery. The effects of such contracts in restricting the competition of smaller firms are similar to those of tying contracts.

5. **Restrictive uses of patent licensing.** If one firm (or a group who pool their interests) controls patents covering product designs or productive processes that must be used for successful operation in an industry, it may and often has shared its patent monopoly with other firms by granting them licenses (at a royalty) to make the patented products or use the patented processes. If the firm or group does this, and in addition grants licenses to only a selected few firms, it effectively excludes the entry of further competitors until the patent grants expire or until alternative and effectively competing products or processes not covered by its patents are developed. Also, the licensees of the patent holder may be restricted as to the outputs they may produce or the prices they may charge by the terms of the licenses, with resultant limitation and control of their market shares. Such licensing systems have been in effect, for example, in the electric light bulb industry, mentioned in a preceding section, and in the gypsum products industry, where, prior to 1951, the number of producers of and the production of plasterboard was controlled under licenses granted by U. S. Gypsum. There has been an increasing tendency of late on the part of the courts to find industry-wide schemes for the control of competition via patent licenses to constitute an illegal extension of the basic patent monopoly, and a violation of the antitrust laws.

The preceding list of examples is not exhaustive of the whole range of "predatory and exclusionary" practices discovered in various markets, but it serves to illustrate their general content. Most such practices or policies are dually effective in (*a*) restricting or weakening existing competition, and (*b*) preventing or discouraging the entry of new competitors. The predictable proximate effects of these lines of conduct are of course various, but their general tendency is to create and preserve more concentrated market structures than would otherwise exist, and to elevate the barriers to the entry of new sellers to various markets. Their indirect effects on market performance are essentially those of increased seller concentration and heightened barriers to entry.

As to the association of such market conduct to market structures, one obvious link is that it tends to create and perpetuate certain types of market structure, generally favoring higher seller concentration and higher barriers to entry. Market structure, in other words, is to some extent created by conduct, although the conduct in question generally is feasible because of certain basic environmental or structural characteristics of industries that various sellers can exploit to their advantage. Predatory and exclusionary conduct is important mostly in industries of oligopolistic structure in which vertical integration by large firms is feasible and financially attractive, and in which scale economies and investment requirements deter other and smaller firms from accomplishing the same vertical integration.

The incidence of predatory and exclusionary practices—if these are broadly construed to include normal and prudent business policies oriented to the exploitation of the inherent advantages of larger firms— is evidently widespread. The principal issue from the standpoint of regulatory law and policy is to what extent these practices *per se* are strategic to the maintenance of existing market structures and market performance, and to what extent they are simply superficial and more or less automatic manifestations of more basic structural conditions. This issue will loom large as we consider, in later chapters, the appropriate character and orientation of a governmental antitrust policy.

The Market Conduct of Buyers

In discussing the market conduct of firms we have emphasized almost exclusively their conduct as sellers in the markets in which they offer their products, and have given little attention to the related conduct of the buyers to whom they sell. The reason for this initial emphasis is that in the great majority of markets throughout the economy the role of the buyer is passive whereas that of the seller is active. Sellers are active in the sense that they set prices (or outputs), design products, promote sales, and so forth. Buyers are passive in the sense that each individually reacts to what is offered him without being able to make a policy regarding the price he pays, or perceptibly influencing it or the product alternatives available to him.

This is because, in the great majority of markets, buyers are many and individually small, each purchasing so small a fraction of market supply that he cannot assume more than the passive role described. Atomistic buying markets are extremely common, and much more common than atomistic selling markets. Even in such atomistic buying markets, to be sure, the details of buyer conduct can be studied: what attracts buyers, what motivates them, and how price-conscious they are as opposed to being influenced by advertising or by product brand or quality. But these details are not of great analytical interest from the standpoint of our aims in this book. In a minority of markets, however, buyers are few in number and individually purchase large enough fractions of total market supply that they can play a more active role. In particular they can either influence or dominate the determination of the prices at which they buy, by virtue of their ability to withhold individually significant amounts of purchases from sellers in the industry. In these cases, the market conduct of buyers deserves separate attention.

It simplifies matters at the outset if we recognize that in nearly all cases of nonatomistic and nonindependent buying, the buyers in question are not consumers but producers—that is, business firms purchasing materials or equipment for use in production, or merchandise for resale. In general they are thus presumably influenced in their conduct by the same profit-making motives that influences the sellers who supply them. The minor sort of individual negotiation or higgling by consumer buyers that goes on in some markets with more or less atomistic buying structures may safely be neglected for purposes of a broad and general analysis.

With respect to the price-determining conduct of nonindependent buyers in concentrated buying markets, the same general range of questions may initially be raised as was raised regarding the market conduct of nonindependent sellers: what are the patterns of inter-buyer coordination (collusion, simple interdependence, and so on), and what are the effective aims of price calculation pursued. It is unnecessary here to reiterate the obvious classifications of alternatives with special reference to buyers, but two differences in the general analysis and interpretation of alternatives must be noted.

First, the predictable consequences of given aims of price determination as applied by nonindependent buyers will generally tend in a reverse direction from the predictable consequences of the same aims as pursued by nonindependent sellers. For example, joint profit maximization by buyers will tend to be *price-lowering* to some maximally profitable point (monopsonistic rather than monopolistic in its orientation). Hybrid profit maximization with the introduction elements of independence of pricing action by buyers will tend to result in a lesser depression of buying price, and so forth. Joint profit-maximizing action by sellers tends to bring prices above a competitive level whereas by buyers it tends to bring price below a competitive level. In both cases, elements of independent profit-maximizing action tend to bring price (down or up) closer to the competitive level.

Second, as we consider cases of concentrated buying, we encounter a special order of situation generally describable as bilateral oligopoly—where both sellers and buyers are few and relatively large, or where there is a significant degree of concentration on both the seller and the buyer side of the market. Here market conduct expresses the active antagonism of seller and buyer interests in some sort of a bargaining or negotiation process, and a special analysis is required.

Otherwise, the same difficulties noted in the case of seller conduct are encountered in deciding from available evidence of buyer conduct *per se* what price-determining aims have been pursued and what performance tendencies might be predicted. Again, direct reference to market performance is generally essential as a basis for inferring the guiding aims of conduct. We may therefore abbreviate our treatment of buyers' price policies by commenting on some superficial evidence of performance and conduct with nonindependent buying in two main sorts of structural setting.

Oligopsonistic Buying from Atomistic Selling Markets

The first of these, involving a concentrated group of buyers facing a large number of small sellers, is found in at least a limited number of instances wherein the member firms of a concentrated processing industry purchase a raw material from an essentially atomistic supplying industry. The purchase of leaf tobacco by a few large cigarette manufacturers, or of a substantial part of the crude petroleum supply by a relatively few large refiners, exemplifies this sort of buyer-seller relationship. Individual instances range from those with very high buyer concentration to those in which buyer concentration is only moderate, with a substantial fringe of small buyers present.

From general observation of a scattering of cases, the following impressions emerge. First, with highly concentrated buying, patterns of tacit collusion implemented by buying price leadership by the largest buyer are frequently in evidence. If not, close interdependence in the buying price policies of the principal buyers is found. Performance evidence concerning the height of price relative to suppliers' costs or to a hypothetical competitive level of price frequently suggests a lowering of price roughly consistent with the maximization of the joint profits of the buyers, and little independent or competitive action on the part of individual buyers.

Second, with only moderate buyer concentration and a fringe of small buyers, collusive and parallel buyer action is usually not in evidence, and the record of performance suggests that a price close to the competitive level is frequently attained by virtue of buying price policies which are strongly influenced if not dominated by independent and competitive action. But the body of evidence so far assembled is far from sufficient to support any firm, general conclusions.

Bilateral Oligopoly—Large Buyers
versus Large Sellers

Where there is a significant degree of concentration on both the buying and the selling sides of a market, as happens with some minor fraction of markets for manufactured and other goods—we find two active sets of price-making policies in opposition: the sellers' policies and the buyers' policies. Then the usual total conduct pattern is one of bargaining or negotiation between buyers and sellers, resulting in the determination either of a single general price applying to all transactions or of a variety of prices paid by individual buyers or in individual transactions. (In the latter event, a "general market price" does not emerge, but rather a complex of different prices reflecting a sort of "chaotic discrimination" in price among different buyers and different transactions.)

One interesting question in actual cases of bilateral oligopoly concerns the usual form of the bargaining pattern. In particular, is there ordinarily solid-front or group action by organized sellers, organized buyers, or both—possibly leading to a single industry-wide bargain on price applicable to all transactions—or is there a complex pattern of many individual bargains by various pairs of seller and buyer? What the pattern would be in "classical" cases, in which a very few large buyers opposed a very few large sellers—say, four or five of each—and no others, is hard to determine from evidence, since such classical cases seldom seem to occur in fact. The actual bilateral oligopoly situation is usually one in which there are, on both the selling and the buying sides, concentrated cores of large firms that supply or purchase significant individual shares of the total market supply, and in addition numerous smaller sellers and buyers who supply or purchase relatively insignificant shares of the total volume. This situation constitutes a rather poor setting for solid-front or cohesive action by either the combined sellers or the combined buyers.

The market for automobile tires in the years immediately following World War II provides a fairly good example of the usual bilateral oligopoly situation. On the supply side, the Big Four of the tire industry produced about 80 per cent of the total tire output, but about 30 smaller firms of varying sizes produced the remaining 20 per cent. On the buyer side of the market, about 30 per cent of the total tire output was sold to automotive manufacturers (for original equipment on vehicles), with the three largest auto firms accounting for about 90 per cent of these purchases. The largest, General Motors, might have bought over 10 per cent of all tires produced, and Ford and Chrysler roughly half this much apiece. In addition, another 30 per cent of the total tire output was sold to so-called mass distributors, including national mail order houses and large petroleum refiners operating or controlling chains of service stations. The number of such mass buyers was in the neighborhood of twenty, and the largest few of them probably accounted for several per cent apiece of total tire sales. Finally, about 40 per cent of all tire volume was sold to independent tire distributors and dealers (or through manufacturer-owned retail outlets), and the buyers in this market numbered in the thousands and were in general individually small. A moderately concentrated oligopsonistic core including buyers of varying sizes, plus a very substantial competitive fringe of small buyers, faced a concentrated oligopoly of sellers surrounded by a significant fringe of small sellers. This example is cited at length because it represents, *roughly*, the sort of actual bilateral oligopoly situation that is usually encountered.

In this more or less typical sort of bilateral oligopoly setting, several things are notable about market conduct and performance in determining price. First, solid-front bargaining for a price by organized sellers or buyers or both is at least uncommon—group negotiations do not generally appear. Second, we find instead a pattern of individual negotiations of single large buyers with both large and small individual sellers, in which bargaining or negotiation the large buyer uses his relatively massive purchasing power as a lever to secure more favorable prices, and in which the sellers, as best they can, attempt to "hold a line" on price.

The outcome of this bargaining procedure is likely to depend in considerable part on the relation of overall market demand to productive capacity at a particular time. In periods of short demand and excess capacity, large buyers frequently secure substantial price concessions relative to the prices paid by small buyers and relative, perhaps, to a long-run competitive level of price. In periods of burgeoning demand and fully utilized capacity, the bargaining power of large buyers may avail them little in the way of advantageous prices. Prices to the small buyers in the market are likely to be set by the sellers, with individual bargaining playing no important role, though they are set at various levels depending on the degree of independence of action of sellers relative to this small-buyer market. The usual overall result is that a wide variety of different net prices are charged to different buyers or in different transactions, with a general tendency being for small buyers to pay more than large buyers. It is extremely difficult to say—although the hypothesis has been advanced without much support—that the overall or average effect of bilateral oligopoly negotiations is in fact or should be generally to produce a competitive price of the sort that might rule if both buyers and sellers were numerous and individually small. The variance of individual results overwhelms the meaning of any statistically observed average tendency.

Predatory Tactics of Buyers, and Other Matters

The emergence of price discrimination between small and large enterprise-buyers, attributable to the exercise of superior bargaining power by the latter, may give the large buyers a competitive advantage over small competitors in their own selling markets. Thus the large automobile manufacturer might purchase tires or other components at lower prices than small competing automobile manufacturers, and be able to sell autos profitably at a lower price. Or a national retail chain store might purchase groceries or electrical appliances for less than smaller competitors and be able to undersell these small competitors in the retail market until the latter were weakened or eliminated. Thus it is not difficult to identify discriminatory buying advantages of large firms with "predatory and exclusionary" practices aimed at smaller firms that compete in the same selling markets.

Federal legislation has been passed to prohibit any seller from discriminating in price between buyers who in turn compete in selling, except on the basis of actual differences in the costs of supplying the different buyers. (The Robinson-Patman Act of 1936, amending Section 2 of the Clayton Act, contains these provisions.) Although this legislation has had some effect in eliminating "unjustified" price discrimination, it seems fair to say that, by various devices, the larger buying firms in bilateral oligopoly markets still frequently obtain buying-price advantages based on their bargaining power, and corresponding cost advantages over competitors in their own selling markets. Whether or not the securing of such advantages by large enterprise buyers constitutes "predation" or "exclusion" is a semantic and a legal question, and not one of economic analysis.

Another sort of allegedly predatory or exclusionary policy by buyers may emerge when integrated firms producing, let us say, both a raw material and a finished good made from the material, are also purchasers or potential purchasers from nonintegrated producers who produce only the raw material. Then, if there is a "tapered" integration, so that the integrated firms control a larger fraction of the finished-good market than of the connected raw-material market, the nonintegrated suppliers of the raw material may find that the integrated firms are their essential customers. They are dependent on the integrated firms for a market, and the integrated firms can subject them to unfavorable prices or other terms for the sale of their raw materials.

Suppose, for example, that the integrated producers of refined petroleum products, such as gasoline, supply 80 per cent of the market for refined products, but produce only 50 per cent of the crude oil required to make these products, purchasing another 30 per cent of the total crude-oil supply from nonintegrated producers. Since the nonintegrated crude oil producers then depend on the integrated firms for three-fifths of their market, the integrated firms might be able to set crude-oil buying prices below a competitive level, thus weakening or restricting the growth of their nonintegrated competitors. Or, integrated movie producers, controlling the bulk of first-run exhibition facilities as well as ample facilities for producing films, might exclude or limit the growth of potential or actual nonintegrated film producers (who lack exhibition facilities) by refusing to exhibit, on favorable terms if at all, the films of these nonintegrated producers in their integrated exhibition facilities. Both of these sorts of "predatory and exclusionary" tactics of integrated buyers have in the past been alleged in the instances cited. Whether or not the particular allegations are true, the possibility is clearly present. Vertical integration, especially of the "tapered" or unbalanced sort, may clearly provide a pivot for disadvantaging nonintegrated competitors who sell to integrated firms, as well as competitors who purchase from them. The sort of policy indicated, however, may usually just as well be viewed as reflecting a normally prudent, selfish exploitation of the inherent advantages of integration, as it may be viewed as reflecting an illegal intent to eliminate or exclude competition.

The careful reader will note that the conclusions that may legitimately be derived from actual observations of market conduct per se are generally *taxonomic* in character and lacking in genuine analytical significance. It is thus appropriate that we turn now directly to the observation of the market performance to which market structure and conduct lead, and to the inferences which can be drawn from observation of this performance.

SUPPLEMENTARY READINGS

Oxenfeldt, A. R., *Industrial Pricing and Market Practices*, 1951.
Adams, W., *The Structure of American Industry*, 1961, (3rd ed.), Ch. 2–14.
Kaplan, A. D. H., J. B. Dirlam, and R. F. Lanzillotti, *Pricing in Big Business*, 1958.
Bain, J. S., *Price Theory*, 1952, Ch. VI.

10

Market Performance in American Industries

Market performance encompasses the strategic end results of the market conduct of sellers and buyers. For sellers it is measured by the character of their adjustments to the effective demands and for their outputs; for buyers, by their adjustments to the supply conditions for the goods they purchase. It is the crucial indicator of how well the market activity of firms has contributed to the enhancement of general material welfare.

On the old principle that "handsome is as handsome does," the long-term performance tendencies of an industry are sufficient criteria of its effectiveness in fulfilling material-welfare goals. Market structure and conduct patterns are significant only to the extent that they are systematically associated with market performance, and they can be evaluated ultimately only in terms of the performance patterns to which they lead. It is thus appropriate that we examine evidence both of the market performance of various industries and of the associations of structure and conduct to performance.

A full appraisal of the market performance of industries is difficult because performance has many dimensions. The adjustment to effective demand that the sellers in any industry make has numerous aspects, and the same is true of buyers' adjustments to supplies. Moreover, the particular set of performance dimensions which are analytically significant varies from industry to industry. Each industry is in some degree a special or unique case requiring a "tailor-made" appraisal not fully applicable to other industries. As a result, market performance patterns could be *completely* appraised only by an interminable series of intensive, detailed studies, each devoted to one of the many hundreds or thousands of individual industries in the economy.

A certain few broad aspects of market performance, to be sure, are important in all industries. These include, for instance, the "technical" efficiency of the organization of the industry as judged by the scales of plants and firms, the "allocative" efficiency of the industry as measured by the relation of price to cost (and reflected in the profit rate), and the size of selling costs in relation to sales revenue. But in each of many groups of industries some additional or "special" aspect of performance, not significant in most other industries, will be of great importance.

In the petroleum industry, for example, performance in the "efficiency dimensions" are important, but an overwhelming aspect of market performance involves the sort of conservation of crude oil deposits the industry accomplishes. Yet in 90 per cent of all industries, conservation performance would be of negligible importance, since the exploitation of a scarce natural resource would not be primarily involved. In the automobile industry, efficiency is again important, but product performance is at least equally so. The level of quality and design of the product that is attained relative to alternatives, alternative costs being considered, has a strong impact on consumer welfare. Yet in the great bulk of industries—producing more standardized, simple, and slowly changing products—product performance would be a minor aspect of the total performance pattern. Or, in the steel industry, which has disparately located production centers and a product with a high weight and shipping cost relative to its value, we find that the relationship of delivered prices among various buyer locations is a performance dimension of substantial importance. But for the great majority of goods and industries the geographical pricing pattern is a minor matter. In sum, individual industries or groups of industries have so many peculiarities that even reasonably complete appraisals of market performance could emerge only from long series of special studies.

This route to ultimate enlightenment regarding the total performance of industries is thus long and slowly traveled—so slowly up to now that, with many hundreds of industries needing investigation, it would be difficult to find intensive and competent studies of market performance in as many as a dozen cases. The few adequate case studies available, moreover, provide no valid basis for generalization about all industrial performance, because almost every case appears to be in a significant degree unique.

There is thus a strong case, in the present state of investigation and knowledge, for not taking the easy road of presenting a few isolated case studies and encouraging facile and unsupported generalizations from them. Instead, we find it scientifically more satisfying to emphasize the cross-sectional analysis of certain basic dimensions of performance in numerous industries, striking directly at the goal of valid generalization. This is true even though the dimensions of performance considered must be very few in number, and though a great deal of the unique and sometimes important detail concerning individual industries is neglected in the process.

We will emphasize here the so-called efficiency dimensions of market performance. These include technical efficiency and allocative efficiency. An industry's market performance in the dimension of technical efficiency refers to how closely it approaches (or how far it misses) the goal of supplying whatever output it produces at the minimum attainable unit cost of production. Technical efficiency thus construed is then determined by:

1. The extent to which the firms in an industry and their plants attain or closely approach optimal scales—or the proportion of industry output that is supplied by plants and firms of at least approximately optimal scale.

2. The extent to which these firms and their plants attain or closely approach optimal degrees of vertical integration of successive processes or functions.

3. The extent to which the firms attain or closely approach the most efficient rates of utilization of their plant facilities—in effect, the extent, of any, of "chronic" excess capacity in the industry.[1]

Allocative efficiency, as pointed out in Chapter 2 (pp. 23–24), concerns essentially the rate of output of the industry, or the amount of scarce productive resources allocated to producing its ouput—relative to the outputs produced and resources committed in other industries. Optimal allocation of resources among all industries would involve all industry outputs being such that each productive resource had the same marginal productivity in every industry. Subject to some simplifying assumptions, the allocative efficiency attained by an individual industry may be judged by the long-run relationship between its selling price and its marginal cost of production that results from the particular rate of output it produces. An industry tends to contribute best to the most efficient long-run allocation of resources among uses if its long-run out-

[1]The most efficient rate of utilization of plant, as noted below, is subject to several alternative definitions. A rate simply involving no chronic excess capacity, it will be argued, is the most desirable, all things considered.

put is such that its long-run selling price equals its long-run marginal cost of production. It tends to lessen overall allocative efficiency to the extent that its output is smaller, so that its price exceeds its long-run marginal cost, or is greater, so that its price is less than is long-run marginal cost. The allocative efficiency of an industry may thus be appraised (to a close approximation) by:

4. The relationship of the industry's long-run selling price to its long-run marginal cost of production—by how close to or far from equality this price and marginal cost are.

Because long-run marginal costs are usually not directly measurable, and also because the long-run average cost of production is typically about the same as the long-run marginal cost,[2] the allocative efficiency of an industry is in practice best judged by the relationship of its long-run selling price to its long-run average cost of production. And the most convenient available indicator (if properly interpreted) of this price-average cost relation is the long-run average rate of profit that firms in the industry earn on owners' investments. Thus allocative efficiency is for practical purposes judged by observing:

4'. The long-run average rate of profit on owners' equity that firms in an industry earn. As we will see later, a long-run industry accounting-profit rate that is equal to the market rate of interest indicates optimal allocative performance; higher or lower rates suggest that too few or too many resources have been allocated to supplying output from that industry.

A related aspect of industry performance to which we will also give some emphasis is the size of sales-promotion costs, or ratio of such costs to total sales revenue. This might also be viewed as an efficiency dimension of performance, since it involves the efficiency of the allocation of resources between producing goods on the one hand, and promoting their sales on the other. Much briefer attention will be paid—because of a lack either of data or of economy-wide importance—to the following additional dimensions of market performance: progressiveness in production techniques; product quality, variety, and improvement; conservation; and price flexibility.

For each of the dimensions of market performance examined, we will take a cross-sectional view of a considerable number of industries, with a view to ascertaining any prevalent general tendencies. The sample of

[2] This is because the firms supplying the bulk of output in most industries have larger than minimum optimal scales, and thus long-run average costs that are constant with long-run variations in output, in which case long-run average and long-run marginal costs are identical.

industries considered will be only in the manufacturing sector, though some remarks on performance in other sectors are added in Chapter 12.

Technical Efficiency in Manufacturing Industries

A dominant aspect of the performance of any industry is its relative technical efficiency in producing and distributing goods. This efficiency is measured by how closely the firms in the industry approximate the lowest attainable costs for the actual outputs they produce and distribute. Both attained and attainable costs, for this purpose, should refer basically to real costs in terms of human and physical resources used, or to the money value of such resources as valued at uniform prices. Then the cost measure of efficiency is not influenced by "strictly pecuniary" considerations revolving around possible variations in the money prices that firms may pay for given real resources.

For example, if each of two firms produces one unit of the same product with two hours of labor of the same grade and quality, they have the same efficiency in real terms even though one firm pays $2 per hour for labor and incurs a money cost of $4 per unit, and the other pays $1.50 per hour for labor and has a money cost of $3 per unit. Similarly, if the minimum attainable cost of the output in question is one and a half hours of labor, both firms have the same relative inefficiency in real terms. Their costs are one-third above minimum attainable—regardless of any differences in money wage rates. This matter is of some importance in evaluating differences in the historical accounting costs of different firms.

The technical efficiency of an industry, broadly construed, is subject to two main sorts of influence: the technical efficiency of its organization and the internal efficiency of its individual member firms.

The efficiency of market organization is primarily reflected, as noted above, in three things: the horizontal size or scale of the plants and firms in the industry, relative to the scales which would permit lowest unit costs; the degree of vertical integration of plants and firms, relative to the cost-minimizing degree of integration; and the long-run rate of utilization of existing plant capacity, relative to the most economical feasible rate of utilization.

The internal efficiency of individual firms, on the other hand, refers (given existing plant and firm scales, patterns of integration, and degrees of excess capacity) to the relative efficacy of the internal organization and management of the firms in minimizing costs. It thus reflects the degree of managerial wisdom in selecting and using productive techniques and methods, in selecting cost-minimizing combinations of productive factors or agents, in designing administrative organizations, and in administering operations.

As suggested earlier, we will be concerned here only with the first aspect of technical efficiency—that is, with the efficiency of existing market or industry organization, taking as given whatever sort of internal performance of enterprises may be experienced. Let us consider how well existing market organization serves the ends of efficiency in American industry.

Relative Efficiency of the Scales of Existing Plants and Firms

In Chapter 6 we have already developed some qualitative and quantitative analysis of the relationship of the size or scale of the plant and the firm to its efficiency. Before proceeding with the present section, let us review the passage in question, since the concepts and terms developed there are directly applicable at this point. In brief, the crucial notions set forth were the following:

1. For plants in general (a plant being defined as a unified body of productive facilities) there is usually a systematic relationship of the scale of the plant to its efficiency as measured by unit costs of production and distribution. This relationship is such that increases in the scale of a plant from zero up to some "minimum optimal" scale are accompanied by successive reductions in unit cost because of the realization of economies of large-scale production. But after the plant exceeds this minimum optimal scale, further increases in its size will neither further reduce unit costs nor increase them.[3] Thus it is possible in any industry to have plants that are *(a)* too small for efficiency, *(b)* just big enough (of minimum optimal scale), and *(c)* bigger than need be for efficiency (of superoptimal scale), though no less efficient for this reason.

2. The relative importance of economies of large-scale plants in different industries may be measured by determining for each industry *(a)* the percentage of the total market output that would be supplied by one plant of minimum optimal scale, and *(b)* the extent to which unit costs will be elevated for plants of successively smaller scale—or, to put it another way, the rate and pattern of decline in unit costs as plant scale increases up to the minimum optimal scale. Evidence presented in

[3]Specifically, such increases in plant scale beyond the minimum optimal scale should not affect unit production costs in any event, and increases in plant facilites controlled by one firm should not lessen efficiency in physical distribution if successive increments of efficient plant units can be strategically (and perhaps disparately) located so as to minimize unit distribution costs.

Chapter 6 suggested that the importance of plant-scale economies, as evaluated in these terms, varies widely among industries because of differences in technology and in size of market.

3. For firms controlling one or more plants, there may be additional economies of large-scale production or distribution as the firm grows to some point beyond the minimum optimal scale of one plant, although the existence of such economies is debated. In any event, if or where there are such economies, we can conceive of a minimum optimal scale for the multiplant firm which is larger than the scale of one optimal plant. The importance of economies of the multiplant firm can be measured in the usual terms: percentage of the market supplied by one firm of minimum optimal scale, and extent of elevation of unit costs for firms of successively smaller scales. Findings presented in Chapter 6 suggested that economies of multiplant firms are found in some but by no means in all industries, and that these economies are in general relatively slight.

4. With the growth of firms beyond some critical size, there may possibly be diseconomies of very large-scale production, unit costs rising in response to "excessive" growth. The actuality of this phenomenon is debated, however, and, as seen in Chapter 6, available evidence does not demonstrate that it occurs.

Evidence bearing on two questions related to efficient performance as affected by scales of plants and firms has already been presented in Chapter 6. Those concerned the extent to which existing firms are larger in scale than need be for technical efficiency, and the extent to which seller concentration in various industries is greater than the minimum required for optimal efficiency. Our tentative conclusions were that, in varying degrees among industries, the principal firms are very frequently larger—and seller concentration thus higher—than would be required for producing going outputs at the lowest attainable unit costs. In the same chapter, a third question, directly concerning efficient performance, was also tentatively disposed of by the finding from evidence that in general the largest firms in our manufacturing industries appear not to be so large as to lose efficiency by suffering perceptible diseconomies of very large scale.

Here we address ourselves to a further and perhaps more crucial question concerning technical efficiency, as follows. To what extent are existing plants and firms in our various industries big enough for optimal efficiency? That is, to what extent are they either of minimum optimal scale or larger, or if below minimum optimal scale still large enough to suffer no significant diseconomies of insufficient scale? And, con-

versely, what proportions of the outputs of various industries are supplied by plants or firms that incur appreciably higher than minimal
costs because of their unduly small scales?

Evidence related to this question has been drawn almost entirely
from the study of a sample of twenty manufacturing industries (discussed in other respects in Chapters 6, 7, and 8). It concerns, first, efficiency as affected by the scales of plants, and second, efficiency as influenced by the scales of multiplant firms.

A first finding regarding plant scales was that for every one of the
twenty industries, the great bulk (but never all) of industry output was
supplied by plants of "reasonably efficient" scale. It was supplied, that
is, by plants that either were of at least minimum optimal scale, or were
smaller by only such an amount that their unit costs were not significantly above the optimal level (in light of the shape of their plant scale
curves). The proportion of industry output supplied by such efficient
plants ranged, over the twenty industries, from about 70 per cent at the
minimum to 90 per cent at the maximum. (A few of the largest plants
in most industries were of substantially greater than minimum optimal
scale because large firms had duplicated efficient plant units on single
geographical sites. But these very large plants were not apparently
either more or less efficient than plants close to the minimum optimal
scale.)

Second—and this is simply a reflection of the first finding—the industries studied typically have an "inefficient fringe" of inefficiently small
plants that supplied from 10 to 30 per cent of the output of the industry.
The size of this fringe, as measured in terms of fraction of industry output supplied, is an effective measure of the degree of inefficiency due to
insufficient plant scale found in our manufacturing industries (so far as
they are fairly represented by the sample in question). The variation of
the size of the inefficient fringe among industries (between 10 and 30
per cent of industry output) did not appear to be especially related to
the most prominent structural characteristics of the industries (seller
concentration and the condition of entry), though the fringe did show
some tendency to be larger in industries with strong product differentiation.

Third, most of the inefficiently small plants in these inefficient fringes
appeared to belong to one-plant firms. Thus insufficient firm size and insufficient plant size to a considerable degree went hand in hand. It
might be added that these fringes of inefficiently small plants (and
firms) show a strong tendency to persist over time, not only in the collective but in the individual sense. Inefficiently small plants in general, therefore, are *not* young, expanding plants that later grow to ef-

ficient scale. The condition is chronic, and not apparently an incident of a process of healthy growth.

If evident or claimed economies of the multiplant firm were taken into account (in the six industries of the twenty sampled such economies were held to exist), the overall efficiency picture was not greatly altered. That is, the bulk of industry output still appeared to come not only from plants of optimally efficient size but also from multiplant firms of optimally efficient size. The multiplant organization of the dominant firms was roughly sufficient to fulfill all scale requirements for efficiency. So far as this was not exactly so, the cost disadvantages attributable to possibly "undersized" firms was generally slight. It was slight enough, moreover, that our previous judgments concerning the proportions of industry outputs that are supplied with reasonable efficiency were not appreciably altered.

The findings from this small sample of industries could only by accident be exactly representative of the tendencies toward efficiency in scales of plants and firms in manufacturing industries in general. But they lend support to the thesis that large proportions of the output of most American manufacturing industries are supplied by plants and firms of reasonably efficient scale.

Relative Efficiency of Existing Degrees of Vertical Integration

The same sorts of questions can be asked about the degrees of vertical integration of firms as were asked about their horizontal scales above and in Chapter 6. That is, we can ask how important and pervasive are the economies of vertical integration, how fully the potential economies of integration have been realized in existing firms, and whether and to what extent there is more integration in being than is strictly required for purposes of economy. Unfortunately, we cannot answer any of these questions on the basis of systematized information now available. (The lack of systematic research endeavor in this area is in part explained by the fact that vertical integration is a much more complex and many-dimensioned phenomenon than the extension of horizontal scale, and correspondingly harder to study.) In the present state of knowledge, we confine ourselves to a few remarks based on miscellaneous scraps of evidence.

First, there are evidently numerous instances in which vertical integration of successive processes or functions in the single firm has been found to be more economical than the alternative of having the processes or functions carried out separately in independent firms.

However, the cases of clear economies of integration generally involve a physical or technical integration of the processes in a single plant. A classic case is that of integrating iron-making and steel-making to effect a saving in fuel costs by eliminating a reheating of the iron before it is fed to a steel furnace. Where integration does not have this physical or technical aspect—as it does not, for example, in integrating the production of assorted components with the assembly of those components—the case for cost savings from integration is generally much less clear.

Second, whether firms in the various industries are usually integrated enough to realize the genuine available economies of vertical integration is a question to which we are simply not in a position to give any meaningful answer. On the one hand, a great deal of vertical integration has developed in the last hundred years, affecting numerous industries. On the other hand, there are many unexploited opportunities for integration which *might* be economical, and a small scattering of cases in which the failure to integrate has been alleged to be a source of relative inefficiency. We are not in a situation where we can generalize on this point.

Third, the trained observer tends to form a considerable suspicion from casual observation that there is a good deal of vertical integration which, although not actually uneconomical, is also not justified on the basis of any cost savings. This is apparently true in particular of the integration of distributive facilities by manufacturing firms. In most cases the rationale of the integration is evidently the increase of the market power of the firms involved rather than a reduction in cost. It is also apparently true of the integration of resource deposits by processors (of iron ore, aluminum ore, copper ore, and petroleum deposits by the corresponding processing firms), or of specialized transport facilities by processors (iron ore, petroleum).

There are some instances of integration of successive manufacturing processes within the firm—exemplified by engine and body component production for automobiles being integrated with auto assembly—where the explanation and justification of the integration appears very clearly to involve mainly market advantage rather than increased efficiency. And, unfortunately, the systematic adoption of a given integration pattern not justified on efficiency grounds may impose a greater horizontal scale requirement for the production of the final product than would be required with a less integrated productive organization. We may tentatively conclude that there is a significant incidence, in manufacturing industries and elsewhere, of degrees of vertical integration which are "unnecessarily high" from the standpoint of efficiency, and thus of firm sizes which are "unnecessarily large."

Fully Utilized versus Excess Capacity

A third aspect of the technical efficiency with which an industry performs involves the relationship of its total productive capacity to the aggregate market demand for its product. Given whatever scales and degrees of integration the plants and firms of an industry have developed, there is the following question. Is the aggregate capacity "just right" in the sense of being present in such an amount as to supply the demand in the most efficient way? Or is there either redundant capacity that raises costs above the minimum attainable level, or insufficient capacity that is used to fulfill demand only by utilizing it with uneconomically high intensity?

Aside from the fact that available evidence bearing on these questions is rather scanty, the fundamental definition of ideal efficiency in capacity utilization raises complex issues and is in some degree arbitrary. Suppose that an industry experiences periodic fluctuations in demand, in connection with general business cycles or otherwise. Is the most "efficient" adaptation of capacity to demand one that gives the lowest unit costs for the aggregate of output over all stages of the demand fluctuation, and that thus involves some shortage of capacity and either rationing or acutely elevated prices at times of peak demand? Or is it the adaptation that permits the high levels of demand to be met without price-elevating shortages, so that capacity is fully adequate for "boom" periods? Is the latter the best adaptation even though it involves more redundant capacity in slack or depressed periods, with a probable elevation of the average cost of supplying any given aggregate demand through time?

We are inclined to support the latter definition of "most efficient" capacity—thus justifying somewhat larger capacities in the case of most industries. The provision of capacity in such amounts in many industries will generally permit high-demand or boom periods to be sustained for much longer periods in the economy as a whole, and the resulting gain in the total employment and output of the economy should outweigh any nominal increase in unit costs that is due to a poorer cyclical load factor on plant capacity. We cannot say that the capacity which minimizes the unit costs of supplying a *given* aggregate demand over time in a fluctuating environment is the most efficient, simply because, for all industries together, the course of demand through time and its aggregate over time is not independent of the amount of capacity available to supply goods.

A second issue concerns the treatment of obsolete capacity. In the usual industry, plant capacity will be of various ages, states of repair, and degrees of technical "up-to-dateness." A plant is properly considered *obsolete*, however, only when because of age, old-fashioned technology, or other factors, the cost per unit of output for simply maintaining and operating the existing plant exceeds the alternative cost per unit of output for building as well as operating and maintaining a new plant. Even according to this strict definition, obsolete plant capacity does persist in some industries, though often on a "standby" nonoperating basis or with a very low rate of utilization. The main question is whether truly obsolete plants should be counted in appraising the desirability of adjustment of capacity to demand. The answer is, generally, "No."

That is, there is an optimal adjustment of capacity to demand when all nonobsolete plant capacity is just sufficient to supply demand in the most efficient way. Correspondingly, a situation in which a part of total demand (in periods of high demand) must be met from obsolete capacity is a situation of insufficient investment in plant. A redundancy of plant capacity consisting entirely of redundant obsolete plant is not truly one of excess capacity. This is so in spite of the fact that redundant obsolete capacity may in practice be operated, with a resultant loss of efficiency, to supply some of the market which efficient plants could otherwise supply. The inefficiency in this case is not attributable to excess capacity in the strict sense, but to other deficiencies in the structure of the industry.

If we employ the standards just suggested, what is the apparent incidence of deviations (in the direction of either insufficient capacity or excess capacity) from the norm of an efficient adjustment of capacity to demand? For manufacturing industries only, as judged largely on the basis of our sample of twenty industries, the following general impressions are gained.

First, insufficient capacity to meet high-level demands does not seem to be encountered in a significant proportion of cases, at any rate as a *chronic* phenomenon. To be sure, transitory insufficiencies of capacity are not infrequently encountered, these being attributable to misestimations of future demand by the firms of an industry, or to lags in expanding capacity to match a steadily growing demand. But the industry in which there is a persistent and chronic failure to provide sufficient nonobsolete capacity to meet high-level demands without encountering overutilization and "bottlenecks" appears to be a rare industry indeed.

This is not to say that nearly all industries provide enough capacity to meet the demands which would be forthcoming if their selling prices were persistently reduced to a feasible minimum, or made equal to average costs of production. The "adequate" provision of capacity is frequently adequate to meet only the demand forthcoming at the elevated or quasi-monopolistic prices that the firms in the industry customarily charge. It might be inadequate to meet the demands encountered if selling prices were at a competitive level. This latter type of maladjustment, however, is properly attributed to monopolistic pricing policies and not to technical inefficiency in the stricter sense.

Second, the incidence of *chronic* excess capacity is perceptible, but it probably affects only a relatively small minority of manufacturing industries. (By chronic excess capacity we refer to an adjustment of capacity to demand where *persistently, over considerable periods of time,* there is a redundancy of nonobsolete capacity at times of high-level or peak demands.) In our sample of twenty manufacturing industries, there were only three—shoes, flour, and cement—in which a significant degree of chronic excess capacity clearly appeared to be present. (There were one or two others for which adequate data on possible excess capacity were unavailable and which might fall in the same category.) Where chronic excess capacity does exist, it is sufficient to elevate costs of production by a significant amount. The writer would be surprised if significant chronic excess capacity were encountered in as many as 20 per cent of our manufacturing industries, though it does not seem unreasonable to suppose that it may occur in at least 10 per cent of them.

Excess capacity "other than chronic," however, very evidently has a much higher incidence in manufacturing. It may be argued, however, that this other sort of excess capacity is not necessarily undesirable from the standpoint of overall efficiency. First, there is, over the course of general business fluctuations, a considerable amount of "cyclical excess capacity," especially affecting industries producing durable goods. This reflects the fact that in times of depressed demand the plant capacities of numerous industries are not fully utilized. If we are to have fluctuations, however, in spite of all governmental efforts to eliminate, control, or dampen them, it does not seem reasonable to charge with inefficiency an industry which has a capacity that is "just about right" for meeting high-level demands and which therefore has unutilized capacity in slumps. For example, in a very minor business recession beginning in 1956 and extending through 1957, the steel industry slid from a consistent ten-year high level of nearly 100 per cent utilization of capacity to a 60 per cent or lower utilization. It is not evident that this reflects an uneconomical adjustment of steel plant capacity to demand over time.

Second, there are a number of industries in which an overhang of obsolete capacity—physically in being but either unutilized or used at very low rates—creates an appearance of excess capacity. If these fringes of obsolete plants which "are dead but won't lie down" persist and are operated so as to impose under-utilization on some nonobsolete plants, they are indeed a source of inefficiency.

Third, there are some industries in which product policies and other market policies are such that plants are utilized for only a part of the year and are "redundant" for the rest of the year, when feasible alternative policies would permit year-around use of plant and the satisfaction of total demand with a smaller amount of plant. In the automobile industry, for example, plant capacity is geared to produce the total required supply of autos in nine or ten months of the year, even in years of high demand, with a shutdown of plants for two or three months to accommodate the "retooling" necessary to effect annual model changes. This is in a sense inefficient, but the inefficiency is really chargeable to the wastes of a product policy of annual retooling for model changes, rather than to a failure to adapt capacity to demand. Avoidable wastes may thus occur from an underutilization of plants which is not strictly a result of "chronic excess capacity."

The preceding refers mainly to manufacturing industries. It is not clear from available evidence to what extent the conclusions reached are applicable to other sectors of the economy. There is a strong suspicion, however, that excess capacity is a more serious problem in the retail distributive trades than in manufacturing—a matter to which we will refer in Chapter 12 below.

Workable Performance in the Dimension of Technical Efficiency

Is the performance of American industry sufficiently good to permit us to say that, in the matter of technical efficiency at least, we have "workable" or socially satisfactory competition? If the workability of competition is judged in terms of its performance results, a "workable performance" on the part of industry would be one which reflected an adaptation of enterprises to the effective demands for their outputs which was reasonably close (in the light of prevailing uncertainties in economic affairs and of the intrinsic limitations of the human intellect) to that ideal adaptation which would maximize the general welfare. In the dimension of technical efficiency, ideal performance would involve all output being produced by plants and firms of optimal scale, with an optimal degree of integration and without any chronic excess capacity. "Workable" performance would not miss these ideals or goals by too much, although deviations from the ideal within certain limits of tolerance would be accepted as consistent with workability.

Just how wide these limits of tolerance should be, however, is not easily stated in general terms. It is safer and scientifically more proper simply to specify the degree to which ideal performance is missed in a particular respect, and to consider workability or unworkability of performance a matter of degree. If we follow this procedure, our summary evaluation of technical efficiency in manufacturing industries (as based primarily on our twenty-industry sample) is as follows.

Although there is probably a fairly close approximation to ideal efficiency in scales of plants and firms in the production of 80 per cent of industrial output, there are probably significant inefficiencies, resulting mainly from insufficient plant sizes, in the production of the other 20 per cent. To this inefficiency may be added some further wastes attributable to chronic excess capacity in certain industries, so that in the aggregate it would not be surprising if about one-fourth of all manufacturing output were produced at unit costs which exceeded the minimal attainable level by 5 or 10 per cent. Some fraction of this inefficiency seems to affect nearly all industries. For example, some fringe of inefficiently small plants is discovered even in those with the most efficient organization. Such inefficiency is more acute, however, in some minor fraction of all industries observed. The common structural or other characteristics of the group of industries with the more acute inefficiency are not easily identified from available evidence. Moderate to low-moderate seller concentration, relatively easy entry, and strong product differentiation all seem to be possible contributing factors.

The bulk of the inefficiencies noted—at any rate, in the more acute cases—seem to be potentially remediable by some policy device consistent with the maintenance of an enterprise economy. It is therefore reasonable tentatively to designate some fraction of manufacturing industries as having unworkable performance in the dimension of technical efficiency, and as being proper subjects for the searching attention of public regulatory policy.

Allocative Efficiency: Price-Cost Margins and Profit Rates

A second efficiency dimension of the market performance of an industry concerns the size of its output as judged by the relationship of its long-run selling prices to its long-run marginal cost of production. And, as noted above, this price-cost relationship is feasibly measured (directly or indirectly) by the ratio of its selling price to its long-run average cost, or by the ratio of long-run average industry profits to the value of owners' investments in the firms in the industry. Before examining and interpreting the pertinent evidence, we should deal, initially or in greater detail than earlier, with three basic matters:

1. The definition and measurement of profits and profit rates, and the properties of profit rates as measures of price-average cost margins.

2. The various reasons that the size of profit rates (and thus of price-cost margins) has or reflects significant impacts on overall economic welfare.

3. Elaborated criteria for evaluating the size of actual price-cost margins or profit rates.

Thereafter, we will consider and evaluate evidence on actual industry price-cost margins and profit rates.

Definition and Measurement of Profits and Profit Rates, and the Relation of Profit Rates to Price-Cost Margins

We should initially distinguish between profits as a concept in economic analysis and "accounting profits" as measured by traditionally accepted methods of business bookkeeping.

Profits in the first sense—variously designated as "economic," "pure," or "excess" profits—are simply defined as the residual excess, received by or for a firm's owners, of the sales revenue of the firm over all cost incurred to earn the revenue. The sales revenue of a firm (what it receives for output sold) is an amount equal to the quantity of goods sold multiplied by its average selling price per unit. The costs incurred to earn the revenue represent the value of all goods and services used by the firm in order to produce and deliver the output from which the revenue has been earned. They include all "contractual costs" of such goods and services that are incurred as payments to "outsiders" other than the owners of the firm, and "imputed costs" equal to the values (in the best alternative market) of such goods and services that are supplied directly by the firm's owners rather than being bought from others. The most important imputed cost is generally the value of the services of funds invested by owners. It is measured as an interest return on owners' investment or "equity," calculated at the best net interest rate they could earn elsewhere. Economic, pure, or excess profits for any time period are simply the excess of revenue thus defined over total costs thus defined. Profits are thus a share of business income (and, in the aggregate, of national income) that goes to owners of firms, over and above all payments made to reimburse them for the costs they incur.

Schematically, we can represent the calculation of the economic or excess profits of a firm for any period, such as a year, as follows. Let R be the aggregate sale revenue of the year, and let C be the aggregate of the *currently incurred* costs of earning this revenue. (These would include, for example, costs incurred in the same year for materials, wages and salaries, plant maintenance, and so forth that are allocable to the earning of this revenue.) Let D represent the aggregate of costs incurred in past years that are allocable to the earning of this year's revenue. They would include, for example, the past cost of that part of plant and machinery, bought in previous years, which was "used up" in producing this year's output (*depreciation*), and the past costs of previously acquired stocks of resources and materials that were used in producing this output (amortization). Further, let V represent the value of owners' investment. V is appropriately calculated (for purposes of a first approximation) as their original investment plus reinvested past net earnings or minus past net losses. This amount is equal to the excess of the cost value (after deducting past depreciation and amortization) of all assets of the firm over all of its liabilities. (This measure of owners' investment will serve nicely in the absence of changes in the price level or value of money through time, which we will momentarily neglect.) Finally, let i represent the net interest rate (net of "risk" returns) that funds can currently earn in the best available capital markets if invested for time periods comparable to those for which owners' funds in the firm are invested.

The economic or excess profit of the firm, if any, is then simply expressed as:

$$R - C - D - i \cdot V$$

That is, such profit equals revenue minus allocable current cost minus allocable past costs minus the arithmetical product of the interest rate and the value of owners' investment.

Suppose that for the firm annual revenue (R) were \$100,000; current labor, material, and similar costs (C) were \$50,000; depreciation and amortization of past costs (D) were \$25,000; the value of owners' investment (V) were \$300,000; and the net interest rate earnable by these funds elsewhere (i) were 5 per cent (0.05) per annum. Then excess profit should be calculated as:

$$\$100,000 - \$50,000 - \$25,000 - 0.05(\$300,000) = \$10,000$$

The accounting profit (as generally calculated by business firms and published in all available statistics) differs from the economic or excess profit mainly in that the interest cost on owners' investment $(i \cdot V)$ is not deducted. Thus the accounting profit is represented schematically simply as:

$$R - C - D$$

In the preceding example, accounting profit would be calculated as:

$$\$100,000 - \$50,000 - \$25,000 = \$25,000$$

The \$15,000 of interest on owners' investment has not been deducted as a cost.

It is thus clear that accounting profit is "not all profit" in the economic sense. It includes the imputed interest cost of owners' investment. In fact, that is, if accounting profit just equals interest on owners' investment (if $R - C - D = i \cdot V$), there is no economic or excess profit. The firm has charged prices just equal to its full average costs.

So much for the measurement of aggregate profits. These profits are interesting and have some usefulness in analysis. But for many analytical purposes profit data are more easily interpreted if the aggregate profits of the firm are expressed as ratios to or "rates on" certain related magnitudes, such as the associated aggregate sales revenue or aggregate owners' investment. Expression of profits in certain ratio or rate terms is especially useful if we wish to compare different firms or different industries, and also if we wish to determine quickly, from accounting profit records, the incidence of economic or excess profits.

One of the most useful ratios for purposes of comparing firms or industries is that of economic or excess profits to the sales revenue from which they are derived—that is:

$$\frac{R - C - D - i \cdot V}{R} = \text{excess profit rate on sales}$$

In the preceding example, this excess profit rate on sales should be calculated as follows:

$$\frac{\$100,000 - \$50,000 - \$25,000 - 0.05(\$300,000)}{\$100,000} = 0.10$$

There is an excess profit rate on sales equal to 10 per cent of sales.

This ratio, as a measure of the ratio of aggregate excess profits to aggregate sales, also effectively measures the ratio of average price to average cost. Thus the 10 per cent excess profit rate on sales indicates effectively that average costs are 90 per cent of the average price at which sales were made.

An alternative ratio measure of profits, and one more easily calculated from available statistics, is the ratio of excess profits to owners' investment, or *equity*, (V)—that is:

$$\frac{R - C - D - i \cdot V}{V}$$

In the preceding example, this should be computed as:

$$\frac{\$100,000 - \$50,000 - \$25,000 - 0.05(\$300,000)}{\$300,000} = 0.0333$$

Excess profits per annum equal 3⅓ per cent of owners' investment.

In the form almost always encountered, however, this ratio is expressed as one of *accounting* profit to equity, that is,

$$\frac{R - C - D}{V}$$

This is in effect the ratio to owners' equity of the excess profit plus the interest return on equity. In our example it would be 8⅓ per cent on equity, calculated as follows:

$$\frac{\$100,000 - \$50,000 - \$25,000}{\$300,000} = 0.0833$$

The relationship of this rate of accounting profit on equity to the corresponding rate of excess profits on equity is easily seen if we recognize that the excess profit rate on equity always equals accounting profit rate on equity minus the interest rate. That is, algebraically,

$$\frac{R - C - D - i \cdot V}{V} = \frac{R - C - D}{V} - i$$

Thus, in our preceding example,

$$\text{Accounting profit rate on equity} = \frac{\$25,000}{\$300,000} = 0.0833$$

$$\text{Excess profit rate on equity} = \frac{\$10,000}{\$300,000} = 0.0333$$

$$\text{Interest rate} = 0.05$$

$$\text{Accounting profit rate} - \text{interest rate} = 0.0833 - 0.05 = 0.0333$$

Any accounting profit rate on equity is thus readily convertible into an excess profit rate on equity by simply deducting the applicable interest rate.

From the preceding, we can derive certain simple rules for interpreting the published data regarding the accounting profit rates on owners' equities.

1. If the accounting profit rate on equity exceeds the applicable outside interest rate on loanable funds, there is an excess profit (some true excess of price over full average cost).

2. If the accounting profit rate on equity is smaller than the applicable interest rate, there is a net loss (some excess of full average cost over price).

3. If the accounting profit rate on equity equals the applicable interest rate, price equals average cost (as it would with a long-run competitive adjustment).

4. *Other things being equal,* larger accounting profit rates on equity indicate larger excesses of price over average cost.

On the last point, however, we must recognize that other things are not necessarily equal. In comparing accounting profit rates on equity between firms or industries, in order to arrive at inferences concerning differences in cost-price margins, we must allow for differences in the ratios of R to V, or in the rates of "capital turnover." Effectively, excess profit rates on equity will be smaller, relative to excess profit rates on sales, for those firms which have a higher ratio of owners' equity to sales ("slower capital turnover"). Profit rates on equity must be interpreted accordingly.

This proposition becomes clear if we recognize that the excess profit rate on sales (measuring the relation of price to average cost) is equal to the excess profit rate on equity multiplied by V/R—by the ratio of equity to revenue. Thus, in the preceding example:

$$\text{Accounting profit rate on equity} = \frac{R - C - D}{V} = 0.0833$$

$$\begin{array}{l}\text{Excess profit rate} \\ \text{on equity}\end{array} = \frac{R - C - D}{V} - i = 0.0833 - 0.05 = 0.0333$$

Excess profit rate on sales = excess profit rate on equity times

$$V/R = 0.0333 \times \frac{300,000}{100,000} = 0.10$$

The effect of the ratio of V to R on the relationship of the excess profit rate on sales to the excess profit rate on equity for any firm or industry is illustrated further by the following example. Consider two firms in the same industry, for which the following is true:

(1) Sales revenues are identical, that is,

$$R_1 = R_2 = \$100,000$$

(2) Current costs are greater for firm 2 than for firm 1:

$$C_1 = \$50,000 \qquad C_2 = \$60,000$$

(3) Depreciation costs are greater for firm 1 than for firm 2:

$$D_1 = \$25,000 \qquad D_2 = \$20,000$$

(4) Owners' equity is greater for firm 1 than for firm 2:

$$V_1 = \$300,000 \qquad V_2 = \$200,000$$

(5) The applicable interest rate in both cases is 5 per cent (0.05).

Then, first, the excess profits of the two firms are identical. That is:

$$R_1 - C_1 - D_1 - i \cdot V_1 = \$100,000 - \$50,000 - \$25,000$$
$$- 0.05(\$300,000) = \$10,000$$

$$R_2 - C_2 - D_2 - i \cdot V_2 = \$100,000 - \$60,000 - \$20,000$$
$$- 0.05(\$200,000) = \$10,000$$

Second, the excess profit rate on sales of both firms is thus 10 per cent (0.10), and the ratio of price to average cost is the same. That is, for both firms,

$$\frac{R - C - D - i \cdot V}{R} = \frac{\$10,000}{\$100,000} = 0.10$$

Third, however, the rates of profit on equity of the two firms are different because of differences in their V/R ratios. This is true of their accounting profit rates:

$$\frac{R_1 - C_1 - D_1}{V_1} = \frac{\$100,000 - \$50,000 - \$25,000}{\$300,000} = 0.0833$$

$$\frac{R_2 - C_2 - D_2}{V_2} = \frac{\$100,000 - \$60,000 - \$20,000}{\$200,000} = 0.10$$

And it is true of their rates of excess profit on equity:

$$\frac{R_1 - C_1 - D_1 - i \cdot V_1}{V_1}$$

$$= \frac{\$100,000 - \$50,000 - \$25,000 - 0.05(\$300,000)}{\$300,000} = 0.033$$

$$\frac{R_2 - C_2 - D_2 - i \cdot V_2}{V_2}$$

$$= \frac{\$100,000 - \$60,000 - \$20,000 - 0.05(\$200,000)}{\$200,000} = 0.05$$

Thus, if we are comparing two firms or industries in terms of the differences between the ratios of their profits to their equities, the comparison is a good indicator of the corresponding differences between the ratios of their excess profits to sales (or of their prices to full average costs) only if $V_1/R_1 = V_2/R_2$. If the rates of capital turnover differ significantly, relative profit rates on equity are not completely accurate indicators of relative excess profit rates on sales, or of relative price-average cost relationships. Let us keep this in mind as we proceed to the interpretation of actual profit data.

Economic Importance of Profit Rates

The usefulness of industry profit rates (viewed as reflectors of the relationships of prices to costs of production) in revealing the degree of allocative efficiency attained by industries has been noted earlier in this chapter. Given the subsequent analysis of profit rates, our earlier argument concerning profit rates and allocative efficiency may be restated as follows.

Assuming always that an industry's long-run marginal costs and long-run average costs are at least approximately equal, so that the relation of price to average cost will be about the same as that of price to marginal cost, then the following is generally true of the long-run average profit rates of any industry:

1. An excess profit rate on sales that is equal to zero, revealing a long run equality of price to both marginal and average costs, is indicative of ideal allocative efficiency for the industry—that is, an industry output of just the right size relative to other industry outputs. When the excess profit rate on sales is zero, the excess profit rate on equity must also be zero (the numerators of both ratios are zero), and the accounting profit rate will equal the market rate of interest. Therefore, an accounting profit rate on equity that equals the interest rate (and an excess profit rate on equity that is zero) also indicates ideal allocative efficiency.

2. A positive excess profit rate on sales (one that exceeds zero) reveals a long-run excess of price over both marginal and average costs, and measures the amount of the excess. It thereby also reveals an allocative inefficiency (misallocation of resources) reflected in the fact that the industry's output is too small relative to other industry outputs. A larger output would be required to equate price to marginal and average cost, though the size of the industry's output deficiency is not measured by the size of the excess profit rate on sales alone.[4] Similarly, a positive excess profit rate on equity—an accounting profit rate that exceeds the market rate of interest—reveals the existence of the same allocative in-

[4]The size of the defficiency in output or misallocation of resources depends also on the price-elasticity of demand for the industry's output.

efficiency, though rates of profit on equity do not directly measure the amount of the excess of price over marginal and average cost .

3. A negative excess profit rate on sales (some rate of net loss after deducting the interest cost of owners' investment) reveals a long-run excess of both marginal and average costs over price. It thereby also reveals a misallocation of resources resulting from the fact the industry's output is too large relative to other industry outputs, since a smaller output would be required to equate price to marginal and average cost. Similarly, a negative excess profit rate on equity—an accounting profit rate that is smaller than the market rate of interest—reveals the existence, qualitatively, of the same allocative inefficiency.

It should be understood that in the preceding propositions, the terms "ideal," "too small," and "too large" as applied to the output of an industry refer to the relationship of actual industry output to that output which would be consistent with an ideal allocation of resources among all industries—that is, with an allocation (or composition of the total output of all goods) that would maximize the economic welfare of consumers. It should also be reemphasized that the propositions refer only to long-run average profit rates over many years (persistent and prolonged profit tendencies), and not to the short-run profits of one or a few years.

Given this rather formal appraisal of the allocative significance of long-run profit rates, we should add a few common-sense comments, and also recognize another impact of profits on overall economic welfare.

All firms in the economy, or all in a particular industry, should on the average in the long run earn a profit rate at least equal to a basic interest return on owners' investment if efficient production under free enterprise system is to be maintained. The system will not work well, *in the long run* in a given industry or sector, unless on the average

$$\frac{R - C - D}{V} \geq i$$

(accounting profit is equal to or greater than the interest charge on owners' investment).

This, however, is a necessary condition for workability of the system only in the long-run sense and for substantial groups of firms averaged together. It is quite consistent with the maintenance of a viable and efficient capitalism that there may be short-run losses to individual firms, individual industries, or even to the whole economy of enterprises—provided that these are in the long run balanced by subsequent short-run excess profits which bring the long-run average at least up to "normal."

It is also consistent that some individual firms should suffer persistent net losses (and probably go bankrupt and disappear), provided that other more successful firms can make compensating extra gains that are sufficient to counter-balance these losses and to attract an adequate supply of business investment over time. It is further consistent that even all the firms in some industries might lose persistently and vanish, if the demand for the good in question is insufficient to cover the costs of producing it in any volume. Short-term losses in any sphere, and persistent losses for some firms and perhaps some industries (to the point where they vanish), are consistent with the long-run average ability of the enterprise system as a whole to earn a normal interest return on owners' investment and to satisfy all demands for goods that are sufficient to cover costs. But, given all of the preceding qualifications, a basic return equal to a normal interest rate on owners' investment is necessary, "on the average and in the long run," for the maintenance of production by any firm or group of firms.

Let us look further at losses, or accounting profits that provide less than a normal interest return on owners' invested capital. These will not persist in the long run and on the average for all firms in the economy, if an enterprise economy is to persist. But we may accept as justifiable and even therapeutic not only short-run depression losses for the economy as a whole, but also:

(*a*) Short-term losses to firms or industries resulting from a transitory imbalance of supply and demand, and

(*b*) Losses to firms or industries that are sufficiently persistent or prolonged to eliminate relatively inefficient firms, to induce reduction of chronically redundant industry capacity, or even to eliminate all production in a "redundant" industry where prices will fail to cover costs at any output.

Since losses are ideally a penalty imposed by the market to force an efficient adjustment of supply to demand—and thus, ideally, are therapeutic in their effects—it follows that net losses are undesirable mainly when both of two things are true. The losses are prolonged or chronic over long periods, and in spite of the persistence of losses, a desirable adjustment of supply to demand is not forced through the removal of persistently losing firms or through the reduction of the capacity of the persistently losing industry. Such truly chronic losses are indicative of a failure of the market mechanism to force an elimination of overinvestment and oversupply. This sort of failure in turn is generally attributable to some undesirable impediment to the mobility of human or physical resources from one use to another.

Some added comment is also needed concerning supernormal or excess profits. Like short-run losses, short-term excess profits are generally justifiable and therapeutic for the economy in booms which alternate with slumps, at least to the extent necessary to counterbalance depression losses. They also provide the industry with an inducement to enlarge a supply which is short relative to demand, and the firm that is superior or exceptionally efficient (compared to its rivals for some period of time) with an incentive reward.

Persistent, prolonged, or chronic excess profits must be judged somewhat differently. As already noted, they signify inefficient allocative performance. In addition, they have a potentially undesirable impact on income distribution. They result in a larger share of the national income going to business owners, who in general are relatively few and relatively wealthy, and in a smaller share going to all other recipients (for example, hired labor) who in general are relatively many and relatively poor. Unless or except so far as the payment of these excess profits is necessary to induce the performance of a useful function by business firms (and it may not be in many cases), this increase in the inequality of income distribution may be counted as a deleterious effect of excess profits.

Criteria for Evaluating Profit Rates

Our third basic question concerns criteria for evaluating the departure of accounting profit rates from the mean water mark of a normal interest return on owners' investment. In this evaluation, we may neglect the phenomenon of short-term excess profits or net losses, on the previously stated ground that they are in a general way justifiable or therapeutic. We therefore center on the phenomenon of prolonged or chronic departures from a basic interest earning on equity, as reflected in long-term average accounting profit rates on equity which significantly exceed or fall below the interest rate.

Little need be added to what has been said about the evaluation of chronic net losses (for the industry of the firm) that fail to induce a restriction of capacity and supply that would bring these into balance with demand. Such chronic losses must be deemed undesirable from a social standpoint. They reflect a failure of the general price and market mechanism to function efficiently in the allocation of resources. And they introduce inequities in income distribution between enterprise owners in chronically "distressed" industries and those in other industries.

These chronic losses, which are encountered in some minority of extractive and manufacturing industries, usually can persist because of two factors. First, there are industries with redundant capacity (that has developed because of declining demand or increasing productivity per unit of capacity) in which the basic capacity is extremely long-lived (as in agriculture or coal mining) and in which, additionally, there is a supply of both enterprises and laborers who will not be induced to move to other occupations even by definitely substandard profit and wage earnings. Second, there are other industries (like shoe manufacturing or corner grocery stores) in which redundant capacity persists mainly because of a never-ending oversupply of new small firms that continually enter the industry to replace defunct firms as the latter go bankrupt. This occurs in spite of a clear statistical showing that the chances for loss outweigh the chances for gain for any small entrant so long as capacity is maintained at so high a level. The endless supply of misinformed or unduly sanguine "cannon fodder" in such industries brings about continual overcapacity, continual net losses, and a continually high rate of small business mortality.[5]

The evaluation of supernormal or excess profits is intrinsically more complicated, but can be simplified by categorizing the general possible sources of profits in excess of a normal interest return on owners' investment. In brief, all excess profits should result from one or more of the four following causes:

1. Misestimation of future demand or cost, or lagging adjustment to changing demand or cost, resulting in positive "windfalls" to firms or industries (but also in negative windfalls).

2. The riskiness of business investment in various lines, resulting in the payment of "risk rewards" to successful risk-takers (but also in losses to the unsuccessful gamblers).

3. The introduction of innovations (of lower-cost techniques or more popular products) by some firms, resulting in "reward to innovation." These rewards are earned so long as the innovators cannot be instantaneously and fully imitated by an adequate group of competitors, and

[5]It may be added that in these cases, on the average, chronic losses by all firms in the industry do not really endanger the maintenance of a desirable supply of the good, although this specious argument has sometimes been advanced in support of proposals for governmental interference with competition and pricing. (If we leave farmers' milk prices too low, babies will suddenly be without milk because all dairy farmers will simultaneously shoot their herds and convert them into hamburger?) If only the penalties of the market would work, losses would induce the withdrawal of enough capacity that the output of the remainder would sell at a profitable price, and supply would be automatically preserved. The difficulty in these cases is not a danger of total failure of supply; it is one of failure to restrict supply sufficiently, through transfer of resources, to support a normal rate of return on remaining investment.

instead enjoy a period of competitive advantage before they are successfully imitated.

4. Monopolistic or monopsonistic restriction of output and raising of selling prices in relation to costs by the industry, generally based on a restriction of interfirm competition plus some impediment to the entry of new competitors.

Which of these types of excess profits are justifiable from the standpoint of their impact on the general welfare? Some of the types are quickly disposed of. Consider first the windfall profits that a firm or industry makes because it has underestimated a future rise in demand or decline in cost, or because considerable time is necessarily consumed in expanding capacity to meet an experienced increase in demand or a decline in cost. These profits are justifiable as a necessary incident of the efficient working of a market system under dynamic conditions with uncertainty, and desirable as incentives to hurry a more appropriate adjustment of supply to demand. In the same way, windfall losses are justifiable and desirable when the errors of anticipation or lags in adjustment operate to produce an excess of supply relative to demand. This applies to economy-wide windfall profits and losses in the face of succeeding phases of the business cycle, to the individual industry faced with fluctuating or secularly changing demand or cost, and to the firm. But windfalls in their essence will not generally be the source of persistent or chronic excess profits to the economy, the industry, or the firm. Over long periods of time, we should expect that windfall profits to any unit would be sporadic and intermittent in their occurrence. Moreover, in considerable part at least, windfall profits should be offset by windfall losses, so that the usual long-term average profit rate should not be interpreted as reflecting net windfalls to an appreciable extent.

Second, risk rewards may be appropriately regarded as a possible component of observed excess profits only in a restricted sense. The argument is as follows. Owners' investments in general are made with some uncertainty as to the earnings they will yield. There is some possibility of loss to the investors because either of a failure to earn as much as a normal interest return or, worse, of the loss of part or all of the invested capital. There will be some relative probability of "winning" with a successful investment, and some relative probability of "losing" with an unsuccessful investment. In this situation, the prospective owner, in order to be induced to invest, will require the prospect of a sufficient extra gain "if he wins" to counterbalance the possible loss he will incur "if he loses."

For example, suppose an investment of $1,000 is made for a period of one year only, with the prospects being 20 to 1 in favor of success, and 1 to 20 for failure. Out of twenty-one such investments, that is, twenty will succeed by earning the basic interest rate of, let us say, 4 per cent on the $1,000 plus regaining the original thousand, while one investment will fail entirely, returning neither interest nor any principal to the investor. The odds being 1 to 20 for such failure, each investor will presumably require, as an inducement to invest, the prospect of earning *if he wins* an excess return (above interest) equal to one-twentieth of what he would lose if he loses. The total loss to the loser for the one year investment would be $1,000 plus 4 per cent interest on that amount, or $1,040. Therefore, investors need the prospect of an excess profit of $52 per $1,000 of investment (an extra 5.2 per cent return) *if they win*, to counterbalance the 1-in-21 chance of losing.

Generally, investors "require" a risk reward in the event of success sufficient to counterbalance the risk of loss. And they will also restrict the volume of their investments, relative to demand, to such a level that risk rewards will be earned by successful investors that are sufficient to offset the losses suffered by unsuccessful investors. These risk rewards to winners are essentially justifiable as a payment for the "cost of uncertainty," just as the risk losses of the losers are similarly justified as unavoidable.

Many individual firms within the economy as a whole or within individual industries should thus earn, for short or long periods, excess profits properly describable as risk rewards. But *not all firms* in the economy or in an industry should do this, for the existence of the risk that is being rewarded should be evidenced or proved by losses to other firms which have been less successful. (If every firm in an industry persistently earns 10 per cent per annum on equity in excess profits, it is a little hard to describe these earnings as risk rewards, or to call the industry a "risky" one for investment.)

This brings us to the crucial point in explaining excess profits in terms of risk rewards. For the enterprise economy of firms at any time, or for a single industry of firms over any prolonged period of time, the risk rewards earned by successful firms should be at least roughly offset by the losses of unsuccesful firms. Therefore, a weighted average profit rate for all firms in the economy or in the industry (all losers as well as all winners being included) should include a true net risk return of roughly zero. There should be no obvious "risk-reward" explanation of group-average excess profits. Although risk rewards may thus be a valid explanation of individual firm excess profits, they are not a valid explanation of long-term group-average profits for industries, sectors, or the whole economy.

Two remarks should be added. First, long-term excess profits to a group could of course result from a "systematic overestimation of risk" that caused investment to be so restricted that the excess profits of the successful firms outweighed the losses of the unsuccessful ones. But such an excess return is more appropriately described either as a "windfall" (already discussed) or as a "monopolistic excess profit."

Second, the general necessity for risk rewards to some firms, counterbalanced by risk losses to others, applies not only to investments in productive facilities using accepted techniques for the production of known products, but also to investments in the development and introduction of new techniques and new products. Investments in research and development activities, and ultimately in "innovations" brought to the stage of production, are intrinsically risky. A minimum necessary stimulus to these socially beneficial activities is that successful endeavors along this line are expected to make sufficient extra profits to counterbalance the losses of the unsuccessful attempts. Risk rewards of this type should not result in long-term average excess profits for industries or larger groups of firms, but they may well explain and justify long-term extra gains to some firms, and shorter-term gains to fortunate industries.

Aside from a "risk reward" to successful research, development, and innovation that is sufficient to compensate for the losses of unsuccessful activities, a third justification for excess profits is that innovation (and the research and development behind it) can be induced only by promising the potential innovator at least "something extra"—net of risk—as a reward for developing and undertaking innovations. Otherwise, he would have no incentive to disturb the *status quo* by introducing new techniques or products. There is a need for and a justification of some excess profits in the form of a true or *net* "reward to innovation," over and above the risk reward just mentioned and not fully counterbalanced by losses of unsuccessful innovators. Such rewards should emerge as the successful innovator "leads the parade" in lowering production costs with a new technique or increasing revenue with a new product, enjoying some period of extra profits until he has been fully and successfully imitated by other firms in his industry.

This general argument for "rewards to innovation" as a justifiable type of excess profits seems valid, but there are difficulties in deciding just how much of such a reward is needed, or justifiable on the grounds that it provides an adequate incentive to useful innovation. This is particularly true because innovations frequently lead to at least temporary monopolies as an immediate source of the excess profit, and because the amount of justified or necessary monopoly profits which are pivoted on innovation is not readily described in quantitative terms. What we can say is (1) that *some* rewards to innovation in the form of excess profits are justified; (2) that we may expect such necessary rewards, for the usual firm or industry, to be sporadic and intermittent in occurrence rather than persistent through time; (3) that when observed excess profits are to be justified on this ground, there should be accompanying evidence of actual innovations; and (4) that under normal circumstances, true rewards to innovation (as distinguished from monopolistic excess profits *simpliciter*) should not favor all firms, or even all principal firms, in an industry equally.

The final possible source of excess profits is plain and simple: monopolistic (or monopsonistic) price-output policies on the part of the members of an industry, directed essentially at restricting supply so as to create an extra margin between price and average cost. These, strictly, are the only excess profits that measure allocative performance by an industry, and two things may be noted about them.

First, except to the extent that they may be classified as necessary returns to innovators, these excess profits apparently are not needed to induce the performance of any useful economic function, but are simply a reward paid for the production of an artificial scarcity of goods. True monopolistic excess profits bias the distribution of income and reflect a distortion of the allocation of resources among uses without giving society anything specific in return. Second, the only sort of excess profits that tend to be reflected in long-term average profits for entire industries are monopolistic excess profits. All other types of excess profit are likely to occur sporadically and irregularly, or to be confined to only part of the firms of an industry.

Nevertheless, a functional justification of at least some monopoly profits has been claimed, by some economists and many noneconomists, on two principal grounds. The first of these is that a desirably high rate of new business investment through time requires, or at any rate is importantly encouraged by, an economic climate in which excess profits are earned by a considerable proportion of all firms. A full theoretical analysis of the issue involved, however, suggests that this conclusion is not uniquely true as a generalization, but only might be true under a rather special set of assumed and not necessarily realistic conditions.

The second asserted justification of monopoly profits is that they provide enterprises with necessary investment funds—both for expanding capacity in a growing economy and for financing research, development, and innovation. The implied assertion is that needed investments of both types will be made in adequate volume only if they can be "internally financed" (out of accumulated excess profits), rather than being financed by "outside" money acquired through borrowing from creditors or through new capital contributions by existing or new owners. Some large corporations with a developing consciousness of public relations have published newspaper advertisements "justifying" their patently excess profits on the grounds that, after dividends have been paid to owners, "half of every profit dollar" goes to expanding capacity to meet the needs of a growing economy. The implication is that expansion would not take place unless these excess profits furnished a fund for investment. In general, this asserted justification is no justification at all. Well-organized capital markets could supply the needed investment funds just as well. Although it may be convenient to them, it is not necessary to permit existing owners to receive an excess profit in order to create a supply of funds for investment. The fact that excess profits are reinvested in expansion or in research and innovation does not justify them. The alternative of lower profits plus "outside" financing should accomplish at least equally desirable investment behavior, while at the same time providing a more desirable income-and-wealth distribution and a better allocation of resources.

On the basis of the preceding evaluation, let us now attempt to describe a general norm for socially desirable profit behavior. First, the long-term average profit return for the industry or the economy ideally should have a tendency to approach (and approximate) a basic interest rate on owners' investment, being neither persistently larger nor persistently smaller. Second, this does not imply that sporadic or short-term excess profits or net losses to individual industries and firms are other than desirable. Windfall profits or losses, and risk rewards and losses, should be accepted as necessary incidents of the working of a market system. Moreover, some net excess profits as rewards to innovation are similarly acceptable. It would be foolish to say that any particular firm, or any particular industry, should earn exactly the basic interest return on owners' investment each year—all sorts of variations among industries and firms are both natural and desirable. Third, in order to qualify as desirable, supernormal or excess profits to industries should normally be periodic or sporadic (as windfall, risk, and innovation rewards would make them), rather than persistent over long periods of time. Chronic excess profits are *prima facie* suspect of resulting from simple monopolistic output restriction, and if so are undesirable.

Evidence on Profit Rates in American Industry

Given the conceptual background just developed, let us turn to evidence on the profit performance of American business. This is available in the form of accounting profit rates on equity. Such a profit rate shows for any single year the ratio of the annual accounting profit of a firm or group of firms to the value of owners' investment or equity. For longer periods of time, an average of annual accounting profit rates can be calculated.

As seen above, the annual accounting profit rate on equity corresponds to

$$\frac{R - C - D}{V}$$

—annual revenue minus annual current cost minus annual depreciation, all divided by the value of owners' investment for the year in question. This measure should give us a good general notion, for any firm or group under examination, of the incidence and size (relative to equity) of excess profits. By mentally deducting the applicable interest rate from the accounting profit rate, we arrive at the rate of excess profits on equity. That is, as we have shown above:

$$\frac{R - C - D}{V} - \text{interest rate} = \text{rate of excess profits on equity.}$$

One amendment to the preceding interpretation of accounting profit rates is required, however, because in periods following any considerable change in the general price level, accounting profit rates give a systematically biased picture of true economic profits. This bias results from the fact that, in dealing respectively with current revenues and costs and with past costs and owners' investments (R and C on the one hand, and D and V on the other), accountants typically measure in terms of dollars with different purchasing power.

Current revenues and costs are appropriately measured in terms of current dollars that have whatever purchasing power prevails at the moment. But past costs and investments are measured in terms of past dollars which, at the time they were spent or invested, had a higher or lower purchasing power than current dollars—higher if the price level has risen since the date when past costs or investments were incurred or made, and lower if the price level has since declined. The current dollar and the past dollar, that is, are dollars of different value, but the accountant counts either one as just one dollar.

In other words, accountants typically do not attempt to make price-level adjustments in stating the dollar amounts of past costs and investments. Appropriate adjustments would result in measuring each past cost and investment as the number of current dollars which has the same purchasing power that the dollars which earlier went into past costs and investments had when they were spent or invested. When past costs thus adjusted were deducted from current revenues—along with current costs—a true measure of annual profit (before deducting an interest return on owners' investment) would be obtained. And when this "true" annual profit was expressed as a ratio to owners' investment thus adjusted, the resulting annual profit rate would reflect the true economic rate of profit on equity. But accountants do not make these adjustments, and as a result accounting profits and profit rates are typically biased upward if the price level has been rising, and downward if it has been falling.

Suppose, for example, that a firm in the present year has a current revenue (R) of $1,200, and currently incurred costs (C) of $400—both clearly measured in terms of current dollars. Suppose further that its past-cost depreciation (D), is based solely on the use of one-tenth of the life of a single machine which was purchased five years ago for $3,000. And suppose that the total owners' investment in the firm (V) is $5,000, also made five years ago. Finally suppose that in the last five years the general price level has risen by 20 per cent.

The accountant's profit and profit rate would be calculated by including past cost and investment both at their original dollar amounts. Therefore, depreciation (D) would be one-tenth of the $3,000 original cost of the machine, or $300, and the owners' investment (V) would be valued at $5,000, its original dollar amount. Then the accounting profit ($R - C - D$) would be $1,200 − $400 − $300, or $500. The accounting profit rate would be:

$$\frac{R - C - D}{V} = \frac{\$1200 - \$400 - \$300}{\$5000} = 0.10 \text{ (or 10\%)}$$

In a proper measure of economic profit, however, we would not measure either past cost (D) or investment (V) in their original dollar terms. Instead we would measure each as the number of current dollars which have the same purchasing power now as those original dollars had when the owners spent or invested them. Because the general price level has risen 20 per cent over the five years since D and V were incurred, we should wish to measure each as the original dollar amount multiplied by 1.2. Therefore, adjusted depreciation is $360 ($300 × 1.2), and the adjusted investment is $6,000 ($5,000 × 1.2). These adjustments are made on the ground that the enterprise has not really recovered its depreciation cost until it has secured enough dollars ($360) to put it in the same purchasing-power position that it had prior to acquiring one-tenth of the machine, and similarly that its interest cost and rate of profit are properly calculated on a number of dollars ($6,000) having the same purchasing power as its original investment had when it was made. The revised or true profit figures are thus:

$$R - C - D = \$1,200 - \$400 - \$360 = \$440$$

$$\frac{R - C - D}{V} = \frac{\$440}{\$6,000} = 0.0733 \text{ (or } 7\tfrac{1}{3}\%)$$

The adjusted, and economically meaningful, profit rate on equity is 7⅓ per cent as against 10 per cent. The accounting profit rate is biased upward (with a rising price level) because of its measurement of past costs and investments as a number of dollars having smaller current purchasing power than was originally sacrificed to incur these costs or make these investments. Following a period of declining price level, the accounting profit rate would have a corresponding downward bias.

The foregoing analysis of systematic bias in accounting profit rates has been emphasized because the reported profit rates we are about to examine embody this sort of bias—generally a downward bias in the 1930's and an upward one for at least a decade following World War II. Therefore, although we are unable to calculate, from available data, just how much bias there is at any time, we should make a mental allowance for price-level bias in interpreting accounting profit rates for various periods of time.

A first question regarding them concerns the average size of profits (relative to equity) for the aggregate of all firms in the economy. The *Statistics of Income* of the Treasury department gives us average annual profit rates for all *incorporated* firms, based on corporation income tax returns. The average annual accounting profit rate on equity for all American corporations in various periods from 1931 to 1962 is described in the following tabulation. Each annual rate entering into an average is the aggregate accounting profit after deducting income taxes of all corporations (total profits minus total losses) expressed as a percentage of the aggregate of owners' investments in all corporations.

Years	Average Annual Profit Rate on Equity of All Corporations (after income tax)
1931–1935	—0.02 (loss)
1936–1941	4.7
1942–1946	8.2
1947–1952	10.5
1953–1961	6.7

The time periods for which average annual profit rates are shown are of unequal length, selected to correspond to periods with differing general economic conditions. The period from 1931 to 1935 represents most of the great depression of the 1930's, and that from 1936 to 1941 the period of gradual recovery from that depression. From 1942 to 1946, the economy of the United States was geared to its participation in World War II. The interval from 1947 to 1952 was one of postwar reconversion, prosperity, and substantial price inflation. From 1953 to 1961, we observe a period of postwar and cold-war "normalcy," with a generally high level of economic activity (varying somewhat with some very minor recessions) and with only a slowly increasing price level.

In interpreting these profit data, the following tendencies toward price-level bias should be allowed for. The general price level from 1931 to 1935 was substantially below that of the 1920's, and the accounting profit rates tend to be biased downward (to understate the true economic rates). The period from 1936 to 1941 witnessed rising prices, to a general level well above that of the depression but below that of the 1920's. Considering the average age of the assets on the basis of which depreciation costs and equities were calculated, the accounting profit rates for this period should not be influenced by much price-level bias. In spite of wartime price controls, there was a moderate amount of price inflation from 1942 to 1946, and a corresponding upward bias in accounting profit rates, tending to overstate true profits. From 1947 to 1952 there was a very large inflation of the price level, and the upward bias of the rates and overstatement of true profits must be substantial. In the period from 1953 to 1961, a much milder and decreasing upward bias in accounting profit rates is predictable.

If we make mental allowances for the preceding, it appears that for the thirty-year period in question the overall average profit rate on equity for all corporations, *adjusted for price level changes*, probably lies between 5 and 7 per cent. Moreover, though it is subject to some cyclical and year-to-year variations, it has not evidenced any systematic upward or downward trend over time.

The next question is what these average accounting profit rates indicate about the overall incidence of economic or excess profits—of profits above a normal interest return on owners' investments. In this connection we must recall that the accounting rates include any such interest return. To arrive at an excess profit rate we must deduct from any accounting rate the applicable market interest rate. Thus if the accounting rate from 1936 to 1941 averaged 4.7 per cent per annum, and the applicable interest rate was 3 per cent, the excess profit rate equals (4.7 − 3.0), or 1.7 per cent—unless some adjustment for price-level bias is indicated.

The basic interest rate to be deducted should *not* include any specific risk return, which has hopefully been washed out in deducting losses from profits in calculating the all-corporation profit rates. It should not exceed 3 per cent per annum for the 1931–1946 periods, 4 per cent for the 1947–1952 period, or 5 per cent from 1953 to 1961. If we deduct these tentative interest rates from the corresponding accounting profit rates for all corporations, and then make appropriate mental allowances for price-level bias in the profit rates, we conclude provisionally that for all corporate enterprise the long-term rate of excess profits on equity has in recent times generally been from 2 to 3 per cent per annum. The rate does not indicate an exceptionally large overall average size of excess profits, relative to the investment base of owners' equities, though the excess profit margin is not negligible.

A better notion of the effect of accounting and excess profits on over-all income distribution may be gained by expressing aggregate corporate profits as a percentage of all net national income originating in or distributed from corporations. Satisfactory data are available here only for the period after World War II. For about the same postwar periods as those for which profit rates on equity were shown above, the share of corporate accounting profits in the corresponding part of national income was as follows.

Years	Total Corporate Profits, after Income Tax, as a Percentage of Net National Income Originating in the Corporate Sector
1947–52	12.5
1953–62	9.4

For earlier periods, we have data only on corporate profits expressed as a percentage of *all* net national income; these are obviously some-what lower than the corresponding percentages of income originating in the corporate sector. For the period 1936 to 1946, corporate profits on the average were almost exactly 7 per cent of all net national income.

The share of income going to corporate profits has been remarkably stable over time, except in an unusually severe depression. For example, corporate profits accounted for 6.2 per cent of all net national income from 1936 to 1940, and 5.8 per cent from 1952 to 1956. Even year-to-year variations in this share are rather small. From 1953 to 1962, the annual shares of corporate profits in net income originating in the corporate sector fluctuated only between 8.5 and 10.7 per cent. And before World War II, the share of these profits in all net national income was between 6.4 and 7.9 per cent in four of the five years from 1936 to 1940, dropping to a lower level (3.4 per cent) only in a recession year.

The percentages of income going to corporate profits that have been described above refer to corporate accounting profits, inclusive of an interest return on shareholders' investments. How much of this share consists of economic or excess profits, over and above a normal return on investment? After appropriate allowances are made for price-level biases in reported accounting profits, and estimated interest earnings are deducted, it appears that excess profits for all corporations tend to account for 4 or 5 per cent of income originating in the corporate sector. The share of the excess profits of all business firms (including proprietorships and partnerships as well as corporations) in all net national income is evidently about the same or a little less.

The 4 or 5 per cent share of national net income apparently going to excess profits is significant but not very large. Total elimination of all excess profits would not change the national distribution of income, or the average relation of prices to costs very much. From this we do not conclude that excess profits are a quite unimportant economic phenomenon, although their aggregate effect on income distribution may be comparatively small.

We do find that excess profits are quite important in certain industries and sectors of the economy, and that their varying importance among industries is indirectly indicative of significant misallocations of resources among uses. Some attention to the variation of profit rates among sectors and industries is therefore in order.

Some systematic variation in accounting profit rates on equity is observable among corporations in the several major sectors of the economy. In 1962, for example, when the reported average profit rate for all corporations was 5.7 per cent, the dispersion of the average profit rates of corporations in eight sectors was as follows:

Sector	Average Profit Rate on Equity, after Tax (all corporations) 1962
Finance	6.4
Manufacturing	6.3
Wholesale and retail trade	4.9
Public utilities	4.8
Services	4.3
Construction	3.1
Mining and quarrying	3.0
Agriculture, forestry and fisheries	1.2

These data engender the suspicion that in some average sense the relationships of price to marginal and average costs vary significantly among some sectors of the economy.

The sector, of course, lumps together many individual industries. As we move to slightly smaller industry groupings (though groups still generally larger than individual theoretical industries), the dispersion of profit rates becomes more distinct. For example, in the manufacturing sector in 1962, we find the general range of profit rates among "subsectors" illustrated by the following instances.

Subsector	Average Rate of Profit on Equity, after Tax (all corporations) 1962
Tobacco manufactures	13.2
Motor vehicles and equipment	10.4
Chemicals	9.9
Beverages	7.1
Electrical machinery and equipment	6.5
Apparel and related products	6.0
Furniture and fixtures	4.7
Primary metals	4.6
Textile mill products	4.3

Among individual Census industries (groups approximating theoretical industries) differences as large or larger in profit rates are found. For example, the annual average profit rates on equity for the five-year period 1957 to 1961 for a sample of seven industries was as follows.

Industry	Average Annual Profit Rate on Equity (after taxes) 1957–1961
Cigarettes	14.3
Motor vehicles	13.8
Petroleum refining	10.3
Steel	8.5
Linoleum	8.2
Meat packing	5.8
Rayon	4.7

A similar or greater dispersion is noted for larger numbers of industries, and for earlier periods. In general, we find that excess profits are not spread evenly and thin "like butter" over all the firms, industries, and sectors of the economy. Rather, they occur in only some fraction of all possible instances, and with varying intensity in those cases where they do occur.

Thus for the years indicated above we can contrast the manufacturing sector, which had an overall average excess profit rate of modest magnitude, with the mining sector, which apparently had no excess profit and some net loss on the average. Or we may compare the cigarette and motor vehicle industries, with steep excess profit rates; the steel industry, with a moderate rate; and the meat packing industry, with very low or negligible excess profits. Similar, though generally lesser, differences would be noted among the profit rates of different firms in the same industry.

The irregular and varying incidence of excess profits among sectors, among firms, and particularly among industries thus stands out, as does the fact that apparently large and very significant excess profits are earned in some proportion of individual industries. In these industries, any large deviation of the profit rate from the norm of a basic interest return on owners' equity may represent a very significant aspect of market performance.

Before we can make even a tentative evaluation of the social consequences or desirability of observed excess profits, however, it is essential that we devise some means of determining the sources of the profits observed. Are they explicable as windfalls, risk rewards to particular firms, or necessary rewards to innovation, in which event they would be potentially justifiable from the standpoint of overall economic efficiency? Or are they in large part functionless and undesirable monopolistic excess profits, of the sort that tend to persist chronically through time?

This is a very hard question to answer directly except by the painstaking analysis of the earnings records of many individual firms and industries over very long periods of time. Unfortunately, such analyses have not been made nor does time permit us to make them now. Some useful clues to the answer to this question, however, may be developed by an indirect route—by ascertaining the way in which industry excess profits are associated with industry market structures.

We may ask, that is, whether or not high excess profits for industries are strongly associated with those characteristics of market structure (especially high seller concentration and high barriers to new entry) that would theoretically be expected to lead to chronic monopolistic excess profits. If such a strong association is in fact found, we then have some reason to believe, on the basis of underlying economic theory, that observed excess profits are in considerable part actually monopolistic excess profits—not simply windfalls, rewards to innovation, and so forth. They are thus, by this reasoning, opprobrious rather than acceptable from the standpoint of the general economic welfare.

In the following chapter, the results of some tests of the association of market structure to the size of the profit rate for manufacturing industries will be described. We may anticipate the findings there by revealing that a significant linkage is found between high seller concentration and difficult entry conditions on the one hand and high industry profit rates on the other.

The very tentative judgment may therefore be offered that, for some significant fraction of all industries in the American economy, market performance is poor or "unworkable" in that substantial monopolistic excess profits of the chronic sort are found. These excess profits result from monopolistic output restrictions and result in an increased inequality of income distribution without rewarding any useful economic function. For another larger or at least equally substantial fraction of industries, however, average profit rates in the long term come reasonably close to the normal interest return on owners' investments, and a more "workable" performance is found. More evidence on this matter will appear in the next chapter. The incidence of chronically subnormal industry profits, though significant, is much lower than that of excess profits. We will refer to typical instances of subnormal profit patterns in Chapter 12. Needless to say, they also distort income distribution and reveal allocative inefficiency.

How large is the social loss—that is, the reduction of consumers' satisfaction—that results from the inefficient allocation of resources which is revealed by the incidence of monopolistic excess profits and subnormal profits throughout the economy? Nobody has been able really to measure this loss. In order to measure it, it would be necesary first to calculate from the long-run excess profits rates and subnormal profit rates of all industries earning such rates (once all these rates had been measured and adjusted) the implied excesses of price over long-run average and marginal cost (and excesses of average and marginal cost over price). Then it would be necessary to determine at least approximately the price-elasticities of demand for the outputs of all of these industries. This latter information would be needed because the amount of restriction of output (misallocation of resources) that will result from any given excess of price over cost for a good depends directly on the price elasticity of demand for the good—and conversely for excesses of cost over price. If information on all of the relevant price elasticities of demand and on all of the discrepancies between price and cost could be assembled, it could then be analyzed to determine the probable size, measured in physical terms, of the total misallocation of resources in the economy. Thereafter, it would only be necessary to contrive a means of placing a value on the corresponding loss in consumer satisfaction.

The foregoing outline of what would be needed to measure the total loss from inefficient resource allocation clearly suggests why it has not been measured. Some slapdash attempts have been made in this direction, but we will not discuss them here.

Size of Selling Costs

Another aspect of the market performance of industries is the magnitude of costs incurred for sales promotion. "Selling costs" may be defined as expenditures made by firms to stimulate the sales volume of their products in two general ways: by informing potential customers of the availability, characteristics, and prices of the products; and by inducing or persuading them to buy. The aims and accomplishments of sales promotion activities are thus both *informational* and *persuasive*.

Selling activities and costs are different from those associated with the production and physical distribution of goods. The latter activities include the physical tasks of extracting, creating, or fabricating goods, of providing services, and of distributing goods to customers. The corresponding costs are appropriately labeled as production and distribution costs.

A rough line distinguishes these activities and costs from those of sales promotion. The line between selling costs and distribution costs, to be sure, is a hazy one, since the character and quality of distribution services may be increased above some basic minimum as a means of promoting sales. For example, when petroleum refiners build a very dense system of service stations on expensive locations, thus increasing the costs of distribution considerably, they apparently do so largely as a means of promoting gasoline sales. On the other hand, they thereby provide a higher quality of "product" or service in the form of increased convenience to motorists. Although there is this sort of ambiguity concerning what proportion (if any) of distributive costs should be considered promotional costs, the general distinction between selling costs and production-and-distribution costs is nevertheless meaningful.

Selling activities and connected costs may be grouped under three general headings:

1. Advertising of all sorts.
2. Personal sales promotion (the use of salesmen to promote sales, as distinguished from the employment of clerks to take orders).
3. Increments in distributive services (above a basic level) that have a sales-promotion orientation.

Measurement of Selling Costs, and Their Significance

In what terms should selling costs be measured, for purposes of appraising market performance? A superficially attractive measure is simply one of the aggregate number of dollars spent annually for sales promotion by the firm, industry, or economy. Although the recitation of total dollar expenditures of this sort is spectacular, the aggregate-expenditure measure is not very meaningful from an analytical standpoint. The fact that one very large firm spends $40 million annually on advertising does not mean very much (except that the firm is a big one) until we interpret this aggregate expenditure in the light of the firm's annual sales volume. That is, if we find that the firm has an annual sales volume of $2 billion, so that 2 per cent of its sales revenue is going to advertising, we are in a much better position to interpret the relative place and true importance of advertising costs in its market performance.

The most illuminating measure of selling costs would express them as percentages of all costs (of production, distribution, and sales promotion) of the firm or industry. Such a ratio would give a rough indication of the proportion of productive resources used that are being devoted to sales promotion rather than to producing and distributing goods. This ratio of selling costs to all costs is fairly well approximated by available data that express selling costs as a percentage of sales revenue.

What is the significance of the size of selling costs as measured in this manner? What difference does it make if it is large rather than small? Various standards of evaluation might be adopted, but the one tentatively offered here is developed from the following propositions.

First, a modicum of selling activity and cost devoted to *informational* purposes are functionally justified, or essential to the effective working of a market system. It is necessary and useful to inform potential buyers of the availability of goods, of their specifications and qualities, and of their prices.

Second, selling activity and cost with a persuasive orientation are not similarly justified from the standpoint of aggregate economic welfare. They reflect, in large part at least, a diversion to sales promotion of productive resources which could otherwise be devoted to producing and distributing a larger volume of useful goods and services. This proposition rests essentially on the rejection of the oft-made but unsupported assertion that persuasive sales promotion is really needed to stimulate an expenditure of available purchasing power sufficient to sustain full employment and production in an enterprise economy.

We deny, that is, the idea that we must have persuasive sales promotion to induce people to buy all the goods and services we are able to, or optimally should, produce. If persuasive promotion is not required, then it is basically wasteful, and more so as selling costs become larger. It is not only wasteful from a social standpoint, but in general not even beneficial to the firms and industries engaging in it (except as a defense against the going promotional efforts of competing firms and industries). Competitive promotional activities tend to be largely self-canceling in their effects on sales, both as among competing firms and among competing industries.

A large proportion of observed promotional activities and costs have, to all appearances, a dominantly *persuasive* orientation, and this emphasis is generally greater as selling costs are larger in proportion to sales. Therefore, a substantial portion of all sales-promotion costs probably are socially wasteful in character. And this wastefulness is evidently acute in industries in which selling costs are relatively high in proportion to sales revenues.

Advertising Costs in Manufacturing Industries

Most systematic data on selling costs refer to the cost of advertising only, and this largely for the manufacturing sector. They measure the expenditures of manufacturing firms and industries for television, radio, periodical, newspaper, billboard, and direct-mail advertising. A general idea of the magnitude and variation of such advertising costs is supplied by a survey of findings for the sample of twenty manufacturing industries previously referred to, the specific reference being to advertising costs just before and shortly after World War II. According to these findings, the twenty industries could be roughly classified, according to size of total advertising costs for all firms, as follows:

Advertising Costs Less Than 1 Per Cent of Sales Revenue

Copper	Meat packing
Cement	Tin cans
Rayon	Farm machinery
Steel	Tractors

Advertising Costs 1 to 2 Per Cent of Sales Revenue
 Gypsum products   Canned goods
 Rubber tires   Shoes
 Petroleum products

Advertising Costs 2 to 4 Per Cent of Sales Revenue
 Typewriters   Flour
 Automobiles

Advertising Costs 5 or 6 Per Cent of Sales Revenue
 Cigarettes   Fountain pens
 Liquor

Advertising Costs About 10 Per Cent of Sales Revenue
      Soap

The sample of industries is a small one, and in all probability not precisely representative of manufacturing industries as a whole. It appears to be sufficiently representative, however, to lend some support to the following tentative conclusions, which are based also on broader and more casual observation of advertising costs in many manufacturing industries.

First, among different manufacturing industries, advertising costs represent widely varying percentages of sales revenue. They range from a small fraction of 1 per cent up to 10 per cent or more. Second, a substantial majority of manufacturing industries have rather low advertising costs (below 2 per cent of sales revenue), whereas a distinct minority of them have significantly higher advertising costs (5 per cent or more of sales revenue). In our sample of twenty industries about three-fifths of them had advertising costs at or below 2 per cent of sales, and only one-fifth had advertising costs that were 5 per cent or more of sales. The incidence of large wastes of excessive advertising appears to be confined to a minor fraction of all manufacturing industries.

Third, producer-goods industries generally (but not always) have low advertising costs. There is also, however, a significant group of consumer-goods industries in which advertising costs are small. It is difficult to identify these latter industries in terms of any common attribute of market structure.

Fourth, practically all industries with very high advertising costs (costs equal to 5 per cent or more of sales revenue) produce consumer goods. They also have high or very high seller concentration, and a strong product differentiation which is largely *created* by advertising. In them, the opportunities for physical product differentiation (in design or quality) are generally rather limited, and nearly all advertising effort has a persuasive rather than an informational orientation.

Fifth, all or most of the industries with relatively high advertising costs are seriously suspect of undesirable or "unworkable" performance in the matter of selling costs. That is, wasteful promotional costs have exceeded the "limit of tolerance" or "margin for error" that should probably be allowed in evaluating the social desirability of market performance.

Promotional Costs Other Than Advertising

The costs of sales promotion, of course, do not stop with advertising, or with firms in manufacturing industries. It would thus be desirable to obtain systematic data bearing on two further matters: selling costs in manufacturing industries other than those of advertising, and selling costs in sectors other than manufacturing.

With respect to nonadvertising promotional costs in manufacturing, the available evidence is very scanty. As reported, these selling costs are typically buried in a broad category such as "selling, general, and administrative expense," so that it is usually not possible to determine the magnitude of the selling costs alone. From casual observation and from more detailed scraps of evidence concerning some individual industries, however, two impressions emerge.

First, a certain base level of expenditure on personal sales representation is common to most or all manufacturing industries. This is indicated by the fact that firms in most or all cases operate sales departments, employ salesmen to develop and serve customers, and so forth. At a basic level, this sort of selling activity and its connected cost are justifiable and necessary in the same sense that informational advertising is needed.

Second, there is evidently at least some minor proportion of manufacturing industries in which nonadvertising promotional activities and costs substantially exceed this basic level, and represent waste. These include some industries in which advertising costs are not especially high. Among our sample of twenty industries this would appear to be true of the typewriter, automobile, farm machinery, and petroleum refining industries.

The most prominent device for nonadvertising sales promotion is the development by manufacturing firms of elaborate and expensive systems of wholesale and retail outlets, for sales and for service to final buyers. When this device is prominent in an industry, each principal competing seller establishes his own exclusive chain or system of outlets. Costs are thereby elevated both by a duplication of distributive facilities and labor force, and by intensive promotional activity within individual facilities. Much of this substantial increment to cost is plausibly identified as sales-promotion cost incurred with a persuasive orientation, and as socially wasteful.

The development of systems of exclusive distributive facilities for manufactured products is sometimes accomplished by actual vertical integration of distribution with manufacturing, with the manufacturer owning the distributive facilities. More commonly, manufacturers encourage, sponsor, and subsidize the development of exclusive distribution outlets that are owned by independent merchants but have contractual ties with the manufacturer. Whatever the device, excessive selling costs apparently develop in this manner in a small but significant portion of our manufacturing industries. An alternative way of describing the result, of course, is to say that the "product" of distributive facilities in these cases (namely, the provision of convenience and service to customers) is made elaborate and expensive as a result of the sales-promotion policies of the manufacturers.

Selling costs have some place in almost every sector of enterprise activity, but outside of the manufacturing sphere are likely to present a problem in market performance chiefly in the retail distributive trades. Let us put aside those retail trades in which facilities are integrated or controlled by the manufacturer, and consider the trades in which firms are more or less fully independent of supplying manufacturers. These include food stores, clothing stores, drug stores, and so forth.

First, although significant amounts are spent on advertising by firms in these trades, the advertising (usually in newspapers) usually has a strong informational emphasis and function, and by and large seems to be justified from a social standpoint. Second, the main possible waste of sales promotion in these trades is likely to emerge, if at all, in the form of distributive excess capacity, taking the form of unduly numerous outlets and unnecessarily large labor forces that have been developed essentially for sales-promotion reasons.

Although the latter is a possibility, and is one of the reasons frequently offered for the "high cost of distribution" in the United States, we are substantially lacking systematic evidence that would reveal how frequently and to what extent this possibility is realized. Evaluation of scraps of evidence that are available is difficult, moreover, because of doubt concerning the extent to which expensive distribution is economically supplying an actual demand by consumers for convenience and elaborate service. In at least some extreme cases, however, a fairly clear aberration from distributive efficiency is present.

That is, in lines where extremely high distributive markups (margins of retail over wholesale prices) have been maintained jointly by resale price maintenance contracts between manufacturers and retailers and by state "fair trade" laws that make these high markups enforceable on all competing retail sellers, the resulting suppression of retail price competition has induced excesses of nonprice competition. It has also induced excessive entry, creating fairly acute distributive excess capacity and elevating costs accordingly. This tendency appears, for example, in fields of drug stores, electrical appliance dealers, and liquor stores in states where private firms retail alcoholic beverages. For most of the distributive trades, however, this tendency is not significantly in evidence.

In summary, it appears that in the majority of industries in the manufacturing and distributive sectors, the costs of sales promotion are roughly justified in terms of function and are not excessive. But there is a significant minority of industries in which selling costs are excessive in an important degree and in which market performance is, to a corresponding extent, "unworkable." The structural bases of excessive selling costs will be considered in the following chapter.

Market Performance in Other Dimensions

There are several other dimensions of market performance which are significant and about which systematic evidence would be instructive. Four of them are: technological progressiveness, product performance, conservation performance, and price flexibility. Unfortunately, we are unable to report very much in the way of meaningful empirical findings with respect to any of these dimensions of performance, for two major reasons.

First, with respect to all except price flexibility, there is a simple lack of systematic factual evidence of a meaningful sort. This lack is attributable in large part to the fact that the data required for a useful measurement of performance are extremely complex and, under ordinary circumstances, either unavailable or impossible to obtain for nearly all industries. Second, in the case of at least two of these dimensions (technological progressiveness and price flexibility), we are substantially without adequate operational criteria for evaluating the performance observed. Then, even if some relevant empirical data are available, we are unable to interpret the evidence in terms of established norms of desirable performance.

It is therefore idle to engage in an extended description of the sort of evidence that is available. Nevertheless, it may be useful to comment briefly, with respect to each of these four dimensions of performance, on the fundamental economic issues involved and on the little we do know about actual performance.

Progressiveness in Production Techniques

Production techniques in any sector or industry of the economy are continually or intermittently improving or progressing, with the general result of lowering the real costs of producing various goods and services. The overall advance of technology has been rapid the past two centuries, with a consequent great increase in the productivity of basic resources. The development and introduction of improved production techniques generally involves two distinguishable stages of human activity. The first is *invention or discovery* of new techniques, which thus became available for use by business firms. The second is *innovation* of newly discovered and available techniques—their actual application in production or introduction into commercial use. Individual business firms are typically responsible for nearly all technological innovation, and for much of invention—especially for inventions that apply basic scientific discoveries to the development of applicable techniques of production. It is thus natural that we should consider one important aspect of the market performance of firms and industries to be "how well they do" in the matter of invention and innovation. Are they "adequately" or ideally progressive in developing and applying new techniques, and thus contributing to the increased productivity of the economy?

But how should we proceed to establish whether the performance of a firm or industry in the matter of technological progressiveness is good, bad, or indifferent? There is one way in which we should not *and legitimately cannot* evaluate the "progressiveness" performance of industries. This is by a simple enumeration and comparison of the number and importance of inventions and innovations made over a certain time period in various different industries, or by measuring "inventive effort" in terms of a gross count of "research and development" expenditures and personnel. This procedure is faulty because the adequacy of the inventive effort, inventive output, and "output of innovations" of an industry has no necessary relationship to its expenditures on research, the number and kind of inventions it patents, or the frequency with which it makes significant technological innovations. That is, the rate of "gross progress" of an industry is not a good index of how effectively it has performed in the dimension of progressiveness. And this is because an industry's progressiveness can be properly evaluated only in terms of how progressive it has been *relative to its opportunities.* The question is how well it has exploited the available opportunities for invention and innovation. Each industry should be judged in terms of how well it did relative to what it was possible to do.

Reliance instead on a criterion of "gross progress" can lead to non-sensical conclusions. Application of this criterion, for example, would find that the petroleum refining industry showed "good" progress in the last forty years, with a steady stream of technological developments. The flour-milling industry, however, would be rated as evidencing "poor" progress because over the same period firms in that industry were able to find or introduce only minor improvements in a technique which was fully developed by the early years of this century. The comparison is unfair, and the conclusions are meaningless, because both of the wide difference in the intrinsic complexity of the manufacturing processes involved, and of the wide difference in the ages of the two industries.

A number of economists in recent years have nevertheless made comparative studies of either a few or many industries that emphasize precisely gross inventive effort, gross output of patented inventions, and gross rate of technological (and product) innovation as measures of comparative progressiveness. Because of the fundamental disabilities of their approach, their findings will not be reviewed here.

If we shift the criterion for evaluating progress to one of accomplishment relative to opportunity, however, we immediately encounter other difficulties. The greatest of these involves the appraisal of observed rates of discovery or invention of new techniques. What an "adequate" rate of discovery or invention is, economywide or in an individual industry, is not knowable. There is no way of knowing, *a priori*, what unknown things can reasonably be expected to be discovered. The "potential" rate of discovery, against which the actual rate might be measured, cannot in any way be systematically guessed or approximated, especially for the individual industry with its individual characteristics of age and general function. Therefore, the absolute rate of discovery is not susceptible to meaningful evaluation, and its relative acceptability from a social standpoint is not subject to meaningful measurement. In this context, observations to the effect that one industry has progressed in technology more slowly than others over the last fifty years, or that "they should have discovered more," have no obvious meaning or validity.

The second difficulty, involving the appraisal of industry performance in the matter of innovation of previously discovered techniques, is of a different order but nonetheless pressing. In this case, it is possible to define a general standard of adequate or ideal performance that is at least potentially subject to empirical application. That is, an ideal rate of innovation through time in an industry is one that promptly exploits every available technological change that would reduce the costs of producing the goods or services in question (the costs of innovation being taken into account). Conversely, it is also one that foregoes or delays technological changes that, if made currently, would increase production costs over time.

The difficulty comes in applying this standard to judge observed rates of innovation in various industries. A fantastically complex body of information—of the sort which is either unavailable or protected by secrecy—would be needed as the basis for such a judgment. In particular we would need to learn, for any industry examined, not only the long-run cost-reducing impact of each technological change adopted (a *relatively* easy thing to learn), but also the identities of all available opportunities for technological change which were rejected, and the estimated effect on cost of each rejected opportunity. Only then could we tell if the observed innovation record reached or reasonably approximated the ideal.

For nearly every industry, this sort of essential information is simply unavailable. As a result, meaningful appraisal of performance in the dimension of innovational progress is not possible. We cannot honestly do much more than acknowledge the record of technological change in each industry, being grateful for gifts received from progress where it occurs, and omit any evaluation of "progressiveness" performance for the moment.

Since we are unable to distinguish good from bad performance in the dimension of technological progress, we are unable to establish empirically the conditions of market structure which might favor good progress. An alternative is to theorize about the effects of market structure on progressiveness. Unfortunately, the indications of such theorizing are so inconclusive as to be almost useless. We therefore drop the matter of technological progressiveness, and turn to other matters.

Product Performance

The general issue concerning the product performance of industries is how well the firms engaged design, determine the quality of, vary, differentiate, and progressively improve their products—all relative to that performance in these several regards which would achieve the best attainable balance between buyer satisfaction and the cost of production. Or, to what extent could the relationship of buyer satisfaction to the cost of production be significantly improved by lowering or raising quality, altering design, increasing or decreasing the real variety of quality or design among competing products, changing products more or less frequently, and so forth?

From the preceding it is clear that product performance itself has numerous dimensions, among which may be emphasized:

1. General level of quality or character of design of the products offered by an industry at any time.
2. Rate and pattern of product change and improvement over time.
3. Frequency of product change and improvement over time.
4. Variety among competing products at any time.

All of these aspects of product performance should be judged relative to alternatives, the comparative costs of the alternatives being taken into account. Let us consider them briefly in turn.

The determination of the general level of quality or character of design of the product offered by the firms of an industry is appropriately viewed as a selection among available alternative qualities and designs. The efficacy of discovery, invention, or creation of better alternative products is for purposes of evaluation not considered. Performance in that regard (like performance in the invention of techniques) cannot be judged against any firm standard concerning what was "possible" or could be expected. Attempts to set standards for adequate inventiveness with respect to products end up essentially on the level of bromides like these: "What this country needs is a good five-cent cigar"; or "Why can't they produce a cigarette lighter that works every time?".

Given some set of known alternatives of design and quality, however, a fairly clear criterion of ideal product performance in choosing among them is available. Firms should elevate quality (starting at some minimum base level) so long as the resulting addition to buyer satisfaction outweighs the resulting addition to cost of production, but should not continue to elevate quality through a range where the addition to satisfaction is insufficient to compensate for the connected addition to cost. Alternative designs of the product should be chosen according to an equivalent principle.

This criterion is not particularly ambiguous in any essential way, but it is terribly difficult to apply to actual cases. The difficulty is basically the same as that encountered in trying to evaluate observed rates of technological innovation—the data required for evaluation are intricate, complex, and practically unobtainable. Measures not only of the costs of all relevant available product opportunities, but also of their relative satisfaction-providing power, would be required to decide how observed product performance compares to the ideal, and all or most of these data cannot be, or have not as yet been, revealed.

To be sure, there are prominent individual cases in which, judging from horseback, economists have suspected that the quality or design of available products diverges significantly from that which would best serve buyers (costs considered). For example, electric light bulbs *may* be designed, relative to known alternatives, with too short a life, in the sense that a small added cost would effect a disproportionately large increase in useful life. Or, American passenger automobiles *may* be too large, too powerful, and too fancy for the maximum advantage of the average purchaser, considering various cost-saving alternatives in automobile design.

Moreover, some *a priori* theoretical models explain how and why competing firms in various structural situations may, in the interests of profit maximization, be led to produce goods of either insufficient or excessive quality (costs considered), or of inappropriate design. Aberrations from desirable performance in the dimension of the level of product quality and design are thus probably present in some instances, and to be expected on theoretical grounds. The unfortunate fact is that we do not have access to that quantity and type of empirical data which would permit us to derive any general conclusions concerning this aspect of the product performance of American industries.

The rate and pattern of product change over time raise issues similar if not identical to those just discussed. First, there is really no solid basis for evaluating the degree of inventiveness or ingenuity in developing new and possibly better products. The manageable question concerns the rate and type of response to known alternatives for change. Again, a standard of ideal performance can be stated in general terms, and again the requisite data are not available for evaluating performance, except perhaps in isolated instances. Again also there are suspicions to the effect that the rate and the pattern of product change in some cases diverge markedly from the social optimum. This divergence could be reflected in insufficient or excessive product quality or in inappropriate design at any given time. It might also be reflected in inconclusive style variations through time (see the rediscovery in the auto industry in the early 1950's of the outboard spare-tire mounts of the 1920's, or the more recent reintroduction of the stick shift). We are in the same position here as we are with the immediate levels of quality and design. General standards can be stated, but data are not available to implement these standards in evaluations of observed performance.

A third aspect of product performance involves the *frequency* of product changes in various industries (whatever the average rate of change over time). The difference between average rate and frequency of change is easily illustrated with reference to the automobile industry. Within a period of ten years, the body design of a typical automobile may be changed from a box-on-a-box motif to a true "fastback." There are at least two ways of accomplishing this change, however. One is by holding more or less to the box design for ten years and then suddenly converting to the fastback (thus making only one major body change in ten years). The other is by making smallish changes in the body design each year over the ten, and eventually arriving at the same fastback design. The rate of change, per decade, is potentially the same; the route by which the change is accomplished is different.

The reason that the frequency of change is important is that higher frequencies of change are generally more expensive than lower frequencies that may well reach the same goal at the same time "in the long run." This is because of the repetitive expenses of redesigning and retooling associated with frequent product changes. Therefore, high frequencies of change tend to result in higher costs and higher product price than lower frequencies. If we are to decide which frequency of product changes contributes more to buyer welfare, the added costs of frequent product change must be balanced against such added satisfaction as buyers may derive from having "a new model every year" as opposed to "a new model every five or ten years," the rate of product change per decade being identical.

Our situation here, with respect to empirical evidence, is much the same as it was for other aspects of product performance. First we lack, for any representative cross-section of industries, the requisite data for evaluating the observed frequency of product development and variation. This is mainly because of a lack of any measure of the effects on buyer satisfaction of different frequencies of product change. Then, there are "straws in the wind," or suspicions, to the effect that some observed high frequencies of product change (due either to general industry strategy or to competitive sales promotion) add much more to costs than they add to buyer satisfaction. (See the automobile industry, or durable consumer goods industries in general). Finally, there are theoretical indications that wastefully excessive frequencies of product change may be expected to develop in various oligopolistic market situations. Beyond the preceding we are not prepared to go, and available evidence helps us very little.

The fourth aspect of product performance concerns the extent of *variety* among competing products offered by firms in any particular industry. A theoretical argument may be developed to define ideal product variety, along the following lines. First, buyers from any industry will generally have diverse tastes regarding the quality-design-price combination they most prefer. Some, for example, prefer a higher quality or more elaborate design even though it must carry a higher price, whereas others will prefer a lower priced good even if to get it they must sacrifice perceptibly in quality or design. Second, the overall satisfaction of buyers will be best served, other things being equal, if the sellers of the industry provide a variety of product-price alternatives equal to the variety of buyer tastes in this regard, with each of the several alternatives offered being optimal for the particular group of buyers it serves. Third, it may be necesary, however, in the interests of efficient production, and on balance desirable from the standpoint of buyer welfare, to restrict variety below the level just indicated. This will be the case if economies of scale in producing individual product alternatives are such that wastefully small-scale production would result from producing a variety of products equal to the variety of buyer tastes. Where such scale economies are significant, some compromise must be struck between variety and efficiency, but a considerable variety should still be possible in a large proportion of cases.

Whether the actual variety of product alternatives offered is adequate in various industries (especially those in which wide variations in the design and quality of products are possible) is indeed an important issue in the assessment of market performance. We are again, however, lacking sufficient systematic data—on the character of buyer preference patterns and on the actual alternatives of product design and quality and their alternative costs—to support any general evaluation of industry product performance in this dimension. It has been noted in some industries, for example the automobile industry, that the highly imitative product policies of rival oligopolists seem to lead to a substantial uniformity of available products and to a suppression of the potential variety in products. Even in such individual instances, however, no conclusive evaluation of the observed variety pattern from the standpoint of buyer welfare has ever been made, and we are restricted for the moment to rather general speculation on the issue.

Conservation Performance

For any of a group of industries whose operations involve extraction of natural resources (mining, petroleum production, agricultural cultivation, lumbering, commercial fisheries) a significant dimension of the market performance of the firms engaged involves how well they do in the matter of "conservation" of resources. To paraphrase the popular literature on this matter, conservation in an economic sense of course does not mean non-use or simple deferment of use, but "wise use" of the resources being exploited. In technical terms, good conservation requires a choice of technique of exploitation, time pattern of production, and time pattern of investments and other costs, which together yield an optimal net social benefit relative to costs over all future time periods in which society is interested. In determining this optimum, distant future benefits and costs should be appropriately discounted by whatever rate of "time preference" society wishes to assign in assessing the relative importance of current as opposed to future benefits and sacrifices. And conservation performance is poor to the extent that enterprises deviate from this abstract ideal.

An adequate operational definition of ideal conservation performance is extremely complex and next to impossible to apply fully in the evaluation of actual performance. Using the definition just given as a guide, however, it is possible to identify certain types of gross departure from good conservation which would have to be censured under any acceptable criterion. These include:

1. Exploitation of resources by a technique that raises both present and future costs above the obtainable minimum while reducing or not increasing the amount of resources ultimately recovered, or the amount of use obtained from resources over time.

2. Unduly rapid or intensive current use of resources which has the result of impairing (or eliminating) future use of the resources to a degree not compensated by current additions to output.

3. Pinching on current costs or investments in the use and development of resources in a way that curtails future use or raises future costs of use to a disproportionate degree.

What of the actual performance of industries in regard to conservation? Of course, only a minor proportion of all industries are sufficiently involved in extraction to make conservation an issue, and for these we do not have highly organized, systematic information on which to base an overall appraisal. However, a broad scattering of evidence on individual cases suggests that, among extractive industries, conservation performance is or has very frequently been poor.

Thus we observe in petroleum production in the United States a history of gross elevation of recovery costs coupled with a substantial reduction of ultimate recovery of available petroleum, attributable largely to the selection of techniques in the context of competitive exploitation of individual oil pools by antagonistic interests. In both lumbering and commercial fisheries, and in some agriculture, we find that a serious long-run depletion of resource productivity has resulted from overintensive immediate rates of extraction or exploitation of the available resources. In much of agriculture, a history of pinching on current costs for or investments in the preservation of the land (against erosion or reduction in fertility) has resulted in long-run losses in soil productivity.

These deviations from reasonably good conservation performance seem in large part attributable to four things: (1) antagonistic exploitation of resource deposits by competing interests, in which a competitive race to capture the resource or its output before others do results in a disregard of long-run yield considerations; (2) an inherent "sort-sightedness" of firms engaged in exploiting resources—firms that attach much less importance to distant future production than society would, or than they do to immediate profits; (3) competitive conditions which bring about such low returns to firms in some extractive industries that they cannot afford to invest in the long-run maintenance of resource yields; and (4) stupidity. Whatever the cause, poor market performance in the matter of conservation has evidently been chargeable against firms in many extractive industries. It is encouraging, in the light of this, that in the past twenty or thirty years there has been a rapidly increasing body of governmental regulations designed to encourage or require better conservation performance on the part of these industries.

Price Flexibility

During the decade of the 1930's, there was intensive statistical study of the flexibility of commodity prices for both manufactured and agricultural goods, centering largely on the *frequency* and the *amplitude* of price change for various goods in response to economywide increases and decreases of (*a*) the total money demand for goods, and (*b*) the general level of money costs. These studies succeeded in establishing that (in the absence of government interference) agricultural prices are generally much more flexible than manufactured-goods prices, and that among manufactured-goods prices there is a wide range of differing degrees of flexibility. We may conclude from casual observation that this continues to be true today.

The relative flexibility of the selling prices of an industry, in response to short-term shifts in demand and cost, is indeed an aspect of the industry's market performance. The reason that we shall not present evidence on such price flexibility here is that we are substantially without clear criteria to judge it by. That is, we cannot say what degree and type of short-term price flexibility is most satisfactory from a social standpoint, or what difference it makes if a price is more or less flexible in response to short-term changes in demand and cost. Theoretical indications on the point are conflicting, contradictory, or inconclusive, and it is thus impossible to justify attention to the voluminous statistical information on price flexibility.

Long-term or secular price flexibility—for example, the responsiveness of an industry's price to a long-term reduction in its costs—can be more clearly evaluated. Such responsiveness is socially desirable, and a lack of it deleterious to economic welfare. Since this aspect of performance is already reflected, however, in the long-term profit margins of firms and industries (considered earlier), we need not give further attention to it here.

Workability of Observed Market Performance— Summary

In this chapter we have posed the general question of how well American business firms perform, from the standpoint of their impact on aggregate material welfare, in adjusting to the markets for their products, or to the effective demands for the outputs they offer. Answering this question at all fully would involve a large program of theoretical and empirical research activity—identifying the crucial dimensions of market performance, measuring actual performance in each of the relevant dimensions, establishing norms of ideal or satisfactory performance against which actual performance might be tested, and evaluating actual performance in terms of these norms. This is indeed a big program and far from completed. In most aspects of it, our reach exceeds our grasp.

In identifying important aspects of market performance, we are reasonably well off. Available theory permits us to identify the numerous significant dimensions of performance in a fairly conclusive fashion, and we have done this. In establishing norms, ideals, or standards of performance, we do not fare as well. Some sort of general *a priori* standard, to be sure, can be established for technical efficiency, profit rates, selling costs, product performance, and conservation, although not (to this time) for price flexibility and technological progressiveness. However, except for the standard of technical efficiency in scale and utilization of plant and firm, the norms are essentially stated in such a general, qualitative, and potentially ambiguous form that testing of actual performance against them involves a variety of difficulties. Such difficulties at the worst lead to temporary defeat because of inability to secure the requisite data for testing. At the best they lead to reliance on quasi-arbitrary horseback judgments, designed to compensate either for the lack of really adequate empirical data or for the range of potential ambiguity of the standards in question. Nonetheless, we "chug along" with a combination of scientific findings and informed guesses, in order to determine (as best we can) how well enterprise in various industries is performing.

As regards measurement of actual performance, we have reasonably adequate systematic data, especially for the manufacturing sector, on technical efficiency, profit rates, and selling costs. Concerning other dimensions of performance except price flexibility, we have only a scattering of isolated observations. And for price flexibility, we lack any definite and meaningful standard of evaluation.

The findings reported above reflect these limitations. On the positive side, however, certain important things stand out. First, in the matter of technical efficiency in scale and utilization of capacity, there is an indication from a sample of manufacturing industries that although efficiency performance is in general reasonably good, there is usually a significant fringe of inefficiently small plants and firms in individual industries, this fringe varying in size from industry to industry. Second, in the matter of price-cost margins as reflected in profit rates, although the overall average profit rate for all firms and industries does not diverge very much from a competitive norm or ideal, there is a significant minor fraction of industries in which long-run chronic excess profits are realized. These profits are strongly suspected of being mainly the result of monopolistic output-restriction and price raising, and therefore indicative of allocative inefficiencies and functionless distortions of income distribution. Third, there is a similar indication that, in a significant minor fraction of industries, selling costs are excessive from the standpoint of material social welfare. Finally, the product performance and conservation performance of some undetermined minor proportion of industries are in all probability seriously at odds with the social ideal.

This is to say that various important aberrations from socially acceptable, or "workable," performance are definitely or probably present in a considerable minor proportion of our industries. The next question is whether these confirmed or probable deficiencies in performance are simply "a fact of life," which we must live with in the light of ineradicable imperfections in the structure, information, and intelligence of the modern world. Or are they attributable in important part to specific conditions which are "remediable" within the general framework of modern society? We may make some progress toward answering this difficult question by inquiring, in the following chapter, into the extent to which "unworkable" market performance is associated with practically alterable or remediable conditions of market structure.

SUPPLEMENTARY READINGS

Bain, J. S., *Barriers to New Competition*, 1956. Ch. 7.

Kaplan, A. D. H., *Small Business: Its Place and Problems*, 1948. Ch. V.

Crum, W. L., *Corporate Size and Earning Power*, 1939.

Nelson, S., and W. G. Keim, *Price Behavior and Business Policy*, T.N.E.C. Monograph 1, 1941, Part I, Ch. 1, 2.

11

The Relation of Market Structure to Market Performance

In preceding chapters we have dealt in turn with salient aspects of the market structure, conduct, and performance of industries. Part of our concern has been with identification and definition. That is, we have identified and defined (1) each of a few principal dimensions of market structure, (2) each of several typical patterns of market conduct, and (3) each of several aspects of market performance. Another part has been with description, as we have presented and interpreted empirical evidence concerning the actual market structures, market conduct, and market performance in various cross sections of American industries. A third purpose, however, has been paramount in our discussions of market structure and market conduct. This has been to present a body of theoretical hypotheses concerning the relationship of the market structures of industries to their market conduct and thus to their market performance.

These hypotheses predict in general that the market structure of an industry determines or strongly influences the crucial aspects of its market conduct and thus indirectly determines certain strategic dimensions of its market performance. If we analyze them in detail, we see that they have predicted first certain relationships of structure to conduct, and then certain relationships of conduct to performance. And in so doing, these hypotheses have also predicted certain direct relationships of market structure to market performance—the "link" of market conduct being implicitly subsumed.

These structure-conduct, conduct-performance, and structure-performance relationships, however, have so far only been theoretically predicted. The most crucial analytical task is that of testing these hypotheses with empirical data.

This chapter is concerned mainly with reporting on the results of empirical tests that have been designed generally to accomplish two purposes. The first is to confirm or disconfirm the existence of a number of theoretically predicted structure-conduct-performance relationships. The second is to implement predicted qualitative relationships by estimating statistically their quantitative strength or importance. Because, as we have seen in Chapter 9, the crucial aspects of market conduct are in general not empirically measurable independently of associated market performance, emipirical tests for structure-conduct and conduct-performance relationships have not been (and do not promise to be) feasible. Therefore, all of the systematic empirical tests referred to below are concerned with relationships of market structure to market performance.

There is no reason, of course, that empirical tests for the association between market structure and market performance have to be confined to tests for theoretically predicted relationships, and in fact they have not been. We will therefore also report on the results of tests for some structure-performance relationships with respect to which *a priori* theory has made no definite predictions—on pragmatic as distinct from theoretically oriented tests. In both sorts of tests, one general question is posed. To what extent and in what ways is the market structure of industries related to their market performance?

Empirical tests for actual relationships of structure to performance—and their results—are of vital interest to economists for two main reasons. First, they may contribute to scientific knowledge by establishing from evidence what relationships of this sort probably exist—and also by estimating the quantitative values of actual relationships. Second, they may furnish factual information that is essential as a guide in formulating public regulatory policies toward industry. The argument supporting the latter assertion is the following.

The market performance of industries is the ultimate test of how well they fulfill their social function of enhancing material welfare, and the aim of regulatory policy should be to improve performance in those instances where it is "unworkable." But actual public policy in a capitalist economy cannot feasibly proceed by directly regulating or dictating the character of market performance in most or all "miscreant" industries. Such direct regulation (especially if it is widely applied) tends to impair essential enterprise incentives or profit motivations, to induce and to protect inefficiency, to engender "evasive" behavior on the part of enterprises, and to stimulate endeavors by the regulated firms to capture or control the public agencies set up to regulate them. Though performance is crucial, therefore, it does not follow that extensive direct public regulation of performance is consistent with the maintenance of a viable capitalist economy.

On the other hand, a feasible way of exercising regulatory influence on market performance is to impose restrictive regulations or requirements on market structures (and possibly on market conduct) in order to create or preserve market situations that are conducive to good market performance. The distinction here is one, for example, between (1) insisting on a relatively unconcentrated market structure but otherwise leaving sellers free to compete according to their own discretion, and (2) requiring each enterprise to produce a certain output and sell at a certain "fair" price sufficient to yield a minimal profit. The former procedure is feasible in the sense of being consistent with maintaining adequate enterprise incentives and drives for efficiency; the latter is not.

This being the case, an essential body of knowledge for the governmental policy makers concerns the character of the association of market structure to market performance. For it is only on the basis of such knowledge that they can know what patterns of market structure are associated respectively with poor and good performance, and can therefore know what sorts of revisions of existing structure to seek in order to eliminate poor performance. Economists therefore push for as complete as possible a knowledge of what are the necessary structural conditions for good market performance by industries, as a guide to policy-making action. It is essential, moreover, to derive this knowledge as far as possible from empirical evidence, especially because the indications of relevant *a priori* theory are frequently uncertain or inconclusive.

We thus turn to empirical evidence on associations between market structure and market performance. Minimally, we would like to have on hand at least fairly conclusive tests of theoretically predicted associations of the seller concentration of industries to their price-cost margins or profit rates (measuring allocative efficiency); of their conditions of entry to the same and related aspects of performance; and of the degree of differentiation of their products to the size of their selling costs and possibly to other dimensions of performance. We should also wish to have conclusive pragmatic tests for the possible association of various dimensions of market structure to aspects of performance such as technical efficiency, progressiveness, product performance, and so forth.

Ideally, we want a set of empirical findings so complete that they would establish the more important market-performance tendencies in all of the 14 terminal sub-categories of the following market classification:

I. Industries with high seller concentration
  A. With blockaded entry
    1. With homogeneous products
    2. With differentiated products
  B. With effectively impeded entry
    1. With homogeneous products
    2. With differentiated products
  C. With ineffectively impeded entry
    1. With homogeneous products
    2. With differentiated products
II. Industries with moderate seller concentration
  A. With blockaded entry
    1. With homogeneous products
    2. With differentiated products
  B. With effectively impeded entry
    1. With homogeneous products
    2. With differentiated products
  C. With ineffectively impeded entry
    1. With homogeneous products
    2. With differentiated products
III. Industries with low seller concentration (and generally easy entry)
    1. With homogeneous products
    2. With differentiated products

Unfortunately, economists at present are several light years distant from fulfilling this ideal. Manifold difficulties in securing adequate data (or any data at all bearing on many matters), together with the sheer magnitude of the implied research task, have deterred them from proceeding very far with establishing the complex interrelationships of the several leading dimensions of market structure with several most prominent dimensions of market performance. In fact, economists have so far succeeded in conducting empirical tests that yield only tentative findings concerning the central relationships of market structure to market performance in the dimensions of allocative and technical efficiency.

We will report on such findings as have emerged from meaningful and statistically valid experiments in the two following sections, which deal with the relation of market structure first to technical efficiency and second to price-cost margins or profit rates—commenting on methodological problems as the occasion may require. Thereafter we will offer some comments on apparent relationships of market structure to other dimensions of performance, and conclude the chapter with some observations on related matters.

Relationship of Market Structure to Technical Efficiency

A first question concerns the association between the market structures of industries and their performance in the dimension of technical efficiency. What is the relationship, if any, of an industry's degree of seller concentration, degree of product differentiation, and condition of entry to its efficiency as affected by the scales of its plants and firms and by the rate of utilization of its plant capacity?

This technical efficiency is an important aspect of market performance. And, as indicated in Chapter 10, the study of a sample of manufacturing industries has suggested (1) that in most or all industries there is a significant minor incidence of inefficiency attributable to plants and firms that suffer diseconomies of insufficient scale, and (2) that the extent of this inefficiency varies considerably among industries. The same study also suggested that there is among industries a lesser and more scattered incidence of inefficiency due to chronic excess capacity. We will consider the relationships of market structure to the occurrence and the extent of these two sorts of technical inefficiency in turn.

Are some market structures more conducive to efficiency in scale of plant and firm than others? Reasonably sophisticated versions of price theory offer no definite prediction on this point, other than the rather limited one that in atomistically competitive markets product differentiation should be conducive to the development of firms of slightly less than minimum optimal scale. (This prediction is not readily tested with available data.) A number of *ad hoc* hypotheses concerning the relationship of market structure to efficiency in scale have been suggested, however, of which we may first mention three:

1. Higher seller concentration tends to reflect the growth of firms to relatively larger sizes, and thus tends to reduce the incidence of inefficiently small plants and firms. Industries with high or moderate concentration should therefore tend to have higher proportions of their outputs supplied by plants and firms of reasonably efficient scale than industries with relatively low concentration.

2. Industries to which entry is exceptionally easy are more likely to attract and maintain a substantial group of inefficiently small plants and firms than industries to which entry is more difficult. Therefore, high or

moderate barriers to entry to industries should be associated with greater technical efficiency in the scales of plants and firms than low barriers to entry.

These two hypotheses suggest that low concentration and easy entry are conducive to comparatively poor technical efficiency in the respect mentioned. They are, however, contradicted by another *ad hoc* hypothesis:

3. Low seller concentration and easy entry are both more conducive to effective price competition than are higher concentration and more difficult entry. And effective price competition tends to enforce efficiency in scale on the firms of an industry as a condition for survival. Therefore, industries with low seller concentration and easy entry are likely to have greater efficiency in the scales of plants and firms than those with higher seller concentration and higher barriers to entry.

It is clear that the indications of these *ad hoc* hypotheses are not only contradictory, but also essentially indefinite or inconclusive. Empirical evidence on the association of market structure to technical efficiency as affected by plant and firm scales is badly needed.

The only available empirical test for such an association is one based on our sample of twenty manufacturing industries. Since the sample is small and only manufacturing is covered, the results of the test must be viewed as extremely tentative. Its indications concerning the relationship of seller concentration and the condition of entry to the proportion of industry output supplied by plants and firms of efficient scale are negative or inconclusive, and as follows.

First, there is no evident association of the degree of "top-level" seller concentration in an industry to the relative size of the fringe of inefficiently small plants and firms. Whatever the degree of concentration among the larger firms supplying the bulk of industry output, a fringe of inefficiently small plants and firms seems to persist. It persists, moreover, in a degree that is not systematically related to top-level seller concentration. Further, the incidence of this sort of inefficiency does not seem to be systematically related to the importance of scale economies as measured by the percentage of the market supplied by one plant or firm of minimum optimal scale.

This, however, means only that the relative size of the inefficient fringe of small plants and firms seems unrelated to top-level seller concentration within the industry, as measured, for example, by the proportion of industry output supplied by the largest four or eight firms in the industry. It is obvious that whenever there is a fringe of inefficiently small firms, the "overall" degree of seller concentration in the industry—

as measured by the total number and size distribution of all firms—is by definition too low for optimal efficiency. Consolidation of the operations of the several or many smallest firms into fewer plants and firms—which would increase overall concentration—would permit their output to be produced more efficiently.

Second, there is no evident association of the height of the barrier to entry to an industry to the incidence of inefficiency due to uneconomically small scales. The occurrence and the size of an inefficient fringe of small plants and firms seems as likely to occur with difficult entry conditions to the industry as with easy ones.

It would thus be impossible to affirm, on the basis of such evidence as is available, that seeking either higher or lower seller concentration or more difficult or easier entry for our industries would have a significant effect on the aspect of efficiency in question.

Given these negative findings, one further *ad hoc* hypothesis concerning the relationship of market structure to efficiency in scales of plants and firms remains to be tested. The hypothesis is briefly that strong product differentiation within an industry leads to the existence and survival of a comparatively larger fringe of inefficiently small plants and firms, whereas slight (or no) product differentiation is conducive to a comparatively smaller fringe. The argument underlying it is that a pattern of strongly developed consumer preferences for various company names, brands, or product designs is more likely to afford a number of inefficiently small firms limited markets at favorable prices than is a pattern in which consumer preferences among competing products are weak.

A study of our sample of twenty industries lends some support to this hypothesis. Within the sample, the industries with the largest fringes of inefficiently small firms are usually those with high degrees of product differentiation among established sellers. On the other hand, some fringe of inefficiently small plants and firms finds a means of surviving in all of the industries sampled, including those with relatively slight and negligible product differentiation.

These findings suggest that a part of the continued survival of inefficiently small sellers is attributable to product differentiation. This survival results from the fact that they supply odd "corners" of the market—usually by providing special products or designs that are demanded by limited groups of buyers, or by supplying regions that are geographically remote from the main producing centers. If this is the case, their "inefficiency" may be more apparent than real.

It would appear, however, that another and perhaps larger part of the survival of inefficiently small firms probably is attributable to two other things:

1. The ability of inefficiently small firms in some industries to make normal profits in competition with larger rivals that establish high prices so as to earn considerable excess profits.

2. The almost endless supply of small firms that are willing to succeed each other in entering some other industries, incurring net losses, and ultimately going broke (only to have their ranks filled by new candidates for financial destruction).

Thus the monopolistic pricing policies of large firms, and excessive or unwise entry by small firms, both help to account for the persistence of fringes of inefficiently small firms in many industries. This observation indirectly suggests that there should be some observable association of the size of the inefficient fringe with seller concentration and the condition of entry, but none is apparent in the sample of industries studied.

The remaining question concerns whether and how the incidence of chronic excess capacity in relation to demand is related to market structure. The principal theoretical hypothesis bearing on this issue is that such excess capacity is most likely to occur in industries with perceptible but relatively low barriers to entry, provided that established sellers develop enough concentration to make oligopolistic price-raising feasible. In this setting, they might find it unattractive to set prices low enough to forestall new entry, and attractive instead to raise prices enough ultimately to induce excessive entry and excess capacity.

As indicated in Chapter 10, systematic evidence on the incidence of chronic excess capacity is very scanty. It may be worth noting, however, that in all three of the twenty manufacturing industries sampled in which there was reasonably clear evidence of chronic excess capacity (flour, shoes, and cement) the structural conditions were roughly those described in the hypothesis just noted.

In brief summary, the tests that have been made fail to reveal any noticeable relation of efficiency in scale to seller concentration or to the condition of entry, or of efficiency in the use of capacity to seller concentration or to product differentiation. The findings suggest some relationship of the degree of product differentiation to efficiency in scale, and of the condition of entry to the incidence of chronic excess capacity. But in neither case has a statistically significant relationship been established. The main impact of market structure is probably on dimensions of market performance other than technical efficiency.

Relationship of Market Structure to Price-Cost Margins and Profit Rates

Another major issue concerns the structural determinants of the allocative efficiency of industries. Since, as we have seen in Chapter 10, the performance of an industry in the dimension of allocative efficiency is roughly measured by the relationship of its selling price to its long-run average costs of production,[1] the question may be reduced to the following form: What is the association of the market structure of industries to the long-run differences between their prices and average costs? And, to the extent that the long-run profit rates on equity earned by industries are indicative of the sizes of these price-cost differences, it may be further reduced to ask: What is the relationship of the market structures of industries to the size of their profit rates?

However stated, these questions reflect our interest in the relation of market structure to the incidence and the size of monopolistic excess profits. We should like to know what structural situations are conducive, or more conducive than others, to the allocative inefficiency (and to connected distortions in income distribution) that are reflected by the earning of such excess profits.

Price theory, moreover, has provided us with some reasonably definite hypotheses concerning this relationship of market structure to performance. Specifically, it predicts that the size of long-run price-cost margins and profit rates will be determined or strongly influenced by the structure of industries in two dimensions: (1) the degree of seller concentration within the industry; and (2) the condition of entry to the industry. Theoretical hypotheses concerning these two relationships of market structure to performance have been developed above in the earlier parts of Chapter 5 and 8. A part of our interest in determining the actual relationship of market structure to profit rates thus stems from a desire to subject these hypotheses to an empirical test—to see if the ascertainable facts confirm or disconfirm them.

In the following pages, we will deal in turn with the relationships of seller concentration to profit rates and of the condition of entry to profit rates. With respect to each relationship, we will first briefly reexamine the hypotheses that are to be tested, and then present and interpret the results of empirical experiments that have been conducted to test them. Finally, since seller concentration and the condition of entry presumably operate as co-determinants of profit rates, we will consider their interaction in influencing profit rates, and the extent to which they exercise independent or separate influences.

Relationship of Seller Concentration to Profit Rates

The theoretical argument presented in Chapter 5 suggested that there should be some long-run tendency for high seller concentration within

[1] Generally about equal to its long-run marginal costs.

industries to be associated with relatively high profits (monopolistic excess profits) and for lower concentration to be associated with lower profits, these differences in profits reflecting differences in the excess of price over average costs, and corresponding differences in the degree of monopolistic output restriction. In a more specific form, this hypothesis should read about as follows:

High seller concentration within industries should be associated with substantial excesses of selling price over long-run average (and marginal) costs, moderately high or moderate seller concentration with appreciable but lesser excesses of price over cost, and lower seller concentration with no excesses at all—all this subject to two provisos. The first proviso is that the price-elasticity of demand for industry output should be about the same for industries with different degrees of seller concentration, or at any rate should not turn out to be progressively smaller (less elastic) as the degree of seller concentration within industries is smaller. (Otherwise, the height of a monopolistic price relative to average cost would be lower in highly concentrated industries than in less concentrated ones—because of a more price-elastic market demand—and the virtual influence of seller concentration on price-cost margins might be counterbalanced by the influence of elasticities of demand for industry outputs.) The second proviso is that the barriers to entry to industries should not turn out to be lower for highly concentrated than for less concentrated industries. (Otherwise, the influence of the condition of entry on price-cost margins might counterbalance the virtual influence of seller concentration.)

Both provisos are especially important so far as the hypothesis refers to differences in price-cost margins between highly and moderately concentrated industries. We should note in passing that both seem ordinarily to be fulfilled "on the average" for industries with various degrees of seller concentration, but are not necessarily fulfilled for every individual industry. Therefore, the hypothesis as stated should hold "statistically" for groups of industries with different levels of seller concentration, but not necessarily for every individual industry.

If one further proviso is fulfilled, the hypothesis in question can be converted into the following form: High seller concentration within industries should be associated with long-run average accounting profit rates on equity that substantially exceed normal interest returns, moderately high or moderate seller concentration with profit rates that are appreciably lower but still include an element of excess profit, and lower seller concentration with profit rates that are about equal to normal interest returns on equities. The crucial added proviso here is that the ratio of owners' investment or equity, V, to annual sales revenue, R

(i.e., V/R) should not turn out to be appreciably and progressively greater as the degree of concentration within industries is higher—that is, larger with high seller concentration and successively smaller with successively lower seller concentration. For if it were, the difference in accounting profit rates among industries with different degrees of seller concentration would not reflect fully (and might not reflect at all) the corresponding differences in the relationship of price to average cost— these differences being reflected directly only in the rate of excess profits on sales revenue. (The reader may wish to refer back to the development of this point on pp. 391 to 393 of Chapter 10.)

This last proviso is evidently somewhat less than completely fulfilled in fact. There is an observable tendency, on the average, for the ratio of V to R to be greater (for "the rate of capital turnover" to be smaller) in industries of higher concentration. So far as this is true, the variation in profits rates on equity associated with variation in industry seller concentration will not fully reflect (may at least partly conceal) the corresponding and analytically much more significant variation in the ratio of price to average cost (the rate of excess profits on sales). It follows that the basic hypothesis, concerning the relationship of seller concentration to price-cost margins, is not tested in a fully satisfactory way—and is perhaps not conclusively tested—by determining the actual relationship of seller concentration to profit rates on equity. Corresponding allowances should be made in interpreting the results of tests for the association of concentration to profit rates.

Five other things should also be noted about the character of the hypothesis to be tested, before we consider actual tests. These are:

1. *The hypothesis does not specify the quantitative degrees of seller concentration that correspond to "high," "moderate," and "lower" seller concentration.* For example, it does not identify high seller concentration as involving supply by the largest four firms of 50 per cent or more, 60 per cent or more, or 80 per cent or more of industry output. What high and moderate and lesser concentration correspond to quantitatively therefore remains to be discovered statistically in any empirical test of the hypothesis, at the same time that the validity of the hypothesis itself is being tested. If a test confirms the hypothesis at all, it should also implement it by converting its qualitative predictions into quantitative ones. A test may thus provide indications, for example, of how high seller concentration can become before severe monopolistic excess profits tend to be encountered. The fact that the hypothesis does not describe quantitatively various "types" of concen-

tration becomes especially important in view of another of its characteristics, namely:

2. *The hypothesis does not predict a necessarily "continuous" relationship of the quantitative degree of seller concentration either to the long-run ratio of price to average cost or to the long-run profit rate.* That is, it does not predict that there should necessarily be a tendency toward a gradual and continuous decline of profit rates in response to a gradual and continuous decline in the degree of seller concentration. It does not rule out such a continuous relationship, but it certainly does not specify that one should be found.

The hypothesis clearly comprehends as one of its equally valid alternative predictions the following sort of relationship of concentration to profit rates: In a certain top "zone" of seller concentration (in all industries having seller concentration as great or greater than a certain minimal degree), profit rates should be high and about equally high; in a lower concentration zone or band (limited by some maximum and some minimum degree of concentration), industries should have profits rates significantly lower but not greatly different from each other; and so forth. That is, one of its alternative predictions is that profit rates may differ significantly among two or three "concentration classes" of industries, without varying continuously in response to varying concentration within the classes. This possibility is clearly suggested by the logic of oligopolistic pricing (discussed in Chapter 5) which indicates that above and below certain critical levels of seller concentration, cooperative or joint-profit-maximizing and antagonistic or independent-profit-maximizing motives may be respectively dominant.

This being the case, tests of the hypothesis that seek only to determine the existence and the strength of a *continuous* statistical relationship between seller concentration and profit rates are not necessarily conclusive. (Such tests determine the coefficient of correlation between concentration and profit rates, the slope of a regression line that measures the average variation of profit rates in response to variation in concentration, and the closeness "fit" of actual profit-rate observations to the regression line.) If tests of this sort find a negligible continous relationship, they have failed to confirm the existence of one, but they have not disconfirmed the hypothesis that there are significant differences between the average profit rates of industries in different concentration classes. A different sort of statistical test, not involving standard correlation and regression techiques, is required to determine whether or not a significant discontinuous relationship of seller concentration to profit rates exists. Nonetheless, a number of empirical experiments have tested only for the existence and strength of a continuous relationship. Their findings should be interpreted accordingly, as potentially inconclusive tests of the central hypothesis, and also as tests that may fail to reveal the actual strength of association between concentration and profit rates.

3. So far as the hypothesis may offer as one of its alternative predictions the existence of a continuous relationship between concentration and profit rates, *it certainly does not predict that this relationship should assume an arithmetically rectilinear (straight line) form.* A continuous relationship, if it does exist, could equally well be described by a logarithmic linear or any of a number of other arithmetically curvilinear regression lines. Testing only for the existence of an arithmetically rectilinear relationship of concentration to profits may fail to reveal the existence or strength of a more complex continuous relationship, and failure to find a significant rectilinear relationship does not necessarily disconfirm the hypothesis. Yet the bulk of published studies to date that bear on this matter are confined to testing only for an arithmetically rectilinear relationship and a corresponding coefficient of correlation. (Testing for this relationship is by far the simplest statistically, and requires the least statistical knowledge.) The results of such studies should be interpreted accordingly—with caution and with reservations.

4. *The hypothesis refers only to long-run tendencies in the relationship of seller concentration to profit rates,* such as might be revealed by the statistical relationship of the concentration of industries to their average annual profit rates for at least a decade, and preferably longer. Even in the long run, moreover, the condition of entry should be expected to exercise a simultaneous influence, and partly to obscure the net relationship of concentration to profit rates, so far as it is examined in isolation. (This difficulty is remediable by analyzing together the multiple and partial relationships of the two structural variables to profit rates.)

Over shorter periods, the average annual profit rates of industries (at a foolish extreme, individual annual rates) are clearly influenced by many things other than seller concentration and the condition of entry. Short-run profits systematically tend to reflect positive and negative windfalls, rewards to innovation, and so forth. Therefore, even if the hypothesis that seller concentration (or the condition of entry) strongly influences long-run profit rates should be entirely true, for any short period of years seller concentration should be expected to "explain" statistically only a minor part of the variation of profit rates among industries. Wide dispersions of actual profit rates around those associated with any long-run relation to seller concentration are automatically to be expected, and have little to do with the validity of the hypothesis. In testing the hypothesis with profit data referring only to a short term, the numerous other influences on profit rates should be regarded as "random" independent variables, and the statistical findings interpreted accordingly. The finding in experiments referring to a few years of low statistical correlations of concentration and profits, or other associations of marginal statistical significance, should thus not be viewed as disconfirming the central hypothesis (even though they fail to confirm it)— but they have on occasion been interpreted in this way. In fact, a test made for a short period of years that finds any statistically significant relationship of seller concentration to profit rates probably should be viewed as supporting the hypothesis more strongly than the bare figures indicate. What such tests may more reliably determine, of course, is the extent of the influence of seller concentration on short-term profit behavior.

5. *The hypothesis refers strictly to the relationship of seller concentration to profit rates for theoretical industries*—that is, for industries delineated so as to include all sellers of a group of close-substitute products supplying a common group of buyers, and exclude all others. Only when both the actual concentration ratios and the actual profit rates used in an empirical experiment correspond to or closely approximate those for theoretical industries is the hypothesis being subjected to a valid and meaningful test. This condition is clearly not fulfilled when the concentration ratios and profit rates used are calculated for an "unfiltered" sample of Census manufacturing industries, or for all such industries as a group.

As noted early in Chapter 5, Census industries typically do not correspond to theoretical industries, and the concentration ratios calculated for a majority of them do not approximate the individual concentration ratios of the theoretical industries they contain, or even an average of those ratios. Therefore, seller concentration measures for Census industries are more frequently than not variously and unpredictably different from the concentration measures that would be relevant for testing the hypothesis in question. They do usually register a downward bias, as compared to concentration measures for component theoretical industries. But the amount of this bias is so variable among Census industries that there is little reason to expect that they would— for all Census industries or for a random sample—display any association with connected long-run profit rates, even if a strong association existed between concentration and profit rates for theoretical industries. Roughly the same is true of a sample of Census industries which has been winnowed only by eliminating those whose markets are geographically segmented. It will still contain a large proportion of industries for which calculated concentration ratios are analytically meaningless, because each includes firms producing several nonsubstitute products and because the firms specialize by products.

It follows that all tests of the central hypothesis that use concentration ratios and profit rates for an unscreened sample of Census industries, or for one screened only by eliminating geographically segmented industries, are substantially irrelevant or meaningless. The finding for such a sample of a statistically meaningful association of concentration to profit rates should come as a statistical surprise. The finding of no association has substantially no bearing on the validity of the hypothesis. Nevertheless, a number of tests using such samples of Census industries have been conducted, and their results seriously reported as having some relationship to the hypothesis. They do not.

If Census industries and concentration ratios are to be used meaningfully in testing the hypothesis, a prerequisite is that all Census industries be screened and winnowed (in the light of extensive further information on individual industries) until in the sample finally chosen each remaining Census industry concentration ratio either (*a*) is a ratio for a theoretical industry, or close approximation thereto, or (*b*) approximates the concentration ratios for all theoretical industries that it contains. (The use of an actual screening process in a research experiment is referred to below.) If then the concentration ratios for such a sample are associated with profit rates that are similarly meaningful, the central hypothesis can be tested, subject to the cautions set forth above.

Almost needless to say, some or all of the various errors in sample selection, statistical procedure, and interpretation of findings that have been discussed above frequently are found in combination in a single statistical study. There is also one other questionable procedure that has been frequently combined with one or more of the preceding ones. This involves abandoning the attempt to associate the concentration ratios of individual Census industries (however reliable they might be) with corresponding profit rates, and instead associating the *average* industry concentration ratios for each of a number of groups of Census industries with corresponding average profit rates. In this procedure, each concentration ratio used is typically a weighted average of the concentration ratio of the several Census industries contained in an industry group, and each profit rate a weighted average profit rate for all

Census industries in the group. Thus, in an industry group *A*, we might have Census industries *w*, *x*, *y*, and *z*—with Census concentration ratios (expressing percentages of industry output supplied by the four largest firms), of 80, 60, 50, and 30, and profit rates on equity of 20, 15, 10, and 5. Assuming that the Census industries are equally weighted, all that enters into the statistical test would be the fact that an average concentration ratio of 55 was associated with an average profit rate of 12.5 per cent. And so it would go with each industry group in turn.

The reasons for adopting this peculiar procedure are obvious once the limitations on available data are known. The most comprehensive source of profit-rate data for manufacturing industries, the U. S. Treasury Department, makes available profit data (from corporate income tax returns) for only 100-odd industry groupings, which contain on the average about four Census industries apiece. In order to use these easily available profit data, various economists have tried to "match" them with corresponding concentration ratios, and the matching ratios have turned out to be averages of concentration ratios for the component Census industries in the various industry groups.

This expedient and superficially innocuous procedure, however, is in great danger of depriving the subsequent test for association of concentration to profit rates of any meaning. The averaging procedure as applied to concentration ratios and to profit rates tends to suppress or conceal the variance in both, and also (except in the unusual case of an arithmetically linear relationship and a very high degree of correlation between concentration and profit rates) to conceal or at least minimize any existing association between industry concentration and industry profit rates. It is therefore more surprising statistically that some studies employing this procedure have come up with any association of concentration to profit rates than that others have come up with none. None of them has much chance of discovering a statistically significant association of concentration to profit rates if it is there. The chance is reduced to nothing if the Census industries whose concentration ratios are averaged, group by group, have not been screened properly to eliminate meaningless ratios.

On the preceding background, we may report the findings of several empirical tests for the relationship of the seller concentration of industries to their profit rates.

The writer made one such test for a sample of 42 manufacturing industries, attempting to ascertain the relationship of seller concentration in 1935 to average annual industry profit rates on equity for the period 1936–40. The 42 industries were selected after a careful screening of all Census industries for which adequate profit data were available. They

included all of those that remained after eliminating all Census industries for which the Census concentration ratios failed to measure the
degree of seller concentration within theoretical industries.

That is, the remaining sample included all Census industries (for
which profit data were available) for which the Census concentration
ratio either measured seller concentration in a single theoretical industry—as it did infrequently—or was approximately the same as that of
each component theoretical industry that the Census industry contained.
Great pains were thus taken to secure a sample of industries for which
the Census concentration ratios approximated the measures of seller
concentration referred to in the central hypothesis—that is, seller concentration for theoretical industries.

For this sample, tests for the association of seller concentration to the
five-year average annual profit rate on equity did not reveal a strong
"continuous" relationship of either a rectilinear or curvilinear form (the
simple coefficient of correlation was only 0.28), though a positive association of concentration and profit rates was indicated. However,
dividing the industries into two concentration classes resulted in finding
a stronger relationship. There appeared to be a critical degree of seller
concentration above which industry profit rates on the average were
significantly higher and below which they were significantly lower. The
dividing line between the two concentration classes of industries fell at
about 70 per cent control of the market by the largest eight sellers in
the industry. In 21 industries in which the eight largest sellers supplied
more than 70 per cent of industry output, the average annual profit rate
on equity was 11.8; for 21 industries in which the eight largest sellers
supplied less than 70 per cent of industry output, the average annual
profit rate was 7.8. There was, as expected, a substantial dispersion of
individual-industry profit rates in each of the two concentration classes,
but standard statistical tests indicated that the difference in average
profit rates was statistically significant. (That is, it was attributable to the
difference in seller concentration between the two classes, and had almost no chance of being due to a sampling or other statistical accident.)

One related finding was that although average profit rates were significantly higher in the high-concentration than in the lower-concentration category, there was within either category no significant
variation of profit rates in response to variation in seller concentration.
In the high-concentration group, the percentage of the market supplied
by the eight largest firms ranged from 71 up to 100 per cent; in the
lower-concentration group, it ranged from 68 down to 8 per cent. But
within either group, the profit rate was not significantly related to concentration.

Another finding of some interest was that the significant difference between the average profit rates for the two groups was caused almost entirely by differences among the profit rates of the larger firms in the various industries. The profits of the smaller firms did not seem to be much associated with the degrees of seller concentration in the industries of which they were members. This finding is not surprising in view of the prevalence of intra-industry advantages of large over small firms resulting from product differentiation, absolute-cost advantages, and more efficient scales.

It should be noted that the sample of industries which "fell out" of the screening process described happened not to be fully representative, with regard to seller concentration of manufacturing industries as a whole. In 38 of the 42 industries, 30 per cent or more of industry output was supplied by the eight largest firms. Thus the proportion of industries in the sample which were in some degree oligopolistic was substantially greater than the comparable proportion for all American manufacturing industries. The tendency of comparative profit rates for industries of low and very low seller concentration was therefore not adequately tested.[2]

The test just referred to involved an extensive and full-fledged statistical experiment. A much more casual and less extensive test was made for 20 of the 42 industries used in the first test. It related seller concentration to average annual profit rates in the period 1947–51, but used as measures of industry profit rates only those of the largest 2, 3, or 4 firms in each industry. The indications were that the same general relationship of concentration to profit rates continued to hold after World War II as held before it. That is, above a critical concentration level in the neighborhood of 70 per cent control of the industry by eight firms, industry profit rates were on the average significantly higher than they were below this level of seller concentration.[3]

A recently published study has reported on a comparably casual test for the relationship of seller concentration to average annual profit rates for the period 1950–60. The test was based on a sample of 30 industries, including 17 of the 20 used in the test referring to 1947–51 just mentioned, and 13 additional industries. Again, the industry average profit rates on equity used were only those of the few largest firms in each industry. The results confirmed previous findings. For the period 1950–60, 21 industries in which the largest 8 sellers supplied 70 per cent or

---

[2]This study referred to is J. S. Bain, "Relation of Profit Rate to Industry Concentration: American Manufacturing, 1936–40," *Quarterly Journal of Economics*, LXV, 3 (August, 1951), pp. 293–324.

[3]See J. S. Bain, *Barriers to New Competition*, 1956, pp. 195–197.

more of industry output had significantly higher annual average profit rates than did 9 industries in which seller concentration was lower.[4]

The results of these tests should be viewed as tentative, since the samples of industries covered were not large and the latter two tests used profit data for only a few largest firms per industry. Subject to this reservation, two principal indications of the tests may be emphasized:

1. A significant association between the profit rates and degrees of seller concentration of industries, with substantial excess profits being earned mainly in highly concentrated industries, strongly suggests that observed high excess profits are monopolistic excess profits, rather than windfalls or rewards to innovation. This characterization of their origin is at any rate the most obvious explanation of their association with high seller concentration.

2. The finding that two concentration classes of industries, with seller concentration respectively above and below some critical level, earned significantly different average profit rates, but that industry profit rates within the classes were not noticeably associated with seller concentration, suggests the following. There may in fact be two sorts of oligopolies: (a) those sufficiently concentrated that joint profit-maximizing price policies usually are successful and produce substantial excess profits; and (b) those sufficiently unconcentrated that independent or antagonistic motives outweigh or seriously undermine joint profit-maximizing motives, lead to more or less competitive price policies, and result in profits not greatly in excess of a competitive level. (In terms of the concentration classification set forth in Chapter 5, industries with "very high" and "high" seller concentration appear to have undesirable monopolistic tendencies; those of "low-moderate" and lesser concentration seem to be relatively free of these tendencies; and those of "high-moderate" concentration are somewhere on the borderline.)

Other published studies of the relationship of seller concentration to profit rates have in general not employed seller concentration measures and profit rates for individual Census industries in their tests, but rather averages of industry concentration ratios for small or large groups of industries (or an equivalent) and corresponding averages of profit rates. This is unfortunate, as noted on pp. 444 and 445, because the statistical procedure tends to conceal the variance in concentration ratios and profit rates and may very well also conceal all or part of any actual as-

---

[4]The average of industry average profit rates for the high-concentration group was 13.3, and for the lower-concentration group 9.0. See H. Michael Mann, "Seller Concentration, Barriers to Entry, and Rates of Return in Thirty Industries, 1950–1960", *op. cit.*

sociation between concentration and profit rates for individual industries.

Levinson[5] made a test involving a very high degree of aggregation, calculating concentration and profit measures only for 19 major groups of manufacturing industries, these groups containing on the average over 20 Census industries apiece. The usual concentration measure used for each of the 19 industry groups was the percentage of the total value of shipments for Census industries in the group which was made by Census industries in which the eight largest firms supplied 50 per cent or more of industry output—calculated for 1954. The profit measure for each group was the average annual profit rate on equity (after income tax) for all industries in the group, calculated individually for the eleven years from 1947 to 1957. The test then consisted simply of calculating the simple coefficients of correlation between 1954 concentration and annual average profit rates for each of the eleven years; thus, it tested for the existence and strength of continuous arithmetic linear relation between concentration and profit rates. Since in addition to using broad average measures of concentration and profit rates, Levinson engaged in no screening or winnowing of the Census-industry concentration ratios that entered into his averages, one would not expect the test to discover any relationship between concentration and profit rates that might be there. It was surprising, therefore, that he found a modest but statistically significant positive correlation between 1954 group concentration ratios and the group profit rates of ten individual years (all except 1947)—the annual coefficients of correlation ranging from 0.34 to 0.76. Although these findings seem to lend confirmation to the central hypothesis, how much relevance to it they really have is not clear.

Weiss[6] also employed average concentration measures for the same 19 major groups of manufacturing industries in 1954, and average annual group profit rates on equity (after income tax) for the ten-year period from 1949 to 1958. His concentration measure for each major

[5]Harold M. Levinson, *Postwar Movement of Prices and Wages in Manufacturing Industries,* Study Paper No. 21, prepared for the Joint Economic Committee, U.S. Congress, 1960.

[6]Leonard W. Weiss, "Average Concentration Ratios and Industrial Performance," *Journal of Industrial Economics,* **XI**, 3 (July, 1963), pp. 237–254. When Weiss found an "overaggregation" of products in a Census industry, he used an average of the concentration ratios of the individual products contained in the industry. When he found an "overaggregation" of geographically separate markets in a Census industry, he made uniform upward adjustments in the Census industry ratio, based on overall average relations of regional or local concentrations to national concentrations. When he found "underaggregation" of products in a Census industry, he made an *ad hoc* adjustment in the Census concentration ratio.

group of industries, however, was a weighted average of the concentration ratios for selected Census industries (actually equivalent Census product groups) in the group, the ratios having been adjusted for bias due to "over and under aggregation." Although these adjustments were made, only a small proportion of Census industries were winnowed out before calculating group-average concentration ratios.

He then tested for the existence of a continuous linear relationship between group-average concentration ratios and group-average profit rates. Somewhat less surprisingly, in view of his adjustments of average concentration ratios, he found a strong linear relationship (with profit rates rising continuously with increasing concentration), and a statistically significant positive correlation coefficient of 0.73. The results may appear to lend strong confirmation to the central hypothesis. Considering the aggregative statistical procedures employed, they indeed lend more support than might reasonably be expected by one who supposes that the central hypothesis is correct, and suggest that the aggregation process itself might produce somewhat capricious results.[7]

Stigler[8] undertook a more extensive experiment aimed at ascertaining the relationship of seller concentration to rates of return on investment. This also involved the use of group-average concentration ratios and earnings rates, but for more numerous and individually smaller groups of industries. He used 119 such groups in all, containing on the average about four Census industries apiece. For each group, he calculated (for each of three years—1935, 1947 and 1954) a concentration ratio which was the weighted average of the concentration ratios of the Census industries contained in the group. In so doing, he apparently did not "screen" or eliminate any Census industries, accepting all of them and their concentration ratios at face value. For each industry group, two averages of average concentration ratios were then calculated, the first an average of the average concentration ratios for 1935 and 1947, and the second an average of the average concentration ratios for 1947 and 1954. The 1935–47 group average ratios were related to earnings rates from 1938 to 1947, and the 1947–54 group averages ratios to earnings rates from 1947 to 1956.

His next step was to identify industry groups as having either

[7]This suspicion is given some support by Sherman's finding of a correlation coefficient of 0.66 between group-average concentration ratios and profit rates for 20 major groups of manufacturing industries for the year 1954 alone, even though no winnowing of component Census industries had been undertaken. See Howard J. Sherman, *Introduction to the Economics of Growth, Unemployment, and Inflation*, 1964, Ch. 8.

[8]George J. Stigler, *Capital and Rates of Return in Manufacturing Industries*, 1963, pp. 66–71 and Appendix C.

"national" markets (all sellers potential suppliers of all buyers in the country), or regionally segmented markets. Given this identification, he proceeded arbitrarily: (*a*) to designate as "concentrated industries" all those industry groups with national markets and with average 4-firm concentration ratios (referring to the average percentage of industry output supplied by the four largest firms) greater than 60; (*b*) to designate as "unconcentrated industries" all those groups with national markets and with average 4-firm concentration ratios less than 50, plus all those groups with regionally segmented markets and average 4-firm concentration ratios less than 20; and (*c*) to designate as "ambiguous" (unclassified) all other industry groups. This classification was made separately for 1935-47 and for 1947-54. The choice of these arbitrary rules for classification was not really defended, nor is it readily rationalized.

Given this three-fold classification of industry groups—concentrated, unconcentrated, and ambiguous—Stigler proceeded to calculate a rate of return on investment for each group, and an average of group rates for each of the three concentration categories. These were expressed as annual average rates for intervals of three or four years extending from 1938 to 1957. The rates of return used, however, were not ratios of profits to owners' equity, but ratios of profits plus interest payments to total assets (that is, to equity plus total liabilities to crediors). This measure of earning power is at least as capricious as the more familiar rate of profit on equity.

A test was then made to determine if, in general or at any time during the period studied, the average annual rates of return on investment in "concentrated" and "unconcentrated" industries were significantly different. The general finding was that they were not different by statistically significant amounts, and further that there was no significant linear correlation between industry-group concentration and rates of return on investment.

In this case, at least, the negative findings were in accord with expectations based on a review of the statistical and other procedures employed in the experiment. That is, since Stigler accepted all Census industries and their concentrations ratios uncritically, then concealed much of their variance (and that of corresponding earnings rates) in computing group averages, and thereafter applied a set of rules invented for the occasion for classifying industries as concentrated or unconcentrated, one would scarcely expect that any existing association between concentration in individual theoretical industries and any plausible measures of their rates of return on investment would be revealed by his experiment. His findings neither confirm nor disconfirm the central hypotheses. They simply have substantially no relevance to it.

A general conclusion based on studies published to date is that there are numerous straws in the wind which suggest that, among individual industries, a significant positive relationship of seller concentration to profit rates on equity indeed exists. More experimental work, however, will be required to confirm or disconfirm the central hypothesis in question. This work, moreover, should if possible avoid the pitfalls of aggregation and of unquestioning acceptance of Census concentration ratios into which a number of earlier experiments have fallen. The writer has seen several as yet unpublished studies of the relationship of market structure to profit rates that employ more satisfactory and more advanced or sophisticated statistical and other procedures than any of those reviewed above, but refrains from reporting in detail here findings that may be subject to revision prior to publication.[9] It may be indicated, however, that some added evidence seems to be forthcoming which supports the hypothesis that there is a significant relationship of seller concentration to profit rates.

Relationship of the Condition of Entry to Profit Rates

In Chapter 8 we developed a theoretical argument concerning the long-run relationship of the condition of entry to an industry to its price-cost margin and profit rate. One essential concept employed in this argument was the maximum entry-forestalling price—the highest selling price that established firms in an industry could charge in the long run without attracting new firms to enter the industry. Related to this concept was a classification of industries according to the condition of entry, distinguishing: (1) blockaded entry, wherein the maximum entry-forestalling price exceeds the price that would maximize industry profits; (2) effectively impeded entry, wherein the maximum entry-forestalling price is below the industry-profit-maximizing price but high enough that established firms can maximize their own joint profits by charging an entry-forestalling price in the long run and excluding entry; and (3) ineffectively impeded entry, wherein the maximum entry-forestalling price is low enough that established firms can maximize their own joint profits by charging a higher price in the short run and inducing entry—with a possible variety of consequences for ensuing long-run pricing. Barring some unusual and perverse strong relationship of the price elasticity of the demands for industry outputs to the condition of entry, maximum entry forestalling prices should be

[9]Prominent among these are studies by Frank J. Kottke of Washington State University, Boyd Fjeldsted of the University of Utah, and William S. Comanor and Thomas A. Wilson of Harvard University.

highest relative to minimal average costs with blockaded entry, lower with effectively impeded entry, and lowest with ineffectively impeded entry. Within each of the three categories, however, a limited range of different relationships of the maximum entry-forestalling price to minimal average cost should be found.

Employing the terminology just reviewed, the central hypothesis concerning the association of the condition of entry with the relationship of price to long-run average cost can be summarized as follows: Among oligopolistic industries with seller concentration high enough to create a strong recognized interdependence among sellers,[10] the excess of price over long-run average cost should be greatest with blockaded entry, less with effectively impeded entry, and (on the average) least with ineffectively impeded entry. Moreover, among such industries with effectively impeded entry, the excess of price over average cost should be lower as the barrier to entry (the excess of the maximum entry-forestalling price over minimal average cost) is lower.

The hypotheses should hold generally on the supportable assumption that the actual long-run average costs of at least the principal firms in oligopolistic industries are at or close to the minimum attainable level. Moreover, if we can assume that the ratio V/R (of owners' equity to sales revenue) does not tend to be progressively higher as barriers to entry are higher, the hypothesis may be reformulated to predict that the condition of entry should have the same sort of relationship to profit rates on equity as to price-average cost margins.

As a prelude to testing the hypothesis, and also as a guide to designing a test, several of its properties should be noted, as follows:

1. *Like the hypothesis concerning the relation of seller concentration to profits, it refers only to a long-run relationship—of the condition of entry to long-run average profit rates.* In short periods, numerous other determinants of profits may be expected to counterbalance or obscure its influence on profit rates.

2. *The hypothesis does not specify a quantitative relationship of the condition of entry to profit rates.* The ratios of the maximum entry forestalling price to minimal long-run average cost that are respectively sufficient to establish the lower limit of blockaded entry, the upper and lower limits of effectively impeded entry, and the upper limit of ineffectively impeded entry, are not quantitatively specified.

In addition, the underlying theory suggests that whether entry is effectively impeded or ineffectively impeded depends not only on the re-

[10]That is, among oligopolistic industries in which intra-industry competition is not likely to result in a price well below the joint profit-maximizing level.

lation of the maximum entry forestalling price to minimal average costs, but also on the length of the lag periods required for entrant firms to become established. And whether entry is blockaded or effectively impeded depends also on the height of the industry profit-maximizing price relative to average cost. This makes direct testing of the hypothesis difficult if we lack information on entry lags and on levels of full monopoly price (as we do) unless we simplify it by disregarding these other things.

Because of these difficulties—which could be resolved only with information we do not have—we actually can test the hypothesis only in a derived and simplified form. In its simplest form, it would state that, for sufficiently concentrated oligopolistic industries, the height of the barrier to entry (measured by the ratio of the maximum entry forestalling price to minimal average costs) should be positively associated with the profit rate—the higher the barrier to entry, the higher should be the profit rate. If this simplified hypothesis is tested, moreover, we can attempt to implement it in quantitative terms.

3. *The relationship between the height of the barrier to entry and the profit rate that is suggested by the basic hypothesis is at least somewhat discontinuous.* Within the range of effectively impeded entry, a continuous positive relationship between the height of the barrier to entry and the profit rate is predicted. But it is also predicted that successive elevation of the barrier to entry above the minimal level required for blockaded entry should not influence the profit rate, nor should its successive lowering beneath the maximum level associated with ineffectively impeded entry.

This reveals that the most simplified form of the hypothesis, described above, is indeed oversimplified, because it predicts a continuous relationship of the barrier to entry and the profit rate for all heights of the barrier to entry. We should therefore not expect this simplified relationship to hold more than roughly in fact.

Indeed we should (if the sample of industries were large enough) wish to test instead for a complex relationship of the condition of entry to profit rates. This relationship should be such that long-run profit rates were high but not much different among industries with barriers to entry that are all very high but of differing heights, low but not very much different among industries with barriers to entry that are all relatively low but of differing heights, and intermediate but varying with the height of the barrier to entry among industries with high, substantial, or moderate barriers to entry. Lacking such a large sample, the simplest sort of test for a continuous or semi-continuous relationship may be all that is feasible. If such a simple relationship of the predicted sort is found to hold roughly in fact, the finding lends some support to the basic hypothesis.

4. *Testing of the hypothesis calls for the "creation" of data on the condition of entry, one industry at a time for many industries, through painstaking research and analysis.* This is necessary because no governmental or other agency compiles or publishes data on conditions of entry to industries. Extensive valid experiments to test the hypothesis concerning the relationship of the condition of entry to profit rates are thus unlikely to be undertaken very frequently. It should be noted in this connection that the problem posed by the huge amount of basic research work involved in such experiments is not solved by casually observing a number of industries and assigning *ad hoc* ratings to their conditions of entry. The results of tests employing "data" thus obtained are of highly questionable validity.

On this background, let us consider the results to date of empirical testing of the hypothesis. The first published results were the product of an experiment that involved a sample of 20 industries (23 industries or segments of industries) referred to in preceding chapters.[11] As indicated in Chapter 8 (pp. 278 to 280), the height of the barrier to entry in 1952 was estimated for each of these 23 industries. An estimate was made in each case, that is, of the percentage by which established firms could in the long run elevate selling price above minimal average costs without attracting new entry. Then, because the individual estimates were evidently too imprecise for their individual numerical values to be employed in testing, the industries were grouped in three entry-barrier classes. This classification distinguished industries with entry barriers designated as (*a*) "very high," (*b*) "substantial," and (*c*) "moderate to low"—corresponding to maximum entry-forestalling prices that were estimated to exceed minimal average costs respectively by (*a*) 10 per cent or more, (*b*) about 7 per cent, and (*c*) 1 to 4 per cent. The resulting classification of industries was presented on p. 279.

The test of the hypothesis consisted simply of ascertaining differences in average industry profit rates among the three entry-barrier classes of industries, for 1936–40 and 1947–51. (Each industry profit rate was calculated as the average rate for the largest 2, 3, or 4 firms in the industry.) The findings for both time periods included the following:

1. Industries with "very high" barriers to entry had on the average

[11]Bain, *Barriers to New Competition*, pp. 190–201.

substantially higher profit rates than all other industries, and the difference in average profit rates was statistically significant.

2. There was no statistically significant difference in average profit rates between industries with "substantial" and with "moderate to low" barriers to entry.

In brief, the condition of entry appeared to make a difference for profit rates only if barriers to entry were "very high."

A comparable later experiment determined the differences in industry average annual profit rates among 30 industries, grouped in the same three entry-barrier categories, for the period 1950–60. Its results confirm the earlier findings. Industries with very high entry barriers had substantially higher average profit rates than other industries from 1950 to 1960, but the profit-rate differences between groups of industries with substantial and moderate-to-low barriers were slight and probably not statistically significant.[12]

As we juxtapose these findings with the hypothesis being tested, it should first be emphasized that the samples of industries were definitely too small and the individual estimates of barriers to entry too imprecise to permit any test of the hypothesis except in its most oversimplified form. Thus the predicted variation of profit rates with the height of the barrier to entry within the zone of effectively impeded entry (which could not really be identified) could not be tested. The rather crude results, however, are potentially subject to the variety of interpretations as related to the hypothesis.

One is that both blockaded and effectively impeded entry were found only or predominantly in industries with "very high" entry barriers, in which event the predicted difference between their profit rates and those of industries with ineffectively impeded entry would be confirmed. Another is that blockaded entry was generally found with "very high" entry barriers, and effectively and ineffectively impeded entry with "substantial" and "moderate to low" barriers. In this event, the predicted difference between the profit rates of industries with blockaded entry and those of other industries would be confirmed, but the predicted profit-rate difference between industries with effectively impeded and with ineffectively impeded entry would be disconfirmed. This interpretation might suggest an alternative hypothesis to the effect that the height of the barrier to entry does not systematically influence pricing and profits unless entry is blockaded, and the corresponding rejection of much of the theory underlying original hypothesis. Finally, it might be concluded that the estimates of all entry barriers other than

[12]Mann, *op cit.*

obviously very high ones were sufficiently inaccurate that the experiment did not provide a valid test of most of the theoretically predicted relationships. We are not in a position to say with much confidence which of these interpretations can be considered correct, and leave the matter there.

Another finding of this experiment was that, to the extent that it influences profit rates, the condition of entry exercises an influence which is distinguishable and separate from the influence of seller concentration. It is conceivable, of course, that high concentration and high entry barriers could be intercorrelated to such an extent that any industry that had one also had the other. Then we could only say that high concentration and difficult entry *in combination* were conducive to high profit rates. This is not the case, however, since among industries with "high" seller concentration (above 70 per cent control by 8 firms), we can identify industries protected by very different heights of entry barrier. For example, 12 of the 23 industries sampled in the first study mentioned had "high" seller concentration, but only 5 of them had "very high" entry barriers, the remaining 7 having "substantial" or "moderate to low" barriers. Within this restricted sample of 12 highly concentrated industries, the 5 industries with very high entry barriers had substantially higher profits, in both 1936–1940 and 1947–1951, than the 7 industries which had lower barriers to entry. There was a tentative indication, therefore, that very high entry barriers provide an independent, contributing structural cause of monopolistic excess profits.[13] Moreover, the conjunction of high seller concentration *and* extreme entry barriers provides a less desirable structural situation than high concentration alone. Extremes both of seller concentration and of difficulty of entry may be tentatively viewed as at least quasi-independent characteristics of market structure that are conducive to unworkable performance in the matter of profits.

One interesting hypothesis which we have so far been unable to test systematically is that the conjunction of high *buyer* concentration with high seller concentration, effecting a situation of bilateral oligopoly (or "countervailing power" of sellers and buyers), will tend to result in less monopolistic restriction and a better profit performance than high seller concentration alone. A few individual instances might be adduced in support of this proposition, but we are unable to confirm or disconfirm it with organized and impartially selected evidence. We will thus dis-

---

[13]This finding was confirmed in the second study mentioned (Mann, *op. cit.*), dealwith 30 industries from 1950 to 1960. Of 21 of these that were highly concentrated, the 8 that had very high entry barriers had substantially higher average profit rates than the rest.

miss the matter here with the observation that the hypothesis is reasonable though not axiomatic, and substantially untested.

The search for empirical generalizations concerning the association of market structure to price-cost margins or profit rates has produced some suggestions concerning the structural conditions for workable competition, so far as the latter is revealed by profit performance. Monopolistic pricing and profits are favored both by high seller concentration and by high entry barriers, and are especially likely to be acute if these two structural conditions exist together in the same industry. The adverse consequences of high seller concentration, in terms of monopolistic price and profit tendencies, are likely to be mitigated significantly if the barriers to new entry are more moderate or low. And, oligopoly with seller concentration only in the moderate range or lower and with more moderate entry barriers may well tend to provide a reasonably competitive pricing performance, or at any rate one a good deal better than is provided by highly concentrated industries with high entry barriers. The implied suggestions for a public policy are obvious.

Relationship of Market Structure to Performance in Other Dimensions

Systematized evidence on the relation of market structure to other dimensions of performance is generally deficient or unavailable at this time. However, we may submit certain impressions, based on casual observation, concerning the association of structure to performance in the dimensions of selling cost, product, progressiveness, and conservation.

A first and unsurprising regularity is that selling costs tend to be greater in industries with higher degrees of product differentiation among established sellers and higher product-differentiation barriers to entry. This type of relationship is evident, for example, in the sample of twenty manufacturing industries previously referred to. Industries with slight product differentiation (such as copper, cement, steel, meat packing, and standard canned goods), have small or negligible selling costs; industries with "medium" product differentiation (such as rubber tires, tin cans, and higher-priced men's shoes) have middle-sized selling costs; those with extreme product differentiation (including cigarettes, liquor, and automobiles) have high costs of sales promotion.

This finding, however, is not only unsurprising but also not very meaningful. It is at least equally appropriate to say that industries *develop* more extreme product differentiation and higher product-differentiation barriers to entry *because* selling costs are high, as to say that extreme product differentiation barriers *lead* to high selling costs. Since the relative seniority of the chicken and the egg is not readily established, we end up at this level with little more than the observations that (*a*) high selling costs are where we find them, and (*b*) that they are usually accompanied, at least as much by way of result as by way of cause, by a high degree of product differentiation.

To get further with this issue, it is necessary to go behind the superficial characteristic of market structure (degree of product differentiation) to the basic structural characteristics of an industry that determine how attractive it is for firms to incur large selling costs and thus strongly differentiate their products. We must refer, that is, to the basic conditions for profitable "differentiability" of products. Some rough indications concerning these basic conditions are the following.

First, the opportunities for profit from extreme product differentiation and large selling costs are particularly good in the case of products which are "prestige," "conspicuous consumption," or "gift" goods. In each of these instances price tends to be a relatively less important consideration than product reputation, "glamor," or asserted quality, all of which can be successfully built by concerted promotional efforts. (Quality fountain pens, liquor, and automobiles all fit this description.)

Second, extreme product differentiation and high selling costs tend to go well with products which, because of their complexity or other characteristics, consumers are unable really to evaluate or appraise, even after repeated use. They thus become dependent on product reputations to protect themselves against unwise purchases. (Pharmaceutical products and, again, automobiles would qualify for inclusion in this class.)

Third, the same opportunities for intensive differentiation via selling costs are present for very durable consumers goods which are purchased infrequently and with large unit outlays, so that the consumer has at best very limited opportunities to experiment by purchasing and comparing different brands of the same product. (Most consumers' durable goods fall in this class.)

Conversely, the best basic settings for slight product differentiation and low selling costs are found for goods that are purchased for their basic or functional utility, that the consumer can easily evaluate and appraise, and that, being nondurable, are purchased frequently and in small amounts, this allowing the consumer a maximum opportunity for experimentation with and comparison of alternatives. Most food and many clothing products clearly fit into this category.

These structural conditions for various sorts of selling-cost performance are indeed so basic that, for purposes of public policy making, they must also be viewed as relatively immutable and not in any important degree "remediable"—even though programs for consumer education and grade-labeling, as well as direct regulations of the volume and content of promotional activity, might remedy the more adverse situations somewhat. It may be noted in conclusion that not every industry with high selling costs has the basic characteristics outlined above. We are at a loss to explain, for example, in terms of the preceding argument, the very high level of selling costs that persists in the soap industry. More empirical and theoretical investigation is thus indicated.

The structural conditions for various sorts of product performance are at present far from clear. Some *a priori* theorizing has been done on this issue, but its results are inconclusive. The same applies to empirical findings, where the added difficulty of substantial inability really to measure or appraise product performance is also encountered. About the most that can be said is that a relatively broad range of product-performance alternatives is found mainly in the realm of large, complex, durable goods, and that it is in this area that there is a maximum opportunity for significant aberrations from a good or "workable" product performance.

The situation is similar when we turn to the putative relationship of market structure to technological progress. Theoretical indications on the issue are extremely inconclusive and ambivalent. Empirical exploration for structure-performance associations is fatally hampered by difficulties both of definition (of adequate progressiveness) and of measurement (of what progressiveness has been relative to alternatives). Avoiding these difficulties and testing for the association of market structure to gross expenditure on research, gross output of inventions, and gross rate of innovations has produced findings that are not very meaningful.

We must be aware, of course, of popular *ad hoc* hypotheses that relate high seller concentration and connected high profits to rapid progressiveness, and low concentration *cum* low profits to inadequate progressiveness. Neither theory nor observation really supports such hypotheses, except to the extent that industries with chronic subnormal profits or net losses—possibly in some degree connected with atomistic market structures and very easy entry—frequently appear to evidence some technological backwardness. This is perhaps attributable to a chronic lack of funds for research, development, and innovation. Putting aside these extreme cases, no regularity of association of technological progressiveness to market structure is either in evidence or predictable, given the existing state of empirical research and theorizing.

The structural conditions for good and poor conservation performance have not been adequately explored on either the theoretical or the empirical level, but some general observations are in order. Poor resource conservation by business firms, as we have noted, generally results from the choice of poor techniques of exploitation, from undue "shortsightedness" of private enterprise in balancing present against future resource yields and earnings, and from the unwillingness or inability of firms to make appropriately large current investments in enlarging or sustaining future production. The only obvious link of market structure to these aberrations from satisfactory conservation performance involves the potentially adverse effects of very low concentration among producer-sellers engaged in exploiting a natural resource. This is not to say that atomistic resource exploitation is always bad in its conservation effects, but it may be bad in two ways.

First, competitive exploitation of *a single common resource deposit or "pool"* by several or (worse yet) many individual producers—in a setitng wherein how much each competing firm can capture of the yield of the common resource deposit depends on how quickly it extracts or captures output from the deposit—is generally conducive to:

(*a*) Adoption of inferior techniques of exploitation, and

(*b*) Extreme shortsightedness on the part of individual producers, such that the effect of present outputs and techniques on future yields is substantially neglected.

A convenient but inadequate simile that comes to mind involves the situation in which each of twenty competitive children is given as many straws as desired with which to suck from a single two-gallon container of ice-cream soda, each being able to drink as much soda as he can get before the container is emptied. The possibilities of unduly rapid use of the resource, consequent indigestion, wasteful use of straws, and later regrets are obvious.

In a more realistic vein, we may consider the results of giving several or many antagonistic interests a common right to exploit a single natural resource deposit, such as a single underground petroleum pool or a single forest, under conditions in which each may enlarge his own share of the output of the common oil pool or forest by drilling more oil wells or using more lumbermen, power saws, and other equipment. The results in such situations are usually (*a*) elevation of costs without corresponding increase in yields, as each producer vies to capture the common resource before his competitors do; (*b*) consequent adoption of production techniques that are generally injurious to future yields, or yield-cost ratios, since no one producer can attach much importance to the future; and (c) a general disposition to discount heavily or overlook future yields in comparison to present yields, in the general race to capture present yields before someone else does. (These tendencies are well substantiated in the histories of the American petroleum and lumber industries.) This is not to say that competition or atomism in the exploitation of resources necessarily has injurious effects on conservation performance. Such injurious effects emerge when there is competitive and antagonistic exploitation of a common resource deposit or unit by antagonistic interests. For exploitation of a single resource unit, single-firm or monopolistic exploitation promises the best conservation results. And if there are enough such units of the same sort, an effective competition among "monopolistic" producers exploiting different units would still be possible.

Second, atomistic market structure may be "bad for conservation" if it leads to, or is partly responsible for, a chronically excessive or destructive competition that leaves producers so short of funds that they are financially unable to pursue good conservation practices which involve current cost outlays to enhance future yields. (This difficulty has evidently been encountered at times in various agricultural industries, with reference to soil conservation.) Destructive competition, marked by chronic net losses to enterprise, has adverse effects on conservation performance. Such destructive competition is usually associated with atomistic market structures, but a majority of such atomistic structures evidently are not plagued with truly destructive competition. We will refer to this matter further in the following chapter.

Relationship of Market Conduct to Structure and Performance

Since many comments were made in Chapter 9 concerning both the predicted and the verifiable associations of market conduct to either structure or performance, we will confine ourselves here to one main finding.

The only aspect of market conduct that can be empirically related to structure and performance involves predatory and exclusionary tactics. These are more easily observed and evaluated than other aspects of conduct, and their effects on structure and performance are more visible in actual cases. From a relatively unorganized scattering of observations, it is possible to conclude that actual predation and exclusion frequently have been effective in developing and maintaining more highly concentrated market structures, and markets to which new entry is more difficult, than would develop in the absence of such tactics. Predacious attack on small competitors or prospective entrants—through price wars, discriminatory price cutting, or aggressive preemption of necessary resource deposits—obviously has these effects, although such attack is most seriously discouraged by existing interpretations of the federal antitrust laws.

More important in fact are subtler exclusionary practices and devices, many of which will be defended by their users as "normal and prudent" business practices. Preemption of distributive channels through integration or exclusive-dealing contracts with retailers, and refusal by integrated firms to furnish nonintegrated competitors either with material supplies or with market outlets on favorable terms, are important phases of exclusionary practices that influence market structures. In these respects, there is a clear and identifiable influence of market conduct on market structure—an influence that is very appropriate subject-matter for consideration by public regulatory authority.

By influencing market structures directly (that is, by developing higher seller concentration and more difficult entry), predatory and exclusionary conduct may of course influence market performance indirectly, since higher concentration and more strongly impeded entry are conducive to a more monopolistic performance. The extent of these indirect effects will depend on the actual impact of the practices in question on market structures, and on the general relationship that holds between structure and performance. About the most that can be said on this point is that there is evidence concerning a number of individual industries in which "successful" predation and exclusion have had substantial direct effects on structure and indirect effects on performance.

The necessary and sufficient original structural conditions for the emergence of predatory and exclusionary tactics are not entirely clear. It might be suggested, however, that favoring structural conditions include the following: (*a*) dependence of the industry on a natural resource which is largely restricted in its geographical distribution to one or a few locations, this facilitating the development of concentrated ownership or control of the necessary resource; (*b*) durability and complexity of the good, requiring the existence of specialized distributive-service outlets, this facilitating the development of integrated or exclusive chains of outlets by individual manufacturers; and (*c*) dependence of producers or distributors of the good on specialized transport facilities (for example, oil pipelines) that require huge investments and are conveniently integrated by firms engaged in production or distribution. In industries with one or more of these characteristics, exclusionary conduct seems especially likely to develop, the law permitting.

Structural Conditions for Workable Competition

The available empirical findings on the relationship of market structure to market performance are incomplete, often inconclusive, and based only on rather small samples of industries. Therefore, definitive statements cannot be made concerning those conditions of market structure that are and are not conducive to a reasonably good or "workable" performance. Some tentative indications on this point are nevertheless available, and it may be useful to summarize them briefly here.

First, "high" or "very high" seller concentration in an industry generally seems to be conducive to poor performance in the crucial matter of price-cost relations or profits, without evidently bestowing offsetting advantages in other dimensions of market performance. Tentative indications are that if seller concentration exceeds that in which the largest eight sellers supply from two-thirds to three-fourths of the output of an industry (the number and sizes of smaller sellers occurring as they usually do in these cases), there is a strong disposition toward significant monopolistic price-raising and excess profits. On the other hand, in industries where seller concentration is "moderate" or less, so that, for example, the largest eight sellers supply less than two-thirds of the output of an industry, there is on the average a disposition toward much slighter excess profits and a much closer approximation to a competitive price-cost and output adjustment. At the same time, performance in other respects is not evidently poorer on the average than it is in highly concentrated industries.

Thus, as a matter of public policy, it would be salutary to preserve and as necessary create market structures that are no more than moderately concentrated on the sellers' side. This rule is applicable, at any rate, to all industries execpt those in which economies of large-scale production are so great as to require high or very high seller concentration in order to secure plants and firms of optimally efficient scale. And it appears from evidence that this sort of exception will arise only in a very small minority of cases. In these exceptional cases, of course, high seller concentration may have to be accepted and dealt with in order to secure technical efficiency, and there is a fundamental impossibility of securing a market structure which is conducive to good performance in all important respects.

It is not evident from available findings that market performance in industries with low seller concentration or relatively atomistic structures tends to be systematically better or worse than that in industries of moderate concentration. That is, moderately concentrated oligopolies seem to tend toward desirably competitive performance about as much as industries of relatively atomistic structure. The important structural distinction is not between atomistic and oligopolistic industries, but rather between highly concentrated oligopolies and all others, the "all others" including both moderately concentrated oligopolies and relatively atomistic industries.

Conversely, it is not evident that very low seller concentration, where it occurs and is consistent with efficiency in scale, is *generally* inferior in its performance tendencies to somewhat higher degrees of concentration. It is, however, possible that very low concentration has undesirable performance tendencies in certain cases. These include industries engaged directly in natural resource exploitation and others wherein very low seller concentration may aggravate adverse performance tendencies that are basically attributable to other causes. In such instances, atomistic structure may in some sense be practically an inferior alternative to moderate seller concentration, but these are more or less special cases and require special treatment. We will refer to them further in the following chapter.

There are some theoretical but very few and indistinct empirical indications that the adverse performance tendencies of high seller concentration tend to be mitigated if there is at the same time relatively high buyer concentration on the "receiving end" of the market. Because the theoretical indications are substantially inconclusive, and because the counter-balancing of concentrated selling with concentrated buying is a practical alternative at best in only a small minority of cases, it seems unrealistic to view the establishment of buyer concentration to oppose seller concentration as an important alternative way of securing workable market structures. High buyer concentration alone (not conjoined with high seller concentration) seems in general to be an undesirable structural development, to be opposed on grounds similar to those on which high seller concentration is opposed.

A second suggestion is that high barriers to entry tend to have an adverse effect on market performance, as compared to more moderate and low barriers to entry to an industry. This shows up at least among highly concentrated industries, in which nearly all cases of extreme barriers to entry are understandably found. Highly concentrated industries protected by very high entry barriers seem to perform worse in general than highly concentrated industries to which entry barriers are more moderate. The worst structural situation is usually one of quite high seller concentration combined with very high barriers to entry. High seller concentration alone seems generally less noxious if its potential effects are tempered by a considerable threat of new competition.

In the same vein, moderate seller concentration in oligopolistic industries probably is associated with more desirable market performance partly because it is generally linked with no more than relatively moderate barriers to entry. The lowered concentration and lowered entry barriers in fact typically interact to effect a reasonably competitive market performance. The policy implications of this finding are clear. Reduction of high entry barriers, as feasible, should produce structural conditions conducive to moderate concentration. The overall aim should be to secure or preserve both moderate or lower seller concentration and moderate or lower barriers to entry. The reduction of existing barriers to entry, however, may in practice be difficult to accomplish, especially if the impediments to entry inhere mainly in the product-differentiation advantages of established firms.

There is a remaining question as to possible adverse effects of "unduly easy" entry. We have already referred to extreme cases in which there is a chronic oversupply of new-entrant enterprises that continue to crowd into an already overcrowded industry without regard to the fact that, statistically, their major prospect is for net losses and ultimate bankruptcy. This sort of "condition of entry" is in general undesirable, though it seems more attributable to lack of knowledge or judgment on the part of entrant enterprises than to any basic structural condition. The appropriate character of remedies may be suggested by this fact, although public or other programs to eliminate the physical redundancy of obsolete plant or of immobile labor attached to a particular industry might often lessen the inducement to excessive entry.

A more subtle difficulty may arise in industries where entry is quite easy but where nevertheless a substantial oligopolistic concentration among established sellers develops. Then established sellers, finding it relatively unprofitable to set prices low enough to forestall entry, may elevate them for immediate profits and subsequently attract excessive entry and excess capacity. A few instances of this apparent tendency have been noted in our sampling of manufacturing industries. In such cases, the creation of a moderate as distinct from a very low entry barrier would probably be conducive to better industry performance over time. But a superior practical alternative may be deconcentration to secure a more moderately concentrated and more competitive market structure among established sellers.

A final characteristic of market structure to be evaluated from the standpoint of "workability" is the degree of product differentiation. Although some degree of product differentiation within the industry is frequently an essential device for providing buyers with a desirable variety of product alternatives, high degrees of product differentiation, as they occur or *sui generis*, are generally inimical to good market performance. As high degrees of product differentiation develop, they do not appear to augment progressively the real variety of product alternatives available. Rather, buyers tend to choose among closely similar products on the basis of persuasion, reputation, and the like. Furthermore, extreme product differentiation (or the effort to create it) is generally linked with wastefully high selling costs and with the creation of excessive barriers to new entry, so far as established sellers succeed in creating strong buyer preferences favoring their products over new-entrant products. It is thus difficult to accept at face value, or even at a fifty per cent discount, the oft-repeated assertion that strong product differentiation is a circumstance tending to make competition more "workable" than it otherwise would be. The empirical indications are contrary. However, it is extremely hard to devise practicable ways of remedying existing situations of undue and undesirable product differentiation, and this difficulty poses a major dilemma for public regulatory policy. If product differentiation is excessive in certain cases, by what psychologically, economically, and politically practicable means can we really lessen it?

We have spoken above of the structural conditions for workable competition, but not of the conduct conditions—of the sorts of market conduct which are and are not conducive to good performance. The reasons for this omission should be clear from our earlier discussions. Although on an abstract theoretical level we can specify some conduct conditions for good performance, these conditions are not operational in the light of our powers to observe and appraise actual conduct. So long as we are practically able to ascertain only the superficial forms of interseller coordination in market conduct, and unable to ascertain independently the aims of price policy or of promotional-and-product policy, we are also unable to establish any operationally useful or practically applicable criterion of desirable observed market conduct. We cannot honestly say, for example, that collusive conduct of one variety or another is bad as compared to noncollusive conduct, until we are able to distinguish the numerous different aims of policy potentially applied under the myriad subvarieties of both collusive and noncollusive conduct. The view just stated is not traditional, but it is supported by our analysis of market conduct in Chapter 9 above. We eschew, therefore, any general attempt to state an operational criterion of the conduct conditions of workable competition, and adhere in the main to a suggestion only of structural conditions.

The only significant exception to this position involves predatory and exclusionary conduct. In general predation and exclusion—except as occasionally justified on grounds that they are necessary adjuncts to realizing actual efficiencies such as those of vertical integration—tend to be at least indirectly inimical to good performance. Their elimination should be one of the conditions for workable competition.

SUPPLEMENTARY READINGS

Bain, J. S., *Barriers to New Competition*, 1956, Ch. VII.

Bain, J. S., "Relation of Profit Rate to Industry Concentration: American Manufacturing, 1936–40," *Quarterly Journal of Economics*, **LXV**, 3 (August, 1951), pp. 293–324.

Mann, H. Michael, "Seller Concentration, Barriers to Entry, and Rates of Return in Thirty Industries, 1950–1960", *Review of Economics and Statistics*, **XLVIII**, 3 (August, 1966), pp. 296–307.

Scherer, F. M., "Firm Size, Market Structure, Opportunity, and the Output of Patented Inventions", *American Economic Review*, **LV**, 5 (Dec., 1965) pp. 1097–1125.

12

Excessive Competition in Unconcentrated Industries

The last seven chapters have presented an extensive cross-sectional description and analysis of market structure, conduct, and performance in American industries But their coverage of such industries is uneven in that, while emphasizing oligopolistic industries, they have given much less attention to industries of atomistic or unconcentrated structure.

This is attributable to two main deficiencies in data available for analysis. First, most of the systematic data on hand refer to the manufacturing sector of the economy, and provide much less information on other sectors. And since such other sectors as agriculture and the distributive and service trades are the primary strongholds of industries of atomistic structure, the relative neglect of these sectors has implied some corresponding neglect of unconcentrated industries. Second, the available studies of individual manufacturing industries on which much of the cross-sectional analysis can be based refer to a sample of industries that are predominantly concentrated. As a result, there has been an insufficient emphasis on atomistic industries even within the manufacturing sector. These deficiencies may be remedied in part by considering evidence on performance in some individual industries of very low seller concentration, particularly in the nonmanufacturing sectors of the economy.

Special attention to industries of this sort is particularly needed because of frequent allegations that atomistic market structures in these sectors are associated with and perhaps responsible for (*a*) excessive or destructive competition, and therefore (*b*) socially undesirable market performance. To be sure, there is not a systematic connection between atomistic competition and poor market performance. In a great majority of manufacturing industries of relatively atomistic structure,[1] in many industries in the distributive and service trades, and in at least some extractive industries, low seller concentration has clearly been associated with reasonably good market performance. However, there are numerous instances, some of them quite important in the total economic scene, in which actually or seemingly poor performance has occurred in conjunction with and has been at least partly "blamed on" atomistic market structures.

For purposes of brevity, we may classify the major types of actual or alleged aberration from good performance that are associated with atomism under three headings:

1. Chronically subnormal earnings to enterprise and to labor in an industry, linked to a "destructive competition" which is, in turn, based on a chronic redundancy of plant capacity and labor force relative to demand.

2. High rates of small-business mortality and chronically subnormal small-business profits, resulting from a process of structural change in an industry which generally features the displacement of small firms by large ones as seller concentration increases.

3. Poor conservation, resulting from the antagonistic exploitation of common resource pools by numerous small enterprises, or from the insufficiency of enterprise incomes to finance and induce the use of good conservation practices.

Good examples of the first sort of phenomenon ("destructive competition" in a genuine sense) have been found in bituminous coal mining and in most basic-crop agricultural industries. The second (small-business losses in a context of progressive structural change) is exemplified in some industries in the distributive trades. The third (poor conservation) is found, for example, in crude petroleum production, in some fisheries, and in some lumbering.

All three sorts of "problem case" in the atomistic sphere are especially interesting from a public-policy standpoint because of one thing they have in common. This is that in each instance the "excesses" of competition have had a sufficiently unfavorable impact on the earnings of enterprises or labor that the interested parties have usually solicited and fre-

---

[1] Including, for example, the various garment industries, the furniture industry, the printing and publishing industry, and numerous others.

quently obtained special governmental regulations of their industries, designed to lessen or eliminate free market competition.

These pleas for public interference seem in general to have been motivated by the simple desire to increase the incomes of enterprise and/or labor in the industries involved, and the types of interference obtained have generally had the same purpose. The ostensible justifications of governmental interference, on the other hand, are usually preservation of the public interest in an assured supply of necessary goods, in good conservation practice, and so forth, though these ends have generally been served only incidentally and inadequately by the types of regulation actually obtained.

The presence of the corresponding policy issue, concerning the relative merits and demerits of a public limitation competition in "distressed" markets of atomistic structure, further justifies giving special attention to the types of problem case enumerated above. Specific public regulatory measures applied to such cases will be reviewed in Chapter 15; at this point, we will be concerned with the economic problems of atomistic industries with which public policy has been asked to deal.

"Destructive Competition" under Conditions of Chronic Overcapacity or Oversupply

In the light of predictions in many textbooks on economic theory, it seems paradoxical that a number of important industries of atomistic market structure have been plagued with a chronic overcapacity of plant and a chronic redundancy of labor force. This sort of distress is at any rate inconsistent with the conclusion of a simplified economic theory that atomistic market structures should generally lead to socially ideal resource allocation, income distribution, and efficiency.

Lack of a real paradox, to be sure, is revealed when we recognize that the theory in question actually refers to (*a*) an economy in which all industries, rather than just some of them, have atomistic structures; (*b*) an economy in which nonspecialized, potentially transferable resources like labor are rather freely mobile among all industries in response to varying employment and income opportunities; and (*c*) industry performance after a long-run equilibrium has been reached for both the industry and the economy. Conversely, the "destructive competition" which atomistic industries sometimes actually experience are apparently attributable to (*a*) the coexistence in the economy of concentrated and atomistic idustries, with different conditions of entry; (*b*) serious degrees of resource immobility, reflected especially in the undue attachment of potentially transferable resources to employment in certain atomistic industries; and (c) the fact that the industries in question are observed not in a long-run equilibrium, but in an unfortunately prolonged process of adjustment to some initial imbalance. For atomistic market situations thus described, an elaborated theory would indeed predict a performance which departed seriously from the ideal.

An added reason why the paradox is more apparent than real is that not all which is claimed to be destructive competition really reflects a chronic maladjustment or malfunctioning of markets. Destructiveness of competition may be alleged because enterprises and labor in an industry are dissatisfied with the subnormal earnings that the market has imposed as a device for inducing a needed reduction of capacity or of labor supply, even though chronic maladjustment is not actually threatened. It may also be claimed simply because "competitors don't like competition" of the thoroughgoing sort associated with atomistic market structure, beneficial as this competition may be to aggregate economic welfare.

Whatever the theoretical and semantic issues are, the available facts concerning the superficial and the essential content of destructive competition in atomistic industries deserve examination. Three cases in point from which illustrations may be chosen are agriculture in its basic-crop industries, bituminous coal mining, and the cotton-textile industry.

Symptoms of Chronic Maladjustment

In speaking here of destructive competition in atomistic industries, we will confine ourselves to the "real article" of chronic maladjustment of supply to demand. We will neglect the synthetic variety that lacks any more substance than the dissatisfaction of enterprises with the normally low profits earned in competitive markets, or of enterprises and labor with the temporarily reduced earnings received in relatively brief periods when supply is being restricted to put it into competitive balance with demand. Referring to cases of actually chronic maladjustment, the following seem to be the major specific symptoms of destructive competition.

First, selling prices of the industry output tend persistently (over a period, let us say, of one or two decades or more) to be driven to abnormally and unprofitably low levels relative to the average costs of production of many or most firms in the industry. This is basically because of the persistent maintenance of an industry supply so large relative to demand that normal competitive profits are impossible for many or most firms. In "perfect" markets, in which the seller simply determines his output relative to a going market price impersonally established in a central exchange,[2] the low price is the more or less auto-matic result of a market supply which is chronically excessive relative to demand. In atomistic markets which are somewhat "imperfect" as regards organized buyer-seller communication and exchange of market information and in which individual sellers may thus quote their own prices,[3] the mechanism for reaching and holding subnormal levels of selling price may involve competitive price cutting by individual sellers. But such price cutting—frequently referred to as destructive, cutthroat, or unfair—is only a superficial manifestation of a basic imbalance of market supply and demand, and not a real problem in itself.

Firms continuing to supply at least a substantial fraction of industry output therefore earn chronically subnormal profits or incur net losses. In the chronically distressed industry, this inability by many firms to earn minimal profits has been experienced at the same time when most industries in the economy were enjoying exceptional prosperity. This was true of coal, cotton textiles, and much agriculture in the prosperous 1920's, for example, as well as in the more depressed 1930's.

Second, the poor profit record of enterprise is generally matched by chronically subnormal returns to the productive factors the industry em-ploys, including nonspecialized and potentially transferable factors like labor, both hired and self-employed. The hired coal miner or the self-employed farmer, for example, for a long time tended to earn less per hour and especially per year than was earned by labor of comparable skill in most other industries. In the case of hired labor, subnormal wage rates have been frequently reached via "competitive wage cut-ting" by hard-pressed enterprises dealing with a redundant labor force, as in coal mining. In the case of self-employed labor, important in small farming, a similar effective wage reduction resulted from falling crop prices coupled with the reluctance or inability of the labor to shift oc-cupations even in the face of subnormal earnings.

Third, the principal impact of the chronic distress in an atomistic in-dustry (in the form of subnormal profits and wages) very frequently, though not always, falls mainly on some particular regional or other segment of the entire industry, with the rest of the industry faring better. For example, the major (though not entire) incidence of chronic distress in agricultural industries has been on small farms in the south-eastern quarter of the United States, and the principal impacts of mal-adjustment in the cotton-textile industry have fallen on the New Eng-land area rather than on the South. This suggests that the processes of industry evolution and adjustment in these cases have frequently de-

[2]As in the case of prices for basic agricultural crops.
[3]As in the cases of bituminous coal and cotton textiles.

veloped a stronger and a weaker regional or other segment in the industry, with effective redundancy of plant capacity and labor force being centered mainly in the weaker segment. Where the economic activity of an entire region has been heavily dependent on one or two distressed industries, the industry distress has on occasion led to a more general regional distress (or localized depression), affecting the regional business community and labor force in general. This sort of development has been observed, for example, in textile and shoe manufacturing towns of central New England.

Fourth, potentially transferable factors, including both labor and enterprise, have been extremely slow or laggard in shifting out of these industries even though under the pressure of subnormal earnings. The attached labor forces have shown a low or insufficient degree of mobility to other occupations and other geographical regions where earnings should be better. Similarly, the ranks of enterprise have tended to remain overly full in spite of persistent losses. This is not to say that there has been no outward mobility of redundant resources, since over time there has been a substantial mobility from distressed industries like coal mining, agriculture, and textiles, but only that the mobility has been at too slow a rate to accomplish a desirable economic balance except over a rather long period of time.

Fifth, the long-term "average" distress in the atomistic industries in question has been complicated in the course of economywide business cycles by the fact that outputs in these industries have been much more stable or insensitive, and prices correspondingly much more unstable or sensitive, than outputs and prices in the rest of the economy. This has meant that the incomes of both enterprise and labor in these distressed industries have fluctuated more violently than comparable incomes in the rest of the economy. And although at the top of business fluctuations, such enterprise and labor may have suffered *relatively* little from the chronic maladjustment of their industries, they have correspondingly been in very acute distress in general business depressions. Thus we find, for example, that whereas enterprise and labor in coal mining and in agriculture were in only a moderately disadvantaged position during the 1920's when the economy in general was very prosperous, they suffered abnormally acute distress in the great business depression of the early 1930's.

Causes of Chronic Maladjustment

Let us turn from the symptoms of destructive competition to its basic causes. Why do chronic maladjustments occur in atomistic industries, and, in particular, why do they occur in some of them but not in others?

In general, a certain combination of circumstances underlies the development of chronic maladjustments. A number of conditions are simultaneously present which together induce and sustain the maladjustment. Although we will not pause to speculate on precisely how many or which conditions are theoretically just sufficient to generate chronic economic imbalance, historically it appears that five conditions generally coexist and are jointly responsible for the sort of destructive competition under consideration. These are:

1. *An atomistic market structure in the industry* (and technological conditions favoring the maintenance of such a structure). This structural setting is important because it leads to a maximum of independence in price-output determination by individual enterprises and because, correspondingly, it practically precludes successful efforts by private enterprises to restrict industry output and raise prices to overcome the effects of chronic overcapacity and oversupply. Privately organized collusive price-output determination is effectively unavailable as a counter-measure against general industry distress. This has been amply proved in all the examples mentioned: agriculture, coal mining, and cotton-textile manufacturing.

2. *Very easy entry to the industry,* in the sense that new entrants are not at a perceptible disadvantage as compared to established firms, require only minor amounts of capital to finance entry, and can accomplish entry rather quickly. This condition of easy entry is important mainly in that it facilitates rapid expansions of industry capacity and output in response to increases in demand, including even transitory increases. It may also be important in that would-be enterprisers, discouraged from entering many or most industries because they have perceptible barriers to entry, tend to crowd into the areas of very easy entry to an unreasonable extent. There are abundant evidences of very easy entry in all three of the examples mentioned earlier.

3. *Very slow exit* of enterprise from the industries involved when overcapacity and oversupply emerge. Enterprises come in easily and quickly when demand increases, but leave slowly and reluctantly when demand declines. This lagging exit is due in turn to the fact that the productive plant, once established, is extremely long-lived (so that redundant plant is not soon eliminated by its wearing out) and that the plant is specialized in function, or not convertible to alternative uses. Coupled with this condition, and related to easy entry, is an almost endless supply of new owner-enterprisers to take over and run existing redundant plant if earlier owners depart because of financial failure. The long-lived plant attracts owners and operators so long as it survives, though it may

"live through" several sets of operators. This slow exit condition and the circumstances on which it is based are evident in agriculture, cotton textiles, and coal mining—but not, for example, in the garment industries.

4. *Unusually slow exit mobility* of labor attached to the industry, reflected in the reluctance of a redundant labor force that has customarily been employed in the industry to shift to other occupations or regions when employment opportunities decline. The basic causes of this impeded labor mobility are complex, but the phenomenon is acute principally in cases in which a single industry supplies a large fraction of all employment opportunities in a given community or region, so that the workers attached to the industry do not have adequate alternative employment opportunities nearby. In such cases, opportunities for occupational mobility are slight unless a geographical move is also made by the workers. In the absence of a willingness and ability to make a geographical move, the labor force of the industry becomes effectively immobile, attached to the industry, and chronically redundant in supply when the demand for labor services by the industry declines. Poor geographical mobility of labor, that is, coupled with the specialization of a community or region largely to one distressed industry, is at the heart of the usual difficulty. The phenomenon has been observed in the "coal towns" of the bituminous-coal-producing regions, in the "shoe and textile" towns of New England, and in predominantly agricultural areas, especially that of the Southeast.

The preceding four conditions set the stage for a prolongation of industry maladjustment if once a maladjustment emerges. Evidently necessary to an explanation of the emergence of destructive competition, however, is a fifth condition, in the form of a "trigger" which creates an initial imbalance. We thus come to:

5. *Some historical event* or events which initially induce the creation of excess plant capacity and redundant labor force in the industry. Important types of such events in the recorded cases are the following:

(a) Large wartime expansions of demand for the output of the industry, followed by subsequent returns of demand to normal levels. The role of exceptional temporary increases in demand during major wars has been unmistakable, for example, in initially (and recurrently) developing excess capacity in agriculture and in coal mining.

(b) Secular declines in the demand for industry output over time, often associated with the development of substitute products (petroleum for coal, synthetic fibers for cotton and cotton textiles) or with the loss of export markets by a domestic industry, as in the case of some basic agricultural crops. Such declines require a downward adjustment in industry capacity and labor force, and this may be slow in coming.

(c) Increases in the productivity of existing capacity, resulting in the need for less capacity to supply existing demands (as in agriculture generally).

(d) Regional shifts in the location of industry, involving expansion of capacity in new locations to exploit their advantages, but leaving redundant obsolescent plant and redundant immobile labor force in the old locations. The regional shift of the cotton-textile industry to the southeastern area, leaving redundant capacity in New England, and the development of cotton production in newly irrigated lands in the Far West in the face of a surplus of cotton land and farmers in the Southeast, are examples of this sort of phenomenon.

When some such historical change has its impact on an atomistic industry with the other characteristics just described, the industry directly and the economy indirectly have usually been faced with a prolonged and painful process of readjustment. In this process, the automatic corrective forces of the market have worked so slowly and imperfectly that severe social inequities and severe misallocations of resources were experienced for unduly sustained periods of time. The market works inevitably in these cases, but it works very sluggishly. Therefore, the prolonged processes of readjustment impose social costs that the general populace may be unwilling to bear or have levied against the major losing groups.

In this connection, it is pertinent to inquire to what extent and in what sense atomism *per se* on the seller side of the markets involved is at fault. In a basic sense, atomistic market structures as such are not to blame. The ultimate culprits are retarded exit of plant capacity and immobile labor resources in the face of historical events which create a redundancy of capacity and labor force. It is true, however, that atomism with its associated extreme of competition intensifies the effects on enterprise and labor incomes of such dislocations as do emerge. The practical impossibility in atomistic markets of private organization to restrict industry output and investment and to raise selling prices, and thus to accomplish short-term income relief and long-term rationalization, means that enterprise and labor alike are hard hit by typical dislocations and more defenseless than they would be with more concentrated market structures. And it is not clear that the atomistic market generally makes its adjustment to a dislocation more rapidly or efficiently than a more concentrated market would. Yet, as we have pointed out, atomism is not the primary or "real" trouble. The preceding poses interesting issues when we turn to the matter of public policy remedies for destructive competition.

Basic Difficulties, Remediability, and Remedies

The adverse social consequences of the sorts of chronic maladjustment under discussion are clear. First, there is a persistent misallocation of productive resources among uses, and a corresponding distortion in the composition of total output. Relatively too many resources, in the form of both capital and labor, are being used in the chronically distressed industries, and relatively too few in all other industries. Correspondingly, the aggregate welfare would be increased if, by transferring resources, the economy received less output from the distressed industries in return for more output from other industries. The allocation problem is only worsened, moreover, if the redundant resources in the distressed industries are confined to partial utilization in order to limit output and raise selling prices. So long as they are not shifted to other uses, enforced partial employment is more wasteful than full employment and resultant "surplus" production.

Second, there is a persisting inequity in income distribution within the economy. Productive factors like labor receive smaller incomes in the distressed industries than in other industries for comparable work involving comparable skill. Owner-investors receive smaller returns on their investments in the distressed areas, and frequently suffer negative returns. The inequities in the distribution of interest and profit returns, moreover, are increased because of the earning of monopolistic excess profits by enterprise in many concentrated industries, just as wage inequities are increased by the exercise of greater labor-union monopoly power in other industries. Finally, the adverse income position of labor and enterprise in the distressed areas is complicated by the excessive cyclical instability of their incomes. All of these inequities represent genuine social problems if they are more or less indefinitely prolonged, without the income disparities in question forcing the desired reallocation of resources which would also lessen or eliminate these disparities.

Third, the adverse income effects, so far as they leave enterprise and self-employed labor in the distressed industries without the necessary funds to finance efficient operations, may produce undesirable side effects on conservation and on the efficiency of operations generally. The lack of normal profits or other earnings to furnish funds or support credit for needed investments in natural-resource conservation and capital equipment may result in the pursuit of poor or "short-sighted" conservation practices and in the perpetuation of inefficient methods of production. This tendency is noted in at least some of the distressed industries already discussed—for example, in the small-farm agriculture of the Southeast.

The next question is to what extent these chronic maladjustments are remediable, either by ordinary market processes or by direct public interference. We advance the following propositions.

First, the basic remedy, if it can somehow be administered, is the movement of redundant resources from the distressed industries to other occupations, so far as these resources are at all transferable. Redundant labor and enterprise should be shifted out of these industries, thus encouraging the earliest feasible abandonment of nontransferable redundant plant and natural resource deposits. We would, for example, envisage the transfer to other occupations of redundant labor force and enterprise in coal mining or in farming, hastening the shutdown of redundant marginal coal mines and the return of redundant marginal agricultural land to other uses.

Second, even the most vigorous sort of competitive pressure by the unregulated mechanism of the market accomplishes this remedy so slowly that society, being subject to the persuasion of the immediately affected groups, is unwilling to tolerate the prolonged and adverse "transitional" income-distribution effects that are experienced if the market is relied on for remedies. In this sense, unregulated market competition in these distressed industries is "unworkable," or unacceptable to the general populace, largely on the grounds that it permits prolonged inequities in the distribution of income.

Third, supplements to the market process in the form of governmental interference are thus perhaps needed and at any rate widely desired. If no effective limits are placed on the relevant regulatory powers of the government, it should be able in some way to accomplish the basic remedies of a reallocation of resources among industries and of a desired restoration of an equitable balance in income distribution. But a resource reallocation is the primary goal. This reallocation should be such that, once it is accomplished, unregulated competitive market forces will result in the payment of normal incomes to resources and enterprises still employed in the previously distressed areas. Redressing the income difficulty without transferring resources tends to impede the needed resource transfer and to abet and increase allocative inefficiency. Measures of governmental interference should thus be designed above all things to hurry the reallocation of resources that the market would "eventually" accomplish, and should never deal with the income difficulty in such a way as to retard this reallocation.

In Chapter 15 we discuss the sorts of governmental interference in distressed industries that have been secured through the solicitation of the immediately interested parties. It may be worth noting here that actual public-policy remedies have been addressed mainly to improving the incomes of enterprise and labor in the distressed industries, by the use of measures which make the prevailing misallocation of resources more comfortable. Thus they virtually retard the desired reallocation of resources that would eliminate excess capacity and redundant labor force. So long as chronic distress in certain atomistic industries tends to produce this type of short-sighted and uneconomic public regulation, the overall picture of destructive competition becomes worse than has already been painted. Chronic dislocations of resources are actually perpetuated by governmental action aimed at redressing inequitable income positions.

Small-Business Distress in the Context of Structural Changes in Atomistic Industries

A second major sort of atomistic-industry problem may arise from the displacement of small enterprises in an initially atomistic industry by much larger enterprises, as the industry undergoes a structural revolution. Instances of this phenomenon are not uncommon in the last century of the development of American industry. For example, in the major "merger movement" from 1870 to 1905, there were numerous instances in which the development of plants and firms of much larger scales and degrees of integration, frequently in part for sound technological reasons, involved the elimination of many small firms from the market, sometimes by bankruptcy and sometimes by absorption by large firms. Furthermore, the process of eliminating small firms frequently involved the use of exclusionary and predatory tactics by the ascendant large firms.

On the general rule that increasing concentration led to greater efficiency (up to a point), and that one "has to break eggs to make omelet," the historical process of eliminating small firms in many industries has usually been condoned as a necessary consequence of desirable change and progress in a capitalist economy. Nevertheless, two issues must be faced in connection with the type of process in question. The first involves the equitable position of the eliminated small enterprises in the matter of their wealth and income—should the problem be dismissed or dealt with? The second concerns the extent to which the reduction in the ranks of small business is actually compensated for by increases in economic efficiency.

Such intrinsic issues are important in any "reorganization process" affecting an industry. But they attract widespread public attention and are dramatized mainly when the industry affected is large and when, in addition, its locational pattern is such that the effects of the reorganization process are observed in all parts of the nation, rather than being confined to a relatively small locality or region. Also, the issues become more pressing when the small-business interests affected can organize sufficient political power to seek and secure governmental interference aimed at arresting or modifying the reorganization process. This is especially so because the sorts of interference sought and obtained ordinarily involve limiting *competition* in order to preserve *competitors*. Then, in effect, the new issue is raised of the effects on industry performance of the types of governmental interference with competition that the interested parties can obtain.

Structural Evolution in the Distributive Trades

The outstanding instance in America of small-business distress in the face of structural change is found in several parts of the distributive trades, including the wholesaling and retailing of groceries, pharmaceuticals, auto accessories, household goods, and some other items, over the time period since the end of World War I. The general initial setting and subsequent developments in this area have been roughly as follows.

Prior to World War I, the distributive-trade sector of the economy was made up of a larger number of separate "industries" (in the theoretical sense), most of which were quite atomistic in structure. The sector in general was divided and subdivided on the basis of merchandise lines, of wholesaling and retailing function, and of geography. Thus, nationally, largely separate groups of distributive firms dealt in groceries, drugs, hardware, clothing, and the like, with little competition between the groups. Furthermore, the firms within any line were divided more or less clearly into wholesalers and retailers, with each group supplying an essentially different market (the wholesalers sold to the retailers and the retailers sold to the final customers). In general, wholesale and retail functions were not combined or integrated in an individual firm. Finally, wholesaling or retailing in any line was divided among numerous small regions, metropolitan areas, cities, or towns, with the sellers of a particular line in any region constituting a more or less isolated theoretical industry. Competition was active among themselves, but negligible with sellers in other regions. A typical industry within the distributive trades, for example, might be comprised of retail grocers in Harrisburg, Pennsylvania, or hardware wholesalers in New Orleans.

There were (and still are) obviously very numerous individual distributive industries according to this definition. And a dominant characteristic of these industries was that they were, in the bulk of the more important cases, atomistic in structure, or populated by a relatively large number of relatively small sellers. This was especially true of retailing industries in the cities and metropolitan areas. In wholesaling industries seller concentration was somewhat greater though still relatively low; only in retailing in small towns and rural distribution centers (which might support only one or a few firms apiece in a given line) was significantly high seller concentration encountered. As to other aspects of market structure, entry to the typical distributive industry was extremely easy. In retailing there was generally some degree of product differentiation among competing sellers, based on location, service, personal goodwill, and the like. Looking especially to the important urban markets, we find typically unconcentrated industries subject to easy entry, made up of large numbers of rather small enterprises.

Another broad characteristic of these industries, moreover, should not escape notice. This is that distributive trade enterprise, by reason of its form and function, was spread thoroughly over the whole country, so that small distributive firms were located in every region, state, city, and town, generally being owned and run by local citizens. This fact provided the basis for the widespread political influence of small enterprise engaged in these industries, when the time came that they wished to solicit governmental interferences on federal, state, and local levels.

The revolutionary change that thereafter struck many parts of the distributive trades was initiated by and involved as its principal incident the development of "mass distribution" through large-scale firms which generally took the form of "chain stores." Several changes in the charcter of the distributive firm were represented in the emergence of the large chain-store enterprises in the grocery, drug, auto accessory, and general or department-store line (the last represented in Sears, Roebuck or Montgomery Ward). First, there was generally the acquisition by the firm of a multiplicity (or chain) of retail outlets—an extensive multiplant development in the retail level. In the case of the larger and more powerful mass-distributors, these chains of retail outlets covered major regions of the country or the entire nation. Second, the multiplant retailing firm generally integrated its own wholesaling function in large part, becoming a wholesaler-retailer which largely dispensed with the services of existing nonintegrated wholesalers. One of the consequences of this integration was that the wholesaling function of an integrated firm with very numerous retail stores could now be carried out on a much larger scale than had previously been attained, with consequent economies of large-scale wholesaling evidently being realized. Third, the larger mass distributors often integrated "backward" even further to acquire or control manufacturing facilities to provide themselves with some of the merchandise they retailed. This is noted, for example, in the acquisition by the larger grocery chains of their own bakeries, dairies, coffee roasting and canning plants, and the like.

Fourth, the chains usually were innovators of a different retail distributive "product," by introducing self-service by customers and eliminating credit and delivery services. This simplified service product could be sold at a lower price than its predecessors, and offered consumers a hitherto unavailable price-product alternative. Fifth, the big mass distributors frequently established their own brands of merchandise, labelling their canned goods or aspirin or tires or refrigerators with the "private" brands of the distributing firms rather than (or in addition to) purveying merchandise bearing the nationally advertised brands of established manufacturers. (This practice has often been followed even though the mass distributors actually purchased the physical merchandise from the self-same manufacturers.) This procedure tended to upset existing patterns of product differentiation, and also to operate to the virtual disadvantage of national-advertising manufacturers, who thus to some extent shared with displaced independent wholesalers and retailers a common grievance against the mass distributors.

Finally, evidence indicates that in at least some lines (for example, groceries) the mass distributors employed various predatory tactics against independent competitors in the early period when they were winning away a substantial share of the market. Local price-warring was prominent among these tactics. (Such tactics have not been at all uncommon in the history of numerous structural revolutions of manufacturing and related industries, but they received a good deal more publicity than usual in the case of the distributive trades.) Once the mass distributors had won a satisfactory share of the market for themselves, predation in general became uncommon or vanished, although the passage meanwhile of various restrictive legislation may have contributed to this result. From the preceding evidence it is generally clear that the process of structural change in the distributive trades was quite complex, involving much more than the simple emergence of very large firms with chains of retail outlets.

The basis of this structural revolution was evidently the existence of certain previously unexploited opportunities for technological and organizational changes in the distributive trades. These changes could realize important potential economies of a simultaneous vertical integration and increased horizontal scale of firms (together with a change in the service product offered at retail), and offered exceptional profits to the innovators of the changes. The results of the revolution were observable on both the structural and the performance level, as well as having noticeable impacts on the welfare of various groups of individual sellers.

As to market structure, seller concentration increased significantly in the distributive industries which were most affected by the chain-store development. The atomistic market structure was in effect replaced by one in which an oligopolistic core of relatively few mass distributors supplied either a major or an important minor part of industry output, and in which a large number of relatively small sellers survived to constitute a competitive fringe supplying the rest of industry output.

The first phase of this structural change involved the capture of a significant but not dominant share of each of several types of distributive markets by a few very large "nationwide" chains which operated either nationally or throughout a major region of the country, this share being gained in considerable part through displacing or reducing the sales volume of a multitude of small independent wholesalers and retailers. In the grocery trades, for example, chain.stores controlled only 2 to 3 per cent of national retail sales in 1920, but by 1930 five large "national" chains had developed which together made about 25 per cent of national grocery sales (a market share which they have neither increased nor decreased very much subsequently). Since in most local markets fewer than all of the national chains were present (there being a good deal of regional specialization by firms), this meant that in the typical local grocery-store industry, one or two or three nationwide chains accounted for about a quarter of the market, the rest being supplied by a large number of smaller firms. In other distributive trades affected by the chain-store movement, the immediate impact on seller concentration was in some cases greater and in some less, but always a substantial competitive fringe remained, and easy entry.

The second and later phases of the structural change involved numerous repercussions to the intrusion of the large national chains, as smaller enterprises adapted their own organizations to cope with the new competition. Some principal developments have been the formation of numerous local chain-store firms, generally confined to a single urban area or limited region and undertaking a part of the integration of wholesale functions exploited by the big chains; the development of supermarkets with very large volumes in individual retail units (these have been developed ultimately both by local and national chains); and the formation of alliances of large numbers of independent retailers to conduct cooperative and large-scale wholesaling operations within a sort of quasi-integrated structure. The general effect of these repercussive changes has been to add considerable numbers of medium-large distributive firms to the relatively few very large national chain-store firms, and further to increase seller concentration in most local markets. Even with this addition, however, the typical concentration pattern in the local distributive industry has remained one of a moderately concentrated oligopolistic core of principal suppliers (including both national and local chains) with a substantial competitive fringe of numerous smaller wholesalers and retailers of varying sizes. The place in the market of the old-fashioned single-unit small corner grocery store or drug store has been substantially reduced but remains important. With some division of distributive markets among chain and nonchain firms of varying sizes, the very small nonintegrated retailer has maintained a position through specialization of function, convenience of location, and the like.

As to market performance in the distributive trades, there is little question but that it was generally improved by the structural revolution just outlined. The weight of evidence strongly supports the assertion that, as compared to the nonintegrated small retailers and wholesalers who occupied most of the market before they entered, the large chain stores were markedly more efficient. Through advantages of integration and large-scale management they attained substantially lower operating costs than the old style independents could, and they augmented this advantage through lower "invoice" costs of merchandise obtained by exploiting their mass purchasing power to secure lower purchase prices for what they bought. And though some part of the reduction in invoice costs was probably attributable to the exploitation of buyers' monopoly power rather than to real increase in efficiency, the substantial reduction in operating costs reflected a real gain in efficiency. So great was the advantage of the large chains that they could (and did) sell at retail prices 5 to 10 per cent below independent competition and still reap a supernormal profit. Consumers unquestionably gained through the invasion of nationwide chain stores. Moreover, the repercussive adaptations of independent firms to the competition of the national chains have to all appearances greatly increased the efficiency of small and middle-sized enterprise in the distributive trades, with the result of a virtual lowering of overall distributive costs and charges to customers in several of the major distributive trades. This is not to say, of course, that the distributive efficiency picture is as yet close to ideal in many distributive lines, but the structural revolution in question was in the net a favorable change.

A final aspect of the change which deserves note concerns "the eggs which were broken in order to make the omelet." That is, many small and nonintegrated independent wholesalers and reatilers suffered from the change. Their vested positions were imparied or destroyed as they faced a competition by larger integrated firms which they could not economically meet, with the result that their profits were reduced or eliminated, and in many cases the firms themselves perished. A reduced number of these very small enterprises could and did survive by fulfilling specialized functions in their markets, but many of them were marked for destruction or relative poverty unless they adapted rapidly to change their own organizations, and this a great many were unable to do. Thus the economy was in general faced with the dual problems of (1) accelerated mortality of small independent distributive firms, and (2) a revised competitive situation in which many very small firms could make at best starvation earnings in the face of the competition of more efficient larger firms. All of this was complicated by the fact that in their earlier stages of growth the large chains did employ some predatory tactics, and that they did benefit from buyers' monopoly positions in purchasing merchandise. However, these phenomena seem to have been more incidental than central to the fundamental problem.

An issue in social or economic "equity" was thus posed. The price of increased economic efficiency via structural reorganization seemed to be the imposition of "inequitable" losses of income or wealth upon large numbers of small, independent enterprisers. Should these losses be accepted as a necessary and inevitable cost of desirable change? Should public interference of some sort be employed to prevent or compensate for these losses? If so, what sort of interference was consistent with the general goal of ever-increasing economic efficiency?

Governmental Interferences with Structural Evolution

As is usual in public economic policy in America, regulatory interferences in the distributive trades were not initiated or designed by some impartial public tribunal, but by the immediately affected economic interests which sought relief. The interests in these cases were of course largely the old-line, small, and nonintegrated independent wholesalers and retailers, aided to a certain extent by nationally advertising manufacturers who had been adversely affected by the chain-store development.

The considerable distress or impairment to their incomes which these groups felt during the later 1920's, aggravated by the severe depression at the outset of the 1930's, was the origin of a number of organized pleas for public restriction of competition in the distributive trades. In particular, legislation was sought which would reduce or eliminate the competitive advantages and tactics of the chain stores. (The major organized supplicants for such interference were national trade associations of retail druggists and grocery wholesalers.) The principal grounds offered for public interference were first that "monopoly" in the distributive trades was threatened unless the chains were checked (a poorly substantiated prediction), and second that certain unfair methods of competition by the chains should be restricted in the public interest (a valid point so far as predatory tactics and buyers' monopoly pressures were concerned, but hardly at the heart of the problem). The real difficulty, which was not cited as a ground for public interference, was that numerous small enterprises were losing much or all of their incomes in the face of competition from new types of business organization which were intrinsically more efficient.

In any event, the organized political presure of the independent-distributor groups was successful in securing a variety of restrictive legislation on both federal and state levels, aimed at restricting or compensating for the competitive advantages and tactics of chain stores. These restrictive laws fall under the three main headings of chain-store taxation, prohibition of discriminatory buying-price advantages of large purchasers, and local fixing of minimum retail prices. Antichain-store tax laws, which simply imposed an arbitrary and discriminatory extra tax burden on the distributive firm with multiple retail outlets, were initially passed by a considerable number of states, though subsequently many of these laws have been repealed or found invalid. On the federal level, Congress passed the Robinson-Patman Act (1936), effectively forbidding sellers (such as manufacturers) to charge large buyers (such as chain-store firms) lower prices than were charged to smaller buyers, unless the sellers could themselves demonstrate that the lower prices were justified by actually lower costs of supplying the big buyers. Back to the state level, the legislatures of all but two or three of the forty-eight states passed so-called "fair trade" (resale-price-maintenance) laws, permitting retailers to establish minimum retail prices on any branded product by entering into resale price maintenance contracts with manufacturers, these privately established retail prices to be binding on all competing retailers, whether or not they themselves were parties to such contracts. Application of such laws had the effect—in trades where most or all of the supplying manufacturers would cooperate in writing resale-price-maintenance contracts—of permitting and sponsoring the private and unsupervised establishment of legally enforceable minimum retail prices on whole lines of merchandise.[4] These laws had wide application and effect in drug-store retailing, electrical appliances, and some other lines, but much less effect in the retailing of food and clothing.

These types of legislation will be discussed in more detail in Chapter 15, but for the moment we may comment on the evident intent and effect of the governmental interferences which were obtained. The major intent of the organized independent distributors who proposed and largely drafted the laws was evidently first to impair the competitive advantages of chain stores or to prevent chains from competing freely in terms of selling price, and second to restrict price competition in general within the distributive trades. This goal was pursued in some part by limiting allegedly unfair advantages and predatory tactics of the chains (as in the Robinson-Patman-Act limitation on the exploitation of buyers' monopoly power by mass distributors), and in some further part by trying simply to suppress retail price competition (as in the "fair trade" laws). The latter approach, involving suppression of competition in order to preserve competitors, is clearly undesirable in its tendencies, since the social *raison d'etre* of having competitors is to reap the benefits of competition. In general, restrictive legislation in this area has elevated the goal of protecting the income positions of small merchants above all more general social goals such as promotion of economic efficiency.

The effects of these types of governmental interference have fortunately not been as socially noxious as might have been feared, largely because they didn't work very well in the sense of accomplishing their evident purposes. Both the Robinson-Patman restraints on chain-store buying prices and the "fair-trade" restraints on the retail prices of manufacturer-branded merchandise have been to a considerable extent "avoided" by the chains, in the first instance by purchasing the whole output of suppliers or by integrating them, and in the second instance by introducing and promoting "private" brands on which no binding resale price-maintenance contracts could exist. Furthermore, the widespread use of resale price maintenance has for a variety of reasons not proved to be practically workable in such important lines as food and clothing retailing, so that a large fraction of all retail sales has not been seriously affected by this sort of suppression of competition. Finally, there have been serious and increasing difficulties of enforcement of "fair trade" prices, so that a good deal of retail price competition which

[4]Reference may also be made to "unfair practices" or "minimum markup" laws passed in a number of states, prohibiting the sale of merchandise at a retail price lower than cost of the merchandise plus a "fair" markup to cover cost of retail operations.

these laws were intended to prohibit has survived. In consequence, the mass distributors in general have been well able to thrive and to maintain their market positions, and to pursue competitive price policies which passed on part of the advantages of their intrinsic efficiency to the consumer. Competition has by no means been frozen or heavily suppressed in the distributive trades generally.

On the other hand, the restrictions in question, and especially the "fair trade" laws, have in some distributive trades placed a perceptible drag on the effectiveness of competition, maintaining distributive margins at somewhat higher average levels than would be associated with free competition, and thereby inducing excessive entry (or retarding exit) to the end of propagating and maintaining some distributive excess capacity.

In the history of small-business disadvantage or distress in the distributive trades, it appears generally that most of the legal remedies secured have been worse than the disease, or at any rate would have been if they had had their intended effects. This is to say that a general suppression of competition is not a wise or justifiable remedy for the inequities in income distribution that are engendered by a structural revolution which introduces greater efficiency into a sector of the economy. It should be emphasized, moreover, that the disease in this and related cases is not one of "destructive competition" in the strict sense of a chronic malfunctioning of unregulated competition that perpetuates a serious misallocation of resources. The evidence is, on the contrary, that competition tended to work very well, or all too well from the standpoint of those business interests which this competition tended to weaken or eliminate. The grounds for extensive public interference of any sort are correspondingly weaker than in cases of true destructive competition. And if interferences are to be had in order to redress transitional income difficulties, great care should be taken to design them so as not to impede the orderly progress of efficiency-increasing economic change.

Atomism and Conservation Performance

Since we have discussed conservation performance and its possible relationship to market structures in the preceding two chapters, we may deal quite briefly here with our immediate issue. This is the allegedly deleterious effect of atomistic market structure on conservation in the exploitation of natural resources. To what extent is it true that an industry engaged in extracting or exploiting a natural resource is likely to have a poorer conservation performance if it has an atomistic rather than a concentrated population of producers and sellers? We may argue briefly as follows.

Let us postulate first that, from a social standpoint, optimal conservation in the exploitation of a resource requires the choice of a technique of exploitation, of a time pattern and total quantity of cost outlays, and of a resultant time pattern and total quantity of resource yields which will, over all relevant future time, maximize the aggregate net satisfaction[5] which the general public can receive from the use of the resource.[6] Given this standard, departures from optimal or good conservation are principally attributable to three things: (1) choice of inferior or wasteful techniques of exploitation; (2) selection of nonoptimal time-patterns of resource recovery, usually involving unduly rapid exploitation of the resource, or undue emphasis on obtaining present as compared to future yields; and (3) selection of inferior time patterns and total quantities of cost inputs for exploitation, usually involving a failure to make sufficient current cost outlays to secure the most desirable amounts of future yield. All three sorts of aberration from good conservation performance have at least occasionally been observed among our extractive industries.

One question then is whether such aberrations are generally chargeable to ignorance, stupidity, or blunder—all of which are encountered frequently in the activities of men. Or, on the other hand, is there some systematic and intrinsic tendency on the part of profit-seeking enterprises to turn in a conservation performance which is deficient from a social standpoint? In brief, if enterprises engaged in exploiting natural resources attempt intelligently to maximize the profits from their operations, and succeed, will their conservation performance tend systematically to deviate from the social optimum?

There is only one possible reason that private enterprises *generally* may tend to deviate from socially optimal conservation performance. This is their possibly inherent "shortsightedness" in placing relative values on present or early as compared to future or deferred resource yields and derived incomes. It seems likely, that is, that private firms generally place a somewhat higher relative value on present or early returns, and a correspondingly lower relative value on future or deferred returns, "than society would" if it were to decide by ballot on the relative weight to be given to future resource yields to be realized by the children, grandchildren, and great-grandchildren of the present

---

[5] Excess of total value of yields over total cost sacrifices.

[6] In the implied calculation, future yields and costs should be discounted at a rate reflecting the social rate of preference for present or earlier over future or later resource yields.

generation of adults. If this is so, the profit-seeking enterprise essentially applies a higher rate of discount to future returns and costs in deciding upon the most profitable plan of resource exploitation than society would use in deciding on the conservation plan which would maximize social welfare over time. An optimal private conservation (to the profit-seeking firm) deviates correspondingly from optimal public conservation (to the welfare-seeking populace).

Then we may expect in general that, from a social standpoint, private enterprises will have a tendency to depart somewhat from optimal public conservation. The departure will be in the general direction of enhancing present or early yields at the expense of future or deferred yields, of making insufficient current cost outlays for the enhancement of future yields, and of adopting techniques that are suboptimal from the standpoint of ideal public conservation. This general tendency stands out, for example, in numerous episodes of the history of the exploitation of our agricultural and forest lands. On the other hand, the sources of the biggest deviations from socially good conservation are probably to be found elsewhere.

The other tendencies of private enterprise to deviate from good conservation practice are attributable not to intrinsic properties of enterprise psychology or motivation, but to certain special circumstances within which enterprise exploitation of resources may take place. As suggested in preceding chapters, two such circumstances or settings stand out as especially important. First, private enterprises in an extractive industry may operate persistently or for long intervals of time in market situations in which they are unable to earn a normal interest return on investment, and are generally "starved" for current income. In this circumstance, the struggle from year to year to maintain financial solvency, and in the case of the self-employed enterpriser-laborer to earn enough to maintain a certain standard of living, may outweigh other considerations such as the impact of present production practices and rates of extraction on future returns. Then future prospects for resource recovery and earnings therefrom may be heavily overdiscounted or neglected althogether. This may lead in turn to the expansion of current yields from the resource at the expense of larger losses of future yields. It may lead to the restriction of current cost outlays that should be made to enhance future returns, and to the employment of inferior techniques because of the lack of funds to finance the introduction of better ones. The specific difficulty in this case is, as indicated, a market situation in which firms are chronically unable to realize normal returns on investment.

Second, the private-enterprise extraction of natural resources may lead to bad or even disastrous conservation results in physical-technological settings in which a number of competing interests engage in *antagonistic* exploitation of a common resource pool. By "antagonistic exploitation" we refer to the behavior pattern which may emerge when several or many separate enterprises have a common right to extract resources from a single physical unit of resources, under conditions such that their several shares of output recoverable from the common unit are determined by the relative rapidity with which they appropriate the resource for themselves "before someone else gets it." Then each firm, in the absence of public regulation or private agreement, is motivated roughly to capture a maximum share of the common resource yield at the earliest possible time. It is correspondingly inclined to neglect or discount very heavily the effect of current techniques, cost outlays, and rates of recovery on future yields, or on the relationship of future yields to future costs. The classic example of antagonistic exploitation arises in the competitive exploitation of a single underground oil pool. The crude petroleum is sufficiently movable or "fugacious" that adjacent oil wells on the land surface can capture more or less of the underground oil in the pool, depending upon the relative rapidity with which they permit oil to flow to the surface under natural pressures, or upon how rapidly they pump it up. But there are other examples equally appropriate, including the antagonistic exploitation of a common commercial fishery by several or many fishing boats.

The adverse conservation consequences inherent in antagonistic exploitation of common resource units are clear. (1) Future yields being largely disregarded or heavily discounted, the time pattern of withdrawal of yields from the resource tends to be drastically foreshortened, resulting in early "surplus" and later "scarcity" of outputs from the resource, relative to the social optimum. (2) This distortion of the time pattern of recovery, involving very intensive exploitation or withdrawal in the early stages, often results in a substantial reduction in the total amount of resource yield which is ultimately recoverable. (3) The techniques of exploitation employed, reflecting or implementing a competitive race for current withdrawal or yield, generally involve both an excessive investment in capital equipment by competing interests and an unnecessary spoilage of the future yield potential of the resource. All of these tendencies are, for example, evident in the earlier history of the American petroleum industry.

The next question is to what extent atomistic market structures in extractive industries are responsible for those aberrations from good conservation performance that stem from chronically deficient enterprise earnings and from antagonistic exploitation. In general, it appears that atomism in an extractive industry does not *necessarily* engender poor conservation tendencies of these types, but that atomism may be and frequently is a contributing cause of these tendencies.

As we have seen above in considering chronic destructive competition, chronically deficient industry earnings will not tend to occur simply because an industry is atomistic in structure. Thus there can be many atomistic industries, including extractive industries, in which enterprise earnings records are normal and satisfactory. Then there will be no deterrent to good conservation resulting from deficient earnings. On the other hand, when atomism is combined with longevity of plant, immobility of potentially transferable resources, and historical incidents which create an initial redundancy of plant and resources attached to the industry, chronically deficient earnings tend to occur. And, if an extractive industry is involved, poor conservation performance may result. In this combination of circumstances, atomistic market structure may be an essential contributing cause of poor conservation. That is, with a concentrated market structure enterprises would probably succeed in restricting outputs and raising prices enough to maintain normal earnings, and would thus be more able and more likely to pursue good conservation policies.

Thus a fairly high degree of seller concentration in a "maladjusted" industry would probably be more conducive to good conservation than would an atomistic market structure. This is not to say, of course, that the development of oligopoly or monopoly is therefore the remedy "of choice" for poor conservation tendencies in distressed extractive industries with atomistic market structures, although it may be a remedy of sorts. The preferred remedy (which would permit elimination of conservation difficulties without inducing the noxious "side effects" of monopolistic price policy) should generally consist of various direct measures to hurry the transfer of redundant resources to other industries and the elimination of excess capacity. This would make the retention of atomistic structure consistent with good performance in conservation and other respects. It is not surprising, however, that the easy and expedient remedy of restricting competition, whether by structural revision or direct governmental interference, is the one usually chosen in practice.

Most of the basic-crop agricultural industries of this country have over considerable time periods typified the case of chronic maladjustment *cum* atomism in which deficient earnings were in part responsible for poor conservation performance. Since the middle 1930's, there have been systematic attempts to remedy these performance tendencies, though largely (at least until very recently) through the limitation of

output and restriction of competition rather than through the reloca-
tion of redundant resources.

Antagonistic exploitation of common resource pools, and its adverse
consequences for conservation, of course requires that there be several
or many separate ownership interests competing in the exploitation of a
common resource unit—under conditions such that the current output
recovered by each is significantly expansible at the expense of the
others. Atomistic exploitation of a common resource pool probably tends
to maximize the essential antagonism and to engender the worst performance tendencies. Exploitation by a concentrated oligopoly on the
common pool should result in a lessening or elimination of adverse conservation tendencies. Monopolistic exploitation *of the single pool* should
be the conservation ideal.

This is not to say, however, that monopolistic *industry* structure is
necessarily required for good conservation, or that atomistic industry
structure is necessarily linked with antagonistic exploitation of common
pools. The basic resource on which the extractive industry is based may
occur, and often does, in a large number of separate pools or units.
Then, even though each unit were exploited by a single firm, there
could still be enough different units and enough different firms to provide an atomistic industry structure with competition among a large
number of sellers. Such an industry organization would be geographically and technically feasible, for example, in the American petroleum
industry, which is based on a large number of different oil pools. Even
with only one firm on each pool, and provided that individual firms were
not permitted to operate on several or many pools at once, a relatively
atomistic crude-petroleum industry would be possible. On the other
hand, there are industry cases in which the common resource pools are
few, and in which an atomistic industry organization almost ineviatably
implies antagonistic exploitation. This appears to be true, for example,
in the case of some principal ocean fisheries. In such instances, high
seller concentration within the industry seems to be a prerequisite for
good conservation performance, unless detailed direct governmental
regulations of conservation practice are to be imposed on a larger number of firms.

Even if there are numerous resource pools, so that atomistic industry
structure is potentially consistent with monopolistic exploitation of individual pools, the actual unregulated development of atomism tends
in the cases observed to involve antagonistic exploitation of common
pools. This undesirable result again can be averted only by extensive
governmental regulation both requiring "unitized" or monopolistic development of single pools and prohibiting the exploitation of multiple

pools by a single firm. In brief, *unregulated* atomism is likely to have poor conservation results in extractive industries which present common-pool problems. This has certainly been the case in the American petroleum industry.

One way of averting these poor conservation tendencies would be to foster much higher concentration in the extractive industries in question. Another would be to subject private enterprises within an atomistic structure to rather detailed governmental regulations of their resource-using operations, while still preserving competition among them in the sale of their outputs. The superiority of the latter alternative is contingent on the ability of government economically to devise and administer effective regulations of market structure and of conservation practice and performance.

Turning to governmental regulations actually adopted to promote better conservation, we again encounter the tendency toward the promulgation of measures which do not deal adequately with the basic economic difficulty. This tendency stems from the fact that, politically, the principal proponents and designers of regulation are enterprises engaged in the afflicted industries rather than representatives of the general public interest. These vested interests ordinarily seek immediate improvement of their own earnings primarily, and better conservation only as a secondary end. Thus we find that the sorts of governmental interference sought and obtained ordinarily emphasize limitation of output and raising of price under conditions of restricted competition. They are seldom addressed to the central problems of elimination of chronic redundancy of investment in the afflicted industries, or of antagonistic exploitation of common resource pools. Although limited incidental conservation benefits may accrue from the improvement in earnings which is effected, it is rare for the conservation difficulty to be directly attacked or adequately remedied. Thus if we include in the total behavior pattern of extractive industries of atomistic structure the sorts of governmental regulation they typically solicit and obtain, we must conclude that their performance tendencies in the matter of conservation are frequently poor. This situation might be remedied, of course, by the adoption of different sorts of governmental interference.

The preceding difficulties with actual governmental policy are apparent in American agriculture and petroleum production. With agriculture, crop control and minimum price maintenance have been used to improve farmers' earnings without effectively attacking the basic redundancy of resources invested in agriculture. Improved earnings have favored better conservation practices (which have also been encouraged by governmental subsidies for this purpose), but the real basis of poor conservation has not been adequately dealt with, and the present remedies have serious offsetting disadvantages.

The principal measures adopted to deal with petroleum conservation have involved governmental output control ("prorationing") affecting the numerous oil pools being developed under conditions of antagonistic exploitation. They have the primary aim of improving the earnings of oil producers, though with the ostensible legal justification of promoting conservation. Conservation performance in petroleum production has indeed been somewhat improved by these measures, to the extent that restrictions on current output rates check some of the more extreme adverse tendencies of antagonistic exploitation. But the measures themselves do substantially nothing to eliminate antagonistic exploitation itself, or many of its attendant wastes in the form of competitive over-investment and inefficient overall technique in the exploitation of common oil pools. Antagonistic exploitation has been made comfortable from an earnings standpoint, without eliminating many of its major adverse consequences for conservation. We will have occasion to refer to the governmental policies in question again in Chapter 15.

SUPPLEMENTARY READINGS

Adams, W., *The Structure of American Industry*, 1961 (3rd ed.), Ch. 1–3.
Hoffman, A. C., *Large Scale Organization in the Food Industries*, T.N.E.C. Monograph 35, 1940, Ch. II, VII, X, XI.
Wilcox, C., *Public Policies Toward Business*, 1960 (rev. ed.), Ch. 13–14.

13

The Problem of
Public Policy Toward
Business Competition
and Monopoly

This book has so far examined the behavior, as producers and sellers, of business firms in the American economy. Viewing these firms primarily as members of various industries, we have analyzed the market structures of industries, the market conduct of sellers in them, and their resulting market performance. Attention has been focussed on (1) the market performance of enterprise and its impact on general material welfare, and (2) the relationship of market structure and conduct to market performance. A major aim has been to discover what sorts of structure and conduct are likely to lead to a socially satisfactory or "workable" market performance.

Two findings of some importance have emerged. First, a significant proportion of industries exhibit poor or unworkable performance in at least some respects, even though most industries perform satisfactorily in most regards. Second, the quality of the market performance of industries seems to be strongly associated with their market structures. Certain types of market structure—as defined in terms of seller concentration, the condition of entry, and so forth—seem likely to engender performance that is undesirable in certain ways, whereas other types of market structure do not. Therefore, though indications concerning structure-performance relationships are tentative and incomplete, a beginning has been made in distinguishing between market structures which are and are not "workably competitive."

These findings are obviously relevant to the formulation of public policies designed to improve the working of the American economy. Similarly, they assist us in evaluating existing policies, to determine if these policies are properly oriented and adequate in scope. In Chapter 14 and 15 we present a critical review of the present American policy that affects the behavior of business firms acting as producers and sellers, in particular by influencing or controlling market structure, conduct, and performance in their industries. Prior to this review, let us consider briefly the appropriate general and specific goals of this policy and the available means of attaining them.

General Goals of Public Economic Policy Affecting Business Enterprise

Most citizens will probably agree that the primary general aim of government economic policy in the United States should be to promote a good overall performance by the whole economy—one that would foster an optimal level of aggregate material welfare for the general populace. The overall performance sought should embody: (1) a high or "full" level of employment of productive resources, including labor; (2) an efficient use of employed resources in production, leading to a maximization of the value of aggregate output obtained from the employed resources; (3) reasonable stability of aggregate employment over time, or freedom from undue fluctuations in economic activity; and (4) a reasonably high rate of progressiveness, reflected in the growth of the value of output per unit of resources employed.

Given this main goal of economic policy, we must note that there is an essential restriction on the means by which it should be pursued. This restriction is that, so far as regulations affecting business firms are involved, it should be sought in the main through devices that foster and maintain impersonal market processes as the main direct regulators of enterprise activity. The policy, in other words, should with a minimum of exceptions preserve a "workable" degree and form of competition that is sufficient to induce good performance by various firms and industries, rather than imposing direct governmental regulations on the performance of business.

This restriction may be viewed as axiomatic on the supposition that we are discussing a governmental policy consistent with the maintenance of a viable capitalistic economy. If such an economy were subject to widespread direct governmental regulation, it would no longer be recognizable as capitalism; by adopting such a regulatory policy, we would actually change economic systems. Departing from the axiom, it may be argued substantively that impersonal regulation by the market is preferable to extensive bureaucratic regulation by men, and more consistent with our democratic political system. Moreover, a heavily regulated "private enterprise" system is an undesirable hybrid that will not function well and will combine the main shortcomings of both capitalism and socialism while attaining few of the virtual advantages of either.[1]

Are there any parallel goals of public policy that have equal generality and stature? So far as policy affects private business enterprise, one important parallel goal is often put forward: the prohibition of undue size on the part of business enterprises, and the preservation of a large population of relatively small firms. The usual rationale of this goal is the prevention of an undue concentration of political and social "power." Whether this goal deserves at least equal rank with that of good overall performance is a matter for argument and of opinion. We will take the position here that an *adequate* public policy toward business directed at maintaining workable competition will incidentally or automatically place sufficient limits on excessive business size and concentration that no separate or special attention to size *per se* as a politico-social problem is required. Maintenance of a degree of competition adequate for good performance *implies* maintenance of an enterprise economy which is sufficiently unconcentrated from other standpoints. As noted, this is an arguable proposition.

Specific Policy Goals
Affecting Business Enterprise

If the general aim of public policy affecting business is to promote high employment, efficiency, progress, and stability for the whole economy, what are the corollary specific goals to be sought in dealing with firms acting as producers and sellers of goods and services?

These specific goals generally involve securing a desirable market performance from the various industries of the economy. And desirable market performance is defined as embracing, for the firms involved, those sorts of adaptation to the effective demands for their outputs that best contribute to high employment, efficiency, progress, and stability

[1]For more extensive discussion of general policy goals, see Carl Kaysen and Donald F. Turner, *Antitrust Policy*, 1959, Ch. 1.

for the economy as a whole.[2] The specific market performance goals are mainly discoverable by a theoretical deduction rather than by observation. We will not explore the deductive process here, but may review some of its indications.

Let us note first, however, that these indications are incomplete. The underlying theory is not sufficiently developed to identify the sorts of specific market performance by industries which best contribute to optimal performance by the entire economy in such respects as the overall level and stability of employment. We are thus limited at best to judging the effects of specific industry performance on efficiency in resource use, on progressiveness, and on the distribution of income. Given this limitation, the specific market performance goals which can be set up appear to include principally the following:

1. *Technical Efficiency in Scale and Rate of Utilization of Plants and Firms within the Industry.* Policy should promote situations in which all, or as much as possible, of every industry output is supplied by plants and firms of optimally efficient size, and in which there is no chronic excess capacity of plant. The relationship of this goal for each industry to the overall goal of efficient use of resources for the whole economy is obvious.

2. *Absence Both of Chronic Monopolistic Excess Profits and of Chronic Net Losses.* Profits of every industry should tend in the long run toward equality with a basic interest return on investment. They should deviate from this norm only sporadically and for acceptable reasons such as rewards to innovation, windfalls, adjustment to changing demand and cost conditions, and the like. Individual-firm profits may deviate further to reflect inter-firm differences in efficiency and the varying rewards and penalties of risk-taking.

This market performance goal is related to two overall goals for the economy—*allocative efficiency* and *equitable income distribution.* If chronic excess profits and chronic net losses are both avoided by an industry, there should be an approximate long-run equality of the selling price of its output with its long-run average and long-run marginal costs of production. And if this price-cost relation is secured simultaneously in all industries, the composition of total output will be to the best advantage of consumers—which is to say that the allocation of resources

---

[2]This definition is subject to the restriction that the range of feasible adaptations is limited to those consistent with the maintenance of private enterprise production in the long run, which implies that as a group enterprises at least "break even" by receiving prices which in the long run and on the average cover their full costs of production.

among uses is the most efficient possible. If such profits and losses are not avoided in some industries, on the other hand, there will be a misallocation of resources among the production of different goods. Thus, the absence of chronic excess profits or chronic net losses is needed to secure allocative efficiency.

Furthermore, the absence of these profits and losses controls the distribution of income between profit recipients on the one hand and hired factors like labor on the other, averting possible functionless rewards as well as inequitably small returns to enterprise. The limitation of profits and losses, however, is by itself hardly sufficient to deal with the general problem of income distribution.

3. *"Adequate" Progressiveness in the Development and Innovation of Improved or New Techniques and Products.* This market performance goal for the industry has an obvious relation to the overall goal of adequate progressiveness for the whole economy. However, as we have noted in Chapter 10, we really lack an empirically applicable standard for adequate progressiveness, and in practice the policy maker will be unable to evaluate progressiveness in the usual industry. The goal in question thus has little current operational meaning for purposes of policy-making.

4. *Absence of Excessive Selling Costs.* This market performance goal is obviously corollary to the overall goal of efficient use of resources in the economy at large. Again, however, a definitive and empirically applicable distinction between desirable and excessive selling costs is not available. The goal lacks an operational meaning for policy-making except so far as we rely on *ad hoc* judgments or rules-of-thumb to identify excessive selling costs.

5. *Desirable Level and Variety of Product Qualities and Designs.* The market performance goal here, requiring a welfare-maximizing selection among alternative product characteristics and variety in the light of connected alternative costs, is linked to the overall goal of efficient use of resources. Again, an empirically applicable or operational standard is lacking in the present state of information and theory.

6. *Pursuit, in the Case of Extractive Industries, of Desirable Resource Conservation Practices and Policies.* This market performance goal, which does have a substantial operational content, is obviously a corollary of efficient overall resource utilization.

The preceding six market performance goals all represent legitimate aims of a public policy toward business. The policy should attempt to promote performance of the sorts designated in the various industries of the economy, and if possible should take remedial measures in industries where there is a serious aberration from good performance in any of these dimensions.

In practice, however, we have noted that only three of the six goals are operational. In only three cases could the governmental regulatory authority systematically distinguish good from bad performance and thus know when and where positive promotion of better performance was required. These three goals are technical efficiency in scale and utilization of plant and firm, absence of persistent monopolistic excess profits or chronic net losses, and acceptable conservation practices and policies. In the present state of knowledge, the goals of adequate progressiveness, lack of excessive selling costs, and desirable product performance are not easily implemented for purposes of practical policy. The general goal of securing good market performance for our numerous industries can thus actually be sought by relying on only a partial and incomplete set of indicators of the quality of performance. This is the unsatisfactory state of affairs which we occupy.

Given the limitations noted, the immediate problem of public policy is largely how to promote good performance by industries in the dimensions of technical and allocative efficiency and conservation. Meanwhile, the policy maker should pray that his measures do not inadvertently worsen performance in the practically unassessable dimensions of progressiveness, selling cost, and product. Under our system, policy will as a matter of practice usually proceed by remedying undesirable situations. It is thus pertinent to summarize our earlier findings regarding the principal observed aberrations from good industry performance in the strategic dimensions mentioned. The major aberrations are four in number:

1. Aberrations from ideal technical efficiency. These are reflected mainly in the existence, in many or most industries, of fringes of inefficiently small plants and firms, usually supplying an important minor fraction of industry output. They are reflected also, to a lesser extent, in chronic excess capacity in some industries, and in inefficiencies of technique in distressed industries.

2. Chronic monopolistic pricing tendencies. These are reflected in persistent monopolistic excess profits to the industry, with adverse effects on allocative efficiency and income distribution. They are encountered in some significant minor share of industries.

3. Chronic net losses to many or most enterprises in the industry, reflecting destructive competition and a chronic misallocation of resources. The occasional occurrence of this sort of aberration in atomistic industries has been noted.

4. Poor conservation performance in some extractive industries, generally industries of atomistic structure.

Remedy of these sorts of aberration would appear to constitute the main immediate goals of public policy toward enterprise producers and sellers, just as, constructively, the broader goal should be to maintain good performance in all the respects mentioned where it is already found.

Means of Implementing the Goals
of Public Policy

Given these goals, how should governmental policy proceed to attain them? As already noted, the policy cannot, consistent with the maintenance of a viable capitalism, proceed largely through extensive direct regulation of performance. It must employ more indirect means, aimed in general at securing and maintaining market situations and behavior patterns which will lead otherwise unregulated enterprises to achieve a reasonably good market performance. It should in short promote, through both negative restriction and positive measures, the attainment and maintenance of workably competitive markets.

The obvious line of approach for policy, therefore, is three-fold:

(*a*) Control of market structures, involving in a constructive vein securing and maintaining market structures which are conducive to good performance, and in a remedial vein alteration of market structures which are linked with and apparently a factor causing poor market performance.

(*b*) Control of market conduct, both constructively and remedially, largely through prohibitions on conduct which tends to lead to poor market performance.

(*c*) Direct remedial measures to reallocate resources among industries in order to hurry the attainment of competitive adjustments that the market should eventually accomplish but is unduly slow in bringing about.

And, in addition, the policy may wish to undertake:

(*d*) Possible "relief" measures to redress inequitable income positions during prolonged processes of market adjustments.

For guidance in this policy approach, we must rely heavily upon available indications of the relationships of market structure and conduct to market performance, and also (for purposes of remedial policy) upon an identification of cases of technical inefficiency, adverse profit and conservation performance, and chronic misallocations of resources.

Control of Market Structures

Control of market structures should be a major tool of policy in remedying or averting monopolistic price and profit tendencies. It should also be used to remedy poor conservation in extractive industries where this results from antagonistic exploitation of common resource pools.

There are general indications that high seller concentration, high barriers to entry, and high degrees of product differentiation are all generally conducive to monopolistic tendencies, whereas moderate or lesser concentration, lower barriers to entry, and lesser product differentiation should lead to better albeit not necessarily perfect performance. These findings imply several related things for public policy affecting monopolistic tendencies.

First, for the *remedy* of performance in markets in which chronic monopolistic price and profit tendencies are already observed, and in which such tendencies coexist with characteristics of market structure which generally might be expected to cause them, the policy should be to seek or require an alteration of market structure. This might proceed, as appropriate, (1) by requiring dissolution or dismemberment of existing dominant firms into several parts, to effect a lower degree of seller concentration; (2) by reducing entry barriers so far as this is possible; and (3) by adopting any feasible measures to induce lesser degrees of product differentiation, especially where existing high differentiation rests on intangible bases. Such structural remedies should be sought only to the extent that they do not interfere with economical production. For example, deconcentration by splitting up large firms should not proceed so far as to create plants and firms of uneconomically small scale, or firms without reasonable prospect of survival. But, within these limits, structural revision should be a primary measure against observed monopolistic performance tendencies, where these tendencies are already coupled with market structures that appear to propagate them.

Second, for the purpose of *preventing* the development of monopolistic price and profit tendencies, the policy should be to scrutinize pending or developing structural changes which threaten to lead toward unduly high concentration, high entry barriers, or extreme product differentiation, and to discourage or prohibit those changes which are not justified on the basis of increased efficiency or on comparable grounds. Such measures should presumably not inhibit the growth of firms by virtue of superior efficiency or other real advantages over competitors. But they might be directed against structural revisions through mergers which increase either seller concentration or vertical integration, so far as these revisions threaten to effect high seller concentration or high entry barriers without compensating increases in efficiency.[3]

Third, the policy could go further and attack potentially undesirable structural situations (for example, very high seller concentration with an industry) *as a precautionary measure*, even though adverse monopolistic performance tendencies were not currently in evidence. This constructive approach, emphasizing the promotion of structural situations in which workably competitive performance is more or less "compelled" by structure (rather than, for example, occurring capriciously or through the largesse of dominant firms) has certain virtual advantages of logical consistency. But it places an especially heavy burden on the underlying generalizations, both *a priori* and empirical, concerning the association of market structure to performance. This avenue for policy development may thus be considered marginal, or open for further consideration.

As to adverse conservation tendencies in extractive industries, of the sort that result from antagonistic exploitation of common resource pools, the following is apparent. For the purposes both of remedying existing poor conservation and of preventing its development, the policy should develop constructive requirements for the monopolistic exploitation (by a single firm or management) of every single resource pool on which antagonistic exploitation does or would have adverse conservation consequences. (A generally inferior alternative to this would be very detailed regulation of the operations of antagonistic resource extractors.) It would probably be desirable for the policy also to include restrictions against monopolistic exploitation of multiple resource pools or deposits by a single firm in the same industry, in the interests of restricting the degree of seller concentration in the extractive industry in question.

The preceding considers the possible use of regulation of market structures to remedy or avert undesirable market performance in the dimensions of monopolistic price-profit patterns and of poor conservation. What of the possible impacts of regulation or revision of market structure on technical efficiency, or on the elimination of inefficiency? Let us consider in turn technical inefficiencies due to the persistence of a fringe of inefficiently small plants and firms, to chronic excess capacity of plant, and to subnormal enterprise earnings resulting from a chronic misallocation of resources.

The fringe of inefficient small plants and firms which seems to be found in nearly all industries sampled has no ascertainable strong relationship to any principal dimension of market structure.[4] In conse-

---

[3]Cf. Kaysen and Turner, *op. cit.*, Chs. 3, 4.

[4]There are some very tentative indications that inefficient fringes might tend to be larger with high degrees of product differentiation, but they are not conclusive.

quence, no simple general measures for structural revision—such as promoting higher or lower seller concentration, or higher or lower barriers to entry—would seem to be indicated as a means of eliminating this rather pervasive sort of inefficiency. All that could be suggested would be specific measures, tailored to the individual industry, to force or encourage the consolidation of the inefficiently small plants and firms to form larger and more efficient units. This policy would increase "low-level" concentration, decreasing the total number of plants and firms. But it would be generally consistent with a policy of not increasing, or even decreasing through deconcentration actions, the proportion of the market controlled by the few largest firms in the industry. A serious limitation on this policy, of course, is that it verges into a detailed industry-by-industry regulation of structure, rather than confining itself to the imposition of broad general rules concerning structure.

As to chronic excess plant capacity *simpliciter* (without chronic deficiency of earnings) this again is not demonstrably enough related to market structure to support positive proposals for structural remedies. To be sure, the conjunction of rather easy conditions of entry with a fairly high degree of seller concentration appears as a possible explanation, and the indicated structural remedy might be deconcentration through dismemberment of the existing largest firms. Otherwise, only direct controls of capacity would seem feasible.

For inefficiencies connected with chronic low earnings in "distressed" industries (those afflicted with true destructive competition), the appropriate remedies do not generally appear to be structural. Unduly small scales of plant or firm or unduly easy entry do not appear to be the basic difficulties. The fundamental trouble is immobility of resources from the afflicted industry, and the preferable remedy is to be sought elsewhere, in measures to promote resource movement. Promotion of increased concentration seems generally to be an inferior instrument of policy.

Control of Market Conduct

Control of market conduct offers a possible indirect method of remedying or averting monopolistic tendencies, but there are fairly severe limitations on its efficacy in securing desirable performance. A general limitation is that control of conduct must proceed almost entirely by prohibitions of certain types or patterns of conduct—particularly the prohibition of collusion among competitors and of predatory tactics. The alternative of active governmental supervision and the dictation of price-output policies of sellers would be tantamount to direct control of market performance, and generally inconsistent with a public policy oriented toward maintaining a viable capitalism.

Given this limitation, other difficulties are encountered with respect to each of the two main phases of conduct that are relevant to the performance goals previously outlined. With respect to conduct in determining price and output, the primary difficulty was anticipated in Chapter 9. What is empirically observable and thus useful for guiding public policy affecting such conduct is largely confined to the patterns of interseller coordination in determining prices and outputs. And the relationship of such conduct patterns to performance is sufficiently uncertain or indeterminate that it is difficult to know what sorts of conduct to permit and what sorts to prohibit in the interests of a market performance that will be reasonably free of monopolistic tendencies. A proper general attitude toward the several varieties of collusive activity, for example, is hard to establish and defend, in the light of prevailing uncertainty as to whether or not various particular patterns of collusive or quasi-collusive conduct will actually tend to have deleterious effects on performance.

Furthermore, there is a serious question about how much or in what proportion of cases the prohibition of specific sorts of conduct, such as collusion, will really affect performance, even though poor performance is initially ascertained. This is because unless the underlying market structure is altered, superficial conduct may often be readily altered to comply with specific prohibitions without really altering the effective aims of price-output determination or the performance outcome. In concentrated oligopolistic markets, for example, simple interdependence of sellers without visible collusive activity may replace elaborate and visible collusive activity without much if any effect on performance tendencies. Finally, with respect to simple interdependence patterns which are suspected of being responsible for monopolistic price-output tendencies, remedies in the form of prohibitions on patterns of conduct are not readily available, since there is nothing tangible to prohibit or enjoin. The government can hardly enforce a ruling upon sellers that they should not be interdependent or should not act as if they were, when the market structure remains such as to make interdependence inevitable.

Conduct prohibitions directed at collusion and related patterns of interseller coordination are therefore likely to be uncertain and inadequate tools for maintaining or restoring a workable competition. Structural remedies and requirements seem to be the basic and reliable tools, and if these remedies are adequately applied it may be argued that conduct remedies are at best only supplementary and perhaps often unnecessary. Nevertheless, some case may be made for a general prohibition of most visible or express forms of collusive activity, on the general ground that such a blanket policy will probably have salutary effects in some proportion of cases, and do little harm, if no good, in the other cases. Prohibition of collusive behavior, however, cannot properly be viewed as a sufficient public policy toward monopolistic tendencies, or as the keystone of a general policy with this orientation.

Prohibition of predatory and exclusionary tactics as a phase of market conduct can be a useful indirect device for discouraging the emergence of market structures with unduly high seller concentration or unduly high entry barriers. Such prohibitions, however, have a limited scope as devices for controlling market structures. At any beginning point in policy there will be numerous undesirable market structures already in being that are maintained without the current use of predation or exclusion, any earlier predatory and exclusionary tactics being well buried in past history. It is also quite possible for unduly high concentration or entry barriers to develop in many industries, currently, without the use of predation or exclusion. Prohibition of exclusionary and predatory tactics (as defined in some way) can thus be viewed as no more than a supplementary measure in a general policy of controlling market structures. A further practical problem, to be discussed in Chapter 14 when we consider actual regulatory policies of this sort, involves the general difficulty in developing an adequate legal definition of predatory and exclusionary tactics, or an adequate and defensible line between permissible and prohibited tactics which disadvantage actual or potential competitors.

There is one further area in which control of market conduct can serve as a useful supplement to other policy designed to deal with basic market performance problems. This is in the prohibition of unethical market practices, or "unfair" methods of competition, such as are found in misrepresentation, commercial bribery, defamation of a competitor's reputation, and the like. Such prohibitions, carefully restricted in content so as not to limit legitimate and beneficial forms of competition, may make a useful contribution to the overall policy of promoting a workable competition.

Direct Measures to Reallocate Resources

Neither controls of market structures nor limitations on market conduct appear as especially appropriate measures to deal with the problem of chronically deficient industry earnings stemming from a chronic redundancy of plant, labor, and other resource capacity devoted to an industry. Since these difficulties are ordinarily encountered in industries of relatively atomistic structure, propagation of greatly increased seller concentration (if feasible) might provide relief to deficient earnings by creating a good setting for monopolistic pricing policies, but such a policy would impose on society the disadvantages of monopoly pricing without necessarily eradicating the basic misallocation of resources. (The same criticism applies to governmental price and output control to accomplish the ends of private monopoly.) Control of market conduct, as for example by prohibitions of "destructive" price cutting, again does not go to the seat of the trouble, and in addition is likely to be difficult to enforce.

In instances of chronic distress, therefore, there is much to be said for an alternative policy of limited direct governmental interference to force or induce a reallocation of transferable resources and an elimination of redundant plant capacity at a more rapid rate than the market will induce them. Such a policy would induce a structural revision in the allocation of resources among industries of such character that, once it was made, unrestricted competition in the previously distressed (and still atomistic) industries would lead to acceptable market performance. The possible specific measures with this general aim which might be pursued are so numerous we will not attempt to review them here. As examples, however, we may mention government expenditure to subsidize geographical movement of redundant labor from distressed areas or to finance re-education of labor for alternative occupations, government subsidy to convert redundant physical resources to alternative uses (as in the "land bank" program to convert surplus agricultural land to forests or game preserves), and government purchase and removal from the market of redundant obsolete or obsolescent plant capacity. Measures of this type may accelerate the "recovery" of distressed industries by more quickly bringing them to the point where they will perform effectively under conditions of unrestricted competition. The resulting improvement of enterprise earning positions, moreover, should tend to remedy poor conservation tendencies attributable to subnormal earnings.

A question remains concerning appropriate governmental measures to relieve inequitable income positions of enterprise and labor during possibly prolonged periods of readjustment in distressed industries. As we have already argued in Chapter 12, general government programs for output restriction and price maintenance tend to be undersirable because, although they may protect earnings, they do not encourage and may even retard the needed reallocation of redundant resources. So far as there is a general public desire to provide income relief, it would appear that such relief should be provided in the form of direct income subsidies not connected with mandatory output restriction and price raising. Furthermore, the subsidies should be administered in such a way as to provide an incentive for the movement of redundant resources to other industries, rather than supporting the incomes of such resources in the lines in which they are presently employed. We will return to these issues in our review of actual policies toward distressed industries in Chapter 15.

Unresolved Problems and Exceptional Cases

The general directions for public policy set forth above are obviously incomplete and subject to various actual or potential deficiencies, which we may now consider briefly.

First, there is a certain lack of "coverage" of the suggested policy, if it is viewed as one addressed to all of the major deficiencies of market performance that are actually or potentially present in industries of the contemporary economy. Because of shortcomings in the theoretical definition of ideal performance, in the analysis of its relation to market structure, and in practical ability to measure performance, we are substantially without positive suggestions concerning measures which would promote better performance in the dimensions of progressiveness, selling costs, and product design and variety. In the present state of knowledge, we necessarily confine our attention to measures affecting technical and allocative efficiency and conservation. With respect to the propagation of greater technical efficiency and of better conservation, moreover, our analysis suggests that rather direct and positive governmental interferences with market structures (as distinguished from more passive negative prohibitions) may be required to secure more desirable performance in the usual problem cases, and that this may create rather severe political and administrative problems. Allocative inefficiency, as revealed by monopolistic price and profit tendencies, is evidently the aspect of performance which is most readily handled by public policy.

Second, there is the general problem of possibly undesirable "side effects" of some measures that have been recommended for the elimination of monopolistic price-profit tendencies. To remedy or avert such tendencies in performance, we have suggested certain primary controls on market structures, and certain supplementary controls on market conduct. The question is whether the suggested controls would inadvertently have adverse effects on progressiveness, selling costs, and product performance. Because of numerous deficiencies in theoretical and empirical knowledge concerning the relation of market structure and conduct to performance in these respects, we cannot answer this question in any definite manner. What can be said is that the general indications of *a priori* analysis and empirical observation are that the measures proposed to control monopolistic tendencies (including certain restriction on the degree of seller concentration and on the height of entry barriers) would probably not have adverse effects on performance in the dimensions of progressiveness, product, and selling cost. But this is a speculation rather than a solid finding.

Third, we must consider "exceptional cases" of actually or potentially poor performance for which our proposed remedies would be inappropriate, and for which extensive direct governmental control of performance (or of conduct and performance) is required. We have attempted to restrict this area of exceptions to the "competitive policy" to the maximum extent consistent with economic logic and observed reality, as in rejecting "distressed industry" situations as appropriate cases for extensive direct regulation. An inescapable minimum of exceptions remains, however, in the form of industries in which seller concentration is (or, for purposes of efficiency, should be) so high as to lead almost inevitably to monopolistic price-profit tendencies, and in which any meaningful reduction of concentration below the present or the efficient level would entail serious technical inefficiencies of plants or firms of unduly small scale. In instances of this sort, a workably competitive market structure is inconsistent with technical efficiency, and an alternative mode of regulation must be sought.

The alternative of direct regulation of prices, outputs, and investments has been applied widely to "public utility" industries supplying electric power, gas, telephone service, public transportation, and the like—all cases in which, actually or allegedly, either monopoly or very high seller concentration is requisite for efficient service. Fortunately for the feasibility of the policy of preserving and promoting workable competition, the occurrence of "dilemma" cases of extreme scale economies is relatively rare outside the sphere of the conventional public utilities. But any general public policy should anticipate the existence, in the manufacturing or other sectors, of a small proportion of cases in which maintenance of a workably competitive market structure is inconsistent with the realization of scale economies. In these cases, direct governmental control of market performance within a highly concentrated or monopolized industry structure is the obvious alternative means of securing good performance. The viability of a general competitive policy clearly depends upon the limitation of such exceptional cases to a small proportion of the total.

One further "exceptional" case involves the grant of a temporary monopoly over novel products, processes, or productive devices to their inventors (or to firms which purchase the rights of the inventors) under the patent laws. Such patent monopolies, which run officially for 17 years under the law of this country, may be justified as incentives to the invention and innovation of new products and techniques of production. Public policy permits the existence of such temporary patent monopolies, and of their effects on market structure and performance, subject to a careful scrutiny of the appropriate scope and content of the patent grants. The determination of what is appropriate with regard to patent monopolies is a very complicated and special matter, however, and one which we cannot explore here. Some reference will be made to the issues involved in the following chapter.

Standards of Workable Regulation

We have so far considered in general terms the appropriate goals of a public policy toward business enterprises in their capacity as producers and sellers, and the preferred means through which the policy may attain these goals. With respect to the means, however, we have not considered in any detail the precise content of a desirable regulatory policy as it might be embodied in legislation, administration, adjudication, and enforcement. And it is not our purpose here to spell out the details of the desired policy. It may, however, be useful to indicate in broad terms certain principles of law and administration that should be observed in implementing a general public policy of controlling market structure and market conduct (and of reallocating redundant resources) to the end of securing and maintaining workable competition.

A first necessity is that the requirements of the law, as stated in the legislation establishing regulation, should be reasonably simple and easily understood both by firms subject to regulation and by interested members of the general public other than expert economists. Such simplicity and understandability are essential to securing needed public support for the regulatory policy, and to encouraging a reasonable degree of voluntary compliance with the law by those subject to its regulations.

Second, the application of the law, in the sense of discovery, identification, and treatment of firms or industries that are in violation of its provision, should be predictable, impartial, and so far as possible relatively automatic—as distinct from being unpredictable, discriminatory, capricious, or heavily influenced by administrative discretion. Fulfillment of this condition in turn generally requires that the basic statute should express, so far as possible, clear and definite legislative standards of what is required of enterprises and industries, of what situations and lines of behavior violate the law and are proper subjects for regulatory interference, and of what measures should be undertaken by the administrative agency to remedy noncompliance with the law. Such extensive legislative specification should reduce to a feasible minimum the scope of administrative discretion in identifying violations of the law and in selecting remedies. A similar and desirable restriction on the scope of judicial discretion in interpretation of the law should also result.

Finally, both the purpose of the regulatory policy and the specific regulatory devices employed should be such as to receive general public approbation, and thus engender a climate of public political opinion conducive to securing widespread voluntary compliance and widespread support of necessary enforcement measures. In the United States, it is fortunate that the general purpose of a pro-competition, anti-monopoly policy already has widespread public support. Specific regulatory measures, however, must be chosen in the light of public opinion concerning their fairness, their impartiality, and their necessity as means for accomplishing broad regulatory purposes. Clear and detailed legislative provision of standards of violations and definitions of remedies may assist along this line.

Applying these political principles along with the economic standards for regulation previously developed, we might at this point propose a detailed regulatory program. Such an endeavor would be clearly premature, however, until the policy proponent had considered the general character and content of existing American regulatory policy concerned with business monopoly and competition. Initially, it is important *per se* that this policy be understood, and be evaluated in terms of the general standards set forth above, to the end of determining its strengths and weaknesses as a means of securing workable competition in our economy. Study of the existing policy, moreover, will necessarily bring to attention, and subject to critical scrutiny on the basis of experience, many of the alternative devices that a revised and improved regulatory policy might employ. Our past regulatory experience contains many indispensable indications concerning the efficacy of alternative means or methods of public regulation of business. Finally, positive proposals for new public policy may most logically and conveniently take the form of suggestions for revision and amendment of existing regulation, rather than that of a complete new policy conjured fully armed from an historical vacuum. This is at any rate true so far as existing policy has salient strengths along with its weaknesses, and is susceptible to progressive development into a generally adequate policy toward monopoly and competition.

In the succeeding two chapters, therefore, we will undertake a compressed review and analysis of existing American regulatory policy toward monopoly and competition, dealing in Chapter 14 with the federal antitrust policy directed toward preserving competition and preventing monopoly, and in Chapter 15 with various federal and state regulatory policies directed toward restraining competition. In Chapter 16, finally, we will consider to what extent the goals outlined in this chapter might be more fully implemented by development and revision of existing regulatory policy.

SUPPLEMENTARY READINGS

Clark, J. M., "Toward a Concept of Workable Competition," *American Economic Review*, June 1940.

Mason, E. S., "Market Power and Business Conduct," *American Economic Review* (Proceedings), May 1956.

Brewster, Jr., K., "Enforceable Competition," *American Economic Review*, May 1956.

Kaysen, Carl, and Donald F. Turner, *Antitrust Policy*, 1959, Ch. 1.

14

Existing Regulatory Policies: Preservation of Competition and Prevention of Monopoly

The American public policy toward monopoly and competition by business firms is composed in general of two main parts. The first of these, expressed principally in three main pieces of federal legislation, is the policy of maintaining competition by prohibiting private restrictions of it, and by preventing the development of monopoly. Historically and in terms of the dominant emphasis still prevailing, this may be viewed as our original and basic policy affecting enterprise monopoly and competition. The second part, expressed in the legislation of individual states as well as in various federal laws, is the policy of restricting or preventing competition in some "special" industries in which unregulated competition is allegedly unworkable, and in most instances of imposing some direct governmental regulation as a substitute. Policy measures in this category are often referred to as exceptions to our general competitive policy, yet such "exceptions" have perhaps become numerous enough to constitute a second main facet of the general policy. They are potentially reconcilable with the basic policy, on the grounds that they apply only to areas of destructive competition and of natural monopoly. But the extent of their true compatibility with the basic policy can be determined only be detailed examination of individual regulatory measures.

We will deal in this chapter with the basic general policy of maintaining competition, and in the succeeding chapter with the complementary policy of restricting competition in exceptional cases.

The basic competitive policy rests on three main federal "antitrust" laws: the Sherman Act, passed in 1890; the Clayton Act, passed in 1914 and significantly amended in 1936 and 1950; and the Federal Trade Commission Act, also passed in 1914 and importantly amended in 1937. The strategic provisions of these laws will be discussed below; their substantive content may be described briefly as follows. The Sherman Act generally declares (1) agreements in restraint of competition and (2) monopolization of any market to be illegal. The Clayton Act names as illegal three important sorts of business policy or conduct which might be conducive to monopolization or the restraint of competition. The Federal Trade Commission Act proscribes unfair methods of competition and (since 1937) unfair or deceptive acts or practices in commerce.

The Sherman Act is primarily enforceable by the Attorney General of the United States, by initiating lawsuits against alleged violators in the federal courts. Such litigations may be either "criminal," aimed at establishing guilt and assessing fines or other penalties, or "civil," aimed at securing court decrees requiring cessation of illegal practices or remedial changes in illegal situations. The substantive prohibitions of the F.T.C. act against unfair competition are enforceable by the Federal Trade Commission, a quasi-administrative and quasi-judicial body empowered to make investigations, hold hearings, and issue orders requiring violators of the law to "cease and desist" from their illegal practices. (Orders of the Commission are subject to appeal to the federal courts.) The substantive prohibitions of the Clayton Act are generally enforceable either by the Attorney General through direct court litigation, or by the Federal Trade Commission through its investigative and hearing procedures.

In discussing the competitive policy that is based on this legislation, our purpose here is only to summarize and evaluate the substantive content of the policy as of the present time. Although all of the laws in question have long, fascinating, and extremely intricate administrative and judicial histories—from which the contemporary interpretation and application of these laws evolved—we have no time here for a detailed chronological treatment of the evolving administration and judicial interpretation of any of them. (For that, the student is referred to any of several excellent works, some of which are listed under "Supplementary Readings" at the end of this chapter.) We will also forego a detailed analysis of individual laws, and will instead treat the substantive contemporary content of existing legislation with respect to each of the four main sorts of regulation which it imposes, as follows:

(*a*) The prohibition of restraint of competition through collusive agreements among competitors.

(*b*) The prevention of monopolization or monopoly.

(*c*) The prohibition of other business conduct that may tend to restrict competition or create a monopoly.

(*d*) The prohibition of unfair or unethical competitive practices.

With respect to each of these phases of the competitive policy, we will follow a uniform sequence of treatment, considering in turn: (1) the applicable laws and their relevant provisions; (2) the interpretation of these laws by the courts; (3) the legal remedies that have been employed and that are available, under the legislation in question, to terminate or forestall violations of the law; (4) the economic effects of the enforcement of the applicable laws to date; and (5) the fundamental characteristics, strengths, and weaknesses of existing law and policy.

Prohibition of Collusive Agreements among Competitors

The simplest and most widely applied regulation of business under the federal antitrust laws is the prohibition of collusive agreements among competitors which restrain or eliminate competition among them. We refer for the moment strictly to so-called horizontal agreements among sellers (or among buyers) who are selling or buying the same sort of good or service in competition with each other. An example might be an agreement to fix prices among several sellers of cigarettes. So-called vertical agreements, as embodied for example in contracts between sellers and buyers, are discussed in the third main section of this chapter. Also, we refer here only to so-called loose-knit agreements—in general agreements between or among firms which are and remain separately and independently owned and controlled. These are distinguished from "agreements" which are accomplished by merging or consolidating the agreeing firms into a single ownership unit subject to a single unified control. Such mergers or consolidations are considered in the next two main sections of the chapter. The prohibition in question is thus against collusion by competitors to restrain competition among themselves.

This prohibition is embodied mainly in Section 1 of the Sherman Act, which states that "*every contract, combination . . . or conspiracy, in restraint of trade or commerce among the several States, or with for-*

eign nations, is hereby declared to be illegal." This is an apparent blanket prohibition of the sort of horizontal collusive agreement just described, so far as interstate commerce is involved or affected. (It applies as well potentially to a considerable variety of other types of agreement or combination, to be discussed later.) The Sherman Act prohibition is reinforced by Section 5 of the Federal Trade Commission Act in its statement that, *"unfair methods of competition are hereby declared unlawful."* This rather vague provision has application to horizontal collusion, in the light of the judicial determination that *one* sort of unfair method of competition is indeed an agreement in restraint of competition. (The other main sort of "unfair method" is unfair or unethical competitive practice, to be considered toward the end of this chapter.) The Federal Trade Commission, in enforicng Section 5, thus more or less shares with the Attorney General the latter's jurisdiction over collusive agreements as established in Section 1 of the Sherman Act. The essential prohibitions of Section 5 of the F.T.C. Act in this regard are not visibly either greater or less than those of the Sherman Act, and in practice procedures against collusive agreements have been left largely, though not entirely, to the Department of Justice.

The prohibition in question applies generally to firms or individuals operating in any industry or market where interstate commerce is affected, and at the time of the passage of the Sherman Act in 1890 there were no exceptions to this rule. In legislation subsequent to 1890, however, horizontal collusive agreements in certain specified industries or sectors of the economy have been exempted from the prohibitions of the act. Labor unions are not to constitute illegal combinations or conspiracies in restraint of trade among their members, nor shall the antitrust laws prohibit them from lawfully pursuing their legitimate objective, such as bargaining collectively or striking for higher wages and shorter hours. (And unilateral actions by any single union, even where these actions have considerable indirect effects on competition in commodities, have been very broadly exempted in judicial rulings in various antitrust cases.) Agricultural cooperatives, and agricultural marketing agreements approved by Secretary of Agriculture under an act permitting and encouraging such agreements, are likewise exempt devices of collusion in restraint of competition. So-called export associations of domestic firms, formed to facilitate joint or collusive action in selling to foreign markets, are also exampted. Railroads are exempt if their agreements are approved by the federal regulatory agency having jurisdiction over them, and a similar exemption is in practice afforded to other directly regulated industries. The principal areas of exemption within the domestic economy are thus labor, agriculture, and the directly regulated industries, with most of the rest of the enterprise economy, excepting strictly intrastate markets, being generally subject to the prohibitions of collusion.

Interpretation of the Law

The content and meaning of the legal prohibition against horizontal collusion to restrain competition have necessarily emerged from judicial decisions, initially of federal district courts but ultimately of the Supreme Court, in a long series of cases or lawsuits, primarily those brought by the Attorney General to enforce the Sherman Act. About 1880 cases were instituted by the Department of Justice to enforce the antitrust laws between 1890 and the end of 1965, and a very large proportion of these were directed against horizontal collusive agreements. Crucial interpretive rulings by the Court, of course, appear only in a very small proportion of these cases. In addition, there have been a few significant judicial rulings on Federal Trade Commission actions affecting collusion, emerging as Commission orders under Section 5 were appealed to the federal courts.

The first step in the procedure leading to judicial decisions interpreting the Sherman Act is generally that the Attorney General brings a suit against firms or individuals alleging violation of the Sherman Act (and asking that the prescribed fines be assessed, or that the court decree remedies to terminate the violation, or both). Second the defendents generally deny guilt under the law;[1] and finally, the courts, after examination of the evidence, interpret the law to determine if a violation has been committed. With respect to allegations of horizontal collusion, a crucial question facing the courts concerns what varieties of allegedly collusive activity are and are not prohibited by the general proscription of "every contract, combination, or conspiracy, in restraint of trade." In the case of Federal Trade Commission actions, the situation is similar, except that the courts are asked to rule upon appeal by the defendants[2] of a Commission order that they cease and desist from allegedly illegal collusive methods of competition. In the following paragraphs we will attempt to describe briefly, and without reference to chronology of cases or to the evolution of court opinion, the prevailing judicial interpretation of the prohibitions affecting collusion among competitors.

The doctrine initially stated and subsequently reinforced and elabo-

---

[1] Less frequently, defendants may plead *nolo contendere* (no contest) to the charge, not admitting guilt but declining to defend themselves, and exposing themselves to such penalties and remedies as the court may decree.

[2] Or, occasionally, appeal by the Commission to enforce an order.

rated by the courts in applying Section 1 of the Sherman Act to loose-knit agreements of the horizontal type is in its broad outlines relatively simple and unambiguous. All such agreements which have the evident purpose and effect of restraining competition among the agreeing parties are *per se* illegal. This prohibition applies clearly to all of the principal types of agreement affecting price-output determination, including agreements to fix or maintain prices, to limit outputs or productive capacity, to divide and share markets, and so forth. (The prohibitions seem logically applicable also to collusion to restrain nonprice competition in terms of selling cost or product, but there is little or no precedent for this sort of application of the law in the case histories.)

In applying the prohibition, moreover, the courts have not been disposed, at least nominally or semantically, to distinguish between reasonable and unreasonable agreements to restrain competition, or thus to excuse reasonable restraining agreements. If a loose-knit agreement to restrain competition is found to exist, it is viewed as *per se* unreasonable, and thence illegal. In particular, an agreement to restrain competition will be found illegal in spite of the reasonableness of the performance results which ensue, of the praiseworthy intent of the agreeing parties, or of the elimination of the alleged evils of unrestrained competition. And such an agreement will be illegal in spite of the alleged inability of the agreeing parties fully to suppress competition in their market. If they have acted together and in agreement with the evident purpose and effect of limiting competition among themselves, they have violated the law.

It may be noted that, under this doctrine, the criterion of illegality is squarely one of collusive market *conduct*, and not in any direct sense one of undesirable market performance potentially stemming from such conduct. Evidence concerning market performance is relevant in the eyes of the court, but only as one of numerous bases for drawing inferences concerning the character of market conduct. (Thus conspicious price uniformity among competitors together with the raising of price to unusually high levels are not illegal *per se*, but such performance tendencies may provide a partial basis, along with other evidence concerning the acts or practices of the defendants, for inferring that they have been acting in agreement.) The preceding doctrine refers directly to interpretations of the Sherman Act, but the judicial construction of Section 5 of the F.T.C. Act as applied to collusion is substantially consistent.

In its detailed application, of course, the doctrine affecting collusion among competitors is not quite as simple as the preceding brief statement might suggest. There are certain complexities and possible ambiguities in the doctrine, and these arise in large part from the intrinsic difficulties frequently encountered by the courts in defining and identifying illegal "agreements." To understand these difficulties, we must recognize that it is relatively rare that a charge and finding of illegal agreement can be based upon the discovery and introduction as evidence of a written contract in which the parties agree, for example, to fix price or restrict output, or upon an open admission by the defendants that they did agree, orally or in writing, to restrain competition. The plain prohibitions of the Sherman Act obviously discourage written agreements or other similarly overt collusion, or the voluntary admission of either. Practical collusion is in effect forced underground, to the level of the *sub rosa* gentleman's understanding, or of the adoption of numerous indirect devices for fostering a tacitly collusive limitation of competition.

In consequence, the illegal agreement in the courts is typically something which is inferred from an assemblage of evidence bearing on some or all of a great many matters, including the associative activity of the defendants, the character and content of communications they have exchanged, the nature of agreements or cooperative arrangements they may have entered into which do not necessarily in themselves constitute agreements to restrain competition, the character and effect of numerous business "acts, practices, and policies" they have pursued in common or in parallel fashion, and the character of their market performance during the existence of the alleged agreement. And in the typical process of drawing inferences from evidence, the courts naturally have some latitude for the exercise of judicial discretion, and for introducing, as if through the back door, some distinction between reasonable and unreasonable collusive restraints of trade. In effect, although the courts find any (inferred) agreement to restrict competition to be unreasonable *per se* and illegal, they may refuse to infer the existence of such an agreement from the fact that defendants impose certain limited restraints on competition. And such limited restraints (being insufficient to warrant the inference of agreement to limit competition) are expressly or implicitly declared to be "reasonable" and not illegal.

This fine line of distinction between legal and illegal market conduct need not be drawn in a great many cases in which there is convincing direct and indirect evidence of the formation, observance, and private enforcement of an agreement bearing directly on the determination of prices, outputs, market shares, and the like. The main issue in such cases concerns the body of evidence required to support the inference of such an agreement; this is a matter better left, for our purposes, to students of the law.

The fine line has become relevant, however, in numerous "trade association" cases, in which the allegation of illegal collusion is typically based on the facts that the defendants are all members of an industry trade association, and that through the trade association they establish certain cooperative arrangements or agreements which may have the direct or indirect effect of inducing a restriction of competition. The most prominent cooperative arrangements in the case histories of antitrust involve agreements by the members of trade associations to file regularly with the associations detailed information on their listed prices, volumes of sales, customers, and so forth, such information being available (usually in digested form concealing firm identities) to all members of the associations, and possibly also to customers and other "outsiders."

In such cases, the courts have developed a somewhat wavering line between legal and illegal trade association activities. Collection and dissemination of trade information from members is not illegal *per se*, which is to say that these activities appear legal so long as the information is made available to customers and other nonmembers of the association, and so long as there is no evidence that the arrangement to collect and distribute information is part of a broader agreement directly to restrain competition. If, on the other hand, there is evidence that the collected information serves as a pivot in a scheme to control prices or price changes, to limit outputs, and so forth—as it might be, for example, if the participating firms agreed not to sell at prices below those they had listed with the trade association—then the scheme as a whole is illegal, as is the use of collection of trade data with the recognized illegal purpose and effect. A comparable distinction is drawn with respect to other cooperative activities of the members of trade associations.

In distinguishing between legal and illegal cooperative activities, the courts generally place great weight on evidences of overt activities of the association or its members, from which the existence of an actual agreement to restrain competition (as distinct, for example, from a simple arrangement to collect and disseminate information) may be inferred. Lacking evidence of such overt actions or practices, the courts would appear generally unwilling to infer an illegal express or tacit conspiracy from the mere existence of the trade association and of the superficially innocuous cooperative activities conducted under its aegis. This distinction, rooted in the judicial view that actual violation of the law involves intent or purpose to restrain competition as well as the effect of restraint, is interesting from the standpoint of economic analysis. Such analysis would point out that the mere systematic exchange of trade information by competitors in oligopolistic markets should tend to increase the strength of the oligopolistic interdependence of the sellers, discourage competition through the normal channels of more or less clandestine price reductions, and facilitate the pursuit of a more concerted and "more monopolistic" price-output policy by the group of sellers. In the present state of interpretation of the law, in effect, a certain range of activities indirectly conducive to an increased restraint of competition appear to be legal.

A related aspect of interpretation concerning horizontal agreements, and one relevant to market conduct in a broad range of oligopolistic markets, concerns the inferences of illegal action which the courts are prepared to draw from "mere parallelism" in the pricing or other market policies of competing firms. Suppose that all sellers in an industry charge identical factory prices, and change prices identically and concurrently by following a "price leader." Or suppose that all of them pursue an identical "basing-point" formula for determining delivered prices at the many locations where deliveries are made, with the result that the quoted delivered prices of all sellers at any given delivery point will be identical. Is this evidence of parallelism in pricing policies, in and of itself and without support of further evidence of overt collusive activity, sufficient to support the inference than an illegal agreement (express or tacit) exists? If it is not, what evidence *in addition* to that of parallelism of policy is required to support such an inference?

The questions just stated are simpler than any answers that can be given, since the "fine line" which the courts have drawn here between legality and illegality is both tenuous and wavering. At one extreme, the traditional view of the courts has been that *mere* parallelism of market policy, as represented, for example, simply in a well observed price-leadership system not buttressed by anything more in the way of visible collusive activities, is not sufficient evidence of the existence of an illegal agreement. At the other extreme, it is clearly the view of the courts that the finding of an illegal agreement does not require discovery of a formal agreement among the firms which are acting in parallel, or of their meeting together with the implied purpose of arriving at an agreement. All that is required is "some character or manner of communication, sufficient to enable them to reach a definite, mutual understanding—of unlawful purpose." And the inference that such communication took place may be drawn from an assortment of scattered scraps of evidence of overt activities apparently directed toward securing a limitation of competition. Given a certain minimum pattern of such overt acts (as embodied, for example, in individual communications, application of suasion or pressure to price cutters, commonly pursued programs of purchasing the surplus outputs of sellers who might otherwise cut prices, and so forth), illegal agreement to restrain trade may be inferred, and the inference may be importantly bulwarked by evidence of concurrent parallelism among defendants in pricing and other market policies. This is to say that parallelism *plus* some quantum of other evidences of the existence of a conspiracy to restrain competition will suffice to sustain a finding of illegal restraint of trade.

The prevailing uncertainty concerning this interpretation of Section 1 of the Sherman Act and Section 5 of the F.T.C. Act results from a possibly evolving change in the judicial doctrine, in the direction of making parallelism alone a ground for inferring the existence of an illegal conspiracy, if this parallelism is conspicuous and detailed and extended to many matters. In several relatively recent cases, the courts have held, expressly or in effect, that an illegal agreement may be legitimately inferred from "a concert of action . . . all parties working together understandingly," even though no overt activities of inferentially collusive purpose are discovered. In the actual cases involved, however, the concerted actions or parallelisms were especially conspicuous, sustained, and elaborate, extending to numerous matters other than the setting of a uniform single selling price, so that the courts perhaps could not believe that "all that much" parallelism would be likely to result in the absence of an agreement. It does not appear, at present, that the courts would view "mere" parallelism of a simple sort, such as might involve only simple selling-price uniformity among competitors, as a basis for inferring an illegal concert of action. But it is impossible to say just how detailed and how complex parallel action needs to be before such an inference will be drawn.

The doctrine just described obviously leaves those tacitly collusive or highly interdependent price-output policies which are common to the more highly concentrated oligopolistic markets in a somewhat ambivalent position under the existing law. Some such policies, with extreme characteristics, may be found illegal if the Attorney General brings action against them. Mere parallelism in pricing, of a simple type and unaccompanied by various "supplementary collusive uniformities" of a visible sort, is evidently not illegal *per se*. In the range between these extremes, the legality of the tacitly collusive or highly interdependent market conduct of oligopolists is uncertain.

In the light of prevailing judicial interpretations, it is clear that although existing legal prohibitions against horizontal agreements in restraint of competition have a fairly wide application in the control of collusive market conduct, they are applicable only uncertainly and partially to the tacitly collusive and interdependent conduct patterns that are common to oligopolistic markets of relatively high concentration. We will return to the implications of this line of interpretation as we consider the economic effects of antitrust enforcement in a succeeding section.

Remedies under the Law for Illegal Collusion

The next question concerns the powers held by the federal government to restrain firms or individuals which are found to have been parties to illegal collusive agreements from continuing their illegal activities, and generally to discourage violations of the relevant law. The available deterrents to and remedies for illegal collusion are of two main sorts: the assessment of fines, and the issuance of injunctive decrees or orders requiring the offending parties to terminate specified illegal activities.

Under Section 1 of the Sherman Act, violations of the law are punishable by fines not exceeding $50,000[3] (assessable against each guilty firm or individual that is party to an illegal agreement), or by a year's imprisonment, or by both. In practice since the early days of application of the Act, only fines have been employed as penalties except in one or two cases. The Attorney General may bring so-called criminal actions in the courts, alleging violation of the law and requesting that the courts assess penalties; upon determination that a violation has occurred, the courts will in their discretion assess fines upon the offending parties. These fines, or the prospect of incurring them because of illegal activity, serve as some deterrent to engaging in illegal collusion. But the deterrent effect of fines of the size provided upon large firms whose extra profits from illegal collusion might be ten or a hundred times the size of any probable fines is doubtful. A great deal would depend here upon the size of the firms concerned, and upon how frequently the Department of Justice sees fit to sue persistent violators.

A second avenue open to the Department of Justice is to bring so-called civil actions in the courts, again alleging violations but in this case requesting the courts to issue orders enjoining the defendants from continuing their illegal activities. In practice, it is not uncommon for both criminal and civil actions to be brought more or less simultaneously against the same set of defendants for the same offense—the criminal action to assess penalties, and the civil action to secure injunctive relief against continued violations. In any event, the major regulatory power of the Department of Justice under the Sherman Act stems from its ability to secure injunctive orders or decrees in civil

---

[3]That is, $50,000 for each separate violation or "count."

actions, rather than from the threat of the comparatively nominal fines which may be assessed. Such injunctive orders are effective indefinitely against the defendants in the immediate case. They require specified alterations in the pattern of market conduct which has been found illegal, and violations of these orders are subject to potentially considerable penalties for contempt of the courts. The real "teeth" in the Sherman Act are thus found in the power of the Attorney General to seek and obtain remedial orders in civil actions.

The Federal Trade Commission, in the enforcement of Section 5 of the governing act, is not empowered initially to assess fines for violations. After holding hearings, it may simply issue injunctive "cease and desist" orders against parties found in violation if the law, these orders being comparable to court orders resulting from civil actions under the Sherman Act. Penalties for violation of Section 5 of the F.T.C. Act can emerge only after the issuance of civil cease and desist orders. They are subject to contempt penalties after being confirmed by the courts, or to penalties of $5,000 for subsequent violation if appeal to the courts has not been brought within 60 days. Again, the primary regulatory power inheres in the injunctive order to cease violations of the law, although the path toward a final court order is perhaps a bit more torturous than it is under the Sherman Act.

The essential content of either court of Commission orders which propound remedies for illegal collusive agreements is more or less prescribed by the legal view of the essential offense involved—that it is the creation of restraining agreements, or otherwise the pursuit of acts, practices, and policies having the purpose and effect of restraining competition. If this is the essential offense, the corresponding remedy is simply to enjoin the offending parties from continuing their agreements or from further pursuing specified acts, practices, or policies which have resulted in an illegal restraint of competition. Conversely, the "obvious" remedy is not, in the eyes of the courts, an enforced structural change in the market of the sort that might make collusion impossible or ineffective. For a "conduct" offense we get a "conduct" remedy, in the form generally of an order to terminate an agreement or to desist from specified acts and practices which are viewed as having been essential to the illegal restraint of competition.

The general efficacy of this sort of remedial procedure as a device for securing improved market performance in industries where collusive activity has been found is open to serious question. This is in part because only limited negative restraints on conduct are imposed, in lieu of any positive or constructive remedy. But it is more largely because of doubts concerning the effectiveness (in improving performance) of the control of market conduct, if the market structure or situation is to be left relatively unchanged. We will return to this matter shortly in the following section.

Economic Effects of Enforcement of the Law against Collusive Agreements

What have been the actual effects upon business conduct and performance in the United States of the legal prohibitions of collusive agreements among competitors, and what, at the maximum, could their potential effects be?

The actual effects to date depend not only on the content and judicial interpretation of the relevant legislation, but also upon the character and the intensity of the enforcement of the law by the responsible administrative agencies. Intensity of enforcement, in fact, seems particularly important. Collusion to restrain competition is an obvious device whereby enterprises may improve their profits. In an economy of profit-seeking enterprises, there is a more or less natural tendency toward collusive agreements. And collusion, though illegal, is not in our society generally viewed as morally opprobrious. Therefore, collusive arrangements will tend to proliferate and multiply throughout the business economy unless they are discouraged by an enforcement of the relevant legal prohibitions which is sufficiently intensive that potential participants in the illegal arrangements run a substantial risk of being detected, penalized, and subjected to remedial orders. A past head of Antitrust Division of the Department of Justice, Thurman Arnold, likened the anticollusion provisions of the antitrust laws to traffic laws dealing with speeding or with observing boulevard-stop signs. In both cases, violations will tend to occur almost automatically in great numbers unless there is such active enforcement that the potential violator of the law always has a real fear of detection and arrest. It is thus relevant, in evaluating the effectiveness of the antitrust-law prohibitions in question, to look briefly at the record of past enforcement.

The intensity of past enforcement of the prohibitions against collusive agreements is at least roughly suggested by the record of the number of actions or law suits filed by the Department of Justice for enforcement of the Sherman Act and the Clayton Act. After the first fifteen years of the Sherman Act (1890 to 1905), during which less than two cases per year were brought to trial, we find that from 1906 through 1910 an average of about 10 cases per year were brought to trial, and that from 1911 through 1930 the average number of actions per year was about 14. After the period of the great depression of the earlier 1930's, during which there was an even less intensive enforcement of the antitrust laws, a revived and intensified program of enforcement was instituted, and from 1937 to date there has been an average of roughly 50 cases per year brought by the Justice Department to enforce the Sherman and Clayton Acts. Of these actions, a very high proportion were for enforcement of the Sherman Act, and a major share of the Sherman Act cases in turn involved the application of Section 1 to collusive agreements among competitors. A fair guess might be that such anticollusion actions averaged at least 8 to 10 per year from 1911 through 1930, and at least 30 to 35 per year from 1937 to date, although even these numbers are somewhat "inflated" because in numerous cases two actions, one civil and one criminal, have been brought for the same offense. To these may be added a relatively insignificant number of comparable actions under Section 5 of the F.T.C. Act.

From the preceding it appears that enforcement of the prohibitions in question was very "unintensive" until 1937, and has been somewhat more but probably not adequately intensive since then, if we judge adequate intensity in terms of the ratio of the number of actions to the probable number of violations. In this connection, moreover, we cannot argue that if there had been more violations there would have been more actions. The Department of Justice is effectively limited as to the number of actions it *can* bring by the budget appropriations it receives from Congress, and the small number of cases brought reflects budgetary limitations rather than any paucity in the number of violations. The number of actions brought even in the period of somewhat intensified enforcement since 1937 has not been large enough to reach more than a small fraction of the continually recurring probable violations of the law. Nor has it provided a strong and active deterrent to the formation of collusive agreements in restraint of competition. This seems true in spite of the fact that the Department of Justice, especially in the last thirty years (being aided by the progressive clarification of judicial interpretation of the relevant law), has secured conviction or remedies in a proponderent proportion of actions brought.

The character of the remedial and deterrent effects of anticollusion actions is also influenced by the fact that these actions have not been spread over the various sectors and industries of the economy in proportion to the probable incidence of collusion to restrain competition, but have been concentrated disproportionately in a few sectors or industrial groupings. For example, about half of all the 1350 actions brought by the Department of Justice to enforce the antitrust laws between 1890 and the middle of 1957 applied to firms in three industrial groupings: food processing and distribution, building materials production and distribution, and the service trades (including transportation). By contrast, numerous important industries in several other groupings including basic metals production, chemicals, electrical goods and machinery, industrial machinery, and transportation machinery and equipment, were touched only very lightly by antitrust actions of any sort. Since this was a long-run and fairly persistent pattern, the implications concerning the substantial lack of deterrent effects by antitrust enforcement (*vis a vis* collusion) in the lightly covered sectors or industry groupings seem fairly obvious.

This apparent unevenness in the application of the laws affecting collusive activity among various sectors and industries of the economy is presumably in part attributable to the disposition of successive Attorney Generals to concentrate their limited funds on actions involving consumer-good "necessities" (like food) or other goods for which there is a very numerous and geographically widespread group of buyers (like building materials). Such a bias in application may be politically expedient so far as public and Congressional support for the enforcement program is being sought. It also may result from the facts that, under administrative procedures followed, actions typically originate from complaints filed by customers or others who have been injured by alleged restraints of trade, and that a high proportion of complaints are received relative to industrial groupings which deal with many small customers.

But this is hardly the total explanation. The observed bias is in at least considerable part attributable to the prevailing judicial (and derived administrative) views concerning those sorts of collaborative or parallel activities of competitors which do and do not violate the law. As suggested above, the obvious offenses in the realm of collusion involve composites of various overt activities of allegedly offending firms, from which the existence of agreements to restrain competition may be inferred. Such overt activities are essential to the effective restriction of competition mainly in industries of moderate to relatively low seller concentration, where the force of oligopolistic interdependence alone is insufficient to induce all or most competitors to restrict price competition. Thus these more obvious violations of the law tend to occur mainly in the sphere of relatively unconcentrated industries, because in these cases they are really needed if competition is to be restrained. Correspondingly, the attention of the relevant antitrust enforcement policy is drawn toward this sphere.

Conversely, proportionate attention is not given to the effective restraint of competition in the more highly concentrated oligopolistic industries. In this sphere, with oligopolistic interdependence generally strong, restraint of competition is very frequently secured without elabo-

rate and overt supplementary devices. Nothing more may meet the eye
than a parallelism of action in pricing and other matters, and the most
that can ordinarily be inferred is the existence of some sort of tacit collusion among the firms involved. Given the traditional view of the courts
that "mere parallelism" of market policies is insufficient to sustain a
charge of illegal collusion—or even under a tentatively revised view
that sustained, detailed, and conspicuous parallelism may serve as a
basis for inferring such collusion—the enforcement agencies are generally loath to wager any considerable part of their limited funds on
actions primarily involving parallel action in concentrated oligopolistic
markets. This is partly because the illegality of various patterns of
parallel action is at least questionable, and partly because of the prolonged and expensive nature of litigations necessary to elicit a decision
on the alleged illegality.

In consequence, interdependent parallel action or tacit collusion in
the more concentrated oligopolistic markets has not received sustained
attention in the enforcement of the antitrust laws, while attention has
been devoted mainly to more overt forms of collusion, mostly in relatively unconcentrated markets. And market conduct in concentrated
oligopolies, and its consequences in the form of monopolistic pricing
tendencies, have not been effectively modified or deterred by applications of the law to date.

Somewhat greater deterrent effects upon express or overt collusive
activities, largely in the less concentrated industries, may be credited to
past enforcement policies, but even here the enforcement usually has not
been intensive enough to come close to eliminating express collusion
within the enterprise economy. In general, we must conclude that the
control of collusive market conduct in general, both express and tacit,
has been at best only partially effective, and that the enforcement of
Section 1 of the Sherman Act and Section 5 of the F.T.C. Act has not
even distantly approached the possible goal of securing substantially
competitive conduct within a very great many industries in the American economy.

On the other hand, it would be wrong to conclude that the enforcement of the legal prohibitions against horizontal collusion has accomplished nothing. The major positive accomplishment of American antitrust law, as written and enforced, is that it has thoroughly discouraged
"cartelization" in American industries.

The cartel, commonly found in the countries of western Europe, is
ordinarily a binding contractual agreement among competing firms
to fix prices, limit outputs, share markets, and even redivide and share

profits. Cartels are agreements in restraint of trade *par excellence*, and under legal systems which permit or encourage their formation, they have flourished. The potential scope of the cartel is such as really to introduce a basic structural change into the market affected, in the sense that the participating firms contractually surrender a part of the control over their operations to a super-firm agency, which may at the extreme direct their combined operations more or less according to the principles of a single-firm monopoly. Thoroughly effective suppression of business competition, potentially culminating in the operation of all or most major industries according to monopolistic principles, can be a result (and has resulted) in countries where cartels are permitted or encouraged.

In the United States, agreements in restraint of trade were found unenforceable in the courts, under the common law, even before the passage of the Sherman Act. Since that act was passed, anything resembling a formal cartel has been recognizable as a blatant and flagrant violation of federal law. As a consequence, full-fledged cartelization has never developed in American industry. Thus this type of structural evolution toward increased concentration and centralization of the control of industries has been averted, and American industry has retained a distinctly more competitive structure than its western European counterparts. A considerable proportion of our industries are indeed oligopolistic, but they are not oligopolies under the control of centralized cartel organizations.

This is not to say that collusive tendencies have been entirely or even largely suppressed. But collusion has been effectively driven underground, to the level of the *sub rosa* gentleman's understanding or of the tacit coordination of policies of interdependent firms, and even here it is subject to attack under the law. The result is that practical collusion in the American scene is generally quite incomplete and imperfect, and subject to general weakening and disruption by the independent actions of member firms in the various industries involved. In the net, monopolistic tendencies are much more checked and weakened by countervailing competitive tendencies than they would be under a system of legal cartels, and, in this sense, we have a much more competitive economy than we otherwise would. This seems on balance true even though the prohibition of cartels has probably engendered the development of somewhat higher seller concentration, largely through mergers, as an alternative device for restricting competition. The moderately or highly concentrated oligopolistic industry is still a good deal more competitive than a cartelized industry of similar or lesser concentration. This broad contribution of American antitrust policy is important and should not be discounted, even though it has not resulted in any thoroughgoing suppression of collusive activities of one sort or another.

Fundamental Limitations of the Policy of Prohibiting Collusive Agreements

Granting the importance of the antitrust laws in averting the development of cartelization, we return to an earlier observation. Partly because of insufficiently intensive enforcement and partly because of judicial interpretations which have made it difficult to attack tacit collusion as evidenced by simple parallel action, the legal prohibitions against collusive agreements among competitors have been only partially effective in deterring collusive market conduct. Let us now consider the potential future efficacy of the enforcement of a law against collusive agreements. In particular, is it true that a much more intensive enforcement policy, together with a revision of the law or its interpretation so as definitely to proscribe tacit collusion or parallel action, would make the prohibition of collusive agreements a major instrument for securing more effective competition?

The answer apparently is negative, and this because of fundamental limitations of the type of regulation involved and of the remedies available under the law. The focus of the antitrust law here is directly on market conduct, specifically in the form of a prohibition of collusive conduct. The only obvious remedy for disregard of this prohibition, aside from penalties that are unlikely to be made large enough to provide serious deterrents, is the issuance of injunctive orders or decrees requiring termination of the specific objectionable acts, practices, or policies. And it is by no means evident that even a very intensive application of orders restricting market conduct will, within the market structures in which objectionable conduct occurs, suffice to secure desirable market performance.

The first difficulty is that of really deterring, by any conceivable succession of injunctive orders, the pursuance of essentially collusive conduct and the attainment of essentially monopolistic performance in industries where the market structure is conducive to joint action aimed at restraining competition. As the aphorism goes, there is more than one way of skinning a cat, and as soon as one specific set of collusive practices is found illegal and enjoined, another set may be invented (not nominally violating the first injunction) to accomplish the original purpose of restraining competition. Or, to continue on the aphoristic level, if "love will find a way," so may collusion, in spite of the issuance of numerous injunctive orders. This line of argument would suggest that even a greatly intensified program of enforcing provisions against collusive agreements would not obviously result in a major revision of market performance in our industries, so long as their market structures remained unchanged. In this respect, the prohibition of collusion might be likened to the prohibition of the sale and use of alcoholic beverages, which generally made "drinking" more secretive, possibly more expensive, and more ingeniously devised, but did not stop it.

To the preceding argument, the usual reply of genuine enthusiasts for a primary policy of attacking collusive agreements is that a sufficiently intensive enforcement policy—involving not only many more antitrust actions per year but also a persistent "followup" or surveillance of industries already placed under injunctive decrees—would ultimately do the job of enforcing active competition. Carried to a modest extreme, however, this proposal is perilously consistent with an informal remark of one official proponent of such a policy that "the main effect of an antitrust action (on industry performance) is probably during the period of the trial." It might imply that the anticollusion policy would work in the main by "scaring" prices down through an unending series of numerous antitrust actions and of active investigatory followups of recently concluded actions. In other words, a continual policing action of market conduct of extremely large scale, involving at all times a significant fraction of all industries in the economy, is the alternative offered in counter-suggestion to the objections previously stated. Such a policy would not be impossible, and it is conceivable that it would have noticeable and widespread effects on market performance. It does not seem either politically feasible or economically advisable, however, especially in view of the very high administrative cost that would be involved, and of the existence of a clearly superior alternative policy—securing revisions of market structures to the point where collusive endeavors would be either impossible or ineffective in securing a monopolistic market performance. The latter sort of remedy is simpler, more basic, and in the long run much less expensive.

Thus a clear case cannot be made for an antitrust policy involving mainly a super-intensification of actions against collusive activities of competitors. It is possible that a somewhat more intensive enforcement along selected lines would bring good returns. In particular, there is a category of relatively unconcentrated industries in which competition is effectively suppressed only by rather overt, detailed, and express collusive arrangements of the sort that are easily attacked under the existing law. In these, an intensified enforcement might have substantial ultimate effects in improving market performance, because the avoidance of specific legal prohibitions through alternative devices may not be very easy. For all the rest of industries, however, including many of moderate to high concentration, intensified anticollusion actions do not appear to embody the policy of choice for securing better market performance. An enforcement sufficiently intensive effectively to discourage outright agreements may suffice.

The mention of essential enforcement difficulties in oligopolies of moderate to high concentration reminds us of the second general difficulty in using restraints on collusive conduct as a major means of securing good market performance. In such oligopolies, overt and express collusive activities are relatively uncommon, or at any rate generally unessential to securing a considerable restriction of competition. In consequence, firms in these industries will—either initially or after revising their activities so as to avoid charges of express collusive activities—at the most be engaged in a tacit collusion, as evidenced in a distinct parallelism in pricing and other policies. We have already noted that the culpability of such tacitly collusive parallelism under the existing laws is uncertain, and that this important phase of collusive conduct is not effectively touched under enforcement of the law to date. But suppose that either the legislation or the judicial interpretation of it were definitely changed so that illegal conspiracy to restrain trade would be clearly inferred from a conspicuous parallelism in pricing, or in other policies of competing firms in oligopolistic industries. Would enforcement of the ban on collusion then become effective in improving performance in the more concentrated oligopolistic industries?

It does not appear that it would, and for two reasons. First, the nature and content of effective remedial orders or decrees in such cases is difficult to conceive. If firms have entered into express agreement to fix prices, or have engaged in systematic overt activities having the evident purpose to restrain competition among them, it is nominally easy enough to enjoin them from continuing the agreement or the overt actions in question. But if they have visibly done nothing more than to act in parallel and concurrent fashion in fixing and changing prices, or in other respects, what injunctive remedy is available? Should the court decree that they should act in an "unparallel" fashion, or act against their own best interests? In brief, in parallel-action cases there is really "nothing to enjoin," within the realm of economic common sense, except possible supplementary collusive uniformities. Thus there is no obvious legal remedy that fits the definition of the offense. Actual control of conduct would really mean detailed direct regulation, and this is inconsistent with the spirit of the whole antitrust approach. The difficulty is obviously inherent in the nature of oligopolistic interdependence, and in the clear possibility that tacitly collusive conduct patterns may emerge without the assistance of any overt collusive activities.

A second reason that the anticollusion ban is hard to apply to tacit collusion in oligopoly is the possibility or probability that potential violators of the law would, once the legal prohibition against conspicuous parallelism were established, deliberately undertake limited evasive action in order to create a record in which full parallelism was not ostensibly maintained at all times. Thus a group of firms in an oligopoly, acting effectively in a tacitly collusive fashion, might be well advised (as they undoubtedly would be by competent legal counsel) to "muddy the trial" by passing the price leadership role from one to another, by engaging in sporadic limited price-cutting tactics, by "rippling" prices a bit rather than holding them constant, and so forth. Such dramatic behavior on the part of tacitly collusive oligopolists, if skilfully conceived, promises generally to be effective in avoiding antitrust actions based on parallel conduct, while at the same time preserving an effective tacit collusion on price-output policies.

For both of these reasons, and possibly for others, it appears that the policy of attacking collusive agreements among competitors will generally be rather ineffective in dealing with monopolistic conduct and performance tendencies in oligopolistic markets. Though it will accomplish something and should be actively pursued along certain avenues, it will not in general be efficacious as a means of securing better market performance in many industries where monopolistic tendencies tend to recur. The obvious alternative is the application of structural remedies, aimed at securing market structures in which competitive forces are sufficiently strong to bring about reasonably good market performance, whatever the superficial aspect of market conduct may be. This suggests that not only a different remedy, but also a different definition of the crucial or primary offense against the antitrust laws, is needed.

Prevention of Monopolization or Monopoly

The second general type of regulation of business established by the federal antitrust laws involves the prevention of monopolization and, perhaps, of the existence or perpetuation of monopoly. This regulation, or complex of regulations, is by no means simple.

The basic complication arises from the varying meanings of monopolization and monopoly, particularly under the existing interpretations of the law. *Monopolization*, which is the thing expressly forbidden in the relevant legislation, is the creation and maintenance (deliberate or conscious in character) of a predominant control of a market by one firm or by several acting in concert, such creation and maintenance involving the elimination, exclusion, or suppressive control of rivals. Monopolization is thus in a primary sense an aspect of market conduct, referring basically to actions undertaken to secure and maintain a monopolistic market position. *Monopoly*, a concept familiar in economic analysis but nowhere expressly forbidden by law, refers instead to the simple existence of dominant market control by one firm, or by a few acting in concert, and not to acts which have been responsible for creating and maintaining such control. Monopoly is thus in essence a structural concept, referring to a market situation rather than, for example, to the predatory or exclusionary conduct that may have created and sustained the situation. (Monopoly in a third possible sense, that of a market performance pattern theoretically attributable to monopolistic structural situations, has a meaning in economic analysis but no significant standing in the interpretation of existing law.) The strategic question raised concerns the present meaning of illegal monopolization and the extent to which, or sense in which, monopoly as well as monopolization is now prohibited or deterred by the law.

A second complication arises from the variety of complementary legislation which has the general orientation of deterring either monopolization or monopoly. The basic prohibition of monopolization is expressed in Section 2 of the Sherman Act. But, in effect, Section 1 of that act, referring to agreements in restraint of trade, is also concurrently applicable in monopolization cases, especially so far as restraining agreements may have an exclusionary purpose and effect.

Moreover, there are three substantive sections of the Clayton Act (Sections 2, 3, and 7) which bear directly upon specified activities that may have the purpose or effect of fostering the development of monopolistic market situations. Understanding of the regulations in question will be facilitated if we deal separately in the present main section of this chapter with the prevention of monopolization or monopoly by the Sherman Act, and in the following main section with Clayton Act prohibitions of acts, practices, and policies which may tend to create monopoly or lessen competition.

Section 2 of the Sherman Act states that *"every person who shall monopolize, or attempt to monopolize, or combine or conspire . . . to monopolize any part of the trade or commerce among the several states, or with foreign nations, shall be deemed guilty of a misdeameanor . . . ."* Subject to the judicial interpretation of "monopolization," this prohibition is enforceable by the Attorney General either through criminal actions seeking to assess fines or through civil actions seeking remedial court orders.

So far as monopolization means exclusion of competitors—and this is a primary meaning of the term at law—certain methods of monopolizing are also effectively prohibited by Section 1 of the Sherman Act through its ban on *"every contract, combination, or conspiracy in restraint of trade."* Two general varieties of agreements (other than horizontal agreements among competitors, already discussed) may restrain trade by effecting the weakening, elimination, or exclusion of competitors of some or all of the agreeing parties. The first of these involves vertical agreements, such as those between sellers and buyers, which may be used to exclude competing sellers from equal access to buyers and thus to needed markets, or competing buyers from equal access to sellers and thus to necessary supplies or materials for production. The second involves horizontal agreements or conspiracies among several firms in the same industry to undertake actions or pursue policies *in concert* which have the aim of eliminating or excluding competing firms. If such collusive restraints of trade (implemented by agreements or conspiracy among two or more parties) have the purpose and effect of monopolizing a market, then the monopolization in question is subject to simultaneous attack under both Section 1 and Section 2 of the Sherman Act, although there may be violations of Section 2 which do not embody simultaneous violations of Section 1.

So far as monopolization involves also predominant occupancy of the market by the offending party or parties (that is, "monopoly"), Section 1 again becomes relevant if the case is one of "joint monopoly" by several firms acting together, rather than one of predominant occupancy by a single firm. For if joint monopoly in the sense of market occupancy is to be shown, there must be implicitly involved the Section 1 offense of a horizontal agreement among the joint monopolists to restrain competition among themselves. Here, the Section 1 offense is a crucial element in establishing a Section 2 offense. Finally, Section 1 is potentially applicable, concurrently with Section 2, to "combinations" in the form of mergers of competing firms to establish dominant single-firm occupancy, on the ground that such combinations accomplish a complete restraint of competition among the parties to the merger. As we will note below, however, the courts have in merger cases for the most part not actually construed or applied the Section 1 prohibitions in this last fashion, centering attention instead on other offenses against Section 1, and on the violation of Section 2.

The nominal exemptions to the prohibitions of monopolization in the Sherman Act are principally those of the so-called regulated monopolies in the public utility and transportation field, in which entry is licensed under franchise granted by public authority and in which market structure, as well as market conduct and performance, is subject to direct regulation by state or federal commissions. Otherwise, the law is in general formally applicable to all sectors and industries of the private enterprise economy.

Monopolization or Monopoly under the Sherman Act—Possible Interpretations

What is it that is really illegal under the Sherman Act prohibitions of "monopolization" in Section 2, as buttressed by the broad prohibition of collusive restraints of trade in Section 1 of the law? Or, aside from its prohibition of horizontal loose-knit agreements to restrain competition among sellers in the same industry, already discussed, what does the act as a whole permit and what does it forbid in the way of market structure, conduct, and performance? We may best develop answers to these questions by first outlining briefly the principal alternative meanings or interpretations of the broad legal limitations on monopolization. In this endeavor, we will not try to include all logically conceivable meanings (for example, we will not consider monopolization as monopolistic performance *per se*, since the courts never have), but will confine ourselves to interpretations which the courts have at least seriously considered.

Under the broadest or most severe of the probable construction of the law, illegal monopolization would be found in "monopoly" in the structural sense—that is, in the predominant occupancy of a market either by a single firm or by several firms acting in concert. Such occupancy or control would require that a very high proportion of all industry sales be made either by one monopolist or by several oligopolists acting collusively and in concert to exploit a joint monopoly. Under this interpretation of the law, illegal monopoly would be primarily a situational or structural concept. The types of market conduct through which the illegal situation was secured and maintained would not be especially relevant to the finding of illegality. In particular, the perpetration of offenses against Section 1 of the Sherman Act in the form of collusive restraints having exclusionary purpose and effect would not be essential to the finding that a given structural situation was illegal. Offenses against Section 1 would be essential only in cases of joint monopolization by several firms, where horizontal collusion to restrain competition among the several firms involved would presumably need to be present. Otherwise the offense would rest squarely on Section 2.

Even under such an interpretation, of course, there could be diverse shades of meaning, of which we may note two. The first is that a specified degree of market occupancy is *per se* (or in and of itself) illegal; this would make the criterion of illegality structural in a strict sense. The second is that a given degree of market occupancy is illegal *be-*

cause it carries with it the inherent or inferred power to exclude competitors by discouraging entry or limiting the growth of established rivals, even though this power is only latent and is not exercised in any overt sense. This would still have the criterion of illegality nominally structural in nature, but would subtly shift the essence of the offense to inherent, implied, or latent market conduct of an exclusionary sort. The relevance of this distinction will appear as we consider alternative interpretations of the law affecting monopolization.

Whatever the nuances of meaning in a possible "occupancy" doctrine of illegal monopoly, however, the actual content of the doctrine would essentially depend upon the character of practical judgments by the courts concerning two interrelated matters: the scope of the market which is allegedly monopolized; and the proportion of control of the market (individual or joint) which is sufficient to constitute an illegally monopolistic occupancy. With respect to the first issue, for example, will the market which is allegedly dominated by one firm or a few acting in concert be broadly defined as including all motion picture exhibition or all transparent wrapping materials, or will it be narrowly defined as including only "first-run" motion picture exhibition or all transparent wrapping materials having the essential physical properties of cellophane? With respect to the second issue, and given the definition of the market allegedly monopolized, how high a fraction of that market may be controlled by a firm or by a few acting in concert before illegal monopolization, in the sense of predominant occupancy, is found? Should the minimal fraction be one-half, three-quarters, 90 per cent, or what? In effect, the courts would be faced in applying a strict occupancy doctrine with the task of making judgments in the application of economic analysis. And, to the considerable extent that these judgments are potentially flexible, the actual content of a strict occupancy doctrine of illegal monopoly would be correspondingly flexible.

Under a second and less severe probable construction of the law against monopolization, predominant market occupancy alone would not suffice as an offense. Such occupancy, whether by one firm or by several acting in concert, would be an essential part of the offense. (And again, in the determination of predominant occupancy, judgments concerning the scope of the market and the critical minimum percentage of control necessary to offend would be involved.) But, in addition, the offense would have to involve, on the part of the monopolizing firm or firms, the commission or pursuit in the course of doing business of various acts, practices, and policies which had the effect, and the inferred purpose, of securing and maintaining the predominant market position in question and thus of excluding competitors.

On the other hand, under this second doctrine, the offending acts, practices, and policies would not need to involve direct predatory attacks on actual or potential competitors, overt actions of specifically exclusionary character, or Section 1 offenses involving collusive agreements aimed at or having the effect of excluding competitors. Rather, the simple and noncollusive pursuit of "normal and prudent" business practices or policies which had the effect and inferred purpose of securing or perpetuating a predominant market position (without there being any direct attacks on others of exclusionary purpose) would suffice as illegal. Such "normal and prudent" practices might include, for example, that of a predominant firm in an extractive-and-processing industry buying up necessary resource deposits in advance of current needs, in such a pattern that potential competitors would have difficulty in securing resources needed for entry; or that of an integrated firm or firms declining to sell goods or services to (or buy them from) nonintegrated competitors on favorable terms, thus denying needed supplies or needed markets to such competitors; or that of a predominant firm or firms reducing their selling prices to match the lower prices of small competitors whenever such lower prices have been resulting in a significantly expanding market share for the small competitors. But whatever the precise nature of such acts, practices, and policies of exclusionary effect and purpose, their commission or pursuit would have to be established in order to sustain a finding of illegal monopolization.

On the surface it may appear that this doctrine, if judged in terms of the practical effects of its application, would not be very different from the "mere occupancy" doctrine previously discussed. That is, in almost every case of single-firm or joint predominant occupancy that might be tried, a related line of "normal and prudent" market conduct aimed at securing and maintaining such occupancy will undoubtedly be present, so that the same potential violators should be found guilty under either doctrine. In fact, however, the shift from the first to second doctrine makes a good deal of difference for practical purposes.

First, the offense against the law now becomes primarily one of market conduct rather than market structure, albeit conduct which has been successful in securing an offensive structure. Second, as a result, the process of litigation to enforce the law thereby becomes vastly more difficult, expensive, and uncertain, as the attention of the Attorney General, the defendants, and the courts is necessarily centered on mountains of conflicting evidence concerning the myriad details of market practices and policies. It is not unusual for five or more years to be consumed in the preparation and presentation in trial court of the government's and defendant's cases in a single action involving monopolization, and to this may be added further years consumed in appeals to higher courts. With limited funds available for enforcing the law, one of the incidental consequences is that the Department of Justice can "afford" to bring and really pursue only a very few monopolization actions, and many fewer than would probably be desirable. Finally, the definition of the primary offense as one of conduct rather than one of structure has in most cases undoubtedly predisposed the courts, when remedies for violations are sought, to apply "conduct remedies" (such as injunctions against speci- fied lines of conduct) rather than "structural remedies" (such as dis- memberment of dominant firms to secure lower concentration). So long as this tendency, inherent in the doctrine in question, is apparent, the actual impact of the law on monopoly as a structural or situational con- dition is likely to be slight.

The third probable doctrine concerning monopolization is like the second in that it requires essentially exclusionary conduct in addition to predominant occupancy as evidence of violation of the law, but dif- ferent in that the required exclusionary conduct must involve express and overt acts of predation and exclusion, rather than simply "normal and prudent" practices. Under this doctrine, monopolization would be in a primary sense overt predation and exclusion. Structure would be involved so far as predominant occupancy was needed as evidence of *successful* exclusion, but predominant occupancy as such would not be offensive. As to predation and exclusion, the most obviously offensive practices or policies would involve violations of Section 1 of the Sher- man Act through agreements or conspiracies having exclusionary pur- pose and effect. But some unilaterally pursued practices of obviously predatory intent, such, for example, as local price warring directed toward the destruction of small competitors, would also offend.

The implication of this most restrictive interpretation of the Sherman Act prohibition of monopolization is that the enforcement of the act would result primarily in a limitation of overt exclusionary and preda- tory tactics. The impact on market structures would be slight so long as the courts found a nominal freedom to compete for actual or poten- tial competitors of the dominant firm or firms, although, failing to find this, the courts could impose structural remedies as well as conduct remedies.

These three varient interpretations of the Sherman Act provisions affecting monopolization embody the major alternatives which the courts in the past have considered, or, under the existing law, are likely to consider in the predictable future. Other points of doctrine are also involved, of course, but it will be easiest to mention them as we turn to a review of court interpretations of the relevant law.

Monopolization or Monopoly under the Sherman Act—Actual Interpretations

The actual interpretation of the Sherman Act with respect to its prohibitions of monopolization has not been completely uniform over time. For a long time after the general coverage of the act was established by the courts (from 1905 until 1945) the prevailing doctrine with respect to illegal monopolization was roughly that designated as the third alternative just above. That is, such monopolization involved overt or express exclusion and predation, with special but not exclusive emphasis on those practices of exclusionary or predatory purpose and effect which would violate Section 1 of the Sherman Act. If such practices were found to be consistently and recently pursued, and if their success was evidenced in predominant market occupancy (generally by a single firm, in the actual cases tried), illegal monopolization might be found, and might be punished by fairly severe remedies.

On the other side of the coin, there was, under this doctrine, a great deal in the way of possible or probable "monopoly" which was not illegal. "Mere occupancy," in the sense of predominant control even by a single firm, was not illegal, as is indicated by the oft-repeated judicial phrase to the effect that "size alone is no offense." This doctrine was in fact not directly pushed to the test of 90 or 100 per cent market control by a single firm, but it clearly applied to cases in which a single firm controlled a substantial majority of the market in question. The illegality of predominant market occupancy (not in the period in question directly tested with respect to several oligopolists acting in concert), hinged on the showing that it had been brought about and was currently being maintained by overt or express predatory or exclusionary practices, including those involving collusive agreements. Conversely, the showing that, in a case of predominant market occupancy, control was not recently created or currently sustained by overt predatory and exclusionary practices, would suffice to escape liability under the Sherman Act. This meant in effect that the accompaniment of dominant occupancy only by "normal and prudent" business practices designed to secure and maintain such occupancy was not illegal.

The most that was required under the act was that, currently or recently, there had been a nominal "freedom to compete" by some smaller firms not defendants in the monopolization action, this nominal freedom being evidenced first by their existence and survival, and second by the fact that they were not being subjected to predatory or exclusionary tactics by the dominant firm. In an oligopoly in which an antitrust action was brought against either the largest firm or against the several largest, and in which the several principal rivals were all surviving nicely under a *modus vivendi* of restrained competition and of the parallel pursuit of normal business policies of essentially exclusionary effect and purpose, it would be hard to find a Sherman Act offense under this doctrine. The legal prohibitions thus applied not to highly or very highly concentrated market structures as such (at least so long as some freedom to compete remained), but rather to certain rather express and overt lines of conduct through which such structures were secured and maintained.

An ancillary but not inconsequential aspect of this doctrine was the treatment of those "combinations in restraint of trade" that take the form of mergers or consolidations which unify previously separate interests under single ownerships and managements. In line with the doctrine that "size alone is no offense," the general attitude of the courts (*vis a vis* the Sherman Act) was that merger alone was no offense, even though the merger was a combination which brought under single ownership and control firms with a majority or more of the total industry capacity. This doctrine is one of the leading results of the so-called "rule of reason" enunciated by the courts, which recognized a category of "reasonable," and hence legal, restraints of trade. The possible reasonableness of restraint via merger apparently inhered in the fact that mergers could have, and generally were conceded to have, laudable purposes (such as the increase of efficiency) other than the restraint of competition. Thus dominant control of an industry by a single firm could effectively not be attacked on the ground that the firm itself had been created by a combination of competitors. Judicial attention focussed instead on the remaining freedom of others to compete with the merger firm, and on the presence or absence of overt exclusionary practices on the part of the merger firm.

Contrariwise, the courts in general did not see reasonableness (that is, the justification of a laudable purpose) to be inherent in loose-knit agreements among competitors which had no greater competition-restraining effect than a merger of the same competitors would have had. As a result, restraint of competition accomplished through a merger of competitors was in effect treated more gently than restraint of competition effected through loose-knit agreements. And the emergence of high oligopolistic concentration was subject to lesser deterrent forces than was the institution of various forms of cartelization.

From this basic beginning, the judicial doctrine affecting monopolization has evolved somewhat since the early 1940's, in the direction of giving greater weight to market occupancy as an essential part of the offense against the Sherman Act, and of considering various normal and prudent business practices of evident exclusionary effect and purpose as sufficient evidence of illegal conduct having monopolistic intent. The current question is just how far the judicial doctrine has evolved, and how much in essence it differs from the old interpretation.

It is not clear that the doctrine to date has ever fully proceeded to the opposite pole of regarding mere predominant market occupancy as an offense against the law. The closest approach to this position was perhaps made in the court decision in the case of the Aluminum Company of America (1945), involving a firm which had long controlled over 90 per cent of the domestic market for primary or "virgin" aluminum. In this, the court clearly rejected the previously held notion that violation of the law required (in addition to occupancy) either Section 1 offenses of conspiracy to exclude, or "manoeuvers not honestly industrial, but actuated solely by a desire to prevent competition." It held the view that only the power and intent to maintain a predominant market position is necessary to offend the law; that such power *is inherent* in the control of most of a market; and that intent may be inferred from a course of market action, devoid of express predatory or exclusionary tactics, which is evidently designed to secure and perpetuate the pre-eminent market position.

This doctrine is at the least fully consistent with the second possible interpretation of the law suggested in the preceding section, to the effect that predominant occupancy together with normal and prudent business practices which effectively create and maintain it is sufficient to offend the law. At places in the decision, the language of the court suggests that it is going still further, to embrace a genuine "mere occupancy" doctrine, but that it actually does is doubtful. Attention is still focused on exclusionary market conduct, albeit on conduct of a routine commercial sort, as an essential element of the offense. And even so far as mere occupancy may be illegal, it is not so *per se* but because of the inherent power it bestows to exclude others.

In subsequent decisions in monopolization cases, of which there have not been very many, the courts have wavered a bit in their doctrine, but the general tendency seems to be toward our second possible interpretation, although perhaps a somewhat more conservative version of that interpretation than was expressed in the Aluminum case. This is clearly a version in which exclusionary conduct, in addition to predominant occupancy, is essential to a violation of the law, although such illegal conduct may consist entirely or mainly of normal business practices or policies having exclusionary effect and inferentially exclusionary purpose, and need not embody Section 1 offenses or other overt predation and exclusion. The offense against the law is primarily or crucially one of market conduct (accompanied by predominant occupancy), although predominant occupancy can be more easily and effectively attacked—indirectly by charges concerning exclusionary conduct—than under the old doctrine.

Complications in and extensions of this doctrine have also developed. A principal extension is that of the prohibitions of Section 2 of the Sherman Act to joint monopolization of a market by several independently owned and managed companies, acting in concert. Whereas in the history of Sherman Act enforcement prior to World War II, monopolization actions had typically been directed against single firms controlling dominant proportions of their respective markets, they have since been directed as well against groups of firms in oligopolies—notably, so far as recorded decisions go, in the Paramount Pictures case (1948) involving seven major film producer-distributors, and in the American Tobacco case (1946) involving the three largest cigarette companies in the country. The decisions in these actions have fairly well established the principle that a group of oligopolists acting in concert may not only violate Section 1 of the Sherman Act by entering into horizontal collusive arrangements, but also Section 2 of the Act by jointly monopolizing their common market.

As to the second offense, which may lead to more severe remedies, the same general criteria seem to apply as in the case of single-firm monopolization, with the following adaptations in meaning. First, evidence of agreement to restrain competition horizontally among the joint monopolists is presumably required, under the same standards applicable in the interpretation of Section 1 generally. Second, the illegal monopolizing conduct, which may still be limited to normal and prudent business policies of exclusionary effect and purpose, will presumably have to involve at least conspicuous parallelism of such policies on the part of the several alleged joint monopolists, although a showing of overt conspiracy to pursue such policies jointly will probably not be required. This complex doctrine apparently extends the prohibitions of the law in such a fashion as to bring collusive oligopolies within the reach of Section 2 prohibitions and remedies, although the emphasis is still on conduct offenses, and the task of demonstrating them in litigation is vastly complicated.

The principal complications in the revised doctrine revolve around the definition of the scope of a market alleged to be monopolized, and around the judgment of what proportionate occupancy (single or joint) is sufficient (given the supporting evidence on exclusionary conduct) to be illegal.

The definition of a market frequently becomes relevant because the alleged monopolist or joint monopolists have predominant control over a commodity or service for which there are imperfect substitutes supplied in significant volume by other firms. In such instances, predominant occupancy might well be found if the market were narrowly defined as including only the specific goods or services supplied by the alleged monopolist(s), but would probably not be found if the market were more broadly defined as including the imperfect substitute outputs of other sellers. For example, in the Aluminum Company case, the company supplied over 90 per cent of the "virgin" aluminum (initially extracted from the ore) which was produced domestically, but only a bit less than two-thirds of the total supply including secondary or scrap aluminum and imports. Definition of the relevant "monopolized" market as being confined to virgin aluminum of domestic origin resulted in an unquestionable finding of predominant occupancy (over 90 per cent); the broader definition of the market would have resulted in finding a degree of occupancy which the courts might not have found to be monopolistic. Or, in the so-called Cellophane case (involving the Du Pont company), definition of the allegedly monopolized market as being confined to flexible packaging materials having the peculiar physical properties of Cellophane would very probably have led to a finding that Du Pont had predominant market occupancy, whereas the broader definition of the market actually adopted by the courts—including all waxed paper, glassine, and sulphite paper along with Cellophane— found Du Pont with less than 20 per cent of the market and thus not a monopolist. The same sorts of issues have arisen in the definition of the geographical limits of regional markets.

Faced with a technical problem in economic analysis, and having generally insufficient technical equipment with which to solve it, the courts have generally "played by ear" from case to case in defining markets, with the not unsurprising result that they have been less than fully consistent with respect to the matter in question. In some cases (for example, those of the Aluminum Company and of Paramount Pictures) the market has been rather narrowly defined, this definition lending support to a finding of predominant occupancy. In other cases (for example those of Du Pont's Cellophane and of Columbia Steel) a fairly broad market definition has been pivotal in finding that predominant occupancy did not exist. Perhaps the most that can be said at present is that the current doctrine affecting monopolization, as applied in actual cases, has a potentially quite flexible meaning or content, depending upon the court's view of the scope of the market in question, and upon its derived determination of whether or not predominant occupancy of the market exists. Considerable uncertainty thus may exist, *a priori*, with respect to the possible illegality of numerous monopolistic or oligopolistic structural situations.

Having defined the scope of a market, the courts must also decide how high the proportionate control of the market defined, as held by a single firm or by several together in concert, must be for illegal occupancy (*cum* illegal conduct) to be found. The doctrine here is far from clear. In most pertinent cases, illegal monopoly has been found only where the defendant firm or firms controlled a very high proportion of the market as defined, such as 80 or 90 per cent or more. In the Aluminum Company case, dealing with a single-firm monopoly, the court commented that whereas 90 per cent control of the market was sufficient for illegal occupancy, it was doubtful whether 60 or 64 per cent control would be, and 33 per cent control would "certainly" not be illegal. In the recent American Tobacco case, joint control by the three defendants of 68 per cent of the total cigarette market sufficed for a finding of illegal monopoly, though judicial mention was made of the fact that the three defendants controlled 80 per cent of the "standard brand" sales of cigarettes. (Thus we observe the essential interdependence of the judicial definitions of the scope of the market and of the critical percentage of control of the market.)

Further cases have not particularly clarified the doctrine with respect to the proportionate market control which is sufficient to establish the existence of illegal occupancy by one or several firms. It seems fair, however, to guess that, under the present interpretation of the law, control of two-thirds or more of the market by the alleged monopolist or joint monopolists would probably be required, in addition to evidence of illegal conduct, to establish illegal monopolization. This means that the actual cases of single-firm monopolization which could be discovered would be very few indeed in the American economy. On the other hand, cases emphasizing joint monopolization by the largest few firms in the industry could be potentially effective against many or most of our highly concentrated oligopolistic industries (so far as the criterion of proportionate market control is concerned), since in such industries three or four or six firms will generally control a predominant proportion of the market. The net effectiveness of the law under this doctrine, however, is limited (as noted above) by the difficulties of establishing the requisite conduct offenses of joint monopolization.

The interpretations of the antimonopolization provisions of the Sherman Act discussed above refer mainly, so far as market structure is concerned, to "horizontal" market occupancy by a single firm or several acting in concert, and otherwise to the exclusionary power which inheres in such occupancy or which has been exercised in creating or perpetuating it. Horizontal occupancy refers to and is measured by the proportion of a single market, such as a market for gasoline, which is controlled by the alleged monopolist or joint monopolists—by the relative reach of the defendant firm or firms "across" a single market. The market occupancy of firms may be defined and measured, however, in other terms as well, and particularly in those of whether and to what extent the firm is vertically integrated so as to occupy simultaneously two or more successive markets in a vertical sequence, interconnecting its operations in the successive markets. For example, a single integrated petroleum company might operate in the three vertically related markets—for crude petroleum (which serves as the raw material for making gasoline), for wholesale gasoline as sold by refineries (which serves as the merchandise purchased and sold by gasoline retailers), and for retail gasoline. Its horizontal occupancy of the successive markets might be registered, for example, by the fact that it accounted for 20 per cent of all crude petroleum produced in the relevant market, 30 per cent of all gasoline produced by refineries in that market, and 15 per cent of all retail gasoline sales in the market. Normally, in such a situation, the integrated firm would supply its refineries with its own crude oil (in addition to purchasing some more), and supply its own retail outlets with its own refinery gasoline (selling any balance not handled in this way to other retailers). Its vertical market occupancy would be reflected in its simultaneous and interconnected operations (of the specified horizontal magnitude) in three successive markets. The legal treatment of such vertical integration, as a phase of possibly monopolistic market occupancy, should now be considered.

Potentially inherent in almost any structure of vertically integrated firms are some implicitly exclusionary effects, or some virtual disadvantages to actual or potential competitors of the integrated firms. This is particularly true if in the successive markets involved there are also sellers who are not vertically integrated, so that nonintegrated firms purchase supplies, produce, and make sales at each of the separate market levels comprehended by the integrated firms. In the petroleum-industry situation mentioned, for example, there might be, in addition to several firms integrated from crude production through refining and through retailing, a number of nonintegrated crude petroleum producers who simply produce crude oil for sale, a number of nonintegrated refiners who simply purchase crude from others and sell refinery wholesale gasoline to others, and a number of nonintegrated retailers who simply purchase gasoline from refineries and sell it at retail. Each of these different groups of nonintegrated firms would be in competition with the integrated firms for shares of the market, and their welfare would be influenced by the intermediate-market and final-market buying and selling prices and policies of the integrated firms.

The possible exclusionary impact on the nonintegrated firms of the integrated company operations is obvious. First, the integrated firm is its own obvious best customer through the vertical sequence, supplying its "higher-stage" operations (for example, refining) from its "lower-stage" operations (for example, crude oil production), and it is disinclined to deal with nonintegrated firms, which are either its potential suppliers or its potential customers, on any more favorable terms than the market forces on it. Thus the integrated firm may refuse to purchase supplies required for its higher-stage operations from nonintegrated suppliers, preferrring to supply itself, or may purchase supplies only on terms unfavorable to the sellers, thereby excluding the nonintegrated supplier firms from equal access to a potential market. Otherwise, the integrated petroleum company may prefer to supply all its retail outlets with its own gasoline, thereby preventing nonintegrated refiners of gasoline from distributing their gasoline through these outlets. Or, the integrated firms may refuse to supply nonintegrated competitors with materials produced in their integrated operations, at any rate on favorable terms, thus excluding such competitors from equal access to a favorable source of supply. (For example, the integrated petroleum company may refuse to sell crude oil to nonintegrated refiners on favorable terms, thus restricting their access to needed materials.) These phenomena are likely to be especially important in cases where the integration of the vertically integrated firms is "unbalanced," so that they control more of the market at one stage of the vertical sequence than another, and so that purchase or sale transactions between them and nonintegrated firms become a practical necessity.

Second, the operation of the vertically integrated firms may in some cases be significantly more efficient than those of a succession of nonintegrated competitors, with the result that the integrated firms can sell in the final market (for example, retail gasoline) at a price which is profitable to them but unprofitable to their nonintegrated competitors as a group, who thus will not survive unless the integrated firms pass on some of their efficiency advantages in the form of especially favorable buying or selling prices to the nonintegrated firms. The structural situation in such cases is unfavorable to the economical continuation of nonintegrated operations, and the apparent effect of "exclusion" may emerge.

Finally, the control by integrated firms of all available facilities at one or more stages in the vertical sequence of operations and markets may effectively make the use of such existing facilities by potential nonintegrated entrants at other stages impossible, and effectively deter their entry because they lack funds to supply their own integrated facilities. For example, if integrated petroleum companies control nearly all of the existing specialized transport facilities for carrying crude oil, and are not disposed to allow their use by nonintegrated refiners on favorable terms, the entry of new nonintegrated refiners may be seriously impeded.

Given these potentially exclusionary effects of vertical integration, what has been the attitude of the courts (under the Sherman Act) to the existence of such integration? First, the proposed doctrine that illegality is found in the practice or agreement between two divisions or subsidiaries of the same firm to the effect that one should be supplied by the other (thus excluding competitive firms from supplying the receiving stage of the integrated firm) has in general been conclusively rejected. The illusive doctrine of "intrafirm" conspiracy thus has little more standing at law than in applied economic analysis. Second, the courts have held that the accomplishment of restraint of trade and monopolization via vertical integration is not exempt from the law as such—that vertical integration which results in specified degrees of restraint or monopolization *can* be illegal—but that vertical integration which imposes some restraint is by no means illegal *per se*. The degree and character of the restraint, and resulting monopolization, is crucial. Third, in conjunction with the preceding, creation (or maintenance) of vertical integration having some restraining effect is not an illegal restraint *per se* under Section 1 of the Sherman Act, as a combination in restraint of trade. Instead, the criterion of reasonableness of the restraint is applicable. This puts vertical combinations having restraining effects on roughly the same footing as horizontal mergers having similar effects. They are not adjudged to be unreasonable combinations in restraint of trade *per se*, and the attention of the courts is thus shifted, under a "rule of reason," to the character of the remaining competition in the market or markets involved, and to whether or not monopolization has been accomplished. Finally, vertical integrations with inherently restraining tendencies are to be adjudged illegal only if the effect is "to unreasonably restrict the opportunities of competitors to market their product" (or to secure essential materials for production).

What this last dictum really will mean in practice is perhaps open to some argument, but a guess might be made along the following lines: (1) that vertical integration with implicitly restraining influences is likely to be found illegal only in cases where it is conjoined with predominant horizontal market control by a monopolist or joint monopolists in one or more of the vertical sequence of markets involved, this being evidence that the integration may have played some role in the creation or maintenance of predominant horizontal occupancy; (2) that the vertical integration, to be illegal, must be in some degree crucial to the maintenance of the predominant occupancy, in the sense that its elimination might undermine the basis of such occupancy; and (3) that the vertical integration, if illegal, has been exploited at least by normal and prudent business practices having exclusionary effect and inferred purpose, though not necessarily by express Section 1 offenses. This suggests in general that vertical integration is not illegal if viewed in isolation, but only as part of a pattern of illegal monopolization involving as well both predominant horizontal occupancy and illegal exclusionary conduct of some sort.

We thus comprehend a general doctrine affecting monopolization under which predominant market occupancy (horizontally measured) by a firm or group of firms acting in concert is illegal, provided that a line of market conduct—possibly confined to normal and prudent business practices—has been pursued with the effect and inferred purpose of creating and maintaining such occupancy, and also provided that, in the case of joint monopoly, a conspicuous parallelism of policies for controlling intra-industry competition and for excluding others has existed as among the several defendants. The crucial emphasis is still on market conduct, although structure, in the sense of occupancy, plays an increasingly important role. Evidence on market performance is relevant, but largely as a means of drawing inferences concerning market conduct.

Monopolization or Monopoly under the Sherman Act—Remedial Devices

If illegal monopolization of an industry is found under the Sherman Act, what then? What deterrent penalties are faced by potential monopolizers, and what remedies may the government secure to terminate existing monopolization?

Just as in the case of Sherman Act violations involving loose-knit agreements, the Attorney General may bring either criminal actions which can terminate in the assessment of fines, or civil actions in which the courts are asked to issue remedial orders. Again (and perhaps especially) in the case of monopolization, the possible fines are nominal from the standpoint of the large business firms usually concerned; they would appear to have at best slight deterrent effects and no direct remedial effects. The main force of the law as it affects monopolization is thus exercised through civil court actions and through the resulting remedial orders which the courts issue when violations are found. Correspondingly, the nature of the remedies which courts can and do apply in such cases is an essential part of the full meaning and content of the Sherman Act as a regulatory device.

The powers of the courts in the matter of determining remedies are very broad and not precisely defined. Section 4 of the Sherman Act simply states that "the several district courts of the United States are hereby invested with jurisdiction to prevent and restrain violations of this act"; that "it shall be the duty of . . . the Attorney General to institute proceedings in equity to restrain such violations"; and that "such proceedings may be by way of petition setting forth the case and praying that such violation shall be *enjoined or otherwise prohibited*" (italics supplied). Both the Attorney General in proposing remedies, and the courts in deciding which shall be imposed, thus have considerable latitude in deciding what remedies will suffice and are appropriate to prevent further violations of the act by the defendants in any particular case.

In monopolization cases, the courts have in practice relied on two main sorts of remedy: first, injunctive and other orders limiting or otherwise directing the market conduct of defendant firms; and, second, orders decreeing a revision of market structure, generally by the dismemberment of defendant firms, and aimed directly at reducing or eliminating the predominant market occupancy which has been an element of the offense.

The injunctive remedies, parallel to those employed in loose-knit agreement cases under Section 1, generally involve orders that specific exclusionary acts, practices, and policies of the defendants (potentially including agreements of exclusionary effect and purpose) be terminated. These are negative prohibitions against monopolization in the restricted sense of exclusionary conduct. Such injunctions may also be supplemented by constructive orders affecting conduct, such as, for example, the order that the defendants must hereafter sell to or buy from smaller competitors on nondiscriminatory terms, or must hereafter make their patented processes available unrestrictively to all comers without charge or with only a nominal charge. It is an essential characteristic of such remedies affecting conduct that they do not attempt directly to alter the structural basis of monopolistic tendencies, but only to place limitations on the market conduct through which predominant market occupancy has been created, maintained, and exploited. It is a further characteristic of these remedies that they are progressively harder to devise, in sensible and enforceable form, as we pass from the realm of overt and express exclusionary tactics and agreements into that of normal and prudent business practices of exclusionary effect and purpose. The difficulty here is akin to that encountered in finding "what to enjoin" in the case of tacit horizontal agreements or conspicuous parallelism in fairly concentrated oligopolies.

Remedies requiring alteration of market structures are clearly more severe in character. Such remedies might require the horizontal dismemberment of a dominant firm (or firms) into several separate and competing firms, or the vertical dismemberment of such a firm or firms by requiring them to "dis-integrate" by divestiture or divorcement of facilities and operations at one or more of the vertically related market levels. The imposition of such remedies by the courts apparently reflects not their belief that an existing predominant occupancy is illegal *per se* or automatically requires removal, but rather the belief that only through the structural revisions required can illegal monopolizing conduct, or the power to monopolize, be effectively eliminated. At least a nominal "conduct orientation" is thus still implicit in the imposition of structural remedies. Whatever the ostensible orientation, application of such remedies with adequate thoroughness and severity could have a fundamental impact on the bases of monopolistic performance tendencies in industry, especially by reducing unduly high seller concentration in numerous oligopolistic markets. Because of this, the possible use of structural remedies (as distinct from conduct remedies) seems to make the Sherman Act a potentially more effective regulatory device for suppressing monopoly and securing workable competition in the economy.

In the history of antitrust cases involving monopolization, however, the tendency of the courts has been to prefer conduct remedies (emphasizing injunctions) to structural remedies, and to resort to the latter only in extremity, with possible attention to the ordering of dismemberments or divestitures in a punitive spirit in cases of exceptionally flagrant violations of the law. And, in the selection of cases in which structural remedies are imposed, the courts have not followed any very consistent pattern which would be explicable in terms of economic analysis. Furthermore, where structural remedies have been imposed, they frequently have not gone far enough in reducing horizontal concentration or integration that the newly created structure has promised to yield a much better market performance than the old. One of the difficulties in this latter regard is that the courts have lacked any legislative or adequate administrative guidance in determining how much dissolution or dismemberment is required to make a real difference from the standpoint of performance, and have thus "played by ear" from case to case, with assorted results.

Summarizing the past application of the Sherman Act to monopolization, therefore, it is fair to say that, in line with the view of the essential offense as one of conduct, the more usual remedies for violation have been conduct remedies. Conversely, the Sherman Act has not provided a solid general basis for attacking and revising monopolistic or concentrated oligopolistic market structures even where exclusionary conduct has been found. And, where such structures have been attacked, the structural remedies imposed have tended to be insufficient to assure greatly improved market performance. Conduct remedies undoubtedly have some limited merits in weeding out specific exclusionary practices, but unless structure is revised in the usual monopoly case, there are serious doubts about any long-run accomplishments in securing improved performance.

Patent Monopolies under the Antitrust Laws

One rather complex phase of the application of the antitrust laws to business monopoly deserves special mention—that involving the exploitation of legal patent grants. Under prevailing law, the inventor of a novel process or method of production, productive machinery, or product, may secure from the federal government an exclusive patent on the process, machine, or product for a period of seventeen years. The patent is essentially a grant of legal monopoly over the specified time interval, made available as an incentive to invention and to the disclosure of inventions. It generally gives the patentee (or those to whom he assigns his rights) exclusive rights in the use of the process or machinery or sale of the product. These rights include the exclusive but limited right to license others to use the process or machinery or make and sell the product, subject to charges and restrictions imposed by the patentee. Thus various processes, productive machinery, and products may be subject legally to exclusive monopolistic control and administration for a period of years. Patent controls are at any time important influences on market structure, conduct, and performance in a significant minor fraction of our industries.

The "basic monopoly" granted by any patent is clearly exempt from the antitrust laws, such basic monopoly embracing potentially the rights of exclusion, of exclusive market occupancy, and of market conduct and performance of a monopolistic sort, in the use, production, or sale of whatever is covered by the patent. Exploitation of patent rights can run afoul of the antitrust laws (the Sherman Act, and also Section 3 of the Clayton Act, discussed below), however, if a patent or group of patents is used as a tool for creating a more extensive monopoly or a greater restraint of trade than has been bestowed in the "basic monopoly" stemming from the patent or patents in question. This is to say in effect that the courts, holding the antitrust laws and the patent law in juxtaposition, interpret the antitrust laws to the end of determining the legal limits of patent grants of monopoly power. They prohibit certain uses of patents for the purpose of restraining trade or creating monopoly. Because the fundamental judicial concepts involved are complex, if not tortured, and the detailed application of these concepts is very complicated, we will not explore the antitrust doctrine with respect to patents at any length, but will note several principal restrictions on the use of patents to magnify monopoly power.

As a preamble to discussing these restrictions, it should be made plain that an individual patentee has clear rights to exclusive use of his patented process or machinery, or to exclusive production and sale of his patented product, in any volume or at any price he may wish to establish. He also has rights to license others for such use, production, or sale, but these latter rights are not unrestricted, since the potentially restraining agreements embodied in patent licenses may extend the scope of monopoly beyond that which stems from the basic patent grant. As to restrictions on the licensing power, we may note the following.

First, the patentee may not, under Section 3 of the Clayton Act, license the use of a patented process or machine on condition that the licensee purchase or lease unpatented goods from the patentee, thus extending the monopoly from a patented to an unpatented good, where the effect would be substantially to lessen competition or create a monopoly in a line of commerce. For example, a company making tin cans could not lease patented can-closing machinery to food canners on the condition that they purchase their supply of unpatented tin cans from the lessor of the machinery, if the specified effects ensued.

Second, if a single holder of a patent or patents licenses the use of a process or machine, or the production and sale of a product, to several others (possibly his competitors) he may *up to a point* impose restrictions on his licensees, limiting their outputs produced, prices charged, and so forth. But he may not, under the Sherman Act, use a licensing system affecting several competitors that includes provisions which effectively eliminate competition among them or within a market. For example, a firm holding patents on strategic processes and products in the wallboard industry could not license each of the several firms in the wallboard industry under a composite of terms which effectively eliminated price and output competition among them. (The firm could, though, legally establish itself as a single-firm monopolist in the patented wallboard.) Furthermore, the terms of a patent license cannot legally include a restriction on the resale of a patented good once sold by the licensee to an initial purchaser, and probably cannot include a restriction on the sale price of an unpatented good made with the patented process or machine which is licensed.

Third, several firms each of which holds different patents covering complementary processes, machines, or products in the same industry may agree to pool or cross-license these patents so that each secures access to all the patents, excluding others, but only if the cross-licensing agreement is not used as a means of eliminating competition among the several patent holders and licensees. If, for example, the members of the cross-licensing pool agree through the terms of the licenses or otherwise to fix prices on their outputs or similarly restrain competition, they are engaged in a united exercise of their individual patent monopolies and violate the Sherman Act.

A fourth area of possible antitrust restriction involves the attainment by a single firm of control over a great many individual patents, covering most or all of the many processes, machines, or products needed for a firm to operate in an industry—the firm thus obtaining a monopoly of individual patent monopolies and an ability to exclude competitors and secure predominant market occupancy of a whole industry. The legality of such a monopoly of patent monopolies is, in the present state of judicial doctrine, at least in question. No clear and simple prohibitions are evident, but great concentration of patent control in an industry may well help to sustain a finding of monopolization under Section 2 of the Sherman Act. The proportion of manufacturing industries in which the sort of development in question is important is quite small, but some major industries are involved.

The remedies for violation of the antitrust laws through the administration of patent rights of course include the standard criminal penalties if the Sherman Act has been violated. The important civil remedies embody, in their simplest form, injunctions against the use of tying agreements, illegally restrictive licensing practices, or illegal cross-licensing systems. Such remedies are focused entirely on market conduct in the administration of patents, and were the main recourse of the courts in patent cases until fairly recently. In the last two decades, however, the courts have shown a considerable disposition in patent monopoly cases under the Sherman Act to use a more severe or even punitive type of civil remedy, with a distinct orientation toward revisions of market structures. That is, they have remedied illegal patent-based monopolization by severely restricting, if not eliminating, existing and future patent rights of the offending firms, so that patents cannot be used further to sustain illegal monopoly. The specific character of such remedies varies, but features generally the requirement of compulsory open licensing of all present (and, in some cases, future) patents to all applicants, either at a "fair" royalty charge or without royalty charge. In addition, it has on occasion been required that the offending firms also supply all licensees with unpatented "know-how" to facilitate use of patented processes. Such remedies essentially abrogate at least a good part of the legal patent monopolies involved by eliminating the inherent exclusionary effects of the patent grants and thus reducing barriers to entry or to the expansion of small competitors. These effectively structural remedies, in monopolization cases involving patents, have in general been preferred by the courts over the more drastic structural remedies of dissolution and dismemberment of dominant firms.

Economic Effects of Sherman Act Enforcement
Affecting Monopolization or Monopoly

In analyzing the economic effects of past applications of the Sherman Act to monopolization and monopoly, it is appropriate to distinguish three levels of effect: on market structures, with especial reference to seller concentration and to conditions of entry; on market conduct, with primary emphasis on predatory and exclusionary practices and policies; and on market performance (indirectly, through effects on structure and conduct). It is also important to recognize that the character and extent of effects secured have depended dually on the content and judicial interpretation of the law and on the intensity and orientation of its enforcement by the responsible agencies.

Because of the content and interpretation of the law, it is unsurprising that most of the *direct* effects of its enforcement have been on predatory and exclusionary market conduct. It has been interpreted primarily as forbidding predatory and exclusionary practices and policies, either *per se* or as connected with dominant market occupancy. Thus the legal actions brought by the Department of Justice have been predominantly actions against offensive conduct, and the remedies obtained have been mainly in the form of injunctions restraining such conduct. In addition there has been a deterrent to firms engaging in predatory and exclusionary activities, in the form of a threat (though one only occasionally carried out) that the courts may, under the Sherman Act, remedy illegal monopolization by dismemberment or dissolution of the offending firm or firms.

The net efficacy of Sherman Act enforcement in suppressing predatory and exclusionary tactics is difficult to evaluate from available evidence. One consideration is that the antimonopolization provisions of the law have never been very intensively enforced. Only a very small fraction of the 1800-odd Sherman Act cases from 1890 to date have concerned monopolization in a primary sense. Taking this generally unintensive enforcement into account along with prevailing judicial interpretations and applications of the law, we may hazard the following guesses concerning the impact of the law on market conduct.

First, overt practices and policies of predation and exclusion have for a long time been rather thoroughly discouraged, though by no means entirely eliminated.

Second, there has been a corresponding implied encouragement to leading or dominant firms in oligopolistic industries to pursue policies of "live-and-let-live" with respect to smaller competitors, eschewing aggressive competitive tactics in favor of a more restrained struggle for market shares (as through product development and sales promotion). Restrained competition with good survival possibilities for smaller as well as larger firms has thus been encouraged, and the use by the larger firms of their dominant market power to eliminate competitors has been discouraged.

Third, the effect to date on normal and prudent business practices having the inferrable effect and purpose of exclusion (but not involving overt acts of exclusion) is doubtful. The courts began to consider such practices offensive (in conjunction with dominant occupancy) mainly after the mid-1940's; antimonopoly enforcement since then has not been intensive; and it is too early to say what the effects of application of the new doctrine will be. Remedial restraint of such practices, however, does encounter difficulties parallel to those met in restraining conspicuous parallelism or tacit collusion under Section 1 of the Sherman Act.

Let us now turn from effects on conduct to effects on market structure. The major effects of Sherman Act enforcement on market structures have probably been indirect ones, stemming from the impact of restrictions on market conduct on the development of market structures. Thus it seems clear that the general discouragement of overt predation and exclusion, and the corresponding encouragement of "live-and-let-live" policies, have in the net forestalled the development of degrees of seller concentration as high as would have otherwise emerged. Increased seller concentration has been restrained at the same time that barriers to entry have been somewhat lowered by the restraint on exclusionary acts. Our antitrust policy thus has tended to favor oligopoly over monopoly, less concentrated oligopoly than might otherwise emerge, and oligopoly without express predatory and exclusionary barriers to entry. These results stem not only from the prohibitions of overt exclusion and predation, but also from the continually doubtful status under the law of dominant market occupancy which attains or closely approaches single-firm monopoly.

On the other hand, the general effect of our antitrust policy has not been directly to deter the development of relatively high oligopolistic concentration, or to reduce it when it does develop. There are several reasons for this failure. First, during the great merger movement in American manufacturing industries between 1890 and 1905, the Sherman Act, though on the books, was initially interpreted as not applying to monopolization accomplished by merger. Though this interpretation was thereafter revised, a major structural change in our manufacturing industries took place—often with the assistance of much predation and exclusion—before it became apparent that the Sherman Act provided any deterrents to monopolization implemented through mergers. And subsequent interpretations were not such as to support structural remedies on the basis of past sins of predation and exclusion, so long as currently there was a nominal freedom to compete in the markets involved.

Second, as regards current situations of predominant market occupancy by one firm or a few acting on concert, an offense can be found only on the basis of exclusionary conduct of relatively recent date. This means, in effect, that in only a minor fraction of concentrated oligopolies can violation of the law be clearly established, so that structural remedies might be in order.

Third, even where violations involving monopolization are found, the courts have generally been loath to apply the structural remedies of divestiture and dismemberment in order to reduce seller concentration. Thus in only a minor proportion of cases where violation has been established have the courts required deconcentration; generally, they have been content with injunctions against offensive conduct, and let the structure remain.

Fourth, the program of enforcement against monopolization has always been unintensive, so that only a very small proportion of potentially offending industries are ever brought to court. In consequence, the number of structural remedies actually applied is correspondingly reduced. Finally, whatever new effects on concentration may be implicit in the application of the extended doctrine developed since the Aluminum Company case are not as yet apparent, in part for the reasons just mentioned. In general, concentrated oligopolistic market structures under the Sherman Act have to date been attacked or deterred primarily to the extent that the discouragement of overt exclusionary and predatory tactics is conducive to a lesser concentration than would otherwise emerge, and that entry is made somewhat easier. But the continued existence of a significant degree of oligopolistic concentration in an important fraction of manufacturing industries has—because of interpretation of the law and of unintensive enforcement—not been seriously deterred.

The recent applications of the Sherman Act to the administration of patents has placed some fairly severe checks on the enlargement of basic individual patent monopolies to embrace the monopolistic control of whole markets. The doctrine here is discouraging to the increase of concentration of market control through patent licensing and cross-licensing, and various remedies applied in specific cases have clearly eased the condition of entry for new competitors. The antitrust policy toward the administration of patents, however, clearly touches only a small fraction of instances in which undesirable market power seems inherent in high seller concentration.

In the light of the content and interpretation of the law, it is not to be expected that antitrust enforcement would have any *direct* effects on market performance. Under none of its provisions is bad performance (or any specified sort of performance) *per se* in violation of the law. The only direct offenses are those of conduct, or of conduct *cum* structure, and evidence of bad or monopolistic performance tendencies is relevant only, if at all, as a basis for drawing inferences concerning market conduct. Consistently, when violations of the law are found, the courts do not impose remedies in the form of edicts governing market performance. They impose remedies restricting conduct, and occasionally remedies revising market structure, and whatever change is wrought in performance is the indirect effect of the enforced changes in structure and conduct.

How great have these indirect effects in market performance in American industries been? This question can be answered only in the most general terms, with emphasis on the following two points. First, by somewhat reducing barriers to entry and by discouraging our oligopolistic industries from becoming as highly concentrated as they otherwise would have become, the antimonopoly policy has probably secured, in a significant proportion of the business economy, a somewhat less monopolistic or more competitive type of market performance than would otherwise have emerged. This would seem especially so with respect to monopolistic output restriction, price raising, and excess profits. Second, the antimonopoly policy has not had sufficient effects on seller concentration or on entry to prevent a large number of relatively concentrated oligopolistic market structures from legally surviving and thriving (albeit with lesser average concentration than would be reached if there were no antitrust laws). In these oligopolies, on the average, at least modified monopolistic performance tendencies are consistently noted. Tendencies toward monopolistic output restriction and profits, moreover, are augmented by elevated costs of nonprice competition through advertising and product variation, this development being engendered in some degree by the legal discouragements of agressive price competition. Generally competitive performance by American industries is thus not an accomplishment of the antimonopoly policy. If workably competitive performance throughout the economy is our general goal, we may say that the Sherman Act is considerably better than no such law at all, but that it has fallen significantly short of the task of entirely or largely suppressing monopolistic performance tendencies in the economy.

Fundamental Characteristics and Limitations of the Sherman Act Prohibitions of Monopoly

The deficiencies of the Sherman Act as a means of preventing or eliminating monopolistic tendencies in American industries does not seem attributable in the main to a lax or unintensive enforcement policy. Although somewhat better results might have been obtained with a more intensive enforcement, the major difficulty seems to lie in the content of the law and in its judicial interpretation.

The fundamental limitations of the act is that it is "conduct-oriented." As written and interpreted, it places prohibitions on market conduct of a predatory or exclusionary nature, but does not place any direct prohibitions on monopolistic or highly concentrated oligopolistic market structures as such. As noted, the scope of offensive conduct has recently been broadened to such an extent that predominant single-firm or collusive joint occupancy accompanied by normal and prudent business practices having exclusionary effects may suffice for violation of the law, but the offense is still primarily one of successful exclusionary conduct.

One major result of this doctrine is that oligopolistic market occupancy (even of a highly concentrated sort), accompanied only by a parallelism of market policies among the member firms which is quite sufficient to secure monopolistic performance tendencies, cannot be effectively attacked as such under the present law. Offenses of exclusionary conduct have to be "tied onto" the predominant joint occupancy in order to establish a violation of the law. And even though conspicuous parallelism among the oligopolists in restraining competition *inter se* and also in pursuing normal and prudent exclusionary practices and policies might suffice to establish the conduct violation, it would not necessarily be easy in the bulk of concentrated oligopolistic industries to prove such a violation. A considerable fraction of industries with clear monopolistic tendencies are thus not obviously reachable under the law. And, so far as they might be reached, the standard of liability for violation is essentially vague and elusive, and thus tends to shift from court to court and case to case.

A further consequence of the content and interpretation of the Sherman Act as applied to monopolization is that each individual litigation, such as *might* lead toward divestiture or other remedies, tends to be extremely prolonged, and, in terms of time and money spent by the Department of Justice (as well as by the defendants), extremely expensive. This prolongation and expense of antimonopoly actions results in large part from the fact that establishment of conduct offenses generally requires almost endless exploration of the minutiae of the business practices and policies of the defendants, and endless arguments about what can be inferred from these practices and policies. Five or ten years from initiation to conclusion of a monopoly case is not unusual. In effect, a conduct offense is much more difficult to establish than a structural offense would be. Because of this great expenditure and consumption of staff time on any "big case" involving monopoly, the Department of Justice is generally loath to deplete its limited budget by bringing any considerable number of monopoly cases per year or per decade. Thus unintensive enforcement of the Sherman Act against monopolization is to be expected as an indirect consequence of the content and interpretation of the existing law.

Another difficulty with the present Sherman Act is that, under it, the courts are generally reluctant to impose structural remedies in the relatively few cases processed in which clear violations are found. Generally, the courts prefer conduct remedies which are of a lesser and rather doubtful efficacy as means of securing improved performance. This tendency of the courts in turn seems to be attributable to two deficiencies in the law itself: the vagueness of the standard of liability, which predisposes the courts to temper justice with mercy, and the lack of any clear legislative direction as to what sorts of remedies the courts should impose. The range of judicial discretion with respect to remedies has proved in practice to be unfortunately broad.

Because of the several deficiencies of the law noted above, it does not seem possible, or at any rate practicable, to secure any widespread structural revisions of unduly concentrated oligopolistic markets under the present Sherman Act. And the conduct remedies which can be imposed, involving both exclusionary conduct and horizontal collusion, are generally insufficient to secure a reasonably competitive performance in this category of industries. In Chapter 16, we will consider possibly indicated revisions in the existing legislation.

Prohibitions of Conduct Tending to Lessen Competition or Create Monopoly

We turn now to the substantive regulations of business conduct embodied in the Clayton Act, as passed in 1914 and subsequently amended. It is appropriate to discuss the provisions of this legislation separately from the antimonopoly provisions of the Sherman Act for two reasons. First, the prohibitions of the Clayton Act apply to specific types of business conduct that may only "tend to create a monopoly," rather than to the accomplished monopolization or monopoly forbidden by the Sherman Act. Second, the standard of illegality of the sorts of conduct named in the Clayton Act extends beyond a tendency to create monopoly, to include also a tendency substantially to lessen competition— a potentially more stringent test of conduct.

The relevant regulations of the Clayton Act, contained in its Sections 2, 3, and 7, are miscellaneous in content and not closely interrelated. They deal consecutively with price discrimination, with agreements between sellers and buyers, and with mergers. It is therefore convenient to discuss them separately, considering for each in turn statutory provision, judicial interpretation, legal remedies for violation, economic effects, and strengths and deficiencies.

Price Discrimination under the Clayton Act

The provisions of Section 2 of the Clayton Act, dealing with price discrimination, became long and complicated in 1936 when it was amended by the so-called Robinson-Patman Act—so long that we will not quote all of them here. The central provision of the amended Section 2 is that *"it shall be unlawful for any person engaged in commerce . . . to discriminate in price between different purchasers of commodities of like grade and quality . . . where the effect of such discrimination may be substantially to lessen competition or tend to create a monopoly in any line of commerce, or to injure, destroy, or prevent competition with any person who either grants or knowingly receives the benefit of such discrimination, or with customers of either of them . . . provided that* (discriminatory price differentials are permitted) *which make only due allowances for differences in the cost of manufacture, sale, or delivery . . . ."* The section continues to impose various restrictions on indirect means of price discrimination, with particular attention to means of granting lower prices to large buyers.

Section 2 thus singles out one of the many types of practice or policy— price discrimination among buyers, not based on differences in the costs of supplying them—which may have the effect of lessening competition and possibly of leading toward monopoly. The possible lessening of competition or tendency to monopolization is to be tested first at the level of the selling market of the discriminating seller, as to whether competition between him and competing sellers is restrained or whether he tends to attain a monopoly through use of discriminatory pricing. It is to be tested second—and this is the major thrust of the section as amended—at the level of the reselling market of the buyer. Price discrimination is illegal if a buyer who benefits from discrimination, in purchasing goods for resale or materials for producing goods for resale, gains an advantage over competing buyer-resellers that impairs their ability to compete with him or that is conducive to his monopolization of the reselling market.[4]

The legal prohibition affecting price discrimination is far more stringent than any corresponding prohibition implied in the two main sections of the Sherman Act. First, illegal discriminatory practices under the Clayton Act need not be collusive in origin (as they would have to be to violate Section 1 of the Sherman Act), but can be simply the unilateral practices of single, independently acting sellers. The attack of the law is on a specified market practice or policy, and not on collusion as such. Second, the minimum test of illegality is not effective monopolization of a market or substantial lessening of competition throughout a market, but simply some "injury" to competition between as few as two sellers or buyers in markets where sellers or buyers are potentially many. The act is thus designed to protect *competitors*, whether or not this is necessary in order to protect *competition*. It therefore appears that Section 2 of the Clayton Act is designed to discourage a good deal more than out-and-out monopolization or restriction of competition via price discrimination, and embodies a detailed sort of regulation of enterprise pricing practices. The consistency of this sort of regulation with the general overall goal of preventing monopolization, however, is often argued on the grounds that the practices prohibited have the incipient tendency (which might be fulfilled in a long process of oft-repeated acts) to foster monopoly. This argument poses questions of fact which are definitely debatable.

As interpreted by the courts, Section 2 has application to three main uses and effects of price discrimination. First, a seller may not discriminate among his buyers (except on the basis of cost differences) with the purpose and effect of injuring or eliminating one or more competitors of the seller. This prohibition applies mainly to so-called predatory price cutting, in which discrimination may emerge from the fact that the predacious seller cuts prices to some but not all of his buyers

---

[4]The act provides that price discrimination having these effects is not illegal if granted in good faith to meet the prices of competing sellers.

(for example, to those in certain areas) in order to take them away from a competing seller. But since only a probable injury to a competitor, and not a substantial lessening of competition in the market generally, is presumably required for such discrimination to violate the law, the most embryonic and tentative of incipient tendencies to create monopoly will suffice. There have been very few actions against this sort of price discrimination.

Second, a seller may not discriminate in price between buyers (except on the basis of cost differences) where the probable effect is to injure competition between the buyers, as by lessening the ability of one buyer to compete with the other. This prohibition applies to any case in which the buyers in question are firms that resell what they acquire in competition with each other, either in the form purchased or as embodied in products they make. The major intended application of the law was to discriminatory selling of merchandise by manufacturers to wholesalers or retailers, but it applies as well as to such transactions as the sale of tinplate steel to the competing manufacturers of tin cans. Again, substantial lessening of competition in a market generally is not essential for a violation, but only a probable injury to one or more competitors.

Third, a group of competitors may not concurrently adopt identical patterns of price discrimination—such as may be embodied in various geographical pricing formulae—where such concurrent adoption results in identical and noncompetitive delivered prices to each of several classes of buyers. This application of Section 2 clearly attacks one type of horizontal agreement in restraint to competition. Such agreements may also be illegal under Section 1 of the Sherman Act and Section 5 of the Federal Trade Commission Act.

The remedies for violation of all sections of the Clayton Act, including Section 2, are primarily civil. Criminal penalties are not provided; the Federal Trade Commission may issue cease and desist orders against illegal discrimination, (subject to appeal to the federal courts), or the Department of Justice may bring actions in the courts seeking similar injunctive remedies. Once secured from or approved by the courts, these injunctive decrees have the same force as comparable decrees under the Sherman Act, and violation of the decrees is subject to the usual penalties for contempt of court. It is not apparent that, in addition to the appropriate injunctive remedies, the government is empowered to secure the structural remedies of divestiture or dismemberment on the basis of violations of Section 2 of the Clayton Act. For such more severe remedies to be secured, a violation of Section 2 of the Sherman Act would also have to be established. In terms of prohibitions and remedies alike, the antidiscrimination provisions of the Clayton Act are thus conduct-oriented.

Section 2 of the Clayton Act has been rather intensively enforced since it was amended by the Robinson-Patman Act in 1936. What economic effects has it had? Aside from creating a good deal of extra employment for cost accountants and attorneys, it seems to have had the following results. First, it has induced considerable revisions in the differential pricing and discount policies of American business generally, aimed at eliminating inter-buyer price differences which were not based on differences in cost. Second, these revisions in pricing policies have strengthened the competitive positions of smaller firms appreciably in a number of cases, largely through depriving their larger competitors of certain monopsonistic buying-price advantages that stemmed from the discriminatory pricing policies of suppliers. This effect seems economically beneficial.

Third, however, the resulting suppression of the granting by sellers of special price concessions or discounts has tended to restrict an important device through which sellers in oligopolistic industries have engaged in price competition. Competitive price cuts in such industries tend frequently to be made not by reducing announced prices, but by offering clandestine price concessions to individual buyers or on individual orders, thus resulting in a sort of "chaotic" price discrimination. Making such discrimination illegal has tended to suppress one of the more important vehicles for actual competition. This economic effect of the law seems to be definitely undesirable.

Fourth, the law has induced some considerable revisions in industrial structure as large buyers—and particularly chain stores or mass distributors—have avoided possible impacts of the law on the cost of their supplies by "backward integration" to secure their own exclusive sources of supply. Large grocery-store chains, for example, not only have integrated all wholesaling functions but also have acquired their own bakeries, dairies, and coffee processing and packing plants. Increased vertical integration has thus been encouraged in some sectors of the economy.

Finally, a reduction of concentration in the distributive trades or weakening of mass distributors—the essential aim of the Robinson-Patman amendment to Section 2 of the Clayton Act—has not been secured. This failure of intended accomplishment seems attributable in part to the avoidance of impact of the law by backward integration, but in larger part to the fact that the competitive advantages of the mass distributors inhered much more in their superior efficiency than in any monopsonistic buying advantages they may have enjoyed.

As drafted, the amended Section 2 of the Clayton Act (i.e., the Robinson-Patman Act) seems to have been an undesirable piece of legislation. Its adverse economic effects appear substantially to outweigh any favorable effects. In addition, it is unduly oriented toward the preservation of competitors as opposed to the preservation of competition, and preserving competitors tends to require suppressing competition. Predictably, it has promoted some lessening of competition, largely outside the distributive trades. The fact that it was not successful in limiting competition to the extent intended hardly supplies a ground for retaining it in its present form.

Tying and Exclusive Dealing Agreements under the Clayton Act

Section 3 of the Clayton Act imposes restrictions on another variety of market conduct, of a sort which may introduce quasi-structural changes into markets. This conduct involves the use of tying contracts and exclusive-dealing agreements. The section provides that *"it shall be unlawful for any person engaged in commerce . . . to lease or (sell) goods (for use or resale) . . . or fix a price charged therefor . . . on the condition, agreement, or understanding that the lessee or purchaser thereof shall not use or deal in the goods . . . of a competitor or competitors of the lessor or seller, where the effect . . . may be to substantially lessen competition or tend to create a monopoly in any line of commerce."* Involved here are two main sorts of vertical agreement, between buyer and seller or between lessor and lessee, which may have the effect of excluding competitors of the lessor or seller from equal access to customers.

The tying contract is typified in the agreement whereby the seller or lessor of patent-protected machinery, equipment, or other goods—for which there may be no adequate alternative sources of supply—sells or leases his patented wares only on the condition that the buyers or lessees also acquire from him only (and not from his competitors) certain other goods which are not patent-protected and of which he is not the sole available supplier. Thus the producer of a patented riveting machine might lease or sell it only on condition that lessees or buyers bought all their rivets from him, even though there were many suppliers of rivets. The exclusionary potential of this sort of vertical agreement is obvious.

The exclusive-dealing agreement, ordinarily between a manufacturer and a merchant, is usually simply one in which the buyer, in return for being supplied by the seller, agrees not to purchase or resell the products of competitors of the seller. Such exclusive dealing arrangements have been common features, for example, of franchise agreements between automobile manufacturers and their retail dealers. They can clearly impose some restriction on the access of competitive manufacturers to markets, and in extreme structural settings can have serious exclusionary effects. It will be noted that the test of violation of the law under Section 3 of the Clayton Act is not simply some "injury" to competition (as under the amended Section 2 of the same act) but either a substantial lessening of competition in a market or a tendency to create a monopoly.

The major issue in interpretation, correspondingly, concerns the degree of market occupancy that must be obtained by a seller employing tying or exclusive dealing agreements before an illegal tendency to lessen competition or to create monopoly is ascertained by the courts. In a considerable succession of cases before World War II, the general position of the courts was that such vertical agreements should be forbidden only if a single seller using them had gained control of a predominant proportion of a market—usually 70 per cent or more. If, on the other hand, at least several competing sellers of comparable size were all employing them in rivalry with each other, as in an oligopolistic market, an illegally substantial lessening of competition or tendency to create monopoly was not found, even though still other sellers might be denied access to considerable groups of buyers. In effect, predominant occupancy of the market by a single firm was an essential part of the offense against Section 3.

In several cases after World War II, the courts tentatively shifted in the direction of not requiring predominant proportionate occupancy of the market for an offense. They on occasion found an illegally substantial lessening of competition where a seller using vertical agreements of the sort in question controlled only a minor fraction of the market, and also had rivals who employed similar agreements, so long as a substantial *absolute* amount of trade was affected by the agreements of the offending seller. This interpretation would broaden the law (to some as yet undefined extent) to comprehend prohibition of tying and exclusive dealing agreements which have only an incipient tendency to create monopoly via exclusion, even though predominant market occupancy has not as yet been secured by an offending seller. It could also support legal attack on concurrent use of vertical agreements by several oligopolists in a market. If this interpretation were sustained, the prohibitions would be in general somewhat more stringent than those of the Sherman Act against monopolization via restraining vertical agreements, where predominant single or collusive joint occupancy are generally required for an offense.

It is not clear, however, that the courts have definitively altered the standards of illegality of such vertical agreements by shifting the meaning of *substantial effect* on competition from one of "proportional substantiality" (referring to the connection of such agreements with very high seller concentration) to one of "quantitative substantiality" (referring only to a large absolute amount of trade). In a case under Section 3 subsequent to those just mentioned, the courts apparently reverted at least partly to the pre-war doctrine of proportional substantiality, validating the exclusive dealing contracts of one principal seller where several other rivals in an oligopoly used similar contracts. Their recent position has been vacillating or ambivalent, and a clear doctrine interpreting Section 3 is yet to emerge.

The legal remedies for violations of Section 3 of the Clayton Act are similar in all essential respects to those under Section 2. They are civil remedies in the form of injunction of illegal agreements, either imposed by the Federal Trade Commission subject to court review or secured by the Justice Department through litigation. In the case of tying agreements involving patented products, more drastic remedies—such as reducing or limiting the patent rights of offending firms—can evidently be secured only if a concurrent violation of the Sherman Act is established.

The enforcement of Section 3 of the Clayton Act does not appear to have been sufficiently intensive—even since some judicial decisions after World War II tentatively gave the section a broader application—to do more than discourage such agreements in a small minority of potentially offending cases, these largely in industries in which predominant market control is held by a single firm. Under a court doctrine of "quantitative substantiality" of effect on competition (by no means clearly accepted as yet) it might be broadly and intensively applied to exclusive dealing arrangements. This application might break up numerous quasi-integrations of a vertical sort that have impeded entry in numerous oligopolistic markets in which no one firm has predominant market control. It might also lead indirectly to reduced seller concentration in a significant though rather minor fraction of markets. It would hardly be expected, however, to have a broad and general impact on most or many oligopolistic industries in the American economy, since the particular devices subject to attack do not have a wide enough use.

Mergers under the Clayton Act

Undoubtedly the most potent and significant regulation of business conduct imposed by the Clayton Act is that affecting the merger of firms—often accomplished by one firm acquiring another. The importance of this regulation stems dually from the provisions of the law and from its interpretation by the courts. Yet its economic significance is still in the process of determination, since it really has become effective only since the passage of the Celler-Kefauver amendment of the Clayton Act in 1950.

As thus amended, Section 7 of the act declares that: *"No corporation engaged in commerce shall acquire . . . the whole or any part of the stock . . . (or) of the assets of another corporation engaged also in commerce, where in any line of commerce in any section of the country, the effect of such acquisition may be substantially to lessen competition, or to tend to create a monopoly."* This is directly a prohibition of any changes in market structure accomplished by merger or acquisition that would have the specified tendencies of substantially restricting competition or tending to create monopoly. The prohibition is more stringent regarding mergers than any implied by the Sherman Act, and it fills to some degree a gap left by the reluctance of the courts to regard firms formed by the merger of competitors as illegal combinations in restraint of trade under Section 1 of the Sherman Act.

In interpreting Section 7 and applying it to particular mergers, the courts have had to rule on a number of relevant issues that either always do or may arise with respect to any merger. These include:

1. The scope of *the relevant market*—i.e., of the "line of commerce in any section of the country"—in which a merger does or doesn't substantially lessen competition. Judicial attention has been particularly directed to this issue by the quoted language of the law.

2. The proper meaning of *substantiality* of a merger's effect on competition in the relevant market. Given the fact that the law forbids mergers whose effect "may be substantially to lessen competition," one issue is whether an illegal effect must be "proportionally substantial" (that is, increase seller concentration in the market significantly by giving the merged firms a significantly larger proportion of the market than either had before), or alternatively need only be "quantitatively substantial" (that is, give the merged firms an absolutely large amount of assets or sales volume). Another issue, of course, involves how large either a proportional or an absolute effect must be to be considered substantial. Though these issues arise also in the interpretation of Section 3 of the Clayton Act, the courts have explored them much more fully in interpreting Section 7, and moreover have generally applied a more stringent doctrine of substantiality in Section 7 cases.

3. The question of whether a violation of Section 7 requires that an actual lessening or suppression of competition in the market be accom-

plished by the merger, or only a reasonable *probability* that competition will be lessened. The courts have made this an issue on the ground that the language of the law forbids mergers whose effects *"may be"* substantially to lessen competition. Although the language of Section 3 is identical in this respect, the courts have emphasized the issue of probability of effect mainly in connection with Section 7.

4. The related but perhaps not identical issue of whether or not a merger is illegal if it only reflects, contributes to, or implements *an incipient tendency* toward the lessening of competition in the market, as distinct from accomplishing a significant lessening in and of itself. An incipient tendency of this sort might be found, for example, if a merger appeared as one in a recent series of individually not very important mergers in an industry which threatened to have the cumulative effect of substantially lessening competition in the industry, or if a given merger was important enough that if several other mergers of the same magnitude thereafter occurred in the industry, a substantial lessening of competition would result.

Although we have had to date less than a dozen Supreme Court decisions interpreting Section 7 of the Clayton Act as amended in 1950, a reasonably clear line of judicial interpretation bearing on the issues just mentioned has been emerging. By and large, it is a line that supports a feasible maximum deterrent to merger activity.

In the crucial matter of defining relevant markets, the courts have displayed a rather systematic tendency from case to case to construe the scope of the market in such a way—whether broadly or narrowly—as to provide more or less maximum support for finding a substantial lessening of competition. Thus in some cases the relevant market has been defined narrowly—as confined, for example, to only some of the steel products and some of the geographical areas supplied by merging firms. This sort of definition confined the issue of the lessening of competition to a selected submarket in which the firms were competitive, thereby providing a "market definition" basis for finding a substantial lessening of competition. Or, markets have been defined as narrowly as local retail markets in individual towns or cities, in order to find areas in which a merger of firms selling on a nationwide basis might result in a lessening of competition. In other cases, a rather broad definition of the relevant market has been essential to the finding that a merger would lessen competition—as in the finding that glass containers and tin cans were sufficiently in the same broad market that a merger of a glass-container company with a can company would substantially lessen competition. In sum, a tendency of the courts has been to construe the term "in any

line of commerce in any section of the country" flexibly in such a way
as to support a finding of illegal lessening of competition if any plausible market definition would support it.

In determining the meaning of substantiality of effect on competition
within relevant markets, the courts have in some cases rested their findings of illegality of mergers on proportionally substantial effects on competition (significant changes in seller concentration) when such effects
were evident, although relatively small proportional changes in market
shares have sufficed to violate the law. In other cases, they have found
that quantitatively substantial effects are sufficient to violate the law,
even though the mergers in question did not appreciably alter seller
concentration in an industry. It should be noted, however, that the
courts have usually been able to equate quantitative substantiality of
effect in an industry with proportionally substantial effect on competition by defining the relevant market much more narrowly than that for
industry output as a whole, so that a quantitative substantiality doctrine
simpliciter is perhaps not fully established. Moreover, the invocation of
a quantitative substantiality doctrine has been regularly linked with or
buttressed by simultaneous reliance by the courts on the finding of
probable or incipient substantial effects on competition. In this context,
an illegal lessening of competition needs really to be no more than
quantitatively substantial, involving large absolute amounts of commerce, and does not have to affect concentration significantly.

The courts have more or less consistently taken the line that a merger
is illegal if it only results in a reasonable probability of lessening competition in the relevant market, and also that an incipient tendency to
lessen competition is sufficient to violate the law. Various judicial opinions have stated that the purpose of Section 7 is to "nip in the bud" tendencies to lessen competition or create monopoly, and that the standards
of liability under this section are thus much more stringent than those
applicable under the Sherman Act. Taking together their stands on incipiency and probability of effect and on the meaning of substantial
effect, the courts have indeed developed a doctrine which provides
extremely strong deterrents to mergers.

The mergers most obviously exposed to the law are "horizontal"
mergers of firms selling in the same industry or market, and the majority of legal actions have involved such mergers. It has also become
clear, however, that mergers that accomplish vertical integration, as
between two firms that stand in a seller-buyer relationship or are in industries that have this relation, can also violate Section 7 if an illegal
lessening of competition results. For example, acquisition by a manufacturer of a chain of retail outlets belonging to another firm has been

found illegal largely on the ground that it reduced retail competition. And control of a dominant purchaser of certain supplies (General Motors) by a firm supplying them (Du Pont) has been terminated on the ground that the control foreclosed competing suppliers from a substantial part of their potential buying market.

Prior to the rendering of a significant Supreme Court decision in April of 1967, one might have conjectured that *conglomerate* (as distinct from horizontal and vertical) mergers were not vulnerable to Section 7. That is, if a firm selling some product (e.g., aircraft) merged with or acquired another firm that (*a*) did not compete with the first firm because it sold an entirely different product (e.g., typewriters), and (*b*) had no actual or potential supplier-customer relationship with the first firm, then an illegally substantial lessening of competition presumably could not result.

This presumption was severely shaken, however, by the aforementioned Court decision that ordered a dissolution of the merger of Procter & Gamble Company and Clorox Chemical Company. Proctor & Gamble, the largest seller of soaps in the United States (and one of three firms dominating the American soap industry) had acquired Clorox, the largest American producer of household liquid bleach (supplying about half of the bleach market). The Court ruled that the merger threatened substantially to lessen competition in the bleach industry, largely because Proctor & Gamble could use its huge advertising budget to promote Clorox bleach in such a way as to deter new entry to the bleach industry and to dissuade smaller firms selling bleach from "aggressively competing." It could allegedly do this because Clorox bleach complemented or extended its line of soaps, and could be advertised concurrently with these soaps, at a lower promotional cost than a single-product bleach firm could attain.

The opinion of the Court distinguished the merger from a true or ultimately "conglomerate" merger, identifying it as a "product extension" merger, because of the complementarity of soap and bleach products. But in an *obiter dictum*, is said that this distinction was incidental, and that "all mergers are within the reach of Section 7 and all must be tested by the same standard, whether they are classified as horizontal, vertical, conglomerate, or other." At this time it therefore appears that fully conglomerate mergers may violate Section 7 of the Clayton Act, and be enjoined or dissolved, if some probability of a resultant lessening of competition in any line of commerce is perceived by the Court.

It is worth noting, finally, that the present attitude of the courts is that mergers of firms in "regulated" industries, like commercial banking and natural gas production and transportation, are subject to attack under Section 7, even though special regulatory bodies established by other laws have approved such mergers.

Section 7 of the Clayton Act is jointly enforceable by the Federal Trade Commission, through its usual procedures, and by the Department of Justice through litigation in the courts. Since the passage of the amended Section in 1950, the latter agency has devoted progressively increasing amounts of its attention and budget to its enforcement—recently instituting a rather large number of investigations of mergers and a substantial number of court actions annually. In fact, its activity in enforcing the Sherman Act appears to have been curtailed somewhat as a result of its increased attention to mergers. The remedies for prospective or actual violation of Section 7 are civil but truly severe—injunctions prohibiting contemplated mergers that have not yet been consummated, and decrees of divorcement or dismemberment of firms already created by illegal mergers. The legal controls are obviously controls of changes in industrial structure, and they are definitely strong. The deterrent effect of Section 7 on merger activity, moreover, is not adequately reflected in the number of cases brought by the enforcement agencies and the number of mergers denied or dissolved by the courts. The intensive pursuit of investigations of both proposed and accomplished mergers evidently discourages the consummation of many contemplated mergers without legal action being taken. This result is attributable not only to the stringent doctrines of enforcement adopted by the courts, but also to the fact that many contemplated mergers are only marginally attractive to one or both of the participants, so that a little legal hazard may be sufficient to discourage them.

It is perhaps too early to appraise the prospective economic effects of the enforcement of the amended Section 7. In its first seventeen years of application, a rather substantial number of mergers have been enjoined or dissolved, with appreciable effects on market structures in various industries. Many more mergers that would probably otherwise have occurred have not taken place because of the interpretation and enforcement of the section. Its judicial interpretation to date has been such as to impose extremely broad restrictions on merger activity. If this sort of interpretation is sustained, and if the section is vigorously enforced, two things are tentatively predictable. First, increases in seller concentration in various industries or markets should be strongly deterred. Second, so far as continuing merger activity is in many markets necessary to maintain existing degrees of concentration—to counteract the growth of markets and of smaller firms—the enforcement of the section in the long run could lead to appreciable decreases in concentration in many industries. Even so, however, such enforcement would not much affect existing concentration in a considerable number of markets in which concentration is already very high.

Some economists have raised questions concerning the net economic desirability of the provisions of Section 7 as judicially interpreted. One prominent criticism is that the doctrine of quantitative substantiality of effect on competition is too severe, and can result in prohibiting mergers that would not harm competition and might have beneficial results. The suggested alternative is a shift—in the legislation itself or in its court interpretation—to a doctrine of proportional substantiality. This would be oriented to preventing the development in any market of more than rather moderate concentration via mergers, but would exempt mergers that did not greatly increase concentration in relatively unconcentrated industries. A related suggestion is that the legislation should specify, or the courts should develop, a "rule of reason" applicable to mergers, which would permit mergers upon a showing by the merging firms that they would result in the realization of real economies of large scale or of vertical integration. Some exceptions of "reasonableness" to temper the existing prohibitions of mergers indeed seem needed at present. Exceptions on the ground that the growth by merger of the second, third, or fourth largest firm in a concentrated oligopolistic industry would strengthen competition, however, do not appear to deserve serious consideration.

Unfair or Unethical Competitive Methods

The fourth general phase of the policy to preserve competition involves the maintenance of an ethical "plane of competition," by imposing legal prohibitions on such things as fraud, bad faith, and deception on the part of firms in the course of their competitive activity. These prohibitions are derived almost entirely from Section 5 of the Federal Trade Commission Act, which in its original form (1914) forbade "unfair methods of competition," and as amended (1937) also forbids "unfair or deceptive acts or practices in commerce." We have already alluded, in the first main section of this chapter, to the fact that "unfair methods" under Section 5 include agreements in restraint of trade, and have discussed this application of the law. Here we are concerned with the application of the section to "unfair competition," in the form of such specific activities as disparagement of competitors, commercial bribery, commercial espionage, passing off, and (especially, in practice) misrepresentation, misbranding, and false advertising. We will content ourselves here with a very brief and synoptic review of this aspect of the antitrust laws.

Interpretation of and Remedies for Violation
of the Law against Unfair Competition

In the interpretation of the law, the major issue before the courts has been the scope of the methods of competition or the practices in commerce which are to be deemed unfair. In this respect, the courts have not given to the Federal Trade Commission much latitude for creating administrative law that would constructively broaden the range of unfair methods. The attitude in general has been that the antecedent concepts of unfair competition under the common law (prior to the passage of the F.T.C. Act) were largely governing, and the range of illegal methods has thus been largely restricted to the roster outlined just above, with the emphasis on fraud, bad faith, and deceit.

Prior to the passage of the Wheeler-Lea amendment of 1937, unfair methods of competition were even more restrictively construed, the courts insisting in key cases that violation of the law required not only such a thing as deception which might damage buyers, but also the existence of competitors of the deceptive firm, damage to these competitors by reason of the deception, and (in effect) a situation in which the competitors had not engaged in comparable deception. The added prohibition of "unfair or deceptive acts or practices" in the Wheeler-Lea amendment overcame this restrictive judicial construction of the law, so that since 1937 misrepresentation, false advertising, misbranding, and the like are illegal if only they deceive and are harmful to buyers, regardless of the impact on actual or putative competitors.

In the interpretation of the law, a certain reasonable latitude has been allowed to firms in the matter of advertising and representation of products. For exeample, ordinary exaggeration or "puffing" of the merits of a product is admitted in ordinary cases, and a test of strict factual accuracy in advertisements or representations is not applied. (The claim that a certain cigarette is rounder, firmer, and more fully packed is not strictly accurate, and may be contested by the Commission, but the courts are reluctant to strike down such innocuous, if exaggerated, claims.) On the other hand, the test with respect to representation of foods, drugs, cosmetics, and curative devices—misrepresentation of which might have direct and definite effects on the health or welfare of buyers—is generally more severe, and substantial factual accuracy in representation is required.

The usual remedy is an injunctive (cease-and-desist) order of the Commission, subject to appeal to the courts. Criminal penalties in the form of fines are incurred if the violation continues for a period of time without appeal to the courts being taken, or if a court-confirmed order is violated. In the case of foods, drugs, cosmetics, and curative devices, however, false advertisements or representations are immediately subject to criminal penalties (fines or imprisonment) if the Commission brings before the courts *prima facie* evidence of the falsity of representation and if the use of the commodity advertised may be injurious to the health of users. Here, the jurisdiction of the Federal Trade Commission both supplements and complements that of other agencies under the various "food and drug" acts of the United States.

Effects of Enforcement of the Law Affecting Unfair Competition, and Connected Issues

There has been a continuing fairly vigorous enforcement of Section 5 against unfair competition by the F.T.C., especially since the Wheeler-Lea amendment of 1937 and especially against misrepresentation and false advertising. The merits and accomplishments of this enforcement are that it has gone a considerable distance toward establishing an ethical plane of competition, in which ordinary lying and cheating are discouraged (though not entirely eliminated) as competitive devices. The advantages of this tentative establishment of a plane of competition are first that consumers and other buyers are afforded a substantial measure of protection against misleading or fraudulent claims or kindred practices, and second that competition should favor the survival and success of the more efficient firms, with the actually better products, if inferior firms are deterred from securing custom or gaining other advantages through various shady devices.

This is not to say that the enforcement of the existing law imposes any important restraint on persuasive as distinct from informational advertising, or significantly restricts the wasteful uses of nonprice competition. But it does establish a modest mean level of ethical market conduct by forbidding gross and harmful misuses of representation and promotion, as well as other doubtful commercial practices.

On the negative side, there is of course always the question of whether and to what extent the total force and effectiveness of competition as a regulator of market activity will be weakened by forbidding various devices of competition, however unethical these devices may be. No serious threat to the general effectiveness of competition seems to be imposed by the present interpretation and enforcement of Section 5 of the F.T.C. Act. There is a continuing danger, however— illustrated in the content of advisory "trade practice regulations" sponsored by the F.T.C. in the 1920's, but not subsequently—that the concept of "unfair competition" will be extended to include direct or indirect sorts of price competition, in which case the elimination of "unfair" competition might go a long way toward eliminating competition itself. In this event, preservation of competition could easily be perverted into elimination of competition in order to preserve competitors. There seems to be no current threat of this development under Section 5 of the F.T.C. Act, but the emphasis of the enforcement of Section 2 of the Clayton Act (against discrimination) tends suspiciously in this direction.

Finally, there is inescapably found in the administration of a law affecting misrepresentation and false advertising a good deal of trivial action. Commission attacks on advertising claims that two out of three tobacco experts smoke X-brand cigarettes, or that Y-brand perfume has aphrodisiac effects on the inhaler, are not likely to be regarded as essential to the attainment of major antitrust goals. In spite of these shortcomings, however, the law against unfair or unethical market practices plays a significant minor role in our overall policy affecting business competition.

Summary

Eschewing any extended recapitulation of the preceding discussion of the content, interpretation, and effects of existing American laws aimed at preserving competition and preventing monopoly, we may note that whereas these laws have had substantial virtues in checking monopolistic conduct and in lessening otherwise inherent tendencies toward monopolistic structure and performance, they are seriously deficient as a basis for securing workably competitive market structure and performance throughout the enterprise economy. The deficiencies of the statutes inhere primarily in their orientation to market conduct as the essence of violations of the law; in the inadequacy of injunctions against collusive or exclusionary conduct as means of securing competitive performance; and in the general impossibility, under the laws, of securing essential widespread revisions of market structure in concentrated oligopolistic industries. Further difficulties with the statutes involve the unduly wide range of administrative and judicial discretion which is left open by their language, and the ambivalence of standards of liability under them. We will return to these difficulties as we consider directions for revision of existing laws and policies, in Chapter 16.

SUPPLEMENTARY READINGS

Stelzer, I. M., *Selected Antitrust Cases*, 1966 (3rd ed.).
Lyon, L. S., M. W. Watkins, and V. Abramson, *Government and Economic Life*, Vol. I, 1939, Ch. X, XI.

Purdy, H. L., M. L. Lindahl, and W. A. Carter, *Corporate Concentration and Public Policy*, 1950 (rev. ed.), Ch. XIV-XII, XXX.

Mason, E. S., "Monopoly in Law and Economics," *Yale Law Journal*, November, 1937.

Martin, D. D., "The Brown Shoe Case and the New Antimerger Policy," *American Economic Review*, June, 1963.

Wilcox, Clair, *Public Policies Toward Business*, 1960 (rev. ed.), Part II.

15

Existing Regulatory Policies: Restraint of Competition; Imposition of Direct Regulations

As we have seen, the main orientation of American public policy affecting enterprises acting as producers and sellers is toward preserving competition and preventing monopoly. This general policy is applicable to all sectors and industries not specifically exempted or set aside for special treatment. Exemptions have been made, however, and importantly in the period since 1930. The usual policy of the federal and state governments toward exempted sectors and industries, moreover, has not been confined to—although it incidentally involved—removal of anti-trust-law prohibitions of private restraint of competition or monopolization. It has also included direct public restrictions of competition, active public support and encouragement of private restrictions, or direct governmental regulation of market performance.

Thus, distinctly anticompetitive policies have been pursued with respect to a number of segments of the economy which have unusual or exceptional characteristics or present unusual problems. The number and importance of the "exceptional" areas are great enough, moreover, that it is no longer possible to regard the various anticompetitive policies as merely an assortment of unusual and special departures from the general competitive policy. Rather we must recognize that these anticompetitive policies as a group embody a second orientation or line of emphasis in American public policy toward business, that is in important part potentially in conflict with and inconsistent with the general competitive policy.

Public measures to restrict enterprise competition or to substitute direct governmental regulation for competition have been imposed in two main types of industry. The first type, singled out for special policy treatment since before the turn of the century, embraces the "public utility" industries, including those providing electric power, natural or manufactured gas, public transportation, and communications via telephone and telegraph. The distinguishing characteristics of these industries (actual or alleged) are that they provide widely used necessities of individual or commercial life for which there are no close available substitutes, and in addition that they are in some degree "natural monopolies" (or, by etxension, "natural oligopolies"). They are held to be natural monopolies or oligopolies because (*a*) advantages to large-scale firms are such that unrestricted competition would lead to exclusive occupancy of individual markets by one or a very few firms, with greater efficiency and monopolistic pricing tendencies both resulting, and/or (*b*) unrestricted competition among several or many firms in a market would, because of technological characteristics of the industries involved, have seriously deleterious effects on the welfare of buyers. These effects may include inferior service, such as might result if two rival telephone companies served customers in the same city, or widespread price discrimination.

Where these conditions prevail, the tendency of public authorities has been to declare the industry a public utility, to license or franchise the operation of firms in a restrictive fashion (so as to allow only one or a few firms in a market), and to subject the franchised monopolists or oligopolists to direct regulation of their prices and services. The regulation is generally administered by specially constituted governmental commissions. The general rationale of this sort of exception to the competitive policy is the asserted existence of a group of industries in which competition would serve very poorly as a regulatory device in the public interest. The nominal main emphasis of the resultant regulatory policy is generally the protection of the buyers from the consequences of inevitable monopoly or from undue wastes or other disadvantages of competition, although the protection of sellers also inevitably enters in as a consideration.

The second category of industries for which anticompetitive policies have been developed—mainly since 1930—include relatively atomistic industries in which unregulated competition has resulted in one or more of the untoward consequences discussed in Chapter 12 above. These consequences include true destructive competition, disadvantages to small business resulting from the ascendancy of larger firms, and poor conservation performance. The primary economic difficulty with which policy deals in these cases is not really the adverse effects on buyers of seemingly inevitable monopoly nor any disadvantage to buyers of oligopolistic rivalry. The occasion for public interference is rather the persistence of comparatively low enterprise and labor earnings in the areas involved, together with resulting pleas that the sellers involved be protected from the rigors of a competitive market. The main aim of resultant public policies has been to restrict, modify, or interfere with competition enough to improve the earnings positions of affected enterprises and laborers, thus giving them equality or parity with enterprise and labor in less competitive fields. Additional goals of improving efficiency or conservation are also frequently announced and pursued, but these aims are in general secondary to that of redressing inequalities of enterprise and labor income. In sum, the emphasis has been mainly on the protection of *competitors* (enterprise and labor) at the expense of restricting *competition* in markets.

Neither the public utility policy of regulatory interference nor the policy of restraining competition in atomistic markets has as yet been carried as far as logical consistency might dictate. Evidently and perhaps fortunately, neither policy has been applied to more than a minor fraction of the cases to which it might be by analogy from cases already covered. Thus, the competitive policy still rules in general. But the future is before us, and possibilities of serious conflict between competitive and anticompetitive policies are present.

What is the character of the actual and potential inconsistency of various competition-restraining policies with the general competitive policy? Any potential inconsistency of the policy toward naturally monopolistic public utility industries stems nominally from the identification of a limited minority group of industries in which competition is not feasible either because it leads inevitably to monopoly, or because the rivalry of several firms would be injurious to the welfare of buyers. The policy is then at least nominally consistent with one of preserving competition *wherever it will serve the interests of the general public*, but rests on the finding that the public will not be well or effectively served by competition in a limited category of cases. More serious or general inconsistencies with the competitive policy may tend to develop so far as certain alleged "natural oligopolies," in which competition actually is or would be reasonably workable, may be designated as public utilities and subjected to public restriction of entry and regulation of price.

Existing policies involving restriction of competition in atomistic industries cannot so easily claim consistency with an overall policy of preserving competition wherever it serves the interest of the general public. To be sure, it is alleged in most relevant instances that the public suffers from the inefficiency or poor conservation performance associated with atomistic competition, and that public interference with competition will ameliorate these adverse performance tendencies. But it is not generally clear that such amelioration needs to be accomplished, or is most effectively accomplished, by the restriction of competition. In this sort of case, competition is not fundamentally inconsistent with good social performance. Other feasible governmental measures—not involving the restriction of competition—should suffice to remedy adverse performance tendencies and to make competition a workable device for industrial self-regulation.

This being true, the remaining justification for restriction of competition in such industries is patently the preservation of competitors and their incomes through the elimination of competition among them, even though the general public (given alternative remedial measures) could be well served by the competitive process. Since the policy of preserving competition must generally contemplate as one of its consequences the exposure of individual competitors or groups thereof to the danger of losses or of elimination from a market, along with their exposure to the opportunity for supernormal profits, these competition-restricting policies in atomistic industries have a fundamental inconsistency with the competitive policy.

We may therefore raise the question of why our legislative bodies have been willing to embrace such a fundamental inconsistency in policy. Aside from the force of powerful pressure groups (such as organized farmers or retail merchants) that seek and get special legal treatment, several explanations may be advanced. All reflect some lack, on the part of the public and its elected governments, of an unwavering faith in competition as a solution for economic problems.

First, there is at least some ambivalence in our basic antitrust laws, as written, applied, and interpreted, as to whether the major legal purpose is to preserve competition or to protect competitors from unjustified damage at the hands of other competitors. Both purposes are there in some part, as is clearly suggested by the Sherman Act prohibition of monopolization and by Sections 2 and 3 of the Clayton Act. And given the initial recognition of the protection of competitors (from each other) as at least one aim of the basic procompetitive law, it has not proved too difficult to stretch this phase of the doctrine to cover the protection of competitors from competition itself.

Second, the special treatment long afforded labor organizations under the antitrust policy has provided some basis for arguing that very small enterprises are entitled to comparable treatment. Labor unions have been expressly exempted as combinations in restraint of trade since 1914, and their exercise of monopoly power in collective bargaining and related activities is clearly legal. This exemption is justified in general on the ground that laborers must be allowed to organize and combine to eliminate competition among individual laborers and to act concertedly in the markets where wages are determined, if they are to secure fair wages. It is but a short step from the individual laborer to the individual small farmer or small retail merchant, either of whom may be essentially in large part a self-employed laborer. It is a similarly short step in reasoning to the conclusion that these very small enterprisers should be able to enhance their incomes by restricting competition under the same legal privileges enjoyed by laborers. This line of reasoning by analogy prevails, even though the typical market situations of laborers and small enterprises differ in significant respects, and though the extent of monopoly power granted to unions has not been scrutinized carefully enough that the prevailing policy toward labor can be justified offhand as a standard for treatment of small enterprise.

Finally, the previously dominant political-economic philosophy which generally supported competition because of its putative advantages to the public, and because of the freedom of action it left to enterprise, has been seriously qualified in the last thirty years by a contrary philosophy which emphasizes economic security as a main end–particularly the security of laborers and enterprises in sustained incomes. This philosophy can be implemented (as it has been) in social insurance schemes and in governmental fiscal policies designed to maintain full employment, without doing violence to the general program of preserving competition. It can be implemented in the labor field without doing much violence to the maintenance of competition in the enterprise sector of the economy. As implemented in the restriction of competition in atomistic industries, largely for purposes of protecting incomes, it introduces a basic conflict with the competitive policy as applied to enterprise, and a conflict which could become acute and destructive if the scope of interferences with market competition were significantly broadened. Governmentally "directed" equality and security in the economic realm thus potentially clashes with the policy of relying on the regulatory effects of the impersonal competitive market.

Against the preceding background, let us undertake a brief review of the principal instances of departure from the competitive policy (as applied to enterprises) in the United States. We will give most of our attention to the content and effect of policy in four principal instances in which competition in relatively atomistic industries has been restricted: in the agricultural industries, the distributive trades, coal mining, and petroleum production. A briefer and more synoptic review will be made of the character and effect of existing policies affecting public utilities.

Restrictive Policies Affecting Agriculture

The governmental interference with enterprise competition which has for some time been best known to the public and most debated in political forums is that affecting agriculture. A substantial part of the electorate is generally acquainted with the long-standing federal policy of supporting crop prices and restricting the output or sale of crops, and has been exposed to arguments concerning the merits of various alternative forms of public interference in the agricultural sector. Before turning to the content and effects of current agricultural policy, we may first comment briefly on the setting and character of the agricultural "distress" problem with which the policy has been designed to cope.

The agricultural sector is made up of a considerable number of different industries, distinguished mainly on the basis of identity of crop (wheat, cotton, cattle, peaches, lettuce, milk, poultry, and so forth), and to a lesser extent (in the case of perishables) on the basis of region. The typical agricultural industry has three important structural characteristics. First, it is truly atomistic in structure, with a very large number of relatively or absolutely small producers and sellers, none of which supplies a significant fraction of the total output reaching his market. Second, it is subject to very easy and rather rapid entry of new producers and sellers, so that, given some increase in demand, supply can be substantially and quickly expanded by new firms.[1]

Third, the typical agricultural industry is perversely subject to a much more difficult, slow, or lagging exit of firms and productive capacity when crops are in oversupply relative to demand and agricultural incomes are consequently subnormal. Rather long periods of subnormal incomes are generally required to induce the removal from the agricultural sector of redundant land and human resources. Thus the forces of the market work fairly rapidly to expand agricultural outputs when expansion is called for, but they work quite slowly to contract output when contraction is indicated. The result is that prolonged periods of inequitably low incomes to farm enterprise and labor tend to be encountered once a situation of oversupply develops.

[1] The speed of entry, of course, varies among crops. Expansion of fruit output requiring orchard planting takes longer than expansion of dairy herds to increase milk supply, and the latter takes longer than expansion of the output of an annual crop like wheat.

Since the end of World War I, or for over forty-five years, American agriculture has evidenced a general tendency (interrupted only by the abnormal wartime demands of World War II) toward oversupply. That is, the unrestricted or competitive output of the land and human resources invested in in agriculture has been large enough relative to demands for farm products that competitive market prices for crops would provide only subnormal incomes (relative to those earned in other sectors) to enterprise and labor employed in agriculture. Thus there has been a redundancy of resources devoted to agricultural production, and one that yielded only very slowly to the pressure of low incomes. To probe the difficulty a little further, it may be noted that the critical redundancy of farm work-force and capacity has been centered, as a matter of emphasis, in certain regions where marginal land is widely employed by many very small farmers (such as in the Southeast generally) and that the critical shortage of incomes has been encountered in the same regions. However, some degrees of oversupply and income deficiency have been at least periodically present (in the absence of governmental interferences) throughout most of the regions and crops of the agricultural economy generally.

The historical reasons for the development of this general maladjustment are fairly complex, but a few major factors stand out.

1. Two periods of major wartime demand for food and fiber, before 1920 and again in the early 1940's, induced substantial and rapid increases in agricultural supply and capacity to supply, and thereafter agriculture in general was quite slow in bringing capacity and supply back to peacetime levels. In fact, the overcapacity stemming in part from World War I had not been adequately "worked off" when World War II came twenty-odd years later. And though the latter war temporarily provided demand greater than the output of available capacity, it was by the same token responsible for the creation of a more acute agricultural excess capacity.

2. Progressive increases in the productivity of agricultural industries, as measured in terms of output per acre cultivated or per man employed, have meant that fewer agricultural resources are required to provide a given total output. Thus resources previously employed have tended to become redundant except so far as the secular growth of demand could absorb the added output.

3. There was a long period after World War I in which export markets for important basic crops were progressively lost, partly because of the development of alternative supplies in other countries, and partly because of nationalistic trade policies and international political schisms. This downward trend in the export market for American farm

products has been arrested and to some extent reversed in the last decade.

4. Finally, the maladjustment of supply to demand resulting from the factors just outlined has been prolonged and perpetuated by governmental interferences with competition that raised and protected the incomes of resources invested in American agriculture, but did not provide an adequate positive incentive for the shift of redundant resources to other occupations. We will speak in more detail of the effects of our public policies toward agriculture as the chapter progresses.

Given these tendencies toward a chronic excess of supply relative to demand and a lagging exit of superfluous agricultural capacity, the character of market performance has been in accord with theoretical expectations. There has been, that is, an actual or virtual secular tendency toward agricultural crop prices that would be insufficient to provide normal incomes (comparable to those in other sectors) to enterprise and labor in the agricutural sector. This is not to say that subnormal incomes have persistently been earned in fact. The Second World War demand was great enough temporarily to sustain satisfactory or even exceptionally high farm prices. And the systematic governmental interference with agricultural competition since the war (and, to a lesser degree, in the latter 1930's) has sufficed to sustain relatively high farm prices and incomes through artificial restrictions of output and marketing, governmental purchase of surplus crops, and direct income subsidies. But it is fair to say that in peacetime periods before extensive governmental interference was instituted, farm prices and incomes as determined in competitive markets tended to be subnormal, and that subsequently they would probably have been subnormal if competition had been permitted to operate in an unrestricted fashion.

Thus the relation of agricultural capacity to demand (wartime periods aside) either presents the actuality or poses the threat of subnormal farm prices and incomes, presuming that competition might be unrestricted. The actual or threatened deficiency of income, to be sure, does or would tend to have its most serious impact on a very large number of very small and relatively inefficient farmers who are, for the most part, concentrated in certain regions. But the possibilities for at least initial moderate deficiencies of income for the relatively larger and more efficient farmers in general, were competition to be reinstituted, also seem relatively strong.

In its broad outlines, therefore, the agricultural sector in general has been, in the absence of public interference, subject to "destructive competition" as described in Chapter 12. This general problem, moreover, was complicated by further specific difficulties. First, farm prices and incomes tend to be, under competition, exceptionally unstable in the face of major cyclical movements in the economy as a whole. This instability is attributable to the inelasticity of the demand for farm products in response to price changes, and to the insensitivity of supply to price changes (especially downward changes) in the short term. Thus uncontrolled farm prices and incomes tend to fluctuate much more violently in response to cyclical fluctuations than do prices and incomes in general, and especially tend to collapse spectacularly in major depressions.

This tendency was reflected, for example, in the depression of the early 1930's, when the agricultural sector in general suffered from extremely low prices and insufficient incomes for several years, and when widespread economic distress in rural areas resulted. In the long run, to be sure, the "famine" of depression farm prices may tend to be offset by the "feast" of high prices in prosperity or in war. But this is a minor solace to the individuals involved during a depression, and the secular maladjustment of supply to demand may, under competition, prevent the "feast" periods from providing compensating rewards. To the difficulty of cyclical instability of farm prices and incomes under competition is of course added a further instability attributable to weather-induced annual crop fluctuations. In brief, the farmers' actual or potential price and income troubles are not confined to those resulting from secular maladjustments, but include those resulting from cyclical and random fluctuations in prices and incomes.

A second complicating difficulty is that, under conditions of uncontrolled competition, there has tended to be a high incidence of technological inefficiency and of poor conservation performance in the agricultural industries. These have been encountered at any time in the myriad very small farms of certain regions, and in the farming community more generally in periods of depression. These adverse performance tendencies seem to be rooted in considerable part in acute deficiencies of farm income, such that the farm enterprises involved cannot afford or finance the use of the most efficient techniques or the pursuit of conservation practices which would preserve or enhance future yields. A side-effect or consequence of destructive competition has thus involved inferior performance in technical efficiency and conservation.

Public Interference with Agricultural Competition—General Outline

Governmental interference with agricultural competition has a long and busy history—busy especially ever since the institution of extensive intervention under the New Deal administration in 1933–and the legacy of this history at present takes the form of a rather complex body of legislation and derived policy. It is not our purpose here to trace the evolution of the present law through a long succession of legislative experiments and developments, nor even to explore contemporary agricultural policy in intimate detail. Instead, we will be content to describe the main features of the principal policies of interference with agricultural competition now in effect, and to indicate in a general way the extent to which they are continuations or revisions of policies pursued in the past thirty years.

The basic American policy toward agricultural competition is federal, and has three main parts. The first is a program of limitation of farm acreage and output and of support of farm prices and incomes. Under it, the government induces farmers to restrict the acreages devoted to producing various specific major crops, and indirectly to reduce the outputs of these crops, below competitive levels. Farmers "cooperate" with the acreage restriction program by accepting acreage allotments for growing the crops involved, and further—with respect to several basic crops—by diverting some of the allotted acreage from crop production to "conserving" uses. The government induces farmers to comply with nominal acreage allotments and to reduce them through diversions in two ways. First, it guarantees that the prices of various crop outputs produced in conformity with prescribed allotments and diversions will not be allowed to fall below specified minimum levels, in effect by standing ready to purchase any "surplus" crops that are unsold at these minimum prices. Second, the government pays direct income subsidies to the cooperating growers of several basic crops in return for both required and added optional diversions of nominal acreage allotments to conserving uses. This program, or complex of individual-crop programs, will be examined further below.

The second program is similar but not identical to that of subsidizing the diversion of acreage from growing specific crops to conserving uses. Under it, the government has entered into medium-term contracts (running from 3 to 10 years) with farmers under which (1) the farmers agreed to divert acreages of *any* crop-producing land (type of crop unspecified) from all crop production to conserving uses variously described, and (2) the government agreed to pay the farmers income subsidies equal to some percentage of the value of crops foregone on the diverted acreage. The extent of these diversions of cropland has been limited by the amount of Congressional appropriations provided to finance them. This program, designated as a "soil bank" conservation program in its first version (1956–60) and as a "cropland adjustment" program in its second version (from 1965 until terminated), is aimed at reducing at least temporarily the amount of agricultural land in general that is available for producing crops, at subsidizing farm incomes, and incidentally at encouraging at least temporary alternative uses of part of our redundant acreage of agricultural land.

Under the third program, the federal government sponsors agricultural marketing agreements among handlers, processors, or distributors of various agricultural products, or issues equivalent marketing orders to them. These agreements and orders are aimed in part at restricting the actual supply of such products reaching the market, and in part at regularizing the flow of products to the market. They have been important primarily for perishable crops and those with local and regional markets.

In addition, there are miscellaneous interference policies of state governments, the most important of which—and the only ones to be discussed here—are embodied in various state laws to control the price of milk. Let us now examine these several phases of policy in somewhat greater detail.

Role of "Parity" Prices in the Farm Prices and Income Support Program

A crucial concept employed in designing past and present federal policies to support farm prices and income is that of so-called "parity" prices for farm products. In general terms, the current parity price per unit of output for any farm commodity is a hypothetical price that bears the same relationship to the current prices of all other goods as its actual price bore to all other actual prices during a designated historical "base" period when the ratio of farm to other prices is held to have been "fair." In other words, it is an imaginary money price of a farm good that would currently have the same real purchasing power that the actual price of the farm good had during some long-past period when farm prices were relatively quite high.

The simplest way of calculating the current parity price of any farm good is to multiply its price in the chosen base period by an index showing the ratio of the current average prices of other goods to their prices in the same base period. For example, suppose that the price of wheat in base period was $1.00 per bushel, that the average price of other goods in the base period is represented by an index of 100, and that the current price index of other goods is 300—which means that the current average price of other goods is three times as great as their average price in the base period. Then the parity price of wheat is $1.00 multiplied by 3, or $3.00. This $3.00 price would give a currently produced bushel of wheat the same real purchasing power it had in the base period. Let us call a price so calculated the "simple" parity price.

Until quite recently, the parity prices used in determining the level of federal price supports of farm commodities were computed in the preceding simple way. The base period price used for any crop was ordinarily its average price from 1909 to 1914, and the price index for other goods by which the base price was multiplied was an index showing the relationship of the current average price of goods purchased by farmers to the average price of the same goods from 1909 to 1914.

Under a recently adopted "modern" parity formula, the parity price of any crop is an adjusted version of the simple one just mentioned—adjusted to reflect differences in the proportional changes of individual crop prices between 1909–14 and recent years. A crop the recent average price of which has risen above its 1909–14 price by a greater proportion than has the recent average price of all agricultural commodities since 1909–14 has its "simple" parity price proportionally adjusted upward. A crop the recent average price of which has risen above its 1909–14 price by a smaller proportion than has the recent average price of all agricultural commodities since 1909–14 has its "simple" parity price proportionally adjusted downward.[2] These adjustments effectively make an arbitrary allowance for changes in the relative demands for different crops over time.

The application of the term "parity" to a hypothetical price arrived

---

[2]A modern or adjusted parity price would be calculated in the following way, or an arithmetically equivalent way. First, compute the "simple" parity price—i.e., multiply the 1909–14 average actual price (e.g., $1.00 per bushel) of the commodity (e.g., wheat) by the current price index relating the current average price of goods purchased by farmers to the average price of the same goods in 1909–14 (e.g., 300), and divide the result by 100. Thus ($1.00 × 300) ÷ 100 = $3.00. Then compute the price relative that shows the relation of the average price of wheat in the most recent ten years to the price of wheat in 1909–14; let us suppose that this relative is 230, indicating that the recent average price of wheat was $2.30, or 230 per cent of its price in 1909–14. Then compute the price index that shows the relation of the average price of all farm commodities in the most recent ten years to their average price in 1909–14; let us suppose that the index is 276, indicating that the recent average price of all farm commodities was 276 per cent of their average price in 1909–14. Finally, multiply the simple current parity price of wheat by the ratio of the wheat-price relative to the all-farm-price index, and arrive at the adjusted parity price. Here we would multiply $3.00 by 230/276 and arrive at an adjusted parity price of wheat of $2.50. The adjusted parity price of wheat is lower than its simple parity price because its price has risen less rapidly since 1909–14 than farm prices in general. If for another commodity, at the same time, its own price relative showing its increase in price from 1909–14 to the average of the last ten years were greater than 276—e.g., 290—its adjusted parity price would be arrived at by multiplying its simple parity price by 290/276. Its adjusted parity price would be higher than its simple parity price because its price has risen more rapidly since 1909–14 than farm prices in general.

at in this way is evidently meant to imply that the price would be fair or just. It would be more accurate to say that a parity price is just a price that is arrived at through a complicated computational procedure, the magnitude of which is strongly influenced by the arbitrary choice of a base period. It is true that parity prices as calculated reflect in a broad and loose way inflationary (or deflationary) price movements in the economy as a whole. But there is no theoretical or empirical reason to suppose that parity prices should correspond at all closely to the current competitive market prices for individual crops that would just permit normal enterprise and labor incomes (equivalent to those in other sectors of the economy) to be earned in the agricultural sector. For a variety of reasons, parity prices have tended and tend to be at supercompetitive levels, or well above what would be required to provide normal farm incomes under a fully competitive adjustment. These reasons include the selection for parity-price calculations of base periods during which farm prices and incomes were supernormal, and the fact that huge increases in farm productivity since the period before World War I have produced a situation in which maintenance of normal farm incomes does not require the maintenance of prewar relative prices per unit of farm commodities sold.

A related property of parity prices (or prices equal to major fractions of parity prices) is that they have consistently been higher, especially for basic farm commodities, than corresponding world prices as established in a more or less free world market. Correspondingly, programs to support American farm prices at near-parity levels have become involved with serious problems of crop surpluses that were nominally "priced out" of the world market, as we will see further below.

The parity price is thus mainly a political concept, reflecting the attempt of a particular economic interest group to gain as much income as possible through governmental interference. It is not a concept derived from any careful economic analysis of the requirements for equitable income distribution through competitive markets. Nonetheless, parity prices, crop by crop, have been and continue to be held forth as ultimate goals of governmental interference with agricultural competition.

Parity prices of crops, as calculated by the Secretary of Agriculture, have played two interrelated roles in federal programs to support farm prices and income. First, they have been used as a basis for calculating the "minimum prices" of basic and other crops which the federal government would guarantee in return for the acceptance by farmers of restrictions on (allotments of) acreage to be planted to these crops. Each federal "support price" for a crop has generally been defined as some percentage of its parity price—e.g., 90 per cent of parity price. Or, if the guarantee was to support a crop price within a given range, the limits of the range were defined as percentages of parity price—e.g., support at between 75 and 90 per cent of parity. Second, parity prices have been used, especially in recent years, as a basis for calculating the direct subsidy payments made to farmers for diverting to conserving uses acreage otherwise devoted to raising specific crops or crops in general. The amounts of such subsidies, or alternatively their lower or upper limits, have been computed directly as certain percentages of the support prices of the crop yields foregone because of acreage diversions, and thus implicitly as certain percentages of the parity prices of these unproduced crops.

The "Traditional" Farm Price Support Program

In its thirty-year history to date, the federal program of supporting farm prices and incomes has undergone many changes in detail, most of which are at present just as well forgotten. In broad outline, however, it has successively assumed two general forms—first a relatively simple one, and in recent years a form that is very complex. Moreover, the present program, which is still in the process of evolving from the earlier one, is sufficiently complicated that it is more easily understood if one first understands the broad characteristics of the old program.

Under the old program, which was almost brutally simple, the government mainly (1) guaranteed to support the prices of designated crops at some minimum percentage of parity, (2) imposed on farmers acreage allotments for growing these crops as a *quid pro quo* for the price guarantees, and (3) in effect bought at the guaranteed or support prices any amount of the resulting crop outputs that private buyers would not purchase at those prices. Since in general its acreage restrictions were not severe enough to restrict crop outputs to amounts that the private market would take at the support prices, the government accumulated in storage stocks of surplus farm commodities that it had bought in order to support their prices. It then had to look for ways of disposing of these stocks outside of the domestic market.

The level of price supports and the number of crops the prices of which were supported varied over time. From 1938 to 1941 there were mandatory price supports only for certain "basic" crops (wheat, corn, cotton, tobacco, and rice), at levels generally between 50 and 75 per cent of parity. During World War II, price supports for a greatly enlarged variety of crops were raised to 90 per cent of parity (though under wartime demands actual market prices were higher), and a guarantee was made that supports at this level would be maintained for two years following the end of the war. From the beginning of 1947 until 1955, farm-group political pressure kept mandatory price supports on basic crops and some designated "non-basics" (oats, barley, butter, cheese, dried milk) at 90 per cent of parity, with optional or permissive price supports for other farm commodities at any level not above 90 per cent of parity. Thereafter, until the beginning of the 1960's, there was a movement toward introducing "flexible" price supports that should vary within limits depending on the relation of current crop supplies to arbitrarily defined "normal" supplies. The price support range for various basic crops was either 65 to 90 per cent of parity or 75 to 90 per cent of parity; it was from 60 to 90 per cent of parity for some designated non-basic crops.[3]

Two aspects of mandatory price supports during the whole course of this traditional program are worthy of note. First, the program supported at the designated percentage of parity the price of the entire domestic output of every supported crop, or all of its output produced subject to prevailing acreage allotments. Second, the mandatory support prices (except during World War II) were systematically above the corresponding world or export prices, so that any surplus outputs that were not saleable in the domestic private market at the support prices would be "sold" to the government by farmers rather than sold in the export market.

As the prices of various crops were supported at various percentages of parity over time, acreage allotments for growing these crops were simultaneously established—nationally and for individual farmers—with conformity to these allotments being a condition for eligibility for price supports. The general aim from the outset was ostensibly to restrict the acreage growing any price-supported crop sufficiently that the entire resulting crop output would be demanded in the domestic private market at a price as high as the support price. The desired output was eventually defined as a "normal" supply, calculated in a somewhat implausible fashion. But as noted above, politically feasible acreage allotments systematically turned out to be too large to accomplish the intended crop output restrictions, in part because allotted acreages were simply too large and in part because of unanticipated increases in crop output per allotted acre.

How did the government "take out of the market" the surpluses of supported crops that were not saleable privately at its support prices? It did this mainly by having its Commodity Credit Corporation make "non-recourse" loans to farmers on their price-supported crop outputs. That is, the CCC would loan to any qualifying farmer (one who had ob-

---

[3]Tobacco continued to be supported at 90 per cent of parity, and wool was also given special treatment.

served his acreage allotments) an amount equal to the support price on all his output not already sold at or above the support price, receiving and storing this unsold output as collateral for the loan. Then, on any amount of this stored output that they could not sell at or above support prices, farmers were free simply to default on their loans (hence the term "non-recourse"), letting the CCC keep the stored surplus output instead. Through the CCC the federal government thus ended up in essentially purchasing (through unrepaid loans) the surplus output of any price-supported crop.

For example, the government would set a support price on commodity X of $2.00 per bushel, and find that whereas the private domestic market would take only 500 million bushels at $2.00, acreage allotments had been sufficient to reduce the crop supply only to 600 million bushels. The CCC would then acquire and store the "surplus" 100 million bushels, through non-recourse loans on which farmers defaulted, at $2.00 per bushel, thus supporting the domestic price at that level.

Given the persistent failure of the government to restrict acreages and outputs for supported commodities enough to avoid surpluses at the support prices, the government's CCC persistently tended (except during World War II), to accumulate staggering surpluses of stored farm commodities that it had bought in order to maintain domestic farm prices. Even in the period from 1938 to 1941, when only a few crop prices were supported at relatively small percentages of parity, it acquired very large surpluses. Then, from the end of World War II through 1955 (a period when farm prices were supported at 90 per cent of parity), the CCC increased its holding of stored surplus farm commodities from a value of about $500 million to a value of $7 billion.

This increase of $6.5 billion worth of surplus farm commodities purchased and stored by the government, moreover, was only a net increase. This net was smaller than the gross acquisitions of the CCC by the amounts that it had been able to dispose of by "dumping" at low prices in foreign markets, by gifts for relief of distress in foreign nations, by gifts or cut-price sales to domestic public institutions or school lunch programs, or by cut-price domestic sales for inferior uses—as by the sale of a potato surplus back to farmers for restricted use as cattle feed.

In the later 1950's and subsequently, therefore, increasing attention was given to systematic programs for disposing of stored surplus commodities in the export market, frequently involving government-to-government agreements for the sale of these commodities at distress prices or for unconvertible foreign currencies. Under these programs in general the government of course incurred substantial financial losses by disposing of stored commodities for much less than it had paid our farmers for them, and to this extent the general taxpayer ultimately subsidized farmers by absorbing the losses.

With some easing of world political tensions, increased world prosperity in the era following postwar reconstruction, and the reduction of artificial barriers to trade and to the exchange of national currencies—together with the growing world demand for food and fiber resulting from population increases—less desperate measures for disposing of American agricultural surpluses in export markets have become progressively more feasible. Corespondingly, the major problem of accumulating and trying to dispose of stored surpluses that was an adjunct of our traditional farm price support program seems to be diminishing. At the same time, our traditional program has recently been in the process of a considerable alteration aimed at accommodating it to changed world circumstances. Therefore, let us now consider some major characteristics of the contemporary program, and how they differ from the traditional one.

Contemporary Farm Price and Income Support Program

Since 1961 a related series of alterations have been made in the federal farm price support program applied to several basic commodities. These changes are sufficiently great that, for these commodities, the program has been significantly altered, embodying a "new" policy. To be sure, we still have in effect for other price-supported commodities the "last model" of the traditional program described above, so that at this writing we are operating with a combination of the new policy as applied to some basic crops and the old policy as applied to other crops. But if the program were further modified to bring other crops under the new policy—a development that would be consistent with recent trends in Congressional action—we would shortly have in being a new generalized program for supporting farm prices and incomes. It is thus important to examine the new policy now applied to certain basic commodities not only because of its own significance, but also because it suggests the possible character of general policy in the near future.

The major characteristics of the new program and its differences from the old one may be described briefly as follows. First, it continues for the crops affected to assign acreage allotments that must be accepted as a condition of eligibility for price and income supports, and in addition requires (also as a condition for such eligibility) that specified fractions of allotted acreages be diverted from crop production to conserving uses. The new policy concerning acreage restrictions therefore differs from the old mainly in that the total restrictions are greater (the net acreage allotments smaller), because some acreage normally allotted for growing the specified crops must be withdrawn from crop production.

Second, the basic support prices for the designated crops are set at substantially lower levels than under the traditional program—in general approximately at the levels of world or export prices. These low prices are guaranteed for all "cooperating" growers (those observing acreage allotments and diversions) by the familiar non-recourse loans of the Commodity Credit Corporation, and may be referred to as "loan prices." These loan prices are generally so determined that exporting any domestically unsold crop output should be equally as attractive to farmers as selling it to the CCC.

Third, the cooperating growers of the designated crops receive direct income subsidy payments in either or both of two forms:

1. An extra payment (over and above the loan price) per unit, in an amount designed to yield a total "price" for domestically sold output equal to a designated higher percentage of parity. (Each farmer's domestically sold output of a crop is effectively calculated as his prorata share of all domestic sales of the crop.)

2. A payment for diverting part of the acreage nominally allotted for growing a designated crop from crop production to conserving uses, this payment being calculated as some percentage of the value of the crop that could have been grown on the diverted acreage. These payments are subsidies for withdrawing acreage from the production of given crops and putting it to noncrop-producing uses.

Fourth, no price or income support is provided for exportable surpluses of the designated crops other than the loan price support set approximately to equal export prices.

The payment of income subsidies calculated as a certain amount per unit of crop sold domestically (presently for two crops, wheat and cotton) effectively creates a two-price system at least from the standpoint of farmers, who receive in total distinctly higher prices for their prorata shares of domestic sales than for their prorata shares of export sales (or of surpluses acquired by the CCC). In the case of wheat, it also creates a two-price system from the standpoint of American wheat buyers and users, who themselves effectively pay a price that includes the income subsidy. An obvious and announced objective of the two-price system is to provide support to farm incomes earned from domestic sales without discouraging exports through general price supports above the levels of export prices.

The full content of the new policy may be revealed more fully if we outline the provisions of the specific programs for wheat, cotton, and feed grains.

Under the wheat program, farmers become eligible for price and income supports by accepting acreage allotments and then diverting a required minimum percentage of the allotted acreage to conserving uses. For all of their wheat production, a loan support price is set about equal to the export price–specifically, at a level based on the world price and the value of wheat as feed grain. This loan price becomes a domestic "base" price, since the CCC stands ready to make non-recourse loans at this price on all eligible production. Then cooperating wheat-growers are guaranteed income payments on their prorata shares of domestic wheat sales in an amount sufficient to bring the total price of domestically sold wheat (loan price plus added payment) up to 100 per cent of parity or as near thereto as practicable. [4]

The added income payments on domestically used wheat are accomplished by issuing "wheat marketing certificates" to farmers for their shares of domestic output, these certificates having a value per bushel about equal to the difference between the loan price of wheat and a price equal to 100 per cent of parity. Domestic wheat buyers and processors must then purchase these certificates as well as paying the loan price for all wheat taken, thus providing the farmers with the full parity prices and themselves paying the subsidy. Since the full cost of wheat to domestic processors is then the full parity price, this high price is more or less automatically passed on to the domestic consumers of wheat products.

Wheat in excess of the domestic share can be sold by farmers to exporters at the export price or surrendered to the CCC at the approximately equal loan price. So far as it acquires wheat, the CCC sells grain to exporters effectively at the world price (nominally the loan price plus an export-certificate charge if the world price is higher, or the loan price minus an export subsidy if the world price is lower). In recent years, the export price has been a little over 50 per cent of the full parity price, so that farm incomes respectively from domestically sold and exported wheat tend to differ dramatically.

Cooperating wheat growers receive no extra income subsidy for the required diversion of allotted acreage to conserving uses. For acreage diversions greater than the required minimum, up to 25 acres per farm, they are to be paid amounts up to 50 per cent of the loan price of the wheat that could have been grown on the extra diverted acreage.

---

[4]The domestic share of wheat output eligible for this support must be at least 500 million bushels per year.

Under the cotton program, farmers become eligible for price and income supports by accepting previous total acreage allotments reduced by a 12½ per cent diversion to conserving uses in 1966, and by 0 to 12½ per cent from 1967 through 1969. Each cotton farm further has its total acreage allotment separated into a "domestic allotment" and a residual allotment, subject to the stipulation that domestic allotments must be at least 65 per cent of total allotments. All cotton produced subject to acreage allotments and required diversions is supported at a loan price of not more than 90 per cent of the world price—i.e., is eligible for CCC non-recourse loans at that price. In addition, on cotton grown on acreage within their domestic (not total) allotments, growers are to receive a direct subsidy payment of 9 cents per pound or at least enough to bring the total price (loan price plus subsidy) up to 65 per cent of parity. This extra subsidy payment is not evidently passed on to domestic processors. Cotton grown on allotted acreage other than that within the domestic allotment is supported at a price below the export price, to encourage its movement into world markets.

Additional subsidy payments, for diverting allotted acreage to conserving uses, are more substantial under the cotton program than under the wheat program. On the 12½ per cent of allotted acreage that must be diverted for eligibility for supports, cotton farmers receive not less than 25 per cent of the parity price of the cotton that would have been grown on the diverted land. For additional diversions of allotted acreage beyond the required percentage, they are to receive not more than 40 per cent of the parity price of the crop yield foregone. Acreage diversion would thus become a comparatively attractive alternative to cotton production , in particular for cotton lands on which production costs are relatively high.

The feed grain program, covering corn and grain sorghum and introduced in 1961, is much simpler. Under it growers could become eligible for price supports if they diverted at least 20 per cent of their 1959-60 acreage devoted to feed grains to soil-conserving crops or practices. In return, prices are supported through loans and payments at between 65 and 90 per cent of parity, with the stipulation that part of the payments may be made in kind from stored CCC surpluses. In addition, cooperating growers are paid income subsidies in amounts up to 50 per cent of the support prices of the crops that would have grown on the diverted acreage. This program embodies some but by no means all of the complex provisions of the wheat and cotton programs.

The wheat, cotton, and field grain programs of the 1960's are the major vehicles to date of the new policy of farm price and income supports. For the rest of price-supported crops, we are still pursuing some variety of the traditional price-support program, usually involving flexible price support for the whole crop. This applies to the "basic" commodities rice and peanuts, and to designated "non-basics" including oats, barley, and dairy products adapted to storage. Special provisions include export subsidies paid to rice growers, the maintenance of tobacco price supports at 90 per cent of parity, and the payment of direct subsidies to wool producers sufficient to bring their total incomes up to about 100 per cent of parity. The possibility that the new policy may be applied to at least some of these crops in the near future is suggested by the fact that legislative provisions have already been made for the application of an acreage diversion program to rice whenever the rice acreage allotment falls below that of 1965.

Specific and General Cropland Diversions

One of the effects of the new price and income support programs for wheat, cotton, and feed grains is that "reserves" of croplands that would otherwise be used to grow these commodities are diverted from crop production and devoted to conserving uses. A considerable amount of acreage suitable for growing crops is thus currently being withheld from crop production under these programs, curtailing crop supplies correspondingly. The diversion programs are scheduled to continue to 1969. The diversions of acreage that created this reserve, however, are made essentially on a year-to-year basis, so that the reserve at any time is potentially quite temporary in character. Therefore, application of the diverted acreage to those sorts of conserving uses that would permanently or semi-permanently commit it to uses other than crop production, and would thus reduce the more or less immediately available supply of cropland, is not encouraged by these programs. The types of conserving uses to which the diverted acreage is likely to be put are thus definitely limited. Converting diverted cropland to woodland, for example, is implicitly not encouraged.

There is, however, another federal program for diverting croplands to "conserving" uses that is designed to secure permanent or semi-permanent conversion of the land from crop-growing to other uses. It was begun as the so-called "soil bank" program, which was in effect from 1956 to 1960, and was renewed in 1965 as the "cropland adjustment" program. Under the soil-bank program, the government subsidized farmers, under contracts running from three to ten years, to withdraw any sort of cropland from crop production and place it in a "conservation reserve," for use as woodland, grassland, duck preserves, and the like. This conservation reserve was to build up to a certain maximum national acreage, and could not be harvested or grazed except by specific authorization. The announced intent of the program was to retire some cropland permanently from crop production, for devotion to other uses.[5] By 1960 when the program was terminated, 28.7 million acres had been contractually placed in the soil-bank conservation reserve. The extent to which even semi-permanent conversion of the acreage to other uses was accomplished may be judged in part by the fact that in 1965 only 13.3. million of these acres, or 46 per cent, were still in the soil-bank conservation reserve. The balance had evidently been either returned to crop production or shifted to reserves under other diversion programs.

The "soil bank" program was revived in substantially unaltered form in the so-called cropland adjustment program, adopted in 1965. Under it, the federal government enters into contracts with farmers, running from five to ten years, for the conversion of cropland to uses that will conserve water, soil, wildlife, or forests, or will protect open spaces or natural beauty or recreation, or will prevent air or water pollution. Under the contracts, farmers thus converting the use of croplands are paid not more than 40 per cent of the value of the crops that would otherwise have been produced on the land. For the first four fiscal years of the program, payments made under it are limited to $225 million per year. The extent to which relatively permanent conversion of croplands to other uses will be secured under this program is open to the same question raised in connection with the soil-bank conservation reserve, although retirement of croplands from production for periods of from 5 to 10 years is of course secured.

Two major questions arise concerning the soil-bank and cropland adjustment programs. The first concerns the extent to which they will tend to secure permanent conversion of redundant farm land to other uses, and conversely the extent to which they will only acomplish a stop-gap withholding of surplus croplands from use in growing crops, leaving us in the medium term with surplus cropland capacity. They tend to accomplish the desired reallocation of resources from farming to other uses only to the extent that they induce permanent conversion of land use. Unfortunately, it appears that only a minor percentage of

[5]The program referred to was only one of two parts of the total soil-bank program adopted in 1956—that establishing the conservation reserve. The other part established an "emergency acreage reserve," which was created by paying farmers annually for temporarily withdrawing from crop production and devoting to conserving uses land previously devoted to growing wheat, cotton, corn, tobacco, peanuts, and rice—all "acreage allotment" crops. This program lapsed in 1958, and no acreage is currently withheld under its provisions. It was, however, obviously the parent of the acreage diversion provisions of the new wheat, cotton, and feed-grain programs.

the croplands that they immediately divert from growing crops will be permanently converted to other uses.

A second and interrelated question concerns the extent to which the two programs have attracted into a conservation reserve marginal or relatively unproductive croplands, and conversely the extent to which they have induced diversion of the more productive farmlands. Diversions of marginal croplands would be preferred both *per se* and because marginal lands diverted would be more likely to be permanently converted to other uses. It is unfortunate that the supporting legislation for both programs lacked provisions designed to implement the selective diversion of marginal croplands, making any grade of land equally eligible. A saving consideration is that perhaps farmers will be disposed to offer for diversion mainly marginal lands on which crop earnings would not exceed the subsidy payments offered, but this outcome is not assured.

In 1966, the diversions of cropland acreage in effect under specific crop programs and under the soil-bank and cropland adjustment programs were as follows:

Program	Millions of acres diverted
Feed grain	32.0
Wheat	8.2
Cotton	4.7
Soil bank	13.3
Cropland adjustment	2.4
Total	60.6

A little over 60 million acres of cropland were diverted from crop production under the combined programs, and of this about 16 million acres were diverted on a comparatively long-run basis. These 60 million acres represent about 21 per cent of all cropland harvested (excluding cropland used for pasture) in the United States, and about 14 per cent of all U.S. cropland.[6] It is clear from these numbers that the various cropland diversions are in the aggregate large enough to make a sizeable "dent" in the surplus of land immediately devoted to growing crops, and in the potential crop surplus. They evidently accomplish a much less significant permanent conversion of surplus farm lands to other uses.

[6]That is, cropland harvested plus cropland pastured plus cropland neither harvested nor pastured.

Agricultural Marketing Agreements

The policy of encouraging agricultural marketing agreements is simpler in both outline and detail. Since 1937 the Secretary of Agriculture has been empowered to implement marketing agreements among the handlers, processors, or distrbutors of any agricultural commodity, or apply marketing orders to them, in order to regularize and restrict competition in the marketing of farm products. Such marketing agreements and orders have been applied mainly to perishable products (particularly those with limited local or regional markets), including various fruit, nut, and vegetable crops, and especially fluid milk—in general, a class of agricultural goods for which government purchase and storage under a price-support program would not be feasible.

An agricultural marketing agreement is formed when the farm producers of the crop in question agree upon a scheme for regulated marketing, and submit it to the Secretary of Agriculture for drafting into an agreement (after public hearings on the proposal have been held), and when the Secretary then secures the assent to the terms of the agreement of all or most of the handlers, processors, or distributors of the commodity. The latter then contract individually and voluntarily with the Secretary to observe these terms. Marketing orders are issued when there is substantially less than full concurrence among the producers or handlers. The Secretary may issue such orders (having the same general provisions as agreements but binding upon dissidents), generally if two-thirds of the producers plus half of the handlers vote to accept the terms of the order. Such an order then becomes a compulsory rather than a voluntary agreement in restraint of trade. The terms of the agreements or orders are not subject to any general legislative restriction other than that they implement the purposes of the basic legislation (that is, the securing of parity prices for farm crops), and there is no effective consumer representation in their formation or subsequent administration.

Except for orders involving milk (which constitute about half of those outstanding), prices paid to farmers or charged by handlers on resale are not directly fixed. But provisions can be and have been imposed to restrict supply reaching the market, either by assigning sales quotas to each producer or by imposing flexible grading regulations (as, for example, in the diameter of fruit) which allow only a specified "high-grade" fraction of the crop to reach the regular market, the remainder being diverted to secondary uses or destroyed. Such provisions are clearly indirect devices for elevation and maintenance of price through marketing quotas, and are given considerable latitude by the law. In addition, provisions regulating the rate of flow of seasonal crops to the market, in order to lessen price fluctuations, are incorporated in a number of orders. Orders affecting local markets for farmers' milk—which currently cover most of the major metropolitan or urban markets for fluid milk—also generally incorporate detailed provisions fixing the price for consumers' fluid milk paid to the farmers (compulsory on all involved), with substantial latitude being left to the Secretary, the producers, and the handlers as to what milk price is a fair one.

In general, the purpose of the government in supporting agricultural marketing agreements and orders is to raise the prices and incomes received by farm producers of various crops (toward "parity"), by sponsoring or enforcing agreements in restraint of competition and thus giving farm producers and product handlers the benefit of a certain measure of monopoly power. In the areas designated, the policy has in general been quite successful in this respect.

The control of milk prices by federal marketing orders has been supplemented or replaced in about fifteen states by state milk control laws. These laws generally provide for the fixing, by an appointed commission representing dairy interests and some others, of the prices of consumers' fluid milk paid to farmers. They also, in all but a few cases, provide for fixing the retail prices of such milk as sold by distributors, this on the ostensible theory that the farmer's interest in a fair milk price to him is thus doubly protected. Interference with commercial competition some distance removed from the farm is thus combined with restriction of agricultural competition, under an assortment of standards of varying laxity or rigidity.

Effects of Governmental Interferences with Agricultural Competition, and Basic Issues

We should now give some attention to (1) the broad economic effects of recent and contemporary agricultural policy; (2) its desirability relative to alternatives; and (3) the fundamental issues encountered in devising an appropriate policy. In the appraisal of policy, some distinctions must be drawn between the traditional and the new price and income support programs.

The basic programs of price and income support and of sponsoring marketing agreements have been and continue to be effective devices for increasing farm prices and incomes. They thus have averted an inequity to agricultural enterprise and labor that, in the absence of intervention, would have taken the form of chronically subnormal earnings. The programs have therefore been effective in attacking one of the economic problems that arises in a sector of the economy which tends to be afflicted with destructive competition.

There is a strong suspicion, however, that in adjusting farm incomes upward we have in general overadjusted so as to create incomes above a normal competitive level. This tendency was most evident under the traditional price-support policy as pursued from 1947 to 1955, when the prices of the whole outputs of basic and some other farm commodities were supported at 90 per cent of parity.[7] It was only slightly less evident with the continuation into the 1960's of the same policy as altered to provide price supports "flexibly" between either 75 and 90 per cent or 65 and 90 per cent of parity for most price-supported crops. Parity prices as calculated—or relatively high percentages of them—are obviously unreliable indicators of what modern farmers require to receive normal incomes for self-employed and hired labor and for invested capital. They seem on the average to be substantially higher than the prices necessary to provide such incomes.

The new support program that has so far been fully applied to wheat and to cotton also seems to provide unnecessarily large farm incomes. The essential abandonment of price support for the exported share of wheat production is compensated for by a total price support for the domestically used share at a fantastic 100 per cent of parity. The effect on incomes of the essential termination of all price support for cotton seems to be largely offset by the multiple direct subsidies paid to cotton growers. And although the related feed-grain program embodies whole-crop price supports at potentially modest levels, it also involves the payment of substantial direct income subsidies. The total contemporary support policy, embodying these three new programs and a continuation of the traditional policy with flexible price supports for most other supported crops, appears to support farm incomes at levels about as high as those attained since 1958, though not as high as those of the period from 1947 to 1957.

Resulting farm incomes are above a normal competitive level for the multitude of relatively efficient farmers who supply the bulk of the nation's agricultural output. On the other hand, only normal or subnormal incomes are earned by a larger number of very small farmers who operate inefficiently on marginal or submarginal land and supply a minor fraction of our total farm output. These farmers need parity prices or equivalent direct subsidies, or more, to bring their incomes up to normal. And it is their plight that has provided the most effective political arguments in favor of our price and income support programs. Yet it would seem foolish to expand the incomes of all farmers through

[7]And at 82½ per cent of parity from 1955 to 1957.

relatively high price supports and subsidies simply in order to rectify the income positions of this marginal group of farmers, especially when we have an oversupply of good land managed by relatively efficient farmers.

In effect, the policy of supporting crop prices at relatively high levels plus paying large direct income subsidies to farmers turns out to be a device for subsidizing the inefficient use of inefficient land—and land that contributes appreciably to a chronic surplus of output or productive capacity in agriculture. This is done by subsidizing the incomes of *all* farms and farmers, efficient and inefficient alike. Unneeded or excessive subsidies are paid to efficient farmers who supply most farm output. It has been calculated, for example, that the great bulk of all "extra" income received by farmers because of price supports or through subsidy payments goes to only about 20 per cent of the nation's farmers—the 20 per cent that in general need it least. At the same time, the policy imposes on consumers either or both of two burdens—unduly high prices for food and fiber, and extra taxation to finance direct farm subsidies. Although the preceding comments apply mainly to effects of the federal program of supporting farm prices and incomes, the marketing agreements program is subject to at least part of the same criticisms. It also generally leads toward an upward "overadjustment" of potentially subnormal prices and incomes.

If farm incomes in general are to be subsidized at the expense of the general public, past and present federal programs have embodied ways of doing it that were or are wasteful in varying degrees. Under both past and present policies, the imposition of restrictions on the acreages planted to various crops, as a part of the overall program of supporting prices and incomes, has clearly undesirable effects. It tends to confine our agricultural resources, both physical and human, to a state of partial utilization. This denies the public the benefit of real wealth, in the form of greater agricultural production, that it might otherwise have. And, very importantly, it does this without shifting very much of the partially idled resources to alternative productive uses.

This criticism applies generally both to the traditional price-support policy and to the new policy adopted for certain crops. Acreage withheld from crop production because it is in excess of acreage allotments is generally held in ready reserve for crop production, and not converted to the next-most-valuable genuinely alternative use. The same applies to acreage diverted to conserving uses, generally in return for income subsidies, under the wheat, cotton, and feed-grain programs. The diversions are essentially temporary, and the conserving uses are of nominal importance. Rather, a "bank" of cropland is held in reserve on a year-to-year basis, producing little meanwhile. Even the general reduction of active cropland acreage attempted under the soil-bank conservation reserve program and the cropland adjustment program does not promise to result in the permanent or semi-permanent conversion of much of the acreage involved to real alternative uses. Again, the main effect is to hold more cropland in reserve, ready for use. Thus a needed major reallocation of land from crop-producing to genuine alternative uses is not really being accomplished through the various acreage allotment, specific cropland diversion, and general cropland reserve programs.

The contemporary and traditional programs, moreover, have both failed to provide adequate incentives to reallocation of redundant labor and capital from agriculture to other occupations. In fact, they have provided noticeable disincentives to this sort of reallocation. Price supports and income subsidies make it possible for self-employed farmers to earn adequate incomes while remaining in farming, being paid to produce less than they could and thus comprising an excessive labor force committed to farming. This payment counteracts economic pressures that would otherwise induce them to move. In this connection, it is notable that whereas numerous subsidies are paid for withdrawing land acreage from crop production, none of the subsidy programs is designed to induce a comparable withdrawal and shift to other uses of redundant labor and capital resources. Although there has indeed been a significant shift of population away from farming in the last two decades, this seems to have occurred in spite of rather than because of the federal farm program. Increased mechanization in farming plus changing cultural attitudes are probably the main causes of the shift.

To summarize the preceding argument, the traditional and current programs of restricting farm output, supporting prices, and directly subsidizing incomes have provided no adequate incentive for the elimination of the basic maladjustment that provides the occasion for governmental interference. They do not force or provide adequate incentives for the removal from agricultural production of the redundant land and human resources whose presence tends to make unregulated competition destructive.

Although it retains this basic deficiency, the new or revised policy as applied so far to wheat, cotton, and feed grains represents a distinct improvement over the traditional policy as pursued from 1947 to 1957. Imposition of more severe acreage restrictions, coupled with the policy of ceasing to support the prices of the export component of these crops at levels above world prices, tended to terminate the stupid policy whereby the government accumulated huge surpluses of stored crops. It is certainly more sensible to move our crop outputs in excess of domestic needs into world markets than for the CCC to buy and store them. It is correspondingly more sensible (if not absolutely defensible) to pay direct income subsidies to farmers to compensate for the reduced income from export sales than to conceal the same subsidy in a high support price that deters exports. That some constructive accomplishments have been made along this line is indicated in part by the fact that from 1955 to the end of 1965, the value of crops held in storage by the CCC declined from about $7 billion to about $4 billion.

We are not as yet, however, at all fully shifted to the new policy, and can reap its full comparative advantages only after it is applied as well to other basic and non-basic supported crops. Also, we should remember that the best that can be said of the new policy is that it has fewer deficiencies than the traditional one; it still retains quite basic defects.

In fairness to the traditional and current farm policies, it should be noted that they have had incidental benefits. By increasing farm incomes they have provided a setting for increased efficiency and better conservation practices, which the now more affluent farmers are much better able to finance. (It is not clear, however, that these programs have been even moderately efficient means of securing these desirable results.) Furthermore, the programs have provided a ready-made means for cushioning the farm community against the cyclical and random price instability it previously experienced, and against the corresponding instability of income.

Let us now turn to general issues. We have already implied that existing public policy toward agriculture is, because of numerous adverse effects noted, clearly inferior to conceivable alternative ways of treating destructive competition in the farm sector. If some or all farm incomes require at least temporary bolstering or subsidization in the interests of equity, this relief should not be accomplished by competition-restricting measures of the sort which engender serious wastes of national productivity or of produced output. It is possible to arrange subsidy plans that do not have these injurious side effects. Furthermore, any rational subsidy plan should be designed to provide definite incentives for the quasi-permanent transfer of redundant resources from agriculture to genuine alternative uses or occupations, rather than providing either no incentives or disincentives. Finally, the calculation of the needed subsidy should clearly not rest on an artificial political concept such as parity price. Much more refined and defensible methods of arriving at an estimate of a competitively normal income to farm enterprise and labor are available.

A revision of policy to eliminate the deficiencies just outlined is clearly in order. It is not our purpose here to suggest the details of such a policy. But in broad outline it should proceed directly to secure a large enough selective reallocation of resources invested in agriculture that the output of resources remaining in agriculture will sell at free market prices sufficient to provide them with normal competitive incomes. The emphasis should be on the transfer of redundant resources, and not on the restriction of the productivity of redundant resources in place. This is to say that restriction of competition via restriction of output or marketing is not a desirable device. So far as restriction of competition is employed at all, it should be employed in a carefully limited fashion and only in cases where agricultural sellers need to counterbalance the monopsony pressure of large buyers in marketing their output. Income subsidies may need to be used in the period of transition while redundant resources are being transferred to other occupations, or to compensate for undue cyclical instability of income. But such subsidies should not in general be derived from or tied to output restriction and price support. And subsidies should be administered in such a fashion as to provide direct incentives for the movement of redundant resources for the agricultural sphere.

Restrictive Policies Affecting the Distributive Trades

The occasion for governmental sponsorship or adoption of various devices to restrict competition in the distributive trades has beeen discussed in Chapter 12. Briefly, numerous industries engaged in the wholesaling and retailing were affected by the emergence of mass distributors, usually of the "chain-store" type. These firms brought large-scale operation and vertical integration to a sector where atomistic market structure and small-scale, nonintegrated wholesale and retail firms had previously been typical. They introduced multiple retail units under a single management, integration of retailing with wholesaling and some manufacturing functions, streamlining and simplification of the retail distributive service, and private merchandise brands. They also engaged in aggressive pricing tactics (at least in the early stages of rapid growth), and had some ability to secure discriminatory pricing advantages in purchasing merchandise in large lots.

In general, they proved more efficient than their small nonintegrated competitors, and could and did sell profiitably at lower prices. In a period of about a decade after World War I, a limited number of very large mass distributors captured significant minor fractions of various national and local distributive markets, including those involving groceries, drugs, auto acessories, and the like. Their intrusion either displaced or seriously reduced the earnings of numerous small and non-integrated wholesalers and retailers. It introduced more vigorous competition into the distributive trades generally, and forced numerous structural adaptations by the small and medium-sized enterprises that survived in these trades. It also had virtually adverse effects on the sales and earnings of numerous established manufacturers, whose nationally advertised brands now faced the private-brand competition of the mass distributors. It is not evident, moreover, that the structural changes in question actually threatened the development of monopoly or concentrated oligopoly in any of the distributive industries involved.

Of all this complex of effects, the one which served as the basis of pleas for public-policy interference was the displacement of or loss of earnings by small retailers and wholesalers. These groups were vociferous and politically effective in securing public intervention of a sort generally designed to preserve competitors (themselves) by restricting competition in the distributive trades. The most effective organized groups were retail druggists and independent grocery wholesalers. But they had many allies in the distributive trades, and some qualified support from groups of manufacturers of consumer goods with nationally advertised brands. With this background, let us turn to the main sorts of interference with competition which were secured.

Restrictive Measures Applied

The first restrictive measure generally applied did not embody a limitation of competition *per se*, but rather a directive punitive attack on chain stores in the form of special state tax laws. Such laws, ultimately levied in 29 states, generally required any chain store to pay a certain annual tax on each retail store operated, the amount of the tax per store increasing progressively either with the number of stores operated in the state, or with the number of stores operated nationally. Maximum taxes per store, for large chains, ranged in various states from $100 to $750. Such special assessments, however, were generally not effective in eliminating mass distributors or reducing their market positions. This, together with the obviously discriminatory character of the tax laws in question, was responsible for the fact that they remained on the books in only 14 states by the early 1950's.

A second attack on mass distributors was embodied in the Robinson-Patman amendment to the Clayton Act in 1936. This federal law, which we have already discussed in Chapter 14, was designed primarily to deny to chain stores unfair discriminatory price advantages which they had allegedly obtained in buying merchandise for resale. The strategic provision was that any price discrimination by a seller which might tend to injure competition between or among his buyers was illegal unless the discrimination could be justified on the basis of a difference in the cost of supplying different buyers. To this it was added that discounts to buyers (generally large ones) in the form of allowances for brokerage services performed by or for the buyers could not be made, regardless of cost justification. Furthermore, the seller could not provide advertising and similar services or allowances to buyers unless he offered such services or allowances to all competing buyers on proportionally equal terms. All relevant provisions of this law were clearly aimed at the buying advantages over smaller competitors which the chain stores had actually or allegedly enjoyed, although the actual effects of the law, as we have seen in Chapter 14, have spread considerably beyond the distributive trades. The effects on the distributive trades as such will be discussed in the following section. It may be noted, meanwhile, that the Robinson-Patman amendment as written did not impose any direct restrictions on distributive-trade competition, but was largely confined in purpose (with the main exception of the outright proscription of brokerage allowances) to the elimination of unfair or monopsonistic buying-price advantages such as the chain stores might enjoy.

A third and major attack on chain-store competition, and indeed on distributive trade competition in general, was embodied in the so-called "fair trade" laws, or, more descriptively, resale price maintenance laws, which (beginning in 1931) were ultimately enacted in 45 states.

The typical "fair trade" law proceeds from a seemingly rather innocuous postulate: that the manufacturer of a branded good should be permitted to protect the reputation and value of his brand or trademark against such loss as might be inflicted if various retailers sold it at "substandard" retail prices. He should be able to secure this protection by placing retailers under contractual obligation not to resell the good below a specified minimum retail price. (The probability of manufacturers actually incurring losses because of retail price cutting on their merchandise is debatable, but it has been claimed that they may stand to lose because consumers judge the quality of a good partly by its retail price, and come to deprecate its quality if the price is frequently or sporadically cut. Also, some retailers may be reluctant to carry and promote branded goods that are likely to be subject to aggressive retail price competition.)

The economic effects of such vertical agreements to maintain resale prices, however, are not necessarily innocuous. In order to protect the manufacturer's equity in his trademark, consumers are denied the possible benefits of retail price competition which might bring them a particular good at lower retail prices. And if all the manufacturers of a given sort of good simultaneously insist on resale price maintenance contracts—for example, if all available brands of toothpaste are price-maintained—consumers are further denied the possible benefits of re-tail competition in the entire market for a commodity. In addition, price competition at the manufacturers' level may also be restricted. For such reasons as this, resale price maintenance contracts were initial-ly and properly found to constitute illegal agreements in restraint of trade under the Sherman Act (and remained illegal until they were specifically exempted in federal legislation designed to implement the state "fair trade" laws).

It should be noted, however, that so long as in the distribution of any class of good there are a number of manufacturers who do not choose to use resale price maintenance contracts and a number of retail-ers who refuse to sign them, the net restrictive effects of such con-tracts on retail competition would tend to be slight unless further con-trols were imposed. "Full coverage" of entire lines of merchandise and of most or all competing retailers by contracts would be required for an effective suppression of retail competition.

The provisions of the state "fair trade" laws—which were promoted principally by associations of independent retailers—reflected an aware-ness by their promoters that simply legalizing resale price maintenance contracts would not effectively suppress retail competition. Therefore, in addition to making resale price maintenance contracts fully enforce-able against retailers who signed them, they further ruled that all non-signing retailers (who had not entered into such contracts) were also bound not to sell any branded product at a price below that set for it in any resale price maintenance contract in effect in the state. If non-signers sold below such contract prices, they were guilty of "unfair competition" and were subject to private suit by any damaged parties (including both manufacturers and distributors) to secure court injun-tions and damages.

The notorious "nonsigners'" clause in state "fair trade" laws made it hypothetically or actually possible, in a given line of retailing in a state, for an organized group of retailers—potentially even a small minority—to impose minimum retail price fixing on all competing retailers. This price fixing could apply to any individual branded product, or even to an entire stock-in-trade of competing or complementary branded prod-ucts, if only one or a few resale price maintenance contracts were writ-ten covering each branded product in question. All that was required was the willingness of the numerous manufacturers involved to write the contracts. If they were reluctant, they could be and sometimes were persuaded by threats not to carry their merchandise unless it was "fair-traded." Under one of the two main versions of the state laws, moreover, wholesale distributors could set up binding resale price maintenance contracts with retailers on branded goods, even though they were not empowered to do so by the manufacturers whose brands were at stake.

It is worth especial note, finally, that this scheme for legalizing retail price fixing involved an unrestricted delegation of power to the private parties who stood to gain by the price fixing. No legislative provisions defining "fair" retail prices (or fair markups of retail above wholesale or manufacturers' prices) were contained in the laws. Private retailers might, subject to negotiation with their suppliers, use their discretion and follow their monopolistic impulses in determing minimum retail prices. On the other hand, both the organization of retail price fixing in a trade and the enforcement of it (through private damage suits) was left in private hands and to private initiative, without administrative assistance from the state. This has been a saving weakness of the laws, as we will see in reviewing their effects below.

The state "fair trade" laws could be really effective means of restricting retail competition, however, only if the resale price maintenance contracts written under them did not run afoul of federal law in the form of the Sherman and F.T.C. acts. The states could legally exempt from state antitrust laws any contract between two parties both resident in the same state. But they could not exempt from federal antitrust action contracts between parties in different states, where interstate movement of the goods affected was involved. Resale price maintenance in interstate commerce had been found to violate Section 1 of the Sherman Act, and most manufacturer-retailer contracts would be between parties in two states and would directly involve interstate commerce. Therefore, amendment of the federal law to exempt resale price maintenance contracts from federal antiturst prosecution was a necessary step in building a nationwide system of "fair trade" laws. This was accomplished first in the Miller-Tydings Act of 1937, amending Section 1 of the Sherman Act. It legalized interstate resale price maintenance contracts in any state that had a "fair trade" law which exempted such contracts.

Essentially an enabling act designed to implement state-by-state legalization of resale price maintenance, the Miller-Tydings Act served its purpose until 1951. At that time the Supreme Court held (in reviewing a decision in a private damage suit under the Louisiana "fair trade" law), that the federal act, which made no mention of the nonsigner's

clause or its uses, did not legalize the use of interstate resale price maintenance contracts to impose price-fixing on parties who were not sig-
natories of such contracts.

This decision undercut the whole structure of the "fair-trade" system, but the situation was quickly remedied by Congress, at the behest
of organized retailer interests. In 1952, the McGuire-Keogh Fair Trade
Enabling Act was passed as an amendment to Section 5 of the F.T.C.
Act. It exempted from all federal antitrust laws all interstate resale
price maintenance contracts operative in states with "fair trade" laws,
and permitted the enforcement of such contracts against nonsigners.
A firm federal support of state resale price maintenance laws was thus
reinstituted. The laws are subject to continuing attacks in state courts,
however, and several have been found unconstitutional,[8] on a variety
of grounds including undue delegation of legislative or police power.
At this writing, the number of states with "fair trade" laws in effect
has dropped below thirty.

A fourth sort of law restricting retail competition, also passed at the
state level and also initially aimed at chain-store competition, is found
in the "unfair practices" acts, more adequately described as minimum
markup laws, in effect presently in 28 states. These laws are more
various in their specific provisions than the "fair trade" laws of the
various states. But in general they provide that in any retailing trade it
is illegal to make sales below cost, this cost to include not only the purchase cost of the merchandise to the retailer, but also a markup or
margin sufficient to cover the other costs of doing business. Thus, in
effect, retailers are required to charge prices which include a minimum
markup over the purchase cost of the merchandise sold. This requirement applies to all merchandise handled by retailers in a given line,
whether branded or not, and no resale price maintenance contracts
need be involved. Under most of the laws, moreover, the legal minimum markup is left to be privately determined by trade associations of
the retailers involved, through such surveys as they may choose to conduct. But the markups are enforceable by the officers of the state, with
violations subject to fine or imprisonment, although violations are discovered and brought to official notice through the private "policing"
activities of the trade association. And retailers brought to bar for selling with subminimum markups can in general escape liability only by
showing that their own costs of doing business require a smaller markup than that established by the trade association.

The ostensible original aim of this sort of legislation was to terminate
the use of "loss leaders" (special items priced below cost in order to at-

[8]Either the entire act has been found unconstitutional, or only its nonsigner clause.

tract customers to a store), which had been widely employed as a competitive device by chain stores. More generally, the minimum mark-up laws have provided an alternative device (in addition to the resale price maintenance laws) for a publicly sponsored private fixing of minimum retail prices, and for a restriction of price competition in retailing. The laws have had their main application in certain retailing lines, like groceries, in which resale price maintenance did not prove feasible because of frequent fluctuations of manufacturers' prices and the general unwillingness of the manufacturers to participate. As such, they have been supported and used by principal chain stores and small independents alike.

One noteworthy difference of the minimum markup laws from the resale price maintenance laws is that the former do not require all retailers to sell at the same price. The retailer with a lower purchase cost of merchandise, may, after adding a standard markup, legally charge a lower price than a competitor with a higher purchase price of merchandise could, although the latter may generally meet the legal competition of the former. Another difference is that the legal retail price minima established can presumably include distributive margins which only cover costs, whereas there is no such restriction on prices established under resale price maintenance contracts. A similarity between the two sorts of law, on the other hand, is that under both there is an undue delegation of legislative power to private groups, a lack of adequate legislative standards, and a total absence of provisions for representation of the general public or the consumer in the determination of "fair" prices.

Economic Effects of Restrictive Measures in the Distributive Trades, and General Issues

In appraising the economic effects of and problems raised by competition-restricting legislation affecting the distributive trades, it is convenient to distinguish three related issues: (1) the effect of the laws on the relative competitive advantages of mass distributors and independent competitors; (2) their effect on the character and workability of competition in the distributive trades generally; and (3) the relation of existing laws to ones which would be most desirable from the standpoint of the general public.

These issues can be discussed in any detail only with reference to specific items of legislation, but we may initially state a broad view of the effects and merits of the combination of restrictive legislation described above.

First, this composite of restrictive laws, together with the private organizations for restraint of trade built on some of them, have not been especially effective in reducing the market shares previously attained by mass distributors or chain stores, or, apparently, in retarding their normal course of development. Although these laws were at their inception aimed primarily at chain stores, the mass distributors have generally been able to avoid their potentially punitive provisions (and even turn them to their own advantage), at least sufficiently to maintain or increase the market positions they occupied by 1930. Whether they would have increased their positions further in the absence of legislation is open to debate. But the indications are that the mass-distributor group was in the net not significantly damaged profit-wise, or appreciably retarded in its attainment and consolidation of significant market shares, by the restrictive legislation. This is also to say that we probably do not have today much lower concentration or much less "monopoly" in the distributive trades than we would have had in the absence of existing restrictive legislation. This result is attributable in part to the numerous possibilities for ingenious avoidance of various restrictive legal provisions, and in part to the essentially weak compliance of enforcement provisions embodied in the "fair trade" and "unfair practices" laws of the various states.

Second, the vigor and effectiveness of competition in a considerable share of the distributive trades has been perceptibly reduced by the restrictive legislation and its uses, particularly through resale price maintenance and minimum markup regulations. This reduction has been only a fraction of the potential, because of the use of numerous avenues for avoidance of legal restrictions, and of the cumbersome and relatively ineffective enforcement machinery. But there has been a perceptible restriction of the force of competition in wholesale and retail trades. By and large, this restriction has added to the profits of the chain stores or mass distributors at least as much as to those of non-integrated independent distributors. The mass distributors have used restrictive legal provisions to their own advantage more than enough to compensate for any virtual losses these provisions might have tended to impose on them. If they have indeed sacrificed potential further growth in their market shares, they have gained in their profits on existing market shares. In this development, the consuming public has been denied the legitimate advantages of more vigorous competition in the distributive trades.

Third, the composite of existing laws affecting the distributive trades do not seem to be in the general public interest. No real threat of monopoly was or is present to be forestalled. Rather, the laws attempt to interfere with a socially beneficial change in market structures, by preserving small competitors who are due for displacement. No genuine case of destructive competition, such as might involve chronically subnormal earnings to all or most of enterprise and labor in an industry, can be presented as a justification of sustained interferences by the government. The problem is rather one of the normal structural evolution of an industry in the process of technological or organizational change.

Finally, so far as transitional relief to the incomes of enterprises in the process of displacement may be involved, the appropriate governmental technique is clearly not that of general restriction of competition in the distributive trades. On this background, let us turn to specific items of legislation.

The various state anti-chain store taxes do not appear to have had much effect on the growth and success of mass distributors, or on the general character of distributive-trade competition. On the level of principle, however, the imposition of any arbitrary punitive tax on one group of competitors in order to assist another group is doubtful public policy, however much the end may seem to justify the means.

The effects of the Robinson-Patman Act on the distributive trades have also not been very great. The competitive advantages of mass distributors have apparently not been seriously reduced by this law, nor has their ability to make good profits while holding a significant share of various distributive markets. The main reasons that this legislative denial of discriminatory buying advantages to chain stores failed in its ostensible purpose were discussed in Chapter 12. Contrary to the theory underlying the Robinson-Patman Act, the major part of the competitive advantages enjoyed by mass distributors did not inhere in discriminatory buying-price advantages. Most of their advantage resulted from greater efficiency and from innovations in the design or content or retail services offered. Even though deprived of some discriminatory buying advantages, they still retained superior competitive strength in the market. Furthermore, mass distributors were able to retain advantages of lower buying prices for merchandise by adjusting their structures or practices so as to avoid the provisions of the Robinson-Patman Act. They could do this by contracting for the entire outputs of supplying manufacturers, by contracting for the production and supply of merchandise to their own specifications and bearing their own brands,[9] and by integrating backward to acquire their own manufacturing facilities.

Given their superior efficiency and the various avenues for avoiding

[9]The specified products being sufficiently distinguished from other products of the manufacturers that antidiscrimination provisions could not apply.

the intended prohibitions of the Robinson-Patman Act, the competitive strength of the mass distributors was in general not seriously impaired. Nor was the general character of competition within the distributive trades greatly affected. On the other hand, the Robinson-Patman law did have the significant side effects of inducing structural changes such as increased vertical integration by mass distributors.

As to general issues, there is a good deal to be said for the endeavor, embodied at least roughly in the Robinson-Patman Act, to put distributive-trade or other competition on a plane such that large firms cannot gain advantage from the exercise of monopsonistic power to buy materials or merchandise at discriminatory prices. The competitive mechanism in resale markets would operate more efficiently if the prices charged to different reselling buyers differed only by the amount of actual differences in the cost of supplying them. On the other hand, extensive control of the discount policies of sellers is likely to have a generally restrictive effect on price competition. And if restrictive laws of the Robinson-Patman variety do not actually succeed in denying monopsonistic buying advantages or their equivalent to large firms, the case for perpetuation of this sort of law seems rather weak.

The effects of the state "fair trade" laws on competition in the distributive trades have been somewhat more significant. They might have been much greater were it not for the fact that resale price maintenance has become an important factor only in a limited number of retailing lines—including drugs and cosmetics, photographic equipment, small electrical appliances, books, sporting goods, and liquor—which together account for only about 10 per cent of all retail sales made in this country. In the other 90 per cent of retailing, including importantly most food and clothing, resale price maintenance has not proved feasible because of frequent fluctuations of manufacturers' prices and the general unwillingness of manufacturers to participate. In the retailing industries in which resale price maintenance has been widely employed, however, the following tendencies are notable.

First, distributive margins, and thus final retail prices to consumers, have tended to be significantly higher on the average with resale price maintenance contracts than without. This appears both from "before-and-after" comparisons and from comparisons of the retail prices and margins of merchants in states with and without "fair trade" laws. This elevation of retail prices—attributable to the general practice of contracting for resale prices which include a high retailer's margin—is not confined to independent retailers who specialize almost entirely in a stock of "fair-traded" items. It extends also to chain stores, who in addition to observing contract prices on price-maintained items which they carry in stock, are able to undersell such items with their competing private brands of nonprice-maintained goods, while still maintaining large margins on these private brands. Being protected from independent competition, that is, by the contractual fixing of the independents' retail prices, the chains are encouraged to compete in only a restricted degree in pricing their private brands. The same applies to "discount houses" and other specialized distributors in certain lines. They persistently offer price-maintained merchandise at below "fair trade" prices, but the sizes of their discounts are smaller than they would be were not their independent competitors adhering to contractually fixed resale prices. In general, therefore, an influence of the "fair trade" laws, in lines where they are effective, has been to restrict retail competition in the market generally, and to result in higher prices generally, this influence extending to mass-distributor and discount-house competition as well as to independent competition.

Second, the market position and competitive strength of mass distributors in the lines involved has not been visibly lessened by the operation of the "fair trade" laws. Through the widespread use of private brands, not subject to resale price maintenance, and of market strategies which involve the joint offering of these brands in conjunction with price-maintained ones, the chain stores appear to have adapted nicely to a "fair-trade" environment and to have maintained or increased their market shares without difficulty. Since their profits have benefited from the restriction of independent price competition by resale price maintenance contracts, it appears highly probable that the mass distributors have gained in the net from the passage of the "fair trade" laws.

Third, independent retailers in the lines involved have nevertheless been afforded some degree of protection in certain shares of their markets, and have possibly maintained somewhat larger shares than they would have in the absence of the legislation. It is not clear, however, that resale price maintenance has given them a significant measure of profit protection. So far as their profits may initially be raised, they tend to be eroded by the easy entry of additional independent retailers to share their markets. High unit margins, wasteful distributive excess capacity, and low profits on investment are thus combined. In addition, they have been increasingly plagued with "discount-house" competition, and with the private-brand competition of mass distributors. The weak enforcement provisions of the laws, as well as obvious avenues for avoiding them, have left the independent retailers with a rather defective instrument for retail price fixing or elimination of retail competition.

The general public has thus not suffered even approximately as much as might have been feared from the application of state "fair trade" laws. The actual scope and degree of restriction of retail competition have been minor fractions of the potential. Nevertheless, there has been some loss to the public as a result of these laws, and without obvious compensating benefits. The consumer has been in some degree denied the benefits of competition (both in lowering retail prices and in forcing increased efficiency) in some of the distributive trades, with the only evident justification of protecting some competitors from the competition of others. This is not a legitimate objective consistent with a general policy of relying on a market regulation of the economy, and not a very sensible objective under any policy. If income subsidies need to be granted as relief to merchants who tend to be displaced by an efficiency-inducing technological change in their industries, they should clearly be made available through means other than restricting distributive-trade competition. They should take forms which accelerate rather than retard desirable technological change and resource reallocation.

The actual affects of "unfair practices" or minimum-markup laws on distributive-trade competition have not been thoroughly studied and are not too evident. By and large, the publicized application of such laws has been mainly in the grocery trades (where resale price maintenance is unimportant). It is also notable that the large grocery chains (against whom this sort of legislation was initially aimed) have been prominent supporters of trade-association activity directed toward calculating and policing minimum markups under these laws.

In general, these laws do not seem to have disadvantaged chain stores. Unless the true "loss leader" were some strategic and indispensable competitive device of chain stores—which it very evidently is not, in view of their overall advantages in efficiency—there is no reason the minimum-markup laws should penalize mass distributors. In fact, it may help them, since if a uniform minimum retail markup is made mandatory for a whole trade, the chain stores, with generally lower costs of acquiring merchandise, begin with lower legal retail prices than their independent competitors (though these may usually be met in competition by the independents). They are thus in some degree protected from aggressive price competition by independent retailers. The chains have usually had more to gain than to lose from minimum-markup conventions, and it is not evident that they have lost at all.

Minimum markup laws also do not appear to have had significant effects on general competition in the distributive trades. This is in considerable part because the minimum markups established by trade associations under the law have in general been rather low (ranging from 6 to 12 per cent of inventory cost), and lower than the average markup obtained under unregulated competition. The main effect has thus been felt on traditionally fast-turnover, low-markup items within a stock in trade. Overall, price competition has been affected mainly to the extent that independent price-cutting competition with the chains has been limited, and price-cutting tactics generally restricted in range.

Although the minimum-markup laws have so far been relatively innocuous devices for restricting retail competition, it is clear that they could become dangerous to the public interest if more effectively implemented by private agencies and more vigorously enforced. And they share with the "fair trade" laws the lack of any real justification for attempted restriction of retail competition. They are also, like the "fair trade" laws, politically unsound in their undue delegation of legislative power to private groups, and correspondingly subject to attack on constitutional grounds.

In the composite of federal and state legislation just discussed, we have seen evidence of an organized attempt by interested parties to secure governmental interferences (or governmental sponsorship of private interferences) with the competitive process to two main ends: (1) the limitation or reduction of the market position and competitive strength and tactics of groups of mass distributors who, in the course of introducing efficiency-increasing technological changes into the distributive trades, were displacing previously established independent merchants; and (2) the limitation of price competition within the distributive trades in general, in the interest of preservation of competitors and the increase of profits. From this composite of efforts the general public has been deprived in some degree of the benefits of competition in the distributive trades, though only in relatively minor degree because of deficiencies in the character and use of the legislation in question. There have been numerous "saving weaknesses" in the legislation passed and the policies it implemented, for which consumers may be grateful.

The broad question, however, is whether or to what extent there is or ever was valid occasion for this type of interference policy. In general, the answer must be in the negative. First, there has been in the distributive trades no imminent threat of monopoly developing from the growth of mass distributors. Dilute oligopoly was in prospect and did develop, but with adequate or workable competition as its corollary. No policy was needed to forestall monopoly; if one had been needed, it certainly was not that of suppressing competition. The policies adopted tended to deny the consuming public some share of the benefits accru-ing from the structural change which was in any event taking place.

Second, there has been in the distributive trades no general phe-nomenon of destructive competition. Normal displacement of some firms by others in a process of structural change was what was mainly involved. And if destructive competition had been present, general re-striction of competition was no more appropriate as a remedy here than in the case of agriculture.

A third possible ground for restricting competition requires more thought, and may be suggested by posing a question. Should small mer-chants, being similar in their income status to semiskilled or skilled laborers, be afforded the same opportunity to raise their incomes by restricting competition *inter se* as is afforded to unionized laborers? This question, which arises also with respect to small farmers, concerns the grounds for a certain type of special treatment to the "little man" in a concentrated industrial society. An at least nominally persuasive case can be made for an affirmative answer to the question, to the effect that small corner grocers or druggists should be given the same opportunity as machinists or teamsters to act collectively to restrict competition among themselves and thus to increase their earnings.

Against this case, however, the following may be noted. Small mer-chants, unlike laborers, do not generally face monopsonistic buying of their services, such as needs to be counteracted through seller organiza-tion. Progressive extension of the special treatment of labor into the en-terprise field would presage general abandonment of a market-con-trolled economy in favor of a substitute with deleterious impacts on efficiency. And the existing boundaries of public labor policy are suf-ficiently flexible that, even arguing from analogy, we do not necessarily arrive at a justification for restrictions of enterprise competition which have inherent in them severe adverse effects on efficiency. The question is indeed a delicate one, but a plausible general conclusion is that actual or alleged deficiencies of income to small enterprises in industries in which they are important should be redressed, if at all, by means other than general restrictions on competition in these industries. The preser-vation of the public interest in efficiency and low prices requires that other devices should be used.

Restrictive Policies Affecting Coal and Petroleum

Briefer mention may be made of two other instances of public inter-ference, on a nationwide basis, with competition in relatively unconcentrated industries. These industries are the suppliers of our two major fuels, bituminous coal and petroleum. Special federal interference with coal-industry competition (aside from wartime and other emergency interference which affected all industries), was undertaken only temporarily, from 1937 to 1941, but the regulatory measures then imposed are interesting enough to merit brief discussion. A composite of state interferences with competition in the production of crude petroleum (complemented by some federal actions) were instituted in the early 1930's and are still in effect. The control of destructive competition was primarily involved in the case of coal. In the petroleum industry, the reduction of competition and the elimination or mitigation of extremely adverse conservation tendencies were the goals. Let us consider the two cases in turn.

Bituminous Coal—the Problem and the Remedy

The bituminous coal industry presented, in the period between the two great wars, an almost classical example or prototype of destructive competition. The industry was and has remained extremely atomistic, with several thousand small sellers, and is subject to easy and rapid entry of added sellers. At the beginning of the 1920's it found itself with a substantial margin of excess capacity developed in response to World War I demands. It proceeded to increase this excess in the 1920's as producers in southern areas expanded capacity when northern production was restricted by labor strikes, or generally to take advantage of cheaper nonunionized southern labor. At the same time the demand for coal declined progressively, mainly because of shifts to the use of petroleum fuels as a substitute for coal, and of increasing efficiency in the use of coal to produce heat and power. Progressive displacement of coal-mine labor therefore took place, with the number of laborers employed declining by over 25 per cent during the generally prosperous and expanding period from 1920 to 1929, and further in the depression of the 1930's. At the same time, the mine labor force, typically situated in relatively isolated one-industry towns, evidenced an insufficient and lagging mobility into other occupations. Even employed labor was only partially employed, and subnormal wage incomes were widely accepted.

As to enterprise, it was also laggard in withdrawing the increasingly redundant (and long-lived) mine capacity from production. It continued to produce and offer coal in quantities well in excess of what would be bought at a normal competitive price, and thus to engage in a destructive price competition of such intensity that the industry as a whole had a net loss every year of the 1920's, with about 60 per cent of firms showing individual net losses in 1929. This was while the economy in general was enjoying unprecedented prosperity. The situation was complicated and prolonged, moreover, by the fact that competitive price cutting was followed by competitive wage cutting, a practice which permitted the perpetuation of oversupply by passing on a large part of its burden to labor in the form of subnormal wages. In general, there was a chronic deficiency of both enterprise and labor incomes, resulting from a serious redundancy of both plant and labor resources which were relatively immobile toward other uses. The income distress of course became much more acute with the advent of a deep general business depression in the early 1930's, and was still chronically in evidence at the outbreak of World War II. In many respects, the experience of the coal industry from 1920 to 1942 parallels that of the agricultural industries, but destructive competition was more severe in the case of coal.

Several unsuccessful attempts were made in the earlier 1930's to administer private agreements to limit competition or fix coal prices, including a government-sponsored scheme for private price fixing under the short-lived NRA depression-emergency plan. Thereafter, a special federal act was passed in 1937 by Congress, providing for imposition of minimum bituminous coal prices by a governmental commission. This law (the so-called Guffey-Vinson Act) generally provided for a commission determination of the weighted average cost of producing coal by all firms in various designated districts and areas, and for the fixing of minimum coal prices roughly equal to such weighted average costs. These prices were enforceable through a heavy penalty tax on sales at prices below the legally established level. The weighted average costs on which prices were based of course included wages paid, and this meant that such wage increases as organized or other mine labor could secure would be automatically reflected in corresponding increases in minimum coal prices. Furthermore, only price fixing was involved, and the necessary corollary restriction of output was essentially left to the discretion of the various mine operators.

As a type of regulatory law dealing with destructive competition, the Guffey-Vinson Act had many merits, especially as compared to comparable laws affecting the distributive trades or agriculture. It contained clear and explicit legislative directions as to the level at which price should be fixed, and it gave authority for price fixing to a governmental commission rather than delegating it to private parties. The basis for fixing price (at the level of weighted average costs of production) was rationally justifiable as coming as close to a competitive level of price as was possible while averting net losses to the industry as a whole, rather than being an arbitrary basis like that embodied in farm "parity." There was provision for regular consumer representation in the administrative proceedings through which prices were fixed. The price-fixing formula was explicitly framed in such a fashion as to accommodate and encourage the raising of coal-mine wages toward normal levels. And the determination of minimum prices on the basis of the weighted average costs of all producers tended to set a price below the specific average costs of the more inefficient or high-cost producers, thus perhaps in the long run encouraging their departure from the industry.

Nevertheless, the law shared with inferior pieces of restrictive legislation some of the basic common faults of all attempts to remedy destructive competition by restricting competition or fixing price. The basic difficulty was the failure to provide any adequate incentive for the removal from the industry of redundant plant and redundant labor force, such as might restore the industry to a status in which unrestricted competition would tend to be workable. Weighted average costs as determined necessarily reflected the average elevation of costs due to partial utilization of redundant plant, and a minimum price was set which on the average made such inefficient utilization of redundant facilities profitable or free from loss. As a result, the existing misallocation of resources was made more comfortable to the enterprises involved, and the desired exit of redundant capacity was thus probably retarded rather than hastened. To be sure, a fringe of high-cost, inefficient producers would tend to lose money under weighted-average-cost pricing, but it would be less than they would have lost otherwise. Also, possibilities for padding reported costs further insulated this group from pressure for elimination. Finally, no provisions were made for encouraging redundant labor force to leave the industry, and the easing of the way to wage increases tended, in the absence of such encouragement, to dampen competitive forces which were tending to force the desired reallocation of labor.

These adverse effects or insufficiencies of the Guffey-Vinson Act are for the most part predicted rather than learned from actual experience, since the Act was fully in operation for less than two years. Although it was passed in 1937, full administrative operations were not under way until late 1940, and a year later the entry of the United States into World War II drastically increased the demand for coal and at least temporarily eliminated distress conditions in the industry. Thus the Act was allowed to expire at the end of the initial term provided by Congress, and has not been renewed.

In spite of the very brief actual experience with the Guffey-Vinson Act, however, the theoretical indications are that it constituted an inadequate and unsatisfactory device for dealing with an industry in destructive competition. Price fixing alone is a weak expedient in such cases, in that it alleviates the symptoms without doing much to cure the disease. And if income relief ito enterprise and labor in the distressed industry must be granted, the granting of such relief needs to be tied to positive measures which promote the reallocation of redundant resources.

Since World War II, destructive competition in the bituminous coal industry (or in most of its several regional segments) has been alleviated or largely averted through the policies of the very strong industrial union which represents the bulk of coal-mine workers. These policies involve first the establishment of a high, firm floor under wages, which prevents price cutting in coal from leading to and feeding on competitive wage cutting; and second the severe limitation of the length of the working day and working week for coal miners to the point where an excessive supply of coal is unlikely to be produced. This combination of policies has more or less stabilized the industry and facilitated the earning of at least normal wages and profits by labor and enterprise in the industry. Yet again, the policies in question are not working to solve the fundamental misallocation of resources. Employed coal miners are in effect only partially employed under work-week restrictions, and the way is made easy for the perpetuation of excess mine capacity. Further interference to encourage and hasten the reallocation of redundant labor and physical resources is indicated.[10]

Crude Petroleum—the Problem and the Remedy

The petroleum industry—with emphasis on that part of it engaged in extracting crude oil from the underground deposits where it occurs—has never had a chronic problem of distress or destructive competition, though there have been short periods in which sudden increases in supply have led to very low prices. On the other hand, it has presented and continues to present a severe problem in resource conservation, stemming largely from the adverse conservation effects of the antagonistic exploitation of individual oil pools. Moreover, these poor conservation tendencies can be, in the absence of public interference, linked with or responsible for instability in crude-oil prices. In an endeavor to deal dually with price and income instability and with the conservation

---

[10]A recent study finds that conditions of destructive competition have not prevailed in the midwestern region of the bituminous coal industry in the period since World War II, largely because of structural changes going far beyond wage stabilization. (It is not clear that comparable changes have occurred in the other main regional segments of the industry.) See Reed Moyer, *Competition in the Midwestern Coal Industry*, 1964.

problem, petroleum producers have sought and obtained a composite of federal and state interferences with crude oil production. These have been designed primarily to raise and stabilize oil prices, but justified primarily as necessary for conservation. It is this body of regulatory laws which we wish to examine here.

The general character of the conservation difficulty in petroleum has been discussed in Chapter 12. Under the common law in this country, the rights to subsurface minerals are included in ownership rights to surface land. Also each of several or many owners of adjacent surface land is entitled to recover, by operating from his surface, as much petroleum from a common underground pool of oil as he can, even though the underground oil is "fugacious" (moves around underground) so that each surface holder can easily withdraw oil which originally underlay the surface holdings of other owners. Given these legal precepts, the usual existence of numerous small surface holdings over any discovered oil pool, and the general unpredictability of where petroleum will be discovered, the typical development of oil pools in the United States has involved the joint and essentially antagonistic exploitation of any pool by several or many competing interests. In the absence of regulation, each interest has attempted to withdraw as much oil as possible from the pool as quickly as possible, "before the others could get it."

Such antagonistic exploitation, as indicated in Chapter 12, has led to poor conservation. Present or immediate yields were emphasized to the disregard of valuable future yields, resulting in an inferior time pattern of recovery. The speedy early withdrawal of oil frequently resulted in a substantial reduction of the total oil recoverable over time. Wasteful competitive over-investment in recovery equipment was encouraged. And the density and placement of competitive well drilling resulted in further net losses in the ultimate total recovery from any oil pool. This composite of results has clearly been undesirable from the standpoint of society. The ultimate wealth of the American economy has been perceptibly reduced by poor petroleum conservation as associated with antagonistic exploitation of oil pools.

Antagonistic exploitation has also been generally undesirable to oil producers as a group, in that their aggregate earnings have tended ultimately to be reduced, and acutely painful to them at particular times. There is essentially no means of predicting or planning the long-run rate of development of petroleum-producing capacity or petroleum output, because of the unpredictability of the results of exploratory efforts. In this setting, when large new petroleum deposits have been suddenly discovered and brought into production, the rapid antagonistic exploitation of these deposits has led to huge immediate increments in the supply of crude petroleum offered on the market. These in turn have led to abrupt and "disastrous" declines in the price of the product. Therefore, not only has bad conservation in the several senses mentioned above been involved, but also severe financial losses to petroleum producers in general, as the initial "flush" (free-flowing or non-pumped) production of newly discovered fields expanded in an unrestricted fashion.

Although poor conservation practice has been with us since before the turn of the century, acute and painful price declines for crude oil hit the industry in severe fashion first in the late 1920's and early 1930's, when very large new discoveries and developments of crude oil were made in eastern Texas, California, and elsewhere. The market was flooded with an oversupply of petroleum so great as to induce drastic price declines. This development of new supplies unfortunately coincided with the gathering of a general economic depression, so that the price of crude oil (on the average) declined by between 60 and 80 per cent between 1930 and 1931. Severely depressed crude oil prices continued through the depression, and it was this financial impact on oil producers which led them to solicit and secure governmental interference to restrict crude petroleum output, albeit in the name of a conservation principle which had previously been in large part disregarded.

The type of regulation obtained in the 1930's, and still in force, was directed largely at limiting the rate of output of crude oil, within the existing industry structure and subject to the continuance of essentially antagonistic exploitation of individual oil pools. Whatever conservation benefits were secured were in the main incidental results of the restriction of the rate of withdrawal of oil, and did not stem from any systematic elimination of antagonistic exploitation. The components of the regulatory scheme are roughly as follows.

First, the federal government, through the Bureau of Mines, issues monthly forecasts of the demand for crude oil in the United States, in each of several districts and in each oil-producing state, the demand being generally or roughly calculated as the amount which will be bought or used at going prices. It estimates roughly, in other words, how much crude oil the industry should produce and offer if it wishes to maintain existing prices. (These going prices are presumably at some level satisfactory to the industry. They have been reached through a process of competitive adjustments and administrative pricing decisions of the large integrated firms which both produce crude oil and purchase large amounts of it from nonintegrated producers.) The federal demand estimates, or suggested output quotas, are not binding on anyone, but they are clearly advisory to the several state regulatory agencies in the principal oil-producing regions.

Second, all of the principal oil-producing states (with the exception of California) have established regulatory agencies that have the power to require curtailment of state petroleum production to a given quota, and to "prorate" this state quota among the various oil fields and individual producers of the state. (In California, the same functions have been carried out, on the basis of private agreement and coercion, by a private organization of oil producers in the state.) In general, the state agencies accept the estimates of the Bureau of Mines as the basis for establishing their monthly production quotas, although minor deviations of quotas from estimates are not uncommon. The state agencies cooperate and coordinate their activities through the Interstate Oil Compact Commission, established by federal law.

Third, the federal government, under its so-called "hot oil" laws, backs up the enforcement powers of the state oil agencies by prohibiting interstate shipment of petroleum produced in violation of legally established state quotas.

This scheme of regulation has proved over a period of more than thirty years to be a reasonably workable device for raising crude oil prices to levels deemed adequately profitable by most petroleum producers. It has also stabilized prices at such levels by preventing large new discoveries from flooding the market with extra oil, and by adjusting production quotas to changes in demand. The actual process by which crude-oil prices are arrived at and maintained, however, is rather hard to trace.

There are no legislative instructions in the relevant laws as to the level of price at which curtailment policies should aim. Only output restriction is involved, and this in general "to balance supply with demand." But the demand will vary with price, and some price must be presupposed in the Bureau of Mines estimates and in the state production quotas derived from them. We have suggested as an initial approximation that the price presupposed in the estimates (and quotas) is a going or pre-existing price. But a good deal of private price-policy making is involved in arriving initially at a reference price, and the system has clearly permitted upward adjustments of crude petroleum prices in response to general inflationary movements in the economy, and to broad changes in supply conditions. In general, demand estimates and production quotas have been manipulated over time to accommodate general upward (and occasional downward) price changes as these emerge from the price policies of principal integrated petroleum firms. Determination of oil prices by the private industry, in other words, has been to a considerable extent implemented by the state regulatory agencies and the Bureau of Mines as they arrived at quotas consistent with privately determined prices. On the other hand, the power of the state regulatory agencies also provides some check on the discretionary power of private firms in fixing prices.

Has this elevation and stabilization of crude petroleum prices through public output control been in the public interest? And has the policy followed been the best of available alternatives in the light of the problems posed? The answers to these questions must turn on a distinction between the merits of production curtailment and proration as (1) a measure to raise and stabilize oil prices *per se*, and (2) a device to further conservation.

On the first point, the case is reasonably clear. The petroleum producing industry is not and never was chronically distressed or afflicted with destructive competition. Its income difficulties were cyclical or otherwise temporary in character, and no long-term deficiency in enterprise or labor earnings was ever observed or seriously threatened. In consequence, there has been no case *per se* for governmental relief of chronically adverse income positions in the industry, through restrictions of competitive production or otherwise. Production curtailment or other measures to protect oil-producers' incomes have not been needed as such, and stabilization of oil prices *per se* has no greater merits in this case than in that of numerous other industries with cyclically or randomly fluctuating supplies or demands. Nor has there been any chronic problem of overcapacity or overinvestment in the ordinary sense, which an interference policy might need to remedy. Thus, on the usual grounds of redressing subnormal income situations in distressed industries, we cannot justify either a curtailment policy which has on the average supported substantial excess profits for crude oil producers as a group, or a stabilization policy which has minimized the fluctuations in these supernormal enterprise incomes.

The case for the curtailment-proration policies in fact must rest not on their merits as income-relief measures (although income relief was their primary intended function when they were instituted), but on their virtue as measures to improve the conservation performance of the petroleum industry. Are they justified on this latter ground, and sufficiently so to overcome any legitimate objections to their "side effects" in raising and stabilizing the incomes of oil producers?

It must be allowed that the curtailment-proration policies have had some significant absolute merits from the standpoint of conservation. Given a general setting of antagonistic exploitation of numerous individual oil pools, they have mitigated the adverse conservation consequences of such antagonistic exploitation in two ways. First, the general curtailment of oil output has checked the tendency, under antagonistic exploitation, to emphasize present at the expense of future oil outputs, and has brought about some degree of postponement in the use of oil resources which is probably desirable from a social standpoint. This check on the rate of immediate withdrawals of available petroleum, moreover, has at least in some degree enhanced the prospect of an ultimately larger total recovery of oil resources, so far as unduly rapid immediate production may tend to damage underground oil reservoirs in such a way as to subtract disproportionately from future production. Second, the stabilization of production in the face of new discoveries of immense productive potential has tended to avert huge early production from new fields that would otherwise tend to create "surpluses" of petroleum that would go to low-valued present uses rather than higher-valued deferred uses, and that also would be damaging to the ultimate recovery prospects from the new oil pools.

In both of these ways, the curtailment-proration policy has served the interests of conservation, albeit at the price of an otherwise unneeded "incidental" elevation of the incomes of petroleum producers. The remaining question is whether this sort of regulatory policy adequately serves the requirements of oil conservation, or is as good as available alternatives. The answer here is clearly negative. The basic difficulty is that although the policy restrains some of the adverse conservation tendencies of antagonistic exploitation of oil pools, it really does not eliminate such exploitation or many of its adverse consequences. The general procedure involved is to give each producer or each oil well on a given oil field a production quota, but not to restrain adequately the number or location of producers or wells operating over the pool. Individual quotas may be calculated according to various principles, including those based on estimates of the effect of individual withdrawals on ultimate recovery from the pool, but in general quotas are dominated by the "equitable" consideration of giving each producing firm or well its fair share of the field quota.

In consequence, the following adverse conservation tendencies remain. First, uneconomically intensive drilling by competitive interests (resulting in too many wells) is not significantly restrained; by some quota systems, it is definitely encouraged. Therefore, the capital costs of extracting a given amount of oil from a pool remain unnecessarily and seriously elevated. Second, the locational pattern of drilling and production on a field is not controlled according to the engineering requirements of the underground pool or reservoir of oil, and there are consequent losses in productive efficiency and in ultimate recovery. Tendencies toward overly intensive drilling have been checked to a certain extent by supplementary state regulations controlling well-spacing, but these do not control well locations and are generally inadequate to secure even a distant approximation to optimal engineering plans for the exploitation of oil pools. In general, therefore, the curtailment-proration policy has succeeded only in mitigating some of the adverse conservation effects of antagonistic exploitation of oil pools. Such antagonistic exploitation remains and still is a source of serious adverse results in the realm of conservation.

The obvious superior alternative is a legal requirement for "unitization" of the exploitation of each individual oil pool, all ownership interests over the pool being required to agree to a single central management and engineering plan for the pool (with sharing of the combined profits). This would eliminate the waste of investment, the loss of ultimate recovery, and the disregard of future as compared to present yields that are consequences of antagonistic exploitation. Given such a requirement, proration would become otiose and legal curtailment of output might not be necessary for good conservation.

Generally, then, the curtailment-proration policy espoused dually by the federal and various state governments, essentially a system of restricting competition through control of output, is a weak and deficient means of promoting good conservation in the petroleum industry. But it is perhaps a good deal better than nothing at all from a conservation standpoint.

In reviewing the major cases of interference with competition in unconcentrated markets—whether the main nominal or actual occasion for interference be chronic destructive competition, displacement of small by large enterprise, or poor conservation tendencies—we have observed that the measure usually adopted is one of restricting competition through price fixing or output control. This sort of measure is generally deficient to deal with the fundamental economic problems involved, has adverse side effects, and should be replaced by more direct and specific measures appropriate to the individual problems involved. All or most of our interferences with competition in unconcentrated industries have a doubtful validity, relative to visible alternatives.

The preceding discussions have by no means covered all cases of governmental interference with atomistic competition. Numerous state laws affecting competition among barber shops, dry cleaners, and the like, and restricting out-of-state competition, could be mentioned. The preceding coverage of the "big" cases, however, should suffice to establish the patterns and principles involved in this type of interference with competition. Let us now turn to a different setting for interference, found in the case of public utilities.

Restrictive Policies Affecting Public Utilities

The economic and administrative issues faced in the so-called public utility field, in restricting competition and substituting direct governmental regulaton for it, are so complex that we cannot treat them in detail here. To be sure, the public utility sector is in the aggregate not as large a contributor to national income as the composite of agricultural, distributive, and fuel producing industries just discussed. But the regulatory issues, and the regulation itself, are more varied and complicated in the public utility sphere, with the result that we must confine ourselves here to a broad and very synoptic review of the occasions for imposing public utility regulation to date, of the general regulatory principles applied, and of the strengths and deficiencies of existing regulation.

The concept of a public utility is essentially a creation of legislation. But social scientists have endeavored to rationalize legislative procedure by identifying the common characteristics of those industries which our lawmakers have set aside for special "public utility" treatment—that is, for public restriction of entry and for direct regulation by special governmental commissions. Employing their rationalizations, we do not construe the public utility sphere either as narrowly or as broadly as has sometimes been suggested. We do not confine it narrowly to the major industries in which governmental authorities usually support and regulate single-firm monopolies in individual markets, like the electric power and telephone industries. We do not construe it so broadly as to include every industry in which governments have imposed direct regulation of competition, production, or pricing. We have already purposefully distinguished the regulation of industries with essentially atomistic competition, and exclude these from the public utility sphere. The occasions for and characteristic purposes of regulation in such industries are quite different and deserve special identification and treatment.

Therefore, we construe the public utility sector as including industries which, according to legislative finding, supply widely used consumer or commercial necessities (in practice usually services rather than commodities) for which there are no close or adequate substitutes available. *In addition,* either or both of the following conditions are supposed to be present in these industries:

1. The technological conditions of supply are such that, in any market, either single-firm monopoly or concentrated oligopoly is inevitable or "natural" in the sense that unrestricted competition would, because of scale economies or other considerations, engender the development of monopoly or concentrated oligopoly. (Therefore, the public requires regulative protection against the inevitable monopolistic pricing tendencies which tend to emerge. Also, "nature needs a hand" from government to hasten the development of the inevitable—and more efficient—monopolistic or oligopolistic market structures.)

2. The supply of service by more than one or a few regulated firms would be damaging to buyer interests, either because of technological conflicts (dual telephone networks, overcrowding of air channels with competing radio or television signals), or because of the generally disruptive effects of discriminatory pricing which would emerge in the absence of regulation.

Such a combination of conditions is deemed sufficient to support the findings that unregulated competition (or unregulated monopoly) is not in the public interest, and that entry to or operation in an industry should ordinarily be restricted to one or a few firms per market by public license or franchise. It is usually also found that the franchised monopolists or oligopolists should be subjected to direct regulation by a governmental commission of prices charged and service rendered.

Areas of Utility Regulation, and the Proposed Justifications for Regulating Them

Guided by the considerations just outlined, federal and state legislative bodies have identified and subjected to regulation a group of industries that fall within the public utility sphere identified. Much of the regulation is adopted by state legislatures and administered by state public utility commissions, where the markets in question are intrastate in scope. This is the case with local electric power supply, local telephone service, local transportation, and so forth. Regulation is adopted by Congress and administered by federal commissions where interstate markets or movements of the service are involved. The regulation of interstate railroads and trucking by the Interstate Commerce Commission, of interstate airlines by the Civil Aeronautics Board, and of interstate telephone and radio-TV communications by the Federal Communications Commission are examples.

The principal areas of utility regulation, federal and state, and the occasions for or ostensible justifications of regulating them include:

1. *Electric Power Generation, Transmission, and Distribution, and the Transportation and Distribution of Natural or Manufactured Gas.* The basic case for regulation here is that the industry in any separable market (local or regional) is essentially a natural monopoly, in that technological economies of large scale are such that one firm can supply the market more efficiently than two or more firms could. The general principle followed has been to offer a monopolistic franchise to one firm per market, and thereafter to subject the franchised monopolist to commission regulation of prices (rates) and service.

In the extraction of natural gas, a similar natural-monopoly case can hardly be made, but federal price regulation has been extended to the natural gas producers whose output enters interstate commerce, on the apparent theory that seller concentration is high enough to threaten monopolistic pricing practices.

2. *Telephone Communications.* With respect both to local markets and to the nationwide long-distance market, the finding again is one of natural monopoly based on scale economies, and also on the inconvenience to consumers of parallel competing systems. The solution again has been monopoly franchises plus the regulation of monopolists' rates and service.

3. *Local Street Transport, as by Trolley Cars and Buses.* The natural-monopoly basis for regulation, with emphasis on scale economies and on the inconvenience of duplicate systems in the individual market, is again apparent here. In large urban areas, however, the segregation of an area geographically into several adjacent markets, each served by a different monopolist, has frequently seemed consistent with the realization of available scale economies. Subject to this qualification, the single-monopolist franchise and rate regulation have again been the preferred devices.

4. *Interstate and Interurban Transportation of Freight and Passengers.* The case for regulation presented here was from the outset more complex than in the classic natural-monopoly industries. It has become much more complex with the development of several competing means of transport.

Initially, railroads were the primary vehicle of long-distance land transportation, and the case presented was one involving:

(*a*) A "natural" oligopoly of a few lines performing any crucial long-distance haul (as, for example, from New York to Chicago). Scale economies dictated a single carrier on any one route, but the use of several competing routes by several competing carriers was justified because of the need for enroute service to localities on each of several routes.

(b) The corollary necessity of single-firm monopoly on local or short hauls on each separate route, which however introduced the dangers of monopolistic exploitation of consumers on such hauls.

(c) The possible disruption of the normal competitive relationships of commercial users of rail freight service because of unrestricted and chaotic discrimination in the making of freight rates by a few competing oligopolists.

Thus interference was justified as needed to limit entry by franchise to an efficient number of firms, forestall monopolistic exploitation of users, and control oligopolistic competition so as to avert disruptive rate discrimination.

As highway transport of freight by trucks and passengers by buses and air lines has come to offer serious competition to the rails, the rationale of transport regulation has become progressively more complicated. Limitation of entry in the interest of fostering a "natural oligopoly" on any given air transport route has been a consideration, with both scale economies and public safety favoring this policy. But similar natural-oligopoly arguments have seemed applicable in much lesser degree to interstate highway trucking of freight, or even to interstate or interurban passenger bus lines. The major shift in emphasis, however, has been from one of restricting the monopolistic and competitive tendencies of railroads to one of restricting the potential or actual competition among several types of competing carriers of freight or passengers, or among several carriers of the same type. Here the rationale of regulation is presumably that of simultaneously protecting users from the possibly chaotic price discrimination that might be exercised by an oligopoly of assorted types of carriers, and limiting entry so as to secure the advantages of large scale operations available in the case of each type of carrier.

It is not surprising that an overall policy with so many masters to serve has had its inconsistencies and deficiencies. On the other hand, it is not clear that unrestricted competition in the interstate transport field would be to the public advantage. The picture is complicated, of course, by the simultaneous pursuit of policies of federal subsidization of various transport industries designed to promote their growth, for national security reasons or simply in the general public interest. In any event, the general policies of franchise limitation of entry and of public determination or control of prices (dually oriented to averting monopoly pricing and limiting competition) have been followed by federal agencies in this field.

5. *Radio and Television.* A fairly clear technological case for natural oligopoly exists here. In any broadcasting area there is "room" on the wavebands for only a limited number of broadcasting or telecasting stations, if interference of one station with another is to be avoided on the receiving sets of listeners or viewers. (Also, in the case of "AM" radio, limitations on the power of local transmitting stations are needed in order to avert widespread interference among stations in widely separated areas.)

These technological considerations have furnished the general basis for the imposition, by the federal government through the Federal Communications Commission, of a licensing system affecting all commercial radio and TV stations, and a limitation on the number of stations permitted to operate nationally and in any locality or region. The system of franchised operations imposed in other utility industries is thus also applied here. And, in addition, various regulations designed to secure a proper and nondiscriminatory use of radio and television stations as media of public information have been applied. But regulation of prices or rates has not been imposed, so that in this sense radio and television outlets are franchised oligopolists who remain "unregulated." This omission in the public policy is undoubtedly in part due to the fact that the "buyers" of TV and radio service are a different and much smaller group than the "users." Whereas the users comprise the general listening and viewing public, the buyers are generally business firms which purchase "air time" for the primary purpose of advertising. Protection of the general using public from monopolistic overcharges has thus not been viewed as a crucial issue.

Issues: The Real Need for Some Regulation and the Workability of Existing Regulation

There are two broad issues of public policy to be considered with respect to the public utility sector. First, is governmental interference to restrict entry and impose direct price and service regulation really needed because economic performance in the industries involved would otherwise be seriously unsatisfactory from a social standpoint? Second, what are the strengths and weaknesses of the existing schemes of public utility regulation, and in general do they provide satisfactory substitutes for competition?

To the first question, the answer must be generally affirmative. Promotion of the general welfare does require a restriction of entry and a direct regulation of market performance in the industries in question. Competition would be inefficient and self-destructive, and the public would be adversely affected by the unregulated market policies of the monopolists or oligopolists who would in any event emerge.

The case is clearest with respect to the true natural-monopoly industries, such as those providing electric power or telephone service. Here, the realization of scale economies and the protection of the public against single-firm monopoly pricing are both involved. It is less clear in the transportation industries, considered as an interdependent complex of several sorts of carriers. In this instance there is a good deal of potential competition which might benefit the public, and regulation is largely concerned with suppressing or controlling competition in order to preserve competitors in each type of carrier service. But even in this case, the effects of unrestricted entry and competition would threaten to be chaotic and to damage user interests in various ways, so that *some sort* of public utility regulation seems to be required. It is notable, moreover, that in the industries in question what is involved is not simply some transitory maladjustment that makes competition temporarily unsatisfactory and requires only temporary remedial measures. Truly chronic conditions are involved which make unregulated competition an unsatisfactory alternative more or less permanently, and which call for the development of a long-term substitute for unregulated competition.

To the second question, as to whether existing utility regulation provides a satisfactory substitute for unregulated competition, we cannot give an unqualifiedly affirmative answer. Existing public utility regulation is subject to a number of serious deficiencies as a means for securing the best in market performance from the regulated industries. To date it cannot be considered an approximately ideal device of its type for furthering public welfare. Improvement is possible and needed. Although space will not permit any detailed examination of outstanding deficiencies of existing regulation, we may comment briefly on several of the principal ones.

These deficiencies, of course, represent failures to attain certain normative goals appropriately established for regulatory commissions, and a word must first be said about such goals. Very briefly and roughly, they appear as follows. First, to secure at the lowest possible cost whatever output is to be produced by the regulated industry, the commission should control entry and plant investment so as to secure the most efficient number of plants and firms, scale economies being taken into account. This may be relatively simple in true natural monopoly cases, where the aim would be to secure a single firm with the most efficient number and variety of plant facilities, and it may not be too difficult where a natural oligopoly of producers of the same service is sought. Where an oligopoly of producers of several different but competing services is involved, as in the case of competing carriers of several types in the transportation sector, the implementation of the goal becomes much more complex. It then involves the determination of the most efficient relative number of plants and firms of each of several carrier types and of the most efficient division of the total market among different sorts of carriers. The indicated policy may, over time, require permitting or encouraging elimination of some existing plants and firms as well as control of entry.

Second, the commission should impose a level of prices or rates for the services supplied by any regulated industry which is competitive in the sense that the average price received in the long-run does not exceed full average cost of production (including interest on investment), or furnishes an accounting profit only sufficient to pay a normal interest return on capital investment.[11]

Third, so far as a level of prices or rates roughly equal to long-run average cost is obtainable at two or more different rates of output or long-run scales of operation (costs declining with increase in scale enough to match the lowering of prices obtainable for larger outputs), the commission should require that the largest of the outputs at which prices will cover costs be supplied, and that the scale of operation be adjusted accordingly. In other words, with progressive scale economies present, regulated firms should be required to exploit the elasticity of demand for their services by seeking the largest output at which prices will cover full costs. Otherwise the price obtained is not a competitive price, or as close to a competitive price as the avoidance of losses would permit.

Fourth, in cases where it is no longer possible at any rate of output for the regulated firm or firms to secure a level of price sufficient to cover average costs, so that losses of existing fixed plant and eventual withdrawal of the service (unless publicly subsidized) are inevitable, the regulatory policy should generally be to establish rates as close as possible to the short-run marginal cost of supplying service, thus securing maximum public benefit from the existing fixed plant. There may

[11]Lower prices, equalling marginal cost, would be justified on allocative grounds if long-run marginal costs were below long-run average costs because of progressive economies of the large scale firm, but would be feasible only if governmental subsidization of utility firms were feasible. High prices, equalling marginal cost, would be similarly justified if long-run marginal costs exceeded long-run average costs, but would lead to profit surpluses that should be taxed away.

be instances, however, in which "external benefits" of the service, for which charges cannot be collected, justify provision of the service even at a financial loss. In such cases, public subsidization of the utility may be indicated, and rates may justifiably bear a variety of relationships to costs.

Fifth, the commission should require or otherwise secure optimal internal efficiency from the regulated firms, so far as this is affected by managerial efficiency, choice of techniques, maintenance of equipment, replacement of obsolete equipment, and so forth. Finally, the commission should be able to impose a properly discriminatory structure of individual rates or prices, so far as the use of price discrimination serves such useful ends as securing a higher rate of utilization of equipment and (subject to some restrictions) a larger total output. The theoretical requirements for an ideal system of price discrimination in utility cases are so complex, however, that we will not attempt to set them forth here.

Using these norms as general reference points, it is possible to outline and explain briefly some of the principal deficiencies of existing public utility regulation in various fields. These deficiencies are traceable in considerable part to the lack of sufficient regulatory power in the hands of the commissions. This lack stems partly from the terms of the legislation establishing regulation, and partly from the restrictive interpretation of commission powers by the courts.

A first deficiency is that commissions frequently have not imposed, or have not been able to impose, prices or rates low enough just to equal full average costs—rates at a competitive level. Commission discretion under broad legislative instructions has accounted in part for this tendency. But judicial dicta to the effect that regulated firms must be allowed "a fair return on a fair value" of property have introduced considerable flexibility into the conception of a legally enforceable level of rates. Both the valuation of the investment on which a "fair" interest return should be earned, and the size of such a "fair" percentage return, have become subjects of litigation and, ultimately, of negotiation between regulated firms and the regulatory commissions—in a context in which precise economic concepts often play an only limited role. In consequence, there is a tendency in the case of a considerable share of regulated utility firms for rates to be set which allow a limited but nonetheless perceptible share of monopolistic excess profits. This tendency is accentuated in numerous instances in which state utility commissions, regulating intrastate firms, are unable properly to ascertain the value of equipment or services supplied to intrastate firms by parent firms which operate outside the jurisdiction of the state commissions.

A second and perhaps more serious deficiency stems from the fact that the regulatory commissions in general do not have the power to determine broadly the rate of output or scale of operations of the regulated firms, and thus to force them to adopt, when there is a choice, the socially most efficient of two or more scales of operations at which prices can cover costs. To be sure, they are generally empowered to require the firms to provide service to all bonafide applicants at the prevailing rates. But in fixing the rate, which will effectively determine the number of applicants or volume of demand for the service, they are generally restricted to fixing a rate which will not exceed costs experienced at about the going rate of output and scale of operations. They cannot insist that a much larger output and lower rate be made available, on the theory that costs would also be covered at the larger output.

Suppose, for example, that an electric power company is delivering 5 million kilowatt hours of service per period with a long-run average cost of 4 cents per unit, and that it could alternatively supply (with larger facilities) 10 million kilowatt hours per period at an average cost of 3 cents per unit. Suppose also that the 5 million units can be sold at a price of 4 cents or slightly more, and that 10 million units can be sold at a price of 3 cents or slightly more. The larger output and lower price (which is consistent with revenues covering costs) is clearly preferable from a social standpoint. But the utility commission is limited in its power to imposing a 4-cent rate to equal costs at the going rate of output. It cannot effectively force the regulated firm to double its output and cut rates to 3 cents per unit, even though the firm could also break even at that point.

The initiative for adjusting output to demand, and seeking an optimal output, therefore rests in the hands of the private utility management. But, being in any event limited to earning an approximate interest return on investment, the management may lack any adequate financial incentive to undertake expansions of the sort outlined, especially since they may entail a degree of risk. And thus the desired expansion may never take place or may be long delayed.

The fundamental difficulty is that by placing the price decision largely in the hands of the commission but leaving the long-term output decision with the private firm, we arrive at a situation in which the commission has the possible desire but not the power to undertake major output adjustments, and in which the firm has the latter power but has been deprived largely of the incentive to exercise it for its own or the public's benefit. In spite of the difficulty, of course, desirable output adjustments may still be arrived at in many cases, in one way or another. But in general, the commissioners should clearly have a greater area of decision-making power in order to make the regulatory scheme more workable. One partial remedy to the dilemma is for the commission generally to set rates which allow a perceptible margin of excess profits, thus giving the regulated firms some incentive to adjust long-term outputs in a desired fashion. But this remedy is only partial, and entails the disadvantagse of sponsoring monopoly profits in the regulated industries.

The difficulty just mentioned is closely related to a third and more general deficiency of existing utility regulation—the fact that it seriously reduces private-enterprise incentives for efficiency in general. It depends on private managements to make all or most decisions affecting the internal efficiency of operations, and does not give commissions adequate power to influence or control such decisions. With profits limited to an interest return on investment or a little more, and rates subject to adjustment to cover whatever level of costs is attained through whatever level of relative efficiency, private managements in regulated industries generally lack the strongest of financial incentives to strive for the greatest efficiency. In any event, their incentives tend to be less than those found in unregulated industries which are not protected against losses and are free to enhance their profits without legal restriction. Possibly as a consequence, suboptimal internal efficiency has been observable in a number of regulated firms or industries. The obvious solution, if public utility regulation is to be made more workable, is to give to the commissions further decision-making power to match their price-making powers, so that the unfortunate bifurcation of responsibility and power between regulator and regulated will not continue.

A fourth deficiency is encountered when utility regulation is applied to a complex industry made up of several types of firms whose distinctive services are essentially in competition with each other, as in the case of the regulation of rail, highway, and air carriers in the transport field. Here the commissions involved should arrive at a rational or optimally efficient allocation of the total market among different sorts of carriers, at a rational regulation of the number of plants and firms engaged in each line, and at a rational relative pricing system. But this is made difficult because of the implied responsibility of the commissions to support rates which will secure for firms supplying each type of carrier service a normal interest return on their investments, and thus to perpetuate the provision of each competing type of service as long as possible. Pursuit of this goal seems from experience very likely to involve an uneconomic limitation of intercarrier competition, through maintaining a relative rate structure among carriers which permits the less efficient to survive. It tends to forestall economically desirable adjustments in the relative volumes of services supplied or facilities maintained. Arrival at any really rational solution in this case is further impeded by the fact that, for various reasons, some of the carrier types have been or are being expressly or implicitly subsidized by governmental bodies (airlines directly, highway transport indirectly) so that their comparative strength as competitors has a somewhat artificial basis.

Furthermore, the division of jurisdiction over the transport industry among different commissions—interstate and intrastate operations of the same firms falling respectively under federal and state commissions, and interstate airlines being regulated by a different federal commission than interstate rail and highway carriers—is not conducive to the development of a rational total regulatory scheme. Yet our complex governmental organization and the judicial interpretations of constitutional protections to private property rights engender the development of the sorts of deficiency noted in the transport industry.

A fifth deficiency, closely related to the preceding one, appears when a regulatory commission is faced with a franchised monopolistic firm which, because of a declining market or rising costs or both, is no longer able at any level of rates to cover its costs of production and is thus marked for elimination unless granted a direct public subsidy. (This sort of problem has been encountered with some frequency in the case of local street transportation companies, for example, in recent years.) In this case, the usual solution to which regulatory commissions are forced or persuaded to agree is a progressive increase of rates until the service is almost priced out of the market—losses persisting—in response to the "commonsense" but economically false argument that if losses are being incurred they can always be lessened or eliminated by increasing prices. In the cases in question, the loss in demand consequent upon price rises and the rise in average costs because of restricted output are sufficiently great that losses are not eliminated, or even necessarily decreased. At the same time the public is rapidly deprived of useful services from available fixed equipment. This sort of solution, flowing from protection-of-earnings reasoning, is generally inferior to one of securing full use of economically redundant facilities at low rates until the facilities wear out, or (if perpetuation of the service is justified because of external benefits) of subsidizing the regulated firm to reimburse it for net losses. But regulatory commissions as constituted generally have neither the power nor the inclination to impose this sort of more rational economic solution.

A final deficiency is noted in the case of the radio and television industries, and inheres in the restriction of entry and competition through license or franchise without the corresponding imposition of rate regulation, or very much in the way of regulation of service. In this instance, the government, in the interest of forestalling the clogging of "airlanes" by too many radio or TV signals, establishes and protects many lucrative private monopolies whose earnings it does not in turn regulate. In addition to being generally inconsistent with the underlying spirit of American public utility regulation, this system places the members of the responsible regulatory commission in the unseemly position of discriminating donors (among competing applicants) of public franchises that may have substantial or huge values to the recipients in terms of the capitalized monopoly profits they hope to earn. The resulting total situation constitutes a rather unsatisfactory substitute for competition, even though unrestricted competition is probably unworkable.

In the light of the several main deficiencies of existing public utility regulation outlined above, it is clear that, although unrestricted competition is not a workable alternative in all or most of the regulated industries, commission regulation of these industries has itself been far from ideally workable. In some degree, the deficiencies of the regulatory system could be lessened by appropriate changes in legislation and administrative policy. But these changes would run largely in the direction of creating stronger and more powerful commissions, with considerably more extensive managerial powers over the prices, outputs, and investments of the regulated firms. Infringement of legitimate private management prerogatives would be charged, and quasi-socialism. In addition, the administrative costs of maintaining duplicate managements at the commission and the private-firm levels would be great. Furthermore, the proposed creation of more powerful commissions would encounter not only political barriers at the legislative level, but possible judicial barriers as the courts strove to afford adequate protections to the private-property rights involved. If there is a better way of utility regulation, it is not easy to come by, and even then it would be imperfect in numerous respects.

This is to say that the public utility sector of the economy poses a true dilemma for public policy. Unregulated competition seems generally unworkable, but the sort of regulation we have obtained or can practically get has serious deficiencies as a device for securing optimal overall market performance within the sector. True socialization of utility industries is a general alternative, but this would raise a host of new problems not easy to solve.

If the preceding discussion conveys any valuable lesson, it might be this: The subjection of an industry to public utility regulation is far from being an automatic and ideal solution of the problem of securing socially desirable performance. If any concentrated industry can perform reasonably well under a system of unrestricted competition or rivalry—even though there are some notable minor deficiencies in its performance—we should be extremely slow in applying the sophomoric solution of curing its ills by declaring it a public utility. Restoring conditions for more effective competition should be the remedy of choice, and first tried.

The preceding concludes our discussion of public policies of interference with competition and substitution of direct regulation for it. In coverage, this review has not ben comprehensive or detailed. In addition to overlooking various minor interference policies, we have omitted mention of temporary general interferences with competition in wartime periods (the most extensive version of which was applied during World War II), and in the "great depression" from 1933 to 1935, under the National Recovery Administration. The history of these episodes of interference is interesting *per se* and illuminating for the study of other problems. With primary emphasis here, however, on the contemporary scene, we leave the discussion of these episodes to other works. Let us conclude this volume with some brief suggestions regarding directions for improvement in existing policies affecting enterprise monopoly and competition.

SUPPLEMENTARY READINGS

Wilcox, C., *Public Policies Toward Business*, 1960 (rev. ed.), Chs. 13–25.
Federal Trade Commission, *Resale Price Maintenance*, 1945.
Phillips, Jr., C. F., *The Economics of Regulation*, 1965.
Caves, R. E., *Air Transport and Its Regulators*, 1962.

16

Directions for Revising Existing Regulatory Policy

Current American regulatory policy affecting enterprise monopoly and competition has been analyzed and criticized at some length in the two preceding chapters, with attention both to the general antitrust policy of preserving competition and preventing monopoly, and to various contrary policies of restricting and regulating competition in selected sectors or industries. The composite of existing policies seems to be substantially better than no regulatory policy at all, providing a means of bettering the market performance of business. This is true in particular of the antitrust policy, although some limited merits may also be claimed for at least some of the competition-restricting policies.

On the other hand, certain significant weaknesses appear in existing policies of both sorts. The performance that these policies secure from enterprise is substantially less than "ideal," and feasible alternative policies could probably secure significantly better performance. The question therefore arises as to what developments or revisions of existing policies are called for or would be desirable.

This is potentially a very broad question, since it could open for discussion all possible alternatives for a change in public policy. These could include very sweeping changes in the relationship of government to economic activity, of such character and magnitude that the resultant system would no longer be identifiable as one of free enterprise or capitalism in the usual sense. In the light of the purpose and content of this book, we will forego discussion of such radical policy alternatives. We will confine ourselves to possible developments and revisions of the existing policy, under which most activity is regulated by market forces and individual enterprise decisions rather than by governmental fiat.

Thus we will not attempt to analyze the relative merits of socialism, or of socialization that would involve government ownership and management of productive facilities in a dominant fraction of the economy. Adoption of such a policy alternative would introduce not only a "new deal" but a "new deck" of cards. Its merits as compared to contemporary capitalism could be assessed, if at all, only through extensive analysis of numerous sociological, political, psychological, and organizational aspects of individual and group behavior in various settings. In such an assesment, moreover, numerous "noneconomic" phases of behavior would transcend in importance the more strictly economic aspects of behavior to which we have given most of our attention in this book. Since our analysis here has provided no adequate background for a consideration of the relative merits of socialism (we have in fact centered on the performance of a capitalistic economy relative to its own potential,) we will not attempt to evaluate socialism as a general alternative.

We will similarly forego analysis of direct governmental regulation of the performance of most of all industries in the economy, under a system of private ownership but with "managed management" of productive facilities. Under this alternative, private ownership of enterprises would in general be retained, but the performance of most industries would be directly regulated, more completely and thoroughly than public utilities are at present. This scheme also lies outside the scope of our discussion, since it in effect introduces socialized decision-making for enterprise while retaining private ownership of productive facilities. Such a system is hardly recognizable as a variety of capitalism in the ordinary sense. It may be added that the overall workability or efficiency of the scheme is extremely doubtful on general grounds, because of: (*a*) the inherent wastes of two-layer management (a private management for each firm, and a public management to manage the private managers); (*b*) the tendency of detailed direct regulation to suppress incentives for efficiency and progressiveness on the part of private managements, while not giving governmental management the incentive-plus-power that would be adequate to make up for this loss; (*c*) the encouragement of sabotage of the regulatory mechanism or its working by the regulated firms; and (*d*) the general danger that regulated firms would over time tend to "capture" regulatory agencies by having them staffed in large part by representatives of their own interests, so that regulation might be slanted toward private rather than public ends.

We will also omit any detailed discussion of two extreme policy alternatives that might conceivably be consistent with the maintenance of a free enterprise economy. The first of these would involve governmental permission, encouragement, or sponsorship of private cartelization in most or all industries. Under this policy, the typical industry would be allowed or encouraged to develop a comprehensive agreement in restraint of competition, including detailed provisions for collusive determination of production, pricing, market shares, and so forth. This alternative is passed over here as representing in the main a prescription for public sponsorship of joint private monopolization of most industries. It would in all probability impose the net reduction in public welfare which is generally inherent in a world of monopolies, and other losses as well. We refer particularly to the adverse income-distribution effects inherent in monopolistic excess profits, and to the protection of inefficiency and nonprogressiveness generally inherent in cartel arrangements among all firms in an industry. Also not discussed is a variant of private cartelization in which the government directs or participates in the decision-making of the various legalized cartels, in order to protect and promote the public interest. We eschew discussion of this alternative on the ground that it will represent either (with weak governmental participation) an innocuous elaboration of private cartelization, or (with strong governmental participation) the equivalent of widespread direct governmental regulation of private enterprise, already alluded to.

A second extreme policy alternative that we will not discuss is that of *laissez-faire* (no regulation at all, and no antitrust laws). This we reject offhand as embodying an open invitation to increased monopolization and cartelization of industries, with generally adverse effects on the public weal.

Given the restrictions just outlined, our discussion of policy alternatives will center on suggestions for improving existing policies. These policies have as their global goal an attempt to maintain a viable market-regulated economy, by preserving competition in general and by interfering with or replacing it only in some specific areas where its results are socially unacceptable. For practical purposes, we are thus led to discuss in turn: (a) avenues for elaboration of revision of existing antitrust policies; and (b) avenues for curtailing, extending, or revising existing policies designed to restrict or displace competition.

Possible Revisions in the Antitrust Policy

In considering revisions or elaborations of existing antitrust policy in the United States, a first issue to be faced is whether this policy is in general terms an acceptable and useful one, in terms both of its broad purpose and of the procedures it employs to implement these purposes. In the opinion of the writer, the policy is in general a good one.

First, the general purpose of promoting a more workable market performance by enterprise in various industries, through securing more active and effective competition, is entirely acceptable. Furthermore, it seems generally practicable, in the sense that performance in numerous cases is in need of improvement and that improvements can be obtained. Second, the general device employed under our antitrust policy —fulfilling this purpose by placing certain negative restraints on market structure and market conduct in various industries and then letting competition take its course—seems intelligently chosen and eminently practicable. The device seems clearly superior, on numerous grounds, to that of imposing extensive direct regulations of performance on numerous industries, after the pattern of public utility regulations. Third, the specific procedure of imposing these negative restraints largely through a process of litigation in the courts seems also acceptable, and preferable to visible alternatives in the light of crucial characteristics of our legal system and of prevailing constitutional protections of private property. The superiority of regulation by quasi-administrative, quasi-judicial commissions is not evident from a comparison of the regulatory experiences respectively of the Federal Trade Commission and the Antitrust Division of the Department of Justice.

The issues which concern us therefore do not involve the broad acceptability of the antitrust approach to enterprise regulation. They center rather on the specific content of the antitrust legislation, and on the character and orientation of the administration and interpretation of such law. Without attempting detailed analysis of all possibilities for change, let us consider several important issues in turn.

Treatment of Monopoly and Monopolization under the Sherman Act

While recognizing its significant accomplishments, we saw in Chapter 14 that the basic antimonopoly policy as it stems from enforcement of Section 2 of the Sherman Act has some very important deficiencies as an instrument of public economic policy. Fundamental among these is the "conduct orientation" of the law as written by Congress and interpreted by the courts. The basic offense against the law has been and still is viewed as one of market conduct in the form of business acts, practices, and policies having the purpose and effect of excluding competitors (monopolization), rather than as one of dominant market occupancy by one or a few firms (monopoly in the structural sense). Monopoly can thus be attacked in the main only indirectly through assault on the predatory or exclusionary actions of firms, and not directly as a structural phenomenon with certain undesirable consequences for market performance. A related fundamental difficulty is the failure of the Sherman Act to provide adequate legislative instructions to the judiciary as to what sorts of relief or remedy are to be applied in order to prevent recurrent violation of the law, once an initial violation in the form of monopolization has been found.

As a result mainly of these basic deficiencies of the law, certain weaknesses have been noted in the administrative policy which applies it. First, it is usually difficult to apply the law to the essentially monopolistic phenomena found in most highly concentrated oligopolistic industries, in which market structure is observably conductive to undesirable performance. The firms in such industries must be clothed with a suit of predatory and exclusionary offenses of conduct before being found in violation of the law. This is not usually easy to do, and even if it can be done, the proper direct goal of attacking monopolistic structure and performance can be approached only by an unduly circuitous or devious route.

Second, litigations centering on the details of market conduct, as monopolization cases at present must, are intrinsically lengthy and expensive, as innumerable details of conduct must be explored, defended and attacked, and ultimately evaluated. This extreme length and expense of litigation effectively curtails the ability of the Department of Justice, operating with a limited budget, to bring legal action against many or most of the industries in which monopolistic tendencies are observed and in which illegal conduct might also be established. Enforcement is hampered by the very high cost of each individual enforcement action.

Third, the standard of liability under the law is intrinsically vague, resulting from the fact that its wording is extremely general, and that a great deal is left up to the discretion of the courts in interpreting it. Adequate legislative standards concerning the nature of an offense have not been provided. Mostly as a result of this, the courts' interpretation and application of the law from case to case has been wavering and not entirely consistent. Correspondingly, business firms are to an unnecessary degree uncertain as to what they are and are not permitted to do.

Fourth, the courts in general—given the definition of the offense in terms of conduct and the lack of specific legislative instruction as to remedies—have usually been unwilling to remedy illegal monopolization by requiring structural changes through such devices as dissolution or dismemberment of offending firms. Thus those revisions of market structure that might most strongly assure a more competitive performance typically are not imposed, even after a violation of Section 2 has been thoroughly established. And there is again unnecessary *a priori* uncertainty as to what remedy will be imposed in a particular case.

The preceding criticisms of the content and application of the existing law suggest three promising avenues for legislative change. First, the law might be changed to state that structural situations (involving high concentration and impeded entry) which might be expected to have and demonstrably do have monopolistic performance tendencies are generally illegal, without particular reference to the lines of market conduct through which the undesirable structure has been created, maintained, and exploited. If this change were made, the standard of liability should be spelled out in reasonable detail in the legislation, limiting the discretion of the courts in deciding what is legal and illegal, reasonable and unreasonable. Furthermore, the law might instruct the courts that the usual remedy for illegal monopoly as defined should be dissolution or dismemberment of the principal firm or firms possessing the monopoly (aimed at decreasing concentration and easing entry), provided that there would be no serious untoward side effects of such a remedy and that lesser remedies would not clearly suffice to reinstitute effective competition.

For the suggestion and articulation of this basic approach to revising or replacing Section 2 of the Sherman Act, we are heavily indebted to a work by Carl Kaysen and Donald F. Turner, *Antitrust Policy: A Legal and Economic Analysis.*[1] The student is urged to refer to that book. In slightly more detail, Kaysen and Turner would substitute for the present Section 2 a series of provisions which *(a)* would find "unreasonable market power" to exist in a market whenever typical monopolistic performance tendencies such as persistent abnormal profits and the failure of such profits to induce entry were observed, and whenever, in addition, the market power had not been created and maintained because of great scale economies, legal use of patents, or innovations of product or technique; *(b)* would declare such "unreasonable market power" to be illegal; and *(c)* would instruct the courts to use dissolution

[1] Cambridge, Mass., 1959.

and dismemberment remedies against the offending firm or firms (including vertical disintegration as indicated) to eliminate such unreasonable market power, provided that lesser injunctive remedies would not clearly eliminate it. The offense of possessing unreasonable market power would not be a criminal one, but only subject to the civil remedies that the courts might impose.

Thus the essence of the offense against Section 2 of the Sherman Act would be changed from that of monopolizing conduct to that of predominant market occupancy by one or a few firms, accompanied by monopolistic performance tendencies. The essential remedies would much more strongly emphasize structural revisions tending in the direction of horizontal deconcentration of highly concentrated industries (plus some vertical disintegration), together with reduction of barriers to entry. Adequate protection against the destruction of efficiency would be provided both in distinguishing "unreasonable" from "reasonable" market power, and in requiring that any dismemberment remedies applied should not result in a substantial loss of efficiency. One putative advantage of this new policy would be that a direct attack on the problem of monopoly would become possible, especially with respect to concentrated oligopolies. Furthermore, litigations should be simplified and shortened, with the result that the enforcement of the law should become less expensive and more efficient. The content of the law would become less ambiguous and more predictable, and its application more consistent. Finally, the remedy for illegal monopoly typically applied should be much more effective in inducing workable competition.

In addition, overt predatory and exclusionary practices, from which specific intent to monopolize might be inferred, would continue to be outlawed, but attention would shift away from the maze of acts, practices, and policies having exclusionary effect that are so much emphasized under the present law.

The writer in general subscribes to the Kaysen-Turner proposal just outlined, as the most practicable means of improving our present legal approach to the monopoly-oligopoly problem. Examined in detail, the proposal may have a few deficiencies, but in its general outline it appears to take the right direction in antitrust-law reform, and to provide a practicable alternative to present law and policy. Other proposals are contained in works listed at the end of this chapter.

Treatment of Collusive Activity
under the Sherman and F.T.C. Acts

The existing prohibitions of collusion in the form of horizontal agreements to restrain competition among rival firms, under Section 1 of the Sherman Act and Section 5 of the Federal Trade Commission Act, seem roughly satisfactory. They control a certain variety of market conduct that is frequently undesirable, and severely discourage the development of overt cartelization of American industries.

A difficulty with the application of these provisions, however, is that they have been asked to bear an unduly heavy share of the responsibility for maintaining workable competition in the economy, as compared to the share borne by the antimonopolization of Section 2 of the Sherman Act. Thus the total policy has been unduly conduct-oriented, and not structure-oriented in sufficient degree. A second difficulty is that the boundaries between legal and illegal conduct of a possibly collusive character are unnecessarily indistinct, or open to debate in the process of litigation. Correspondingly, two major suggestions for revision in the legislation involved or in its application may be considered.

As to the application of present or revised anticollusion provisions of the law, the clear prescription is that, given the revision in the Section 2 or antimonopoly provisions proposed above, a much larger share of the time and budget of the Antitrust Division of the Justice Department should go toward prosecuting antimonopoly cases (involving "unreasonable market power") and securing structural remedies. A correspondingly smaller proportion of effort and expense should be devoted to prosecuting collusion cases under Section 1 of the Sherman Act. The primary emphasis of the enforcement policy would shift toward antimonopoly cases and this policy would be only backed up and supplemented by anticollusion actions.

This is not to suggest that anticollusion actions should be largely neglected; there should still presumably be a great many of them. But they would not need to be relied upon primarily in the important cases involving concentrated oligopoly. They might center therefore more on policing the less concentrated areas of the economy, in which predominant market power is not in evidence but where collusion is a form of conduct occasionally employed to temper the forces of competition. It may be added that the success of an intensified enforcement policy of a revised Section 2 would tend to create a congeries of market structure in which collusive conduct would be rarer or less effective, and in which a somewhat less intensive enforcement of Section 1 would, for practical purposes, be needed.

As to the content of the laws affecting collusion, a recurring suggestion is that their application might be clarified, simplified, and speeded if they were revised to list as illegal *per se* a number of specific collusive devices or practices which generally have the intent and effect of restricting competition, and which have usually been found to be illegal in the interpretation of the general prohibition against agreements in restraint of trade. This suggestion may have some merit, but the merit is retained if a list of *per se* offenses is used to supplement the general prohibition of restraining agreements, rather than to replace the general prohibition. That is, the essential basic provisions of Section 1 of the Sherman Act (and Section 5 of the F.T.C. Act) should be retained, but supplemented by a list of *per se* offenses. Under the Kaysen-Turner proposal, the named *per se* offenses would include agreements to fix prices, to share markets, to limit production, or to boycott third parties, and also agreements to conform to reported list prices and to exchange information in ways which would encourage or support the restraint of competition. Both overt agreements of the usual sorts, and specified trade association activities of a certain genre, would thus be named as illegal. There has been considerable support from various commentators for instituting some such list of *per se* offenses, and in principle the general proposal seems a good one.

Enforcement Budget, Procedures, Penalties, and the Courts under the Sherman Act

In the extensive technical literature concerning antitrust policy, there are suggestions aplenty for procedural and administrative changes in the application and interpretation of the law. Space here does not permit us to examine such suggestions in any detail, but a few salient proposals may be mentioned.

As to the amount granted by Congress for the enforcement of the antitrust laws, it is reasonably clear that this is seriously insufficient to support a program of maximum effectiveness in maintaining competition and preventing monopoly. As the primary enforcement agency, the Antitrust Division of the Department of Justice is unable to hire enough lawyers and economists, or finance enough litigations, to make a reasonably complete coverage of probable violations of the antitrust laws from year to year or decade to decade. This could continue to be true if the substantive changes in the law suggested above were made. At present, for example, the budget of the Division permits it to employ about 250 lawyers and 30-odd economists, plus office staff. In view of the demands on the time of attorneys and economists of each individual litigation (especially those involving monopoly charges), this complement is clearly insufficient to support an adequately intensive enforcement program covering the whole United States. An increase of the overall budget of the Antitrust Division by at least severalfold is clearly called for if violations are to be deterred because of the prospect of apprehension and legal action, and if the bulk of undesirable situations and practices are to be remedied as they occur.

As to procedures of enforcement, we have already expressed general approval of the litigatory procedure in the courts as a means of enforcement. We thus would not suggest a shift in emphasis toward administrative procedures, as under the Federal Trade Commission, although the Commission plays enough useful roles outside the area of basic antitrust enforcement to justify its continuance. Procedures of the Antitrust Division in selecting cases for investigation and ultimate litigation, however, might be improved. There is a persistent tendency toward the selection of cases largely in response to the receipt of specific complaints, usually either from competitors of or buyers from allegedly offending firms, or from Congressmen who represent or reflect the opinions of such interests. Application of this principle does not seem to have resulted in a very balanced coverage of probable violations among different sectors and industries of the economy. There is a distinct bias in selection toward relatively unconcentrated industries (where the collusion problem may be apparent but the problem of strong monopoly power is relatively slight), and toward industries supplying basic necessities which are purchased by large numbers of buyers (food, building materials, and gasoline, for example). Thus there has been a tendency toward relative neglect of numerous industries in which very high concentration provides a basis for probable unreasonable monopoly or market power, and too much emphasis on cases involving collusive market conduct that frequently has innocuous consequences. It might thus be suggested that the enforcement policy would be improved if the selection of cases were derived in much larger degree from a general economic analysis of industry structure and behavior within the economy, with attention to the actual incidence of poor market performance and suspect market structure, and in lesser degree from the volume of complaints by private parties. This would imply the strengthening of the function of general economic analysis within the Antitrust Division, as a guide to the policy strategy and tactics of the Division. A more reasoned regulatory policy might then emerge.

The matter of appropriate penalties for violation of the antitrust laws has been debated from time to time for many years, and poses some difficult issues. As we have argued in Chapter 14, the "criminal" penalties for violation of the Sherman Act are hardly severe enough to provide a serious deterrent to violation on the part of the medium- and large-sized enterprises which are most frequently involved in antitrust suits of an important sort. It would be difficult in practice to secure legislative imposition of financial penalties large enough to provide a strong deterrent. The real "teeth" in the enforcement provisions of the Sherman Act are found in the civil remedies which may be imposed, in the form of various injunctions against the continuance of illegal behavior, or of constructive decrees imposing dismemberment, dissolution, or other changes in market structures. Such injunctions or decrees may impose far greater indirect financial penalties on violators of the law than the direct "criminal" penalties in the form of fines, and thus serve as more powerful deterrents to violation. In addition, the civil remedies have the comparative merit of being directed toward securing improved behavior in the future, rather than simply penalizing firms for their past behavior. To draw a parallel, the imposition of a $100 fine for the second offense by an automobile driver for speeding or driving while intoxicated is likely to be less of a deterrent to violation than the suspension of his driver's license for a year; in addition, the suspension remedy at least temporarily removes a hazard from the roads.

In addition, it may be argued that offenses against the antitrust laws are not ordinarily considered morally opprobrious by the average citizen, and may be perpetrated inadvertently or because of the intrinsically complicated and vague standards regarding what does and doesn't violate the law. Both of these circumstances argue against any primary reliance on "criminal" penalties, and for a major reliance on civil remedies. This case would become especially clear if the revision of Section 2 of the Sherman Act suggested above were adopted, so that mere possession of "unreasonable market power" would violate the law. Here imposition of any criminal penalties would be quite inappropriate, and entire reliance should be placed on civil remedies.

It may thus be suggested—as Kaysen and Turner have in the book referred to above—that criminal penalties be abandoned for all offenses except specifically listed *per se* offenses and overt predation and exclusion, and that otherwise entire reliance be placed on injunctive remedies and other decrees secured from the courts in civil suits.

Let us finally look at the federal courts, which stand as the crucial arbiters in antitrust litigations, interpreting the prohibitions of the law and determining what are the appropriate remedies for violations. The major difficulty here stems from the fact that the ordinary federal courts, from the "district" level up, are now called upon to try, and hear on appeal, all antitrust suits brought by the Department of Justice, and that they are in general ill-equipped to pass on the complicated issues of law and economics frequently involved in these antitrust suits. A tribunal with specialized knowledge of and intensive experience in dealing with the legal and economic issues involved in antitrust cases would evidently tend to be more efficient, consistent, and fair than a large assortment of district and higher courts in the regular federal system.

It has therefore been suggested—we refer here again to Kaysen and Turner—that a special constitutional court should be established to handle the initial trial of at least all "big" or antimonopoly cases, with appeal directly therefrom to the Supreme Court. Institution of this arrangement would relieve the regular lower courts of a burden they are poorly equipped to bear. It would also encourage the development of a specialized panel of justices who would accumulate detailed and intensive knowledge of the economic and legal issues posed in antitrust cases, and who would dispose of such cases in an efficient and consistent manner. (Trial of routine *per se* and other cases involving collusion only might be left to the regular courts.) This proposal seems at the least to be worthy of very serious consideration. It seems clearly superior to the proposal for enlarging the function of quasi-administrative, quasi-judicial regulatory agencies like the Federal Trade Commission, since at the outset it places the litigation where it usually arrives anyway, at the level of the federal courts.

Mergers and the Clayton Act

Section 7 of the Clayton Act as amended by the Celler-Kefauver Act of 1950 has been rapidly becoming one of the most potent weapons in the arsenal of current antitrust policy. This has happened mainly because the Supreme Court, in a succession of decisions and opinions, has interpreted its prohibitions of mergers in such a way as to give them a more or less maximum scope of application. It has defined relevant markets in elastic fashion so as to locate almost any possible lessening of competition that may result from mergers. In construing the meaning of an illegally substantial lessening of competition via mergers, it has invoked doctrines of quantitative substantiality, incipiency of effect, and probability of effect in such a way that very slight or only possible effects of mergers on competition provide grounds for finding them illegal. And it has found that every variety of merger—horizontal, vertical, and conglomerate—is subject to the prohibitions of the law. Thus, with a vigorous enforcement policy, very severe restrictions on the alteration of market structures through mergers can be imposed on the whole business community.

The legislation in question, however, is not without its flaws. First, the crucial language of the act, which makes the illegality of a merger pivot on whether or not its effect "may be substantially to lessen competition" is intrinsically subject to a wide variety of interpretations. Given the fact that the Court long construed almost identical language in Section 3 of the Clayton Act narrowly, so as to find that very large effects on competition were necessary for violation of that section, it seems adventitious that this language has so far been so broadly construed in interpreting Section 7. It is entirely possible that a "new" court, with revised membership, could radically alter the present "strong" interpretation of the section. More fundamentally, the difficulty is that the language of Section 7 gives the Court too broad a range of discretion in interpreting its prohibitions.

It would therefore seem desirable to amend the section by inserting in it a general definition of an illegally substantial effect on competition. This definition should have primary reference to the proportion of the relevant market or markets controlled by the merging firms, or to the proportionate change in market structure that a merger brings about. Though it might be wise to indicate that rather moderate proportional effects of mergers on market structures should suffice to support a finding of illegality, the suggested amendment should permanently lay to rest the questionable doctrine of "quantitative substantiality," under which mergers can be found illegal simply because they involve absolutely large amounts of assets.

Second, Section 7 conspicuously omits any "standard of reasonableness" under which potentially offending mergers might be exempted from its prohibitions. The Court, moreover, has not so far come forth with any "rule of reason" in its interpretation of the law. Yet a standard of reasonableness, or definition of the grounds on which otherwise offending mergers could be found legal, is clearly needed and should be set forth in Section 7. The one simple rule that is obviously needed is that a merger which may substantially lessen competition should be allowed if the merging firms can demonstrate that the merger would substantially increase real efficiency in production and distribution. (Demonstration that a merger would simply increase the profitability of the merging firm should not qualify as a basis for exemption from the law.) This sort of amendment would strengthen a very significant piece of legislation, and tend to assure that its enforcement would be in accord with accepted principles of economic rationality.

Section 3 of the Clayton Act

The application of Section 3 of the Clayton Act was for a long time severely limited by judicial interpretation. Exclusive dealing and tying agreements between seller and buyer were found to result in an illegally substantial lessening of competition only as used by a dominant seller that supplied a large majority of the output of its industry. If each of several oligopolists in an industry used such agreements in rivalry with each other, no one of them was in violation of the law. The resulting restriction in the application of the law was unfortunate, because the general use of exclusive dealing or tying contracts by the principal member firms of an oligopolistic industry could foreclose new entrant firms or small competitors from markets or from access to most distributive outlets. Entry could be made more difficult, and existing high degrees of seller concentration protected.

This interpretation of the section was later altered in two or three cases by the finding that the exclusive dealing contracts of a seller were illegal if they only affected an absolutely large amount of sales in a line of commerce (under the so-called "quantitative substantiality" doctrine). Thus the way was apparently opened for finding illegal and enjoining the use of tying and exclusive dealing agreements in a significant number of oligopolies. But the Supreme Court has since vacillated in its interpretation of Section 3, apparently returning toward its original stand by finding these vertical agreements to be legal where used generally by sellers in an oligopolistic industry. As a result, we now have at best an ambivalent doctrine concerning the conditions under which use of these agreements is and is not illegal, and no vigorous program for the enforcement of Section 3 is being pursued.

This unfortunate state of affairs stems basically from the provisions of the law which give the courts a broad range of discretion in determining when such agreements "substantially lessen competition." It results immediately from the fact that in interpreting Section 3 the courts have in effect invoked a narrower doctrine of substantiality of effect on competition than they have in interpreting Section 7, so as to confine Section 3 to a much more limited application. Much more substantial effects on competition are required to find tying and exclusive dealing agreements illegal than are required to find mergers illegal.

One way of remedying the situation would be to amend Section 3 by including in it a general indication of when vertical agreements have an illegally substantial effect on competition—parallel to an amendment proposed for Section 7. Such an amendment might specify that tying and exclusive dealing agreements should be presumed to be illegal (subject to rebuttal by the defendant) whenever used by a firm that supplies more than a given percentage of output in a market or "line of commerce." Use of such agreements by any firm supplying more than 10 per cent of a market, for example, might be made presumptively illegal. An amendment embodying approximately this "percentage limit" should provide a basis for seeking injunction of the use of these agreements by firms in all concentrated oligopolistic industries.

Such a rule, however, should probably be tempered by extending the amendment to exempt otherwise illegal vertical agreements which the defendants could show to be "reasonable" on the sole ground that they significantly increased efficiency in production or distribution. Defendants would then have the opportunity to rebut a *prima facie* finding of illegal use of vertical agreements by showing that their agreements had a countervailing merit that made them reasonable. This suggestion is parallel to one made for the amendment of Section 7.

The more drastic alternative of simply outlawing all tying and exclusive dealing agreements, just as all horizontal agreements in restraint of trade are now outlawed, has also been suggested. This simplified solution has obvious virtual merits, especially at the level of enforcement. But many proponents of legislative reform would not go so far, holding that these vertical agreements may have economic justification in enough instances that they should not be proscribed entirely.

The Robinson-Patman Act

The Robinson-Patman Act of 1936 essentially rewrote and became Section 2 of the Clayton Act. As we have seen in Chapter 14, it was aimed initially at the buying-price advantages of mass distributors as compared to small independent wholesalers or retailers, but has placed severe restrictions on the selling-price policies of enterprises in general. Effectively, any price discrimination not based on cost difference is illegal if it results in some "injury" to competition between any pair of buyers of the discriminating seller, or between the discriminating seller and any one of his competitors—unless the discrimination results from meeting competitors' prices in good faith. The minimum test of illegality in terms of economic effects is thus much more stringent than the conventional one of causing a substantial lessening of competition within a whole market or of tending to create a monopoly.

On the basis both of experience with enforcement of the law and of analysis of its content, there seems to be a strong case for not retaining it in its present form. It has evidently not accomplished its dubious purpose of discouraging mass distributors or depriving them of their essential advantages over independent wholesalers and retailers. At the same time, it has imposed a considerable restriction on the freedom of pricing policy and action of all enterprises, by denying them the right to vary net prices, discounts, and customer classifications at will in dealing with individual buyers or concluding individual sales. The general tendency of this restriction is to shut off or discourage the use of one of the principal and most effective devices for actual price competition in oligopolistic markets—that of freehand or chaotic price discrimination through the making of numerous individual price concessions on individual sales. As a result, the overall vigor and effectiveness of price competition has probably been reduced by the enforcement of the Robinson-Patman Act. This tendency is suggested by the frequent observation of defense attorneys, in antitrust cases charging collusive price uniformity, that a defense against the main charge is most easily made by admitting and proving that actual price policies have violated the Robinson-Patman law.

The major question is whether the law should be repealed in its entirety, thus reverting to old Section 2 of the Clayton Act (which in effect dealt mainly with predacious price discrimination aimed at a competitor of the discriminating seller), or whether it should only be severely amended to eliminate its most objectionable provisions. This is a complex issue which we will not discuss here. The writer would favor on balance a full repeal, with reversion to a better drafted version of Section 2 of the Clayton Act of 1914.[2]

Unfair Competition and the Federal Trade Commission

A main issue involving the Federal Trade Commission concerns the desirable scope and emphasis of its activities in enforcing antitrust laws. At present, it is charged with sole responsibility for enforcing Section 5 of the F.T.C. Act, which in practice deals mainly with unfair or unethical competitive practices but may also be applied to ordinary restraints of trade. And it has joint jurisdiction with the Justice Department over Sections 2, 3, and 7 of the Clayton Act. Except on the argument that "two heads are better than one," or two enforcement agencies better than one, the advantages of this dual jurisdiction are not evident, and it is certainly not efficient in terms of administrative costs. It would seem quite reasonable that, in line with its overall purpose, the Antitrust Division of the Department of Justice (with appropriately augmented staff) should be *the* agency charged with enforcing Sections 3 and 7 of the Clayton Act. Also, restraint-of-trade cases might well be handled entirely by the Justice Department under the Sherman Act, without any recourse to Section 5 of the F.T.C. Act. In addition, the basic provisions of a revised Section 2 of the Clayton Act would be appropriately enforced by the Justice Department.

The law-enforcing activities of the F.T.C. would then reasonably be confined to unfair or unethical competitive practices (false advertising, misbranding, and so forth), and the remainder of enforcement activities would be assumed by the Department of Justice. This change is sug-

[2]See Kaysen and Turner, *op. cit.*, pp. 179–188, for development of a detailed proposal for amending the Robinson-Patman Act.

gested because it is not clear in theory or from experience that investigations, hearings, and orders by a quasi-administrative, quasi-judicial body like the Commission—subject to appeal to the courts—is as efficient a device of enforcement as that of initial direct court litigation instituted by the Justice Department. The staffing of two complementary enforcement agencies does not have advantages which outweigh the clear increase in enforcement cost that results. And, if it is argued that having a specialized agency like F.T.C. enables us to develop a specialized staff that is expert in the economic analysis of antitrust issues, the evident answer is that just such a staff should appropriately be developed or expanded in the Antitrust Division of the Justice Department, where it really belongs. Except on possibly valid grounds of political expedience, therefore, the writer would not argue for retention of real antitrust enforcement activities in the F.T.C. On the other hand, the Commission is well conceived to deal with the very special range of problems involved in the application of the law against unfair competition.

With respect to the content of that law, as it stems from Section 5 of the F.T.C. Act, the writer has no major criticisms or suggestions to offer.

Exemptions from the Antitrust Laws

As noted in Chapter 14, several industries or sectors have over time been exempted from the application of the Sherman Act or related antitrust laws. We will not attempt here any detailed analysis of the economic issues involved in all or any of the existing areas of exemption, but will only comment briefly on three crucial areas with respect to which there has been considerable controversy.

The first area is that of agricultural marketing agreements and orders. These are exempt from the prohibitions of the Sherman Act if approved by the Secretary of Agriculture, whose duty it is to encourage and sponsor such agreements (or impose such orders) pursuant to the legislative purpose of securing parity prices for various perishable and local crops. About such agreements there are two serious questions. First, are they really needed, either absolutely or as superior to alternative modes of alleviating certain types of market maladjustment in agriculture? Second, if they are needed or are preferred to alternative regulatory devices, are the present provisions of the law under which they are encouraged or imposed satisfactory from the standpoint of the general public interest?

As argued in Chapter 15, there is at least serious doubt as to whether, in the area of perishable and local crops, governmental sponsorship of marketing agreements (or imposition of orders) exempt from the anti-trust laws is needed to compensate for any chronic maladjustment in the markets in question. The normal competitive forces of the market, unrestrained by enforceable agreements to limit competition, would promise in many or most of the markets affected to induce a healthy competitive adjustment of supply to demand without undue delays. Furthermore, so far as there are signs of chronic maladjustment, the remedy of choice is not evidently that of sponsoring and enforcing agreements in restraint of trade—which have the general purpose and tendency of raising prices enough to make chronic maladjustment comfortable—but that of in various ways directly inducing or forcing the removal of redundant resources from the affected areas.

Even if a tentative case for marketing agreements is made, however, on grounds such as the one that they represent politically the most feasible mode of interference in maladjusted situations, the law which provides for encouraging and sponsoring them is at present seriously deficient. First, there is no really adequate legislative standard as to when marketing agreements are and are not to be permitted or en-couraged—as to what market situations do and do not qualify for the severe limitation of competition through exempt agreements or orders. The only implied standard is that they should be applicable in any agricultural industry which has not been receiving "parity" prices. This is certainly a loose, arbitrary, and unduly liberal standard, involving no close attention to the crucial question of whether or not a normal competitive return to resources invested in the industry is presently being or shortly could be secured, without suppressing competition.

Second, there is no adequate legislative standard for the prices which should be permissible once agreements are in effect; again, the "parity" goal for prices is loose and arbitrary, and unduly slanted toward enhancing the income of producers and processors at the expense of consumers. Third, adequate procedures are not provided for the representation of consumer and other third-party interests in the negotiation and determination of "fair" restrictive provisions in the agreements. The government is present primarily in the person of the Secretary of Agriculture, generally playing the role of advocate for special farm interests and instructed only to seek for "parity" prices. Consumer and other user interests are not represented in such a way that agricultural prices are effectively controlled (downward) to favor buyer interests as well as being elevated (upward) to enhance producer incomes.

Our general conclusion, therefore, is as follows. First, there is considerable doubt that the agricultural marketing agreements program as a whole should be retained at all. Reliance on unregulated competition plus a few direct interferences to correct market maladjustments may be preferable. Second, if marketing agreements are to continue to be used, the basic legislation should be thoroughly revised to provide adequate legislative standards concerning the grounds for interference and the permissible limits on prices sustained by agreement, and to establish more adequate procedures for the negotiation of agreements, with especial attention to the strong representation of consumer and other buyer interests.

A second area of exemption is that of resale price maintenance contracts affecting the retail distributive trades. We have argued in Chapter 15, and will argue again in the following section, that the entire program of resale price maintenance under state "fair trade" laws has doubtful economic virtue in terms of either purpose or effects, and that there has been no valid occasion for the imposition of this sort of interference with distributive-trade competition. Consistently, it would appear that the amendments to federal antitrust laws which exempt resale price maintenance agreements written under state "fair trade" laws are prime candidates for oblivion.

A third area of exemption embraces the legal use of patent grants to monopolize markets or to restrain competition between a patentee and others. As suggested in Chapter 14, the issues involved here are very complex. The doctrine of the courts which attempts to define the limitations on the use of patents which are imposed by the Sherman Act (and by Section 3 of the Clayton Act) is complicated or even tortured, and correspondingly somewhat ambiguous. In the broadest terms, the general line followed by the courts in limiting the extent of legal monopoly under a patent seems to be a sound one. The aim is to restrict the monopoly to the scope of the patent itself, and not permit this basic monopoly to be enlarged by the use of patents to regiment whole markets through licensing, cross-licensing, and similar schemes.

Without exploring the patent issue at any length, it may tentatively be sugested that a radical legislative requirement that each and every patent must be licensed at a reasonable royalty, unrestrictedly to any and all applicants (compulsory licensing to all comers) would have many theoretical and practical merits. While reasonably protecting the interest of the patent holder in his patented device or produce, by providing for reasonable royalties when he licenses its use or production, it would severely restrict or eliminate the use of patents as levers for collusive market control or as monopolistic barriers to entry. At the same time, it would avert the development of numerous long and costly court litigations involving the concentrated holding and restrictive licensing of patents, thus greatly simplifying our regulatory procedures under the antitrust laws. As an offset to this saving, there would of course have to be developed a specialized commission or tribunal to adjudicate claims concerning, and ultimately to determine, the level of "reasonable" royalties for the licensing of many individual patents. On balance, however, the indicated procedure should produce a net gain in efficiency and effectiveness or regulation, especially since it would largely remove the patent problem from the area of antitrust litigation.

Possible Revisions in Policies to Restrict and Regulate Competition

Only a very brief discussion of current competition-restricting and direct regulatory policies will be presented here. The general lines along which such policies might be revised have already been suggested in Chapter 15, and the introduction of detailed proposals for reform would require lengthy technical discussions which are not within the scope of this book. We may nevertheless present a brief summary of our views concerning the general direction policy reform should take in (*a*) agricultural and other chronically distressed industries, (*b*) the distributive trades, (*c*) extractive industries with acute conservation problems, and (*d*) public utilities.

Distressed Industries

With respect to agricultural and other atomistic industries afflicted with chronic maladjustment of labor force and physical productive capacity to demand, the main guiding rule for policy should be either to abandon entirely or to use only as very short-run emergency measures the commonly employed devices of governmentally imposed restriction of outputs, support of minimum selling prices, and income subsidies. Conversely, attention should be shifted toward direct measures to induce (perhaps with the use of incentive payments) the transfer or redundant resources, both human and physical, from employment in the distressed industries to employment elsewhere.

The customary remedies do not cure the basic disease (that is, redundant physical plant and labor force) in these cases. They only make the disease more comfortable by raising incomes in the afflicted areas, and may postpone any fundamental cure for the disease by removing the market pressure for a transfer of redundant resource. Moreover, the remedies are inefficient in that, in order to raise the incomes of inferior or marginal resources in distressed areas, they generally subsidize the income of more efficient resources in a way which is not required on grounds of equity. A further inefficiency results from chronically confining resources in the afflicted industries to partial employment or utilization.

Direct measures to induce the movement of redundant resources, on the other hand, should within a reasonable time restore distressed markets to such a state of health that they could thereafter operate with unregulated competition, efficiently and without significant aberrations from an equitable distribution of income. The direct approach would have the further advantage that public funds could be channeled mainly toward encouraging genuine removal of the inefficient or marginal resources from the distressed industry, without involvement in a general subsidization of all enterprises in the industry.

Our conclusions concerning agricultural or other distressed industries which are receiving or may apply for relief through governmentally imposed output limitation or price fixing include the following. First, general price-support, output-limitation, and income subsidy policies should be gradually but progressively abandoned over a transitional period of several years, and not granted in new cases. Second, direct measures should be rapidly developed and pursued to induce the transfer of redundant resources to other occupations, with public funds being used mainly to induce or subsidize the transfer of the more inefficient or marginal resources to other occupations, without subsidizing the distressed industry as a whole. Third, the distressed industry should be marked for complete return to the fold of unregulated competition as soon as the direct measures have attained certain economic goals concerning the adjustment of capacity and supply to demand. The suggested policy would clearly involve the directed use of income and other subsidies to enterprise and labor as inducements to the removal of redundant labor force and plant capacity from the over-supplied industry.

The same general conclusion applies to the present program of agricultural marketing agreements. These should in similar fashion be progressively abandoned over a period of several years, and direct measures as appropriate should be substituted in the areas affected, with the ultimate goal of returning such industries to the fold of unrestricted competition. In the preceding section, of course, we have suggested that if the marketing-agreements program should be maintained, the basic legislation should be altered to provide adequate legislative standards for (a) eligibility of an industry for an exempt marketing agreement, and (b) limitation of prices accomplished via agreement, in order to protect the equitable interests of consumers and other buyers. In similar vein, it could be argued that, if the basic price-support, output-limitation, and income subsidy program affecting agriculture were to be maintained, legislative amendments are in order to provide a fairer standard than the present "parity price" standard contained in the law. We will not pursue this matter here, since it appears that miscellaneous efforts to "patch up" the present program are unlikely to provide the basis for a viable and socially satisfactory type of regulation.

Distributive Trades

Whereas there has been considerable evidence of chronic maladjustment and of the consequent needs for some sort of public interference in the agricultural and some other industries, this has generally not been the case in the distributive trades. The occasion for seeking interference in the form of state resale price maintenance and minimum markup laws, and also through the Robinson-Patman Act, was the displacement of numerous small and nonintegrated wholesalers and retailers by mass distributors. It does not appear, after sober reflection on the thirty-odd years since the interferences mentioned were generally obtained, that they were justified on the grounds either of a threat that monopolies would develop in distribution or of chronic maladjustment or distress in the distributive trades. On the contrary, their main rationale was interference with an efficiency-increasing structural change, aimed at averting the losses to certain groups of sellers that this change would automatically impose.

Even in their intended and dubious purpose of arresting the development of mass distribution, moreover, the laws in question have not been visibly very effective, as mass distributors have evidenced great ingenuity in avoiding the adverse effects of their provisions. They have been effective mostly in restricting distributive-trade competition in some significant though minor degree. The laws in question thus embody an unnecessary and unjustified inconsistency with our general policy of promoting effective competition.

We have already suggested in a preceding section that the Robinson-Patman Act probably should be repealed, because of its economic effects outside of as well as within the distributive trades. The same recommendation for outright repeal can be made with even greater force with respect to state resale price maintenance ("fair trade") and minimum markup laws. This recommendation is consistent with our previous one that the related federal "enabling" statutes, amending the antitrust laws, also be repealed.

Given the repeal of the restrictive legislation in question, the problem remains as to whether any direct measures should be taken to alleviate the financial distress of small retailers or wholesalers who may in the future be displaced by further structural changes in the distributive trades. Such measures in general do not seem desirable unless very widespread distress is created by the rapid displacement of large numbers of such small firms. Should this phenomenon be encountered, restrictions of competition would still not evidently be in order, but direct governmental subsidies to ease the transfer of redundant resources to other occupations might be desirable.

Conservation Problems

We have seen in Chapter 15 that there is a certain tendency on the part of public authorities to deal with poor conservation performance in extractive industries by restricting their outputs and, incidentally, raising their prices. This device is chosen primarily because adverse conservation performance is very frequently linked with problems of excessive current supply, and because the enterprises involved ask for and get output curtailment as a means primarily of increasing their earnings and secondarily of improving conservation.

As we have seen in Chapter 15, there is usually a certain limited virtue in output curtailment as a device for enhancing conservation. With an exhaustible resource like petroleum, curtailment may effect a desirable rate of postponement of use, and may also avert the adverse effects of an unduly rapid early rate of withdrawal on ultimate total recovery. With resources capable of supporting relatively perpetual yields, like farm or forest land or fisheries, limitation of the current intensity of exploitation via output curtailment may contribute to averting an uneconomic depletion of the future yield potentials of the basic resources. Thus curtailment schemes cannot be written off entirely as subterfuges for raising prices in the name of conservation, lacking in any conservation merits.

It is clear, however, that in many or most cases output curtailment alone is not enough to induce relatively good conservation performance, and also that the particular degrees of curtailment imposed may be either less or more than needed for conservation purposes. This is because, in the case of exhaustible resources, postponement of use is usually not the only or even the principal conservation problem, and because, in the case of perpetual-yield resources, mere curtailment in the current average intensity of exploitation is often insufficient to bring about highly satisfactory conservation results. A general rule, therefore, is that an adequate public conservation policy should not be limited to output curtailment. The justifiability from a conservation standpoint of the degree of curtailment imposed should be carefully examined, and the basic laws should provide for such an appraisal. Finally, these laws should include important provisions which regulate techniques in some detail and which also eliminate the antagonistic exploitation of common resource pools.

Detailed discussion of possible improvements in existing conservation regulations is outside the scope of this book. It may be noted, however, that the adequacy of existing regulation varies considerably from case to case, and that there are corresponding differences in the degree of need for reform. In the case of petroleum production, for example, the curtailment and proration policy described in Chapter 15 is clearly insufficient. Some general overall curtailment of petroleum output might be retained in the interest of postponing use of a wasting resource, but otherwise the policy should be replaced by on which makes unitized development of every individual oil pool mandatory. This would eliminate antagonistic exploitation, with resultant savings in cost and increases in ultimate recovery. In the case of several ocean fisheries regulations, on the other hand, existing limitations on the intensity, type, and timing of fishing operations seem fairly well designed to control the "technique" of extraction so as to assure a desirable preservation of yields over a long period of years. Policies affecting conservation of agricultural land are complex; they embody numerous desirable direct inducements to good conservation technique. But, in general, they place too much reliance on simple output curtailment as a means of averting the over-intensive or technically inefficient use of farm land.

The general direction indicated for improvement in conservation policy is that of supplanting output curtailment (wherever it is the thing mainly relied upon) with detailed direct regulation which requires improved technques of exploitation and averts antagonistic exploitation whenever it is a problem. The reader is referred to numerous specialized works on conservation in extractive industries for further pursuit of this subject.

Public Utilities

We saw in Chapter 15 that the regulated industries in the so-called public utility sphere (excluding atomistic industries subjected to some sort of regulation) did not tend to perform ideally in significant respects. Deficiencies in performance were seen to stem in large part from limitations on the powers of regulatory commissions, with the result that responsibility, initiative, and incentive are unfortunately divided between regulated firms and regulatory commissions. They result also from the organization of regulation in such fashion that different utilities providing competing or complementary services are regulated by different commissions. Furthermore, there is a lack of clear legislative standards with respect to what goals regulatory commissions should seek, with the result that deficient or inadequate judicial standards have been invented to fill the vacuum.

The issues with respect to possible reforms in public utilities are so numerous and complex that there is no opportunity in this book for discussing them in detail. We will therefore confine ourselves here to a few brief suggestions.

First, the area of public utility regulation should not be extended to presently unregulated industries unless there is a very clear and conclusive demonstration that other regulatory devices will not suffice to preserve or institute a reasonably workable competition in them. Public utility regulation is very far from being a panacea for poor market performance, monopolistic or otherwise. It is likely to introduce as many new problems as the old ones it solves. Unless the problems encountered without regulation are indeed severe and pressing, a proposal to institute public utility regulation in the affected area will in general be ill-considered.

Second, commissions charged with the regulation of existing utilities should in general be given more power so that, instead of in large part simply limiting or supporting rates to cover average costs, they could in addition (under adequate legislative standards) control or establish the scale of operations, rate of output, and investment of regulated firms, to the end of securing socially optimal price-output adjustments. Only by thus increasing the regulatory powers of commissions does it seem possible to compensate for the loss of private management incentives for efficiency, bold expansion, and so forth which results from the rigid control of rates and profits. It is of course not suggested that commissions should be given *carte blanche* to determine utility outputs and investments at their whim. Rather, detailed legislative standards should be provided defining the grounds upon which, and the required information on the basis of which, commissions could order given expansions (or contractions) of investment, capacity, and output on the part of regulated firms. Moreover, the overriding goal or purpose of the commissions in imposing such orders should be given an adequate legislative definition, consistent with the general purpose of obtaining the most efficient possible allocation of resources among uses.

Third, legislation should be revised to relieve commissions of the implied responsibility of progressively raising the rates of chronically losing utility firms in order to reach for a lesser loss, when such firms are in a declining industry or are being displaced by the competition of substitute outputs. In such cases, commissions should be specifically empowered to make findings of fact concerning the declining character of the markets involved, and to determine prices and outputs in line with the purpose of deriving the maximum social benefit from existing fixed plant facilities. (A chronically losing street transportation system, for example, might be required to lower its rates rather than being allowed to raise them progressively, if the commission's factual findings concerning relative passenger volume, revenues, and costs supported this move.) Such a regulatory power would probably have to be supplemented with provisions for a public subsidy to the losing firm in those cases in which there was a factual finding that maintenance of the service was really essential.

Fourth, existing "splits" in commission jurisdiction over utility firms which offer competitive services should be eliminated, by consolidating control of any group of competing services under a single regulatory body. In the case of interstate transportation, for example, all rail, highway, and air transport should be subject to the control of a single commission, rather than having air transport separately controlled. Given this sort of consolidation of regulatory authority, moreover, adequate legislative instructions should be provided to commissions concerning the extent to which it is and is not desirable to manipulate competing rates so as to preserve the market positions of suppliers of each of several types of competing service. An overall policy standard specifying the proper aim with respect to encouragement or discouragement (via rate regulations) of growing and declining groups of competing suppliers should be written into the law, again in the orientation of securing the most efficient overall allocation and use of resources.

Finally, the authority of state regulatory commissions should be extended to make clear their rights and powers to secure without restriction all relevant information on the operations, earnings, and so forth of out-of-state firms which have ownership or comparable affiliations with in-state regulated firms and which serve the in-state firms as suppliers, top managers, or otherwise. They should be free to use such information in establishing legitimate definitions of cost and investment, and in determining fair rates for service.

The preceding is a short and sketchy list of possible improvements in the existing system of public utility regulations. The reader is referred to numerous detailed works on the subject if he wishes to pursue the subject in any detail.

Conclusion

In Chapters 14 and 15 we presented some analysis and evaluation of existing public policy directed, first, toward the maintenance of competition and, second, toward its restriction. In the present chapter, we have outlined briefly some suggestions concerning revisions in existing policies. The latter treatment is extremely synoptic, and far from complete even as an outline. It is intended mainly to stimulate the reader's interest in further and much more intensive study of contemporary policy issues involving industrial organization and control.

The general direction of our argument in this chapter has been to support the maintenance and strengthening of existing policies aimed at preserving competition and preventing monopoly, to recommend a limitation and selective elimination of policies designed to restrict competition (so that the area of exceptions to the general antitrust policy is reduced to a feasible minimum), and to suggest a strengthening of regulatory procedures and a clearer and more satisfactory definition of regulatory standards in those areas which will still be subject to direct public regulation. This all implies a support on the part of the writer of the past accomplishments and future potential of an enterprise economy which is in large part market-regulated through the forces of competition, and his preference for a competitive economy as opposed to one in which there is a great deal of direct governmental regulation. There are many divergent, and even opposite, views on this matter, however, and the reader is encouraged to explore and evaluate these as he continues his study of industrial organization.

SUPPLEMENTARY READINGS

Kaysen, Carl, and Donald F. Turner, *Antitrust Policy: A Legal and Economic Analysis*, 1959.

Edwards, Corwin D., *Maintaining Competition: Requisites of a Governmental Policy*, 1949.

Stocking, George W., and Myron W. Watkins, *Monopoly and Free Enterprise*, 1951, Ch. 16.

Dirlam, Joel B., and Alfred E. Kahn, *Fair Competition: The Law and Economics of Antitrust Policy*, 1954, Ch. 9.

Schultz, Theodore W., *Agriculture in an Unstable Economy*, 1945, Part IV.

Index